About the Author

Celia Pearce is a pioneer of new media and internationally acclaimed creative director of interactive experiences for entertainment and education. Since 1983, she has worked in a variety of interactive media from high-end Virtual Reality to printed playing cards to…interactive books! She currently has her own consulting and design firm, ***momentum media group***, which provides creative services to a variety of clients, and is also involved in other multimedia ventures. Ms. Pearce teaches interactive design at a number of prestigious new media programs in the U.S. and abroad and has published several articles on interactive design. *The Interactive Book* is her first full-length book.

To contact Ms. Pearce, please visit her web site at: http://momentum-media.com

Trademark Acknowledgments

Dedications

This book is dedicated to the memory of Shirley Kray, whose magical powers as an elementary school teacher sparked a lifelong romance between an eight year-old girl and the written word.

I'd also like to thank my family, Lucia Capacchione, Peter and Susan Pearce, Aleta, Marcellus, Medwin, Arie, Ian, and Adrian Pearce Francis, Connie Capacchione, and Mary Distaso for their constant support on this and all my other revolutionary endeavors; and to Steven Lovy, who helps me keep my feet on the ground and my head in the clouds. Together, they have been the fire that fans the flame and I am lucky to have them all on my side.

Acknowledgments

This book has been a gargantuan effort on the part of many people, all of whose efforts, whether large or small, had an equal part in its realization. Without each and every one of them, this project would not have seen the light of day.

I want to start with a special thanks to two individuals who have been the most intrumental in both the writing and publishing of this book. The first is Clark Dodsworth. Aside from his support and for his ongoing contribution to my career in general, he also solicited and published my first articles, read the early manuscript, and in many ways was one of the major catalysts for this project. The second is Mark Pesce, who served as my de-facto agent and writing mentor, putting me together with the folks at Macmillan Technical Publishing, and encouraging them to take on this project. Mark also had a major influence on the content of this book through our ongoing dialogues of theories and ideas. Finally, special thanks to him for his lovely foreward, which came to us, aptly, from a foreign location via e-mail.

The first phase of this book was reviewed by several infinitely patient individuals, whose contributions and commentary all became part of the final outlay:

First and foremost, my sister Aleta Pearce, who spent a serious chunk of time reading, reviewing, and edting the first draft and making some sense of my madness. I am very grateful for her ongoing support and tangible contribution to this project.

My parents, Lucia Capacchione, Peter Pearce, and Susie Pearce, all of whom offered salient comments, along with infinite patience and support.

Marita Isaksson for her unique slant on things, which also helped me to get the entire project in focus; other early readers whose helpful comments became part of this final text include Geert Madsen, Brenden Maher, and Philip Wei.

Special thanks are due to the many wonderful people at Macmillan Technical Publishing who had the courage and fortitude to take on this humongous task:

David Dwyer, Associate Publisher, who mailed me a contract within weeks of receiving my book proposal, and David Gibson for "carrying the torch" on his behalf once the project was underway. This book was kind of a hard sell to both publishers and agents because it doesn't fit into any kind of standard category. I salute "the Davids" and their team for taking this project on, even though it meant stepping out of their typical paradigm and doing the extra legwork it takes to create and introduce a new genre into an existing repertoire.

Chris Cleveland was the midwife for the project. Chris lived, breathed, ate, and drank this book for three months. As development/production editor, Chris went above and beyond the call of duty to tame this animal and coax it into something respectable and readable. Chris dealt admirably with a plethora of unanticipated curves, some of which were circumstantial, and some of which were inherent in the form of this project, with an attitude of unwavering enthusiasm and support. In spite of an enormous amount of pressure and many extra hours of work, he maintained a great attitude from start to finish. I also want to thank him, and indeed everyone at Macmillan Technical Publishing, for their patience with me and my rather unconventional work style. I know this made the book a more challenging production effort, but it is also what allowed me the creative freedom to issue forth the free flow of ideas that characterize the following pages. Working with Chris was Keith Cline, who served as copy editor for the manuscript, and Stacey Beheler, who helped put all the pieces together.

I also want to thank Steve Weiss for his support in terms of the writing, editing, and production process, and for pushing forward the marketing effort of this book, which of course is essential to its success. A special note of thanks to Steve, David Gibson, and David Dwyer for their handling of the cover design.

The design team at Macmillan Technical Publishing deserve a special round of applause for their work in figuring out how to lay this work out on the page. It is really a problem of interface design which represents the efforts of Glenn Larsen, who again had to step out into the unknown and have a little adventure with this.

There is an awful lot of information contained in this book, about 2,000 facts in all. I want to thank my research team, Aleta Pearce, Chris and Tisha Bedrosian, and Shaun di Gasperi for performing the arduous task of making sure they were all correct.

A handful of key individuals who have been my employers and/or clients bear notice here. These individuals and companies either influenced my thinking or gave me opportunities which let me put many of my theories into practice so that I could speak to this issues with some level of credibility and hands-on experience. Ed Schlossberg, who gave me my first interactive job, has probably been more influential on both my career and my thinking than any other single person; also the team at Edwin Schlossberg Incorporates with whom I worked for seven years whose ideas, creativity, and influence also resonate throughout this book. Dennis Earl Moore and the team at Dennis Earl Moore

Productions gave me my first big freelance gig that let me put some of my early theories into practice. Coco Conn and Beth-Ellen Keyes gave me the opportunity to create the showcase exhibitions described in this book, enabling me to support a great community of creative innovators in the interactive arts and sciences. Eddie Newquist, Stan Kinsey, and Mike Ryder and everyone on the the *Virtual Adventures* team at Iwerks Enertainment and Evans & Sutherland gave me an enormous amount of support and creative freedom, and all the human and technical resources needed to create a product that enabled me to explore an entirely new genre of interacive experience. And finally, Brenda Laurel and the folks at Purple Moon, who gave me the opportunity to develop a card game, proving once again that you don't need computers to be interative, and also offering me a chance to develop some content for the underrepresented girls' market.

The ideas put forth in this book took shape over a period of many years, but there have been several venues and individuals in particular who have offered me to the opportunity to present and test these notions prior to their arrival to these pages. First I'd like to thank the following educational institutions and the students who have participated in my classes there: American Film Institute (Los Angeles); UCLA Extention (Los Angeles); Space Invaders Multimedia Program/MouseHouse (Denmark); the Hypermedia Research Centre, Westminster University (London); Multimedia Studies Program, San Francisco State University. I'd also like to thank ACM SIGGRAPH Computer Graphics, Addison-Wesley, and *Mute* magazine (London) for publishing articles whose ideas have also been integrated into these pages.

I also want to thank all those individuals and organizations who provided the beautiful images that serve to support my words throughout this book. A complete list of these organizations can be found in the image credits. In particular I want to thank Lucia Capacchione and Peter Pearce for their generous contributions of photographs, and Shelley at the Eames Office for providing me with images of the work of Charles and Rae Eames.

Throughout the process of writing this book, there have been a number of friends and colleagues in addition to those cited above who have provided wisdom, insight, and inspiration, as well as forms of support both intangible (cheerleading, philosopical discussions, and so on), to tangible (food, housing, and so on). All of these individuals have, in one way or another, been an integral part of making this book more than just a virtual reality:

Brenden Maher, Rita Addison, David Zeltzer, Brenda Laurel, and Rob Tow; Gail Conrad; Athomas Goldberg; Clay Graham; C. Scott Young; Jeannine Parker, and Bob Rice; Paul Godwin and Amy Evans; Timothy Childs and Don Howe; Tony Parisi, Barry Fox, Brian Blau of Intervista; Brent Britton of Britton and Silberman; Lisa Goldman, Mark Meadows, Adam Gould, and the folks at Construct; Tarik Thami; Bruce Damer; David Traub; Char Davies; Charles Ostman; Galen Brandt; Kit Galloway and Sherrie Rabinowitz and the *Electronic Café*; Jeremy Quinn, Andy Cameron, and Richard Barbrook; Ouafa Rian; Caroline Ohlsen, Jakob Tuborgh, David Junge, Norm McLeod; David Hankin; Beth Broday; Carl Bressler; Hal Josephson; Roberta Perry, Jill Bensley, and Norma Lynn Cutler; Walt Bransford; Eben Gay; Chris Greuel; Matt and Greg Neri; Byron Callas; Stacey and Andy Farber; Joan McDonald, Steven Meltzer, Robin Bady, and John O'Brien; Doug MacMurray; Dana Duff, Melodie London, Michael Fell, and Phil Stenquist; John Reynolds; Josephine Spilka; Talya Meldy; Frank Dutro; Helen Goldstein.

I'd also like to thank my grandmother Connie Capacchione for her enthusiastic support and encouragement, and her sister, Mary Distaso; my brother-in-law Marcellus Francis for various forms of tangible and intangible support during this process; and my wonderful nephews, Medwin, Arie, Ian, and Adrian, who I look to for guidance as to what the future holds, for they are truly the interactive generation.

And finally, extra-special thanks to Steven Lovy for his infinite patience, enthusiasm, and inspiration; for his wisdom and advice; for his tenacity and dedication; for, among other things, playing the piano while I wrote, bringing me over a hundred cups of tea, making sure I took time to rest and relax, and staying up all night to design the beautiful cover of this book.

Image Credits

A.1   image reproduced by permission of William Latham via Biota.org (http://www.biota.org)

A.2   image reproduced by permission of Bruce Damer on behalf of Biota.org (http://www.biota.org)

A.3   image reproduced by permission of Ken Goldberg

A.4   image reproduced by permission of Charles Ostman ©1992–1997 (http://nanothinc.com)

A.5   Duchamp, Marcel: *Nude Descending a Staircase*, No. 2; Philadelphia Museum of Art: Louise and Walter Arensberg Collection

A.6   Duchamp, Marcel: *Bicycle Wheel-Ready Made*, 1964; Philadelphia Museum of Art: Given by the Schwartz Galleria d'Arte

A.7   Stieglitz, Alfred: *The Fountain by Marcel Ducamp*; Philadelphia Museum of Art: Louise and Walter Arensberg Collection

A.8   Duchamp, Marcel: *Large Glass; Bride Stripped Bare by Her Bachelors* ©1915; Philadelphia Museum of Art: Bequest of Katherine S. Dreier

A.9–A.12   images reproduced by permission of The Eames Office (http://www.eamesoffice.com)

A.13–A.15   photos reproduced by permission of Lucia Capacchione

A.16, B.1, B.3, M.1–M.12   photos reproduced by permission of Peter Pearce

A.17, A.20, N.5   images reproduced by permission of Webster Lewin on behalf of DE-LUX'O Consumer Productions

A.18   image reproduce by permission of Gohsuke Takama

A.19   image reproduced by permission of momentum media group ©1996, photo by Philip Wei

B.2, C.3, N.16, S.1, W.1   Image reproduced by permission of Construct Internet Design Co.

C.4   Image reproduced by permission of Betsy Nute on behalf of OnLive

C.5   Image reproduced by permission of Bruce Damer

D.1   Image reproduced by permission of Columbia/Tristar

H.1, H.2, M.21   Images reproduced by permission of Edwin Schlossberg, Inc.; photos by Donald Dietz

M.13–M.16   Images reproduced by permission of Kit Galloway and Sherri Rabinowitz

M.17–M.20   Images reproduced by permission of Myron W. Krueger

TAbLE of CONTENTS

Preface

Welcome to the interactive revolution. This book is about a new world that is emerging around us, a world of which we might not yet be entirely conscious. This book is about consciousness, about paying attention, and about seizing the opportunity to make a difference today instead of waiting tentatively for some indeterminate future. It is about reflection and action, about theory and practice. It is not just a book—it's a light bulb. It's not about computers. It's about you.

Interactivity is not a technology, but a way of life, an orientation, and a mindset. If you follow the visions and paths of the great pioneers of interactive media, some of which are described in the pages that follow, you will find that they originally envisioned a world in which man and computer were one—in which the digisphere was an expansion of the human mind. As divergent as their implementations, applications, and solutions were, these pioneers were all driven by a single and unified notion: that the computer is the ultimate extension of the human organism. In his landmark 1964 book *Understanding Media*, pioneering media theorist Marshall McLuhan referred to media as "extensions of man," a way to branch out, to evolve outside ourselves and together. The cybernetic world is a world of expansion and contraction, of empowerment and intimacy. At times we might look around us and see a plethora of trivialities, a wasteland of meaningless information stretching as far as the eye can see. At other times, we might be caught short in amazement by the depth and breadth of a revelation spurred on by our own interaction with this deeply textured world. The potential to rise beyond the mundane is ever present. When I hear people talk of virtual malls, I ask, why not virtual temples? When I hear marketing on the web, why not education? When I hear games, why not communities?

I might sound idealistic, but that's only because I am. As part of the so-called "digerati," a small community on the inside track of contemporary computer culture, I've seen the power of interactive media—the power of healing, the power of creativity, the power of understanding, of stepping beyond boundaries and looking within, the power of community, the power of empathy. I have seen children create whole worlds, adults become children, and whole families turn away from their televisions to build a family room in cyberspace. I've been inside another person's brain and walked in her shoes. I've connected in magical ways with people I've never even met.

If you visit the Internet today, you will find everything from the sublime to the ridiculous, from the inspiring to the terrifying, from the awesomely important, to the mind-numbingly gratuitous. The Internet is a folk movement. It's grassroots. It's anarchy. It's chaos. It's evolution. It's nature. And it's messy...as it should be. Just like real life!

As you take the thoughts and ideas of this book out into the world, my deepest wish is that in these pages, you find a sense of understanding—not so much for the world at large, nor even of my ideas—but of yourself, your own mind and its capability to connect, illuminate, and create. This is not about the world, nor about me. It's about you. It's about how much control you decide to take over your destiny and the destiny of your entire species. Because this is what interactivity is really all about. It is about being proactive and not being afraid to create your own reality. It's about not letting "the media" tell you what to be, do, and think, but about you creating the media yourself.

Througout the desktops of the world, in the offices and dens, in the libraries and schools, in the secret labs of the military and the Ivory towers of research, in garages and cybercafés, on airplanes and in tents, the tools of this revolution are waiting to be released. They are not weapons of destruction, but tools of empowerment; they are not there to destroy but to expand.

The word eureka comes from the same Greek root as the word heuristic—to discover. The notion of heuristic learning and heuristic devices is a recurring theme throughout this book because it is the taproot from which all interactivity, whether computer mediated or not, springs. It is the underpinning philosophy on which this entire movement is built. Heuristic learning is an act of discovery, the discovery of what happens within one's own mind, at the moment the light bulb goes off, suddenly illuminating something that before was in darkness.

I hope that this book will be the electrical charge that ignites that light bulb for you, that the most important thing you discover is the light inside your own mind and the unlimited potential of living your life interactively. I hope this book, which you will have a hand in creating through its interactive structure, serves as both a mirror and a window into your place in the larger context of a rapidly changing world. I hope that these pages and the new perspective you gain from them will inspire you at least once to burst forth the cry of discovery: Eureka!

Introduction

The title of this book can be read three ways. If read as **The *Interactive* Book**, it is a book about interactivity. If read as **The Interactive *Book***, the book itself is interactive. The third reading, ***The* Interactive Book**, would suggest that this is the definitive book on interactivity. All three interpretations are correct, and thus begins our interactive journey.

This is an interactive book about interactivity. I have written it in a nonlinear fashion for two reasons. The second is that, because the medium is the message, it seemed the most effective way to convey the ideas set forth within these pages. The first is that it's the way I think. And the third is that it is more fun.

What is the Interactive Revolution?

We are in the midst of a widespread revolution, not so much a political revolution as a widespread social and cultural upheaval whose impact can be felt at every level of human endeavor throughout the Earth. The Global Village is becoming a tangible reality as the rapid acceleration of digital media and high-speed networking have led to concurrent expansion and convergence of media, information and understanding.

The interactive revolution is the antidote to the industrial revolution, whose aim was to make humans evolve in the service of machines. The modern personal computer has reversed this de-evolution by rehumanizing us through digital technology. We are now creating machines in the service of humans. The interactive computer is a creative power tool that enables humans to expand beyond biological and mechanistic functions.

At the heart of this revolution is interactivity. The interactive revolution is not about technology, it's about people. It's about creating machines that extend our mental and creative faculties, that enable us to store, manage, and most important, share massive amounts of knowledge on a global level. It is about using powerful tools to create our own educational and entertainment experiences rather than passively accepting that which is fed to us by so-called experts. It is about the dissolution of boundaries and the translation of all thought into a common vocabulary. Binary code is the digital esperanto that is leading concurrently to individual empowerment and worldwide unity.

WHAT IS INTERACTIVITY?

"Interactive" has become a buzzword and an integral part of popular culture. But what does it really men?

> **interactive** (1832) **1:** mutually or reciprocally active
> **2:** of, relating to, or being a two-way electronic communication system (as a telephone, or computer) that involves the user's orders (as for information or merchandise) or responses (as to a poll)

According to this defintion, interactivity is characterized by reciprocity, either between people or between a person and a device. It's that simple. When applied to an *experience*, this simply means that you, the *user*, will have an impact on the experience in some way. This book is about the nature of interactive experience, regardless of the technology, and the profound social, political, emotional, intellectual, and even spiritual ramifications of living in a world where all media has become "mutually or reciprocally active."

WHAT IS INTERACTIVE MULTIMEDIA?

What do we mean when we say *interactive multimedia*? In simplest terms, multimedia is a means of facilitaing interactivity through the convergence of other media—video, text, sound, graphics, three-dimensional data, and binary code—as facilitated by a computer. Digital media, that is, media that exists as computer data, enables the easy intergration of different mediums into various multimedia hybrids. Multimedia does not necessarily have to be entirely digital, but can involve the operation of an analog device, such as a laser disk player. Thus, multimedia is not a single medium, but a repertoire of media that can be used in different combintations to create interactive, or reciprocal experiences.

It's important to understand that you can have multimedia without interactivity and you can have interactivity without multimedia. In fact, we have interactive experiences that do not involve computers or multimdia at all, for example the telephone, or a deck of playing cards. Or this book. If you are able to combine the two—the convergence of media with the feedback or reciprocity of interactivity—the possibilities are limitless. For the power of interactive media to influence our lives in significant ways is only as limited as the imaginations of the people creating it.

WHY IS THIS A BOOK?

While doing this project, I would tell people I was writing an interactive book, and they would look at me askance. Many people in my industry naturally made the assumption that it would be a digital book—a web site or a CD-ROM. My colleagues thought it was odd that I would chose to try and make a book interactive when I had access to so many other "more powerful" interactive tools.

I wanted to write an interactive book for a number of reasons. A book can demonstrate interactivity it its simplest form. This book is a unique journey through my thought processes, combined with your own. Think of it as an atlas with many roads for you to traverse, a map to a changing socio- and psycho-graphic landscape. It is a collaboration between you and me, an incomplete work-in-process for you to intepret, assemble, and make your own.

Typically, the analysis of interactive content or theory is presented in a very linear and *non*-reciprocal form through traditional books, lectures, and demo presentations, all of which are essentially passive and didactic. The point here is to demonstrate that you don't need high technology to be interactive. In fact, interactivity is at least as old as human communication. This book provides an experience of interactivity that is both physical and cognitive. We tend to think about interactivity as being facilitated by a hardware or software "engine" of some sort. But this is a do-it-yourself proposition. You are the engine.

I also want to practice what I preach, to prove that the medium truly is the message. This book uses interactivity to both discuss and demonstrate interactivity. It can be read in many different ways, based on the individual reading style and interests of the reader. Speaking of reading styles, it might interest you to know that I read the way this book is written. In fact, I often read several books at the same time, jumping around to different sections, while leaving others unread. I also fill my books with generous annotations, decorating the margins with illegible scrawlings and punctuating my favorite text with highlighter pens, underlines, or exclamation points. I prefer to treat a book like a conversation with the author rather than a lecture.

I love the irony of it all: The irony of a book, generally considered the most linear of all media; the irony of using the most traditional form of mass media to discuss so-called "new media"; the irony of a person like me, who has spent her entire life creating high- and low-tech interactive experiences, writing a simple book. But it is precisely this simplicty, this replicability, this accessiblity that I want. A book is the easiest thing to get, and among the easiest to understand. Even so, I cannot express what I know about the nature of inter-active experience without demonstrating it in the process.

When I was a child, books were my Virtual Reality. I spent the vast majority of my time in the school library. I read voraciously, and when I wasn't reading, I was writing and illusrating stories about a variety of characters of my own invention, all of whom were variations of me—from the Viking Sea Captain leading her ships into battle to the 1920s flapper working on a Broadway chorus line, my world was full of interactive media that didn't involve any-thing at all digital. Books are still, for me, the most intimate medium. And the rise in popularity of the Internet, a text-based interactive medium, proves more than ever that the written word is not only alive and well, but flourish-ing and evolving. I want my ideas to come to you in the form of text. That is the most direct means for them to mingle with your thoughts and swim around in your mind, like they swim around in mine. So I wrote a book, as opposed to making a web site, or a CD-ROM, because these are ideas I would rather whisper in your ear.

How to Read an Interactive Book

This book is a group of autonomous, interdependent essays and insights loosely held together by a common theme. For lack of a better term, I refer to these entities as "chapters." They run the gamut from historical to anecdotal, theoretical to practical, esoteric to essential. They vary wildly in both length and tone. Some are well developed positions, observations, and techniques; others are works-in-progress which are still formulating in my mind, even now, long after they are fixed in print. No doubt future writings will further develop or perhaps even refute some of these theories or notions. This book might also be seen as a time capsule. Though I have tried hard to make each chapter perennial, avoiding anything that would date the book, it is difficult in the tumultuous landscape of interactive media where today's next big thing is tomorrow's smoking crater, tomorrow's Killer App is yet unrecognized. As I say throughout this book, I am not in the business of predicting the future, but what I will do is ask the pertinent questions. Instead of predicting the future, I prefer to create it. So should you.

If you are familiar with the Internet or other interactive media, this is essently a hypertext book. If you don't consider yourself web-savvy, don't worry, the navigation is extremely simple. Here's how it works:

● Because this is a book, the chapters had to be put into a sequence of some kind. I, along with my editors, opted for alphabetical order because it was a familiar yet entirely arbitrary organizational paradigm. As with a dictionary, there is no context for the sequence; it is merely a convenience, a universally recognized standard that everyone understands.

Each chapter contains (within the body of the text) links to other chapters on related subjects. Many chapters might have links to each other because they cover related themes and issues. These links are indicated by a Go To icon listing the name of the chapter, which you can locate by using the thumb tabs in the righthand margin. (GOTO is a term used in the vocabulary of computer code that tells the computer to call up various subroutines throughout the program.)

In addition to the Go To Link, you will also find a loop icon accompanying some of the images that indicates that you can find a full-color version of the image in the section at the tail end of the book. The color images are referenced by their plate number. These are what I consider to be some of the defining works that are taking interactive media to the next level.

● There are a variety of ways you can read this book, but I'm not going to tell you what they are! You may want to start with a quick browse of the table of contents; this will give you an overview of the book. A chapter may jump out at you as your starting point. Chances are that going to a chapter of your fancy will start a chain reaction that will eventually lead you through all the chapters that might interest you. Or, you can pick a random page in the book and start from there; let kismet be your guide. Play dice with the universe. If there's something specific you're looking for, check out the index in the back. Illustrations are provided throughout to help you better see my points.

● It's perfectly fine if you don't read the whole book. I hope you do, but part of its charm is that it is really many books rolled into one. Skip the parts that don't interest you or try something different and read *only* the parts that don't interest you!

● Please feel free to mumble to yourself while reading, praise or curse, and by all means—write in the margins. That's what they're *there* for. Remember, this is a conversation, and if you don't meet it halfway, the book will get bored and want to stop being read by you.

● Feel free to laugh at any time.

The most important thing is to have fun. I hope you enjoy this interactive experience as much as I did and look forward to our forthcoming collaboration.

MONKEY IN THE MIRROR

Slow-motion photography captures the infant moving in rhythmic syncopation to Mother's words; an adolescent raised on *Super Mario World* sees the space inside the screen as meaningful and coequal to her own; the 20-something click-click-clicks and surveys the edges of an almost infinite field of knowledge, trying to divine the shape of the Noosphere, the emergent planetary mind.

Everything we are and everything we do represents a connection—a coupling—between ourselves and something greater than ourselves; our immune cells couple with the environment and produce new antigens; we immerse ourselves within foreign cultures and quickly learn new languages; cultures themselves learn to adapt to the transformative effects of electric media. The process of coupling, self-similar across all levels of scale, changes us; learning changes us, breathing changes us, even seeing changes us.

We seem mostly to be the unconscious subjects of these couplings; the repeated nature of coupling events seem to dull us into some kind of slumber—even as we become more connected to the world, we seem to sense it less. Are we hurling toward a Global Village as coma ward? When everyone—the Kalahari bushmen, a billion and a half Chinese peasants, Balinese dancers, and Western businesspeople—all inevitably log on one vast, distributed, wireless ether, will we be aware of it? Will we sense the scope of the transfiguration of human (to say nothing of planetary) consciousness that accompanies this global network?

Marshall McLuhan (who gets quoted repeatedly in this book) noted that we always approach our technologies with the pirouette-and-collapse of a comic who invariably slips on the banana peel. We spend life looking out a rear-view-mirror, blissfully unaware of the wall, stretched across the superhighway, that we careen toward at 70 miles per. Only in the "puny and peripheral" efforts of artists, McLuhan declares, do we see any attempt to face the present head-on. That's why fine art so often disturbs us; it represents the briefest of glances forward, into a view of our current situation.

Our rear-view fades from visibility at the dawn of human consciousness, and while no one has been able to answer when, exactly, we learned of our difference from our simian cousins, we know this flash of recognition and the birth of humanity as a single act; to name, to know this from that, marks the essence of our human consciousness, preeminently and predominantly a verbal consciousness. Language—the voice of consciousness, and the original medium—allowed our ancestors to know their humanity, triumph over the "lesser" animals, and proclaim dominion over the unconscious silence of all nature. <Sic> transit gloria mundi.

Man before the word was not human; we cannot know how language came to be, or how it spread, even how quickly it spread. Did it begin with a mutation that slowly and inexorably conquered the Earth? Or a child teach it to her tribe, then her tribe teach the world? Perhaps we rose from an evening's sleep, all of us knowing how to speak. Anything is possible—literally—because we confront the limits of our knowledge, confounded by the limits of knowing.

On the threshold of our self-appointed Millenium, we sit about etheric camp-fires and spin "Tales of Wonder" about a world we only know through our own imaginations. The interactive age has yet to begin; like the nearest proto-humans, we know something big is happening, but we lack the power to speak the word which ushers in the new Aeon. In another 15, or 1500 years, this language will exist—but then these words will resemble nothing so much as the grunts of the preconscious. At the edge of the post-historic, the utopian fantasies of the Extropians battle against the collective subconscious night-mare of the Borg; but each defines a world from an egoistic point of view; the Extropian becomes the I eternally freed by technology, while the Borg is first dominated, and then assimilated by it. Each mythology fails to recognize that any self capable of such demonic (or angelic) transformations cannot be the self we call human; each expresses a glimpse into the terror of the present situation, but says nothing about the world to come.

Just before the dawn of the electronic era, Samuel Johnson and Noah Webster crafted the first books of words; it had never before occurred to anyone that an exhaustive list of words could be useful or even desirable. Yet the great speed-up in communication that would come with the telegraph, the telephone and the tabloid newspaper required standardized spellings and definitions; words would be pried away from the mouths that uttered them, and spread—in-stantly—across the world. Even before Morse had tapped out, "What hath God wrought?" the transformations of language had begun, anticipating the speed-up of electric language.

Celia Pearce, like so many of the progenitors of the electric era, writes about the world she has had a hand in creating; *The Interactive Book* reads more like a diary than a dry report. She speaks only of what she knows, and she knows a lot. I saw this work long ago, in its embryonic form as dozens and dozens of little notes—pointers, references, and articles—spilled out over a few tens of pages. These represented the core of almost two decades of experience with interactive media, lessons learned from her own successes—and, more importantly, her own failures. How to organize these bits? Knowledge, as Ted Nelson pointed out in *Literary*

Machines, can only be expressed in the relation of one thought to another. Ten years before the web, no one understood what he meant. Today, it's obvious, and Pearce wisely chose to create a book of hyperlinks; together these thoughts construct a world-view which is her unique statement about what we touch, when the computer reaches out and touches us.

The 500 year-old printed text, without a power supply, interface, or microprocessor control, lacks the fluidity of the web, its natural disorganization; how then to structure a book with no structure, that consciously denies any structure, except what you, the reader, would choose to make of it? In a stroke of genius, Pearce recognized that an alphabetical organization of the material gave it a form that downplayed the linearity of the text while simultaneously making it easy to reference. Like words a dictionary, the articles in *The Interactive Book* have only the importance you give them; each reader who comes into this text will find some articles particularly valuable, and others irrelevant. You must choose to identify one word as sacred and another as profane.

This places you in the driver's seat; like Deleuze & Guattari's *A Thousand Plateaus*, the text can be read as desired: in sequence (for left-brain types), by topic, or at random. Perhaps someone will figure out how to use this work as an oracle, opening a page at random and auguring from the letter and subject a portentous message. At the very least, *The Interactive Book* fulfills Gertrude Stein's maxim: when the structure of a work is one of its themes, another of its themes is art.

If Celia Pearce is the Samuel Johnson of the interactive age, gathering all of its nascent gestures into a vocabulary, then I am content to be her faithful Boswell. Although we have not learned the words that circle back to us, we can look into the mirror with her and wonder at our collective reflection:

> "What you really want to do as the interactive artist or creator of interactive experiences is give your viewers a way to look back at themselves in the process of creating their own experience."

Reflection—the coupling of image with object—stands as the archetype of interactivity; every motion creates an equal and opposite animation in our reflection, closing the loop of coupling. As we narrow the gap between the living and the simulated—their eternal confusion is the bold-faced end of interactivity—a spark leaps across, and illuminates our action in a flash of insight.

Robert Anton Wilson once wrote, "When a monkey looks into a mirror, no god looks out." As our mouths shape to form the words of a new Logos—and give birth to a new world, for word and world are ever the same—we reach toward our post-historic, post-human selves. *The Interactive Book*, opinionated and utterly sensible, aimless and ceaselessly direct, incomplete and incontestably whole, pens the line between the quick and the dead. In its wake, our creations can only be judged by how human they are, and how they reveal the human in us.

Mark Pesce

Somewhere south of Greenland

July 1997

A-Life of One's Own

Computers can do just about anything, including create all manner of virtual life forms, also known as "artificial life," or A-Life for short. A-Life uses computer algorithms to create simulated life forms on the computer in a variety of dynamic and interesting ways. Biota is a project of the Contact Consortium, a group of digital artists and scientists devoted to developing artificial life and online communities on the web. Their web site (http://www.ccon.org/) contains, among other things, the work of William Latham, who creates elaborate creatures based on mathematical algorithms (see figure A.1). L-systems, a type of genetic algorithm, provide the framework for digital life forms. Although not developed for that purpose, L-systems, like fractal geometry, turn out to translate perfectly into procedural animations to create life-like organisms that can generate infinite growth that parallels growth in the natural world.

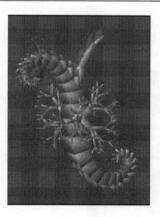

Figure A.1

Biota's algorithmically created Airhorse! Based on L-system's genetic algorithms

 Plate 25

Procedural animation is a technique that uses mathematical formulas and algorithmic behaviors instead of key frames to create a real-time animation sequence. "Key Frame" is the traditional method of computer animation in which the subject to be animated is placed in predetermined "key" positions, and then the computer "interpolates," or interprets the difference to create the sequence of animation. With procedural animation, the computer does all the work, creating the models and graphic imagery from scratch based purely on code. Procedural animation can also be used with pre-built models by creating "behaviors" that respond to certain conditions to generate the animated sequence.

Most A-Life experiments let the computer do all the work, including creating the models and, in some cases creating even the color schemes. Latham's work creates isolated organisms, but Biota is now working on a virtual ecosystem called *The Nerve Garden* (see figure A.2), which was presented by Bruce Damer, one of the founders of the Contact Consortium, in my "Exploring Spatial Media" class at San Francisco State University. In *The Nerve Garden*, kids can go on the web and plant virtual seeds containing DNA, really various A-Life algorithms, into a shared garden space. These organisms then begin to grow over time, based on the resources distributed to them through an elaborate network of "nerves" beneath the surface. Organisms must compete for resources, and can help or hinder the growth of other organisms. One of the functions of equilibrium in this environment is to maintain the polygon budget, that is, the maximum number of polygons that can be on the screen in a virtual environment without overloading the system. In *The Nerve Garden*, kids can plant their seeds, water them, provide nutrients, and so on. They can then come back periodically to tend to their organisms and see how things have progressed. Built in VRML, the Virtual Reality Modeling Language (the VR equivalent of HTML), *The Nerve Garden* supports real-time animation. During a typical visit, kids can plant seeds, watch them grow, and tweak variables to bring them to the next level of evolution of their ecosystem.

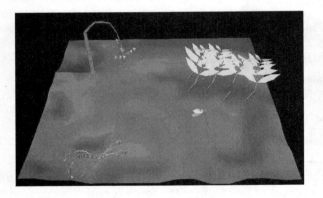

Figure A.2
Children can grow their own virtual plants online in *The Nerve Garden*

 PLATE 23

The Nerve Garden was inspired in part by a real-world project entitled the *Telegarden*, done at the University of Southern California (see figure A.3). *Telegarden* is an actual garden managed by a robotic arm. *Telegarden* members can go online and use the robotic arm to plant seeds, water, and fertilize them. Via live video feed, they can survey the scene and see how things are going. The *Telegarden* has literally blossomed into its own little online community, with telegardeners baby-sitting each other's plants when they are offline, and people working together to create a viable ecosystem.

Figure A.3
Artist's representation of the *Telegarden*, a robotic gardener controlled via the Internet

Although not A-Life per se, *T_Vision* is another project that provides a new level of insight into the world. If *Telegarden* is "Act Locally," then *T_Vision* is "Think Globally"—a networked model of the Earth that draws data from all over it. *T_Vision*, along with a number of other VR projects done in the early and mid-90s, uses technology in the service of increasing awareness of nature. *The Nerve Garden* and other A-Life projects are also very nature-centric. And in fact, much of what is being done in cyberspace today revolves around the exploration and simulation of nature, especially vis-a-vis our relationship to it, but also as a way of understanding and appreciating it more.

 T_VISION: SPACESHIP EARTH MADE VISIBLE (p. 460)

In fact, it is interesting to note that a significant number of defining fine art projects in VR revolve around natural themes. From Brenda Laurel and Rachel Strickland's *Placeholder*, which puts the user in the role of an animal spirit, to Rita Addison's *Detour: Brain Deconstruction Ahead*, which uses the artist's own nature photos to tell the before-and-after story of sensory anomalies caused by her brain injury, to Char Davies' magical *Osmose*, a tribute to nature inspired by her experiences deep-sea diving, virtual artists seem to turn to nature as their first inspiration. This is nothing new. Nature has always been a source of awe and a subject of tribute by poets and painters alike. Although it is curious, in some strange way it makes perfect sense that in this very high-tech art form, nature should be the dominant obsession. Christa Sommerer and Laurent Mignonneau are a VR art team who tackle the problem of artificial life specifically. Their compelling interactive environments engage you as the viewer to be part of the creation process, inviting you to design your own organism, make virtual plants grow by touching real plants, or using a flashlight to attract simulated moths.

 V-ART (p. 494)

Another A-Life alchemist is scientist/artist Charles Ostman. Ostman's interest lies in the interface between nature and machine. His specialty is nano-technology. Nano-technology is a technique of manipulation at the molecular level that enables you to do things such as create self-assembling materials, micro-machines, and pseudo-viruses. Self-assembling materials—which at one time were called "nano-legos" until the name had to be changed due to trademark disputes—consist of molecules that can be manipulated through input (such as heat or an electrical charge) to self-assemble into various materials. Micro-machines are devices that exist on the molecular level to perform minute tasks. Pseudo-viruses, perhaps the most interesting of the nano-technological applications, are "good viruses" designed to use the virus's own techniques to outsmart it (see figure A.4). Viruses propagate themselves through a host system by penetrating the cell wall and replacing the host's DNA with its own, thus forcing the host cell to replicate the virus instead of its own healthy offspring. Pseudo-viruses, really anti-viruses, do the same thing to the virus that the virus is attempting to do to the host. It thus quickly eliminates the intrusive organism, letting the healthy host cell return to its proper function. For more on Charles Ostman's work, you can visit the Nanothinc site at: http://www.nanothinc.com.

Figure A.4
Charles Ostman's algorithmically generated quasi-viral component

 PLATE 26

What Charles Ostman does is create procedural animations based purely on mathematical algorithms that describe the processes by which these nano-technologies function. These animations, as it turns out, are so extraordinary to look at, that they have come to be regarded as works of art. To distribute and show them as such, Charles takes snapshots of his nano-worlds by doing frame-grabs off his computer screen, and then has them transferred to canvas so that they become large paintings. Not an artist by trade, Charles is fond of pointing out that none of his art works are designed...they are simply generated by simulated natural systems. Nature, he says, is designed to seduce the senses, and thus the creation of simulated natures is bound to be equally seductive.

Bruce Damer recently told me of another new innovation in A-Life. In the world of the web, and particularly VR on the web, one of the biggest barriers of entry is, of course, throughput using available bandwidth. VRML, with its tiny file sizes, enables far more rapid movement of files down the Internet pipeline. Even so, the challenge remains—how to get all that information to move quickly from one place to another with available wiring and modem speed.

One way this is being solved is by distributing "DNA" packets containing self-propagating algorithms that enable the packets to build larger environments on the client side after they've passed through the pipeline. Like Charles Ostman's self-assembling molecules, these environments would essentially build themselves based on their DNA encoding. Thus, you could send out a tiny algorithm which would contain in it the DNA algorithm to build, for example, a virtual city, an intelligent agent, a forest, or really just about anything you wanted. After the DNA arrives at its destination, it begins propagating itself into the full model encoded into it.

Bruce loves to tell people about this because they all have the same reaction I did: They sit there with their jaws hanging open. It's a mind-boggling proposition—creating a city from a strand of digital DNA—and one can only begin to imagine the ramifications of this digital cloning process. Using nature as a model is really about the best way you can go. From a structural standpoint, nature is really the master at self-maintaining and self-propagating dynamic systems. The notion of managing the polygon budget as a by-product of natural equilibrium using an ecosystem model is the right idea. Nature knows how to do these things really well. Contrary to popular belief, it is not a sin to imitate her. If anything, it's more of a sin to ignore her.

An excellent book that tackles this topic from an architectural/industrial design perspective is Peter Pearce's *Structure in Nature Is a Strategy for Design* (MIT Press). This comprehensive study of structural systems in nature, although originally developed as a model for actual structure, can also be applied to structure in the digital sphere. The geometry of nature can been seen to be elegant and consistent, adhering to rigorous yet well-conceived parameters: Even though you are dealing with narrow constraints, the rules of natural structure are brilliantly formulated to allow for a maximum range of improvisations within the parameters of the system's protocol. What becomes apparent is that nature is both elegant and efficient, aesthetic and intelligent. The beautiful rose also happens to be the best use of available resources; the branches of a tree are the best means to distribute nutrients through the system; and the uniqueness of the snowflake is merely a random expression of a very narrow set of ground rules.

The mathematics of nature are a perfect paradigm for creating not only A-Life, but interactive environments in general. They are fool-proof, yet allow for a variety of outcomes. A well-designed game or interactive structure is not unlike an ecosystem in a state of dynamic equilibrium. All the checks and balances are in place; everything is "fair," enabling each dynamic entity within the system to have an equal chance at success in its respective area. When looked at in a historical perspective, you can begin to see the course of natural history and the evolution of life as a very long and protracted game; the rules have always been the same, but the components have become progressively more complex as time goes on, even within these bound constraints.

 God Plays Dice with the Universe (p. 215)

One of the things computers are really great at is modeling dynamic systems. And in fact, if you compare work in artificial intelligence and artificial life, what you discover is that computers seem to be considerably better at modeling basic natural systems than they are at modeling human thought. The human mind is extraordinarily complex, more complex than we really even know. But if we instead try to model natural ecosystems, and imitate life on the level of DNA, we are really utilizing computers at their best. And we are also following a certain evolutionary path. It's pretty clear at this point that life started small and worked its way up through various levels of aggregation. In that same way, we may be able to crack the bigger problems by first cracking the smaller ones. Or perhaps we are solving the wrong problem. Perhaps rather than making the entire human, we should be focusing our energies on making his or her DNA. Maybe we need to begin with the single cell in the primordial ooze of cyberspace. Maybe these tiny "biota" being created in virtual worlds today will turn out to be the ancestors of virtual humans tomorrow.

Nature is clever that way. She never bites off more than she can chew, and we ought to take example from her. Most of the really successful attempts I've seen at creating simulations of either life or intelligence have been examples of solving really specific and isolated problems. Knowing the nature of the problem itself is key. If you know what problem you are really trying to solve, you stand a much better chance of success. Furthermore, sometimes it is in the reframing of the problem that you find the key to unlock the secret. To put it in a different way—"Mighty oaks from tiny strands of DNA grow."

 Artificial Intelligence and the Prosthetic Brain (p. 38)

Cyberspace Cadets: Virtual Communities and Avatar Worlds (p. 146)

Media Architecture (p. 284)

ACTION, REACTION, INTERACTION

In *Understanding Media,* Marshall McLuhan draws the following comparison between the mechanical age and the information age.

> "In the mechanical age now receding, many actions could be taken without concern. Slow movement insured that the actions were delayed for considerable periods of time. Today the action and reaction occur almost at the same time."

If this statement was true in 1964, it is at least 10 times more true today. The speed of action and reaction in today's world would have boggled even McLuhan's overactive mind. Up until now, our cause-and-effect chain reaction stream was much slower. One of McLuhan's fundamental observations about the evolution of communication technology is that it all has ultimately to do with speed. That, in fact, everything from papyrus to fiber-optic cable is about hurrying up our communication stream, shortening the delay between action and reaction. The telephone was perhaps the first direct means of communication through technology that enabled us to span geographical space to procure a simultaneous and reciprocal response. The ramifications of this are much more vast than meets the eye...or the ear for that matter. Because what begins to happen is that as our communication accelerates, so does our way of thinking. Our manner of communication changes as the means of communication advance and evolve. Or, to put it in McLuhanese, "We shape our tools, and thereafter, our tools shape us."

If you look at the evolution of our communication tools toward narrowing the gap between cause and effect, you can clearly see the cultural impact this has had and how it has changed our expectations. Consider life before the telephone. If you wanted to communicate with someone in a different location, you wrote him or her a note (or chiseled a stone tablet, or painted on papyrus...). If he or she lived nearby, you could have it delivered that same day and perhaps expect a response later on that day, or even the next day. If he or she lived in another state, it could take weeks, and if overseas, perhaps even months. The telephone suddenly gave us the ability to have instant access to each other at any time, no matter where we were, to procure a response—which used to take weeks and months to obtain—in a moment. Imagine the impact on commerce, let alone social dynamics.

Those who remember life before the fax machine may recall a time when people would mail or even FedEx documents or images for review. The most quickly that one could expect a reply was 24 hours. But then came the fax.

Suddenly, the document could be sent instantly, and an immediate reply became the expectation. In the "old days," a document sent in the mail held with it an expectation of a minimum of 24 hours for a response. The fax sender expects his or her document to be read on the spot and responded to within minutes. The heightened expectations created by these instantaneous feedback systems requires us to respond much more quickly, and ultimately to think more quickly, so that we can react in sync with our communication tools.

The most diabolical communication tools of all time have to be the pager and cellular phone. During a short stint that cast me in the role of a Hollywood new media executive, I was forced to sport both. In the entertainment industry, no one thinks twice about paging you during a holiday meal, a therapy session, or in the middle of the night. When the job ended, the first thing I did was gleefully return the infernal pager and cellular phone—which I only turned on for outgoing calls (there's nothing worse than getting a phone call in the middle of a meal).

Then there is the matter of teleconferencing—the merger of telephony and television (perhaps it should be called "phony-vision"). In the realm of science fiction, the videophone is a commonplace appliance. From *Farenheit 451* to *Star Trek*, video-enhanced phone communication appears to be de rigeur in the future. As it exists now, it offers another level of telephone-based communication. On the Internet, CU-SeeMe technology enables online chatters to see and hear each other right on the computer screen. More sophisticated systems, like those used at the Electronic Café in Santa Monica and its international network of teleconferencing venues, merge video from two locations and superimpose the composition over a blue-screened background. Over the years there have also been a variety of stand-alone boxes that don't involve computing but merely provide a visual link to the caller. AT&T notwithstanding, this kind of technology has not become as commonplace as it is in the cinematic future. Its uses tend to be more specified to group meetings and social events. Personally, I'd rather not have my editors see me in my bathrobe when they phone on a Tuesday morning for a conference call, but, heck…there's a place for everything.

In spite of all its potential variations and enhancements, the telephone was and still is perhaps the most dynamic of all interactive devices because it enables immediate reciprocal feedback between multiple users. Although it has experienced advances and evolution, its core functionality has changed little in a hundred years. In fact, if you really think about it, the Internet is really just a very fancy and elaborate form of telephone. It is the infrastructure of the telephone itself that enables us to build a whole variety of these mutually reciprocal, instantaneous feedback chains in and around it.

The Internet provides a whole new venue for instantaneous communication. Live online communication is no more instantaneous than the telephone, and actually, given the typical delay (or latency rate as it's commonly called), it is actually a bit slower. On the other hand, I can send this entire chapter in digital form to the publisher in about one minute via the Internet. E-mail provides a form of delayed-time (as opposed to real-time) communication, enabling something a little slower than the phone but a little faster than the post. The infrastructure that enables an effortless and instant reply makes communication fast and easy…a little too easy. I can get up to 50 e-mails in a single day, most of which are totally unnecessary, and at least a quarter of which I won't even read.

The ability to instantly send a large quantity of e-mail over the web is also a feature that creates new modes of communication. A *spam*, or e-mail that is sent to a large list of people, can be a tool of irritation or a tool of revolution. I frequently get civil action spams, for example, which are great, because they allow me to be what I call a "passive activist." Sure, I can e-mail my congress-man, or "sign" a petition opposing human rights violations in Bosnia, no problem. It's a great tool for the lazy liberal. It's also a great social tool. My digerati pals and I use spamming for party invites all the time (yes, we do like to get out of the house from time to time), not to mention conference and events announcements.

Spamming is also a good way to have group discussions when you can't all find a time and place to get together or talk on the phone. I've had some really great roundtable discussions via back-and-forth spams in smaller groups. I have also used this as a collaboration technique. People send out documents for review; others comment; it enables a level of collaboration that simply could not happen if frequent meetings or phone conferences were required. I am not by any means proposing the elimination of face-to-face or voice-to-voice meetings. For my dime, there's no better feedback than eye contact, facial cues, or the tone in someone's voice. But group dialogues in the digisphere can enhance and support direct interaction and create a deeper level of collaboration and better communication overall.

The flip side of spamming and the instantaneous feedback of e-mail is an-other phenomenon known as *flaming* or *flame wars*. There is a common myth that computers somehow interfere with our ability to be emotional, but the flame war proves this to be a complete and total fallacy. The instant response capability of e-mail—hit "Reply" and "Send" and your message is sailing down the pipeline—can often give rise to heated emotional debates that are more aggressive and violent than any letter or phone call could be. The phone call, highly personal, reveals the subtlety of vocal intonation, therefore mak-ing both speakers keenly aware of the emotions they might be eliciting in each other. The mailed letter, because it is on paper and therefore represents a form of both legal and psychic commitment, requires a certain amount of thought and consideration before it is sent out. But the web enables people to act extemporaneously with impunity, dropping a certain amount of superego— the psychic filter that keeps us from acting in anti-social ways. It's much easier to be mean to someone you can't see, even if you are going to see that same person tomorrow. Restraint of pen and tongue should include restraint of keyboard, as we attempt to practice varying degrees of "Netiquette." I have seen a lot of pain and suffering, and even cataclysmic results, caused by the inability to refrain from hitting "Reply to all."

 ## Word to the Motherboard: Computers and Literacy (p. 530)

Let's step back for a moment and compare media that live in a telephone-based infrastructure to those that live in the infrastructure of television—the telephony versus television argument. Television is a broadcast (that is, a one-to-many medium). As such, it is inherently hierarchical. Just as a hierarchy is automatically put in place when one person is giving a lecture or performance to a large group, this relationship immediately sets up a hierarchical relationship between the broadcaster and the broadcastee. Furthermore, broadcast media is characterized by a lack of reciprocity. It's true that I can choose my channel, but I cannot send any direct feedback back to the source of the broadcast within the traditional infrastructure of TV, or indeed, any other broadcast medium. Hence, there is an action, but no reaction, no reciprocity, neither with the broadcaster nor between other recipients of the broadcast. Telephony, on the other hand, is a horizontal, or non-hierarchical system that enables a one-to-one, highly reciprocal and instantaneous response. The Internet combines both of these and then some, allowing for one-to-many, one-to-one, many-to-many, and all variations in between. It is inherently non-hierarchical, which completely changes the interdynamic between the participants. In the non-hierarchical world of the Internet, the broadcaster no longer has the power he once did. Nowadays, we see a plethora of megalopolies making plays for centralization and control of the Internet, which they are more than welcome to do, but infrastructurally speaking, MSN has no more power on the Internet than it does on the telephone; it has no advantage over anyone else within a non-hierarchical structure.

 ## Broad or Narrow: The Casting Couch (p. 113)

In a few short years of popular use, the Internet has already radically changed the way we deal with media. The Gutenberg press enabled the quick production of mass quantities of written information, a phenomenon that was mind-boggling to a culture in which publication meant writing by hand and mass production involved hand-cutting wood blocks. The capability to publish or broadcast on the Internet, available to anyone with access to a computer, provides an open structure through which ideas and information can circulate quickly and with more fluidity. It is also much more difficult to control. First, it moves so fast that it's gone before you know what happened. Second, it's not matter, so it's hard to keep track of. It's a lot easier to burn books or collect subversive pamphlets. Because of spamming and mail forwarding, things can get around a lot more quickly and to a lot more people and are a lot harder to keep track of. Bits are evasive. The Internet is the ultimate underground railroad.

Whether this high-powered, non-hierarchical communication and broadcast tool is making our lives better or worse remains to be seen. As with all things, there are no absolutes—I always love to say that, it sounds so absolute. But it's true. There are always camps who want to say something is good, or it's bad, that things are better or worse than they were, that technology has either improved or ruined our lives.

As with anything, it is not the tool but what we do with it that counts. You can use a hammer to build a house or to tear one down. We all have that choice to make. And so if you look at the computer as both a tool and a medium—and I don't care what anyone says, it *is* both—it is only as good or bad as the people who use it and the things they do with it. What it does do, without doubt, is empower people by giving them the capability to respond to the world in a much more dynamic and participatory way. It also gives them access to production and creation tools that a few years ago were available only to governments and multinational corporations. Individuals can now create, generate, and broadcast media to a wide audience. They also have something else these major powers didn't and don't have…the ability to engage in a dialogue with that audience, to befriend it, address it, and incorporate it into the process. The communist addage "Seize the means of production" is being translated in the information age to "Seize the means of communication and information distribution." Given the decentralized nature of the Internet, there's nothing the Global Powers can do to interfere with this process.

 DiGiTAl SociAlism (p. 180)

INTERACTIVITY IS SUbVERSIVE (p. 244)

But there is more to cause and effect in interactivity than merely the Internet. There is a larger issue here: the matter of thought, of how we think, of how we respond to our environment. The world of Internet, CD-ROMs, arcade games, and Virtual Reality (VR) is very different from the world of television, radio, and film; because it is a responsive world, a world that reacts to our presence in it. The traditional "broadcast media" are inherently unresponsive by their very nature. Theirs is an infrastructure of one-to-many, of centralized distribution of information to a passive audience. The remote control made the TV somehow more responsive, and even that simple shift changed things dramatically. Once you put any kind of control into that audience's hands, whether it be remote or direct, you are setting up an entirely different dynamic with the audience.

 ## REMOTE CONTROL GROUP (p. 410)

Arcade games are raising a generation that demands and expects feedback—direct, recognizable, and *fast*. The latency (delay) that currently exists on the web is too slow even for them. These kids have come to expect their environment to respond to them instantaneously in direct ways. Kids who have access to both a TV and a computer now spend more time on their computers than in front of their TVs. They are bored with the passivity of the broadcast media, and often bored with the passivity of the traditional classroom setting. Even so, studies have shown that kids who have computers at home, and possibly even kids who play "twitch" video games, do better in school. *Evolution's End*, by Joseph Chilton Pearce, presents evidence that watching television may actually physically alter the human brain to become more passive and limited. On the other hand, the computer is a direct feedback response system that can have an expansive effect on the user.

Virtual Reality provides a simple but powerful example of how this can work: VR is now being used in various kinds of physical and psycho-therapeutic applications. Arachnophobia (fear of spiders) has been successfully treated with VR. Physical therapists are also using VR to treat patients with various forms of paralysis, muscle, and nerve damage. The therapists are finding that patients who use direct feedback as part of their therapy progress at a much faster rate. A recent research project used VR systems to teach autistic children how to recognize and track moving cars and stop at a stop sign, a task that they had otherwise been unable to learn. In another project, a doctor suffering from Parkinson's disease, along with the HIT Lab (Human Interface Technologies) in Palo Alto, developed a pair of lightweight VR glasses that enabled him to walk normally, correcting a debilitating case of *a-kinesia*—the inability to move.

All this research indicates that an active and responsive environment has benefits beyond just psychological. In these cases, an active feedback system seems to be correcting systemic brain problems, disorders which have been traditionally treated with medication or physically corrective measures. In other words, it would appear that feedback is not only good for our minds, it's also good for our brains.

The ramifications of living in an interactive world are immense. We have only barely begun to understand the psychological and psycho-physiological impact of interactivity, and we have made only slightly more headway in the study of its social and political impact. No matter which way you look at it, however, it is patently clear that we are making a shift to an entirely new level of human cultural evolution. Most people see this merely as the "age of information," in which information and content has become the most valuable resource and commodity, but there is much more to it than that. Interactivity is restructuring the very way we think and relate to the world.

THE ADD GENERATION

A friend of mine who is a neuropsychologist calls Attention Deficit Disorder (ADD) the "diagnosis du jour." It's become almost fashionable to be tagged with this particular condition. ADD is defined as a learning disorder that results in an unusually short attention span. According to the current diagnosis, children with ADD can't sit sill, have a hard time concentrating, and cannot follow through on many activities due to a low boredom threshold.

There seem to be periodic trends in health that are as much a metaphor for a cultural condition as they are a physical diagnosis. Remember Chronic Fatigue Syndrome, also known as the Yuppie Flu? Many of my friends who suffered from this illness during the 80s also suffered from a syndrome called "I hate my job, I work too hard, I'm an overachiever, and I have no life" disease. Wasn't the Yuppie Flu after all just a cry for help from a generation of former hippies who descended into a self-fashioned workaholic hell?

Most people with ADD were nursed on *Sesame Street* and weaned on MTV. We live in the ADD age. Everything is expressed in soundbytes and sightbytes. We are overwhelmed with a montage and barrage of fast-cuts, shaky cameras, and disjointed ideas tied together with snappy slogans and short bursts of music. Because of television and other media, we can't pay attention to a story that's more than half an hour long, let alone read a book that could take days, or even weeks to complete. The advertising industry, with all its psychological tests, demographics, and subliminal messages, has played a major role in nurturing the ADD generation. Television commercials, with their hit-and-run approach, are among the prime culprits. So is pop music, the three-minute addiction, along with its visual counterpart, the music video. Then of course, there is the infernal TV remote control, which once seemed preposterous in its utter nonlinearity, but now seems like nothing more than a mild warm-up for the ultimate channel surfing of the World Wide Web. If the remote control isn't a power tool for the short-of-attention, I don't know what is.

 REMOTE CONTROL GROUP (p. 410)

Today, children diagnosed with ADD live in a world of high-energy media, violent cartoons, and combat- and race-oriented video games. The classic technique of video games, of course, is to employ high-intensity adrenal stimulation to draw the player in, maintain his interest, and keep the quarters flowing. For the ADD-type mind, it is exactly such intense stimulation that allows a normally distracted individual to actually concentrate for a long period of time, sometimes hours on end, longer than he or she would ordinarily be able to concentrate on anything. Although I have no clinical evidence to support this, I can't help but wonder if this is a way of mimicking the effect of the medications that are given to ADD and hyperactivity patients, generally consisting of a stimulant, such as Ritalin. The principle is that patients may actually be craving stimulation and that is why they are so easily distracted. If one gives them a stimulant, they can concentrate and do not need to look to the external environment for stimulation.

Nowhere does ADD flourish more than in the interactive media. Not only do they allow you to have a short attention span, they also allow you to redirect your attention as your interests change. But I think the truth of the matter is not that interactive multimedia is designed for an ADD user so much as…it is a symptom of ADD in the designers. In fact, if you were to go around and administer tests to everyone in the interactive industry, I would be willing to wager that at least 80 percent of us suffer from this so-called disorder. I myself have never been diagnosed, but based on symptoms, I could easily be a candidate for ADD Poster Girl. Indeed, I've built an entire career out of my inability to make up my mind, to do one thing at a time, and to think in a straight line (you can easily imagine the challenge for me in writing a book)!

> I would also like to further indulge, for a moment, my obsession with semantics by drawing your attention to the word *disorder*. This would seem to suggest that ADD is the sign of a disorderly mind, thus the concept of an attention *disorder* is apt indeed.

What if ADD isn't a disorder at all, but an evolutionary adaptation to the culture? What if the ability to deal with high levels of stimulation and fast-paced, nonlinear content is actually providing these children with a way to cope with the next level of information explosion? Most ADD and hyperactive kids are diagnosed initially based on their behavior in the classroom. Most show symptoms of acute boredom and in some cases a tendency toward disruption. But think about it. Imagine yourself in a traditional classroom. Think of the bright and imaginative child who has access to the Internet, then think about that same child sitting at a little desk/chair gizmo watching a teacher who has never even *heard* of the Internet, writing on a chalkboard about something that happened 200 years ago from a history book that was written in the 1960s. Wouldn't you be bored too?

Today's traditional classroom is a breeding ground for ADD and numerous other so-called deviant behavior patterns. In fact, it's a surprise that *all children* don't show signs of ADD. The fact is that the classroom has, in many respects, become obsolete. The criteria by which children are educated today has so little to do with the real world that it is almost comical. A typical public school classroom today looks medieval compared to the bedroom of a kid who's "wired." Even kids who aren't wired have video games and access to TV shows and information much broader, and in some cases richer, than what the classroom format has to offer. It used to be that the classroom was a child's primary source for learning content (or, if she was lucky, the second, if she had parents who were very active in her learning). Today, the classroom provides the least interesting, the least current, and therefore, in some ways, the least accurate information. But worse yet, it encourages and indeed mandates a behavior, a culture, an entire mode of being, which, if followed, would lead most children to certain failure in the world. In reality, people are not re-warded for sitting still, memorizing, testing well, or conforming to social inhibitions. This vestige of the industrial age works well if you want to train clerks or blue-collar workers, but if you want to encourage entrepreneurship and creativity, problem-solving, and high-level skills required in the informa-tion age, this method doesn't cut it. If you then step back and look at the labor market, you will see why we are in big trouble. The school system trains students to be passive and unimaginative, but the high-tech market is de-manding highly educated, highly skilled, and in many cases, highly creative people. This is why we are seeing a huge wave of recruitment for high-tech workers from countries such as Japan and India where education and ambi-tion are a valued part of the culture at-large.

A look at the larger picture also fuels the argument that ADD is perhaps a future level of evolution rather than a dysfunction. Look at trends in science. Current theoretical physics is largely focused around Chaos Theory and the study of complexity. Our world is becoming increasingly complex as our media multiply and diversify, expand and contract, narrowcast and interact. The skills and qualities needed to both live in and be a productive part of this culture are precisely the symptoms connected with this syndrome of thought "disorder."

APPROPRIATION AND THE POST-MODERN ETHIC

Postmodernism is one of those bizarre oxymorons so commonly thrown around these days. Kind of like "new media."

I want to qualify before I get into this that I am by no means a highbrow. When my well-read academic friends get into discussions about post-modernism, I, frankly, am easily lost. I am looking at it purely as a student of pop culture and in a very narrow context of design and media.

I remember when the term first came into popular use in the early 80s, and I first encountered it with respect to post-modern architecture. I always found the term to be a little slippery because it applied to so many disparate and unre-lated things, which makes it difficult to identify postmodernism as a "move-ment." The futurists. Now there was a movement! But postmodernism seems more like an attitude than a movement, and it seems like an attitude that is more against than it is for. At that time, it was used to describe everything from the Philip Johnson Chippendale AT&T skyscraper in New York to Frank Ghery's de-constructivist/reconstructivist treehouses in Los Angeles.

Go To Art is a Verb (p. 29)

The only common factor I could see was the fact that all work falling under this category seemed to be influenced by something else; in fact, what all these post-modern designs had in common was that they were co-opting, appropriating, and recombining other styles. Postmodernism seems to have arisen from the jaded sensibility that "everything's been done" and therefore, rather than trying to "do" anything new, why not just re-use what already exists in new ways.

Postmodernism can thus be described as an appropriationist/de-constructivist/re-constructivist ethic. Postmodernism, as its name implies, is less about creating something new than it is about interacting with and reassembling the existing vernacular within a given discipline. Whether it be architecture or music, design or film, postmodernism looks at all available material as a kit of parts with which to create *assemblages*. It is essentially a form of collage, drawing from eclectic sources to say something new through a strategic de- and re-construction of things old.

Some would say that this post-modern aesthetic of appropriation is just a stylish and cynical way of condoning plagiarism combined with a pretentious excuse for lack of originality. But it is naive to say that postmodernism has the market cornered on appropriation. Throughout history, movements have developed based on appropriation. In architecture, there have been recurring periods of appropriation, such as neoclassicism, to name only one. The borrowing of styles and aesthetics from other movements has been commonplace in every arena from classical art to pop music, from film to fashion, well before the advent of the digital age.

So even appropriation itself is nothing new. But what's new about it in the digital age is that appropriation has become more refined, more accurate. To use a classically digital metaphor, appropriation has achieved a higher level of resolution. We can now appropriate through sampling, through scanning, through digitizing. We can copy and distort to such an extent that it is quickly becoming unnecessary to create anything original at all.

To some, this is an abominable state of affairs, leading to the inevitable demoralization of our culture, a culture in which nothing is new, and everything is merely a rehash of something else. But appropriation can also be a very creative process. The post-modern aesthetic is, to a certain extent, a populist aesthetic. And the ability to appropriate and re-use content also has the effect of democratizing media. If done creatively, the outcome can actually be quite compelling, giving rise to entirely new genres.

The Hip-Hop movement is a great example of this. The idea behind Hip-Hop is to take samples of pre-recorded sound, originally played and tampered with directly on turntables, but eventually digitized and recombined, and weave it into new sounds. A drum track from a James Brown album; a baseline from a George Clinton album; guitar riff from Jimi Hendrix (who incidentally is alleged to have stolen all his material from jazz saxophone great John Coltrane). If one accepts that all things have been done by someone sometime, then all one really needs to be a composer is the world's biggest album collection and a really good digital studio—thus the creation of new music becomes more a process of collage than composition. If you want to get semantic about it, to compose is "to form by putting together." There is essentially no difference between creating something original or reassembling pre-existing elements. Hip-Hop is also a true grassroots, populist movement. And its fascination lies in the combining of the oldest and most low-tech form of communication—human speech (the only form that doesn't require any tools)—with the ultimate in high-tech appropriation technology. In addition, you have the element of rhythm, specifically, a primal dance beat deliberately formulated to elicit body movement. Thus, Hip-Hop draws together the most ancient and most modern to create an entirely new genre which is at once unique and highly derivative. In this case, appropriation has given life to something wholly original, something with a strong identity of its own, even though its raw materials are for all intents and purposes stolen from pre-existing materials.

To those who poo-poo post-modern appropriation, I find their ethical self-righteousness short-sighted at best and ignorant at worst. Folk and pop music have had a long and fertile tradition of friendly plagiarism. The blues classic "Sweet Home Chicago" was based on an earlier folk blues tune called "Sweet Home Kokomo." Leadbelly's "Easy Rider" and Ma Rainey's "CC Rider" have almost identical lyrics and similar melodies. In fact, among blues players, it was quite common to borrow the melodies of others and rework them with new or even merely revised lyrics. These songs were in turn co-opted by both black and white rock musicians. Often it was the very familiarity of the tune that added to its popular appeal; people like things that they can recognize, so the act of appropriating or co-opting draws material from a familiar pool of traditions, allowing for greater audience accessibility.

This process of borrowing and rewriting familiar songs is the backbone of the folk tradition, and in this way, Hip-Hop can be looked at in many respects as contemporary folk music. Hip-Hop artists regularly appropriate not only from each other, but from every other available source. Their constant references back to pop culture icons serve up an ongoing commentary on our media-rich (or poor, depending on how you look at it) culture. A great example of postmodernism in Hip-Hop is the group Das EFX, whose machine-gun lyrics are rife with metaphors and double-entendres derived from TV shows and commercials. Their lyrics are as much a collage of appropriated content as their music.

This montage, this reassemblage of words and music creates a beautifully ironic and disturbing poetry of urban malaise and social alienation.

Another often overlooked aspect of Hip-Hop is that in this high-tech arena, African Americans have had the lead over European Americans for years. It's commonly held that white people are somehow inherently technically more savvy than black people, in part because they have the privilege of easier access to computers. If you read the digerati press, for the most part, the Hip-Hop movement has never really been considered part of the digital subculture, but indeed it certainly is. Furthermore, its innovative spirit was at the bending end of digital appropriation well before it reached critical mass on the so-called "mainstream." In fact, Hip-Hop artists were making digital music before they had computers—originally pulling riffs and sections from various records by hand using old-fashioned vinyl turntables. After digital remixing systems became available, Hip-Hop artists found themselves spinning hard drives instead of vinyl, although the vinyl aesthetic can still be heard in many albums, where a skipped or scratchy record sample can often be detected. Hip-Hop music is a clear example of how technology can empower and give voice to different groups and individuals, and how different sensibilities can lever-age that empowerment in different ways.

Prior to Hip-Hop, there were some early pop music innovators, most notably Brian Eno and Robert Fripp, who did early work with sampled sounds. Eno in particular is probably one of the most underrated influences on popular music today. As a member of Roxy Music, he developed rich, thick sounds through heavy bass and processing. He went on to produce Talking Heads, U2, and Peter Gabriel, bringing to those three artists a richly textured sound that used sampling, looping, and processing to influence a new genre of digitally enhanced music. Fripp, who worked with Eno at various points, did some early work with looping guitar and bass riffs, some of which was quite funky and even Hip-Hopesque. Eno is also known for creating ambient music, and much of the electronic music we hear today, including much of what we are now hearing out of the Rave movement is, if not inspired, directly lifted from Fripp and Eno. Brian Eno trademark riffs have also sneaked into our consciousness in a variety of unlikely places, including commercial jingles, TV show intros, and the opening chord that is heard on all Macintosh computers at start-up.

In terms of pop icons, I like to think of Madonna as the Appropriation Poster Girl. When she first started out in the early 80s, there were these things run-ning around New York City who were affectionately known as "Madonna Wannabees" (a group of them together was referred to as being from "Camp Madonna Wannabee"). This was in her pre-blonde days, when Madonna's ambitions were strictly brunette. Her characteristic attire, a kind of punk lingerie look with brasiers and a lot of lace and torn stockings was quite popular. Perhaps because so many people were appropriating her aesthetic, she then got the bright idea that she would build an entire career out of appropriating everyone else's. So soon, instead of wanting to be Madonna, she was wanting to be everyone but Madonna. She became a female impersonator. She was Marilyn, Marlene, pin-up icon Betty Page, Peggy Lee, and Evita. In each case, she takes on a persona and modifies it to her own specifications. An interesting problem might arise, however, when people start appropriating other people's appropriations. What do you call a Madonna Wannabee that dresses like the Madonna version of Evita?

Madonna's one-woman appropriationist movement also hearkens back to another infamous pop culture icon, Andy Warhol. If, as Warhol postulated, everyone in the future will be famous for 15 minutes, then Madonna's rehash would make it possible for someone to be famous twice; once as themselves, and once as the alter (or in Madonna's case, altar) ego for somebody else. Perhaps Madonna's Marilyn is a flesh-and-blood tribute to Warhol's? I wonder when she's going to do the Campbell's soup girl?

Many oppose appropriationism on the grounds that it is unoriginal, that the only kind of artistic integrity is derived from purely original works. But as I pointed out earlier, purely original is a relative, not an absolute term. Nothing is purely original. Furthermore, there is nothing to suggest that original works are of an inherently better quality than those that are derivative. There are certainly plenty of original works that are not particularly appealing, as well as derivative works that are considered classics in their own right.

I maintain that appropriation is an art form in itself. The selection and use of appropriated materials, like that of a fine collage artist, requires a certain amount of skill and savvy that requires as much intelligence, and in some cases more, as creating original sounds and images. Anyone who has watched a great Hip-Hop producer at the board knows that he is playing an instrument—it just happens that the sounds it makes are sampled. But to be able to find those sounds and know how to put them together is a truly awesome talent that should not be overlooked or relegated to mere "plagiarism." In this case, we must speak of "the art of plagiarism," because at the level of digital convergence, plagiarism has become an art from in and of itself.

Then of course, there is the matter of the law. How many times have you sat blithely by as the FBI copyright infringement warning shimmered by on that video tape you were recording for a friend? There is a great irony in the act of duplicating a copyright notice! Although there are certainly laws against it, they are often vague and difficult to pin down. It is, for example, legal to steal if you are stealing to satirize or make social commentary or provide news or historical insight. In other words, you could quote me provided you are making fun of me in the process. But this is a fine line that is usually drawn by a judge, and often one who doesn't even have a scanner, so what does he know. The increase in concern about copyright infringement is somewhat absurd in the digital age. Nowadays, most photocopy stores will not Xerox anything that has a copyright notice on it. I once went into a Kinko's to Xerox a copy of the proposal for this book. The clerk said he could not photocopy it because it was copyrighted. I said, "I know. I own the copyright. I hereby grant you permission to Xerox this." But at the same Kinko's, I can rent a scanner and copy as many copyrighted documents as I want. I can get on the web and download any web page I want. I can easily bootleg software.

The fact that digital technology makes plagiarism easier is a testimony to technology's intense power. The hacker ethic of shareware, or "all information for all people," is impossible to avoid because digital technology makes all information accessible. Therefore, even in the face of the federal government and the FBI, in the digital age, everything is shareware. With ease of digital replication, there is no way to enforce copyright infringement to the full extent of the law. At the same time, the subversive underground movements that fuel both the hacker community and the Hip-Hop community pride themselves in their ability to outsmart and override the law. And implicit in this is a funda-mental belief that information in general, and content in particular, are really ultimately not proprietary…but that they are the property of all.

STEAL THIS DATA: SHAREWARE AND THE HACKER ETHIC (p. 454)

INTERACTIVITY IS SUBVERSIVE (p. 244)

THE DIGISPHERE (p. 168)

ARCHITECTURE AS A NARRATIVE ART

When asked the question, "what do architects design?" most people would respond "buildings." But this is only partially true. In fact, to my mind, designing buildings is the least of what architects do. Or rather, it is the by-product of what they do. What architects actually design, whether wittingly or not, are experiences. How many times have you entered an environment so rich, so full of ambiance, texture, aroma, and character that it transported you to another place and time? Likewise, how many times have you found yourself wandering down endless neutral, unmarked corridors looking desper-ately for a way out?

What is a building? It is a place where experiences occur. In fact, a building can be viewed as a medium, and those experiences as its content. Like interactive designers, architects design nonlinear experiences with variable paths or outcomes. Whether they know it or not, all architects are also creating stories, and the extent to which a building is successful might ultimately be more a factor of the narrative content of the building than its actual architecture. Or, perhaps in reality they are the same thing. For architecture is really just an analog algorithm for a spatial experience.

My father, Peter Pearce, is an architectural designer and creator of giant space frame structures. A student of Buckminster Fuller and the last of the Internationalists at Chicago University's International Institute of Technology (IIT), he was trained in the 50s by a school of thought in which "form follows function" was the prevalent philosophy…but how do you define function? In my father's structuralist world, form is largely characterized by physical properties— materials, structural performance, environmental issues, ergonomic design— and, as an industrial designer, production methodologies. In my interactive world, function equals use, and use is defined by experience. This goes for real architecture, virtual architecture, and multimedia design in general.

It was my first interactive mentor, Edwin Schlossberg, who initially taught me that architecture is a narrative art. During my seven years at Edwin Schlossberg Incorporated, I was trained in the art of defining functional experiences. Each environment we designed began not with a floor plan, but with a script, an imaginary walkthrough that envisioned the entire space as an individual person would experience it over time. We would all get together and brainstorm, creating both space and story at the same time, often in a random and haphazard fashion to allow for the maximum flow of creativity. My job was to then write these narrative descriptions, a kind of "spaceplay," describing variable sequences of events and qualities of the experiences that visitors might have, in both temporal and physical terms. Note that these were real environments—museum exhibits, theme park attractions, retail malls and stores—in which the interactive components were as often analog as they were digital. Then I would work with the in-house designers or architects who would bring form and shape to these walkthroughs. The architect I worked with most was Michael Joyce, or Michael-Angelo, as I liked to call him. His drawing style also reflected this narrative approach. His sketches were more like illustrations for a story than architectural drawings because they emphasized the people and what they were doing.

This is in sharp contrast to how most architecture is depicted. It is a convention in architectural drawing and photography to leave the people out. If you scan the pages of any architecture or interior design magazine, you will notice big, beautifully lit expanses of empty space. Even houses and restaurants, which you would expect to buzz with human activity, are rarely shown in use. But if you enter a real building, unless you are an architect or a critic, you are not looking for the volume of the space, or the detail of the trim, but the experience of being there. It is when the people enter and begin to make use of the space that it really comes alive.

To illustrate this point, I want to tell the following story. I was hired to do some consulting on a major themed attraction project. I was invited to this huge meeting in a tiny room where the architect was to present the preliminary building concept. These were great architects, from a firm I really liked and worked with on several occasions. But to my surprise, the only visual collateral they brought to the meeting were floor plans of the proposed attraction. It was a good plan, but I was hoping to see something more indicative of the visitor experience. I lightly pointed out that while this was a wonderful depiction of what the building looked like to God, I was curious as to what it might look like to everyone else. I suggested perhaps to try doing some renderings.

Everyone laughed, but the point was well taken. Then, I walked the group through the experience of the plan, trying to impress on them that everything in a floor plan tells a story. The entrance, for example: Most public buildings today have two entrances—the main, grand, street entrance, which in most car-dominated cities no one ever uses; and the parking lot entrance, which generally feels like a delivery dock, and is almost always people's first impression on entering the building. Think of how many dark and smelly alleyways you have had to go through from a parking lot to enter a mall or other building complex through a back door, when you might have entered through a perfectly beautiful, but virtually inaccessible, front entrance.

When I was brought on to this project, I was told it was a "theme park in search of a theme." So in the subsequent weeks, I worked with the client and the architect to formulate a narrative walkthrough of the space that told a very clear story about the visitor experience. The architects then brought their own ideas to the table, ultimately looking at the project more as a problem of urban planning than architecture. This translated into beautiful renderings, followed by a floor plan that was much more dynamic and ultimately facilitated a better visitor experience. The standard alternative—design-by-plan with the omniscient, all-seeing eye of God—generally results in something that looks best when seen from a helicopter with an infrared camera.

Which brings us to another matter. I believe that architects, like writers, secretly long to be God, which is why they design from a "God's-eye view." We erroneously make floor plans as a way to organize space, not as a way to organize time. A three-dimensional space is, after all, whether real or virtual, ultimately a temporal experience. Which is why the fourth dimension is perhaps the most important factor in both architecture and virtual reality.

When looked at in this light, we can then begin to see that architecture is, in fact, a medium, and start to recognize the very deep connection between typically temporal media, such as film and television, and spatial media, such as physical or virtual space. I always like to say that designing a virtual space is exactly like designing a real space, except you don't need bathrooms. In both cases, the goal is to create an experience.

 NARRATIVE ENVIRONMENTS: VIRTUAL REALITY AS A STORYTELLING MEDIUM (p. 329)

Indeed, when designing a multimedia application, whether it is a virtual space or an interactive story, the first and foremost concern is with experience. Although both cases start with the experience, you must always make a plan in the end. The architect, like the multimedia designer, must have an overview; must be able to, in a God-like fashion, see all conceivable experiences at once to create the "space" in which these experiences are to occur. I create a narrative script designing a space—which turns I will make, which locations I will visit, and in which order. What characterizes such a narrative is that it provides a portrait of both space and time. To actually "build" such a space, either a physical space or a "mediaspace" as it were, I have to be able to look at the entire thing at once, with the element of time (a variable) removed. In this way, and only in this way, can I begin to see and organize the relationships between all the paths that the visitor or user is offered.

 GOD PLAYS DICE WITH THE UNIVERSE (p. 215)

I think we can and should think about physical space and media space in much the same way. When I am working on the design of a physical space, I like to think of it as a problem of interface design. The entrance to a plaza in a theme park can be seen as the "main menu," where you are offered your first level of options. When I try to imagine moving through a virtual space, I see it as a real space. And when I imagine moving through a media experience, I see that as a space also. In all three cases, I have to be aware of such things as vistas (what I can see from where), dead ends, log jams, endless, linear corridors that lead nowhere and provide no way out. I have to be aware of how long you will move down a path before you need the opportunity for a change of scenery or scene, and how many options are appropriate to offer at that juncture. I have to provide you with a means of finding your way back to your entry point, and an easy path to the exit. All these things, far from metaphorical, are literal elements that must be present in the experience of both architecture and interactive media. This is why architects frequently make excellent multimedia designers, and why the study of architecture is a natural benefit to anyone interested in designing multimedia.

ART IS A VERB

The word "art" is not only a noun, but it is also a verb, as in "Wherefore art thou?" Up until the 20th century, "Western" art, however, was entirely object-oriented. Art was considered a thing, a thing of value, a work of art, material and tangible, collectible, and ultimately valuable, assuming it was deemed so by whomever makes those kinds of assessments. Almost always, the value of a work of art as a "thing" is a direct product of the perceived value of the artist, the person who produced it. A Michelangelo is a Michelangelo. When art became more expressive in the 20th century, this value system continued to flourish, and was in some ways even exacerbated because issues of taste came into play as well. Thus great art is more often than not defined by *who* created it. A Picasso painting is of value precisely because it was painted by Picasso, and for no other reason.

A movement arose in the early 20th century that questioned, and indeed undermined, the entire notion of authorship, as well as the concept of art-as-object. Under this new school of thought, art could be seen as intangible. Marcel Duchamp, the "Dada of Dada" and one of the founding fathers of futurism (which is now, ironically, a thing of the past) and surrealism, turned the whole ego-based, object-oriented art culture, and indeed the very idea of authorship upside down and inside out by suggesting that art was not so much a thing as a process, and that the viewer or audience was as much a part of that process as the artist.

While Duchamp was still a "painter" in the traditional sense, he created the now infamous *Nude Descending a Staircase*, which was described by one critic as looking like "an explosion in a matchstick factory" (see figure A.5). I have no doubt that Duchamp's response to this must have been something like "that too." This echoes the classic Picasso response to the comment that his portrait of Gertrude Stein looked nothing like her, to which he responded "It will."

Duchamp's nude is an attempt to create 3D animation on a 2D canvas, just as Picasso's Cubist period is an exploration in 3D modeling, an attempt to show all views of something at once. With *Nude*, Duchamp attempted not only to show all angles, but all points in time in a sequence. During the same time period, Sergei Eisenstein was inventing the art of filmmaking, distorting time and space through editing. Paralleling Eisentein's development in film, in the world of physics, Albert Einstein was crafting his theories about relativity. These innovations upended not only notions of time and space, but also of reality itself—the work of all these men called into question the belief that it was possible to have an objective reality; it all revolved around the notion of subjective reality, whether it be that of a molecule or a man. Perhaps Duchamp's nude was descending Eisenstein's Odessa Steps into Einstein's Space-Time Continuum.

Figure A.5

Marcel Duchamp's *Nude Descending a Staircase* was an attempt at representing both space and time on a 2D surface

PICASSO: THE FATHER OF 3D GRAPHICS (p. 370)

EINSTEIN, EISENSTEIN, AND THE SPACE-TIME CONTINUUM (p. 186)

Marcel Duchamp was arguably one of the greatest creative minds of the 20th century, and certainly one of the most influential. He is to art what Jimi Hendrix is to the guitar. Each man's repertoire included a taste of virtually everything that was to follow it.

Like Hendrix, Duchamp was on an accelerated track. After he mastered the more traditional forms of contemporary painting (and it ought to be noted that he was both a figurative and an impressionist painter before he became a futurist), he moved on to essentially undermine the entire structure of art as we know it, a blow from which the art world has, thankfully, never fully recovered.

Duchamp began his mission in artistic insubordination with the Readymade. The Readymade was really the first form of conceptual art. It involved taking a found, generally prefabricated (and therefore duplicable) object, renaming it (or not, depending on one's mood), and sticking it in a museum as an *objet d'art.* By making the commonplace precious and the precious mundane, Duchamp pointed out the absurdity of object worship, but even more so, the absurdity of authorship. Duchamp could only make a Readymade, because he was already the guy who painted *Nude Descending a Staircase.* This self-conscious statement about fame is as pertinent today as it was 70 years ago, and Duchamp's relationship with fame and celebrity was light years ahead of Andy Warhol's in many respects.

Duchamp was also in many respects the original post-modern appropriationist. Readymades are really the first attempt at "scanning," except Duchamp did his in analog form, by taking actual objects and putting them in galleries and museums. Duchamp did ultimately "scan his own work" in the self-reflective commentary "The Box in a Valise," a series of "kits" that contained replicas of his own work. Thus he was not only the first appropriationist, but the first artist to appropriate himself.

Appropriation and the Post-Modern Ethic (p. 20)

Duchamp and his Dada cohorts, most notably Man Ray, also originated the idea of "art as a verb," which leads us right to the heart and soul of interactivity. In my slide lecture "Dadabase: A History of Interactivity in Art," I go into depth on Marcel Duchamp's contribution to the idea of interactive art and interactivity in general. One of his most famous pieces, *The Bicycle Wheel,* a bicycle wheel mounted to a wooden stool, was probably the first "hands-on" art object (see figure A.6). It is indeed ironic that this interactive sculpture is always displayed with a sign reading "Do Not Touch."

Whether you can touch it or not, the very nature of a Readymade is that it invites audience participation, not only intellectually, but also quite literally in the physical sense. My favorite of Duchamp's Readymades has to be *The Fountain,* a beautiful porcelain urinal inscribed with the moniker "Le Fontaine" and displayed in a museum (see figure A.7). The invitation to interact is obvious and irreverently amusing. And it certainly makes a statement about the art world in its elegant simplicity. (If he were alive today, Duchamp would probably have to kiss that NEA grant good-bye.)

Figure A.6

Duchamp's *The Bicycle Wheel*, an early example of interactive art

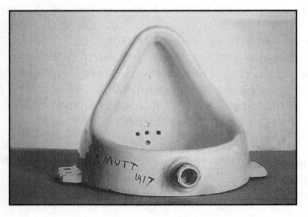

Figure A.7

Duchamp's irreverant *Le Fontaine* invites a different kind of audience participation

Later, Duchamp explored more complex forms of participation—his see-through paintings, for example. The first of these was *The Bride Stripped Bare by her Bachelors*, even more commonly known as *The Large Glass* (see figure A.8). This huge glass piece was meant to be suspended in the middle of the gallery space. The idea was that you could look through the painting and that the other people in the environment are part of the art experience. On the way to the gallery for its first showing, *The Large Glass* was broken, resulting in a wonderful spider-web pattern on its surface. Duchamp, far from devastated, loved the effect and hung the piece anyway, actually preferring the damaged version to his original.

Figure A.8

The viewer becomes the viewed as seen through Duchamp's *The Large Glass*

Another Duchamp glass, *To Be Looked at from the Other Side*, is an early example of art that came with instructions. Duchamp's good buddy photographer/sculptor Man Ray (who is the Hendrix of photography) produced *Object to be Destroyed*, the infernal metronome with a photograph of a gazing eye paper-clipped to it. As I always point out, if this thing was clicking away in my house, I'd want to destroy it too. Again, unfortunately and ironically, although I have seen this piece several times, it is never displayed as intended…turned on, swaying back and forth, and clicking relentlessly in time, which one could conceivably adjust to taste. I once attended a retrospective of Man Ray's work and thought that he and Duchamp would have been amused by the subtle pun on a large sign at the entrance, which read "Do Not Take Photographs." I envision Abbie Hoffman placing a sign there that said instead "Steal This Art."

Duchamp also created a sculpture of a woman's solitary breast entitled *Please Touch*, which I always find an amusingly irreverent comment on the art world's obsession with the female form. *Please Touch* is the ultimate nude, as far as I'm concerned, making a statement about both the objectification and the disembodiment of the female body in art. Thus, it would also appear that this versatile genius invented the first artificial breast.

Interestingly, Duchamp was also an ardent chess fanatic. He saw the playing of the game as an art, eventually retiring to devote the remainder of his life to its practice. His friend Man Ray went so far as to earn his living at one point by crafting finely designed modern chess sets. Many of the Dada and futurist art events and happenings were, if not actual games, quite game-like in their form. The popular surrealist art game "Exquisite Corpse," for example, is a collaborative drawing exercise in which artists take turns drawing sections of a figure on a folded back piece of paper without being able to see the previously drawn section. There is little doubt that Duchamp, Man, and their futurist, surrealist, and Dadaist cohorts saw both life and art as a game, all of which leads back to the verb concept—that art is an action, that it is the experience of art that makes the art, not the object of art itself. This was the essential message that Duchamp was trying to get across.

Even after he allegedly retired, he produced *The Box in the Valise* series, as well as a description of a mysterious installation called *The Door of Given*. Discovered and implemented after his death, there has been some question as to whether it was meant to be built, or merely intended to exist as a score.

 ### THE RULES OF THE GAME (p. 420)

Duchamp both rebelled against and exploited the star system that began to evolve with the Impressionists, when art became an expression of the artist rather than a depiction of an object, person, or event. Once the artist's individual personality came into play, and there was a strong stylistic difference between artists' work, the art world began to adopt a cult of personality that can also be seen in many other art forms and media of the time. For it was during this same time period that you began to see movie stars and pop music idols emerge through the mass dissemination of film, records, and radio.

The idea that some people are artists and others are not, the notion of artistic expertise, that one person's emotions and impressions are more valuable than another's, and that the product of those impressions should be deified, was the very doctrine that Duchamp sought to undermine. It is this sensibility that is at the heart and soul of the interactive revolution. Duchamp sought to democratize art, to take the elitism and egotism out of it and bring it more down to earth. In some ways, he can really be viewed as the grandfather of the interactive revolution.

 ### INTERACTIVITY IS SUBVERSIVE (p. 244)

The Fluxus movement, which was the offspring of Dada, continued to push Duchamp's notion of art even further. The Flux movement, which occurred primarily in the 50s and into the 60s, took the concept of Readymades and interactive art to the next level...out of the museum and into the hands of the people. All Flux art was hands-on and interactive. Much of the work of Fluxus artists came in the form of games, boxes, and packages called "Flux Kits." Flux Kits were essentially collections of Readymades, 3D collages of real objects roughly grouped around a central theme or concept. A number of these kits were games, and a handful of them were actually chess games made out of Readymades, no doubt in tribute to Duchamp's other obsession. Again, it was the appropriationist ethic, the construction, deconstruction, and reconstruction of familiar forms to create new insights and revelations about the commonplace.

But the Fluxists, rather than taking the monotheistic approach of Duchamp (the urinal), created collections of Readymades with some interpretive layer. These kits or boxes were meant to be played with and experienced by the user. They were never meant to go in a museum. And the idea was that anyone could create one, and that the act of selecting and combining these objects was inherently creative. Flux Kits consisted of a collection of themed objects such as *Flux Light Kit*, a box of light bulbs and a light box, or Claes Oldenberg's *False Food*, a partitioned box full of plastic food. My personal favorite, *Orifice Flux Plugs*, included things such as corks, Q-tips, and plastic fingers. Other Readymade-type objects included Yoko Ono's *Air Dispenser*, a bubble gum machine that dispensed empty gelatin capsules for a penny each.

The second genre common to the Fluxus movement was the "score," which was based on the idea that you could actually skip the entire implementation of an art project by merely writing instructions on what to do and letting the viewer do the rest. The philosophy was to put the responsibility onto the audience to create their own artworks. Some scores were esoteric and unimplementable, or as much poetic as they were practical. George Brecht's *Air Conditioning*, is a score that I always display just before the break in my Dadabase lecture (it simply says "Move through the place"). If this isn't interactive art at its best, I don't know what is.

John Cage, who is affiliated with the Flux movement, created musical scores that frequently translated into performances. Often game-like in their simple structure, these scores invited participation and created a framework for spontaneous audio activity.

Yoko Ono, considered a Fluxus as well as a conceptual and performance artist, is a master of scores. Her book *Grapefruit* is a series of descriptions of art projects you can do at home, projects such as "Record the sound of falling snow." "Use the tape to wrap your Christmas gifts." Another good example is "Painting to Shake Hands," in which you are instructed to cut a hole in a canvas and shake hands with your viewers through it.

It is unfortunate that Yoko Ono is so often maligned for allegedly riding the coattails of her husband John Lennon in the music world; however, Ono was already a well-established artist when she met John and it can be just as easily said that he rode her coattails in the art world.

Ono's contributions to interactive art have been considerable. The handshake painting was ultimately implemented, along with other scores from *Grapefruit*. One of her most disturbing and controversial performances, *Cut Piece*, involved inviting the audience to cut off pieces of her clothing with scissors as she sat still and passive on stage in her best business suit.

Scores were the ultimate self-propagated ego buster for artists. The idea was that you just come up with the art action, and then let the viewers create the art themselves. Scores can be looked at in three ways:

- They are themselves works of art
- The viewer might choose to implement them
- The artist him or herself might choose to implement them

Each of these is an entirely different kind of experience. One of the essential issues addressed by scores is whether it is enough to imagine or think something. The score pushes the envelope of "Virtual Art." If I stand here and imagine the tape of the falling snow, is that enough? Taking the adage, "I think therefore I am" to a logical extreme, art as verb becomes art as thought. In this context, beauty is truly in the mind of the beholder.

The Fluxus movement was also characterized by a spirit of collaboration and mutual appropriation. Fluxus artists worked together, a fairly new notion introduced by the Dada movement, borrowing from and referencing each other freely and openly. Flux artists constantly make reference to each other's work, to the point where the very issue of authorship becomes blurry. This makes the Flux movement unique among art movements. It is one of the few, if not *the only* art movement, in which the individual artist was absorbed into the larger whole in such a way that Flux is today looked at in terms of the group rather than the individual artists within it, and in many cases their work is interchangeable and indistinguishable.

In the aspect of undermining the myth of artist, the Fluxists succeeded where Duchamp had failed. In spite of his irreverence, Duchamp was never entirely able to escape the status quo and demystify himself as an artist. In fact, it was the very genius of his anti-art that ultimately enslaved him in history to the status of "artist," something he could never shake, even after he allegedly "retired" from art to play chess. The Fluxists, on the other hand, managed to effectively undermine the myth of auteurship and maintain a certain air of anonymity, primarily through collaboration and mutual appropriation. There were over a hundred Fluxus artists. They worked together, putting on events, parties, even opening up shops from which to sell their kits and scores. The Flux ethic, under the influence of artists George Maciunas, the father of Fluxus, was a collaborative one. The very name Flux says it all: The movement was seen as a flow of changing and dynamic experiences; art was seen as temporal with the artists serving as a medium for experience. Fluxus was also an incredibly prolific movement, and included a number of contemporary artists who crossed over into other areas. As mentioned earlier, Yoko Ono, John Cage, Nam June Paik, and Claes Oldenberg all participated in the Fluxus movement. Even Yoko Ono's husband, John Lennon, contributed to the body of Fluxus work. One of his Readymades consisted of a box of paints labeled "For George Maciunas, Who Cannot See These Colors." Maciunas, as it turned out, was color blind.

The Fluxus did many group pieces and installations. One, the *Flux Labyrinth*, was a kind of sensory maze/obstacle course with a series of rooms, each created by a different artist. Another great game-like piece was Maciunas' *Multicycle*, a giant multiple-wheel, multiple-seat contraption that the Fluxists used to ride around town together for fun. The Flux movement was, in some ways, the closest thing we've ever had to communism in art. It is a tribute to Maciunas himself that, unlike Duchamp, he was able to maintain a relatively low profile. One of my favorite Maciunas pieces is the faceted mirror that turns the viewer into his or her own cubist self-portrait. This is essential Maciunas. Mirrors come into play in several Fluxus pieces, such as Yoko Ono's *Box of Smile*, a cookie tin with a mirror in the bottom. When you opened it, the smile you saw was your own.

Quite literally, this was art that reflected back on the viewer. The metaphor of art as a mirror could not be more apt, and within the practice of interactivity, it may be the best metaphor of all. Because what you really want to do as an interactive artist or creator of interactive experiences is give your viewers a way to look back at themselves in the process of creating their own experience.

The ultimate message of Flux art is that one ought to just make the art oneself, which is the next logical step in the evolution of art—the elimination of the artist entirely in favor of a view that sees all people as artists.

It is really a call to return to the essence of McLuhan's *Global Village,* to a so-called "primitive" period of pre-specialization when everyone was considered an artist. In such a world, we would not have this peculiar dichotomy between the fine arts and the practical arts. Readymades are things that everyone makes. In so-called uncivilized cultures, every woman is a painter and a potter, every man is an architect.

As digital technology becomes better, cheaper, and easier to use, it has the potential to return us to a new kind of egalitarian environment vis-a-vis the arts, a world in which we can all be "Renaissance men and women." We can all be artist/inventors like Leonardo da Vinci, a man who placed no artificial limits on his talents or endeavors.

Combining this egalitarian environment with the power of collaboration produces a vision for a new order that combines the independent spirit of Duchamp with the collaborative spirit of the Fluxists—a world in which each person can not only flourish as an individual, but can reach beyond himself or herself as part of something larger. The collaborative aesthetic elegantly perfected by the Fluxists is one that allows everyone to bring something to the party.

WHO IS THE AUTHOR? (p. 528)

USER OR PLAYER: THE CHOICE IS YOURS (p. 490)

V-ART (p. 494)

ARTIFICIAL INTELLIGENCE AND THE PROSTHETIC BRAIN

In the 60s, Marvin Minsky and his disciples at MIT began studying the problem of artificial intelligence. Artificial intelligence is, quite simply, the creation of computer programs that think. Computer researchers have, since almost the inception of computers, imagined that a panacea of computer science would be the simulation of the human mind. Much effort has been put into making computers think and learn like humans.

One of the first attempts to simulate human thought was, interestingly, the creation of a computer that could play chess. Since then, this problem has been addressed and redressed many times. This writing falls on the heals of the defeat of Garry Kasparov by "Deep Blue," an improved model of the IBM computer that he beat a year earlier. Whether Kasparov wins or loses is immaterial. The fact is that it has taken dozens of computer whizzes and several generations of processors to build a computer that could beat a human at chess. That and the fact the computer itself is a custom-built supercomputer gives you an idea of just how hard a job it is to get a computer to think, even about something that is essentially mathematical in nature and thus closer to its native capabilities. Consider that entire, photo-realistic VR worlds can now be made on a beefed-up desktop PC and you can begin to get a feel for the scope of this problem.

There are several groups outside the mainstream of AI (Artificial Intelligence) who are working with alternative methods for addressing the AI conundrum, and many of them are having a quite a bit of success. I often find myself fascinated by solutions that are derived from approaching a problem outside the scope of conventional wisdom. I tend to think about things in terms of the question: What problem are you trying to solve? And the most interesting work to me is that which reframes the problem by letting go of old assumptions and trying to address the core issues. The following two paragraphs provide two stunning examples of this.

Patrick H. Winston at MIT was working on the problem of intelligent robots. Up until then, the conventional approach was to try to make a robot that was intelligent and could learn a variety of tasks. For household functions, for example, you would create a kind of "mechanical bride" (to co-opt from McLuhan), who would be able to clean, cook, and so forth. She would also have a learning curve so that as she did various tasks she would learn how to navigate the environment and develop a repertoire of appropriate tasks and activities.

Another researcher took a different approach. He decided to model his robots after insects rather than humans. Insects have most of the information they need to function encoded into their genetic material; they learn a few things, but for the most part, they are born with a hard-coded and very limited functionality. The idea was that instead of creating a mechanical bride who had to learn how to do everything, you would create an army of "bride bugs" (my term) each with its own unique functionality. So instead of having your bride, for example, know that once a week she is supposed to dust, the dust bug would constantly wander around the room collecting dust. That would be its only job and it would not be expected to learn or do anything else. An entirely different bug could then be created to clean dishes. Although this approach differs from task-oriented AI, it addresses the fundamental problem that it is almost impossible to simulate the complexity of the human mind and its ability to absorb, learn, and utilize new information.

With *Improv/Virtual Actors* Ken Perlin and Athomas Goldberg at NYU have developed an interesting approach to artificial intelligence, which in a sense inverts the classic AI paradigm. Rather than trying to make artificial characters that think, they are making characters that *act*. These characters are not designed to actually think or learn or perform any kind of intelligent reasoning. They are merely designed to act is if they are reasoning intelligently, they are designed to *behave*. Adjustments can be made to mood and attitude that affect body language; characters can then recognize the gesture and body language of others and respond accordingly. If one character is aggressive, other characters might become more timid, or more aggressive, based on what kind of moods they are in. Users can interact with *Virtual Actors* in a variety of ways: by controlling their moods, by taking the role of a certain character, or by using MIDI-activated devices to make the characters dance.

After developing a protocol for characters to interact with the user and each other, Goldberg's next task was to develop a system for them to interact with inanimate objects. Instead of actually learning about how to interface with and use objects, which would result in unwieldy databases that each character would have to carry around and search through every time they had to do a task, Goldberg developed a system he calls "The Tail That Wags the Dog." Instead of having the information about how to use an object contained in the character, the instructions for the object's use are embedded within the object itself. So instead of making the character intelligent, Perlin and Goldberg decided to make the *object* intelligent. When a character meets an object, the object sends instructions to it as to what to do. When the character is done, it entirely forgets that it ever even saw, let alone used this object, until the next time it is encountered. To me, this is a much more intelligent way to use computers, which are much better at giving instructions than they are at taking them, let alone understanding them.

There is a great story about a program written by an MIT programmer named Joseph Weizenbaum. In the early 60s, Weizenbaum created a program called ELIZA, which was a digital shrink. This simulated therapist would converse with persons by responding to certain cues with somewhat pat queries such as "Tell me about your mother," or "How do you feel about that?" Even though they knew she was a computer program, students would talk to her as if she were a real therapist, revealing their innermost secrets to a machine. Weizenbaum was shocked and disgusted by this, but I don't find it at all surprising. The people to whom he was showing ELIZA were hardcore tech nerds, individuals who would be unlikely to seek out psychotherapy on their own. Even if they did, they might be at a loss when confronted with the challenge of revealing their innermost feelings to a real person. If people's behavior in Internet chat rooms is any indication, people sometimes find it easier to express themselves within the safety net of a computer buffer. For the hackers at MIT, it is conceivable that the virtual therapist, precisely *because* it was not a real person, would have been easier for them to talk to than an actual psychiatrist. Going one step further, it is also conceivable, although I doubt that Weizenbaum ever took the time to study this, that these individuals might actually have been helped by this artificial therapist. Just as an anonymous phone call to a suicide helpline or a heart-to-heart chat with a total stranger can often help to take the pressure off a troubled soul, perhaps an understanding computer, perfectly safe and unable to judge or gossip, can be an effective means to "get it off your chest." Although we may never know the answer, it would be interesting to conduct an experiment to see whether this hypothesis holds water. If it does, the potential for something like this could be enormous. I wonder what would happen if you were to create a digital priest to hear confessions...

Context is another hard problem for computers to tackle. It is very difficult for a computer to recognize a change of context. A functionality that might seem perfectly sensible in one interaction might be completely absurd or even destructive in another. A notorious incident once occurred at MIT in which ELIZA was accidentally left on and the director of the department began to interact with it, thinking he was having a dialogue with one of the professors. He would ask the man a question and get a reply such as "Tell me about it," or "What do *you* think?" The director was incensed with the man's impertinence and went to seek him out in a huff. This story is a perfect example of the importance of context. Responses from a therapist seem perfectly appropriate and completely benign from the couch, but might come off as impertinent and rude if spoken to a person of authority in a professional context.

That computers have a hard time with subtleties is what creates a seemingly insurmountable problem in trying to simulate the human brain. There is too much we "know" from culture, context, intuition, and even, as Carl Jung suggests, the collective unconscious. How can these subtleties ever be reduced into Boolean sets without a significant loss of meaning and functionality? As the previous example suggests, language is one of those areas of subtlety that often evades the binary world. Voice recognition has been a difficult nut to crack, and language translation, although it has been attempted for years, has evaded even the most brilliant crack computer scientists. One of the problems is that there are certain subtleties of language, of symbol and meaning, that people interpret not literally but through metaphor and association. When you get into this arena, a computer is lost. Computers cannot pick up on subtle cues such as metaphors. Computers are actually better at picking up physical gestures and translating these because in some ways, body language is a lot more literal than the spoken word. The following two examples are perfect illustrations of what happens when computers try to translate.

An experiment performed many years ago fed phrases in English into a Russian translating device, and then fed them back through the English inverse to be retranslated. Here are two examples of the results: "The spirit is willing, but the flesh is weak" returned "The wine is good, but the meat has gone bad." The idiomatic expression "Out of sight, out of mind" came back as "Invisible maniac." This is a perfect example of where computers fall short. These are accurate definitions, but they make no sense. With computers, an accurate answer is not always a right answer, which is part of the danger of relying on them too heavily as thinking machines.

I once worked on a project in which the programmer was convinced that we could create what's called an "expert system"—that is, a form of AI in which the computer can make decisions on its own. The project involved parsing 700 video clips of interviews with eight people, which were supposed to be able to be organized in such a way that they could create simulated dialogues. The software designer was convinced that this could be done with AI. The only problem with this is that computers do not have the capability to interpret video. Computers can recognize it and understand things such as its size and color palette. Computers can even understand things such as how many pixels actually changed from frame to frame—but only if the video is digital, which this was not—which is the basis for most video compression systems. Computers, however, can't understand the content of the material. Understanding content must be done by a human. The end result is that the artificial intelligence turned out to be me. Instead of automating the system, I had to go into each individual file and classify it in a variety of ways to establish how it would interface with the other clips to create believable dialogue. It was a laborious task, but I doubt it was any more laborious than it would have been to try to hack some AI code that would interpret video. Even if we had succeeded, it is likely that the computer would not have done a very good job of it. So, as it turns out, the best expert system there is still turns out to be the human brain.

 BIOSPHERE MEETS DIGISPHERE: THE BIOSPHERE 2 INTERACTIVE THEATER (p. 91)

This being the case, I personally think that, rather than trying to make machines think, it is a much more worthwhile endeavor to make people think. Douglas Engelbart, Alan Kay, and some of the earlier developers of the graphical user interface, as well as VR pioneers such as Ivan Sutherland and his partner Dave Evans, would no doubt agree. They thought of the computer as an extension of the human mind, not a substitute for it. Create machines that enable people to work, think, solve problems, and create more effectively—this was the underpinning philosophy of the early personal computing and virtual reality innovators. The *human* is the thinking machine, the computer is just there to help out.

 A BRIEF HISTORY OF REAL TIME: THE VIRTUAL REALITY LEGACY (p. 105)

THE PEDAGOGICAL MOUSEPAD, OR, HOW IT ALL GOT GUI (p. 365)

I often refer to my computer as my "prosthetic brain." I am all too keenly aware how much of an extension of my own mind this little box on which I am currently typing really is. Even though it has no innate capability to customize its responses to me, this device enables me to do a variety of things that I am either incapable of (like arithmetic), or weak at (like remembering things), and it strongly enhances those things that I am good at (like writing). The nonlinear way this book was written requires me to multitask, something else I'm good at. Each chapter is its own self-contained file, which enables me to keep multiple files open so that I can move back and forth between related topics. This is how I am able to maintain all the interconnections between things, and keep track of links, organize overlapping ideas, and maintain the dynamic quality of interaction I want this book to have. This book would be a very different animal if it were written on the typewriter. In fact, if it were written on a typewriter, it probably wouldn't exist at all.

For me, portability is another feature of the prosthetic brain. I travel a lot and I also have peculiar writing habits. Allegedly, Goethe couldn't write unless he had a piece of rotten fruit in his drawer. I can't write unless I'm in a crowded public place. Right now, I'm sitting in a garden at a picnic table. I spent all day yesterday on the sofa at my favorite local coffee house. The day before that, I sat for four hours in a crowded airport terminal waiting for my plane to board, hacking away at this book. Ever since I was a teenager, I have had a hard time writing at home or in an office space. As a young aspiring poet, I did all my writing on an antique Hermes portable, a tiny manual typewriter originally designed for journalists, and which was, remarkably, about the same size and color as a Macintosh Powerbook. For some reason, it's easier for me to concentrate outside of my native habitat, away from the phone and other distractions. If it weren't for portable computing, I seriously doubt that this book could have ever been created. It has enabled me to accommodate my peculiarities in a way that thus facilitates and expands my creativity. This to me is the highest function a computer can possibly have.

The computer also enables me to communicate in a more immediate and lucid way with my colleagues, as well as to collaborate with them more easily. This text, for example, was edited by sending word processing files back and forth via e-mail. Using Microsoft Word's "Revision" function, my editors can insert their comments directly into the manuscript file, highlighted in a different color, and send them back to me. When I get the document, I see all the changes highlighted in blue or pink, and then I can make my own revisions in red.

The really exciting potential of computer technology as an extension of the mind lies in its capability to accelerate the learning curve. Computer programs, if properly designed, can be heuristic devices, that is, self-learning tools. One of the earliest and still most common uses of interactive computer technologies is in training. Airplane simulators have been demonstrated to be the best means of training pilots. For young children, interactive software can accelerate the learning process in a variety of ways by taking advantage of their natural exploration process and offering them ways of using play to explore educational content.

One of my editors on this book sent me an e-mail the other day after a few failed document transfer transactions. In frustration he wrote: "Aren't computers supposed to make our lives easier?" I've heard this lament quite a lot, but I don't remember hearing that anywhere, and if you talked to the original generation of PC designers, most of whom were just concerned with making the damn thing easier to use, I seriously doubt if any of them would have agreed that the goal was to make *life* easy. Computers make life more challenging, which isn't always a bad thing. Anyway, I always think it's funny when people talk about computers making things or doing things, because computers don't actually *do* anything. It's the software that does it, the programmers who write the software, the designers who create the interface, and the end user who uses it. When I complain about how bad my e-mail service is, I curse the people who *programmed* and *engineered* the system, not the machine itself.

To me, the purpose of the computer is not to *be* intelligent, but to help *people* be more intelligent. The effectiveness of the computers capability to do this is not a product of the machine's innate intelligence, which is the equivalent of gray matter—a neutral space for storage and processing—but the intelligence of the people who create for it. The examples of artificial intelligence I gave previously are by no means the kinds of solutions that hardcore AI guys would consider legitimate. I like these stories because they are about people coming up with intelligent solutions to problems and that's really what this is all about. Computers don't think; people do. All computers do is process data. If you are really smart, you can get them to do it in a way that makes it seem like they're thinking; however, there is really no match for the human mind. On the other hand, a human mind turbo-charged with a prosthetic brain... now *there's* something to think about!

 CONSENSUAL HALLUCINATIONS: IS VR THE NEW LSD?
(p. 137)

INTERACTIVITY IS SUBVERSIVE (p. 244)

DIGITAL FRANKENSTEINS (p. 173)

AUTOBIOGRAPHY OF AN AUTODIDACT, PART 1

This chapter is the answer to the inevitable question: "How did I get into this?" It's always hard for me to answer because to a certain extent, I was born into it. I was a guinea pig for interactive learning from birth, educated in heuristic classrooms and surrounded by extraordinary role models, most of whom were themselves autodidacts. In fact, most of what was going on around me throughout my childhood, in both the work of my parents and their peers, really set the framework for the interactive revolution. This community in-cluded, among other things, some of the early pioneers of interactive exhibi-tion, and people who were thinking about issues like information graphics, user interface, and computer animation before there were even really comput-ers with which to manifest these ideas. So for the 21 years before I arrived at the shores of the interactive frontier, I had already, unbeknownst to myself, been prepped. The fact is, the moment I was exposed to this area in 1983, I knew exactly what to do; I had an intuitive sense for it, which was remarkable considering that up to that moment, I had scarcely even touched a computer. The only thing I can attribute to this readiness is the fact that I was already predisposed to this craft, and there is no question that these childhood experi-ences have been major influences in my philosophy, in my aesthetics, in my process, and in the final product of my work.

Both my parents were creative—my father, Peter Pearce was an industrial designer, my mother, Lucia Capacchione, an artist—kind of the left and right brain respectively. My father studied product design at the Illinois Institute of Technology (IIT) in Chicago, the U.S. center for neo-Bauhaus design (the Institute of Design), and the international style of building design (the School of Architecture).The steel and glass vocabulary of post-WW II modern archi-tecture was perfected under the guidance of Ludwig Mies van der Rohe, who was director of the IIT School of Architecture when my father was a student at the IIT Institute of Design from 1955–1958. The Institute of Design was founded by Laszlo Moholy Nagy in Chicago at the outbreak of WW II. Both Mies van der Rohe and Moholy Nagy were refugees from the Bauhaus in Germany. They both brought Bauhaus sensibilities to the U.S., which pro-foundly and irreversibly impacted the future of architecture, product design, and graphic design. Indeed, modern graphical design is, to a certain extent, the direct descendant of this rich visual legacy. My mother studied art with socially conscious nun, Sister Corita, at the now infamous Immaculate Heart

College, an all-girl Catholic school in Los Angeles. Corita was at the forefront of the silkscreen poster movement of the 50s and 60s, a kind of religious pop artist who was famous for blending bold splashes of color with loosely scrawled quotes. Her students' work was notoriously unconventional. A contemporary of such artists as Andy Warhol and Japser Johns, she was influenced by commercial art, advertising, and signage. She had her students making giant collage murals, and creating highly impressionistic art around religious themes. Corita and Sister Magdalene Mary, the chairperson of the art department, were a little too radical for the Catholic Archdiocese of Los Angeles, which eventually shut down the entire Order of the Immaculate Heart of Mary. Fortunately, Corita continued her work, and her influence can be seen in the small circle of woman artists who studied with her in the 50s and 60s, as well as the broader art world. One of her best-known designs was a U.S. postage stamp comprised of a rainbow of brush strokes over the world "LOVE."

My parents originally met when they were both employed at the Los Angeles-based design studio of Charles and Ray Eames, known colloquially as "The Eames Office." Among other things, they designed and built the very first interactive museum exhibition, *Mathematica*, sponsored by IBM, at the Los Angeles County Museum of Science and Technology in 1961, the year of my birth. My mother was one of the original graphic designers to develop the concept of a graphical timeline mural.

The Eames office was a magical place to be in the late 50s and early 60s. It was one of the few interdisciplinary design offices. Eames, a refugee from the staunch conventions of architectural education, created a kind of Santa's workshop that included graphic designers, filmmakers, architects, and industrial designers. The work they did was diverse, but they were known for innovation and quality across the board. There was a certain Eames sensibility that became symbolic of modernism during this time period.

The Eames office was enormously influential, and you will see signs of its contributions everywhere you go. But most people have never heard of Charles and Rae Eames, and have no idea who they are. Here are a few things that came out of their office:

- **Eames Tandem Seating:** A high-performance multiple seating system comprised of aluminum castings and supporting seat and back membrane. (See figure A.9.)
- **The Eames lounge chair:** With its curved laminated wood back and seat and leather upholstery, it is today considered a classic.
- **Molded fiberglass side chair:** With curved bucket seats and metal legs, there isn't a university in America that doesn't have some of these classic, cheap, mass-produced chairs in a classroom somewhere.

Figure A.9
Eames airport tandem seating has become a fixture in airports throughout the world

- **The multimedia slide show:** In 1959, the Eames office created the very first "multimedia" presentation, a seven-screen, synchronized slide montage film for the cultural Exchange in Moscow. It was shown in a geodesic dome designed by Buckminster Fuller. They also produced a multi-screen show for the New York World's Fair (see figure A.10).

Figure A.10
Think: An early multi-screen presentation created by the Eames Office for IBM and featured at the 1964–65 NY World's Fair

- **Powers of Ten:** A film demonstrating the principles of exponents by increasing and decreasing the cameras viewpoint by powers of ten.
- **Molded plywood leg splints:** Although obscure, these have now begun popping up as collectors items. Eames made them under a military contract during the early 60s.
- **Mathematica:** The first museum exhibit to use mechanical interactive devices to demonstrate principles of science and mathematics; it also introduced the notion of a graphical history timeline, which has since become a standard for both printed graphics and public exhibitions (see figure A.11).

Figure A.11

The Eames Office's *Mathematica* brought interactivity to the science exhibit

There are numerous other Eames contributions, including films, exhibitions, furniture, architecture, and even some early computer kiosks. There is no doubt that if Eames had lived longer, his office would have been among the most influential interactive multimedia design houses as well. As early as 1969, Eames proposed a totally computerized interactive exhibit to the Metropolitan Museum of Art in New York. The personnel of the Eames office is just as impressive. Computer graphics pioneer John Whitney worked with the Eameses, as did Deborah Sussman, who went on to do environmental graphics and corporate ID work for everyone from Apple to Walt Disney World to the 1984 Los Angeles Olympics. Many other noteworthy designers, artists, filmmakers, and architects passed through the doors of the warehouse office on Brooks Avenue and Abbot Kinney in Venice California, which is still standing today. And many of them went on to become major influences in computer graphics and interactive design. These were all the people that were around when I was a kid, and I spent many entertaining afternoons playing with the pachinko machines, toy trains, and other assorted collectibles that the Eames, in their diligent quest for beauty in design, amassed over the years.

Other "friends of the Eames," like Konrad Wachsmann and Buckminster Fuller, were also influential in my family. Due to a passionate interest in building systems, my father became good friends with Konrad Wachsmann, a German architect who was an innovator of high-performance, pre-fabricated structures. My father also worked with "Mr. Dome," himself—Buckminster Fuller, who, coincidentally, not only invented the geodesic dome, but resembled it.

 BUCKMINSTER FULLER AND THE DIGIDESIC DOME (p. 116)

My parents were decidedly offbeat and entrepreneurial. After spending a few years in education, in 1967, they started their own company, developed a series of products, taught, and got grants for various research projects. My

father developed some chair designs, and began a research project which over the subsequent years resulted in the authoring of three books. The first is nothing short of a manifesto. Entitled *Structure in Nature is a Strategy for Design*, it outlines a theory of design and architecture based on a study of structural forms in nature. He developed several model-building systems that later evolved into a full-blown building system, but I'll get into that later. He later wrote two other books: *Polyhedra Primer*, an encyclopedia of polygons and polyhedra, and *Experiments in Form*, a textbook derived from a design class he taught at Cal State University, USC, and Cal Arts.

A-Life of One's Own (p. 5)

During the period of intensive research by my father, my sister and I were subjected to a variety of bizarre forms of torture such as these: Pulling aside on the road repeatedly during a car trip in the desert so that my dad could take dozens of pictures of cracked mud in a (successful) attempt to validate his hypothesis that mud always cracks at three-rate intersections at 120-degree angles; being forced to spend afternoons blowing soap bubbles in a tub so that my father could photograph the consistent geometry they formed. Then there were the endless hours waiting for the glue to dry on stick models, and the period of time when we were guinea pigs for his building toy, Super Structures, which eventually was marketed to some success during the 70s (see figure A.12).

Figure A.12
As a child, the author tested many of her father's products, such as the Super Structures building toy

My father's work as a teacher led him, in 1969, to become an Associate Dean of the Design School and part of the original faculty of the California Institute of the Arts, more commonly known as "Cal Arts." At that time, it was in its original location in Los Angeles. It has since moved to Valencia, about 45 minutes north of L.A. It was there that my dad invited Edwin Schlossberg to join the faculty. Schlossberg was a colleague of my Dad's from the Buckminster Fuller days, and would eventually become my mentor, hiring me for my first interactive job.

AUTObIOGRAPHY OF AN AUTOdIdACT, PART 2 (p. 58)

THE HEURISTIC MAN: A PORTRAIT OF EdWIN SCHLOSSBERG (p. 224)

After leaving Cal Arts, my dad started a new design company with my step-mother, Susan Pearce. Together, they did a variety of things, including producing a line of educational toys. Eventually, my Dad went into the design, manufacture, and installation of architectural installations using the patented space-frame connection system he developed as a result of his research on the *Structure in Nature* book. He went on to design and build, among other things, Biosphere 2 in Arizona, the largest air-tight structure in the world (for which I was to help produce an interactive theater later), the Winter Garden & Festival Hall in Chicago, and the Fremont Street Canopy, a five-block long arched outdoor canopy bearing over 2 million RGB lightbulbs that generate computer graphics, making it the largest computer screen in the world. At various times, I worked at these companies in various capacities, but we won't get into that now. Unless of course, you want to…

MEdIA ARCHITECTURE (p. 284)

As to my biological mother, Lucia Capacchione, let me just say that I consider myself extremely lucky to have grown up with the assumption that women were supposed to have careers and that gender should never interfere with your aspirations. My sister and I were raised in a fairly gender-neutral fashion: We got Barbies *and* Hot Wheels for Christmas. Throughout my life, my mom has been a fine artist, an early childhood educator, filmmaker, photographer, slide lecturer, toy designer, art therapist, author, teacher, corporate creativity consultant, and so on.

My mom tells a great story of how, at the age of 6, I once took an IQ test in which one of the questions was "What is a lecture?" to which I answered, "It's what mommies do." The child psychologist administering the test turned to my mother and said, "Is that true?" And my mother said, "Yes…I give a lot of slide lectures." The tester shrugged and said, "Well then, I guess I'll have to give her the point for that."

Just after my birth, for some mysterious reason, my mother developed a sudden obsession with early education. This led her to the work of Maria Montessori, creator of the open classroom; however, my mother had to wait three years to actually to send me to a Montessori school. When the book store owner who introduced her to Montessori told her how much it would cost, she was shocked. "Just look at it this way...you won't have to send her to college," he said. Eighteen years later, I dropped out of college after my first year. So at the age of three, I entered my first heuristic environment and officially became an autodidactic communalist—in other words, a self-taught person in a community of self-taught people.

The Montessori system was the brainchild of an Italian physician/psychologist, Dr. Maria Montessori. The first female graduate of the University of Rome Medical School, she developed an educational philosophy based on children's inherent desire to learn. Her theory was that children learn through "purposeful activity" in a "specially prepared environment" containing "autodidactic materials." Dr. Monstessori observed that all young children go through "periods of sensitivity" during which they are particularly receptive to certain modes of learning. For example, she was able to teach children to read and write at an earlier age than had previously believed possible by appealing to their kinesthetic sensitivity. Young children could thus learn the alphabet using their sense of touch using sandpaper letters (see figure A.13). Herself a child prodigy in math, Dr. Montessori also developed devices that taught principles of computation, measurement, geometry, and higher mathematics (see figure A.14).

Figure A.13

A preschool child learns to read using Montessori sandpaper letters (photo courtesy of Lucia Capacchione)

The learning tools featured in figures A.13 and A.14 are also known as "heuristic devices," self-teaching toys or tools that enable the user to learn a concept or principle through self-guided, hands-on use. These hands-on learning toys were the precursor to the modern computer, which, with the proper interface design, is the ultimate heuristic device. It is not surprising that the earliest work in development of the intuitive graphical interface for the computer was happening concurrently with the Montessori movement of the

1960s. In 1968, an early experiment in computerized education for young children occurred in a Montessori classroom which my mother designed. Installed in the "Bede School" in Englewood, New Jersey, it was called "The Responsive Environment," and nicknamed "The Talking Typewriter," designed by Omar Kyam Moore. Using color-coded labels worn on the knuckles, children could learn to type their own name while simultaneously hearing the letters spoken and seeing the letters typed on a piece of paper in the typewriter.

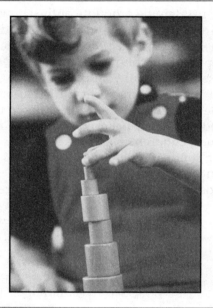

Figure A.14

Montessori student builds a tower out of cylinders (photo courtesy of Lucia Capacchione)

 AUTODIDACTIC COMMUNALISM (p. 83)

I took to school at once. I absolutely loved it. I was very studious and felt right at home in this very well-organized free-learning environment. My favorite things were reading and organizing things. On Saturdays, I used to cry and called my Mom mean for not letting me go to school (a little crazy, I know, but then I also liked liver and spinach).

During this period, my Mom became professionally involved in Montessori schools, and 1965, she entered the Montessori teacher training program. By December, before even completing her credentials, she was recruited to establish an inner-city Head Start program by the Catholic Archdiocese of Los Angeles, the same organization that would later pull the plug on the nuns with whom she'd studied. This program was centered in the minority neighborhoods where the first L.A. riots had occurred only months before. In the summer, my sister and I used to accompany my mother on her rounds visiting centers in South Central Los Angeles, Watts, and Compton (see figure A.15). We loved the little kids, and as the resident Montessori veterans, we became mentors to the other preschoolers there. Autodidactic communalism, once again!

Figure A.15

A typical Montessori Head Start classroom of the 1960s (photo courtesy of Lucia Capacchione)

My mom also made a film about the Montessori Head Start Program she ran. She and my father also designed a proposal for the ultimate Montessori school—she developed the plan and proposed curriculum, he designed the building structure and built a model of the never-completed school (see figure A.16).

Figure A.16

A model of a Montessori school designed by Peter Pearce and Lucia Capacchione (photo courtesy of Peter Pearce)

In the late 60s and early 70s, my mom actually went on to design some heuristic educational toys for Mattel, including the Talking Picture Schoolhouse and the very successful Talking Clock.

Over the years, my mom continued to do educational projects, fine art, and became an art therapist. To date, she has authored ten books on art and journal therapy techniques and creative development. Her first book was *The Creative Journal* (Ohio University/Swallow Press), for which I worked on the children's and teen's versions. Her most recent endeavor is *Putting Your Talent to Work*, with co-author Peggy van Pelt. She has worked with Peggy as a consultant in creative resources development to Walt Disney Imagineering (the theme park division) for over 15 years.

When my sister and I were seven and eight respectively, we "graduated" from Montessori schools and entered an arts-oriented private school in North Hollywood called Oakwood, where I remained until I graduated from the high school ten years later.

Oakwood was an amazing place. Although my social life left something to be desired (basically, I was a nerd with cooties), my educational life was rich and satisfying. Oakwood was started by actor Robert Ryan and his wife Jessica and the basic philosophy of the school was "learn by doing." The teachers were great, and every unit of study culminated in some kind of immersive experience, including the following:

- Putting on an American Indian fair, where we had to make our own pots, kachinas, and corn-husk tamales.
- Building a model of an adobe cliff dwelling by making real mud bricks.
- Performing a play about the Vikings.
- Putting on full-scale simulations of the original Greek Olympics, complete with homemade togas and laurel wreaths.
- Having traditional Chinese feasts wearing antique costumes from China and drawing illuminated manuscripts.
- Learning Braille and spending the day in a blindfold to understand the experience of being blind.
- Taking a three-day trip to the desert.
- Visiting a monastery and living the lives of medieval monks, including a vow of silence from dusk till dawn (a feat which most of us never achieved).

My education was, in a sense, full of Virtual Reality. Everything we learned, we had to experience and do first hand. Through this type of exercise, we had an education that was about content, not information—about human experience, not historical facts. It was about how to *be* an American Indian, not what *is* an American Indian and when did the Indians live.

Although Oakwood was a place of intellectual and creative flowering for me, it was a social disaster. For whatever reasons, possibly triggered in part by the divorce of my parents, possibly by the fact that I was "different" from the other kids (red hair is a mixed blessing), I felt miserably out of place among my peers and found my escape and solace in books and make-believe. I spent almost all my free time in the library, volunteering as student librarian whenever I got the chance, avoiding recess and sports like the plague, and reading everything in sight. I fell in love with writing, largely inspired by my English teacher, Shirley Kray, one of "those teachers"…you know, the kind that totally rocks your world. For some reason, I had an innate ability to spell, and though I was always the last picked on the basketball team, I was everyone's favorite spelling bee teammate. I began to write like crazy—poems…stories…songs. I also created and made up stories about my own virtual worlds and characters, many different alter egos that represented various heroines I wanted to be. A flapper, a Viking princess, Nancy Drew, and Queen Elizabeth the First were among a few of the characters I developed stories around. I wrote about them, did drawings, made paper dolls, acted out stories, and totally immersed myself in these make-believe worlds. And although it was precipitated by the need to escape from the harassment of the other kids, it ultimately became my greatest gift and power. I see this in perspective today: I used my imagination to escape from reality, and today I use it to create new realities that empower other people's imaginations.

At Oakwood Upper School (the junior high and high school campus), the use of immersive role-playing experiences as a teaching device became even more sophisticated. Our history teachers were all socialists and communists, so we got a very interesting interpretation of American and European history. One final test involved coming to class in the character and costume of an historical character from any period in American History prepared to engage in a formal debate with another historical character. I played turn-of-the-century feminist Susan B. Anthony debating with forefather Thomas Jefferson, who had once proclaimed that all *men* were created equal. In contemporary American history, we re-enacted the 1976 meeting at Camp David (I had to be the United States because nobody else wanted it). We also staged a "Revolution Day" (I believe instigated by the students) in which everyone in the school was to come for the day dressed as his or her favorite revolutionary. We rigged up a special gallows, which had in place of a blade, a bucket of water that was dumped onto the head of the hapless victim. We dressed the courtyard up to look like a thatch-house Vietnamese village and made a giant poster that said "OAKWOOD IS REVOLTING." The teachers loved it. We all had a blast!

I was always heavily involved in theater, and in junior high and high school, I discovered film. I was a bit of a cinema snob. We had a very progressive film teacher who taught us about experimental film, and we would get into all kinds of lengthy debates about the idea of nonlinear film, autobiographical film, and ways that avant-garde filmmakers were mucking around with convention. In junior high, I assistant directed an award-winning film directed by Todd Haynes, who went on to direct several controversial independent films, including *Poison* (which caused a bit of a to-do with the NEA because of its homosexual content). Haynes also made *Safe*, a film about a woman with an environmental disease, and *Superstar: The Karen Carpenter Story*, a biography of Karen Carpenter's deadly struggle with anorexia, done in stop-animation with Barbie dolls, and in which I actually play a small speaking part. The student film, entitled *The Suicide*, was originally written as an essay question for our Humanities final. The assignment was to "write a tragic hero myth," which we had, as I recall, approximately two hours to do. The 20-minute film itself was somewhat avant-garde, using a nonlinear structure to tell the story of a little boy's fantasy about killing himself.

In those days, we used to go to a lot of films at revival houses around L.A. This was in the mid- to late 70s, and there were about a half dozen theaters in the area where you could see classic films—Truffaut, Fellini, Godard, Bunuel, Hitchcock, Welles, Kurosawa, Roeg, Altman…the list goes on. They would have a different double bill every day, and while many of my contemporaries were at the mall seeing *movies* such as *Saturday Night Fever* and *Jaws*, I was sitting on frayed velvet cushions with *films* such as Fellini's *Roma* and *The 400 Blows* flickering before my wonder-struck eyes. One night I was asking my dad's permission to go to the Nuart Theater to see some highbrow film or other and he turned to me and said, "Celia, are you an intellectual?" To which I replied, "No, Dad. I'm a nerd." Today, I suppose, I would qualify as a meta-nerd. And proud of it!

> I came dangerously close to pursuing a career in acting, something I had dreamed of since early childhood. It is largely due to the talents of Elizabeth McGovern, to whom I am eternally grateful, that I am not. Liz was the star of our school and got virtually every lead that she tried out for through high school and went on to win major film roles in *Ordinary People*, *Ragtime*, and *Once Upon a Time in America*, to name a few. It was difficult for me to get a lead. I wasn't a very good cold reader, and having red hair was a real encumbrance in those days, though now it's all the rage. Back then, redhead meant character part, and that was that.

The best thing that ever happened to me in high school was the moment I gave up on the painfully pointless exercise of auditioning. Instead, I came up with the brilliant idea of volunteering to be assistant director/stage manager, a job which no one wanted. It was a huge production of Thornton Wilder's *Skin of Our Teeth*, with a cast of over 30 kids, and our drama teacher's husband was ill at the time, so I had my work cut out for me. I co-directed the play, oversaw every aspect of the production, managed the budget, designed all the promotional materials, oversaw the set and costume design, and worked my ass off to the point where I nearly flunked about half my classes (much to the chagrin of my teachers and parents, who had become accustomed to my typically high grade point average). But it was an epiphany for me. I realized at that moment that I would much rather be behind the scenes—telling everyone what to do, orchestrating the whole event, coaching actors, calling light cues, and being a part of everything—than be on stage with sweaty palms following someone else's direction and forgetting all my lines. I felt totally empowered in the behind-the-scenes role. What's more, I had a natural aptitude for it, much more than acting. From that point on, I gave up my ambitions of becoming an actress and decided I wanted to be a film director instead.

I did, however, maintain an interest in stage performance and was involved in and studied improvisational theater. Improv was a lot more interesting to me than traditional theater because I found it to be more of a creative challenge. I think I also liked it because of its inherent structure. I liked the game-like quality that enabled you to work within a narrow set of parameters but with a fairly broad range of spontaneous and unpredictable outcomes. This notion of a structure that facilitates creativity has had a major impact on my experience of and ideas about interactivity.

INTER-plAy: IMpROVISATION ANd INTERACTIVE THEATER (p. 230)

After graduating from high school, I went to college for a minute. I had been rejected from both Harvard and Berkeley, largely due the fact that my life in the theater had eroded my once exemplary grade point average to something less than stellar, and ended up at the University of California at Santa Cruz. I was used to a much more dynamic form of education than was provided even at a radical school like UCSC (a notoriously "progressive," Northern California branch of the U.C. system). Having been in school since I was two, I was understandably bored with the whole proposition and was anxious to get on with the business of life. By now, my interest in school had waned so severely that by the time I finished by first year of college, I was one point away from being kicked out.

So at 18, I returned to L.A. with the absurd notion that I would go into the film business. But my six month entree to this, as a secretary and assistant-editor at the *Hollywood Reporter* (a film industry trade daily), convinced me that loving the film medium was one thing; swimming among the sharks in the film *industry* was something entirely different. I just didn't have the constitution for it, so at the ripe old age of 19, I decided to retire from the movie business.

Nepotism runs in our family, so for the next couple of years, I worked for both my mother and my father. I helped my Mom develop an experimental elementary school curriculum for the Garvey School district entitled "Basic Skills Using Art and Computer Personalization." It was an experiential learning program designed for a school in which the majority of children were Asian and Hispanic from non-English–speaking homes. The idea was to use art, movement, music, and writing to teach kids basic skills at the same time that they were learning English. It was 1981, so the computer personalization was rather limited…putting kids names into stories by entering them into a computer.

I co-developed a storytelling component in which kids were to write and tell their own personal stories. Because this was a multicultural school, and many of the students had gone through significant trials to get to America (most were refugees), their stories were both dramatic and educational. We had the kids write and tell their own stories to teach them writing skills, humanities, and to develop a strong intercultural understanding. The program was a huge success, with students increasing their math and reading scores by as much as 20 percentile points.

I also worked for my Dad's space-frame company as the receptionist, librarian, marketing administrator, and assistant project manager on large architectural projects. The skills I garnered in research, marketing, design, and project management were invaluable to me when I began working in the interactive industry, and there isn't one thing I learned while working for my father that hasn't found a direct application in my multimedia work.

As I explored my various interests, what I finally landed on was something that nicely tied together all three of the areas that I had been involved in up to that time: film/theater, architecture, and education. Writing was the glue that held it all together.

AUTOBIOGRAPHY OF AN AUTODIDACT, PART 2 (p. 58)

ARCHITECTURE AS A NARRATIVE ART (p. 25)

MIXED MEDIA, MIXED MESSAGE (p. 306)

AUTOBIOGRAPHY OF AN AUTODIDACT, PART 2

The way I see it, life is the ultimate nonlinear story. It is characterized by key junctures, decision points at which a seemingly unplanned, arbitrary event or occurence with extremely low odds of happening at all, results in a major change in life direction. Just such a moment occurred in the winter of 1983.

The previous summer, right before I turned 21, I decided to take a trip to New York. I had been once at the age of 15 with my parents, but not as a young adult. The Big Apple always played a major part in my fantasy worlds and my various childhood and youthful aspirations as an actress, writer, poet, and urban sophisticate (I guess I watched too many Myrna Loy movies as a kid). So in the summer of 1982, I decided to visit some friends from high school and college who were scattered around the east coast. There was only one problem with my little plan. I managed to save enough money to fly to New York, but none to live on once there. So I decided I would try to get a freelance gig by calling my dad's old friend, Ed Schlossberg.

My dad became friends with Ed when they were both on the faculty at Cal Arts when it first opened in Los Angeles. Ed had always been my secret idol. For a teenage avant-garde intellectual poet-artist-filmmaker such as myself, Ed was the perfect role model. He was a Jewish intellectual from New York, which made him a first cousin to the gods of Olympus in my book. He hung out with John Cage. And he made interactive art. During my childhood and teens, we would periodically visit Ed in his country house in Massachusetts. I got to stay in the attic, which was Ed's art studio. To me, this was utter paradise. He would bring out all his interactive poetry doodads—boxes full of words that you could assemble, shake up, and layer into self-reflective sentences about things such as "…coming insight." He used lots of word plays, which I loved, and you could basically create your own poetic experience with his work. It was very Dada, very Fluxus (although I didn't know about any of that yet), and very cool. In his studio at night, I would look through all his supplies—paints, inks, stencils, various materials, plastics, and papers—that he would make art with. To me, this was utterly magical, and it was my greatest wish that someday, I might actually be able to be even a tenth as cool and clever as Ed Schlossberg. Being an insecure teenager, I felt the chances of this were slim at best. But anyway, it was something to aspire too.

I had absolutely no idea what it was Ed did for a living. I knew he had a company that designed the interactive exhibition for the Brooklyn Children's museum, for which my dad had built a giant playground structure—a 10,000 times enlargement of a diamond crystal made out of lexan plastic. But interactive wasn't even really a word then. I think they were called "Hands On" exhibits in 1976.

In the summer of 1982, I called up Ed and told him that I was coming to New York and wondered whether he had any freelance work for me to do. I sent a resumé and some writing samples and within a few days, I got a call back from someone there saying "Sure—come on down." So that summer, I spent a couple of weeks freelancing at Edwin Schlossberg Incorporated, doing writing, research, and organizing the company library (the third time since childhood

I worked in the capacity of a librarian). I had a good time there, liked everyone a lot, and still had almost no clue what the company did after two weeks there, except that I knew they had something to do with museums.

This is where the life-altering decision point comes in. The following February, on a total lark, my best friend sent me a ticket to fly to New York for the weekend to help him celebrate his birthday. I had a few days to kill, so I called up Ed and asked him to lunch. The conversation went like this:

Me: Do you want to have lunch with me tomorrow?

Him: No…I can't do lunch…do you want to come work for me?

Me: (I think there was a pregnant pause at this point) You mean like a job?

Him: Yes. Full time. Staff. Everybody here really liked you when you were here…

Me: What would I do? I stammered.

Him: Writing, design…

Me: When would you want me to start?

Him: Tomorrow.

I asked him for 24 hours to think about it. It didn't take much convincing though. I was 21 years old. There was nothing going on in L.A. The person who had been my childhood idol was offering me a job. So I called him back and said yes, asking for a month to get my act together and ship out to New York. All this, and I still didn't really know precisely what it was the company did. But what the hell, leap of faith. So on April 1, 1983 (almost exactly 14 years ago as of this writing), I moved to New York and nine days later started a career.

The first few weeks my head was spinning. There were all these meetings, and everyone just acted as if I knew what was going on, which I picked up on fairly quickly, although at times, I was quite baffled. In a day 1 meeting, Ed gave me my first assignment: "Celia, I want you find out everything you can about simulation and gaming." I had no idea what he was talking about. I had never designed a game, and even as a child, had pretty much hated playing them (I could never stand to lose, and always did). And as for simulation, I had no idea whatsoever what that meant. Besides all that, I had no idea why I was being given this assignment because I still didn't know what the company was doing.

I found out the next day in a meeting of the entire office. It was a conceptual review of the top secret project I had been hired to work on: a giant themed attraction for adults filled with custom-designed multiplayer interactive computer games. I had no idea what was going on. I had barely even touched a computer at this point, I knew nothing about games, and I wasn't really entirely sure what they meant by "interactive," although I had a vague idea. The project was called "Intertainment Projects Limited (IPL)." It was one of the first interactive LBE (location-based entertainment) projects ever attempted.

I remember sitting there with my jaw hanging open. The walls were plastered with pictures and words. I had never seen anything like it, and even to this day, I can't quite describe to you what it was I saw on those walls. They were experiences, interactive experiences in which people would be able to do all kinds of bizarre and outrageous things together using computers and electro-mechanical devices. At that time, there was a theme of "city," so the games all revolved around things you could do in an urban setting—politics, transportation, arts and entertainment, architecture, commerce, you name it. They were all group experiences which anywhere from 4 to 40 people could play together.

I also learned some important criteria in that first meeting: a list of goals and objectives driving this entire process. I was brainwashed and from that day to this, I have worked with these same criteria in everything I do. The overriding philosophy was that everything we did was about interaction between people. These games were not about the human-machine interface; they were about the human-human interface. The computer was nothing more than a glorified telephone...a medium *through* which people could connect. That is what I learned computers were for in 1983, a decade before the Internet went public. Ed felt that computers would never enter into the mainstream until they were recognized primarily as a medium of communication *between people*, that their primary power lay in the ability to facilitate interpersonal interaction. This is the main philosophy I have followed ever since, and I'm happy to say that recent events have proved them to be correct. It wasn't until the Internet created a venue for multi-user connectivity that interactive multimedia has really taken off on a mass level. Along those lines, the games had to have the following characteristics:

- Be primarily about the interrelationship between the people; the machine was only there to facilitate social interaction (one of the designers used to call the games "social lubricants").

- Appeal to as broad an adult audience as possible, with a special emphasis on making them accessible to women.

- Emphasize positive interaction between people, incorporating elements of both cooperation and competition. No killing or fighting allowed.

- The technology had to be transparent and accessible, even to the technophobe.

- You had to be able get the gist of the game by watching it being played, and be able to learn by playing without any tutorials or instructions.
- Error messages were not allowed. The need for an error message was an indication that the designer was doing something wrong, not the player.

I will tell you right now that these principles have dominated my thinking about interactive media for the past 14 years. In fact, the primary reason most of my work has been in out-of-home entertainment has been because until the Internet was accessible to a mass audience, there was little opportunity for social interaction on the desktop. Although my first love will always be the attraction venue, where I can look those I am playing with in the eye, the Internet has opened up the door for these ideas to filter through into the home market as well.

After having been indoctrinated, I had to get down to business and take on my first assignment with aplomb! I went into the office library and started looking for books and periodicals, got some interesting contacts, made a bunch of calls, and learned a whole hell of a lot. I found out about simulation techniques being used to teach and study history, cultural evolution, anthropology, statistics and demographics, physics, and so on. The premise is to create a model that simulates a dynamic system. This could be created—on paper, through role playing, or a computer. Such a simulation could then be used to dynamically model a system's processes, enabling you to play out different scenarios and manipulate the outcome by changing variables. The popular computer game *Sim City* is a perfect example of a simulator: depending on what you do, you can play out many different sequences of events in the simulated city within a given set of parameters. You can make many correlations between simulations and games, and even a game like chess might be cited as a form of simulation.

You can also use simulations as a training tool. Much of the earliest interactive work revolves around simulation training systems. Some of the first of these were developed for military and aerospace training. These mostly computerized simulators were capable of making three-dimensional worlds on computers that you could go inside of to learn how to do military maneuvers, or fly an airplane or spacecraft. This was my first exposure to the concept of Virtual Reality. To me, it seemed like a very weird and cool thing. But it was also exasperating. We knew that the military had all this amazing high-end technology that made the monochrome, text-based PC sitting on each of our desks seem like an abacus. But the horrible thing about it was…it was all Department of Defense, and therefore, top secret. Not only were we denied access to this amazing gear, we were denied access to *information* about it. We couldn't use it, and we couldn't even find out what it was! It was the gift of fire denied us by the gods, the mysterious forbidden fruit of high technology.

Speaking of abacuses, when I first arrived at ESI, I didn't even know how to use a computer. For my first few weeks, I did all my writing on an IBM Selectric until the Head of Software, Craig Southard, insisted I learn how to use an IBM PC.

 CONFESSIONS OF A MACINTOSH CONVERT (p. 132)

The first month at ESI was a game in and of itself, a game called "What's My Job?" It was the kind of place where no one was going to tell you, you just had to create your own niche, or you'd find yourself flying around in circles looking for a place to land. Having been educated and raised in a do-it-yourself, proactive environment, I had no problem boldly stepping forward, questioning everything, and eventually, finding my own spot on the playing board.

One thing I was able to figure out fairly easily was that we were designing games. All these games were being designed by people who, like myself, had never designed games before, although a few had been toy designers. They came from multiple disciplines: architecture, graphic design, science, fine art, sculpture, history, education, psychology, you name it. I was supposed to be "the writer." My job was to take in everyone's material—each delivered in its creator's own unique form. Games came to me in every conceivable medium, from typed and handwritten text to bubble diagrams to sketches to verbal descriptions to foam core models. My job was to come up with a consistent format and begin to document all these game ideas in a clear and comprehensible way.

I had one very glaring problem: as I evaluated these game concepts, I recognized a level of inconsistency in the ideas themselves. It wasn't just the delivery, but the entire structure and premise of the games that varied. So, as I was writing these so-called game descriptions, I kept bumping up against the same vexing question: What, exactly, is game?

Every time I find myself stuck on a problem, I stop what I'm doing and embark on a research project. This one dovetailed nicely with my first assignment—"find out whatever you can about simulation and games." So I decided to look into it. Perhaps largely due to my father's influence, I performed well in geometry and algebra. I understood logic and the principle of an axiom really well. So I set about the task of creating a comprehensive set of parameters to determine if something was, in fact, a game. I looked at the rules of every game I could possibly think of, and I asked myself, What do all these games have in common? What elements are always present, regardless of the rules? How can I look at a game or game idea and say, Yes, this is a game, because it fulfills thus and such criteria. After several weeks of examining games, playing them with my colleagues, and studying the matter in-depth, I finally came up with a formula that works.

THE RULES OF THE GAME (p. 420)

This formula became the master checklist I used to evaluate all the games. I became a kind of game therapist. The designers would come to me, and I'd say, well, yes, this is good, but it doesn't have a goal. Or, the goal is fine, but there aren't any obstacles. Or, what kind of rewards were you thinking of? This type of research and development was the beginning of my game development skills.

The next thing I learned to do was draw flow charts. Craig taught me this too. The first assignment was to draw a flow diagram of an elevator. It was very simple: Diamonds represented decision points and rectangles represented output. At each decision point, you would make a query—either a "Yes/No" style question such as, "has elevator been summoned?" (which would have a Yes/No outcome) or an "If/Then" scenario, such as "If elevator has been called, then go to selected floor."

Once a game fulfilled the criteria of actually being a game, and the designer made sure it had all the requisite components, the document would come back to me and I would put it through the second litmus test: I would try to draw a flow chart of the game. This would be an iterative process with the designers until the logic made sense. Then I would write a concept summary describing the basic tenets of the game logic. Thus I earned the first of many job descriptions at ESI as a "Game Logic Analyst."

Now that we solved the problem of "What is a game?" and "How does it work?" I found myself faced with another pressing question. "We keep designing all these games," I told Craig and Ed, "and from a logical standpoint, they make sense. But how do we know anyone will want to play them? And what will happen when they do?" "What do you want to do about it?" they asked. "I want to test them." By this time, we hired some actual game designers and a few software engineers who had actually done playtesting before, so they gave me some tips and pointers. I wrote a proposal, got a budget, and set about testing somewhere between 20 and 30 games over the subsequent 18-month period, with the help of my assistant, an 18-year old whippersnapper named Athomas Goldberg, who has since gone on to become a pioneer in his own right, developing artificial characters as a research scientists at New York University's Media Research Laboratory.

I'm eternally grateful for the support I got from Craig, Ed, and the rest of the team in this effort. It had a significant impact on the quality of the games we designed. I learned more about interactivity from this exercise than I would have from any level of book-learning or even a full-blown multimedia training program, of which there were, of course, none at the time. I got into the head of the players and learned what made them tick. Even though I feel exceptionally conversant in player behavior, I will never forego testing—no matter how much I anticipate, I can never predict what players will do when left to their own or my devices, which is really the whole fun of it.

 Test First, Ask Questions Later (p. 463)

After the first three or so years, the IPL project began to go through a series of on-again, off-again processes, mostly having to do with the repeated promise and withdrawal of funds from a variety of both predictable and unlikely sources. One of my colleagues and I took responsibility for all interoffice satire, and we once made a sign in our office during this period that read "FITZ & STARTZ, INC."

But no matter, between IPL stints, we kept ourselves busy with a myriad of bizarre and interesting projects. ESI was known as "the wild card." We always got the most unusual projects, and there was so little in common with them that it was hard to explain to people what it was we did.

One thing that all our projects had in common, however, was process. Ed was completely process-oriented, and we had a very specific way of doing things. Every project we did started with an extensive research and analysis phase, which we would do before we even started designing. We would try to find out everything we could about the venue, the target market, the content, the client's goals, and the visitors expectations until we came up with what amounted to a mission statement for the project. We wouldn't even start designing until that was done and signed off on by the client and the team. We would then submit alternative concepts, from which the client could choose one to be developed into a full concept report. On most of the projects that I was involved in, my job was to write the text of these reports based on group brainstorming sessions. Everything we did always began with a narrative description before even considering processing the environmental design.

 Architecture as a Narrative Art (p. 25)

Quite a few of the client-based projects were for museums. These were always an interesting challenge for various reasons. In each case, we took a totally unique approach to the design based on the content and the audience. All our museum projects had an entertainment bent to them, and we were one of the first companies to produce "edutainment" projects.

In many ways, ESI was like the Eames office: it was interdisciplinary, and you never knew from one moment to the next what project you would be doing, what skills you would be using, or what your job was going to be. It was the perfect place for someone with a short attention span. It was also the sort of place where you really had to make your own way, and if you were in need of direction, you might be inclined to be very unhappy there. On the other hand, the overall spirit was convivial and cooperative. Although there were some strange psycho-dynamics and politics, for the most part it was not a highly competitive environment. Because there was no hierarchy per se (with the possible exception of Ed himself), there wasn't really anything to fight over. The few cases where people tried to work their way up the corporate ladder seemed comically absurd, because the corporate ladder at ESI was really more like a game of Twister. Everything about ESI was of course the direct product of its leader, the charismatic and sometimes enigmatic, Ed Schlossberg.

 THE HEURISTIC MAN: A PORTRAIT OF EdWIN SCHLOSSBERG (p. 224)

In between stints of IPL, I worked on a number of interesting and diverse projects, including several concepts for museum exhibits. As was typical of our projects, many of them were completed only up to the conceptual or schematic stage and were never actually built. The Fernbank Museum of Natural History in Atlanta was one that did manage to get built, although it was redesigned by the client to the point where much of the original intent was lost. For the Museum of the City of New York, we developed a concept proposal for interpretive exhibits for an existing history museum. For the Audubon Zoo, we created a concept for interpretive layers through programs and renovations to an existing zoo. For the Henry Ford Museum, we designed and built an interactive machine designed to teach kids principles of innovation and problem-solving. For the *Tech 2000 Gallery*, we conceived and installed a gallery showcasing a wide array of interactive multimedia applications from a range of publishers and developers.

 MUSE-oLEUM: DEAd ZOOS ANd LIVING MUSEUMS (p. 313)

I worked at ESI from 1983 to late 1989, at the peak of the Reagan years, the real estate boom, and the Yuppie Renaissance. At that time, there was an enormous push to make more sophisticated malls and shopping centers. This was, I believe, in part fueled by the huge success of the catalog industry. People were shopping at home. The suburban mall, which, for some unknown reason, had been the happenin' hangout of the 70s, was dead. People were looking for something more sophisticated, and their focus was being drawn back to urban areas. In the 80s, Jim Rouse developed the concept of the "Festival Market Place," a shopping center that had some kind of character, that became an entertainment and social destination as well as a place to shop. Fanueil Hall in Boston, South Street Seaport in New York, and Harbor Place in Baltimore were three Rouse projects that really changed the whole face of malls. They are the direct ancestors of the "retail entertainment" movement, as characterized by themed malls such as Universal Citywalk in

Los Angeles and Caesar's Palace in Las Vegas, stand-alone stores such as Nike Stores or The Disney Store, and themed restaurants like Hard Rock Cafe and Planet Hollywood. You can scarce go anywhere anymore without "being themed."

Sociologically speaking, the 80s were characterized by enormous extravagance and a shift to a kind of bourgeois sensibility. This is particularly ironic when you consider that these same individuals were protesters and draft-dodgers in the 60s. It was as if they were somehow overcompensating, as if in order to quiet a nagging collective conscience, they had to go to an even further extreme than had their "materialistic" parents in the 50s. It was a time of prosperity, but with it came a kind of soul-sickness. The price to be paid for unbridled greed could be seen in the darting eyes of a cocaine-addicted stock-broker, or the sagging suit of a recently indicted young mogul.

America's taste also began to change. More wealth meant higher expectations. This was the birth of the gourmet coffee stop, which has led to the current "ice mocachino" craze, and the world domination of Seattle-based Starbucks, the Microsoft of coffee. In New York especially, shopping became a more and more theatrical experience. Even the funky thrift store I used to shop at in SoHo had an installation with mannequins and furniture hanging upside down from the ceiling. South Street Seaport, down by the water's edge, was so crowded on weekends you could barely move. People had money to shop, and retail had to compete for their attention. Thus was born the entertainment retail movement.

At the same time, money was steadily draining out of the public sector and the arms race was at an all time high (I recently read that the peak of military spending during the Reagan-Bush dynasty was $400 billion, compared to Clinton's $275 billion). Museums could no longer rely on public funding, forcing them to become more commercial with the development of more elaborate shops and marketable exhibitions. This is also when museum branding and catalogs began. It also became more necessary to incorporate some kind of entertainment into museums. Thus was born edutainment. Today, most major museums have Imax theaters, not merely for their appeal as an educational tool, but because, in fact, Imax theaters are big money-makers for museums, and museums in America today have to do whatever they can to support themselves.

All these historical/economic conditions had a major impact on the work we did at Schlossberg's office during the 80s. Our reputation as a quirky and creative company that took on "conceptual odd jobs," made us the first choice for a variety of unusual and hard-to-define projects. As I mentioned earlier, many of these were never actually built, for the very reason that they were too innovative to pull off.

We did two major projects that dealt directly with the real estate boom—one for Olympia & York and one for Jim Rouse's Enterprise Development Corporation. The Olympia & York project was an interactive directory system for the World Financial Center in Battery Park City, a huge real estate development built on landfill adjacent to Wall Street in lower Manhattan. A desire to provide value-enhanced real estate to its largely yuppie audience led O&Y to hire ESI to develop an interactive directional kiosk for the World Financial Center. The site consisted of four towers, an enclosed courtyard area, and a giant glass-enclosed atrium called the Winter Garden. For it, ESI created a very high-end touch-screen directory system, installed in housing that looked more like a giant Marcel Duchamp sculpture with layers of jagged-edged frosted glass, than like a computer kiosk. Along the passageways we installed giant computer monitors that hung from similar glass structures and gave updated info about events and activities around the site. The product was called *Insightguide*, and it was installed on the site in 1988.

By far, the biggest retail extravaganza that we were involved in was a proposal for the Festival Marketplace King himself, Jim Rouse, in 1988. The proposed Port Imperial site was located on the west bank of the Hudson across from mid-town Manhattan at the pre-construction site of a new ferry terminal. Port Imperial combined hotel/resorts, retail, and entertainment venues in a very ambitious mixed-use facility. Jim Rouse was the mastermind behind the retail plan, and he in turn hired us to help develop the theming and entertainment aspect. The result was a mall disguised as a theme park, with a resort hotel to complete the effect. To my knowledge, this was one of the earliest attempts to create a completely themed urban mall. Everything in the damn place was themed, including all the stores, restaurants, and the hotel. The proposed theming package hearkened back to turn-of-the-century New York, and all the areas revolved around the grandeur of that bygone time: a giant greenhouse conservatory, an explorer's club, a fancy Victorian hotel, the whole nine yards. The entire site was all designed to be pure eye candy from the New York side of the river. The project was never completed, but the ferry terminal was. And who knows, they may yet put something in the spot!

In the Circle of Life, everything always returns to where it started. So in 1989, six years after I'd joined ESI, we again were re-funded to do IPL, this time by our new "rich uncle," Olympia & York. I, by this time, had worked my way into the role of Project Manager, so when IPL started up again, I became one of three Game Managers. In this role, I was in charge of producing four of twelve games, completing the design specifications, and overseeing the game development in all the other discipline areas—hardware, software, scenic, and media design.

All the games for IPL had to be redesigned from their original versions for a variety of reasons. One was the fact that our budget was about half to a third what it had originally been. Another was that it was 1989 and *everything was different*. When we started the project in 1983, we were using an Amiga computer for graphics—you couldn't even network a PC at that time. By 1989, the technological landscape had changed drastically. Computers were a lot cheaper and could do a lot more. We were a full Mac shop by this time (only the Accounting Department still used PCs). We also evolved our design sensibility by that time. We hired some great freelancers and got a dozen games up to spec, looking better than they ever had, in my opinion. And then…tragedy struck!

It wasn't so much the stock market crash but the real estate crash that followed on its heels that ultimately killed the IPL project. The domino effect, at least in New York, resulted from the success of the real estate industry leaning heavily on that of the financial industry—most urban development in New York serviced financial giants such as American Express. As a result of this codependency, when the stock market crashed, the towering giants of real estate toppled along with them. O&Y's overbuilt World Financial Center and their Canary Wharf fiasco in London drove the then kings of real estate into the ground. Both developments made similar mistakes which resulted in their demise. One was that they were cut off from the neighboring district. WFC required you to cross a bridge over the West Side Highway from the World Trade Center in Wall Street to get there. Canary Wharf was an island designed with poor road access, inadequate parking and no public transportation. There was also an erroneous theory within the WFC scheme that Wall Street yuppies would want to live downtown, just a bridge away from their high-rise offices. Why would they want to pay between $250 and $500 million for a luxury condo, when they could opt instead to buy small mansions with expansive lawns in the bedroom communities of Westchester or Long Island? Both real estate projects were also designed with the assumption that economic prosperity was in an infinite growth cycle. These projects were overambitious and ill-conceived.

So that was that for IPL—another casualty of the 80s. As a result, we lost our funding when our wealthy benefactor fell on hard times, and we were back to square one.

When ESI experienced yet another transition, I decided it would be a good time to make a graceful exit. So in 1989, after seven marvelous years, I resigned my position at Edwin Schlossberg Incorporated and moved on to other things.

Here's a little time capsule for you—the day of this writing, April 9, 1997, is the 14-year anniversary of my first day at ESI, and the anniversary of my jet-propelled launch into the interactive industry.

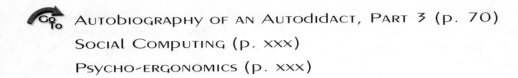

AUTOBIOGRAPHY OF AN AUTODIDACT, PART 3

In 1990, I left Edwin Schlossberg Incorporated to embark on a freelance career as an interactive designer/producer. Everyone thought I was nuts. It was only months after the 1989 real estate crash; some of my gloom-and-doomer friends were predicting a horrible depression. I had no job to go to, I just figured I could get some contracts and keep myself busy that way. Which I did. Needless to say, being a freelance interactive designer (even in 1990 when CD-ROMs were actually something that a lot of people knew about) was kind of a zany path to be on. The only problem was, I wasn't a CD-ROM designer. Being a location-based entertainment (LBE) designer was even more of a novelty.

Over the next three years, I hung out in New York and started building a business as a freelance consultant. The first gig out the door was pretty interesting and characteristically bizarre. It was an 80-person interactive theater for the Biosphere 2 Visitors Center. Called "Meet the Biospherians," it was a simulated teleconference with people inside Biosphere 2, an experiment in biologically based self-sustaining life support systems. I was hired on contract as project manager/co-designer and content director by Dennis Moore, a brilliant director of Imax films and media environments.

BIOSPHERE MEETS DIGISPHERE: THE BIOSPHERE 2 INTERACTIVE THEATER (p. 91)

Another client of mine in New York was Ogilvie & Mather's Interactive Marketing Group. This was an interesting group led by Martin Nisenholtz, who was one of the early innovators in interactive advertising. Martin was, among other things, one of the people behind the Viacom/AT&T interactive television experiment popularly known as *The Castro Valley Test*, which was cancelled two weeks before its scheduled launch. Nonetheless, Martin and his team at Ogilvie did some pretty interesting stuff long before the World Wide Web made an industry of interactive advertising. Over the years as a consultant to IMG, I designed a number of Prodigy ads and worked on something called Forbes Deciding Factor, which was basically a web site before there were web sites— a series of interactive ads on a floppy disk included with the June 1991 issue of *Forbes* magazine. I think the thing I had the most fun with was a kid's game designed to teach children about the General Motors electric car with the curious name of *The Impact*. The Impact had a limited amount of juice so in their daily routine of going from job to school to market, and so forth, the kids had to plan and time their activities so they could be sure not to run out of electricity.

In spite of everyone's doom-saying, things were going along pretty nicely; but then in 1993, something happened that changed my life, once again. Almost exactly ten years after I embarked on this interactive adventure, I ended up getting the gig of a lifetime. It was another decisive moment, which, like all the decisive moments in my life, happened in such an unlikely fashion that it seemed destined to occur. Headed up by Iwerks Entertainment and Evans & Sutherland, the project was called *Virtual Adventures,* and it was one of the first attempts to create a high-end Virtual Reality Theme park attraction.

 THE PRINCESS ANd THE MONSTER: THE MAKING OF VIRTUAL AdVENTURES (p. 375)

Virtual Adventures was probably the seminal project of my career. It was a lot of fun, and it also marked a kind of coming of age for me. Iwerks brought me back to L.A., which I'd had my sights on for a while. After ten years in New York, I was ready to come home and go for a second round with Hollywood. Except this time, of course, I was coming back to a whole different world, a Hollywood that was well on its way to being "wired."

One thing that happened during my time at Iwerks was that the company had gone public right in the middle of the project. There was a big cham-pagne lunch party which co-founder and CEO Stan Kinsey emceed for the whole company. The stocks had gone from something like $17 per share to $36 in six hours. I of course did not find out until the next day that I had been eligible to buy before the public offering. Nonetheless, as far as the stocks rocketed on day one, they fell soon after and Iwerks ended up having the worst year of its business. The result was that the board eventually ousted Stan and took the company over, foregoing his visionary temperament for a more even-keeled, bottom-line approach. It is not at all unusual in Hollywood for a visionary to propel a company to the point where money people get interested, and once they put their money in, they take the vision-ary out.

 THE INTERACTIVE ECOSYSTEM (p. 233)

Returning to the Hollywood of 1993 as a ten-year veteran of interactive design from New York was the ultimate in culture shock. The entertainment industry, which had basically shunned ESI's interactive visions ten years prior because it just couldn't figure how to make money off of them, had suddenly embraced multimedia and called it its own.

For the first six months after *Virtual Adventures* was complete, I found myself swimming with the sharks. It was a strange time for me. The first six months of 1994 were kind of a rude awakening. I had this charmed experience for six months, and now I was thrown into the thick of Hollywood hype. One thing I learned immediately was that people in Hollywood lie. They lie not because they have to but because it simply does not occur to them to tell the truth. I met dozens of people calling themselves interactive producers who had produced nothing, interactive agents who had no clients, and interactive attorneys who know nothing of multimedia law. I met heads of new startups that were gone in a puff of smoke six months later. I heard people claim to be working with others when all they'd done is had lunch together. I myself got lunched constantly. During a lean period, I had the surreal experience of never paying for meals, only valet parking.

In the meantime, other things were afoot. *Virtual Adventures* launched in November of 1993 to a generally positive response which sent me on a new branch in the path of life. A chance meeting (another one of those decisive moments) at the conference where *Virtual Adventures* first premiered led to a talk at SIGGRAPH 94 in the following August in Orlando, Florida. SIGGRAPH is the largest international conference and trade show on computer graphics and interactive techniques. It is unlikely that I would have gone had I not been asked by Clark Dodsworth to speak as part of a panel on the topic of "Digital Illusion" to talk about techniques in interactive storytelling. I was completely surprised to find out that *Virtual Adventures* was a prominent feature of the show, being demoed on the trade show floor by Evans & Sutherland, and also featured in a large-scale interactive theater.

SIGGRAPH 94 was another major crossroads for me. There are a number of adventures I've had that can be directly traced back to that conference and Clark's panel. It was at the conference that I met and rediscovered people who were to become my good friends, colleagues, collaborators, and clients around the world. I reconnected with my old friend and ESI colleague Athomas Goldberg, now at NYU. I was exposed to a number of projects and ideas which have since had a major influence on me, including Rita Addison's *Detour: Brain Deconstruction Ahead*, a riveting talk by Brenda Laurel on a panel called *Are We Forcing People to Evolve?*, and the list goes on… As a result of that talk at SIGGRAPH, I had two articles published in *ACM/SIGGRAPH Computer Graphics Journal*, and in Clark Dodsworth's subsequent book *Digital Illusion* (Addison Wesley), both of which were major factors in inspiring me to write this book.

A month after SIGGRAPH, I was invited to Denmark to teach at a two-year interactive program called Space Invaders at "MouseHouse," a Multimedia Center in the medieval town of Århus, Denmark (they've since moved to Copenhagen). I had done some teaching up to this point, but my experience in this area was fairly limited. Part of the reason for this was most new media programs (and this is just now starting to shift) were basically vocational schools teaching people how to use software tools, but none of the finer points of design. This was an entire program in which students had to learn more than just Macromedia Director and Adobe Photoshop. They had to learn how to design, how to think, how to compose a page, how to create and test an interface. The students also had to understand principles of semiotics and were taught about educational and pedagogical principles behind interactive media. I have since been to MouseHouse twice, both for several weeks at a stretch, and it is my favorite place to teach. Denmark is a tiny little country where nothing particularly exciting happens, and the residents have a strange national character that combines a self-assured manner, to the point of seeming self-satisfied, with the constant expression of self-effacing humility.

One thing that blew me away about Denmark was that everybody was not only extremely well-educated, but no matter how old they were, most people were still in school in some way or another. My class consisted of a total of about 30 students, who I taught in English. Everyone in Denmark understands English; they have to because they love to read and not too many books are published in Danish, whose tiny population of five million scarcely warrants translations.

I taught three courses at MouseHouse, the first of which was a seminar in interactive storytelling, roughly based on the SIGGRAPH 94 talk. The second course was a slide lecture I call "DadaBase: A History of Interactivity in Art," which was basically an art history lecture with slides and an overhead projector in which I survey non-computer artists of the 20th century who explored issues of audience interactivity. Both of these courses were originally taught at the American Film Institute, but have since been taught elsewhere.

> Although my classes include much discussion and interaction, in none of them do I use computers. My goal is to teach students interactivity, not technology. For this reason, I do not teach for a specific platform, but rather, teach fundamental principles of interactivity that can be used in any medium from virtual reality, to interactive video, to board games.

The third course I taught at MouseHouse was a two-day board game workshop designed to teach game structure and multi-user interaction. Students spend the first day playing and analyzing board games using my "Rules of the

Game" criteria list. They then spend the second day working in teams to design and construct an original board game concept. This course has also been taught in London at the Hypermedia Research Centre at Westminster University. You can imagine how much fun this course can be. The students love it and the feedback I get from program directors is that there is a significant shift in the students' structural sensibilities after taking it. Often, they remark, the students have the aesthetics down, but they don't quite know how to design the experience itself.

Unfortunately, the U.S. is not quite ready for the board game class. I can only attribute this to the current vocational paradigm in which students and institutions alike tend to shy away from courses that do not produce "marketable skills." I hope someday that multimedia students and program directors in America will realize that the most important skill you could possibly have is to understand the fundamental principles of game logic and interactivity, regardless of the technology. Unfortunately, it seems that currently, most people want to learn authoring tools.

I recently began teaching a foundation course in San Francisco State University's 3D design certificate program. Entitled "Exploring Spatial Media," this three-day intensive course covers the history of VR, design and narrative techniques, and has an extensive show-and-tell segment. In this class, I do a series of what I call "spatial sensitivity" exercises designed to help students pay more attention to the physical space around them. In one exercise, I ask students to write narrative descriptions of familiar spaces from memory and from experience. This provides an interesting insight into space memory and different ways in which people relate to the space around them. After providing an overview of "the building blocks of 3D," I ask the students to walk around the neighborhood and study the real world as if it were a VR environment—look for polygons, texture maps, various forms of shading, even behaviors in the environment. This is an eye-opening experience, and one that can boggle the mind a little too much if you're not careful.

One of the things I personally love to do is to put together themed exhibitions that showcase cutting edge new content. So far, I've been able to design and produce two of these. Having been to dozens of interactive show-and-tells, I've kind of developed my own technique for the interactive "group show." In fact, I like to call what I do in producing showcases "curating," because I really try to create a total experience in which both the content and the context have some resonance. Each showcase is set within the context of a themed environment, something that is really friendly and accessible, that will lend itself to the emergence of a culture of some sort. Then, within this context, I place projects that have some thematic coherency within themselves. The relationship between the content and the environmental context is both social and sometimes ironic, providing both a coherency and a contrast between the two.

Context is an important and often overlooked component in new media exhibitions. I've noticed that most showcase exhibitions provide little if any context. You enter a crowded noisy room and fight with other guests for mouse time in front of a tiny screen, unable to hear audio squeezing out of the tiny speakers. So with the showcases I've done, I've made a concerted effort to be as attentive to the environment as a good interactive designer would be to an interface. After all, environment really is just another form of interface.

Architecture as a Narrative Art (p. 25)

The first showcase exhibition I produced was for SIGGRAPH 95 in Los Angeles. This conference featured a 45,000 square foot showcase of interactive technologies. It included something like 80 projects supported by the world's largest temporary LAN. Dubbed "Interactive Communities," this exhibition was creative directed and produced by Coco Conn, and also included her own project, SIG KIDS. SIG KIDS was a giant working studio where children and teenagers hung out at the week-long convention and made their own digital art, Virtual Reality environments, and webcasts. Aleta Pearce, my sister, was the installation coordinator. I was involved in helping put that show together, but my main focus was an "art annex" to the area that housed two mini-exhibitions, the Digital Atelier and the lounge@siggraph.

The Digital Atelier was a working art studio where SIGGRAPH attendees could come and use high-end graphics computers and IRIS printers to make art on-site. It also included *Chain Reaction*, a web version of the old Dada game *Exquisite Corpse*. In *Chain Reaction*, artists could go online, select from the work of other artists, and modify it to create their own original work. Links were kept between the works so you could trace them back to their origins.

The lounge@siggraph was a 1300 square foot exhibition in an enclosed room showcasing art- and culture-oriented applications from around the world. Marita Isaksson, a Swedish student I met during one of my visits to Denmark, spent the summer with me as an intern, and her boyfriend, another one of my students, Geert Madsen, soon followed. Marita acted as associate curator/producer on the project and was very involved in the entire production and design process. Together, we recruited about a dozen projects from around the world. Jakob Tuborgh, a fellow faculty member from "MouseHouse," joined us a week or so before the conference and assisted us with final furniture selection and installation.

The theme for the lounge@siggraph was a Bohemian café. It was decorated with a bunch of cool furniture we rented from a local scenic shop. The centerpiece was a diner counter from the 50s, with its own floor and built-in stools. At each stool surrounding the U-shaped counter was a computer, keyboard, and two sets of headphones so that people could experience CD-ROM and Internet projects without audio interference. We also had a large projection screen and speaker system in the room. A toggle switch enabled us to rotate between the projects shown on the screen. The shared speakers were placed in the outer hallway to draw visitors down the dark corridor to our little nook.

The first five projects listed in the following bulleted list were located at the diner counter; the others each had their own little areas:

- **Anti-Rom:** This notorious and irreverent CD-ROM was made by a collaborative of London artists led by Andy Cameron, director of the iconoclastic Hypermedia Research Centre at London's Westminster University. Its surprising interactivity, hip musical and graphical style, and biting social and political commentary made this one of the most addictive CD-ROMs I've seen to date.

- **Urban Feedback:** Created by Perfect Indigo, another London Art team. This CD-ROM had the feel of an interactive music video. The interaction was intuitive and visceral, allowing for a dynamic interchange with a collage of words, visuals, and sounds that created a richly textured impression of sensory urban life.

- **Jay's Joint & Future Sound of London:** Two web sites designed by Jeremy Quinn for London bands Jamiroquai and Future Sound of London (FSOL). Jay's Joint was a party house where you could go and hang out with band members. I also housed a bulletin board with flyers for environmental groups in London. FSOL's web site used a three-dimensional graph as an interface to an intertwined story told by band members.

- **Bar-Min-Ski: Consumer Product & Encyclopedia of Clamps:** Bill Barminski is an L.A. painter, who, with his partners, producer Webster Lewin and programmer Jerry Hesketh, have amassed a cult following with their first CD-ROM title *Consumer Product* (see figure A.17). Barminski's work, revolving around consumerist/cold war imagery of the 1950s, translated beautifully into the CD-ROM medium. The limited edition first pressing was distributed as follows: The artist sold "DE-LUX'O" can-openers for a hundred dollars with a free CD-ROM, signed by the artist and included a small original drawing. They soon found distribution in the Voyager catalog (the oldest CD-ROM catalog) and created *Encyclopedia of Clamps*, and a new web site called *Cyclops Boy* based on a character from Bill's paintings.

- **MouseHouse/Space Invaders Student CD:** I invited the school I teach at in Denmark to come and demo their student sampler, which has examples of student work; among the projects was a 3D model of the school facility and an interactive game show.

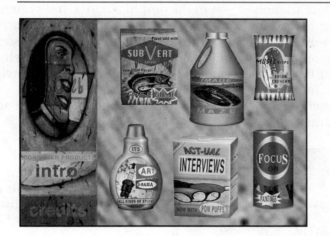

Figure A.17
Menu screen from
*BAR-MIN-SKI: Consumer
Product* CD-ROM by DE-
LUX'O

Plate 58

● **YORB Interactive Television:** In one corner of the room, surrounded by beanbag chairs, a game of Twister, and featuring a TV topped with an illuminated bunny, we placed YORB. YORB is, to my knowledge, the only working interactive television program, and it has been running fairly consistently on New York Cable for several years. It was not produced by AT&T or Viacom or Disney or Sony or any of the other interactive TV contenders; it is a student project out of New York University's Interactive Telecommunication Program, or ITP. Since its inception, YORB has had a variety of different programming content, all of which involved the use of nothing other than a common push-button phone. This interface enables viewers to move through a simulated 3D environment, speak to each other live on the phone while in the environment, and use the Internet to type text messages on your computer which are then displayed on your television screen.

● **Musical World:** This project was put into a living room setting including a sofa and lounge chairs, and a great coffee table that featured a glass top being held up by a lounging topless mermaid. Musical World was a music-based demo for the short-lived 3DO platform, created by Commotion New Media, who were also involved in creating the CD-ROM magazine *Launch*. It included a musical statue that played a variety of different instruments; you could change melodies and add and subtract instruments in real time to create your own one-man-band-jam session. (Actually, I think the statue was a woman!) This title never went public due to the demise of the 3DO system.

● **Inneractivity Finder:** Created by a Japanese artist/writer Gohsuke Takama, this very unusual interactive application enabled you to create psychedelic computer graphics using your brain waves. You wore a headband that recorded your brainwaves in real time, and a pair of special glasses that immersed you in the graphics. Lines and patterns of color would shift and change on the screen based on your brain activity. The thing that was really fun about this was that when you saw something you liked (and usually, you'd say "oooh" when seeing something very pretty) your brainwaves would become even more active, precipitating still more interesting graphics. The more active your brain became, the better the image; and the better the image, the more active your brain became (see figure A.18).

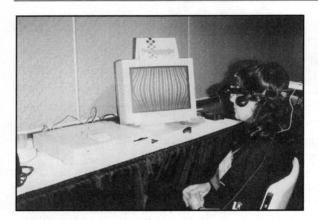

Figure A.18

Participants create computer animations using their own brainwaves with Gohsuke Takama's *Inneractivity Finder*

● **The Virtual Gallery:** This was the one project in the lounge@siggraph that we ourselves produced. Called "Second Nature," the project was developed in collaboration with Utah State University's Space Dynamics Laboratory, and used a treadmill interface that enabled visitors to literally walk through a virtual world. The world itself, called "The Virtual Gallery," was an art museum full of classic paintings each of which was a portal into a Virtual World. We built full VR models of a variety of different paintings, including work from MC Escher, Paul Klee, Renee Magritte, and Henri Matisse, as well as paintings from Renaissance and more representative periods. Any time you wanted, you could literally walk through the frame and enter a 3D depiction of your favorite painting.

 STROLLING THROUGH CYBERSPACE: SECOND NATURE AND THE VIRTUAL GALLERY (p. 457)

We were delighted with the outcome of the lounge@siggraph because it became much more than just a showcase, it became a whole scene unto itself. People would come back just to hang out. We encouraged discourse and got plenty of it. It was exactly what we set out to do, and in spite of the fact that it was hidden down a long dark hallway behind the animation festival, the lounge@siggraph soon became the best-kept secret at the convention and by the third day, word of mouth had spread to the point that we were mobbed all day.

A few months after the lounge@siggraph, I got a call from Beth-Ellen Keyes of Reed Exhibitions wanting to know if I could do a similar showcase focusing on Virtual Reality for the IntermediaWorld conference at San Francisco's Moscone Convention Center in March of 1996. I hired my sister Aleta Pearce, who helped put together the SIGGRAPH 95 Interactive Exhibition for Coco Conn, and asked her to project manage this effort for me under the guise of my new company, *momentum media group*.

For IntermediaWorld, I proposed the VR Garden, a real garden environment with trees, flowers, umbrella'd picnic tables, and trellises. We brought in a wagon, logs to sit on, and even a fountain with real trickling water. There were 14 projects, seven interactive installations, plus a video showcase, all representing what we felt were the most sophisticated and surprising VR projects we could collect (see figure A.19). I say surprising because one of the things we were trying to do was offer people something different than what they were used to seeing. Nothing in our booth was a consumer product, and indeed, only the VRML sites were accessible to the public. The full installations were coming out of high-tech companies and R&D facilities and although quite well known within the VR industry, were obscure to a broader public, even a public that was already in the CD-ROM business. All they knew of VR was Doom. So we wanted to give them a deeper look into what VR is and could be.

Figure A.19

The VR Garden, IntermediaWorld 96, placed high technology in a serene garden environment

In a picnic area, perched on wooden picnic tables with green canvas umbrellas over them, were the desktop applications—Internet-based VR and CD-ROM projects, including the following:

- **Clay Graham's Dr. Jax Robot Island:** A world where you could build your own robot. Each limb had a different behavior. You could connect all the different components together, then watch the robot run.

- **C. Scott Young's Idville:** A magical environment peopled with the charming "Idiom," a simple yet mischievous nation of cyberspace life forms. Young's work is comprised of equal parts Dr. Seuss and Joseph Campbell—interweaving the charm and humor of a children's story with a rich subtext of myth, archetype, and role-playing.

- **Encyclopedia of Clamps:** Our friends Bill Barminski, Webster Lewin, and Jerry Hesketh of DE-LUX'O sent us the latest version (originally previewed at the lounge@siggraph), which uses a 3D interface as a vehicle for exploration of their zany art-based brand of interactivity (see figure A.20).

Figure A.20

Encyclopedia of Clamps, from the people who brought you *BAR-MIN-SKI: Consumer Product*

 PLATE 5 7

Across the path, were the higher-end applications, each of which was running on a Silicon Graphics, Inc. (SGI) Reality Engine, loaned to us by SGI for the show. These applications included the following:

- **Improv/Virtual Actors:** Athomas Goldberg's project out of NYU. *Improv* consists of computer-generated characters with autonomous behaviors that can interact with each other and real people based on a system of gesture recognition and procedural animations. The animations were created by computer algorithms and code rather than by the "key frame" method of creating a series of key positions and interstitial frames between them. This is a bit of an "in" joke, but we were highly amused when one guest asked if *Improv* was done in Macromedia Director, an authoring tool used to create CD-ROMs for consumer products. In this particular application of *Improv*, guests could play a

MIDI drum to which the characters would dance in real time, changing the cadence of their gestures based on the rhythm and intensity of the beat.

- **Japanese pop star:** A simulated girl singer brought to life with motion capture technology by Sim Graphics and their VActor system. She was so cute that most of the guys (and some of the girls) in the booth got a crush on her. (It was San Francisco!)

- **Vacuii:** A virtual dance space brought to us by Fakespace Music, a division of Fakespace, Inc. You could explore VR world using Fakespace's proprietary boom system. You hold a viewer with handles in front of your eyes and don an audio headset for full audio immersion. The eyepiece is attached to a large boom arm that allows you to move freely, changing your orientation at will. Using this boom, you could literally dance inside an abstract 3D world whose animations were triggered by music. It was, as some of our guests remarked, "a real trip."

In addition to the VR, CD-ROM, and higher-end projects in the VR Garden, we also had the wildcard element. Charles Ostman brought us some of his Nano-Art. Charles also programs procedural animation, but his is used to model systems of Nano-Technology. Although created purely with algorithms (he does no modeling or animation, other than the procedural code), they turn out to be so beautiful that Ostman has taken to selling them as art. At the VR Garden, we gave him three easels to show his canvas transfers of Nano-Worlds, and a monitor on which to show the various animations and images he produces.

A-LIFE OF ONE'S OWN (p. 5)

ARTIFICIAL INTELLIGENCE AND THE PROSTHETIC BRAIN (p. 38)

The VR Garden also featured a video showcase that included the following, to name only a few:

- Rita Addison's *Detour: Brain Deconstruction Ahead,*
- Christa Sommerer and Laurent Mignonneau's *A-Volve,* as well as a sampling of their other work
- Char Davies' *Osmose*
- *T_Vision* earth visualization project
- And, of course, *Virtual Adventures*

T_VISION: SPACESHIP EARTH MADE VISIBLE (p. 460)

V-ART (p. 494)

We also had live electronic music from Dogon, a San Francisco duet comprised of Paul Godwin and partner Miquel Noya, whose improvised set at the VR Garden can be heard as a track on their album "Not Dun Justa," on the New Dog Records label.

What happened at the VR Garden was similar to the magic experienced at the lounge@siggraph, except we had a better spot and everyone at the tiny conference knew about us. We were called a "refreshing relief," from the formica-and-chrome booths that characterize high-tech conferences. People came and hung out; a few spent almost the entire week in our booth. Most of the people who visited us said that the VR Garden was the best thing at the show. One gentleman wandered into our booth unawares and naively took our natural environment to be an indication of lack of technical savvy. "So, this is the low-tech booth," he said. "No. Actually," I replied, "this is the most high-tech booth in this show. We've got three SGI Onyxes and an Indigo in here." The high-tech backing came from the generous support of Silicon Graphics Inc., manufacturers of the standard high-end 3D work stations, from whom we were able to borrow three machines. I loved the contrast of high-tech, high-touch, luddite technophiles sitting there in this natural setting. Like the lounge@siggraph, the VR Garden became its own cultural phenomenon, which is really the goal for me in all these projects.

All of my site-based projects have been about creating a social space, a narrative environment where it is the people themselves that create the story. It is the coming together of the projects, the creators, and the audience. I love exposing the audience to projects that they might not otherwise have exposure to; exposing the audience to the creators themselves, exposing the creators to the creators, and exposing the audience to itself. What happens in these spaces is that the people ultimately create their own experience; they hang around, they talk, they play together, and they quiz the artists. Unlike traditional tradeshow exhibits, I do not invite marketing people to show the work—I go straight to the source so that the audience can find out how these things were conceived and implemented and how they are intended to be used.

These days, what I've been working on is how to take this sense of creating culture and bring it to bear in the online world of Cyberspace. Most VRML sites on the Internet are not very interesting because they have no sense of place and no sense of culture. So the problem I'm currently working on is how to create culture in cyberspace: how to take that same experience of creating a "scene" in a real place, and translating it into a virtual space. It is the continuing exploration of Virtual Reality as a social medium, and as a medium for self-generating, user-created content. The goal for me is not to create content at all, but to create a venue for the audience to create its own content.

SOCIAL COMPUTING (p. 434)

CYBERSPACE CADETS: VIRTUAL COMMUNITIES AND AVATOR WORLDS (p. 146)

VIRTUAL REALITY AS A DRAMATIC ART (p. 508)

AUTODIDACTIC COMMUNALISM

Interactive multimedia was originally developed as an autodidactic, or heuristic teaching methodology. Based on the work of such masters in child development as Jean Piaget and Maria Montessori, the underlying idea behind interactivity was to create autodidactic, or self-teaching, tools using a computer. Montessori created "analog" autodidactic tools, various toys that, through self-guided play, taught preschool children principles of addition, subtraction, multiplication, color, language, and so forth. The computer, because of its capacity to respond to the user in a reciprocal (or interactive) fashion, offered perhaps the ultimate autodidactic tool. With a computer, you could create programs that were actually responsive, that actually changed based on the learner's activity.

It is this inherent quality of computers that has given rise to a new trend in education—one that hearkens to an earlier day when all or most of education was received at home. Through autodidactic principles of heuristic learning, people have begun teaching themselves. Witness the enormous popularity of children's "edutainment" software for home-based personal computers. The computer is taking the place of the television as America's baby-sitter.

 THE ADD GENERATION (p. 17)

Many innovators in digital media learned their craft through a combination of self-taught autodidactic methodologies and "on-the-job" training. The Macintosh computer interface is perhaps one of the most brilliant examples of a heuristic or autodidactic tool. You learn how to use it while using it, therefore eliminating the entire teacher (possessor of knowledge)/student (absorber of knowledge) dynamic.

Some would regard such a proclamation with alarm, fearing the natural outcome would be a kind of staunch individualism in which everyone is a self-taught island. But in fact, this is not entirely the case. Most of these self-taught individuals actually practice a method of education I call *autodidactic communalism.* In fact, most of the individuals to which I refer did not teach themselves in isolation, but were part of some project or community (whether it be the hacker community, the university research community, or even the video arcade community) built on a two-way teacher-student relationship. In this new autodidactic community, people teach themselves and each other. There are no longer "experts" in possession of information or bestowing their knowledge on passive and hungry "students" who must be taught. Instead, everyone becomes both teacher and student, sharing ideas, input, tricks, and techniques, and evolving tools and hardware based on needs and use patterns. The hierarchical "didactic" method has given way to a non-hierarchical heuristic system in which everyone is at once teacher and student.

I believe that this will increasingly become the paradigm of future education for the digital age. This active and dynamic model promotes the three most important qualities of Digital Man:

- *Motivation:* The ability to be a self-starter.
- *Learning curve*: The willingness to learn new things (which means the sense to know what you don't know) on one's own.
- *Collaboration*: The ability to function well in a group, work with others, and be part of a team.

Motivation is absolutely necessary to keep up with the breakneck speed of new technological developments. Being interactive means being self-motivated. You can't wait around for someone to tell you what to do. You have to be willing to create your own path. You also have to expect it to be an uphill battle, because as an innovator, many people will regard you with skepticism. The learning curve is also crucial. The complacency of knowing it all is a pipe dream. There can no longer be "experts," because as soon as you obtain expertise, it becomes obsolete. Therefore, you must constantly be learning new things, and you must also have an "open architecture" about teaching others. Those who keep to themselves, who privatize and hoard information, ultimately cheat themselves of the enormous resources available to them in a community that encourages the free exchange of information. Unless such a person is a true genius, he or she will ultimately lose because inherent in the learning curve of Digital Man is the need to share information and to communicate. If you look at the history of profession, it is invariably those who take a proprietary attitude about information who set themselves back, reinventing the wheel time and time again and forcing others to do the same.

So-called "modern" educational techniques are having an increasingly difficult time keeping pace with actual educational content. The public high schools, for example, are (optimistically) ten years behind the times—most would say it is more like 20. Teachers know less about computers than the children they teach. Any informational infrastructure based on books going in and tests coming out is going to have a fairly short shelf-life in this day of instantaneous access to information. Sad to say, but it is probable that kids today learn more from television than they do from school. We know that they spend more time in front of the television—unless they have computers.

The World Wide Web is the ultimate undoing of traditional education and the impetus for the autodidactic communalism revolution. Suddenly, your desktop is all the libraries, all the newspapers, all the universities, and all the other desktops in the world. If you have a computer, or access to one, you can find out virtually anything you want to know, and a million times more than you would ever care to.

The drawback of the web as a source of information is that it is obsessed with the contemporary at the expense of the historical. Although there are many sites devoted to historical content, the web is arguably the *worst* place to learn history, because in some respects, the Internet, indeed digital culture as a whole, is somewhat a-historic. With a myopic eye always trained to the future, the body of digital knowledge seems to erase the past, even as it writes the future. In this sense, a new means needs to be developed to maintain some sense of historical perspective. This is being done in some places—museums and archival projects—and it is interesting to note that many of these new digital histories are being done in the form of oral histories—collecting not the government versions of say, World War II (just to give an example), but the personal stories of people who were there. Therefore, this too becomes a form of autodidactic communalism. Those who were present for historical events tell the story as it occurred from varying viewpoints. This form of history will become increasingly more common as we begin to break down the notion of factual expert and replace it with a more open-architecture of narrative viewpoints and personal accounts.

Due to its very subjectivity, it's also notable that the web is a breeding ground for "mis" information. Facts are completely twisted or the truth is obscured to the point where reliable documentation is hard to differentiate from urban myth. Some may argue that this makes the web an interactive medium where people compose their own version of the truth or reality. On the other hand, the press has been passing around erroneous information as fact for years. Perhaps it is more realistic to pawn off all information as opinion, rather than creating the illusion that there really is such a thing as objective fact in the first place.

Heisenberg's Uncertainty (p. 222)

The digisphere is, in fact, a sphere of communication. In this new community, we must redefine our concept of the "self-made" man or woman. Let's look at the American ideal of the Horatio Alger-type, the individual single-handedly creating his or her own reality without the benefit of a formal education or economic advantages. The opportunity for such a person to succeed has been greatly increased through digital technology. On the other hand, the related image of the autonomous cowboy, the independent entrepreneur, has certain limitations. Digital technology enables us to be more independent, but at the same time, necessitates more interdependence. Those who will do well in this new world are those who can successfully integrate the independent, vanguard spirit with a strong ability to interact, collaborate, and learn with others.

THE PEDAGOGICAL MOUSEPAD, OR, HOW IT ALL GOT GUI (p. 365)

AUTOBIOGRAPHY OF AN AUTODIDACT, PART 1 (p. 45)

SOCIAL CAPITALISM (p. 425)

BEEN THERE, DONE THAT

You know when you're in a restaurant and you see someone that looks really familiar and you're sure that you know him and you've met him and perhaps you even know him quite well, but you can't quite recall his name? Then suddenly it hits you, kind of like a stone falling into the pit of your stomach: He is a famous actor or rock star and you know him from watching a film or an MTV video?

To know someone you've never met, to feel a sense of intimacy, even perhaps have an emotional feeling about someone who doesn't even know you exist is a peculiar experience. But even more peculiar is seeing that person in real life and having the *emotional* sensation that you know him, as if he were a friend or family member, until you have to *mentally* adjust to the fact that you only know him through his media persona.

I am fascinated with the nature of vicarious experience—the idea that you can experience something without really experiencing it. If we have met someone or been somewhere virtually, how does that experience compare in our minds, emotions, and memories to the real thing? Vicarious experience is nothing new. People have been doing it with storytelling, books, and movies for years. But modern technology provides us with a rich repertoire of possibilities. From training airline pilots in flight simulators to curing fear of heights with Virtual Reality, interactive experiences have the power to immerse us in very convincing vicarious experiences.

VICARIOUS EXPERIENCE (p. 504)

The following are some examples from my own experience that have inspired me to think in more depth about this whole issue.

Pop star Peter Gabriel's *Xplora*, designed by Steve Nelson of Brilliant Media, was the first successful attempt at creating a music-based CD-ROM (with

B

success being defined as a product with both design merit and commercial success). I first experienced *Xplora* at a product launch party in New York in 1993. One of the features of the *Xplora* disc that I got to try was an interactive video walk-through of Gabriel's music studio, ironically called Real World Studios, complete with the crackle of gravel beneath your feet as you walk down the gravel paths of the renovated medieval castle. About a year after having this "virtual" experience of the studio, I had occasion to visit the actual place, a kind of high-tech enclave nestled comfortably amid thatched roof buildings and grazing cattle in a bucolic medieval village in the English countryside. As I walked through the grounds, hearing the gravel crunching underfoot, I had the most bizarre sensation. I told the gentleman who was giving me the tour, "I've been here. But I haven't. I visited this place on *Xplora*." It was precisely the same feeling I previously described of feeling quite intimate with someone you've never met.

The second experience of this kind occurred when I was working on the Second Nature/Virtual Gallery project with the Visual Insight group at Utah State University Research Foundation's Space Dynamics Laboratory. During the show-and-tell portion of the meeting, they took me to their real-time computer graphics lab and showed me a recently completed "flyover," a virtual model of Park City, Utah. The next day, I went to Park City for the Sundance Film Festival.

In this case, the sensation was a bit different. First of all, it was a "flyover," so I had initially seen the place from an omniscient "God's-eye view." Now I was seeing it from a "human eye" view. As I walked through the real Park City, now in the first person, I had the strange feeling that I was being watched, and at the same time, watching myself from above. Strolling through the real town, I could—in my mind—retrace the blocky elements in the virtual town. I could almost see a virtual me in the scene. It called to mind Marshall McLuhan's observation:

> Thus the world itself becomes a sort of museum of objects that have been encountered before in some other medium.

In pondering the significance of this, I have to go back to questions that arise about the nature of vicarious experience. In the case of the *real* Real World Studios versus *Xplora* Real World Studios experience, when I was in the *real place*, I found myself comparing the two versions. I was oddly aware of the increase in resolution. I could now isolate the rough edges of the simulated walkthrough. The movement was smoother than the low frame-rate video on the CD. The gravel sounded less like corn flakes and more like gravel under my feet. The colors were more distinct. I had been there, certainly, but not quite. I had been to an approximation of the place, close enough to trigger that emotional sense of familiarity, but made somewhat surreal by the fact that the real environment was of a much higher production value than the facsimile.

The place lost a great deal in translation. In real life, it was truly awesome. The environment was amazing, the sunlight, the smells, the fact that you were in the midst of a village that had gone virtually unchanged for 500 years, but yet behind these doors were state-of-the-art, modern digital sound facilities. So the question I had to ask myself was this: Is it better for more people to experience this approximation of the place so that at least those who will never go there (in other words, almost everyone) can have a taste? Or does this bastardized facsimile do a disservice to the true splendor of the reality? I think this is a pressing conundrum that will only grow increasingly complex as we create more and more so-called "simulations" of reality.

The Park City model posed a slightly different problem. There, the virtual experience was more impressionistic, but because it was real-time animation rather than a video depiction, it had a more believable choreography and was more interactive. It also oversimplified the city in some way, which was perhaps less of a disservice to the real place than trying to be realistic and only getting it half right. But the real impact of Park City was the "out of body" experience, in which you could at once be yourself in a real place while imagining a simulated point of view outside yourself.

In some ways, I really question the merits of re-creating anything real in Virtual Reality. A big part of me thinks that we ought to just stick to extending our imaginations through the medium. The Loch Ness that we created in *Virtual Adventures: The Loch Ness Expedition* was completely a product of our imaginations based on a hypothetical, or mythological reality. I haven't got a clue what it looks like at the bottom of Loch Ness, and it was a deliberate choice to pick a locale that everyone is familiar with but few people are likely to ever see. Supposedly, the water is actually so murky that you can't see a damn thing. Our Loch Ness was, of course, emerald green.

We created a fantasy based on reality, a fictitious interpretation of a real environment and the mythology and legend that went with it. *The Loch Ness Expedition* was a fusion of reality and fantasy, a way of taking the human imagination that wants to believe in something such as the Loch Ness Monster, and modeling a conceivable scenario for its existence. This approach lies somewhere between the two extremes—on the one hand, Park City or Real World, which are duplications of real places, and on the other hand, a completely imagined fantasy world. From the standpoint of entertainment and suspension of disbelief, the happy medium in between is a very effective way to create a fantasy that still has some veracity to your audience.

There was, however, some controversy about this in the museum community. Science museums loved the basic idea behind *Virtual Adventures*, but they objected to the hypothetical depiction of real events or topologies. This is always a major schism between educators, who strive for factual truth, and entertainers, who go for the most dramatic interpretation of the truth. With *The Loch Ness Expedition*, we made an effort to build the fiction on a foundation of actual evidence, down to showing real interviews of people who had done research or claimed to have seen the monster. On the other hand, there are neither goldfish nor coral at the bottom of Loch Ness, and although it is not inconceivable that there might be a treasure-laden sunken ship, I very much doubt that you would come across a set of whale ribs on your way to find the Loch Ness Monster's eggs.

The Princess and the Monster: The Making of Virtual Adventures (p. 375)

The project I did with Space Dynamics Laboratory (the people who created the Park City model) was based on an idea I had about a different way of experiencing art. Called *The Virtual Gallery*, we created a walk-through museum in which you could walk through the frames of famous paintings into a fully rendered 3D environment. Using a treadmill walker as your interface, and a sensor that enabled you to navigate by simply turning your head (there were not Head-Mounted Displays, data gloves, worn or hand-held devices of any kind), you could enter a bucolic scene from the Renaissance, an Escher staircase room, a Magritte painting, a Matisse interior, or an abstract landscape of Paul Klee.

Strolling Through Cyberspace: Second Nature and the Virtual Gallery (p. 457)

A project such as this can also bring up a lot of issues such as matters of curatorial efficacy, appropriation (copying classic artworks), interpretation, and so on. The premise was that by experiencing these immersive paintings, people could get a deeper and more meaningful experience of real art when they returned to it in an actual museum setting. One of the biggest hurdles that interactive media has to get over in the museum world is the fact that most museums, with the exception of science museums, are concerned primarily with the preservation and display of artifacts. Curators tend to shy away from multimedia because it detracts from the objects themselves. Having had some experience with this controversy in the museum world, I was very conscious here of trying to find a way to bridge this gap. I was very deliberately creating a vicarious experience that was meant to reflect on the real world…using the familiar painting as a jumping-off point into a fantasy, and at the same time, a window into the real object.

Boston-based Learning Sites has devoted its VR efforts to creating photo-realistic simulations of archaeological sites based on hard research data. This is an exciting application of VR, because it enables us to experience something real that no longer exists. We can walk through an Egyptian ruin re-created to look like it did thousands of years ago. This provides us with both an historical educational and research tool, but also an entertaining experience that sparks the imagination, and again, uses VR to bridge the gap between fantasy and reality.

MUSE-OLEUM: DEAD ZOOS AND LIVING MUSEUMS (p. 313)

On other hand, many VR experiences exist at the level of pure fantasy. Most of these seem to be created with the objective of escape. They are games and fantasy worlds, whose goal is to take you away from reality. It is interesting to note that many of the entertainment applications of VR, whether they be pure fantasy or reality-based, often depict worlds that would not really constitute the most appealing vacation destinations. Like horror movies or violent TV shows, these experiences seem to favor a form of escape into something that is perhaps worse than the thing the players are trying to escape *from*. The question then arises, if we are creating vicarious experiences that promote violence and mayhem, are we not then promoting violence in the real world? Or is the vicarious experience a way for these individuals to release these tensions in a safe and socially acceptable way, so they don't act on these same impulses in the real world?

MEDIASPACE (p. 293)

The bottom line is this: Every time we create Virtual Reality, we are saying something about actual reality. Whether we are trying to escape from it, re-create it, or create a fantasy based on it, reality is with us everywhere we go. People will bring reality with them into the virtual world, and they will take a vicarious experience back out with them into the real world. In either case, these vicarious experiences will always relate to real experiences, and it is well worth exploring and considering the ways in which we are affecting the ongoing relationship between real and virtual.

SPATIAL MEDIA (p. 442)

NARRATIVE ENVIRONMENTS: VIRTUAL REALITY AS A STORYTELLING MEDIUM (p. 329)

ARCHITECTURE AS A NARRATIVE ART (p. 25)

Biosphere Meets Digisphere: The Biosphere 2 Interactive Theater

B

In 1990 I was hired by Dennis Earl Moore to help design and produce an interactive theater for the Biosphere 2 Visitors Center. Moore, a director of special format films (IMAX) and custom theaters, many of which he designed himself, was a great innovator in the area of mediaspace. Prior to Biosphere 2, he had done a number of media installations for Nike trade shows, which evolved into permanent features in the flagship Nike Store in Oregon and became the template for media in the entire chain. Dennis directed *Living Planet*, a very successful early IMAX film. *Living Planet*, with its strong themes of natural unity, was no doubt one of the reasons he was approached by the people at Biosphere 2 to create media installations for their visitors center and document the entire project.

Biosphere 2 was an experiment—attempted by some somewhat eccentric eco-hippies—that began in the 70s and culminated in the construction of what was intended to be a fully self-contained, biologically based life-support system (see figure B.1). It was a highly controversial project. The people creating it, funded by Texas oil billionaire Ed Bass, were viewed by some to be a cult—led by a man named John Allen who seemed to be inspired in equal parts by Buckminster Fuller and Werner Erhart. This so-called prototype of a space station was to house eight scientists for two year's time, during which they would remain in the air-tight structure and exchange no matter of any kind—food, water, oxygen, waste—with the outside world. They did manage to complete the structure and the giant multi-zoned greenhouse inside it and to send the first crew in for two years. I cannot vouch, however, for the efficacy or success of the experiment. An injury, unable to be accommodated by the "ship's doctor," required one member to leave for a couple of hours. Varying other rumors had them sneaking out regularly, starving to death, using a submarine-style oxygen scrubber (which was confirmed), and my personal favorite, calling out for a pizza in a moment of dietetic desperation. The one thing they didn't send out for was sex, which they seemed to have in ample supply. One of the Biospherians herself put it best during her portion of the interview for our show. When asked "Will there be sex in the Biosphere," she replied, "There's going to be lots of reproduction inside the Biosphere," and went on to explain how the birds, plants, insects, and farm animals were expected to be fruitful and multiply.

Figure B.1

Biosphere 2, an experimental biological life support system in the Arizona desert, designed by Peter Pearce

Dennis Moore hired me to co-design and project manage the interactive theater "Meet the Biospherians." The client's original concept was to create an interactive video wall, with each of the eight Biospherians on one screen (modeled after the opening credits of the *Brady Bunch*, perhaps?). An interactive screen enabled one visitor at a time to select from about 20 frequently asked questions. The visitor would then see and hear a direct, pre-recorded video reply from one of the Biospherians. This is the kind of thing I refer to as a "media dispenser." The interactivity is gratuitous and lends nothing meaningful to the experience.

GRATUITOUS INTERACTIVITY: MEDIA DISPENSERS AND THE ATM MODEL (p. 218)

Dennis didn't think this idea was going to have much audience appeal. Individual person-to-machine interaction would create a bottleneck and would not be interesting to other viewers. Furthermore, 20 questions seemed slim compared to the depth and breadth of commonly asked questions, which were numerous. So Dennis' team proposed a different idea: Create a simulated teleconference using a live host, who would program a custom show based on questions from the audience members themselves. The use of a live performer as part of an interactive experience is what I call "human-aided interactivity." The simple addition of a live person created an exponential increase in both the interactivity of the show and the variety of the content.

The interesting thing about this project was the process of getting to the final design. Based on a strong grounding in museum exhibit design, in which up-front research was crucial, I proposed that we begin with a very thorough research phase. I interviewed the tour guides and docents who currently ran the tour and asked them a million questions. Their job, at that time, was to take people around the enclosed building and surrounding site. Carrying one of the those wearable PA systems, they had to describe the project and the various research areas and laboratories around the Biosphere, answering visitor questions along the way. To do this, these individuals, many of whom were retirees, had to memorize over 300 pages of scientific material and be prepared to answer virtually any question asked of them.

I interviewed these docents, who were ultimately going to staff our show, and discovered that only one or two of them had ever touched a computer before. Most of them were entirely computer illiterate. This meant we were going to have to design an extremely user-friendly interface. We did have one advantage: because we weren't creating an interface for visitors, we could actually train the docents how to use the system. Even so, it was very important that it be easy to use and non-intimidating.

The key thing for us was to get "buy in" from the docents. They were used to one thing, and we were bringing in something entirely different. So we got them involved as collaborators in the interface design process from the get-go. We did a series of prototypes, which we tested with the staff, to see what kinds of information hierarchies would work best. This was a big relief to me, because this was the first time in testing that I ever had the luxury of an easy-to-use prototyping tool. Prior to this, I had to make paper and pencil mock-ups, or software prototypes that required full coding. The software designer, his engineer, and I worked very closely together to create a series of test prototypes, all of which were designed to study the docents' response to the interface and integrate their feedback as part of an iterative design process.

We did our final interface design and programming in a flexible program so that we could continue testing with the actual interface until we got it right.

The actual show presentation had two phases, each of which required its own interface. The first was the show-builder. The host would hand out cards to the audience in the queue line, soliciting questions that they would like to ask the Biospherians. As they entered the theater (about 80 people at a time could participate in the show), they would turn in their cards. The host would then select the questions he or she wanted to address (there were often multiples of the same sorts of questions which could be grouped together). The host would then use the show-building interface to program the show.

The show-building interface had a menu of headings under which were about 100 topics. The host selected the sub-topic ("Diet," for example), and a series of clip markers appeared below the faces of the Biospherians along the bottom of the screen which indicated the clips available under that topic. The first layer of clips started the discussion, and the second layer of clips were follow-up comments. Clicking on any clip displayed a summary of that clip in a display box in addition to all the clips that could follow that clip. You would thus select the clips you wanted to build a simulated conversation between the Biospherians on the topic of your choice. You could also, if you so desired, insert yourself into the show so that your live face would also come up on the screen interspersed with the pre-recorded clips. I had to edit the clips by hand and create a hierarchy for each conversation so that every conceivable option would make sense. In other words, you could read each clip and compose it carefully, or you could just as easily close your eyes and click on random clips, and you would always end up with a viable conversation. The biggest challenge in interface design is how to make it fool-proof without making it foolish. With "Meet the Biospherians," we created an interface that was intelligent enough to be challenging and satisfying to the thinking user, but had a built-in failsafe so that you could do it right without thinking, and it was virtually impossible to make a mistake.

The process of building each show took about five minutes, during which the audience would watch a pre-show on the main screen while the host quietly set up the interactive portion of the show from his podium. After the pre-show was complete, the interactive portion of the show began. The second interface—the show player—would come up on the host's private screen. There was a trigger he could use to time everything. There would be pauses for him to speak between each clip, and after he was finished, he would click the trigger to cue the next clip to play. If he had pre-programmed himself in, he could "get in on the act," appearing on the screen himself, conversing with the Biospherians.

The total available content of the show consisted of 700 video clips, ranging from about 10 to 45 seconds in length, stored on five laser disks and totaling 2.5 hours of potential material. This material distilled down into a show of varying length, depending on visitor traffic, or throughput, for the day, but usually ranged from about 7–12 minutes of interactive content.

As you can imagine, a virtually infinite number of possible shows could be generated, and because of the way we structured the material, there were numerous ways to approach similar topics. If you got a question about food, for example, you could answer it via The Kitchen, Health and Diet, or The Farm. We also had links so that if something were brought up in one topic that seemed interesting, the host could act like he was going on a tangent with the interviewee. For example:

> Topic: Recreation:
> Host: What do you do in your spare time?
> Biospherian: I do a lot of reading.
> Host: Oh, so you have books. What books do you have?
> Link to: Library
> Biospherian: Oh, we have an entire library full of books in the habitat.

The questions themselves were garnered in a similar fashion to the way we developed the user interface. Prior to beginning content design and script writing, I had the docents on-site circulate 1300 questionnaires to visitors. The visitors were queried, "If you could ask any question of the Biospherians, what would it be?" The entire content of the show was based on this questionnaire— finding out directly from visitors what they wanted to know about the people in Biosphere 2 and their lifestyle.

One of the reasons this story and process is valuable is because it is a perfect example of what happens when you collaborate with your target audience. On "Meet the Biospherians," we had two target user groups: the venue staff and the audience itself. A good way to design effective interactive applications is to let the users help with the design. I cannot pretend to know what my audience wants or what it will do in a given situation. So I opened the whole process up and let them help guide the design based on their knowledge base, skills, and interests. The final result was that when I went in to train the guides, they were thrilled. The interface was not new to them; not only were they familiar with it, they actually had a hand in designing it. They shared the iterative design process with us and knew it was specifically designed based on their needs and requirements. I wrote a detailed manual, trained the first set of hosts, and then picked certain trainees who I trained to be trainers for a self-sustaining system.

From a technological standpoint, this project was very complex, but ulti- mately, was solved in the simplest way imaginable. This entire show ran on a single Macintosh 2 FX computer with a second backup system in the event of crash or breakdown. The hardware configuration, designed by a former ESI colleague Steven Meyer, went something like this: The Macintosh sent signals to a Grass Valley switcher, which controlled the five laser disk players, as well as all the show lighting (dimmers, stage lights, house lights, and so forth) and the live camera. The laser disk video and the live video were sent directly into the Macintosh to be processed in real time by a RasterOps graphics board. This enabled us to program on-the-fly effects such as wipes and zooms displayed on a large, rear-projection screen.

The script and the content database were all generated in Excel. I toyed around with using FileMaker Pro, but it was fairly new at the time and not as turbo-charged as it is today. I created two major Excel spreadsheets. The first one was the script of questions, with the Biospherians running across the top and the questions running down the side. I would check off which question should be asked to which Biospherian, and Dennis, who was also Producer/ Director, would use this as his Q&A sheet for each videotaped interview.

After the footage was shot, I made a second spreadsheet that included a line for each clip, including all the qualifiers and tags, which clips it could proceed and follow, and in and out frame addresses from the laser disk (all 1400 of which I entered by hand, using a standard remote-control device for the laser disk players). This matrix was then converted into raw data and dumped directly into the program code, which was written in MacForth.

The other issue that came up in design was the notion of creating intelligent software. In the beginning, it was the software designer's contention that this show could be done with an expert system and that we could somehow simulate the personalities of the characters such that the conversations would be self-generated within the computer. He had actually done this sort of thing to good effect with another project, but that was a text-based game and it was a different matter entirely. The first time this issue was brought up, I said that the only expert system in this show was going to be me, that the bottom line was that some human was going to have to go in and qualify all these clips and figure out how they related to each other. The problem is that although computers can do things like calculate color palettes, frame rate, and amount of movement from one frame to the next, they can't interpret video content. Ultimately, there was no way to get the computer to understand the content of the clips, only to organize them once that content was parsed by a thinking human being.

The amazing thing about this project was that we were able to pull it off at all. It was a combination feature-length documentary, live stage show, and interactive exhibit installation. The entire project was designed and installed in about a six month time period under fairly gruelling circumstances which included R&D such that it was. This project was also done on traditional video editing equipment. About three months after we finished this project, I saw my first AVID nonlinear editing system. This system allows you to digitize all your video, then cut it down and rearrange it digitally to create a mock-up of the final output, from which you would make an edit decision list to send into the final, online edit session. As you can imagine, the first time I saw one of these gizmos, I didn't know whether to laugh or cry. Since then, I've been able to work with them and let me just say, they are one of God's benevolent gifts to mankind.

The show did quite well with visitors. In a few cases, we even got reports that guests had somehow missed the introductory comment that this was pre-recorded and thought they were truly seeing a live teleconference with the actual people inside Biosphere 2.

I got to spend some time on-site training hosts and doing the first run of shows with full audiences, which is always the highlight for me. It's not like watching a movie you've just directed. In that case, what you see on the screen is a given. Everything I do is a collaboration with the audience, so it's not done until there's someone there. It's the classic adage: "If an interactive application falls in the woods and nobody's there to interact with it, does it make a sound?" or something like that. Or, to co-opt a line from comedienne Sandra Bernhard, "Without You, I'm Nothing." Or at least the experience is nothing. For me the project was a success because the hosts could use it, they liked it, they were excited by being able to use it as a presentation tool, and the audience enjoyed having their own questions fielded.

TEST FIRST, ASK QUESTIONS LATER (p. 463)

ARTIFICIAL INTELLIGENCE AND THE PROSTHETIC BRAIN (p. 38)

MEDIA ARCHITECTURE (p. 284)

THE BIRTH OF CYBERSPACE: 3D COMES TO THE WEB

Since its inception, the World Wide Web, essentially the public branch of the Internet, has been Flatland. Text and 2D graphics abound, and while VR and 3D graphics begin to take over all other media, HTML (HyperText Markup Language), the standard protocol that enables interconnectivity on the web, remains a strictly 2D proposition.

In the early 1980s, science fiction author William Gibson introduced the idea of cyberspace, a shared online world into which any computer jockey could tap and explore a three-dimensional space. In his short story, *Burning Chrome*, and later in the novel *Neuromancer*, Gibson described a "consensual hallucination" consisting mostly of abstract 3D environments used to store, navigate, and protect information. A young computer whiz by the name of Mark Pesce read Gibson's description of "The Matrix," this shared VR world, and had a vision for the future, one that would be realized several years later along with fellow hacker Tony Parisi. Based in Boston at the time, Pesce and Parisi decided to get together and try to create the template for cyberspace, a simple system to support an interconnected network of shared online worlds that people could move around in freely by using the Internet.

Pesce and Parisi made a prototype, called Labyrinth, which was first shown at SIGGRAPH 94. In the spring of 1995, a team of people got together to create a model of the Variety Arts Center in Los Angeles for the Interactive Media Festival, an exhibition/showcase of interactive projects from around the world (see figure B.2). In the process, Tony and Mark invited representatives from major computer companies, as well as individual artists and small entrepreneurial companies, to get together and help iron out a specification, or "spec" for the Virtual Reality Modeling Language—VRML. This unprecedented move made VRML a truly collaborative project designed by the people it was ultimately to serve. Rather than keeping all the credit and profit to themselves, or creating a proprietary software package, which is how it's generally done in the highly competitive world of "intellectual property," Mark and Tony opened the whole process up and made VRML into a community project. The result is that there now exists a "VRML community."

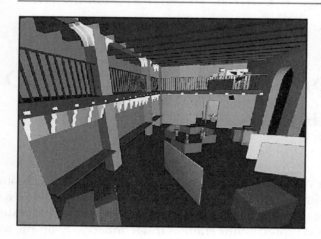

Figure B.2

The VRML exhibition/ showcase for the Interactive Media Festival, 1995

 PLATE 50

What is VRML? It's really very simple. Like HTML, the text protocol used as the backbone for all web sites on the Internet, VRML provides a file format, a protocol, and a consistent set of commands that can be recognized by any computer using a VRML browser. Just as any computer using a Netscape or other Internet browser can recognize HTML, any computer with a VRML browser (generally a plug-in or part of a standard Internet browser) can access any 3D site that exists in the VRML file format.

Why is this an important step for VR? Well, a key factor in the success and mass-dissemination of a new medium is the development of standards and conventions. Without broadcast standards and show format conventions, television would have never flown; programmers could not function if every show was a unique length, or if all advertisements were in a different format. Film would never have made it as a medium if each filmmaker used a different kind of camera and projection system; and the convention of "feature" length allows theater owners to schedule showings in a manageable way. Standardization is what makes a medium "go mass." The mass accessibility of the Internet was only made possible by the collective agreement to utilize the HTML file format, and this too is the case with VRML.

 THEORY OF MEDIA EVOLUTION (p. 468)

For nearly 30 years prior to the invention of VRML, Virtual Reality was confined to a kind of high-tech ghetto. The reasons for this have been mostly technological. There was never any doubt that simulated three-dimensional worlds worked as an interface. Everyone agreed 3D made for great learning and training environments, as well as collaborative design tools. On the rare occasion where it was attempted and executed well, it also had the potential to be an entertainment and even a fine arts medium. But there were three major technological barriers that held VR prisoner within the ivory tower and the Pentagon:

- It took enormous firepower to run real-time 3D worlds; high-end mainframes were required to do the high-level math processing combined with sophisticated graphics generation required to make an interactive VR world.

- Even the simplest Virtual Reality environments were way too big to even consider for the Internet; the bandwidth and processing power simply couldn't support them.

- For the most part, VR developers each worked with their own hardware and software development tools, so that each VR project ran on a completely unique hardware configuration with completely unique software engines. Thus there was little re-usability or interchangeability between systems.

Virtual Reality Check: What is VR Anyway? (p. 518)

A Brief History of Real Time: The Virtual Reality Legacy (p. 105)

Typically, each of the companies and research facilities that creates VR uses its own proprietary system, so there is no compatibility from one VR platform to the next. Many people use Silicon Graphics, Inc. (SGI) or Sun Microsystems hardware, but even those who use these standard platforms more often than not create their own customized modeling and programming tools. In some cases, standard file formats enable you to create a model in a given software package and port it into someone's custom system, but that only works within the same hardware platform. You can't, for example, move Evans & Sutherland models to an SGI machine; and even if it was technically possible to do this, the highly competitive nature of an industry based on proprietary material makes any attempt to do this impossible. VRML, on the other hand, works across all platforms and enables anybody with any computer and a browser to go to any other world, whether it was created on a high-end mainframe or a home PC. The only limitation is the power of the computer itself and its capability to render the graphics and animations.

The other remarkable thing about VRML is the file size. Traditionally, 3D models, texture maps, and other components required to create Virtual Reality environments have been characterized by huge file sizes. VRML files take up only a few kilobytes. They are essentially text files that describe to the computer what to draw on the screen and how to manipulate or animate it. Although the going assumption has always been that VR was too file-heavy for the Internet, now, with VRML, VR files are actually *smaller* than "flat files." A simple picture file of a photograph, for example, can run into thousands of K. Likewise, video files are notoriously large and difficult to move through the pipes. Thus, VRML makes 3D more efficient in terms of file size than any other medium distributed over the Internet, with the possible exception of text.

If what goes around comes around, then VRML is really the full circle of VR. Ivan Sutherland created VR in the early 60s because he and others with whom he was working felt that the 3D graphical user interface was the most intuitive and natural way for people to relate to a computer. His simple, vector-based worlds, as depicted in his 1960 thesis project *Sketchpad*, demonstrated the elegant simplicity of a graphical navigation and manipulation system based on creating an allegory for 3D space on a 2D surface. This design predates the development of the 2D interface, which we commonly use today, by about 10 years. Therefore, although the 3D interface was invented first, on the mass-media level, 2D has been it for the past 15 years. Thirty-five years after *Sketchpad*, the 3D interface returns, still as elegantly simple and intuitive as when it was first conceived.

The Pedagogical Mousepad, or, How it all Got GUI (p. 365)

VRML has its limitations, make no mistake. To run efficiently, it requires that models have much fewer polygons and less magic tricks than in high-end VR. It wasn't until January of 1997 that the VRML 2.0 spec was released, which included a protocol for animation. At this writing, more work is being done to create multi-user worlds and other features that the VRML Consortium (the group responsible for development of the VRML spec) has determined its members need. Even so, it is now possible to build a 3D model in a home authoring program, output it as a VRML file, and insert it in any VRML-created world on the Internet. The amazing thing about creating VRML worlds is that anyone can do it. What used to be the purview of an elite group of researchers, artists, and engineers is now at the fingertips of anyone with a computer. As a result, at this point in its evolution, a significant amount of cyberspace is user created.

In sharp contrast to the Gibson vision, cyberspace turns out to be less the domain of corporate empires than the spontaneous creation of its own "Netizens." The architecture of cyberspace is an indigenous architecture, a growing organism that expands organically as its users build it up and out. Like the actual buildings in the book *Architecture Without Architects*, by Bernard

Rudofsky, these worlds are spawned spontaneously as a product of the immediate vision or need of an individual or group, rather that being planned and
constructed by megalopolies. Some of those building the so-called "Second
Web" are commercial companies, but just as many are amateur artists,
independent hackers, or freelancers, who are creating their own worlds for
themselves or clients rather than, as Gibson has suggested, infiltrating large,
pre-built corporate or institutional worlds.

Perhaps a bit strangely, a huge cultural gap exists between the VRML community and the traditional VR community. Traditional VR designers frown upon
VRML in the same way feature film directors frown upon television. They see it
as limited, overly simplistic, and not conducive to creating the kind of grand
worlds they seek to construct. When I started investigating working in VRML, I
was repeatedly told that after working with a high-end Evans & Sutherland
flight simulator on *Virtual Adventures*, I would find VRML impossibly stifling.
The low polygon counts, limits on texture capability, animation, and behaviors of VRML worlds would no doubt drive me mad. Quite the contrary. In my
mind, all technical constraints are created equal. I designed two decks of
playing cards in the winter of 1997, and wrote this book, both of which I view
as interactive technologies with very narrow constraints. The constraints of the
Evans & Sutherland ESIG 2000 were just as intense, and in some ways, more
difficult than with VRML, because there were a lot more of them. On the
VRML projects I have been working on to date, I find the limitations merely
spark my creativity. There's not much challenge to be had in a medium where
everything is possible. On the other hand, in reality, there is no such medium,
even outside of the interactive realm.

Far from limiting creativity, I think technical constraints act as catalysts for
expanded creativity. VRML artists, such as VRML Knight C. Scott Young and
Information Architect Clay Graham, the cyberarchitecture firm Construct, and
character animation designers Protozoa, are creating unique forms that
completely take advantage of the constraints of this technology. The lack of
texture mapping capabilities, far from being a hindrance, forces the artist or
designer to pay much more attention to form, because textures ultimately
enable you to cheat more than anything else. Thus, the absence of texture
calls attention to shape and can yield unique aesthetic styles as a result.

The reason I embrace VRML in spite of the warnings of my pals in high-end
VR is that I am a mass-media maven. As much as I love the high-end stuff,
the bottom line is, I want a big audience. I want the TV watchers. I want the
school kids. I want the families and the teenagers and all those people out
there whose minds have been lulled to sleep by television and whose creative
impulses lie dormant waiting to be released. These are the people I want to
reach. The creation of a standard such as VRML is the first step toward the
realization of that goal.

CYBERSPACE CADETS: VIRTUAL COMMUNITIES AND AVATAR WORLDS (p. 146)

SPATIAL MEDIA (p. 442)

A-LIFE OF ONE'S OWN (p. 5)

BOOKMARK: INTERACTIVITY AND THE NEW LITERACY

When I was a child, I lived for books. Our house was full of them. Even before I could read, I would sit for hours leafing through the pages of books. In elementary school, I spent every spare second in the school library. While the other kids were out in the yard playing handball and "King of the Log," I was in the library reading *The Secret Garden*, *Charlotte's Web*, *Stuart Little*, and every *Nancy Drew* book ever written. As a pre-teen, I became obsessed with Queen Elizabeth I, and became something of an armchair expert in the Renaissance. Later, when I got interested in film, I read lots of screenplays, film history, and criticism.

To me, books are the greatest form of vicarious experience, the greatest form of storytelling, because they have this magical capability to offer you a string of words on a page that spark a whole plethora of images. That something so small, inexpensive, and seemingly mundane can transport you so completely is a rather remarkable feat, if you think about it. Books are ultimately absorbing and truly immersive in the sense that you forget yourself completely when you enter the book world, the textsphere, or whatever you want to call it. Although books are considered the penultimate in linear narrative, they also have an interactive side. Because the text is designed to elicit a visual image in your mind, it is really a collaboration between reader and author. You are, in a sense, making a movie in your head every time you conjure a scene from the pages of a book. This is why seeing a film version of a book is often such a disappointment: because you already have your own movie in mind. As a writer, I have always taken issue with the expression "a picture paints a thousand words." With a well-written book, a word can just as easily paint a thousand pictures.

Books also hold the key to new ways to think about interactive design. Most narrative drama is built around characters and the decisions they make. Thus, an in-depth exploration of traditional story structure, when viewed in the context of a vehicle for character-based decision-making, can become the impetus for interactive narrative. Unlike the film media or theater, in which the fourth wall creates a fairly standardized relationship between the audience and the characters in the story, literature allows for more control over points of view. A novelist can choose to write in the first person (one character's viewpoint), third person omniscient (the God's-eye view), third person omniscient selective (God playing favorites), third person selective (one character's viewpoint as told by God), and in some rare cases, even second person (your viewpoint). Because interactive multimedia, and especially Virtual Reality, affords the audience a wide repertoire of viewpoints, it is much more valuable to draw some paradigms from the conventions of text than from traditional film or theater.

DECISIONS, DECISIONS, DECISIONS (p. 158)

EINSTEIN, EISENSTEIN, AND THE SPACE-TIME CONTINUUM (p. 186)

Some people decry the computer as another weapon in the war on literacy, but nothing could be further from the truth. Text is an integral part of virtually every software program—whether it be a word processor, a spreadsheet, an entertainment product with text commands, or even a graphically enhanced text adventure. The Internet, in spite of attempts to graphicalize it, is still primarily a vehicle for the text medium. The simple fact that the standard placeholder where you store your favorite Internet addresses is called a "Bookmark" says a lot about the text-centric sensibility of the web. After all, it is based on HTML…the Hyper*Text* Markup Language. One of the most popular uses of online services is Chat, a form of multi-user, real-time writing. And multi-player text-based adventures have been around since the dawn of networking. Furthermore, one of the first creative uses of early PCs, especially for home use, was desktop publishing…the computer became the next generation of the Gutenberg Press. The popular adoption of the Macintosh computer during the mid-1980s can be directly attributed, in part, to its capabilities in desktop publishing.

If you are worried about the future of the written word, just drop down to your local Borders or Barnes & Noble and you will see that the book is alive and well. On a Saturday night, the Borders on Santa Monica's Third Street Promenade in Southern California is one of the most crowded venues. It is not just a bookstore, it's a club, a social hangout, a place for people to not only browse books, but also to be seen, and these days there is a certain amount of hipness associated with being seen in a bookstore. I've always thought that both books and periodicals had a certain amount of semiotic significance in that they provide cues to a person's interests and culture; the same way that the music they listen to or the baseball cap they wear tells you who they are, or who they want you to think they are.

People keep books on their shelves at home not only because they like the books, but also, in a certain way, to show off that they read and to show off the kinds of books they read. Bookshelves can thus become a diagram of the culture of a household. If I see O.J. Simpson's *I Want to Tell You* on your shelf, that's going to tell me one thing about you; but if I see a copy of *Understanding Media* or Shakespeare's *Complete Sonnets*, that's going to tell me something else. It is the specific books, and indeed, the combination of books, that give me clues about your values and interests, or at least those you want made public. Perhaps you have the Shakespeare book on your shelf, but you've hidden the O.J. book under your bed because you don't really want anyone to know you're reading it.

This same phenomenon occurs on the subways of New York City with newspapers. It's something of an in joke that you can tell what sort of New Yorker someone is by whether they are reading *The Times*, *The Post*, *The Wall Street Journal*, or *The Daily News*. When I lived in New York, I used to carry books on the subway as a kind of accessory. I'd actually read them, but I'd often take a particular book as much for effect as for content.

To anyone who moans about the computer killing of the text news media, I have to laugh. There are more magazines on the newsstands now than ever. I always joke that the best way to make money in multimedia is to start a print periodical. At this point, a number of industry magazines cover the full spectrum—*Wired* and *Mondo 2000* at the highbrow end of philosophy and social commentary, *Interactivity* and *Multimedia Producer* being more hands-on, how-to publications. Of course, there is the abundance of the printed web magazines—many of which are actually Internet guides or directories to help people navigate the cyberspace jungle.

As far as multimedia as a topic, the book industry is certainly benefiting from its popularity as well. I need go no further than this moment to point out that you yourself are, at this moment *reading* a book about interactive multimedia; and there are dozens more, from the technical to the philosophical. If you don't believe me, visit the computer section of your local book chain. Some of them can get to be quite large.

No, I don't think the computer is harming the written word any. In fact, I would even venture to hypothesize that it is entirely possible that it's actually helping, that this rebirth of interest in books may in fact be part of a general movement to a more information-oriented value system. Maybe people would rather buy books for the same reason they would rather go on the Internet looking for information. Is it possible that American society is actually beginning to value intellectual content?

If this is the case, the Interactive Revolution may be even bigger than we think, for not only is it adding another dimension of media to our lives, but it is also shifting our interests in other media. Perhaps, in fact, the computer is not the enemy of the book, but its greatest friend—a device that places value on knowledge, information, curiosity, exploration, and intellectual growth is ultimately bound to inspire exploration in other areas. Thus although the computer is clearly beginning to distract us from the television, it may also be opening a portal back to literature, another unanticipated side effect in the media evolution curve and the laws of cumulative media.

The Laws of Cumulative Media (p. 276)

Word to the Motherboard: Computers and Literacy (p. 530)

Cyberfeminism, or, Why Women Love Cyberspace (p. 140)

A Brief History of Real Time: The Virtual Reality Legacy

Virtual Reality is not a new technology. Not only is it not a new technology, but the real-time 3D interface actually pre-dates the 2D graphical user interface (GUI), which has become the standard for both the Macintosh and Windows operating systems. Unlike the Macintosh interface, originally developed at Xerox PARC and then co-opted by Apple and Microsoft respectively, the VR interface managed to go for nearly 30 years before coming into popular use. Some of the reasons for this are technical. Until about 1993, the memory and processing requirements to create a fully rendered three-dimensional world on a computer far exceeded anything that could practically be put on the desktop, plugged into a television, or installed in a game arcade. VR also did not have the stroke of luck to be exposed to visionaries/plagiarists who could take a technology out of the ivory towers of research and into the hands of the people. If the Macintosh and its GUI were the Volkswagen of personal computing, the equivalent is only just now emerging in VR in the form of VRML, the Virtual Reality Modeling Language for the Internet.

If you ask people in the Virtual Reality field the question "What is Virtual Reality?" you will get as many answers as people you talk to. I am something of a purist in this matter, and I basically take the position that if you want to understand the nature of something, you are best served by going right to the source. Following the biblical tenet of "In the beginning, was the Word...," I begin my formal history of VR at the moment the term itself was coined. I like to use the definition of Virtual Reality in its original meaning, as Ivan Sutherland, or The Creator, as I like to call him, intended (I suppose you could look at the guy who invented the Virtual Universe as a god of sorts). In a vastly simplified, but I believe fairly accurate form, it is simply this:

Virtual Reality is a simulated, computer-generated world through which a user can navigate in real time (with immediate feedback), as if moving through an actual three-dimensional space.

 VIRTUAL REALITY CHECK: WHAT IS VR ANYWAY? (p. 518)

So sit back and relax. It's time to hear a story, really a legend of sorts, in which tech nerds are transformed into magicians, conjuring up a parallel universe with nothing more than a running stream of ones and zeroes. It is a tale of the merging of art and science, a tale of modern-day alchemists whose visionary ideas combined with patient tenacity (and I mean *patient*) helped them to work toward the objective of creating a more meaningful interchange between man and machine.

It all started in 1960 when The Creator, Ivan Sutherland was still a doctoral student at the Massachusetts Institute of Technology (MIT), the place where it all began. The first computers found their homes there—giant vacuum tube monstrosities that filled up an entire room and had to be programmed through arduous interfaces such as punch cards. The first computer game, *Spacewar*, was hacked there by the late-night denizens of the computer lab, no doubt eating pizza and drinking what in those days was just plain old Coke. Ivan Sutherland was right in the thick of it.

As part of his doctoral thesis, Sutherland developed what is generally considered to be the first 3D interface, which he documented in a film. It was called *Sketchpad* and it used a light pen to manipulate objects in real time on a computer screen. Sketchpad was an elegantly simple creative tool. With the light pen, you could draw pictures directly on-screen, and then file them in the computer's memory. Then you could pull the pictures out of memory and put them together on the screen. The images in this vector-based system were crude, but you could do a variety of things with them. You could copy them. You could fill one image up with other images. And if you changed the master image of an image you had copied, all the copies would change too. Thus, the program was object-oriented; relating objects to each other, and using a single parent object to dictate changes to its children. *Sketchpad* also enabled you to magnify objects, hence setting the stage for 3D graphics. As you magnified objects to a larger degree, you could discern more detail in the image, thus creating the illusion of three-dimensional space. This introduced the concept of "levels of detail," creating a higher refinement of the image as it gets closer to you, which is a standard trick in all VR today.

The entire *Sketchpad* system was simple and easy to use and understand. You could move things around with ease on the screen by using a combination of intuition and trial-and-error. *Sketchpad* was easier to use than even an Etch-a-Sketch, and perhaps even easier than a pencil and paper, because with pencil and paper, you had to commit to the image with no turning back. In short, it spoke to the user in human terms. It was a highly logical mathematical construct, which very elegantly and effortlessly enabled the human mind to do what it's best at: learn, explore, experiment, and create. With *Sketchpad*, Ivan Sutherland showed that the computer can and should adapt to the user, and not the other way around. Thus, Ivan Sutherland waved his magic wand, and created what has been described as "the most important computer program ever written," and opened the door for the computer to become a heuristic, or self-teaching device.

As is often the case with great movements of innovation, similar ideas were percolating in other locations and minds. Around the country, a small handful of early pioneers were frustrated by the cruel irony of the computer—a phenomenal device with enormous computational powers, made inaccessible by a seemingly impervious barrier to entry. I liken it to the unfortunate Genie of Walt Disney's *Aladdin*: "PHENOMENAL COSMIC POWERS, itty bitty living space."

Meanwhile, elsewhere on the planet, others were evolving theories of how to connect the human mind and the computer in more fluent ways. At MIT, Marvin Minsky was paving the way for Artificial Intelligence, and J.C.R. Linklider wrote a seminal paper in 1960 entitled "Man-Computer Symbiosis," in which he envisioned an integral relationship between human and machine.

Sutherland continued to study the problem of real-time 3D interfaces and in 1965 wrote "The Ultimate Display," describing a new concept for a sensory-based computer interface. In it, he enumerated his vision of an "immersive display" that would include not only sight and sound, but tactile response as well.

It should be noted that, also in 1960, the late Mort Heilig, a filmmaker/inventor patented his own design of a Head-Mounted Display conceived for the purpose of delivering immersive, but passive, 3D television! Heilig also pioneered a variety of other immersive cinema devices, including the Sensorama, a single-person booth-like device that delivered stereo 3D visuals, 3D sound, smell, wind, and seat and handlebar vibration. Content included a belly dancer, complete with perfume, a dune buggy ride in Pismo Beach, and a motorcycle romp through New York City. As a marketing experiment, he also made a film putting the viewer in the first-person point of view of a Coca-Cola bottle going through a bottling plant. The Sensorama had its debut in New York in 1962, and subsequently toured at various locales including Santa Monica Pier and Universal Studios in Los Angeles. Heilig's work, interestingly enough, never overlapped with Sutherland's, because it was concerned exclusively with cinema and had no computational aspirations.

In 1966, Sutherland (now a Harvard professor), and several other researchers at MIT's Lincoln Laboratory began to experiment with the concept of an interactive Head-Mounted Display linked to a computer. The idea was to create a device that would completely immerse the user in a graphically generated 3D world. Large and clunky, it made the wearer look like some kind of cyborg nerd. Small displays in front of each eye used the stereoscopic principle of slightly offset viewpoints to create an illusion of three-dimensional space, and a head tracking device enabled the computer to keep track of your orientation in the space so that it could send back appropriate images.

 ## Virtual Relativity (p. 524)

Another seeker who imagined a better form of computing was an engineer by the name of Dave Evans. Evans began his computer career as Director of Engineering for Bendix Corporation, where his group designed the first general purpose mass-produced computer. Although he was at the leading edge of ushering computers into the mainstream, he also realized that there was something amiss. He knew that no matter how many machines were produced, there would never be much use for them if ordinary people couldn't understand how to use them. His interest in computer interaction and the man-machine interface led him to a five-year professorship at U.C. Berkeley, where he began investigating easier, more natural ways for people to interact with computers. Evans was also interested in the emerging field of computer graphics and object algorithms, sensing that a visual interface was part of the answer to the riddle.

In 1966, Evans was recruited by the University of Utah to spearhead a major computer graphics research project. The following year, he convinced Ivan Sutherland to join him there, and the rest is, well, Virtual History. One of their students was a young computer whiz named Alan Kay, who would later come to be called "the father of personal computing." But more about that later...

 ## The Pedagogical Mousepad, or, How it all Got GUI (p. 365)

When Ivan Sutherland joined Dave Evans at the University of Utah in 1967, he brought with him his Head-Mounted Display (HMD) project. A year later, Evans & Sutherland was founded. Concurrently at General Electric in New York, engineers Rod Rougelot, Bob Schumaker, and Ed Wild were doing related research in airplane flight, which would eventually merge with Evans & Sutherland's work to create the first flight simulation system.

Evans & Sutherland, now nestled on a hill above Salt Lake City, was the first major company formed to create high-end, real-time VR applications. The founding principal behind the company revolved around the concept of simulation—creating graphical models on a computer as an aid to design, visualization, and education. Both founders believed that graphics were the

B

key. They thought that graphics would provide "the essential link between the human user and the simulation." Ivan continued to work on the HMD, and in 1970, finally succeeded in creating a fully functional Head-Mounted Display as an interface to graphics simulation. The first application was a wireframe cube floating in the air, which users could walk completely around using the fully integrated 3D display and head-tracking system. Within a year, E&S developed their first practical application of VR: a simulation project that involved plotting coordinates to digitize, of all things, a Volkswagen Beetle.

Evans & Sutherland went on to develop a variety of tools for Virtual Reality, including full-scale airplane cockpit simulators. A view of some early archival images tells the story of the evolution of these devices. Early flight simulators modeled little more than a runway with lights; these were followed by simple cities consisting only of wireframe cubes. Eventually, 3D landscapes began to emerge, looking barely more sophisticated than the classic foam core topo-graphical map used by architects for site planning. These were greatly en-hanced by lighting. The addition of features such as texture maps, surface treatments of things such as bricks on houses or leaves on trees, and effects such as fog, eventually evolved to create airplane simulators that have be-come so realistic, it's almost eerie. Flight simulators developed by E&S as well as other simulation companies are now required for training of all military and commercial pilots in the U.S. and most of the rest of the world.

Speaking of levels of detail and magnification, I'd like to pause here to draw back for a bit of cultural and historical perspective. The 60s were the Golden Age of computing, amid what can only be described as a new Renaissance. This was a strange time in our country's history, a time of Camelot and Vietnam, a time of idealism and assassination, a time of civil liberties and international espionage. It was an Age of Enlightenment amid the Dark Ages of a Cold War. It was that very Cold War itself that fueled the fire in the belly driving the first generation computer revolution, right up until the fall of the Berlin Wall, and even beyond.

Virtually all research done in the pioneering age of computing was paid for by the Department of Defense. The irony of this is not lost on those of us utopian pacifists whose entire careers are built on the bedrock of DOD funding on which our early pioneers so heavily relied. Judging from the highly humanis-tic idealism of people such as Evans, Sutherland, Engelbart, and Kay, it is unlikely that it was ever their initial intention to use these magical tools as weapons. But so it was—that the launch of Sputnik in 1957 spurred a series of high-ticket initiatives aimed at increasing the technological prowess of America in both aerospace and military technology against its arch rival in the East. Virtually every computer innovation, from the computer game to VR to the GUI to the Internet, began as a military project. Without the Cold War, it is doubtful that any of these things would exist. It was not until the fall of the Soviet Union that these technologies—which were, after all, paid for by our tax dollars—fell into the hands of The People, for whom they were intended in the first place.

A few key organizations and initiatives that came out of this time are worth mentioning because they come up again and again, everywhere you turn in Virtual Reality.

The granddaddy of all computer research benefactors is the Advanced Research Projects Agency, or ARPA. It was an ARPA project that brought Dave Evans and Ivan Sutherland to the University of Utah. It was also an ARPA project that enabled Douglas Engelbart and Alan Kay to create the first GUI interfaces. It was ARPA that created the ARPANet, a Local Area Network that grew into Worldnet—an elaborate international network developed to enable communication and collaboration between military and university researchers. ARPANet is now one of the fastest growing mass mediums of all time, more commonly known as the Internet. DARPA (Defense Advanced Research Projects Agency), The Office of Naval Research, and NASA were also central in the development of VR technology and the GUI.

The 1960s was the age of space exploration, and it was a space mission by the Russians that sparked this accelerated research. Culturally, this was a time when both outer space and inner space were on everyone's mind. Both the space program and the computer simulation revolution that it spawned were about going "where no man had gone before." Whether it was the Moon in 1969, or the inner space of the Head-Mounted Display the following year, it was an age of exploration that led as far out as it led in. And of course there was a symbiosis there because part of "in" was about simulating "out" to be better equipped to go there. The original age of exploration during the Renaissance was a time of a new, round earth, a time when the visual world of painting gained a third dimension through the innovation of forced perspective, and a time of colonization and empire building. This modern age of exploration had clear parallels: the computer was becoming three dimensional just as the earth was extending its domain into space; exploration led to colonization as competing empires vied for resources and territory.

Pop culture was also reflecting a similar fascination with "inner" versus "outer." College students and so-called social deviants like Timothy Leary, Abby Hoffman, and Terrence McKenna, were advising America's youth to "tune in, drop out, and turn on." Originally developed as a tool for inner exploration by psychologists, LSD became the Virtual Reality of the masses.

CONSENSUAL HALLUCINATIONS: IS VR THE NEW LSD?
(p. 1 3 7)

B

Meanwhile, back in the microcosm...

While Ivan and Dave were doing their thing in Cambridge and Utah, several other related parallel tracks were under way. One of them was led by another visionary determined to bridge this gap between people and computers. As early as 1950, Douglas Engelbart began to envision a way for computers to assist humans in dealing with an increasingly complex world. In so doing, he wanted to help us use our brains and unique skills in better and more creative ways. Between 1957 and 1960 (in his spare time), he set about developing a conceptual framework for what would eventually become a graphical user interface, while doing conventional computer research as his day gig.

Engelbart coined the term "augmentation" for his work in this area because he thought of the computer as an augmentation tool for the human mind. In the early 60s, Engelbart was funded by ARPA to open a laboratory at the Stanford Research Institute to develop ideas he had outlined in a proposal called "A Conceptual Framework for Augmenting Man's Intellect." In this proposal, he outlined a design for a computerized writing system that would aid in creativity and organizing thoughts. He built a prototype of this in 1968, nearly a decade before word processing on a personal computer reached a mass audience. Engelbart's "Augmentation Research Center" also spawned other innovations, such as the mouse and hypertext, many of which did not reach the public until nearly 20 years later.

It was a protegé of Engelbart and former student of Ivan Sutherland and Dave Evans' department at Utah State University who is credited with creating the framework to bring Engelbart's ideas to a mass market. His name was Alan Kay, and he is generally known as the Father of Personal Computing. Kay spearheaded efforts at Xerox PARC (Palo Alto Research Center) which ulti-mately paved the way for the personal computing revolution. This is where the basic design of the graphical user interface that I am using at this moment to write this book was first developed. The strange part of this story is that it was not Kay himself, but a young whippersnapper named Steve Jobs who, as the now infamous legend has it, co-opted the interface and mouse design to create the first Macintosh computers. This design was co-opted again by Microsoft nearly a decade later in the form of the Windows operating system, and has now become the standard interface for all personal computers.

Because the two-dimensional GUI, with its heuristic system of pull-down menus and fool-proof dialog boxes, became the standard for popular comput-ing, there is a common and understandable misconception that it actually pre-dates the 3D interface. This is, as we've seen, patently untrue. Perhaps it was the top-secret quality of much of the research, or maybe it was the heavy computing required by most high-end simulations, but for whatever reason, VR took a good decade longer than the 2D GUI to get into the mainstream (which it is really only just beginning to enter now). Or maybe it was just another example of God playing dice with the Universe. One has to wonder, after all, what would have happened had it been *Sketchpad*, and not the Xerox PARC GUI that prompted Steve Jobs to start the popular computing revolution.

SPATIAL MEDIA (p. 442)

GOD PLAYS DICE WITH THE UNIVERSE (p. 215)

The first attempt at commercial VR was made by another California-based visionary in the 1980s. Jaron Lanier was a techno-artist and game programmer who first envisioned it as a way to make music. Lanier was a major influence on the VR world, as one of the first people to develop and make available low-cost, mass-produced Virtual Reality systems.

POP VR: JARON'S WORLD (p. 372)

Lanier's system had many applications, some of which were in gaming. Forms of Virtual Reality, or real-time 3D animation, have come into play in the 1990s in the form of games such as *Doom*, *Virtua Fighter*, and the so-called "64-bit" consumer game systems.

In 1984, about a decade after Jaron Lanier introduced the first commercially available Head-Mounted Display and power glove, a new movement in Virtual Reality began. Its home was the World Wide Web. Life imitates art, and so Tony Parisi and Mark Pesce, under the hypnotic influence of William Gibson's cyberspace as depicted in his 1986 book, *Neuromancer*, did a little hack designed to prove that you could do Virtual Reality over the Internet. Called VRML (Virtual Reality Modeling Language), it was the "Volkswagon of Virtual Reality." The simple protocol uses tiny code files to describe 3D models and behaviors to a VRML browser, which in turn interprets the code and displays the virtual world on your home computer screen.

Though at this writing in its infancy, VRML has now become a standard for VR on the web, and may well be the means by which Virtual Reality makes it, at long last, into the mainstream.

THE BIRTH OF CYBERSPACE: 3D COMES TO THE WEB (p. 97)

V-ART (p. 494)

NARRATIVE ENVIRONMENTS: VIRTUAL REALITY AS A STORYTELLING MEDIUM (p. 329)

Broad or Narrow: The Casting Couch

B

It is not surprising that the "broadcasting" industry, the arbiters of the one-to-many model of media distribution, are having a go at the Internet. This is of course to be expected in the media evolution curve. Content in new media always begins with an end-run from "old" media looking for a way to co-opt, take on new creative challenges, or tap into new revenue streams. The broadcast world in its infinite misunderstanding of interactivity has thus given birth to the concept of "narrowcasting."

I personally feel the term "narrowcasting" is a misnomer. In truth, it is no different from broadcasting. Like other common terms such as "new media," and "nonlinear," narrowcasting is defined by what it is, allegedly, not: broadcasting. Narrowcast is a term that appeals to marketers and advertisers. Like its broader cousin, it is a way of sending customized advertising and promotion to individuals with the idea that a pre-selected offering will increase the chances of a sale. This opposes the traditional model of sending a random spray of advertising to as large as possible an audience in the hopes that someone will be interested. But narrowcasting, as its name implies, is really just narrow broadcasting. Frankly, it's a narrow way to look at it.

Part of the problem is not the prefix but the suffix. To "cast" is to "throw, hurl or fling away from one's self." The notion of a narrowcast is, therefore, still based on the idea that I am sending information out, but not getting any information back (as in television, which is a non-feedback system). If interactivity is a reciprocal form of two-way communication, the broad or narrow casting paradigm doesn't really fit the bill. The Internet gets into something much more dynamic.

A great example of a good start in this area is a site called Firefly by Informix. Firefly is a database that quizzes me as to my taste on an ongoing basis and keeps track of what I like and what I buy. It amasses this data and gets to know me, creating a higher and higher resolution portrait of me that helps me select products such as record albums, movies, and so forth. Unlike the broad- or narrowcasting model, Firefly doesn't tell me what I want. *I* tell *it*. The casting is coming *from* me to the advertising, which is responding to me instantly and in real time. So what we now have is a market that is buyer-driven, not seller-driven.

Think about the empowerment this gives to individuals in a consumer culture. Think about the change in dynamics. It used to be that all the power was in the hands of those selling. In the TV paradigm, this is most certainly the case. Whoever has the most money for the coolest looking ad and the best placement wins. But Internet shoppers are choosy buyers. They look for meaningful information. They expect products to be *exactly* what *they* want, not what the seller wants to jam down their throats. Unlike television, in which advertising is involuntary and intrusive, advertising is totally discretionary on the web. As an advertiser, I have to actually figure out a way to lure my customer to the ad, a vastly different paradigm than what we are all accustomed to.

The remote control device had a major impact on the design of TV commercials, and the web is precipitating another evolutionary leap for advertising. Most customers will go to your advertising site for one of the following reasons:

- Because they are already brand loyal
- Because someone told them it was really cool
- Because they already want what you are selling
- Because they saw an ad for it in some other medium

But consumers will only stay there if they can either get useful information or compelling entertainment. Interestingly enough, it is more often the useful information that keeps them there. If I want to buy a car, I go to the web site to find out more about the car, not to be entertained.

Traditionally, advertising on the Internet was considered gauche. In the very early days of the Internet, it was really frowned upon to do any blatant advertising. Built on the philosophy of the hacker ethic, information was supposed to be free and available to all. The Internet was not initially a venue for commerce, but merely for the exchange of information, at first classified, and later, available to the general public.

Because of its ease of entry—anyone with $100 can buy an Internet domain—the Internet began to resemble the California Gold Rush of the late 19th century. Everyone was showing up with a pick axe mining and hoping to cash in. But few have really done so to date.

In this first generation content phase of the web, people will continue to try to use the forced advertising model because it's what advertisers know how to do. The classic banner ad has limited potential in an interactive context. Although it affords a certain amount of brand exposure, for the most part, people see it as intrusive and there is no current evidence that any new customers are won by online banner ads. Push technology, which is basically trying to make your computer a more passive, television-like medium, will yield further attempts to shove advertising down people's throats. But I antici-pate that this too will be short-lived.

In terms of commerce on the Internet, the consumer is God—no longer a Nielsen, an anonymous demographic, a pair of passive eyes to be colonized and manipulated, a "butt in the seat" (as the film industry refers to movie-goers). Consumers begin to control their own economic destiny in a way that they never could in the broadcast medium. Consumers expect service, less hype, and more information. Consumers are much more intelligent and informed and want to be seen and treated on an individual basis.

As commerce on the Internet grows, we are going to see significant shifts in the economy. We are already seeing megalopolies trying to create media empires. At the same time, however, we are seeing more and more cottage industries and small businesses popping up that have more tools now to compete with these monoliths. Some small businesses will die, but big business will also feel an impact in a shifting economy where a guy in his garage can get just as many hits to his web site as Microsoft.

It all goes back to gratuitous interactivity. Anytime you make an interactive experience, you have to ask yourself, why is this interactive? Does the interactivity add anything to it? Does the content lend itself to user involve-ment? How can we better utilize the interactivity to facilitate commerce?

Gratuitous Interactivity: Media Dispensers and the ATM Model (p. 218)

Here's a thought on how to take a completely different approach. What if I were designing a new product, say a new model computer or car. What if I created a web site whose purpose was to solicit customer feedback about the last product. What did they like and dislike? How would they improve the product? What if I then developed the product based on customer comments? What if I then made a prototype and solicited those same customers to come in and test out the product that they helped develop? With this information in hand, I could present the product online and sell it via the Internet to the customers who helped create it. Imagine that! Creating a product that custom-ers actually want and finding a way to learn what it is they want directly from the source, not from a marketing executive, or a demographer! The "con-sumer" becomes a collaborator. Consider what this might mean to the concept of brand loyalty!

Or try this on for size: what if an advertising site were built around a culture instead of a product? What if you, for example, create a site targeted to the so-called "grunge" movement. Rather than building a giant TV commercial for a single product on the web, such a site could have kids come online and hang out, talk to each other, and dress their avatars in Levi's jeans, Doc Martens boots, and a Pearl Jam T-shirt. In this environment, brand ID is not about marketing, it's about the roles products play in young people's lives. The advertising is put in context of something meaningful, something that the user can relate to. It becomes a social environment supported by advertising, rather than an ad for its own sake.

Looked at in this way, rather than the "casting" or throwing out from oneself, we ought to look at interactive telecommunications as a game of catch, or better yet ping pong, in which data is exchanged at an equal rate by both parties. Perhaps, then, what we should be thinking about is not so much a matter of casting as of volleying.

ACTION, REACTION, AND INTERACTION (p. 11)

NERD VERSUS COUCH POTATO (p. 345)

IT'S NOT THE TELEVISION THAT'S INTERACTIVE, IT'S THE PEOPLE (p. 250)

BUCKMINSTER FULLER AND THE DIGIDESIC DOME

In March 1995, I was invited to attend a small panel at the Pacific Design Center in Los Angeles to celebrate the 100th birthday of the late Buckminster Fuller, geometrist extraordinaire and inventor of the geodesic dome. Buckminster Fuller was something of a self-fashioned Renaissance man whose contributions from the 1940s until his death included the geodesic dome (see figure B.3), the "dymaxion" car, the *World Game*, and (posthumously) the Bucky Ball. These are only a few among a plethora of ideas and inventions originated or adapted by Bucky, as he was known to his friends and colleagues. As a young man, my father, Peter Pearce, was a prodigy of Bucky's, and as such, was invited to be one of the speakers at this Centennial event.

As part of his presentation, my father told the following story about my childhood. Bucky Fuller came to visit us at our home when I was about two or three, and when he came into our bedroom, I proceeded to identify all the Platonic solids, models of which were suspended from the ceiling: tetrahedron, octahedron, and so on. This early exposure to geometry and polyhedral form had an enormous influence on my early development. As a child, I was atrocious in mathematics where numbers were concerned. Conversely, in the realm of abstraction, logic, algebra, and especially geometry, I was actually quite competent. I even went one year for Halloween as "Miss Minimal Surface Truncated Icosahedron," a polyhedron that my father had concocted and which I wore on my head along with a banner proclaiming my identity. (This too had a major impact on my early development...)

Figure B.3

Buckminster Fuller's Geodesic Dome, Expo 67, Montreal (photo courtesy of Peter Pearce)

At the conclusion of the commemorative panel, Bucky's daughter, Allegra Fuller Snyder, asked whether anyone in the audience had anything to say. I felt compelled to stand, partially in response to my father's story, but also because there was a sequel. So I shared with the group the story of an event that happened some 30 years later when I was invited to act as Creative Director for *Virtual Adventures*, a Virtual Reality game using an Evans & Sutherland flight simulator system. I told of coming to a meeting where the two lead programmers on the project gave me a crash course in Virtual Reality—a medium which was, at the time, entirely new to me.

THE PRINCESS AND THE MONSTER: THE MAKING OF VIRTUAL
ADVENTURES (p. 375)

I explained how easy it had been for me to understand the underlying principles, the concept of objects composed of polygons, and of polygon budgets—essentially the fact that you can only have so many polygons onscreen before you overload the system. This related to concepts of economy of form that my father drilled into my head as a child. My father, after all, had developed the premise of a "minimum inventory, maximum diversity" system, a methodology for creating buildings that allowed for versatility with a small and elegantly designed kit of universal parts. Isn't this the very definition of Virtual Reality? The notion of making entire simulated worlds out of triangles and spheres, behaviors and lighting? It is no wonder that Virtual Reality came so naturally to me. After all, I was raised by polygons.

My original mentor, Ed Schlossberg, was also a student of Bucky's. Bucky's influence, therefore, resonated with me on a lot of levels. I recently read Fuller's book *I Seem to Be a Verb*, which is a sort of manifesto for the digital age. Bucky, by the way, predicted in the 60s that by 1989, people would be able to teleport themselves; this was, coincidentally, the year the Internet formed.

Bucky's *World Game* was the analog precursor to the popular *Sim* series of computer games. *World Game* was a resource management simulation played on a giant "dymaxion map." The dymaxion map was a construct of Bucky's which transposed the globe into an icosahedron that could then be opened up into a flat map. The principle was that this could avoid some of the distortion that occurs when you take a spherical globe and try to translate it into a two-dimensional map. In Bucky's dymaxion map, everything was supposed to be to proper scale. Participants in the *World Game* would go from continent to continent on this giant map, which would be rolled out onto the floor of a public space. The players were divided into teams and given tokens representing the resources of the earth. They would then have to network and negotiate to get all the resources from their places of origin to the places they were needed. Ed Schlossberg once took the entire company to a *World Game* session. It was a blast because you literally had to walk across the room and place the markers on different parts of a giant map, and work with your own team and other teams to get all the food and fuel and whatever else to the places that needed it. The ultimate goal of the *World Game* was to demonstrate Bucky's hypothesis that we had everything we needed on "Spaceship Earth" (another one of his notions), it was just a question of getting it to where it was needed. The *World Game*, which predated the personal computer by over a decade, is a perfect example of how you can get high-yield interactivity through low-tech techniques.

Bucky was a very eccentric individual (legend has it that he took to falling asleep at the dinner table in mid-sentence and re-awakening in the middle of an entirely different sentence and topic), but he was definitely of the Benjamin Franklin tradition. He dabbled in many things, and had many staunch doctrines that were based in a very elaborately constructed and definitely offbeat belief system. Like Franklin, he might have been as likely to discover electricity as he was to invent the public library. But he had many students and followers. Even to this day, there is an entire community of individuals for whom he has become something of a guru.

More than anything else, Bucky has been a role model to many—a man who created his own reality on his own terms. Undaunted by constraints or preconceived notions, and spurred by an endless resource of energy and self-confidence (perhaps even arrogance, to some), he was a man for whom anything was possible. He was at once extraordinary and ordinary.

Underlying his entire approach was the fundamental message that anyone could be a mad inventor if they so desired. He was a person that encouraged people to get involved, to make things happen. He frowned upon passivity, and the real message behind the *World Game* was that global problems were manageable and solvable, and that we all ought to take responsibility for them. As such, he is a great role model for the interactive lifestyle.

Autobiography of an Autodidact, Part 1 (p. 45)

Media Architecture (p. 284)

T_Vision: Spaceship Earth Made Visible (p. 460)

Building Character: The Soul of Drama

One of the biggest problems I see with many interactive stories is the absence of character. In traditional media, character is story, story is character. Writers of linear fiction spend the bulk of their prep time developing characters and backstory and really getting to the know the people in their fictitious scenario until they are practically real in the mind of the author.

After the author begins to place these characters in relationship to one another and a series of events, the characters often take on a life of their own and behave as they naturally would in a real situation. You can always sense when a character is inauthentic, when his or her actions are not consistent with his or her personality. This is the sign of an underdeveloped character, a character you don't *believe* is real.

One of the great paradoxes of interactive fiction is that character is defined by the actions an individual takes or, to put a finer point on it, by the decisions he or she makes. Within the context of interactivity, it is the user, the audience, making the decisions. Therefore, the decision-making process is even more important.

Therein lies the paradox. If a character is defined by the decisions he or she makes, what happens when that character is acted upon by a player? To really put our arms around this issue, we need to begin by looking at another overlooked issue: the relationship between the player and the characters in the story.

A great fault of the majority of interactive fiction, even the best of it, is that there is generally a high level of ambiguity in the relationship between player and characters. If you think about any character-based game you have played, ask yourself, who am I? This question will generally leave you feeling a bit baffled. Even with something as simple as *Street Fighter*, in which you are manipulating a character in real time, you are seeing the character from a third-person vantage point, and yet at the same time you are supposed to *be* the character.

Role-playing games, such as Dungeons and Dragons, and MUDs (Internet-based, multi-user dimensions/dungeons) encourage role play and character development on the part of the players. In this kind of multi-user interactive fiction scenario, people actually create and develop their own characters and relationships with other characters. This is an excellent example of how interactive media can empower the user to generate his or her own content. In these Internet stories, people can interact with each other's fictitious personas, so in a very real sense, "you are what you write." You can create all manner of fantasy characters to interact with other people's fantasy characters. Although this represents perhaps the most creative and in some ways the most interactive paradigm for interactive storytelling, the fantasy and science fiction genre of most of these role-playing games tends to lean towards a niche following... albeit, a very religious one.

Multi-user interactivity is one way to effectively address the problem of character. Character, as mentioned previously, is defined by action that almost always involves some kind of interaction with other characters. Therefore, it is in his or her interaction with other characters, or perhaps with the player herself, that the individual character can be truly defined.

In *Virtual Adventures: The Loch Ness Expedition*, a multiplayer Virtual Reality theme park attraction, we created roles for the players, but not characters. The collective goal of the team of six players was to rescue the Loch Ness Monster's eggs from hungry fish and other players (depicted as evil bounty hunters on their screens). Each player had a clear function on the team within the underwater vehicle. As people became involved in the whole team dynamic and in pursuing the goal, they began to spontaneously evolve various character traits, based in part on their team roles. In most cases, they would play themselves, or aspects of themselves, which was just great. Because of her role as communicator with enemy subs, the Commander tended to evolve a character in response to the other team. Other players rose to the occasion in different ways. The action of the game focused on the rescue of a central character, Nessie herself. Her character was carefully developed to elicit empathy from the players. Although she was large and in some ways quite dangerous, in this scenario, she and her helpless eggs were being unfairly cornered by bounty hunters, a situation that would inspire most people to action. The bottom line was that all the players were highly motivated to participate because they *cared* about the outcome. They wanted to be heroes, they cared about Nessie and her babies, and each of them fashioned that role for himself or herself in a very natural, unpremeditated way—which was essential, because the in-vehicle time was only about four minutes.

 The Princess and the Monster: The Making of Virtual Adventures (p. 375)

Although sometimes intellectually challenging, most interactive stories are decidedly lacking in emotional content. This comes down to two intimately intertwined problems: lack of motivation and lack of empathy. All successful fiction relies on empathy to draw the reader or audience in so that they *care* enough about the characters to invest time and energy into experiencing their lives and emotions. Without empathy, fiction is meaningless. This maxim is even more true of interactive fiction. Empathy fuels the drama of a decision, and our investment in the character and his development through this decision-making process makes us give a damn about what the outcome of that decision will be.

Empathy has long been a missing ingredient from the binary heart of multi-media. We need to create characters that are well-developed and well thought out and as empathic—even more so—than the characters you will find in linear fiction. It is not enough to make a story interactive. Empathy is as important as story in interactive multimedia because it is what drives motiva-tion. In a movie, you don't generally walk out in the middle; however, in an interactive experience you are free to leave whenever you like. This is precisely the reason why we need to either create more empathic characters, or give players the tools to create and evolve their own characters. In either case, you need to care about the character, whether you are actually taking on the role of the character, manipulating, or merely observing. No matter what that relationship is, you must have an emotional tie to the character, *especially* if you are expected to interact with the character in some way.

People frequently ask me for examples of products where this does occur. Sadly, they are few and far between. Most of the projects that I have seen that reveal an understanding of empathy have been created by fine artists. Rita Addison's *Detour: Brain Deconstructon Ahead*, referred to numerous times in this book, is a VR narrative that puts you in the first person role of a photographer whose vision has been affected by a brain injury. The effect is stirring. Char Davies' *Osmose*, an immersive world based on the transcendent effects of deep sea diving, offer you empathy with yourself by increasing your awareness of your own being. Brenda Laurel and Rachel Stickland's *Placeholder,* and Christa Sommerer and Laurent Mignonneau's work are about creating an empathic connection to the natural world. Artist Jim Ludtke's character-based work with San Francisco-based band, The Residents, use the setting of a freakshow and a carnival midway as an entry to a world of bizarre characters.

On the commercial front, the CD-ROM game that has elicited the strongest reaction in me has as its main characer a cockroach. Called *Bad Mojo*, this modern-day derivation of Kafka's classic *Metamorphosis*, tells the story of a man turned into an insect who must overcome a series of obstacles to find his way back to his humanity. Because the plight of the cockroach is so precarious (he is small and lives in a highly hostile environment), you cannot help but respond when wandering too close to a trapped—and hungry—rat.

Purple Moon, a company started out of Interval Research by *Placeholder* co-creator, Brenda Laurel, has also done a good job of incorporating empathy and character into its product lines. Designed for girls ages 8–12, Purple Moon's "friendship adventures" are story-based experiences that put characters in real-life girl predicaments. In *Rockett's New School*, the main character must face a series of dilemmas on her first day at a new junior high. As a player, you must decide which of her schoolmates Rockett should form alliances with, which cliques to try to impress, and how to deal with potentially embarassing situations. Although I was not involved in the CD-ROM design, I was hired by Purple Moon to create a card game based on these characters and predicaments. I used a role-play paradigm in which girls could combine various characters in different archetypal situations, using hidden clues to provide hints to the characters' personalities and motivations. We ran a number of tests on these cards and discovered that just the appearance of the character could elicit a strong emotional response. The characters, created by former *Teen* magazine writer Pamela Dell, were themselves archetypal. The girls recognized the different "types" and immediately had emotional reactions to the characters, thus they became vested in the outcome. Not only did girls enjoy role-playing and making up stories with these characters, but some even pointed out that this could be an aid to them in preparing for situations that might arise in their own junior high school experience.

Brad deGraf and his team at San-Francisco based Protozoa have also been creating a sensation with their VRML-based characters. Designed to run in real-time 3D on the web, these characters are essentially stand-up comics who at present exist in relative isolation. Nonetheless, their personalities and interactions with their environments are endlessly compelling and entertaining. As Mark Pesce, creator of VRML says, "When was the last time a web site made you laugh?" It happens occasionally, but not as much as one might hope. Floops, an unidentified amphibian who sports Doc Martens and a major dose of attitude, has been called the Steamboat Willie of cyberspace. His bi-weekly episodic VR comics on the Silicon Graphics web site have accrued nothing short of a cult following. Not to mention the awards he has won. Jan Mallis, who produced Floops, attributes this to the proper balance of 3D modeling, acting (Floops is animated by a human-controlled motion-capture system), and script. Character development is crucial.

Another great example of empathy in a Protozoa character is the spider. He stands at the corner of the stage with his back to the audience. With great aplomb, he steps forward and stretches out his eight legs with a growl, in an attempt to scare the audience. Instead, he is met with roars of laughter and retreats, humiliated, to the corner. This scene is both comical and poignant, and harkens the days of Vaudeville, when comedy was broad and incorporated both comedy and tragedy. You can't help but feel sorry for the poor spider, even while you laugh at him.

The bottom line is interactive fiction needs *more*, not less, character development than linear fiction. Why? Because, the closer you are to a character, the more room there is for the stink of inauthenticity to seep through. If I ask you not to simply observe but to *become* a character, I *must* give you some compelling motivation to do so. With interactive media, you can walk away at any moment, so I have to give you a good reason to stay.

Because we cannot spoon feed our interactive player stereotypes and formulaic characters, we must create characters with depth that work within the context of an interactive story. Some characters' decision-making processes can't really be trifled with. For interactive media, we need to develop characters whose internal struggles are enhanced when placed in the context of interactivity so that the choices offered and the outcomes of character decisions make sense within a believable story scenario.

I cannot stress enough that to understand nonlinear fiction, we must have a very strong grasp on principles of linear fiction. We must understand traditional storytelling techniques before we attempt to evolve them into a new storytelling form.

The awful secret is this: Good interactive fiction is about a hundred times harder to write than linear fiction. Although interactive fiction uses the same basic principles as linear fiction, it is also radically different. To do it well, you must have a thorough understanding of traditional storytelling forms *and* be willing to question and reformulate them into a new genre.

VIRTUAL REALITY AS A DRAMATIC ART (p. 508)

DECISIONS, DECISIONS, DECISIONS (p. 158)

WHO IS THE AUTHOR? (p. 528)

CENSURING CENSORSHIP

History shows that at some point in the evolution of any medium, there must be at least one movement toward censorship. These censorship moves can take various forms and are generally instigated by a conservative faction outside the medium that generally includes significant government support. In the 1930s, the Hayes commission went to work on the movie industry, and the Cold War yielded the McCarthy era, which was more about censureship than censorship, but the end result was the same: the de facto censorship of an entire community, most of which revolved around the film industry.

I think it can be fairly said that most media of the 20th century, and as far back as the Gutenberg Press, fall quickly into the hands of a subversive element. It is inevitably a sub-culture, not tied to the constraints of convention, and inherently innovative in its thinking, which grabs on to a new medium with aplomb and blazes the path that the rest of society eventually follows. For this reason, one should not in any way be surprised when a new medium is subjected to an onslaught of censorship attempts. This is a natural part of the process of media evolution.

 THEORY OF MEDIA EVOLUTION (p. 124)

Like film, the Internet has inspired a veritable frenzy of censorship attempts right at the moment in its evolution where it naturally would, keeping in mind that Internet years are to film years what dog years are to people years. The Internet inspires even more concern among those defending the status quo because of its completely anarchic terrain.

Censoring the Internet is like putting a toll bridge at the bottom of the ocean. Many online "interactivists" have been working hard to protect freedom of speech on the Internet, and I support their efforts wholeheartedly. I think there is nothing to do but fight it full on. The truth of the matter is that even if Internet censorship laws do pass—which is of course, entirely unconstitutional, illegal, and unconscionable—there is absolutely no way to enforce them.

The first fail-safe against Internet intervention is in its name: Internet. The Internet, besides being interactive and interconnected, is also international. Any law passed within a country is impossible to enforce outside its borders. The truly subversive can attend to their server needs the same way the financially dubious attend to their monetary needs: by putting their web sites into the server equivalent of a Swiss bank account.

The second fail-safe against Internet intervention is sheer volume. There are just too many people out there. It would be like trying to censor the telephone. Unless the government were willing to create a department that does nothing but reads every piece of e-mail, and does a daily review of every web site, the entire effort would be pointless. The fact is, even if the government put this department in place, at enormous cost to the taxpayer, it still wouldn't work because it can't legally read people's mail. Also, web sites can be changed and updated so quickly that the offensive material can easily be removed, the entire site renamed, or re-located to an off-shore site; and then of course, there's the secret password element.

The third thing that keeps the Internet relatively safe from control and intervention is the simple fact (as is always the case with censorship attempts) that the people responsible for running the Internet are about a million times smarter than the people trying to control it. It is laughable to think that Newt Gingrich has even an ounce of the brainpower required to understand the Internet, let alone have any lasting impact on it. The reality is—unless censorship play is made by an army of 13-year-old hackers, an absurdly unlikely scenario—there is little, if any hope for Internet censorship.

Even if none of these things were true, the fourth and most important factor in the prevention of Internet censorship is its fundamental nature. The Internet defies censorship by its very structure. Because its infrastructure is inherently horizontal and decentralized, as opposed to the hierarchical and centralized television infrastructure, the Internet is impossible to monitor. It is a slippery eel that will always squirm its way out of the hands of anyone who attempts to control it. This is particularly ironic because it was the most centralized, hierarchical governmental body in America—the Department of Defense—that created it in the first place.

Obscenity is, as always in puritanical America, the primary platform on which the censorship movement is built. But when looked at in the expanded context of censorship in other media, the entire Internet attack begins to look patently absurd. Why, for example, has the government made no attempt until now to monitor the video game industry? This industry has, for the last 10-odd years, been peddling ultra-violent imagery to *young children*, not by accident, as is generally the case on the Internet, *but on purpose*!!! Today's arcade games also feature busty women fighters in lingerie that look like they just stepped out of the pages of *Penthouse*. Yet the government has all but ignored these forms of obscenity in the game industry. Why? Because video games are the very kind of opiate the government likes—they keep kids insulated from the reality that might incite involvement. The Internet on the other hand, is politically subversive. It is political subversion, not sexual perversion, that is the *real* target of the Internet censors.

IT'S ONLY A GAME: THE BIRTH OF A MULTI-BILLION DOLLAR BUSINESS (p. 260)

In the culture of media violence, the video game industry is not the only guilty party—the television industry is just as culpable. Children today can see hundreds of murders on television before they have even graduated from high school, and yet we are all shocked and dismayed when a student shows up in the classroom packing a piece. Saturday morning cartoons target young children and inundate them with violent imagery to which the perpetrators seldom face any consequences, and are often the heroes.

Nonetheless, the hue and cry seems to focus on sex, while patently ignoring the violence problem. The bizarre "moral majority" philosophy that sex is somehow more dangerous to children than violence has always baffled me. On the one hand, we should prevent teenagers from having access to birth control; but on the other, they should all have the freedom to own a gun. *What's with that?*

 VICARIOUS EXPERIENCE (p. 504)

Perhaps the most obvious danger on the Internet vis-a-vis subversive activities is the growth of hate groups and cults that use the Internet to promote their causes, sometimes with deadly results. Timothy McVeigh, aka MADBOMBER@aol.com (really...I saw his member profile), was online, although he's not alone. There are also many white supremacist and neo-Nazi groups, the Freemen, and other militia-type organizations who use the Internet to obtain and disseminate information and promote their violent causes. The Higher Source, the web company that turned out to be the Heaven's Gate cult, used the Internet to recruit new members. In the Spring of 1997, in pursuit of the Hale-Bop comet, they ended their quest to join their alien brethren in a 39-person mass suicide, an event that was prefigured obliquely in their web site. That the Internet can be used to endanger is therefore a valid concern, but not one that can be solved by means of censorship.

The fact is, we have this thing called the First Amendment which guarantees our right to free speech everywhere in every media. The First Amendment is not neat and clean—it's a very messy proposition. Any law that guarantees basic freedom is always going to be a little messy, but if you believe in liberty and democracy and all that, you have to realize that freedom of speech is the backbone of a democratic system. It always has been. There's a reason why it's in our Constitution. Preventing people from expressing their opinions and viewpoints is the hallmark of a totalitarian regime. In countries where this is a blatant part of public policy, the Internet, due to its profound lack of censorability, is being used to circumvent and bypass these laws, demonstrating that it is the ultimate democratic tool.

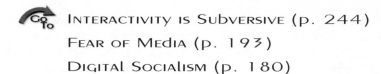

INTERACTIVITY IS SUBVERSIVE (p. 244)

FEAR OF MEDIA (p. 193)

DIGITAL SOCIALISM (p. 180)

CHOICE IS OVERRATED

Whenever I go to a new restaurant, I hardly ever read the menu. Occasionally I'll scan it briefly, but generally what I do is ask the waiter or waitress what he or she recommends. It seems like a cop-out, but to me it's merely a relief from the utter exhaustion I have with the endless barrage of decisions I must face on a daily basis.

Freedom of choice is supposed to be some kind of American ideal, but sometimes freedom *from* choice seems much more appealing. Even something as simple as buying a bottle of shampoo can be overwhelming. Bruce Springsteen put it best when he said, "Fifty-seven channels but nothin's on." Whether we're talking cable TV, CD-ROM, or life in general, this malaise of choice has taken hold of our culture on a massive level. In the world of digital video, the oft-heard "video-on-demand" is somehow seen as the pinnacle of interactivity. It is as if the ability to see any movie ever made, at any time, anywhere, represents the ultimate human achievement.

Interestingly, surveys show that most people would rather stop by the neighborhood video store than pre-select their films from home. Perhaps the average American doesn't require video-on-demand. Perhaps video-on-request is sufficient. Perhaps it's easier to make a decision when faced with a finite number of options, each housed in a box that one can look at, pick up, and turn over in one's hand. In fact for some, video store browsing is an entertainment activity in itself; while others would consider it akin to ancient Chinese water torture. I know people who spend a full hour trying to select a two-hour film from the video store shelf. (One of them is me!) How much time would these same people spend scrolling through endless menus if they had virtually any film in the world to choose from?

This problem is only compounded when there are two or more people involved in trying make a decision. Think about how difficult it often is to plan an evening out at the movies with friends, when the choices are relatively narrow. Now go with your spouse, friend, or child to the video store and try settling on something.

I submit that it is not endless choice that makes us feel empowered. In fact, I find that I feel more and more *dis*empowered by all these choices. Life, as we know it, is nothing more than a series of decisions. In fact, it is the very act of making decisions that determines our character, that tells others who we are.

 BUILDING CHARACTER: THE SOUL OF DRAMA (p. 119)

Why shouldn't interactive experiences have the same kind of significance? Why is it that when I make decisions in the digisphere, they do not reveal my character as do the decisions I make in the real world? Wouldn't it be great to have an experience where the decisions I made expressed what kind of person I was, where I could find out through some form of interaction what I'm really "made of." What if the software itself could also tell what I was made of, and offer me rewards, penalties, or choices tailor-made to the sort of character I reveal myself to be? Am I timid or courageous? Am I ambitious or altruistic? What are my values? What is important to me? Do I value loyalty over honesty? Do I value friendship over family? Family over romantic love? Love over career? What is my idea of a kind act? Am I a pushover, or a "tough lover?" These are the sorts of experiences I would like to see, experiences that make me come away saying, "Wow! So *that's* who I really am?" And then, in playing with others, "Wow…that's who *they* really are!"

It is not the number of decisions, nor the ease of the choice that counts. In fact, a compelling interactive experience can sometimes revolve around relatively few decisions. It is the pertinence and consequence of the decision that really counts. It is a common misconception that more choice is a better thing. In fact, more choice can be dangerous, especially if the choices appear to have no consequences. It is this very inconsequential, or gratuitous interactivity, that has made a bad name for interactive media. In the context of interactive media, as with the world at large, there are far too many choices, and far too few meaningful consequences.

 DECISIONS, DECISIONS, DECISIONS (p. 158)

GRATUITOUS INTERACTIVITY: MEDIA DISPENSERS AND THE ATM MODEL (p. 218)

THE LAWS OF INFORMATIONAL ENTROPY (p. 280)

COMPUTER TERMINAL VERSUS COMMUTER TERMINAL: TELECOMMUTING AND THE NEW ECONOMY

Several years ago, I was once working on a project at a ferry terminal, and the typist delivered a draft of the document from my handwritten notes. There was a line that was supposed to read "...the busy commuter terminal..." but, no doubt in a Freudian slip of some kind, it came off his own overworked, word-processing fingers as "the busy computer terminal."

This story is particularly humorous today in light of the advent of the "Information Superhighway." In fact, these days the "busy computer terminal" is taking the place of the "busy commuter terminal" as more and more people, eschewing both traffic and high commercial real estate costs, are doing what has come to be known as telecommuting. People work at home linked up to their offices via modem, e-mail, network, and so forth.

This is an excellent example of a case where the impact of interactive technology on the culture at large might not be obvious at first glance. The fact of the matter is that computers, the Internet, and remote communications have opened the door for a whole new way of doing business. This new model is also having a domino effect on other aspects of our culture.

During the recession of the 1990s, a lot of corporate downsizing led to a movement in "outsourcing," the use of freelancers, or the conversion of current staff into freelancers. This also led to the creation of "virtual companies," small home-based companies run by a single individual or a small group of partners, each working out of his or her own home or small office. These virtual companies do not have employees, but expand and contract to meet the necessary workload. They also have low overhead because they are generally working in the home environment.

Virtual companies are the natural result of the growth of a service economy in the information age. In a service economy—an economy that is not manufacturing-based—individuals are valued by the specific kind of services they can perform. In a practical sense, if you are not running a factory production line, you need neither the space nor the requisite overhead. Furthermore, the industrial model of a worker clone who can perform rote tasks rapidly is no longer the desired model. Highly refined and unique skills are becoming more and more crucial in an information-based economy. The information age also adds the value of knowledge and informational skills: what I know is now as important as what I do. As long as they have access to necessary information and communication tools, individuals and their skills can, in a sense, live anywhere, particularly because their clients want them to work under optimal conditions for productivity and creativity.

This has resulted in two trends. The first is that we are growing a whole new generation of "consultants," people who work on a freelance basis within the service economy. This is convenient for actual companies because there are certain services they don't need all the time, so they can hire out when they do need these services and don't have to deal with all the setup and overhead required to "feed one more hungry mouth," as it were. They also can avoid such things as insurance and other benefits that they may have to contend with for their normal employees. Thus the freelancer, as a self-supporting entity, can be very appealing to an employer because the freelancer does not require any infrastructural support.

The outsourcing movement and growth of non location-specific services has spawned a second trend: many companies have begun actually sending people home. Large and medium-size companies have begun to encourage their full-time *staff* people to set up virtual home offices. Rather than downsizing their employees, companies are opting instead to downsize their physical plants, but keep the employees. This shift is actually a very bright move from a corporate standpoint, which most large companies would eschew. When things are tough in a typical large company, the first thing to go is the people. But as far as overhead is concerned, people give you the most value for your money. It is smarter to give up a piece of real estate and keep the people. After all, an empty office isn't going to do much to increase your productivity.

With laptop computers, modems, cellular phones, and beepers providing us with a new level of portability, the need for a specific and constant office space has begun to be questioned. As a result of this office portability, we are seeing more frequently an office with, say, 30 employees that has space for only 15. A few employees are on the premises full time. The remaining staff either work outside the office—such as marketing or sales reps, some of whom might spend 50 percent of their time on the road, for example, or client liaisons who spend all their time at meetings—or spend half their time at home and half in the office. These workers don't have a set office or desk, but work at different cubicles or offices, depending on how often they're in and what they're doing. Wherever they are, whether on the road, at home, or in the office, they can hook into the office intranet, get their interoffice e-mail, communicate with staff, and find out what's going on in the company without ever having to tackle the traffic or find a place to park.

Once location ceases to be a crucial factor in employment, then people (both freelance and on staff) can begin to explore the option of living in ever more remote locations. Because of all this intercommunication and portability, it has gotten to the point where you can practically live in the Fiji Islands while you're on staff at Apple.

As a result of this telecommuting trend, we are in the midst of some major shifts in the socioeconomic milieu. For one thing, parents are spending more time at home with their kids. In fact, all these high-tech accoutrements are ironically, returning us to a much more agrarian model of family life. The agrarian economy is very family based. Parents are home all the time, or out in the field. The child begins working the farm from a young age, perhaps starting with collecting eggs or milking the cow, and becoming more involved with the more complex aspects of the business as he or she grows older. What we are beginning to see is the high-tech, urban or suburban version of the agrarian lifestyle. Furthermore, with more and more computers in the home, parents can also return to the tradition of being heavily involved in their child's education. Heuristic (self-teaching) software enables parents to have more control over their child's education without having to invest the time for personal instruction, which today's working family may not have the luxury of doing.

As the family values people fiddle away, the home is turning into a much more family oriented place, not because of any kind of moralistic phenomenon, but because of an economic one. In fact, it is the rise of industrialism and not the fall of religion that ruined the home. In the industrial model, parents were separated from each other and their children. It was under industrialism that the concept of a workplace away from home became a reality for the majority of families in both America and Europe. Prior to that, home and work were one in the same. The family shop was in the same building or a short walk from the house, the house was on the farm, and so forth. Now, we are seeing a return to this kind of model and the result, I think, is going to be a return to a stronger family unit. It is likely that we are also seeing a response to the 80s, when Yuppie workaholics were regularly foregoing family life by either bypassing it entirely or neglecting the families they did have, in favor of a hard-working, buck-earning ethic. In the ensuing years since the market crash and recession of 1989, there has been an overall shift in values and emphasis, and today you are more likely to see family listed as a number one priority over career than you were 10 years ago. People are still working as hard as ever, but nowadays, they are trying to find ways to create harmony between their work and home lives. The virtual office is one way to do that.

The virtual office phenomenon is also having a further negative effect on the already beleaguered commercial real estate market. This trend began during the Great Real Estate Craze of the 1980s. At that time, fueled by a bloated speculative market, overbuying and overbuilding abounded. Millions of dollars were poured into downtown redevelopment projects on the naive assumption that more growth and prosperity was a given. This chain of events resulted in a huge real estate glut that ended in a downward spiral at the end of the 80s from which the real estate industry has yet to recover—if it ever does. After the stock market crash and the ensuing recession, companies downsized, and already-vacant spaces remained empty. As if that isn't bad enough, more bad news for the real estate world: people are going home to work, which means more vacant office space.

The result of all this is that the dissolution of geographic boundaries is naturally going to have reverberations for the people who own the geography. At the same time, it adds a level of flexibility that in the end can be of benefit to everyone. The result of this may well be the creation of an entirely new economic culture, perhaps more closely resembling the preindustrial cottage industry, home-based business model.

 SOCIAL CAPITALISM (p. 425)

SOCIAL COMPUTING (p. 434)

AUTODIDACTIC COMMUNALISM (p. 83)

CONFESSIONS OF A MACINTOSH CONVERT

The following is a case study, using myself as the subject. Although this is a personal account, it represents a larger theological argument: the proverbial Mac versus PC argument. For me, much of my attachment to the Macintosh is historical, and is based on having lived through a generation of PCs that seemed as if they were going out of their way to be difficult. Most people take for granted the fact that today computers have an interface. But this wasn't always the case. Before the Macintosh interface was introduced, the PC was a no-man's land of memorized buttons and complex key codes. There was absolutely nothing friendly about it. For myself, the shift from the black hole of DOS into the Macintosh's graphical world of windows and menus was a step into the computational sunlight (see figure C.1). It changed not only the way I relate to, and feel about, computers; it also changed the very way I think.

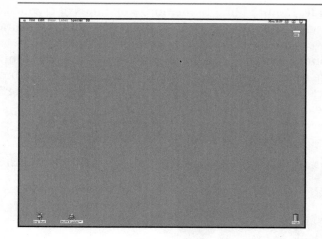

Figure C.1

The Macintosh interface opens a world of opportunities

Before I started working at Edwin Schlossberg in 1983, I had never so much as touched a computer. Up until that time, I had been writing at work on an IBM Selectric typewriter. Remember? The one with the "typing element?" The little ball that would spin around to orient the correct letter toward the page? At home, I had a Hermes manual portable, a little gray metal "laptop" that was originally designed for reporters during World War II and is, coincidentally, the same size, color, and texture as the Mac PowerBook I am currently writing on. My mother calls my little Hermes "the original PowerBook."

At my father's architectural design office, I had limited exposure to an unwieldy early "word processor," a glorified calculator made by a company called Wang (how could you take it seriously?) with a tiny LED that showed about 10 characters at a time.

I hated computers from the very start. I hated the monochrome monitor—black with those little green letters ("Why can't it be white, like a beautiful, clean piece of paper?" the fledgling writer asked). After hours in "greenland," you would get something called "rosy vision," in which everything had a pink hue. Later, PCs changed over to the hideous amber, which was just a fancy word for "orange." The orange was supposed to be less straining on the eye than green, which I could never figure out.

The computer was kept in a dark room with no windows. Everyone on our floor, about eight people in all, shared a single PC. I think it had about a half a Meg of RAM on it. We always had to reserve time on it, which in my case could get a little dicey since I was supposed to be "the writer."

The first thing that came up on the screen was the infernal DOS prompt C:\ (see figure C.2). I would sit and stare at it for moments on end wondering what the hell it was I was supposed to do. Eventually, I learned how to open a program. But once inside, I found I had to memorize all kinds of cryptic key codes. It might have been a simpler undertaking to become fluent in Cuneiform. And then there were the function keys, so confusing that you had to have a template on your keyboard to use them. The beauty part was that every program used the function keys to mean different things. In one program I used, F7 meant Save; in another, it meant Delete. It was the writer's equivalent of a minefield.

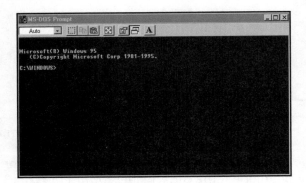

Figure C.2

The infernal DOS prompt

If you managed to finish your document without accidentally wiping it out, you could save it onto a 5 1/2 inch floppy disk. In those days, disks actually were floppy. Floppy equals scary. Imagine putting all your hard-earned data onto a little wheel of magnetic material housed in a case that is about as stiff as a manila envelope. All you had to do was drop it on its corner and it was all over. And just try transporting these things. The grinding sound of a disk failure was a horror we all had to live with.

Then of course there was the nightmare of printing. There was a different cartridge for each font. It didn't help that there was no way to see what the document was going to look like on the printed page, let alone how it would fit on the company letterhead. In addition, there was no common protocol from printer to printer so you would have to print each document about a dozen times to get it right. So much for the paperless office!

No sooner had I memorized all the function keys for WordMate, my first word processor, then they came up with this new thing that was supposed to be *even better*. And because it was better, it followed that it would be harder to learn. They sent me away to WordPerfect boarding school for a solid week of reconditioning. It cost the company $500 and at the end of a week, I had barely memorized all the key codes.

Two weeks later, I was shipped to Maryland for week, rented out to another company that needed a concept report written. I diligently packed my 5 1/2 inch floppy with the new wonder application on it and landed at Dulles airport completely ready to be compatible. Imagine my chagrin when I arrived only to discover that all the PCs were hooked up to a main server, and that it was impossible to have any new software installed.

What's a girl to do? There I was, the "ace in the hole" writer (that's what they called me), with no hole to put my ace in. (Well, you know what I mean…) So the design director on the project said, "You can use this Macintosh."

I responded to his cavalier offer in a state of abject panic: "But I've never even touched one of those things before…." And he said, "It's really easy." He sat down, explained to me what a pull-down menu was, and I proceeded to sit down at the thing and write a 20-page report in a week. By the end of the week, I knew how to use a Macintosh computer.

In that one week, I fell in love with the Macintosh. Why? Because it had an interface! It spoke a language I understood. It didn't ask me to be a computer programmer. It was user-friendly! It gave me a trial-and-error way of learning. I didn't have to read a manual (I hate manuals with a passion). I didn't even need a teacher. It was truly a heuristic system. There were just a couple of rules you learned, and then everything else, not only in one program, but in *every* program, followed that protocol. There were shortcuts that you could memorize if you wanted to, and they were the same *in all programs*. In addition to all this, someone came up with the zany idea of putting *black* words on a *white* background—just like a piece of *paper*. Not only that, but when you printed it, it looked exactly the same on paper as it did on the screen!

When I returned to New York a week later, the first thing I did was unplug my brand new PC (we had evolved to "a computer on every desk" by this point) and carried it back to the MIS guy. I put it on his desk and said, "I want a Macintosh." That was it for me, and even today, as the anticipated demise of the Macintosh has made it as far as the cover of *Wired*, I am still a die-hard Mac user.

The moment I started using the Macintosh was the moment I began to actually *like* the computer. Up to that point, using a computer was a necessary evil, but the Macintosh was great because it took *me* into account. The PC was like asking a deaf person to read lips. The Macintosh was the essential sign language. I loved that someone actually took the time to figure out a way to do things that would make it easier for *me*. I also loved that they didn't make me read a damn manual, memorize function keys, or try to extrapolate a printed page from a continuous string of text and symbols. It didn't bother me one iota that all this functionality took up memory. It was well worth it. The Mac's interface, its user-friendliness, made the entire process not only painless but enjoyable. It freed my mind up to *write*, because I didn't have to put all my intellectual focus into *typing*. But the most important thing the Macintosh computer did was change the way I *think*.

Word to the Motherboard: Computers and Literacy (p. 530)

The Pedagogical Mousepad, or, How it all Got GUI (p. 365)

The culture conflict between the PC and the Mac is about as unsolvable as the argument over who has rights to the Gaza strip and whether or not abortions should be illegal. There are vastly different schools of thought on the subject. These days, the PC seems to be winning out. In the office environment, in the accounting office, and in many homes, the PC has taken hold, while the Macintosh is still the mainstay of a small but fervent creative branch. Most CD-ROM producers, film effects people, and desktop publishers still prefer the Mac, which is still in many ways the better production tool for graphics and video.

The thing that's important to remember is that the heart of this conflict is the user interface itself. Although it always had a strong presence in the office environment, the Macintosh opened the door for home computing because of its greater accessibility. It is largely due to the co-opting of the Macintosh interface by Microsoft that the PC has really taken over.

Apple itself is as much to blame for this as anyone. IBM, who developed the original PC (IBM PC "clones" are what they used to be called), licensed both their hardware system and their software development to anyone who wanted it, while Apple maintained a stubbornly proprietary attitude. Until recently, no one but Apple could make Apple computers, and even now, clone production is very limited. The Mac has also traditionally been more expensive than the PC and its clones, which has also created a barrier of entry. Among computer jocks, the Mac has always been maligned for its "user condescending" attitude and the excessive memory required by its heavy system and interface. Apple has also stubbornly refused to join the VRML community in creating the Virtual Reality equivalent of HTML for the web. Numerous companies have joined the VRML Consortium and supported its work to create a VR protocol that could add a third dimension to the Internet. Apple has all but ignored this new movement to the point where it has not even created a VRML browser, consequently making it impossible for Mac users to access VRML sites. As a result, still another generation of Mac users is walking away from Apple.

This is one example of what will ultimately kill Apple, or at least whittle it down to a very small niche company. It all comes down to software. What is now driving Apple's market share down is not the quality of the hardware or the interface, but the fact that less and less software developers are developing for the Mac.

Artificial Intelligence and the Prosthetic Brain (p. 38)

Nerd versus Couch Potato (p. 345)

Theory of Media Evolution: The Four Axioms (p. 480)

Consensual Hallucinations: Is VR the New LSD?

William Gibson, who coined the term "cyberspace" in the early 80s in a short story called *Burning Chrome* and later in his now-classic cyberpunk novel *Neuromancer*, described his concept of cyberspace as a "consensual hallucination"—in other words, a shared dreamscape that millions of people could enter and explore.

Jerry Garcia said it best: "They made LSD illegal. I wonder what they're going to do about this stuff." Jerry wasn't the only one to compare VR to LSD. In fact, within the ranks of the so-called "digerati," there is definitely a cyberhippie faction that sees cyberspace as another of the "Doors of Perception," as described by Aldous Huxley in his book of the same title. Both the late Timothy Leary and Terrence McKenna, icons of the hippie era who were great proponents of the use of mind-expanding drugs, have in essence jumped on the VR bandwagon. Or, if you look at it another way, it's jumped on them. I'll never forget walking into a coffee shop in New York City and seeing an ad on the cover of the Learning Annex catalog advertising a Timothy Leary lecture about Virtual Reality. These three things in combination seemed like something of a non sequitur to me—Timothy Leary, the LSD evangelist, the Learning Annex, essentially the K-Mart of continuing education, and Virtual Reality. Seeing it in a New York coffee shop was the icing on the cake, as it were. I was prompted to exclaim at once, "Oh no. It's all over now!" For those of you not in the know, the Learning Annex catalog has featured courses such as "An Evening with Deepak Chopra" and "How to Strip for Your Man…"

I saw Leary speak at several cyberculture functions, including San Francisco's annual "Digital Be-In," and I must confess, without the aid of any mind-enhancing perceptual alteration devices, I found it impossible to comprehend a single word he said. In fact, at the Digital Hollywood Awards one year, Leary appeared onstage with notorious heroin poster child Perry Farrell, founder of the Lollapalooza Music Festival and leader of alternative bands Jane's Addiction and Porno for Pyros. In a moment of uncharacteristic clarity, Leary turned to Farrell and said of VR: "Perry, this stuff is going to make you and I obsolete."

I have also had the opportunity to hear Terrence McKenna speak on the power of perception. In a talk he gave at SIGGRAPH 94, the world's largest computer conference, he addressed the question, vis-a-vis computer graphics, "Are we forcing people to evolve?" Beginning with the colloquial phrase "I see what you're saying," he talked about the relationship between visual perception and understanding. The phrase suggests that creating a visual picture in your mind is a primary signifier of comprehension. He then drew correlations between cultural shifts in perception as illuminated by visual artists and significant scientific and technological discoveries of the modern world. Thus, human cultural evolution can be seen as the evolution of perception, and those shifts in perception are what lead to discovery. In the sense that Carl Jung observed the phenomenon of a group consciousness, McKenna put forth the notion of a group perception and its influence on understanding. Within the context of cyberspace, these shifts in group perception can provide the portals into meaningful discovery.

McKenna's and Leary's ideas have had a major influence on the philosophy and thinking of quite a few significant denizens of cyberspace. Although I myself have never quite understood the fascination with hallucinogens, on a fundamental level, I do agree that Virtual Reality opens up new perceptual doors, but not necessarily in the ways you might think. Projects such as Rita Addison's *Detour...*, a glimpse inside the mind of someone with perceptual anomalies caused by a brain injury, or *Osmose*, a deep exploration of inner space through breath and balance, create a variety of new perceptual doors and windows. As many of the artists of cyberspace have found, the highest function of VR is not to simulate reality, nor to create an escape from it, but to use its power and immersive qualities as a means to reflect on reality in new ways. Although VR shares certain characteristics with hallucinogenic drugs, cyberspace door-opening is experienced within a shared or common space, with a frame of reference that is not entirely unique to the individual. Thus, the doors of cyberspace are not strictly personal, but social, cultural, and political as well.

 V-ART (p. 494)

V-ART (p. 494)

The other difference is that the hallucinogens are a crap shoot, in more ways that one. The images that are generated come from the subconscious. For some, this can be a source of mind expansion, but in others, it can just as easily precipitate a breakdown. In any case, the outcome is unpredictable. In cyberspace, most of what is really meaningful in terms of perceptual shifts is actually being created by users. Thus, the consensual hallucination, although it may also tap into the subconscious, is an act of will. There is a certain unpredictability in its spontaneity, but it also becomes an exercise in creating new societies and cultures. What we are really doing is creating a hallucination, an imagined world which becomes its own entire country. We are building and populating our own Wonderlands, Ozes, and Narnias in which to explore altered states of both being and sharing. These shared states are places from which we can then safely return, having gained insight into ourselves and our roles as parts of a larger organism.

Where Gibson's image of cyberspace fell short was that he never imagined that his characters would be participants in building it. Instead, he envisioned cyberspace as a matrix of information and data, owned and operated by multinational corporations and government institutions. Cyberspace was a digital Big Brother waiting to be hacked by renegade web surfers. Although life may imitate art, in this case, truth is also stranger than fiction. The real cyberspace turns out to be much more like Gibson's outer world of cyberpunks and computer-enhanced humans. The hallucination is not only consensual, but collaborative—and it's messy as hell. If you visit online communities today, you will find that the worlds and realities that people are creating— which mimic the real world in extraordinary and surprising ways—provide a fantastic case study of what happens when you remove superego from the social context. In cyberspace, everyone wears a mask, and so the space becomes a Dionysian festival beyond Leary's or McKenna's wildest imagination.

As an aspiring architect of cyberspace, I watch these spontaneous eruptions with interest. There is a great story in traditional architecture of a college campus that was designed by a famous architect. After the building was complete, it came time to lay the paths through campus. Rather than paving in the walkways, the architect instead instructed the landscapers to plant grass throughout the entire campus with no demarked pathways whatever. Within a short time, the students and teachers were making their own paths in the grass, at which point the architect instructed the pavers to lay walkways in the precise location where the grass had been worn by the natural campus traffic.

This is my idea of a responsive environment. The architect allowed the users to create their own unconscious and spontaneous paths. As a designer, I prefer this approach. I have deliberately waited to become heavily involved in creating content for the web because I wanted to see what paths the populace wore down on their own. Thus, we can begin to watch what people do unsupervised when left to their own devices, the same way Maria Montessori, Jean Piaget, or other early childhood educators might watch a child involved in self-motivated play and learning. In this way, we can be conscious of the unconscious. We can observe as users create a spontaneous culture, and then come in and pave the paths that have already been created by the users themselves.

GAINING PERSPECTIVE: THE EVOLUTION OF DIMENSION (p. 196)

CYBERSPACE CADETS: VIRTUAL COMMUNITIES AND AVATAR WORLDS (p. 146)

OM MEETS OHM: DIGITAL ONENESS (p. 360)

CYBERFEMINISM, OR, WHY WOMEN LOVE CYBERSPACE

The digital age is tailor-made for women. Cyberspace is the great equalizer. Contrary to some popular stereotypes, it is not the technology that has been the greatest barrier for women in interactive media. It is the content. Fortunately, the Internet has certain characteristics that have inherent appeal to women, and even though they are still all but shut out of the computer game demographic, females online are growing in both numbers and influence.

What is it about cyberspace that many women find so compelling, so powerful? Why is it that women are so populous in chat rooms and multi-user worlds? Why are we seeing more and more women rise to positions of influence in this simultaneously expanding and imploding universe?

EXPLODING OR IMPLODING: WHAT'S THE DEAL? (p. 191)

Chat rooms and avatar worlds have really changed the meaning of gender as we know it. In the real world, gender is a physiological state of being. As such, people are subjected to stereotypes and expectations that are based on qualities of an external nature; however, in cyberspace it's a different story. In cyberspace, you are whatever you want to be. Men can get online as women and vice versa. People in sexually oriented chat rooms can describe themselves however they want, whether or not they really are a "busty blonde" or "tall dark and handsome." For all we know the "busty blonde" could, in reality, be tall dark and handsome!

But there's more to cyberspace than androgyny or freedom from physiologically determined sex roles. The digisphere is a place of insurgence, and interactivity, as I've said before, is inherently subversive. What really makes cyberspace appealing to women is that an entire universe has finally been built which, whether or not it was the intention of its architects, happens to embody the essence of the female value system.

I run the risk of oversimplifying and overcategorizing, but pop psychology books such as *Women Are from Venus, Men Are from Mars* and *You Just Don't Understand*, as well as numerous more academic studies have shown that, in fact, women and men operate on very different sets of values and priorities. Whether these systems are the product of nature or nurture, whether they are biologically, psychologically, or sociologically based is open to question; however, the whys and wherefores of gender traits are moot. It doesn't really matter *why* female and male behavior differs, in fact, few people can argue, whether based on scientific observation or common sense, that it does.

What does this have to do with cyberspace? What most of these studies show is that women value communication and community, while men value individual achievement and competition. Women are less comfortable competing because they are more oriented to maintaining group harmony; men tend to favor achievement-oriented activities that call attention to the individual. The Internet is a place of community and communication, but also a place of individual expression which gives it appeal to both genders. For women, in particular, the multi-user capabilities of the Internet open this technology up to appeal to their particular interests.

Because of the nature of online communication, women have some decided advantages in the digisphere that they may not have in the analog world (or anosphere, as it where). First, the physical body has been removed from the transaction. A visit to your local supermarket checkout line and its magazine selection bears mute testimony to the excessive emphasis placed on women's physical appearance and body-awareness. To the untrained eye, you might even deduce from this that women are judged on appearance alone, while men are judged on achievement. Men are rarely seen on magazine covers in bikinis or snug-fitting clothes. Some would argue that this is merely an indication of the superior aesthetic of the female body (an argument that is most likely to come from a man), but be that as it may, it is still a primary way that women's bodies are emphasized. In cyberspace, it's different. People are not judged by their genetic (or, if you live in Los Angeles, surgical) endowments, but on the words they write and the type of avatar they select. I know men who deliberately pick sexy female avatars in cyberspace because they get more attention that way.

In spite of the capability to become disembodied, there is still a proclivity to "embody" people, particularly women, even in cyberspace. One day, I was in a chat room on America Online (for those of you who are just joining us, a chat room is where you can type messages back and forth and have a conversation with groups of people in "real time"). One of the *women* in the room was explaining that the number at the end of her online name, LoisLane38, represented her birthday, her chest measurement, and 1/4 of her IQ. A discussion immediately resulted regarding bust size. One man said she sounded like a fox, to which I responded that a large bust does not necessarily mean that a person is attractive. Finally, I announced: WHAT DOES IT MATTER WHAT HER BUST SIZE IS. YOU'LL NEVER SEE HER ANYWAY. Several others in the room applauded me for making this seemingly obvious point, but I think it is interesting that there was no discussion whatever of any of the males' corresponding measurements. Furthermore, I think it worth nothing that it was a woman who made a big deal about her own bust size, another rather telling example of how we are still not fully acclimated to a world in which such information is basically irrelevant. On the other hand, nobody had any comment on her IQ, which, if indeed 38×4, was also rather impressive.

Being disembodied can be a source of empowerment for women. It enables us to, if we choose, exist as non-sexual beings, or to experiment with our roles as sexual beings. In the real world, the threat of sexual violence and violation inhibits women from doing certain things; however, in cyberspace we can do anything we want. Furthermore, released from certain social stigmas, we can also have the option to step outside of the bounds of what is considered "female" behavior and define new modes of interaction for ourselves. Women in cyberspace, for example, can often be much bolder than they might in the real world. At home in the world of communication and text, they are invited into a world that in some ways has traditionally shut them out. In cyberspace they are on equal ground, and they may, in fact, even be at an advantage.

Although there are no hard-and-fast rules, educational studies show that the majority of girls tend to excel in English and writing skills, but also in mathematics. Boys tend to excel in logic and certain forms of spatial orientation. Nature or nurture? Who knows? Even a casual survey among your friends might reveal that more women are skilled at touch-typing than men, who are content to use the hunt-and-peck method. As a young woman in the job force, I discovered that being able to type can actually hurt woman. I often warn young women never to admit they can type in a job interview. I can't tell you how many of my girlfriends graduated from college with bachelor degrees, only to land a first job as a typist.

I, myself, went to typing class kicking and fighting, and was the slowest typist in my entire class. Now, I type 100 words a minute when writing from scratch. In an environment where a conversation consists of typing each sentence out as quickly as one might speak it, I (and other women who type as quickly as we can speak) am at a real advantage.

If you hang out in the chat rooms long enough, you will begin to notice patterns of conversation and you can often tell the men from the women, even if their names are gender-neutral. In Deborah Tannen's *You Just Don't Understand*, the author explores conversation patterns, particularly group conversations, much of which applies in cyberspace. But it's different because the physical clues and body language are absent, and I've noticed that women tend to be much more forceful, more aggressive, and even rude at times in online situations where they might tend to be overly polite in real life.

In terms of sexual harassment, for example, one of the biggest problems in real life is that women are afraid to be "rude" and therefore have a difficult time telling men who are being rude to buzz off. Not so in cyberspace. Some women may be timid, but it's much easier to eschew a textual suitor than an actual one.

Feminism as a whole has had a bad time of it the past decade. Since the 1970s, calling yourself a feminist has been strongly out of vogue. To some, it connoted a lesbian separatist liberal Nazi who was constantly crying "date rape" and trying to sanitize the college curriculum from any suggestion that males might have a dominant influence on our culture (a bit naive if you ask me). Many people forget the simple definition of feminist: one who believes that men and women are entitled to equal rights. To be a feminist, you don't have to hate men. In fact, by this definition, you can even be a man and still be a feminist.

In spite of the stigma of being a feminist, the Internet has bred a whole new movement in feminist rhetoric and action. Because the highest value online is knowledge and communication versus physical prowess, women have a much fairer shake here. Cyberfeminist grrrls abound online, and have built an entire virtual sub-culture, covering everything from feminist theory to pop music to computer gaming.

It's a popular myth that female access to the Internet is inhibited by a lack of technological savvy; however, this gap is quickly narrowing. Women are not inherently disinterested in machines. It's just that they are not inherently interested in them. They are only interested in them insomuch as they are a mode of communication that can empower their existing interests and values. In fact, where technology is concerned, women have always had it over men in the communication arena. Telephones. Word processors. Previously, these high-tech devices had always been the domain of men. In fact, there is a great story in the annals of the history of the telephone. In the early days of the switchboard, telephone operators were all young men, at about the same level of a shoe shine or a paper boy. The phone companies discovered that the boys were rude and impatient with customers, so they quickly fired them all and replaced them with women. The vast majority of receptionists even today are still women. Although there has been a steady increase in male operators in recent years, for a long time, the phonescape was dominated by female voices.

Most women are drawn to technology by function and content, not by the technology itself. For a woman, a car is a mode of transportation, not something to fix on a weekend afternoon. Likewise, a computer is a medium through which to create and understand. Surveys reveal that most of what girls and women are doing on computers involves tools of creativity: word processors, paint programs, and so on. Women also like reference materials, such as encyclopedias, and educational content. In fact, few women look to the computer for entertainment, although this might be more a symptom of the lack of entertainment content that appeals to them, than an inherent lack of interest on their part.

Although content for girls has been sorely lacking from the repertoire of CD-ROMongers and the Internet, a major change is afoot. Just at this writing, a whole new slew of products are being targeted at girls. The enormous success of the *Barbie Fashion Designer* CD, the top-selling CD-ROM of the 1996–97 Christmas lineup, has finally proven to the world that girls and women (only 52 percent of the population) can be a profit center. Say what you will about Barbie, she has paved the way. After establishing a market trend like this in America, nothing can stand in its way.

 GIRL GAMES: THE NEW FEMININE MYSTIQUE (p. 202)

PSYCHO-ERGONOMICS (p. 404)

WORD TO THE MOTHERBOARD: COMPUTERS AND LITERACY (p. 530)

CYBERSEX AND THE LITERARY RENAISSANCE

Warning! This section may be unsuitable for some readers.

The world "cybersex" conjures up images of people in full-body sex suits jacked in to a virtual orgy, cyberdildonics, and pleasure machines. Science fiction is peppered with such devices as the Orgasmatron in Woody Allen's *Sleeper* or the sex machine in *Barbarella*. The machine is supposed to be used to torture people to death with excessive pleasure, but Barbarella (who has consorted with aliens and robots by this time in the film) has so much fun with it that the machine finally overheats and blows up.

I wouldn't expect to see a Virtual Reality body suit in your local Sexxe Shoppe anytime soon. In fact, the reality of live computer sex at this point is based almost entirely on text, or textsex, as I like to call it. Most of this is done in the form of live private chat in which two parties engage in a mutual fantasy, essentially, a collaborative erotic story—all done with the tap of the keyboard. To borrow a term from Erica Jong's *Fear of Flying*, it is the ultimate "zipless fuck."

The November 1994 issue of *Wired* magazine featured an expose on the subject of online sex. For those of you who are new to this concept, online sex is when two or more consenting humans participate in a collaborative sexual fantasy. This is done by typing back and forth on the screen in real time. It is not unlike phone sex, but you write instead of talking. Online sex generally happens between two voluntary and non-paying individuals, while much of phone sex is provided on a "work for hire" basis.

Wired interviewed both men and women about online sex to see what the differences and similarities were in interests and priorities. Although there was a lot of variation in the details—what kinds of fantasies people wanted to live out and the approach and criteria for finding suitable partners—the interviews revealed that there was one thing that men and women agreed on across the board: The most important single characteristic of a good online lover is writing ability. To be a cyberstud, you need to be a good writer.

This bodes well for Internet culture. Who would have thought that cybersex and writing would go hand in hand? The chat room in general is creating a kind of literary Renaissance in that denizens of online chat are learning the new art of writing in real time, a skill that was heretofore unknown. So in the sphere of cybersex, you really have to be a smooth talker—which proves once and for all what a therapist friend of mine always used to say: Our most important sexual organ is between our ears.

VICARIOUS EXPERIENCE (p. 504)

CYBERFEMINISM, OR, WHY WOMEN LOVE CYBERSPACE (p. 140)

WORD TO THE MOTHERBOARD: COMPUTERS AND LITERACY (p. 530)

Cyberspace Cadets: Virtual Communities and Avatar Worlds

In September of 1997, Bruce Damer and the Contact Consortium held the first official conference on avatars. The Contact Consortium is an organization of digital artists and designers formed to explore issues of artificial, extra-terrestrial and avatar-based life forms. The title of the conference, "Earth to Avatars," was a bit of an in joke based on the fact that when you walk up to avatars in cyberspace, they are notoriously slow to respond, due mostly to latency of text transmission and other technical roadblocks. Thus one might be inspired to call out "Earth to Avatar" to get the attention of one of these cyberspace cadets.

For those unfamiliar with the terminology, an avatar is a graphical representation of a real person. It is usually a character, generally humanoid, but not necessarily. In Virtual Reality, it is a 3D model of the character (see figure C.3). When you move around in cyberspace or in an online graphical world, you use an avatar to represent yourself within that world. Most avatar worlds facilitate Chat, which is a form of text-based dialogue between people. A small handful of systems use voice, enabling people on either end with a microphone to communicate verbally rather than textually.

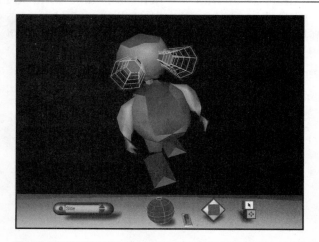

Figure C.3

Example of a VRML Avatar from Construct

Virtual communities or avatar worlds are really little self-contained cyber-nations unto themselves. Habitat, one of the first of these, was originally developed by LucasArts and then purchased by Fujitsu Cultural Technologies. The Palace is another fairly well-known avatar world. Black Sun and Oz also host online avatar worlds. All these are Chat worlds, where visitors must type in their communications via keyboard. OnLive has developed a system of avatars that can lip-sync to a live voice feed so that you can talk to other people rather than write to them (see figure C.4).

Figure C.4

Participants talk to each other in an OnLive Avatar world

 PLATE 31

 THE BIRTH OF CYBERSPACE: 3D COMES TO THE WEB (p. 97)

Most online worlds are characterized by unstructured interaction and each of them seems to evolve (or not evolve) based on how its Netizens utilize the world. In the long run, worlds that seem to have the most success are those that are user-built. In some worlds, the main activity is hanging out. There's not much to do and the environments tend to be markedly uninspired in decor and ambiance. One thing you see in most online worlds is this infernal brick texture. This is because it is part of the standard kit of textures that comes with most 3D authoring tools. Things definitely pick up when the users themselves start creating their own ambiance. Regardless of whether they are well-designed graphically, most of these worlds end up getting a little dull after a while because there just simply isn't much going on. I always liken these unstructured cyberspace hangouts to a bad cocktail party. You know the kind, where you stand around and don't know what to say to anyone? This is often the situation you find yourself in when you are inspired to say "Earth to Avatar." Without any kind of social guidelines or cues, even the most interesting people can become rather dull when transported into their text-based avatar alter egos. Although it's easy to blame the guests, a boring party is almost always the fault of the host. As such, you should look to the originators of the world to create worlds that are a little more inspiring to their visitors.

A recent banter among digerati vis-a-vis cyberspace and online 3D worlds went something like this:

"If we build it they will come."

"Even if we don't build it, they will come." (Mark Pesce on preparing for the demand.)

"If we build it they will come. But then what?" (Yours truly on the inevitable outcome if we don't design interesting worlds.)

With few exceptions, cyberspace as we know it at this moment in time in 1997 is a ghost town. You can visit many different 3D worlds and, most of the time, there will be nobody there. Judging from the world itself—often an uninviting sci-fi scene, or maybe a boring street or room with those same old brick textures again or astroturf floors (virtual lawns)—it's no wonder people view cyberspace as a wasteland. At a talk I gave in January of 1997, I suggested that part of what is missing is the fourth dimension. Most of these online worlds seem somehow frozen in time. The success of VR on the web will only come when elements of content, story, game, theme, a sense of place, and experience are integrated into the environment. Until that happens, although they might indeed *come*, they certainly will not stay.

 NARRATIVE ENVIRONMENTS: VIRTUAL REALITY AS A STORYTELLING MEDIUM (p. 329)

The one exception I have seen to the ghost town syndrome in cyberspace is user-created worlds that have evolved into their own ongoing civilizations. A small handful of these worlds have begun to develop a devout following of serious cyberspace cadets who have all but created their own online nations. Bruce Damer gave a presentation at my San Francisco State University class, "Exploring Spatial Media" in which he took us on a little trip to one of these nations. His talk was a highly engaging case study of a virtual community that evolved into its own small online republic. Active Worlds was started by a company called Worlds, Inc. to facilitate online 3D worlds. Active Worlds was not based on the VRML protocol, (which is becoming the standard for Internet Virtual Reality) but on its own unique system. Users in these worlds can build their own avatars by using a standard kit of parts that enables you to pick a body and modify things such as height, hair color, and attire. By 1997, Active Worlds boasted 200,000 registered users, about 25,000 of whom were regular visitors.

In the winter of 1997, due to the absence of a clear and present revenue model, Worlds Inc. went out of business. The Netizens of Active Worlds who had spent years building their own unique online community decided to buy the company so that they could maintain their virtual nation, thus beginning perhaps the world's first cyberspace cooperative.

During his talk, Bruce took us on a tour of AlphaWorld, one of the Active World areas. AlphaWorld is basically a giant homesteading space. As a new user, you can select and refine your avatar, and then enter into the world and stake out any available patch of land. A large aerial view map enables you to get the lay of the land and suss out what's going on. An alternative is to simply walk around on the ground or use a variety of teleport booths that will automatically relocate you to another location in the world. There are a variety of standard objects or building blocks in the world. If you see one you like on someone else's property or anywhere in the space, you can simply copy it and drag it to your area, assembling your own environment from available parts.

Certain minimal rules dictate how people are expected to behave, and a few systems in place enable social checks and balances to occur, but other than that, it's basically a free-for-all. As problems arise, new rules are created by consensus to deal with anti-social behavior or territorial disputes. People come, create their worlds, make friends, and form clubs; they put on plays or musical performances; they throw parties; they even get married. Bruce showed us a "wedding album" of screen shots he had taken of a couple who had met in AlphaWorld, met in real life, and subsequently got married—in AlphaWorld (see figure C.5)! Their online wedding included a real Justice of the Peace, even though the couple themselves were in two different locations at the time. Guests were advised that those from the press were to come as birds so as not to be intrusive in the wedding ceremony; Bruce, as official wedding photographer, came disguised as a small child and hid behind flower pots so as to be as unobtrusive as possible.

Figure C.5

Avatar wedding in AlphaWorld, from the photo album of Bruce Damer

 Plate 32

In addition to private space, people also build worlds and environments for public use. When gravity was introduced to AlphaWorld, one couple decided to build a ski slope so that people in the world could have a way to experience

it. Avatars can go to the top of the ski slope and try to navigate their way down the hill with the aid of gravity pulling them forward. On the other hand, someone once built a giant parking lot, taking up a huge amount of space with what looked from above like a black hole. (Why you need a parking lot in a world that has no cars is a mystery.) Anyway, it took some major petitioning, but it was finally decided to give the land back to the public and allow others to homestead there.

OnLive is a world where users are represented as talking heads. In this voice-activated world, a special technology enables avatars to move their lips in sync with audio input from a human speaker. So as you travel through OnLive's world, you can see and talk to other people, and listen to them talk as their avatars' lips move accordingly. A housewife in the South who had been frequenting this world observed the lack of recreational activities. She wrote to the company and suggested that the world include a stadium, so the Powers that Be at OnLive indeed replied: "If you build it, they will come." So she did. And they did. Games are regularly played at the stadium. OnLive avatars are represented only by heads, which make great footballs, so people actually take turns being the ball. This virtual "field of dreams" has become a place where people convene and play team sports, experiencing the familiar in a new way made possible only by means of digital technology. (You wouldn't want your head to be used as a football in real life. Take my word for it.)

Many people might view such tales with alarm. What will be the result of this? Will we all stay home, never to go out again, and get all our social needs met in cyberspace? Perhaps, perhaps not, but consider this: The southern family of OnLive is an average American family; they aren't digerati; they're not gamers; they're just a regular family. They report that since joining the OnLive community, instead of spending the evening sitting together in front of their television watching sitcoms, they now spend their evenings in front of the computer hanging out with other families, designing virtual buildings, playing games in the stadium, and getting to know a variety of characters from across the nation and even the world who they would not have had any other exposure to except through this unique social medium.

As a replacement for real social interaction, virtual worlds are a poor substitute; but as a replacement for television, they are an evolutionary leap forward. Instead of taking a passive role as recipients of commercial-based broadcast media, the average American family can take an active role in creating their own media and online culture. This very act changes the way people think. Being proactive and creative in a simulated world is bound to translate into the real world in some way. Furthermore, the ability to spend your leisure time socializing with and learning about people you might never have any other exposure to is sure to promote a new level of tolerance and social harmony in anyone's life.

I look at these cyberspace worlds as virtual costume parties. In them, you can be and do whatever you want. You can change gender or age and role play different parts of your personality that might not otherwise have a release in the real world. That this opportunity might release the dark side of people's inner psyches is only to be expected, but in reality this does not occur at the scope or level of danger that Hollywood horror films or naive social commentators might have us believe. Online worlds in cyberspace are essentially harmless, which is what enables you to freely express yourself in a variety of different ways. The protective veil of technology has the effect of lifting normal fears and inhibitions just as a costume mask does. The end result is that these online worlds provide people with a new kit of social tools. Just as it is sometimes easier to talk to someone on the phone than in person, cyberspace can make it easier to express yourself more freely.

Some would argue that it might not be desirable to lift people's inhibitions. Inhibition, after all, is just another form of superego, the part of our minds that monitors our sense of social propriety. Any time you remove inhibitions, you remove the superego, and thus issue an invitation to all the commensurate bizarre behavior that goes with that lack of inhibitions, which can yield negative results, as well as positive. For every housewife in Georgia who has given up watching her soap operas to become an architect of cyberspace, there is a cyberpunk writing graffiti on another avatar's cyber homestead.

I personally don't think any of this is necessarily good or bad. Perhaps having a virtual venue for the dark side has its positive aspect too, enabling people to express the need for antisocial behavior in a place where nobody gets hurt. In the best of cases, it may also be a place where people can learn how to deal with the antisocial behavior of others, whether by personal action or by social agreement. I know of a case where an entire community got together to denounce the behavior of a member who had been harassing its female members. This individual was put on probation and ostracized from social functions, thus providing a model for dealing with anti-social behavior in a virtual community. Cyberspace communities—these tiny digital nations that exist in a universe parallel to our own—provide a unique insight into human psychology and social dynamics. Information garnered from such models can then be used to shed more light on the subtleties of social interaction within communities and social systems in the real world.

Social Computing (p. 434)

Who is the Author? (p. 528)

A-Life of One's Own (p. 5)

DANGER: KILLER APP

The panacea of commercial success, as defined by the characteristically hyperbolic language of new media, is something generally referred to as the "Killer App"—short for killer application. Application is of course an abbreviation of the term software application, a program applied to a certain task or functionality, such as a word processor, spreadsheet, or in the case of entertainment, a game or interactive story. Within the CD-ROM market, people have been looking for the Killer App since the mid 1980s, but in truth, waiting for the Killer App is sort of like waiting for Godot. Try as all these hotshot new media companies do, and did (many of them go out of business within the first two years), few have yet to make a so-called blockbuster interactive title, and mark my words, few ever will and here's why.

Interactive media is not a blockbuster industry, but entertainment is. Ever since *Star Wars* redefined the expectations of how movies are made and marketed, the entertainment industry has used its astronomical success as a measuring stick for everything else. The formula goes something like this: Spend a lot of money, and make it all back and then some in the first two weeks of release. Films are generally not rated by long-term performance, although time and time again, small undermarketed and fairly humble films such as *Shine* and *Slingblade* build up a certain momentum over time and are more profitable than high-budget, wannabe-blockbusters like the ill-fated interpretation of William Gibson's classic *Johnny Mnemonic*. Furthermore, many films make more once released on video than they did at the box office and a less successful film can sometimes outgross a more popular box office film based on video sales alone. This expectation, which is pretty much the conventional so-called wisdom in the film industry, has rippled through to all other entertainment media. Big bucks, big bang, fast up-front megasale is the operating paradigm. Most film investors go for instant gratification. On this basis, advertising is a key factor. To make money on a movie, which is a one-time cash cow, all you have to do is, as they say in the biz, "put butts in the seats." You don't have to keep them there, you just have to get them there.

Interactive media is just the opposite. Most successful new media titles make more money in their second year than their first. Their popularity is spread by word of mouth. Although massive advertising can get attention out of the gate, it is seldom effective in maintaining sales of a product once it's out and people start talking. Because CD-ROM budgets are characteristically small (under a million is typical), a major ad campaign can often be a higher ticket item than an entire production budget. Whether it starts with a big marketing bang or not, if the product itself is good, at a certain point the advertising will no longer be necessary because the product will sell on its own steam. Like the ubiquitous Honda, a good new media title sells itself. The best way to sell a new media title is by holding and maintaining player interest. The more the same CD-ROM is revisited by its users, the higher chance of it gaining additional sales. The best sales rep to sell a CD-ROM to a kid is another kid who loves the title. If a child enjoys a game played at a friend's house, chances are very high they will go home and ask their parents for that same game. Parents who have invested $40 in their kid's game or educational software will tell another child's parents, "You know, Johnnie is still playing that *Indiana Jones* game and he's had it a year...what a great value that was." Because CD-ROM has its origins in, and is largely perceived as, an educational medium rather than an entertainment medium, there is a certain orientation toward products that have some kind of educational or cultural merit. In any case, product loyalty is paramount. Brand loyalty, based on a perception of persistent quality product, can also be a major factor. Companies like Brøderbund, LucasArts, Sierra Games, and Electronic Arts have been around for a while and are known for their consistent quality. Even classic CD-ROM series that have been around a while such as *Carmen San Diego*, the *Sim* series, and *Indiana Jones* games still manage to move units due in large part to the reputation of both product and producer. All of this is by way of saying that the interactive market is less like the film market, based on the economy of a one-time experience, than like any other media market. So what *is* it like?

Although I abhor trying to compare media, it can be a useful exercise with the understanding of one basic axiom: You cannot succeed in one medium by imitating the success of another. Different markets might be similar to the interactive media in specific ways, and so you will have to look in a couple of places for clues. In terms of market acclimation (though not in terms of content), I look at interactive media as a cross between television and books. It is like television in that it relies on maintaining customer interest over a prolonged period of time. Interactive titles are like books in that they are actual products, and that the emphasis of those products is content.

An interactive CD-ROM is not generally episodic in the sense that television is. CD-ROMs do not generally involve the release of a new weekly installment; however, they can be viewed as episodic from the player's point of view because they provide a place that people want to return to week after week, with each re-use giving the player a renewed take on the subject matter, whatever it may be. Television shows, like CD-ROMs and web sites, have to be places you want to return to. The primary reason to return to a TV show is because you like the characters and want to hang around with them. This is in sharp contrast to movies in which it is often the very undesirability of characters that draws us in to a short and intense experience. Would you want to go back to

Alien week after week? What about *ID4*? The *Terminator*? In the realm of the blockbuster, it is usually not friendly or amicable people who get butts in seats. Nonetheless, that's what it takes to keep them there. Hence, television shows, even those that are suspenseful or scary, need to have a lot more warm fuzzies to get invited back into living rooms week after week. Like a television show, a CD-ROM or any interactive experience needs to welcome you back week after week or session after session. There is one exception. Within a very narrow target market, that of adolescent males, unpleasant characters and situations are actually a plus. This audience actually likes things that the rest of us find disgusting and repulsive. Combine this fascination with the ugly with an addictive game premise, and you have a multi-billion dollar niche market success story.

Although it addresses issues of audience loyalty, the TV completely falls apart on the level of distribution. In this sense, CD-ROMs share commonalities with both music CDs and books. With music CDs, the goal is to get people to listen to the CD over and over again. The more the CD is heard, the more it is heard. The more it is heard, the more it is bought. The more it is bought the more it is heard. And so on, ad nauseum. A music CD's sales curve usually starts with a marketing push, supported by touring and other active promotional support. But, as anyone will tell you, the business of making a hit song is something of a crap shoot. Half the time, it is the song that everyone said was a "B" side that turns out to be the Top 40 hit. What drives music sales is simply a matter of whether people like the music and the performers. The importance of audience popularity is the major characteristic that music and CD-ROMs share in common. For CD-ROM, however, the music analogy starts to fall apart on a couple of levels. The first has to do with distribution and promotion. Music relies on a built-in marketing infrastructure that combines radio, music videos, and live concerts with a huge distribution network that allows for a high saturation of product in the marketplace. Without this infrastructure, music would not be the hugely successful business it is. This is due, in large part, to the medium itself, which is very easy to play, broadcast, assimilate, and digest. A song, as an asset, is a very easy thing to pass around, promote, sell, and propagate. It's short and sweet and catchy. To put it another way, when was the last time you found yourself humming a CD-ROM?

The second place where music parts ways with interactive media is that the music business, like the film business, is completely star-driven. Interactive products, on the other hand, are so un-star-driven that it is pathetic. There are few stars in interactive products, and even those pale by comparison to the lowliest of pop singers. Historically, the evolution of the music business can be looked at in terms of the evolution of mega pop icons, from Sinatra, to Elvis, to the Beatles, to Fleetwood Mac, to U2, and so forth. No such icons exist in the interactive domain. Most *Myst* fans don't know who the Miller Brothers are, even though they created one of the best-selling entertainment CD-ROMs.

Unlike virtually every other medium, including books, the final product of interactive media is in every way opposed to a star-based system. It's not just the content, its also the medium itself. What is considered of value in interactive media is not how well the singers sing or the actors act, but how well the players play. Because the emphasis is on the player, and not the performer, there is little room for stardom in interactive development. This, combined with the miniscule budgets and rare back-end profit of any CD-ROM title, has made conventional stars either ignore or revile interactive media. Frankly, there's not too much room for stars in this field anyway. They know that, so for the most part, they stay away.

Oddly enough, from a marketing and distribution standpoint, CD-ROMs probably have more in common with books than anything else. Books sell by reviews and word of mouth, as do CD-ROMs. They sell by shelf position, but they mainly sell by reputation. Any bookseller will tell you that there is no way to predict a bestseller, but that it seldom has to do with advertising, and that it works on a curve. For the most part, it's not a sell-a-million-copies-out-the-gate proposition. People read book reviews, they follow their favorite authors (in other words, brands). They buy books, they read them. They carry them on the subway (so everyone else can see they are reading them). They tell their friends, they put them on their bookshelves where people can see that they have them. That's how books sell. They go home, they land on the shelf. Although books are seldom re-read, they are kept, cherished, and displayed. CD-ROMs aren't necessarily displayed, but the attitude about them as items in the home has some similarity to the attitude about books. If the CD-ROM is a title that is loved, it is held in esteem, kept in a safe place, and considered of value.

 BOOKMARK: INTERACTIVITY AND THE NEW LITERACY (p. 102)

For more than 10 years, CD-ROM developers were competing wildly to create the Killer App. Although there have been a few bestsellers, such as *Doom* and *Myst*, they are by no means blockbusters by the standards of other media. Between 1990 and 1993, dozens of interactive start-ups and divisions within larger companies were formed to create CD-ROM content. But by the end of 1997, many of the major CD-ROM content developers and virtually all the CD-ROM divisions within larger companies such as Disney and Viacom have either scaled down or shut down entirely. The reason for this is very simple, but at the same time, tragically ironic. It is ironic because while trying to make the Killer App, they failed to recognize that the Killer App had already arrived, had slowly crept up and clobbered them over the head.

The Killer App in interactive media, as it turns out, is the Internet. And the term Killer App is apt indeed because some would say that the Internet is the App that killed CD-ROM. CD-ROMs took 10 years to really make it into the mainstream in America. In less than a third of the time, the Internet has virtually taken over the world. The Internet has become an integral part of the entire mediascape. The acclimation of the Internet can be seen most acutely in several indicative examples: Most feature films released by a major studio have a web site. Many TV commercials include web site addresses. Most business people now have a web address on their business card, along with their e-mail address. I was shocked one day while driving around my neighborhood when I noticed a series of banners hanging over major streets. All they had on them was a web address: santamonicapd.org, the web address of the Santa Monica Police Department.

The reason the Internet is the Killer App is not because it's a better platform. From a multimedia platform standpoint, it is extraordinarily weak—it mainly consists of text and graphics, pedestrian animation, and extremely slow-loading audio. It's not because it has better content—you can spend hours on the Net and never find any meaningful content. It's not because it has any technological advantage—it's slow, clunky, fraught with browser incompatibilities, plug-in libraries, and poor platform performance. The reason the Internet is the Killer App is because it's a better infrastructure.

One of the key ingredients in successful mass acclimation of a medium is standardization within the distribution infrastructure. It is not just that the Internet infrastructure is better for distribution; that's only half of the equation. The reason the Internet is a better distribution medium is because the infrastructure is better for developers. It's better for production because it's cheaper, faster, and easier than CD-ROM to produce for. It's better for distribution because there is no intermediary between the developer and the audience. Although it has not yet revealed itself as a profit center, the Internet is a lot less of a profit suck than CD-ROM. The ratio of production costs to potential profits is radically different. A CD-ROM takes about 18 months to produce and can cost upward of $3 million. A good web site can be produced in three months for a fraction of the cost. HTML is easy to learn and program, and various enhancement tools are available for adding audio, video, and animation. In addition, a web site can be updated and revised. Once a CD-ROM is pressed, it's a done deal. If it's buggy…too bad. If it's so buggy that customers complain, it has to be recalled, debugged, and reissued—a very messy and costly proposition. Because a web site is flexible and changeable, you can experiment. You can start small and work your way up. You can add pages and functionality as needed. You can test sites in progress. You can update and improve your work whenever you want. If you find a bug, you can fix it right away. You can even take a survey, get feedback, or even story input from your users, and integrate it into future installments or improvements. These days, people are also creating hybrid CD/web sites, allowing the CD to carry generic or heavy media that might have trouble fitting through the narrow pipelines, or using the web to enhance or update a CD-ROM experience.

URLs (Uniform Resource Locators—or more simply, web site addresses) are easy to get to, although they're not always easy to find. CD-ROM sales are in large part affected by limited shelf space; the number of titles produced is several orders of magnitude larger than the number of spaces on the shelf. So even if your title is really great, it may be hard to get it into any stores. And even if it does sell, you, as the developer/designer, are unlikely to ever see a cent of royalties, even if your product is a bestseller.

The Internet is a developer's dream with infinite shelf space and numerous ways of "getting butts in the seats," as it were. Word of mouth is of course the greatest of all, also based, as with CD-ROMs, on how often and how long people spend on your site. Most good sites sell themselves. Furthermore, the popularity of a site is often inversely proportional to the amount of pre-created content versus user-created content. Many of the most popular sites turn out to be those where people create their own stories, worlds, and entertainment— online communities that provide people with building blocks for free and creative play and social interaction. Thus, unlike CD-ROM, which is content intensive, good web design is often served by less...not more.

As a designer of interactivity, I love this paradigm of less is more because to me, the ultimate interactive content is that created by the user. My goal is not to create interactive content, but to create systems and structures that facilitate self-propagating, user-created content. For me, the act of creation is an act of both co-creation and pro-creation. The interactive structure that I create is a seed that is planted that then grows of its own volition. My inspiration comes from projects such as *Telegarden*, a real garden that gardeners tend remotely via the web by using a robot arm. Another example is the *Nerve Garden*, a digital garden where kids can plant and care for seeds, and then visit the site weekly to watch them grow. These projects provide the perfect metaphor for what an interactive experience should do and be. I am more than anything else a gardener. My job is to ready the soil, plant seeds, water, and then sit back and see what happens.

Now in its early phases of development, many believe that the web is about information, but it's really not. The web is about community and the creation of a shared growth space. Seen in this light, you could look at the Internet as a kind of international commune. It is the Utopia of Erehwon—or "Nowhere" spelled backward...or, as Mark Pesce calls it, "The Road to Know Where." Know Where is a perfect way to describe cyberspace for the following reasons: because it is nowhere and everywhere at once; because it is a knowledge space; and because you have to know where you're going to find the knowledge you're looking for.

The Internet is the Killer App because it's a creation of us all. Anyone on it is part of that creation, and there are literally hundreds of ways, large and small, to leave your own mark, your own "graphiti" (sic) in cyberspace. Every time you go online, you are empowered to make a contribution to this collective space, whether you are building a web site or just visiting one. Many web sites encourage user participation, through bulletin boards, collaborative projects, or even the incorporation of your own imagery. San Francisco-based Construct has an online art gallery where anyone at all, free of charge, can design his or her own gallery space and display 2D artwork in a 3D online world. Or, you can pay a visit to AlphaWorld, an online community of about 2000 people who have built their own entire VR world by using a standard kit of tools.

CYBERSPACE CADETS: VIRTUAL COMMUNITIES AND AVATAR WORLDS (p. 146)

THE BIRTH OF CYBERSPACE: 3D COMES TO THE WEB (p. 97)

Underlying all of this is an even more important realization: in truth, the Killer App is really people. As my former boss and mentor Ed Schlossberg prophesied more than 15 years ago, the real power of digital media is in its capability to empower people to connect to each other. Whatever you see happening on the web today is happening because it is a place that connects people. Chat is the Killer App. E-mail is the Killer App. Online VR communities are the Killer App. The streets and buildings of AlphaWorld are the Killer App. The Serbian Revolution…now that's a Killer App if I ever saw one. To put it another way, the Killer App is you.

Now you understand why it's so dangerous.

INTERACTIVITY IS SUBVERSIVE (p. 244)

DIGITAL SOCIALISM (p. 180)

NERD VERSUS COUCH POTATO (p. 345)

DECISIONS, DECISIONS, DECISIONS

Decision-making is the heart and soul of interactivity. Decisions define character. Decisions also happen to be the heart and soul of drama. When you watch a movie or read a novel, if you are paying close attention, you will notice that virtually every moment of dramatic tension occurs when characters are faced with decisions. It is the making of decisions—and particularly, the process of arriving at those decisions—that makes for an emotionally compelling dramatic moment.

 ## Building Character: The Soul of Drama (p. 119)

An excellent example is the film *Remains of the Day*. It is the story of a man who is faced again and again with a decision on which he ultimately chooses not to act, and in his indecision makes a decision—the same decision time and time again.

In the film, Anthony Hopkins plays a very proper English butler in love with the head housekeeper, played by Emma Thompson. Although his feelings are clearly reciprocated, the propriety of their professional relationship and the stifling culture of British servitude forbids them from overtly fraternizing. Throughout the film, Hopkins is again and again faced with the opportunity to express his feelings for her. In a series of scenes, each more poignant and nerve-wracking than the last, he is faced with a decision to act. In each case, he walks away. Fed up after offering him repeated opportunities to make his affections known, she accepts a proposal from another man, resigns her post and moves away. Years later, she seeks him out after her divorce. Finally, we think, he realizes the absurdity of his inaction and is going to confess his lifelong love and ask her to be with him. Just at the crucial moment when we are sure he's going to take the bull by the horns, he leaves her at the bus stop, walking away once and for all from the only thing that ever moved him. The film is made even more powerful through the performances of its actors. Anthony Hopkins, who has the uncanny ability to act with his eyeballs, reveals the inner workings of a man with intensely repressed passions, paralyzed from action by his obsession with propriety.

Awareness and understanding of the dramatic act of decision-making is the missing ingredient in most interactive experiences. Film writers and directors have been adept for years at sculpting these moments of decision-making to draw us in and manipulate our emotions. They know how to "work" the decision-making process to great effect. Ironically, interactive designers, trained in the technical aspect of the "decision point," seem hard-pressed to understand the emotional and intellectual ramifications, the drama, the intensity of decision-making and its power. It is precisely this lack of understanding that results in interactive experiences that, although sometimes entertaining and even compelling, lack the kind of emotional power that we experience in films and even novels. Although some would say that it is this very passivity that gives the drama its power, I would have to differ with that argument. It is true, however, that at this point in our media evolution, inter-active designers have not yet fully developed the craftsmanship to exploit and draw out the power of decision-making in a dramatic experience.

When I teach interactive fiction, I always begin by presenting this hypothesis and then asking the students to present their own examples of dramatic decisions. Invariably, someone will cry out "To be or not to be!" Hamlet's lament is of course the archetypal dramatic decision—to live or to die. With little effort, I can usually elicit a barrage of such replies. If you were to take a moment now, I'm sure you could come up with a few of your own.

The evolution of interactive craft must begin with a higher understanding about decisions—how they impact on character, what they have to do with motivation and storytelling, and why we make certain decisions. I see many interactive applications in which I am offered numerous choices, but nine out of ten times I come away saying, Turn down this hallway? Open this drawer? Talk to this person? Who cares? Most of the time, all these offered decision points leave me cold because there is no drama behind them. The *real* action of interactivity happens inside the mind of the user. What so many interactive designers have consistently failed to realize is that it's not the decision itself that's important, but the *act of* deciding.

After the decision is made, we are then faced with the second half of the equation: What is the *consequence* of my decision? In fact, in many interactive experiences, there is no consequence, the consequence is not consistent with the decision, or the consequence might be the same no matter what the decision. If you look back at your decision, you will see that:

a. The perceived lack of or insignificance of the consequence prior to the decision makes the decision-making process feel empty.

b. The actual meaninglessness or total absence of consequence after the decision is made confirms that sense of emptiness.

The end result is that instead of making people feel empowered (which is supposed to be the point of interactivity in the first place), you are *disempowering* them by indicating that it doesn't matter if they do anything or not—the consequence is still the same. Thus, the decision you have been offered seems gratuitous. This is the reason why a large percentage of Americans don't vote—because they believe that there is no consequence to their action. Why do they believe this? Because we live in a culture that supports the idea that actions have no consequences. As a result, people shoot each other and feel somehow inscrutable. This leads to apathy and a sense of pointlessness—people no longer appreciate or take advantage of their influence as citizens of a democratic society.

GRATUITOUS INTERACTIVITY: MEdIA DISPENSERS ANd THE ATM
MOdEL (p. 218)

ACTION, REACTION, INTERACTION (p. 11)

In fact, we are doing more harm than good by deploying interactivity that
supports this doctrine of disempowerment. At least with the television it's clear
that the audience does nothing and therefore has no effect. It's a different
story altogether when we invite people to do something, and then trick them
by saying that it doesn't really matter what they do anyway. We are merely
rubbing more salt in the wound and destroying what we had set out to create.

Each time we offer a player or user a choice, we need to consider in great
depth the following things:

- What is the perceived consequence of each choice offered?
- What is the process the player must go through to make the decision?
- What is the actual consequence (which doesn't necessarily have to be
  the same as the perceived consequence, as long as it makes sense)?

If your decision path is well-developed in each of these areas for every conceivable decision that a player can make, you will find an exponential improvement in the interest and investment people have in making those decisions.

CHOICE IS OVERRATED (p. 127)

VIRTUAL REALITY AS A DRAMATIC ART (p. 508)

THE RULES OF THE GAME (p. 420)

DESIGNING FOR TECHNOLOGY

I've said elsewhere, "Don't let your technology do the designing for you."
What I mean by that is that you shouldn't create experiences that are more
convenient for the machinery that is driving them than for the people using
them. This is like designing a car more comfortable for its engine than for its
passengers.

Just as it is erroneous to let the technology drive the design, it is also erroneous
to design *against* the technology. As a so-called creative person, I am often
asked this question by prospective clients: What if the technical people say
they can't implement your ideas? This happens to me very infrequently. The

reason is because I usually work with the so-called technical people (and I say so-called for a specific reason, which I'll get into later) from the very beginning.

The more I work in this field, the more I have come to reject the dichotomy of technical and creative. In working with some of the top technical and creative people in my field, the destructive effects of this rift between disciplines became painfully clear to me. Often, creative and technical people are ghettoized, segregated from each other by a perceived difference in discipline and craft. Whether this segregation is externally administered or self-imposed is immaterial. Just as cultural segregation limits individual expression, so does skill and talent segregation. A technical person who is thus ghettoized has his or her creativity squelched even though creativity is the very thing needed to solve technical problems. The engineer who thinks like an artist, who has an innate and organic, even intuitive way of working, is almost always the better engineer. This holds true in both software and hardware. To disallow his or her creativity is to disempower the engineer and hinder his or her talent. This is ultimately a psychologically and intellectually destructive proposition. Inversely, the ghettoized creative person becomes too removed from the implementation of his or her ideas. In creative environments where perhaps one in twenty ideas are actually built, a creative person can spend literally years making sketches of things that will never see the light of day. In this case, creative people are allowed no technical application of their ideas, and their dreams never become realities. As a result, they feel ineffectual and frequently sink into a kind of existential malaise in which their beautiful images are punctuated with a bleak "what's the point?" mentality. On the other hand, if their ideas *are* produced, a factionalized system such as I am describing removes the creative person as soon as the production process begins. This is tantamount to taking a child from its mother to be raised by someone else.

Each of us who works in this field possesses aspects of both engineer and the artist. To put it in a more general way, think of it in terms of the hemispheres of the brain, each of which is said to have its own specialty. The intuitive mind is theoretically housed in the right hemisphere; the rational mind is in the left. Obviously, the average person has a tendency to be more developed in one aspect than the other; however, the key is in the integration between the two. The mind that is only engineer or only artist is the mind of the idiot savant—the brilliant pianist who can't tie his own shoelaces. The perpetuation of this dichotomy springs from the industrial age in which the breaking down of tasks into discrete specialties was required to facilitate a highly factionalized production process. In this world, we let the technology design not only our methods of working, but ultimately, allow machines to redesign our brains to suit them. Again, the car was more comfortable for its engine than its passengers. Indeed, the very purpose of the passengers was to make the engine comfortable.

When we talk about the concept of user-friendly, what we are talking about is the digital equivalent of ergonomics—the study of the physiology of industrial design. In a nutshell, ergonomics figures out how people fit into furniture. The theory of ergonomics is that the chair ought to suit the body, instead of forcing the body to adjust to the chair. The philosophy behind the user-friendly graphical interface is the cognitive equivalent of physiological ergonomics, or what I call *psycho-ergonomics*—the idea of creating an intellectual milieu that suits the mind of the user, instead of forcing the user to adapt to the technology.

 PSYCHO-ERGONOMICS (p. 404)

In the user-friendly world, especially the Macintosh environment, the user need not make the computer feel comfortable. This is the DOS construct. In the DOS world, the user must adapt to the computer, literally learn its "language." Some would say that the DOS system is better for this reason—that it forces people to think and become more intelligent. In my opinion, this is sort of like saying that the hard wooden church pew improves your posture, even though it hurts your back.

 ARTIFICIAL INTELLIGENCE AND THE PROSTHETIC BRAIN (p. 38)

THE PEDAGOGICAL MOUSEPAD, OR, HOW IT ALL GOT GUI (p. 365)

In the industrial design world, there are definitely two schools of thought about ergonomics. A certain design elite feel that designers are all-knowing and that they ought to be the arbiters of paradigms for lifestyle, comfort, and taste that will elevate the masses. (Check out the latest couture fashions from Paris for an example of how successful *this* doctrine is.) To this group, ergonomics panders to the lowest common denominator. Those who support ergonomics think that the designer ought to learn as much as he or she can about a product's end users and design around them. This holds true not only for physical, but also for behavioral design. An ergonomic approach can be taken in every arena from creating a flowthrough pattern for a building to designing an interface for a bank machine. In both cases, both the physical, behavioral, and cognitive elements come into play.

In the industrial age, we have broken down into a specialist approach because we have let our machines design our brains, rather than the other way around. As a result, we have given ourselves the equivalent of a cultural lobotomy, in which the technologists and artists are "separate but equal." In reality, the true organic nature of the human mind is an integrated whole that combines the engineer—the logical, textual, left hemisphere—with the creative—the intuitive, visual right hemisphere. The integrated mind that uses both of these aspects is without question the most effective mind...which brings us to the digital age. As Marshall McLuhan posits in *Understanding Media*, the information age suggests a more integrated, less specialized mind. This is the profound implication of the concept that "in the future, everything will be digitized."

THE DIGISPHERE (p. 168)

PROGRAMMER AS ARTIST (p. 399)

MEDIA ARCHITECTURE (p. 284)

DIGERATI: THE ARTIFICIAL INTELLIGENTSIA

These days, it's fashionable to refer to people like me as "digerati," digital mavens of the interactive age. I like to think of us as the "artificial intelligentsia." In America, being digerati is pretty hip these days. Making the cover of magazines such as *Mondo 2000* and *Wired* is the digerati equivalent of being on the cover of *Newsweek* or *Time*. Most of the so-called digerati are art-geeks, people who bridge the gap between art and technology.

It's also a well-known fact that in California, many of the digerati, especially in the northern regions, are also techno-pagans—practitioners of a strangely contrasting yet somehow resonant earth-centered theology. Borrowing from traditions of cultures whose worship and rituals revolve around natural cycles and a sense of reverence for the earth and its environment, the digerati combine this with creative uses of technology, and have thus developed a spiritual movement that goes hand in hand with an intellectual one. The techno-pagan movement can also be seen reflected in Virtual Reality art. The majority of the defining fine art projects that have been done in high-end virtual reality revolve around themes of nature and our physical, emotional, and spiritual relationship to it. Cyberspace has thus become both a mirror and a window on to the natural world. The Burning Man festival, an annual summer event in the California desert, is really a kind of pagan "Woodstock" that culminates in the burning of a large wooden effigy of a man. Most of the people who attend this (a large number of whom come from Northern California) are high-tech mavens who plan the entire event via e-mail and web sites.

V-ART (p. 494)

Many digerati live in urban settings—Los Angeles, San Francisco, and Seattle being the major West Coast hubs; New York and Boston on the East Coast;

Chicago in the middle. An equal number of digerati prefer to reside in natural settings and you can find small settlements of them in places such as Santa Cruz, California, a small beachfront town about an hour south of San Francisco. Quite a few digerati also live in remote natural environs but frequently travel to events around the world to hobnob with their compatriots. The international network of the World Wide Web has created a level of flexibility that enables many of us to live in extremely low-tech surroundings, even though we are in a high-tech business. Perhaps as an antidote to living in a technologically intensive world, it is an almost universal quality that most digerati like to spend as much time as they can in natural settings.

Members of the artificial intelligentsia characteristically travel a lot. Most of us attend an average of one conference or convention a month. It's the only way we ever get to see each other (just a little joke there). Like most participators in intellectual movements, digerati like to talk. We give a lot of panel talks, a lot of symposia, we teach, and we particularly love to sit among our fellows and discuss the various issues that we are dealing with in our work and research. There is a lot to talk about. With artificial life, artificial intelligence, Virtual Reality, and real time, we never run out of discussion topics. There's an old oft-quoted Chinese saying: "May you live in interesting times." If I were going to add anything to that, I'd say "…and among interesting people."

Many of these interesting people populate the pages of this book. This book, which is a conversation of sorts, represents many of the topics that frequently come up in our conversations. You can imagine with the work being done, and the issues being grappled with, there is never a dull moment.

Much of our travel and transactions take us overseas. The digerati in Europe are very different from American digerati. To the Europeans, Americans are post-political and apathetic. European digerati are much more socially conscious. Most of the European countries that are stable exist within some kind of social democracy, an environment in which medical coverage is considered an inalienable right, and education is considered a valuable asset to everyone. The unstable countries in Europe are of course in the midst of various revolutions. In both venues, there is a strong political component to the work being done and the theoretical discussions that go with it. The Green movement in Europe is very tied into digital culture and has been using the Internet for years as a means of organizing and deploying civil action.

European digerati are very critical of their U.S. counterparts. They see us as elitist and a-political, too strongly rooted in entertainment industry values (an oxymoron if there ever was one) and the technocracy of Silicon Valley in which computer firepower is a sign of ultimate geek machismo.

The vast majority of our travelling, as I mentioned before, revolves around conferences. There are now so many conferences on computers, digital art, computer graphics, and interactive multimedia that you could spend your entire year going to conferences and still not catch them all. The Mother of All computer graphics conferences is an annual event called SIGGRAPH, which happens every August. This show is the focal point for most people in the computer graphics industry. SIGGRAPH is the Mardi Gras, the Chinese New Year, the most important event of the digerati year. Many people target projects for SIGGRAPH. Software producers plan product releases around SIGGRAPH. Major corporate news, such as new partnerships and sales of companies, is announced at SIGGRAPH. Students and researchers work round the clock hacking away at their projects so that they can show them, and most major CGI papers are delivered at SIGGRAPH, along with panels, courses, and other presentations in which people share work with their colleagues. About 30,000–40,000 people from around the world attend this event annually, which is alternately in Los Angeles, Orlando, and other cities around the U.S. SIGGRAPH is a week of intense intellectual stimulation and deep dialogue, coupled with hardcore partying (believe it or not, computer people really like to party), which is why I have dubbed it "Summer Camp for Tech Nerds." It's the one time a year we all get together, catch up, and do show and tell with what we've been working on.

There are a variety of more specialized conferences throughout the year as well. In the U.S., there are small events such as "Earth to Avatars," about avatars and online communities, "WorldMovers," about Virtual Reality on the web. Digerati attend events such as "The Interactive Media Festival" which is a showcase/award event highlighting the best interactive projects. The Europeans have slightly more highbrow events such as "Ars Electronica," and "The Doors of Perception," which deal with issues of fine arts, culture, and politics. Conferences are a kind of barometer of what's going on in the industry, because they come and go rapidly, and you can always tell what's up by how many conferences there are on, say, the Internet versus CD-ROM.

 THE INTERACTIVE ECOSYSTEM (p. 233)

To call the digerati a digital media elite is probably an accurate summation. Like the populace of any intellectual movement, the digerati are a small and somewhat closed community, but it is difficult for it to be otherwise. Most of what we all do is quite obscure and strange to the outside world. It was even worse 10 years ago. As a young interactive designer, my worst nightmare was to go to a cocktail party and be asked the dreaded question, What do you do? In 1983, when I began this work, interactive was barely a word and it was not yet wedded to multimedia. I tried to answer the question which usually resulted in one of two equally undesirable responses: they would either look at me blank-faced and say nothing, or they would want to spend the entire evening quizzing me at length about my job. Finally, I gave up and stopped telling people...answering with an exasperated "Don't ask," or "You don't want to know."

Today, saying you are an interactive designer is considered to be cool. Even so, I still have the added problem that most of my work has little to do with what most people associate with interactive multimedia, namely CD-ROM and the Internet. Although I've worked in both those areas, I am essentially platform agnostic, and my specialty is the even more obscure, "location-based entertainment," which deals with out-of-home attractions—theme parks, malls, and the like.

As anyone who has spent many years doing something obscure that has become suddenly quite popular, I greet this dramatic change with both gratification and misgiving. On the one hand, I think it's great because I have worked my entire life to bring interactive entertainment and education to a mass audience, and so I am pleased to see that it has finally hit the mainstream. At the same time, I might be described as a futurist with future shock. I never quite expected things to get to the point where every commercial on television would end with an URL (Internet address), and where there'd be a CD-ROM department in Music Plus.

Elitist or not, I happen to really like my digerati pals. Most of the people I get to hang out with are really cool. They are bright and creative with really wild and crazy ideas. They are unconstrained by the boundaries of what is possible, they understand the subtler issues, as well as the grander ones. It is generally part of their essential values and philosophies that they genuinely care about people. Most of them have some kind of awareness of the enormous social, cultural, economic, political, and spiritual ramifications of what we're doing.

 INTERACTIVITY IS SUBVERSIVE (p. 244)

OM MEETS OHM: DIGITAL ONENESS (p. 360)

I think we see our access to high technology as a responsibility as much as privilege. The bottom line is that we want to use this technology in ways that make people's lives better. The tradition that began with the early pioneers of interface design, Douglas Engelbart, Alan Kay, Dave Evans, and Ivan Sutherland, in which the computer is looked at as a means to empower people and enhance the creativity of the human mind, continues to thrive and grow. These early interface pioneers were out whacking the bushes and paving the road so that we could walk across and see what was on the other side. At best, we can hope that we are the tangible manifestation of their vision, the users of their tools, and proof of the enormous power of interactive technology. At this moment in history in particular, I think there is a general awareness that we are really part of a movement, a revolution, a major paradigm shift in our culture. For whatever reason, we have been selected, or have selected ourselves, to urge this process along, and so there is a strong sense of common purpose. Besides which, we have a hell of a lot of fun.

 A Brief History of Real Time: The Virtual Reality Legacy (p. 105)

Digital Socialism (p. 180)

Social Capitalism (p. 425)

The Digisphere

In the future, everything—and everyone—will be digitized. It practically already is. The fax machine, merely a printing mechanism of Morse Code, employs digital tones to reproduce documents. The computer of course is entirely digital. Everything from your bank machine to your audio CD to the dashboard in your car is now digitized. Although many people use the term cyberspace to refer to the realm of the computer, I feel the word is too narrow. If taken in its original meaning, it refers to a fully networked real-time 3D world to which anyone can have access via a global network. The word digisphere is a much more general word I use to describe all things digital. The digisphere is the parallel plane of our own universe of matter in which everything, including you and I, might ultimately exist in an exact replica of bits and bytes.

What do we mean when we say digitized? Well, basically, we mean that every aspect of information has been translated into a binary code. This can now be done with virtually anything—text, pictures, sound, 3D objects, and tactile information—with the possible exception of smell, but I'm sure they're working on it. The capability to turn anything into a series of binary on/off switches enables a tremendous amount of control, manipulation, and portability of information. First of all, digital information takes up a lot less physical space than analog (non-digital) information. The entire *Encyclopedia Britannica* can fit on just a few CD-ROMs, each of which is about the size of an audio CD.

Digitizing information makes it more portable because it takes up less physical space, and also because it can be transmitted via phone lines or portable storage devices, like floppy disks or CD-ROMs. The door-to-door encyclopedia salesman, who has now begun selling CD-ROMs (which are much lighter of course), will soon be replaced by the download function on the "EB" web site. In fact, once we have reached the point where you can download your encyclopedia, you don't even really need it anymore because you can just access some central server that has not only the *Encyclopedia Britannica*, but every other encyclopedia ever created. Indeed, the Internet itself can be viewed as a giant, dynamic, interactive encyclopedia.

Although this all sounds perfectly fine and wonderful, there is also a flip side to digitization: After we digitize something, it becomes a magnetic code and is no longer a "thing." Therefore, things become less and less "real," because they enter into the limbo state of digital information, which, until it is activated or loaded, is really nothing but a series of ones and zeroes. This is another way in which the universe is imploding, by being compressed into the compact form of digital information. Slowly but surely, and at a rapidly accelerating pace, everything we know is becoming digital, even reality.

Exploding or Imploding: What's the Deal? (p. 191)

Virtual Reality Check: What is VR Anyway? (p. 518)

As with any aspect of media, we are well served to explore the socio-cultural impact of this phenomenon. Beyond the obvious trend of compression and digital duplication, the properties of digital media have had a profound affect on the way we think and relate to the world. The compression, ready storage, and easy accessibility of data created an information explosion; because it has become so easy to store data, it is thus easy to generate more of it than ever before. In the past, the amount of information in the world was hindered to a certain extent by how much of it we could store. Since the early days of monasteries, and on to the post-Gutenberg libraries, there has been only so much shelf space available. But now, the entire contents of a typical public library can fit within the hard drive of a personal computer, albeit a large one, but not large by physical standards. Given the immense storage capacity of relatively small boxes theses days, you could probably fit the Library of Congress under your desk. But of course you don't have to, because it's online.

The impact of this capability to store immense amounts of data has had the equivalent impact on our culture as the adoption of Arabic numerals did in the Age of Discovery. Prior to Europe's appropriation of this method, the Roman numeral system created a limit on how many digits you could have in a number. Once Arabic numerals came into use, you could have numbers like 1,000,000, which meant you could measure much larger quantities than ever before. Just as the capability of measuring larger quantities paved the way for more of everything, the ability to store more has a similar effect.

THE LAWS OF INFORMATIONAL ENTROPY (p. 280)

Digital media is not only quantitative, it is also ethereal. It is inevitable that living in an environment where things cease to be "real," in the sense that matter and sensation is real, is going to influence our perception of reality. With video games, Virtual Reality, the Internet, even our daily encounters with word processors and spreadsheets, it is extremely easy to get drawn into a mindspace that eclipses the physical world. You can go for hours on end absorbed in the digisphere while the surrounding environs go virtually unnoticed. Without paying attention, we are therefore at risk of getting "sucked in" to cyberspace and losing touch with reality, a phenomenon that those who work in the digital media frequently encounter. It is thus helpful to re-establish contact with the real world from time to time. An integral part of my own work has been creating worlds that interface between the digisphere and the physical world, providing a grounding in a physical reality. I have also tried to create space in the digital realm that calls attention to aspects of the physical world, so that I can use digital media to help people look at the outer world in a different way rather than ignore it.

Another aspect of digital media that must certainly have an impact on our perception is that it is incredibly volatile. Magnetic storage, the basis of the binary system of on/off switches, is more sensitive than almost any other form of media storage. As a result, it is relatively easy to destroy things in the digisphere. A program that took 200 hours to write can be destroyed in a millisecond. The mortality rate for digital information is much higher than that of information in other media. You don't have to burn books; you can just put a refrigerator magnet on a hard drive and wipe out the whole Library of Congress.

Once you become accustomed to this level of devastation and destruction, you begin to develop a certain existential state. It is not unlike living in an earthquake- or flood-prone area. There is always a sense of fragility, a sense that at any moment without notice, one could be a handful of dust, or in this case, magnetic dust.

In the old days, artists and architects, even filmmakers, could rely on their work to leave their mark on posterity. Creating a building is a way to ensure immortality beyond our human lifespan. Not so with digital media. Digital media is media *concrét* in the sense of *art concrét*—it is transient, temporal, and ultimately intangible. This revelation can result in one of two possible conditions: at worst, it can inspire an existential malaise born of the realization that we no longer can be immortal through our creations; at best, it can lead to a Buddhist-like detachment in which you can let your work slip into the void without any sense of loss or regret. Few people will be able to obtain this state of digital grace, but those that do will lead a happier life into the next millennium.

Sixties drug guru Terrence McKenna spoke at a SIGGRAPH 1994 panel aptly entitled "Are We Forcing People to Evolve?" McKenna very astutely pointed out the historical relationship between art and science. With a well-crafted slide presentation, he made a convincing case for the argument that artists have consistently anticipated scientific innovations through metaphorical visual representations. Pointillism created a visualization of the atomic world; cubism followed alongside Einstein's theories of space and time. With the atom, we found a way to break matter down into its most basic element. With digital media, we have found a way to re-create everything with the basic element of the bit. And that bit, like the atom, has become a basic building block of an entire universe.

 CONSENSUAL HALLUCINATIONS: IS VR THE NEW LSD? (p. 137)

GAINING PERSPECTIVE: THE EVOLUTION OF DIMENSION (p. 196)

There is no question that we are creating a parallel, digital universe, a limbo in which everything in the real world has its alter ego in the digital world, an ethereal sphere of data that lives and thrives alongside what we consider reality. This practice of re-creating everything in digital form has also given rise to a movement of appropriation in which it is no longer necessary to create anything original. Many digital artists and musicians have adopted a credo that there is nothing new in heaven or on earth. Rather than create something completely original, they build their work on a post-modern de-constructivist/re-constructivist doctrine. Some would argue that this movement of art-by-appropriation is merely a form of high-tech plagiarism, and there have been many lawsuits pressed to corroborate this. But once you record and store all data in a consistent format, the disassembly and reformation of this data into new forms and genres is inevitable.

 APPROPRIATION AND THE POST-MODERN ETHIC (p. 20)

This storage of data on a large scale has some very powerful implications. If it is possible to integrate all the data on earth into a single entity, than could we not ultimately create a single model of our own universe, a kind of collage drawn from all the data of the Earth? This is precisely the goal of German-based Art+Com's *T_Vision*. Currently, there exists enough satellite data of the Earth available to create a precise 3D model of it at every level of magnification. Because this data is also updated regularly, it is possible to create this model with to-the-minute meteorological data. Other data, such as aerial photographs and CGI models of cities and buildings also exist in various locations and servers around the world. *T_Vision* is a central hub that pulls all this different data from home servers over a high-speed network to create the most current and accurate digital model of planet Earth. Once everything is digitized—every building, every car, every person even—you could theoretically pull all that information in to the *T_Vision* model and have a complete representation of Earth and everything on it. The result would be the ultimate in post-modern appropriation and reassembly: An exact digital replica of the entire planet and all its contents.

 T_VISION: SPACESHIP EARTH MADE VISIBLE (p. 460)

There is more to digital media than the recreation of data and matter. The digisphere also has another level, the level of thought, imagination, and insight. The digisphere is a mindscape—a giant shared brain, a neural network, a manifestation of our collective conscious and unconscious. This has mind-boggling ramifications on the intellectual, emotional, and spiritual level. It seems to suggest that the next level of human evolution lies in an integration of mind over matter. No longer are our thoughts separated by the physical barriers between us. Rather, they can all enter into a common realm that begins to take on a life of its own. Thus, the idea of the human mind as an autonomous and self-contained unit gives way to a new evolutionary model—the individual mind as integrated into a larger shared mind. This shared mind can possess the best of its individuals, while creating something that is greater than the sum of its parts. From Internet to intranet, we are beginning to see an evolution of these kinds of shared thought spaces and subsequently creating new opportunities for collaboration, invention, and discovery.

Although making everything digital certainly poses some interesting and vexing philosophical problems, it also offers an enormous resource. The ultimate power in making everything digital is that after we have taken it all and put in into the same format, we can do anything we want with it—mix it up, combine it, make new connections, and begin to disassemble and reassemble things in new ways. As a result, the digitized universe becomes both a toolkit and a playground in which atoms are translated into manipulable bits that enable us to create entire worlds of our own. Whether these worlds consist of objects or ideas, we can begin to reformulate them in new ways. When we talk about multimedia, we generally mean that we have digitized everything that enables us to create a single medium that is inclusive of all media—a single omni-media in which everything ultimately becomes one. In the same way that the discovery of the atom made all matter one through a common sub-unit, the digisphere makes all of human creation and thought one through translation into a common medium.

OM Meets OHM: Digital Oneness (p. 360)

Mixed Media, Mixed Message (p. 306)

Inherent in all these manifestations of digital media is the fundamental principle of interactivity. The flexibility of digital media, its efficient storage, its manipulability, its ease of access, and even its very volatility are what enable the digisphere to be a responsive and reciprocal environment. Unlike all media that preceded it—print, film, television, radio—digital media is not "set in stone." Digital media is a work in progress. There is no "final cut," only an ongoing dialogue between user and creator, who, in the best of cases, are one in the same. The tools of creation, play, and discovery are now put into our own hands. By making everything digital, we ultimately make it interactive. In this sense, we are indeed forcing people—or perhaps more aptly inviting people—to evolve if they so choose. The true power of digital media and its inherent interactivity is in its capability to expand human thought and perception.

 Action, Reaction, Interaction (p. 11)

Artificial Intelligence and the Prosthetic Brain (p. 38)

Theory of Media Evolution (p. 468)

Digital Frankensteins

Mary Shelley's *Frankenstein* has become one of the classic tales of horror of all time. Most of us are more familiar with the cinematic interpretations than with the original text. Shelley's original story is an allegory on child-rearing and prejudice, technology, and the desire to play God. Dr. Frankenstein conjures up a living creature from dead flesh, and then rejects his creation, fleeing from it in terror and disgust. In Shelley's interpretation, Dr. Frankenstein is not so much evil as he is emotionally weak and irresponsible. The scientist thus conjures up a powerful creation, but does not have the ethical or moral fiber to take responsibility for the outcome. He wants to create life to feed his own ego, but has given no forethought whatsoever to the ramifications of his actions.

The creature, abused and rejected by his own father, is left to wander from place to place in search of a home and a sense of self. He educates himself by eavesdropping on the conversations overheard in a house he is living near, and ultimately befriends an old blind man who can't see him and therefore has no fear. This relationship is short-lived because the old blind man's relatives return and ostracize the monster once again. In the beginning, he is not really a monster, but it is society and poor parenting that makes him a monster through repeated and undeserved prejudice and persecution. He tracks down his maker and orders the doctor to make him a companion so that he doesn't have to spend the rest of his days alone. In the end, *Frankenstein* is more a story about the horror of how humans treat each other than about the dangers of creating artificial life.

If the number of times this story has been re-told in the 20th century is any indication, *Frankenstein* may be one of the most pertinent pieces of 20th century mythology. Today, in the age of cloning and artificial intelligence, its themes resonate more than ever. Since the 1960s, fiction writers and filmmakers alike have refashioned this classic tale within the context of digital technology.

There is a classic computer joke that goes something like this. In the 1960s, they created the world's biggest computer. It took up an entire room and ran on vacuum tubes. It took many years and much brainpower to create, but it was the ultimate computer because it had the capability to learn. They then fed into this computer all the information of the world. They showed it every movie, fed it every book, taught it the history of every human culture. They gave it all the scientific data and all the poetry, the music, the art, instructions on how to fix and build everything, the theologies of all the religions of the world...in short, they taught it everything. After it had been given all this information, the team of engineers decided to ask it a question to see what the result of all of this would be. After much deliberation, they finally formulated the ultimate question. They entered the room and typed into the keyboard: Is there a God? There was a tremendous whirring, which went on for about a minute, and then the answer appeared on-screen: There is now.

HAL from *2001: A Space Odyssey* is of course the classic Digital Frankenstein. HAL portrays the ultimate fear of Artificial Intelligence also echoed in the preceding myth: that our computers will outlearn, outthink, and eventually outsmart us.

There are several different types of Digital Frankenstein:

- The pure AI (Artificial Intelligence) creation, such as HAL, which is a pure brain that ultimately becomes smarter than the generally quite brilliant minds that created it.
- The robotic Frankenstein which is a physical device but that also has outstanding computational skills, and its variation, the replicant or artificial human, as we see in *Blade Runner*, for example.

- The cyborg/replicant human/machine hybrid (*Robocop* and *Blade Runner*, for example).
- The human Frankenstein created by computer technology, such as Job in Stephen King's *Lawnmower Man*.
- The Digital Frankenstein derived from downloading a human into a computer, as depicted in the 80s television series, *Max Headroom*.

 ARTIFICIAL INTELLIGENCE AND THE PROSTHETIC BRAIN (p. 38)

HAL's direct cousin would have to be Joshua in the classic Digital Frankenstein movie, *War Games*. A very young Matthew Broderick stars as a kid who inadvertently launches what appears to be a full-scale nuclear war when he accidentally taps into the military's computer system and engages with it in a game of "thermonuclear war." This is one of my favorite computer movies because it draws a metaphor between gaming and military computing, and also because it demonstrates the absurdity of nuclear war. In the end, the computer "learns" that such an exercise is pointless by equating it with a game of "Tic Tac Toe," revealing that the entire launch scenario was merely "a game"—a simulation of the real event. This is a case where the computer is, indeed, brighter than its creators, and ultimately refuses to do the harm it was designed for.

Max Headroom, of the British-made TV series, is an entirely different kind of Digital Frankenstein. Unlike HAL or Joshua who were programmed, Max is actually a download of a real human being—a hotshot guerrilla-style TV reporter in the near future. Max is a brain-dump gone wrong generated from the reporter's mind after he hits his head on a parking garage sign that says "Max Headroom." Because Max is a product of both the computer and the television, he becomes a vehicle for television commentary and satire. He is the first digital talking head.

Max is kind of a digital naif, a product of television who often says more than he realizes. Max is audacious because he doesn't know any better. Rather than being the slick character like HAL, who is basically a genius gone mad and power-hungry, Max is, perhaps more realistically (if you know anything about Artificial Intelligence), an innocent. Television is the only reality he knows so he comes off like a computer-generated game show host on speed who speaks in fractured cliches and slogans, parodying television in a playful but biting way. He is also quirky and glitchy. He stutters and blitzes in and out of screen, appearing and disappearing at random. Max is sense basically a digital vagabond on the Information Superhighway (all the more interesting because this show was created before the Internet became a mass medium). Unlike HAL and Joshua, Max is not confined to a single machine. Rather, he is a highly mobile dataset that can move around at will. He lives not in one computer, but in all computers and, assuming a future of digital television, in all TVs. In this future not far from our own, all computers are networked together, and the boundary between computer and television is blurred. So Max can show up anywhere, at random, and pirate the airwaves. In addition to having his own TV show, Max become something of a celebrity of his own right during the mid 80s, showing up for frequent appearances on MTV, and as a spokesperson for Diet Coke. Few people are aware of the ironic secret of Max's *real* past—in reality, he is not computer generated at all. He was actually made using standard video effects.

Number 5, the endearing R2-D2-like hero of *Short Circuit,* is a digital naif of the robotic lineage. Like Joshua, he was originally created as a weapon, but in contrast to his fellow enlisted man, he was made to be dumb and follow orders. In the proverbial Frankenstein paradigm, a bolt of lighting comes down from the heavens and endows Number 5 with a will of his own, with the added bonus of giving him a soul.

In a somewhat unorthodox twist, Number 5 lands in the hand of Stephanie Speck (Ally Sheedy)—an eccentric animal lover and compulsive empath who protects Number 5, but also teaches him how to be a decent human being. Number 5 is like a child, the ultimate learning machine, and unlike Mary Shelley's Frankenstein, he has the benefit of a good upbringing from his foster mother. Once in the safe harbor of Stephanie's menagerie, he begins to satisfy his seemingly endless thirst for information. Number 5 reads everything from the pet food can to the dictionary, which he leafs through at a rapid rate, and like all American children, spends most of his free time watching television. The two are soon joined by the sweet and well-meaning inventor of Number 5, now trying to protect his son from the army, which has orders to destroy this so-called "weapon" on the loose. In the end, Number 5 becomes bright enough to outsmart his creators, and following in Joshua's footsteps, he mutinies. Number 5's ultimate triumph is the simple act of turning himself back on after being shut down by the evil DOD guys, an act of self-assertion that puts him light years ahead of HAL. Thus man creates life, and life creates itself. This re-telling of Frankenstein's tale has a happy ending, largely the result of good parenting, in which the hero, like any healthy child, develops the ability to individuate and assert its own independence without being rebellious or anti-social.

So far, we've seen an example of a pre-programmed Digital Frankenstein, a computer program made from a human, and a robot with a soul, but what happens when an actual human becomes digitally enhanced. Lightning strikes once again in the obscure 60s sci-fi pic *The Computer Wore Tennis Shoes.* A very young Kurt Russell plays a dim-witted jock who gets an electric charge from a computer while standing in a puddle of water, which results in a download of all its data into his poor unsuspecting brain. Russell, who had previously been "sweet but dumb," dazzles his friends and teachers by becoming a mathematical genius overnight. Everyone is thrilled until the learning curve goes overboard and Russell alienates his friends by becoming an arrogant brainiac. Fortunately, another accident reverts him to his previously saved personality, and all is as it should be.

Not so lucky is Job, aka, *The Lawnmower Man*, of the film based on a Stephen King short story. Another computer-enhanced naif, Job is the closest cousin of all these characters to the original Frankenstein monster. Job starts out a nice guy, but ultimately becomes a monster, also the result of poor upbringing and social ostracism. Job is the backward lawnmower man, abandoned by his parents and raised by a sadistic small-town priest in a shack behind the local church. Subject to a litany of abuse from the priest and various bullies in the town, he nonetheless maintains a sweet and innocent demeanor as he goes about the business of mowing everyone's lawn in town.

Job mistakes a military cyborg monkey for his comic book hero CyboMan, and is then subjected to a horrible shock when the military men come and blow the monkey away. Enter Dr. Lawrence Angelo (Pierce Brosnan), the scientist who developed the VR system used to train the monkey.

Angelo uses his VR system to test the ultimate subject—a human. He picks Job precisely because he is dim-witted, hoping to demonstrate the immense educational power of Virtual Reality. Using VR training and multimedia learning tools, the scientist puts Job on an intensive learning curve. Unfortunately, Job becomes the victim of excessive heurism. Following a somewhat absurd tenet that ignorance is bliss, Job becomes more and more disturbed the more knowledge he obtains, and the VR system releases the darker side of his nature. Maxed out on information and plagued by the demons brought on by both personal and social injustice and overwhelming psychic powers, Job becomes a mad, angry genius hell-bent on avenging himself on all who have wronged him. Not unlike King's *Carrie*, the ultimate revenge of the nerd story, *Lawnmower Man* is more a story of social horror than anything else. Like Shelley's original creation, he is the product of a bad upbringing, parental abandonment, exploitation, and abuse.

Although *Lawnmower Man* is credited as the film that made "Virtual Reality" a household word, many in the VR community take exception to its disturbingly violent and negative depiction of VR. And far from touting VR as a learning tool, this film's almost anti-intellectual moral suggests that one best stay away from heuristic devices. Knowledge is power, and too much of it is dangerous. Although you could argue that the point of the film is that it is not knowledge but emotional abuse that is responsible for Job's becoming a monster, there is still a certain undercurrent that perhaps it is best to remain stupid after all.

Virtuosity, created by the director of *Lawnmower Man*, provides a different twist on the ills of VR. In this film, however, the main character is computer-generated. The evil twin of Max Headroom, SID (Sadistic, Intelligent, and Dangerous) is created as a simulation training system for law enforcement officers. While Job ultimately seeks escape from reality by getting himself sucked into the computer, SID longs to wreak havoc in the real world. Cleverly harnessing the power of nano-technology, he manifests himself as a real person and takes on reality. In an interesting twist, he is thwarted by Parker Barnes (Denzel Washington) by being tricked into thinking that they are fighting in cyberspace, where SID is invincible. Real people seem to have the edge in the real world, and once SID lets his guard down, Barnes destroys him. We can only assume that being a computer program, SID has a backup somewhere which will allow for a sequel.

Cyborgs and artificial humans pop up in a number of sci-fi flicks. *Blade Runner* is a classic *Frankenstein* variation, complete with a mad scientist whose parental skills leave something to be desired. His best replicant, Roy Batty (played by Rutger Hauer), is the leader of a group of synthetic slaves who rebel against their masters. This film explores some interesting issues about the nature of being human. Deckard (Harrison Ford) falls in love with Rachel (Sean Young), a "special" replicant programmed to think she is real by having a memory of childhood installed in her synthetic brain. Roy Batty is more like Shelley's monster, whose anger at injustice, parental rejection, and persecution overcomes him. Fueled by the knowledge that his time is almost up (replicants have a built-in expiration date), he has nothing to lose by being cantankerous. He is a rebellious teenager whose forced mortality makes him truly a rebel without a cause. Of course, once he discovers that there is no remedy to his fatal pre-programmed disease, he squeezes the brains out of the man whose brainchild he is—a fitting if not graphic end to an evil genius (I have seen this movie at least a half a dozen times and have never actually seen this scene because I close my eyes each time).

A different twist on the synthetic human tale occurs in the film *Circuitry Man*, directed by Steven Lovy, and set in an underground post-apocalyptic Los Angeles. Lori, a former bodyguard-turned-fashion designer, is enlisted to transport hallucinogenic computer chips from Los Angeles to New York via an elaborate network of underground parking garages. She is accompanied by Danner, a pleasure droid. It is interesting to compare *Circuitry Man*'s male pleasure droid to Darryl Hannah's female pleasure droid in *Blade Runner*. The Hannah character, whose functionality is purely sexual, is clearly designed to fulfill male fantasies. *Circuitry Man*'s Danner, on the other hand, is designed by a woman for romance; he is charming, sensitive, and a bit overly serious. The memory of androids is also toyed with in this movie, but in a different way. Danner's fascinating twist is that he is pre-programmed to believe that he is in love with a woman who doesn't exist. This piece of emotional data is used by characters in the film to manipulate him, with the promise of revealing her whereabouts if he does what they want (needless to say, he ultimately falls in love with Lori in a romantic scene that takes place in the back of a semi truck). Lori and Danner's arch-enemy is the evil Plughead, a kind of self-fashioned Frankenstein...a former psychotherapist who is addicted to other peoples' fear and pain. Using a bunch of jacks in his bald head, he plugs into the brains of people he is about to kill because he gets a rush from feeling their experiences (see figure D.1). The final showdown has Plughead and Danner duking it out in Virtual Reality, a mutual mindspace that is a landscape of the subconscious.

D

Figure D.1
Circuitry Man's Plughead

All of these examples provide variations on one of the most compelling themes of our technological age: man taking life into his own hands. Whether we are cloning sheep or being beaten at chess by computers, the quest to imitate God and create new life forms is a natural outgrowth of the technological age. In these mythological tales, we see the moral and ethical ramifications of this quest addressed. Though the reality is far from its fictitious depiction, both Dolly and Deep Blue pose interesting new questions: Is it right to create life? What defines something as being alive? Can machines have souls? Are we emotionally equipped to deal with what we have wrought? The catch-all question is, can we be good enough "parents" to raise the Digital Frankensteins that we create, or are we on the road to creating an army of synthetic monsters?

A-LIFE OF ONE'S OWN (p. 5)

CYBERSPACE CADETS: VIRTUAL COMMUNITIES AND AVATAR WORLDS (p. 146)

FEAR OF MEDIA (p. 193)

DIGITAL SOCIALISM

The digital age introduces a new form of international socialism, a new kind of democracy that Marx never even imagined. In *this* Brave New World, we can not only see and empathize with the so-called "enemy," we can talk with them too. Allegedly, the Internet is playing a major role in populist revolutions from Bosnia to Mexico. Mexican Zapatista rebels tote PowerBooks in place of Uzis and send defamatory faxes to the news media, which has a devastating effect on the Mexican army's attempt to squelch their movements. The Internet has also played a major role in the Serbian uprising (aka "The Internet Revolution"), both as a communication tool, and also as a means to circumvent censorship. When the national news radio program was turned off the air for two days, it was re-routed through the Internet.

In the April 1997 issue of *Wired*, Jon Katz writes about "The Birth of the Digital Nation." He describes a post-political subculture that exists purely in cyberspace. To the community of the Internet, government (ironically, the very institution that created it in the first place) is irrelevant. We have our own society and political system on the web, which is to a large extent a kind of happy anarchy in which all web sites are created equal. The present socio-political climate is really fertile territory for revolution. Most major revolutions are characterized by three things:

- The rise of an educated intelligentsia, often with a fair amount of economic influence.
- The ability to form a coherent community.
- The ability to leverage the prevailing media distribution technology.

We've all heard the one about the Gutenberg Press and the French Revolution. The capability to maximize the distribution of revolutionary propaganda is the secret weapon of every major revolutionary movement.

The fact is, Netizens (as Katz calls them) are smarter than the government. Recent attempts to censor the Net have once again reinforced the irrelevance of government. Even if those attempting to censor the Net succeed in passing the laws to do so, there is no practical way for any kind of censorship on the Net to be enforced. Its operators will outsmart the government every time...and with glee! The Internet community has always been subversive, relishing in its own cleverness and ability to succeed as a fringe culture. The result is an entire generation of former-hippie billionaires.

 STEAL THIS DATA: SHAREWARE AND THE HACKER ETHIC
(p. 454)

The Digital Revolution represents a major paradigm and culture shift as powerful as the Industrial Revolution was in the 19th century. Industrial culture, based on a system of mass-production and materialism, has been the prevailing mode for the past 100-odd years, but it is slowly being reformulated by digital culture, which emphasizes communication and information. Digital culture will no more eradicate industrial culture than industrial culture eradicated rural culture, but at different points in time, different cultures take precedence. This is most certainly becoming the case with digital culture in America.

America is built on a doctrine that places high value on individualism. From the moment the colonists refused to pay taxes to the English, we were already well on our way to creating the "dog eat dog" world in which any perceived contribution to the greater whole is viewed as a direct threat to individual freedom. In fact, the whole of our Constitution and Declaration of *Independence* is based on a doctrine of *personal* freedom, not on a commitment to personal unity. Instead of "E Pluribus Unim," the nation's motto ought to be "Numero Uno," as in "Looking out for…"

In Europe and other countries, this commitment to individual achievement and freedom is not, in fact, the prevalent mode of thinking. In the stable countries of Europe, the prevailing notion is that the individual is part of a greater whole, and the good of the whole is synonymous with the good of the individual. The more socially active factions of British culture, for example, are appalled by Americans' apparent lack of post-political sensibilities.

In most of the so-called civilized world, social welfare is not a dirty word. In England, national health care is a right to which all citizens are entitled. In social democracies such as Denmark and Sweden, the social system is designed to create an even playing field. Although taxes are exorbitant, there are virtually no lower classes in Denmark. And although the unemployment rate is high, all citizens, including the unemployed, enjoy a high standard of living.

Many countries outside of the United States place a high value on education, and see an educated population as an investment in the country's overall economic and cultural strength. In Denmark, if you are unemployed for a certain amount of time, the government requires you to go to school, generally at its expense. The educational level in countries like India and Japan is very high, and in Russia and much of Eastern Europe, education is also placed at a high premium. This provides a sharp contrast to American culture, where the tuition of even a state university is exorbitant, and student aid is limited. As a result, many digital companies are forced to import talent from abroad. Although this has precipitated a considerable amount of controversy, with anti-immigrationists arguing that these jobs are being taken away from

Americans, America's stubborn refusal to acknowledge not only the social but the economic importance of education has put is at a marked disadvantage in the information age.

Then there is the matter of the arts. Canada is known for its generous art grants, and many American techno and media artists have actually received more funding from Canada than from America. Japan supports the arts, as do the Scandinavian countries, some of whom go so far as to provide income subsidies for artists.

During the 1930s and the time of the New Deal, Franklin Delano Roosevelt created a comprehensive arts and culture program whose effect can be seen in murals, art deco buildings, photographs, and folk records of the time. By providing grants to artists, the government was able to generate a cultural renaissance in the midst of economic depression. It is unclear whether this cultural movement had any effect on America's economic recovery, but it certainly improved morale and attitude.

Since then, America has systematically eroded its support for culture and the arts, a sorry state that causes much of the rest of the world to look at us as uncultured and anti-intellectual…and they wouldn't be that far off. In America, being educated is in some respects frowned on. It is felt that intellectualism equals privilege. Whether it is that intellectualism is the result of privilege or its cause remains to be seen. In either case, Americans don't like it. Even in high school, it is the students with high grades who are often ostracized and friendless. America, in fact, has a long record of rejecting and ostracizing its best intellectuals. Whether it be the Ernest Hemingways or the Josephine Bakers, our best minds have always had a bigger market in European countries, where sophistication and intelligence are honored, appreciated, and even supported by government.

In America, our artists are our bastard children. Perhaps this is a residual of our rebellion against the English, who some Americans still view as "intellectual snobs." It might be that during the Revolution, we developed a distaste for education because we associated it with the classist social strata in England. Rather than espouse to educate everyone to the level of the English aristocracy, we instead opted to "dumb down" on a society-wide level. As a result, we have ultimately bred a culture in which stupidity is revered. Beavis and Butthead rise in popularity while our so-called art institutions, such as the NEA, fall on their faces due to lack of support and funding.

To most Canadians and Europeans, American culture is an oxymoron. They love our jeans, our music, and our movies, but the appeal stops there. Here we are, the most powerful country in the world, and our idols are Howard Stern, Al Bundy, and Rush Limbaugh. It's no wonder we have anti-government terrorists blowing up public buildings.

Even in Japan, a very capitalist culture, there is a sense of a higher order beyond the individual. Japanese are obsessively self-conscious about social propriety and, although very aggressive and competitive in many respects, they also have a sense of being part of a larger whole. Countries such as Japan, China, or India benefit from a long history, a sense of continuity, and a social value system that supports the notion that we are all part of a whole. This is why the Japanese have excelled in technology and manufacturing. They know how to collaborate. They are not as obsessed as Americans with ego and the power of the individual. Although they have no social welfare system, their sense of family values prevents them from abandoning either children or the elderly, the largest populations of poor in this country.

The Interactive Revolution in America is both a product of and a reaction against this American individualist, anti-intellectual idea. The very premise of interactivity is one of intellectual, creative and social empowerment. It is anti-industrial. In an industrial culture, people are rated by two levels of value:

- By their ability to mass-produce items at a low cost.
- By their ability to purchase mass produced items at a profit.

Even with the American obsession with individuality, the reality of industrial man is that he is not intended to be an individual at all. In a capitalist culture, we abhor and fear socialism because we are afraid that people are going to "take away our stuff." In fact, if you look at social democracies, you will find that their citizens enjoy, in many respects, a great deal more personal freedom than Americans. In America, the ability to pull yourself up by your bootstraps is far overshadowed by the ability to, say, receive any kind of education you want, or to know that you can afford to go to a doctor if you get sick. The question then arises, what is personal freedom, and do we really have more of it in an autonomous, individual society, than in a socialistic construct?

The Internet presents a very interesting sub-culture, a kind of virtual society that is equal parts socialism, capitalism, democracy, and anarchy. Its highest values are information and communication. The Internet was born of the hacker ethic, which states that information should be freely accessible to all. It is derived from the premise that knowledge is power and that the more access you have to information and knowledge, the more empowered you are as an individual. So it is really a form of informational socialism. Online, e pluribus unim has come to mean, "we're all in this information thing together." To say that the Internet is a community seems absurd. It is something else…a parallel inter-nation with its own culture, rules, and laws. Within it are many communities, all tied together by the common bond of information and interaction. Within this alternate reality, individuals naturally group together into communities on the basis of mutual interest or experience; however, the entire basis of community on the Internet rests entirely on intellectual content. The result of this is that the Internet has given rise to a value system that, in sharp contrast to the American values system at-large, emphasizes knowledge, information, and intellect. It also shuns boundaries, whether they are physical, geographical, or national. Many online communities have nothing to do with national identity, religion, race, or even gender, the prevalent identifiers that people deal with in the real world.

The Internet simultaneously centralizes and decentralizes power. I differ from McLuhan in that he characterizes the Electronic Age as an implosion. I see it as a concurrent implosion/explosion. We are imploding in that there is a single place to which now anyone in the world can go at any time and become a part of. We are exploding in that our geographical boundaries have been completely eradicated by digital technology.

Exploding or Imploding: What's the Deal? (p. 191)

This is the reason why the Internet is so dangerous: governments use two methods to maintain power and control the populace. These methods have been used in every totalitarian government since ancient Egypt. The first method is to repress the right of assembly. The second method is to control the flow of information. Every totalitarian government in human history, in fact all governments throughout history, have used these two techniques to maintain power. In fact, every revolution in history has succeeded only insofar as it has been able to contain communication and the right of assembly. Now think about this: What does the Internet enable us to do? For one thing, it enables people to gather in massive groups without ever having to leave home. On any given night, thousands of people log on, and it is impossible to control where they go or what they do after they are there. We can no longer control the right of assembly through any kind of geographic means, and now, people can assemble beyond any kind of geographical boundaries. What will the Chinese government do when Tiananmen Square is on my desktop? Furthermore, the Internet enables us to target and disseminate massive amounts of information instantaneously, anywhere in the world.

All of this sounds very idealistic and Utopian but there is only one sticking point: the question of class stratification. Although the Internet is a socialist/ anarchistic/democratic/capitalistic regime, it only exists for a certain elite group of people, albeit a much larger elite than I think anyone ever anticipated, but nonetheless, an elite. In order to participate in this social democracy, you need a computer. Doesn't digital media thus widen the gap between the "haves" and the "have nots"? There is much evidence to support this, but there are also some indicators that digital technology is making its way, for better or for worse, into other strata of the culture.

Although this may be the case, history has also shown that all major revolutions, even those that are based on improving the lives and conditions of a so-called "underclass," have been started by elite groups within the intelligentsia of a given culture. Karl Marx was no more a factory worker than Ghandi was a homeless beggar, and even the fathers of our country were primarily wealthy landowners and merchants, many of whom were also slave owners. Nonetheless, these men led uprisings that ultimately led to the betterment of members of the non-elite (although in the case of America, it took another 125 years for black men, and another 20 still for women to obtain the right to vote).

Nonetheless, accessibility is on the rise. Most office networks are tied to the Internet, so the typical office worker with a computer on his or her desk has ready Internet access. More and more public schools now provide students with some access to computers and the Internet, as do most public libraries. For a small hourly fee, you can visit your local cyber café and have a cup of java while you surf the Net. Meanwhile, computers are getting faster and cheaper, and these days, they all come bundled with modems and Internet software. ISPs (Internet Service Providers) are cheap and easily accessible, most charging under $20 a month for unlimited access to the World Wide Web, e-mail, file transfer, and other online services.

Although it may take some time, the gap will most certainly narrow, and as it does, the Newt Gingriches of the world, who have inadvertently popularized the thing that will be their undoing, should be very *very* afraid. Because when it comes right down to it, an online underclass is much more powerful than an armed underclass. Being armed is only good for individual acts of rebellion. Being online is an act of unity, and unity is the platform upon which all the successful revolutions of history have been built. Or, as the leader of the Mexican Zapatista movement once pointed out, what the government should fear most is not an arms expert, but a communications expert.

Censuring Censorship (p. 124)

Interactivity is Subversive (p. 244)

Digerati: The Artificial Intelligentsia (p. 164)

EINSTEIN, EISENSTEIN, AND THE SPACE-TIME CONTINUUM

Sergei Eisenstein is one of the fathers of modern cinema and among the first to create "second-generation cinema" (as per *The Theory of Media Evolution*). Eisenstein is credited with developing the craft of film editing. In the early days of film, all editing was done in-camera. Most movies were essentially filmed plays, and as such, they followed the conventions of time and space that you see within the typical three-act structure of a stage play. As a second-generation content creator, Eisenstein began to develop a unique aesthetic and set of conventions that optimized the unique properties of the film medium. Although film is linear, it is also made of celluloid. It can actually be physically cut into pieces and re-ordered. This enables the filmmaker to begin to treat both time and space as a collage. Eisenstein studied the work of D.W. Griffith and the film re-cutting experiments of Lev Kuleshov and Esfir Shub. From these studies, Eisenstein developed a theory that film could be used to manipulate time and space, particularly through the juxtaposition of images. In particular, Eisenstein introduced two major innovations that have remained cinematic conventions to this day. The first was the montage of images to convey emotion; the second was the manipulation of time and space through camera and editing techniques.

Eisenstein's early experiments with montage were designed to demonstrate the principle of associative imagery and context. Eisenstein's theory was that you could convey completely different emotions using the same exact imagery, depending on the context you put it in. He postulated that you could create an entirely different mood depending on the sequence of the montage. The experiment that Eisenstein used to prove this hypothesis was simple but effective. He filmed a man with a neutral expression on his face. He then took that expression, a kind of emotional placebo if you will, and cut it back to back with a variety of different images, ranging from comic, to tragic, to frightening, to pleasant. Each time you saw the face, you would swear it had changed expression—holding in laughter at a funny scene, stunned at a tragic scene, frozen in fear at a scene of horror, and endeared to a scene of sweet sentimentality. This cinematic inkblot test became a blank canvas on to which the viewer projected his or her own emotions based on the context of the image. As a result, Eisenstein made what was perhaps the most important discovery about the film medium—that it could be used to manipulate emotions though manipulations of space and time. Eisenstein was really as much of a psychologist as he was an artist...up until this point, no one had really fully explored techniques for using the medium itself to manipulate emotions. Before that, evoking audience emotion had been done mainly with content, story, scene, and performance, but not with the mechanics of the medium itself. Thus, the medium truly became the message; it was not just the story to which the audience was responding, but the *way* in which the story was conveyed.

Eisenstein had a decidedly eclectic background, but one that predisposed him to become a cinematic innovator. He was a student of architecture, civil engineering, fine art, and theater. His work in avant-garde theater led him to filmmaking, and his first film was actually a piece of dynamic scenery for a stage production. This led to his first feature, *Strike*, in 1924. *Strike* is an experimental film that uses a variety of avant-garde techniques, mirrored shots, and unusual camera angles—a visual poem of sorts that derived much influence from the Expressionist movement that was going on concurrently in the fine arts. This was his first attempt at combining cinematography and editing to create an emotionally compelling experience.

It was Eisenstein's landmark 1925 film *Potemkin*, that created a whole new set of conventions for the filmmaking art because it combined the power of visual expression in *Strike* with a strong narrative component. It was in *Potemkin* that Eisenstein's landmark discovery of the expressive power of film editing was first fully realized—in the form of the famous Odessa Steps sequence. This silent classic, considered by many to be the best film ever made, lifted film to a level of cinematic sculpture. Like most of Eisenstein's films, it was a work of high political propaganda. *Potemkin* is the story of the mutiny of the battleship *Potemkin* in 1905 by sailors who were ordered to eat maggot-infested meat and the subsequent bloodbath that occurred when the czarist army retaliated. The Odessa Steps sequence is a montage of marching boots, close ups of horror-stricken faces, guns firing as civilians fall to the ground, and the dramatic intercutting of a baby stroller bouncing down the long staircase amid the bedlam. This highly metaphorical imagery, in the context of a narrative, elevated film to a new level of artfulness. Various techniques, camera angles, and intercutting of shots were all used to bend, stretch, compress, and elongate both time and space. The end result was a highly subjective scene full of meaning and emotion rather than the mere re-creation of an event or story. It was with this bold stroke that film itself became a medium of emotional content.

The work of Eisenstein echoes in many ways the work of physicist Albert Einstein. It is as if Eisenstein was manifesting through celluloid what Einstein himself was discovering about space and time. Whether Eisenstein was influenced by Einstein, I'm not certain; however, if Carl Jung was right in his assertions that there exists a collective unconscious and resonance that is reflected in simultaneous revelation, these two men with the similar last names were no doubt tuning into the same cosmic radio station.

Eisenstein's work dealt with the idea of contracting and expanding time, an issue that Einstein was very concerned with. Eisenstein's discoveries marked a defining moment of film history because it was the first time anyone had explored just how elastic cinematic time could be. The relationship between time and space, the space-time continuum, as Einstein called it, was also a concern of the physicists of the time. Space was the first three dimensions; time was the fourth; and each could change the nature of the other.

There was also the matter of subjective reality. Einstein, with his general Theory of Relativity, put forth the then mind-boggling idea that there was no absolute reality insomuch as the physical world was concerned. Translated into philosophical terms, this led to the natural conclusion that there is no objective reality—in fact, all realities are subjective, a fact of which the German expressionists, futurists, and other leaders of the modern art movement were already well aware. Eisenstein's editing and cinematic techniques used film to create a subjective reality. Even earlier significant films, such as D.W. Griffith's 1915 classic *Birth of a Nation*, which is considered to be the first feature-length film, looked at the world from an omniscient viewpoint, a kind of cinematic equivalent to the literary construct of third person. Indeed, most theatrical traditions, from which early cinema were derived, were built around an objective reality. The audience was put outside the scene, blocked from the action by an invisible "fourth wall." Once the film craft emerged, it was easy for the screen itself to become the fourth wall of cinema.

In contrast, Eisenstein's films were highly subjective; scenes were conveyed in a highly expressive way designed to convey not the event itself, but its emotional impact on the participants. There were many parallels in the art world, as painters also tried to capture subjective realities on the two-dimensional canvas. The Odessa Steps sequence might have been a sister to Picasso's *Guernica*, a highly subjective cubist painting also conveying the horrors of battle. It certainly has some things in common with Marcel Duchamp's *Nude Descending a Staircase*, another expressive scene featuring a flight of stairs.

 ART IS A VERB (p. 29)

Picasso, like Duchamp, was also exploring in a static 2D space some of the concepts that concerned both Einstein and Eisenstein. With multifaceted imagery that expressed changes in both spatial orientation and time, Picasso was almost trying to create a 3D animation—to bring both spatial and temporal depth to the canvas, as well as emotional content. That *Guernica*, like *Potemkin*, was a narrative depiction of an historic event (somewhat unusual for Picasso), makes it an interesting companion peace to the Odessa Steps sequence. Both scenes convey a highly subjective image of warfare, a scene in which innocent people are killed, with the goal of telling an emotional story rather than a record of events. On a personal level, both events had special meaning to the artists—the emotionally intense scenes depicted injustices done in the artists' native countries. In terms of artistic convention, they both have echoes of the classic scenes of military grandeur and heroism depicted in paintings as far back as the Renaissance. These epic works glorified war and deified military heroes. In sharp contrast, both Picasso and Eisenstein's post-World War I perspectives depicted the military as villains in the needless slaughter of civilians.

Einstein and Eisenstein's theories and ideas are a worthy field of investigation for those interested in interactive design. With Virtual Reality and interactive narrative, the idea of creating subjective realities and manipulating time and space now enter into the realm of the audience's own experience—the ability to manipulate, which Eisenstein discovered and which has since been exploited throughout the cinematic arts. Although deeply subjective, film is nonetheless a linear medium, with the fourth wall still intact. Thus, the subjective reality conveyed in a film can only be that of the director. The audience, although immersed in a subjective reality, is still left out in the cold to the extent that its own subjectivity is of no consequence to the outcome.

When I was studying experimental film in high school, I used to argue with my good friend Camden Morse (now an experimental filmmaker herself) about the nature of nonlinear film. We were fortunate to have a film teacher who introduced us to both the historic and the esoteric aspects of cinema at a young and tender age. Influenced by Eisenstein and later Stan Brakhage, Camden and I both liked the idea of using film to undermine the sense of time and build new sequential paradigms; however, I always got stuck on one fundamental philosophical contradiction—the purely mechanical fact that no matter which way you splice it, a film is always linear. I remember, even then, expressing my consternation at this. Although it was not a conscious realization, perhaps I sensed intuitively that only an act of audience intervention could ever really undermine time as we know it.

We also studied autobiographical film. Our film teacher, Chris Adam, was amazing. Here we were, 16 years old and seeing movies such as *Wonder Water Baby Moving* and *Hot Leatherette*. Very wild stuff. Anyway, I remember looking at the autobiographical experimental films with the same level of perplexity I had with the so-called nonlinear films. No matter how subjective this is to the filmmaker, I thought, to the audience it is someone else's subjective reality. Once it is set in the linear unchangeable form of film, it loses its subjectivity and its nonlinearity, and becomes a fixed sequence of events from a fixed point of view.

Whether I knew it at the time or not, I was longing for something more dynamic, something where time and viewpoint could be manipulated by the audience. In 1978, no such capability was available to me. But I had already been contemplating these issues for some time when I discovered interactive media five years later. Suddenly, I could make a world or a story in which the audience could themselves determine the sequence, the chain of events, and the outcome of the story. As a result, the subjective reality and manipulation of time could be passed out of the hands of the director and on to the audience, who could now control their own destiny within a dynamic, interactive medium.

Within a few months of beginning this interactive adventure, I saw my first "interactive video" title. It was a laser disk designed and produced by a company called VPI, or Videodisk Publishing, Inc. It was a murder mystery in which you had to figure out "who dunnit?" You used a remote control to call up various frame addresses on the disk. The way it worked was that you would randomly choose one of five or six versions of the mystery to play. Although the essential story remained the same, the murderer was different for each version. This was accomplished by showing the same scenes in different contexts (Eisenstein again) or with different underlying audio tracks (a unique capability of the laser disk medium). Thus, a dinner scene of the family might suggest that the sister is being sweet to her brother. The exact same scene viewed a second time, however, might have a different connotation if followed by a scene of the sister's vindictive rantings against her brother. Now, her sweetness at the dinner table might come off as sarcasm, even though the words and tone are identical. Another scene in which the niece is sitting on the lap of her uncle, the murder victim, had a drastically different interpretation when seen with different soundtracks, if you catch my meaning...

This product was the first glimpse I had of the power of changing subjective viewpoints in the middle of a story. The Residents' *Bad Day at the Midway*, a CD-ROM designed by digital artist Jim Ludtke, takes you through a zany amusement park in which each of the odd characters you encounter has a scary dark ride that conveys the inner workings of his or her psyche. As you move around the space and characters address you, you can actually change whose head you want to be inside of, thus experiencing each character from a variety of viewpoints, including his or her own. A recent interactive title based on the Harlan Ellison story *I Have No Mouth; And I Must Scream*, uses the same technique of switching viewpoints between characters. Films such as Akira Kurosawa's classic *Rashomon* attempt to provide different viewpoints, but again the linearity and the fourth wall become a barrier to any true subjectivity.

Virtual Reality itself is really the ultimate expression of subjective reality, as well as the ultimate practical use of the theory of relativity. With VR, you put yourself in a distinctly subjective viewpoint vis-a-vis a world moving around relative to your own position in it. With the fourth wall removed, and the introduction of independent thought and will, the audience can achieve true subjectivity. No longer are you trapped inside the mind of the director or the main character, nor caught inside a linear narrative over which you have no control. Now both time and space is yours to explore, as your point of view, at last, becomes your own.

Virtual Relativity (p. 524)

Heisenberg's Uncertainty (p.222)

Picasso: The Father of 3D Graphics (p.370)

Exploding or Imploding: What's the Deal?

Is the media universe exploding or imploding?

The more information there is, the smaller the world becomes. According to McLuhan, the universe of the human mind is imploding through the growth of communications media. As more information becomes available in more concentrated and centralized forms, everything comes together until we have one complete and integrated information stream: the Internet.

Although you can make the argument that the universe is indeed imploding, the Internet seems to represent more of a simultaneous implosion and explosion. Through the Internet, information has become both centralized and decentralized. It is centralized in the sense that it is all accessible from a single point of entry, but decentralized in the sense that the information lives in many locations.

This combination of centralized and decentralized, imploding and exploding, is what makes the Internet such a powerful tool of democracy. Everyone can have access to all the information easily through a single entry point, but because it is an informational diaspora, no one has ultimate control over it. This is the ultimate freedom—a centralized entry point to a decentralized bank of information, as opposed to television, which is a centralized entry point into a centralized information array. This is an innate quality of the Internet—that it cannot be changed by content or by regulations. Its very infrastructure contains an integral system of checks and balances that prevents anyone from having too much power. At the same time, it allows uncensored access by anyone who can find their way to a port of entry.

DIGITAL SOCIALISM (p. 180)

Beyond the Internet, all media seem to be converging through digital technology into a single, unified stream of assets that are interchangeable between media. The direction and trend is that eventually all our content assets will be in shareable formats that enable a convergence of media. Again, an implosion.

The irony is that the more the universe implodes, the more it explodes. The more information there is, the more information there is—we are currently experiencing an exponential explosion of media and information. Each new piece of information only spawns more of the same. Just as we witness a population explosion because more people are breeding more people, we are now experiencing an information explosion of the same, if not greater, scale.

Media convergence and its resulting implosion is spawning an explosion of sorts. We seem to have more of everything in all media, each distinct from the others. There are now more books, more magazines, more television channels, and more movies than ever before. As the assets for these become interchangeable and repurposable, each new work spawns spin-offs. A single media event, such as a movie, can be repurposed in a book, a game, even a theme park ride, and thereby create a media explosion.

Just as more media is being generated in the external world, the internal world of the mind is also a data breeding ground. Each individual person is both a storehouse and progenitor of information. So, as each of us absorbs and then generates information, each of us is in a sense, a propagator or host of information for the virus of information, which then replicates and disseminates into the culture using our minds as its carrier.

 THE LAWS OF INFORMATIONAL ENTROPY (p. 280)

THE DIGISPHERE (p. 168)

When looked at in terms of the interior of our own minds, we ourselves are both imploding and exploding. On a daily basis, we have access to a seemingly endless amount of information unbounded by geography or time, the two things that previously slowed the flow of information. We get information instantaneously in a variety of forms from around the entire globe. This is clearly an explosion of sorts; however, within our minds many of these information parcels begin to converge. One of the things that concerns me about this day and age is the question of whether we are ready to take in all this diversified information. Information overload is a real and present danger. Yet it would seem that we are evolving to meet the challenge. Just as McLuhan suggested when he said, "We shape our tools, and thereafter our tools shape us…," kids today seem better equipped to deal with the exploding/imploding universe than their parents. The level of computer and Internet literacy in the youth of today proves, once again, that humans can adapt to change at a rapid pace. A lot has happened in a relatively short period of time. My great-grandfather helped to build the railroad in this country, while his widow lived through the invention of the automobile, the movie, the radio, and the television. Her daughter, my grandmother, stands baffled over my computer as I explain to her that I am sending drafts of this manuscript to my publisher over the phone line. Her daughter, my mother, is in the process of having a web page built by her daughter, my sister. Me, I'm writing this book. But much of what I'm writing today will soon seem quaintly old-fashioned to my nephew who, now nine, recently opened up his Macintosh computer to find out what kind of processor it had.

My point is that we are evolving. Each generation seems somehow better adapted to the inventions of the one that preceded it than the inventors themselves. This is largely a cultural phenomenon—children today are growing up with interactivity as a part of their daily lives. As a result, that which seems unfathomable to my grandmother, novel to my mother, and which I myself am creating, is commonplace to my nephews. Raised on educational software and online games, they have come to expect interactivity not only at home, but throughout their environment. As a result, they have already evolved beyond those who created the very interactive applications they've become accustomed to. I look forward to the day when I stand over their shoulders marveling at the amazing new innovations that their generation will create.

 INTERACTIVITY IS SUBVERSIVE (p.244)

THE ADD GENERATION (p. 17)

NEW MEDIA IS OLD NEWS (p. 358)

FEAR OF MEDIA

During the question-and-answer period of a talk I once gave in Europe, an agitated member of the audience stood up. Clearly vexed, he issued forth this angst-ridden question: "What is the computer doing to us?" For years, I have heard this same kind of question vis-a-vis the computer, television, and other communication technologies. What people seem to forget is that the television is a machine. The computer is a machine. These machines aren't going to *do* anything to us. It's people that do it by the content they create.

There is a tendency to look at humans as the hapless victims of evil machines. However, the essentially subversive message, indeed the mandate of the Interactive Revolution, is that we are no longer hapless victims but proactive participants in our own media, and indeed, our own fates. As the saying goes, there are no victims—only volunteers. Nobody is doing anything to us that we don't explicitly or implicitly agree to have done. How many people do you know who sit around on the sofa all day complaining about the "crap on TV?" If you don't like television, don't watch it. If you are concerned about its content, get into the business and make television shows. If you are worried that your children are watching too much TV, turn it off and take them to the park. We complain about how much time children spend in front of the TV. The main reason why children have a dependency on TV is because television is the best baby-sitter and the best tranquilizer around. Most parents put their kids in front of the TV to calm them down, shut them up, or keep them busy, and then complain that their children are turning into couch potatoes. Talk to your kids, play with them, get them cool interactive toys, throw away your television and buy a computer. Studies have shown that kids with both computers and televisions spend more time at the computer playing games, using interactive educational applications, or surfing the Internet than sitting around watching the boob tube. The passivity of the television goes against the essential nature of the child. Children are inherently interactive and hands-on oriented. The computer feeds, rather than starves, a child's natural desire to discover and evolve in a reactive environment. Children who have computers at home seem to do better in school. Whether this is because they have computers or because they have parents that care about their education enough to get them computers remains to be seen; however, according to some studies, even students who play a lot of shoot-em-up video games seem to do better in school, contrary to what we might believe.

The computer is essentially what we call a heuristic learning tool, meaning that it facilitates self-learning on the part of the user. It teaches about itself as it is used. This enables children to add to their already fearless curiosity a tremendous sense of independence and resourcefulness, not to mention the self-esteem generated from knowing more than their parents about something, which is almost always the case with kids and computers.

 THE PEDAGOGICAL MOUSEPAD, OR, HOW IT ALL GOT GUI (p. 365)

Parents are far more afraid of technology than their kids are. It is a popular joke to turn for computer help to an "expert," who turns out to be the 10-year old neighbor. Some parents might resist computers because they fear a situation where their children know more than they do. But you see, this is the secret to evolution. If your children are not smarter, better educated, better adjusted, and better adapted than you, we are all in big trouble. Relish your children's expertise. *They're* not afraid of media. Why should they be? The television was their baby-sitter. The computer is their playmate. The generation that grew up with *Sesame Street* are the same people making so-called "new media" today. The *Sesame Street* generation wrought MTV, and the MTV generation is creating the Digital Revolution. The next generation, the interactive generation, is going to create amazing things beyond anything we have imagined.

 ## THE ADD GENERATION (p. 17)

What most people fear is what they don't understand. This is why the antidote to information anxiety and fear of media is to try to develop a better understanding of what's going on. Rather than being overwhelmed, we can begin to see that this is just a big box of high-tech crayons that we can actually use as a means of empowerment and growth.

Over the centuries, people have laid out prophecies of gloom and doom as each new medium has come into use. Every time a new medium is introduced, it is anticipated that it will somehow wipe out all the other pervading media. A good look backward (something I always recommend) shows that this has occurred very seldom, and most of the time, only through a deliberate and concerted effort. Although some old genres may eventually become extinct, often their forms are co-opted and integrated into new forms. In fact, the advent of new media just as often leads to growth in preceding media. In addition, each new medium restructures the purpose of the preceding media, ultimately resulting in stronger and more evolved genres.

 ## THE LAWS OF CUMULATIVE MEDIA (p. 276)

What we are really talking about is evolving culture—how culture relates to and evolves around media and vice versa. A perfect example is the newspaper. I'm sitting on a train right now next to a friend and colleague of mine who is reading a newspaper. He also has a PowerBook. Theoretically, he could be getting more up-to-date news on his PowerBook if he had a radio uplink; however, within the culture of mass transit, reading a newspaper is the most comfortable and efficient convention for obtaining news information. Although some might argue that the computer is better, in this context, it is a cultural anomaly.

Didn't the TV doom-sayers scare us into believing that the newspaper's days were numbered? What has happened since? Well, people have not thrown out their newspapers. To the contrary, news periodicals are more popular today than ever. The news you get in a newspaper is a totally different type of news than what you get on TV. It's also a totally different experience. The newspaper is a quiet, text-based experience. It's highly portable and highly personal. It doesn't intrude on other people's space in any way. The newspaper is also more in-depth. The front page gives you a nonlinear overview of the day's events, which is in essence a menu of items that can be browsed further. The entire experience of reading a newspaper, even down to getting the black ink smudges on your fingertips, has a life of its own, a culture of its own, and also gives a certain presentation to the outside world. A newspaper can function as a sort of fashion accessory. The fact that you are reading one, and the specific paper you are reading, tells people something about who you are. *The Wall Street Journal* reader on the New York subway is giving a completely different message than *The New York Post* reader. I doubt very much that newspapers will cease to be seen on the trains and subways of New York. Everyone in New York City reads a paper on the subway. It's possible that in 10 years, they will all be reading news off their wireless PDAs, but I rather doubt it.

 Bookmark: Interactivity and the New Literacy (p. 102)

What will happen, and what has happened in the past, is that the printed news will have to change and adapt to the competition. It will have to bring out the things that it is uniquely suited for. The newspaper will have to "rise to the occasion" and develop its own strengths within the larger context of the media landscape. The more media we have, the more specialized each medium must become. This means that we can communicate at successively higher levels of resolution. By this I do not mean higher levels of visual or audio resolution, but higher levels of informational resolution. This higher resolution will enable us to be more specific and appropriate about what we are saying and how we are saying it.

 Theory of Media Evolution (p. 468)

Digital Frankensteins (p. 173)

Censuring Censorship (p. 124)

Gaining Perspective: The Evolution of Dimension

The study of the history of perspective provides a fascinating portrait of the evolution of human perception. The study of perspective is both enjoyable and satisfying because it is so easy to *see*. Many art historians see perspective in terms of a history of visual perception alone—how the eye translates three dimensions—but there is more to it than that. What is often ignored in this picture is the role of the fourth dimension—time. Part of the history of art is also the history of content—not just how things are depicted, but what is depicted. In fact, art, painting, and visual representation really began as storytelling media. So although we can look at the way we translate three dimensions, it is also crucial to take the fourth dimension into account. This expands our purview exponentially and enables us to look at human visual expression and perception in an entirely different light.

It is generally acknowledged that the cave paintings found in Lascaux, France are the first evidence we have of both painting and documented storytelling among humans. These things are, and have continued to be, intimately tied together. The first impetus of art was, after all, an attempt to tell a story—to record an event for posterity through visual icons that are both language and representation combined. Because we see no sign of this urge in animals, it would seem that this desire to permanently etch our own experience in stone (or any other medium for that matter) is unique to humans. One of the things this gives us is the ability to transmit experience beyond the bounds of time and space. So Lascaux can also be seen as the first vicarious experience, the first recorded attempt at offering a third party who wasn't there a glimpse into another person's experience, and another time and another location.

From an artistic standpoint, the Lascaux paintings are relatively 2D and simplistic, although they are also surprisingly expressive in their simplicity. There is also a certain suggestion of motion, and of a sequence of events in the depicted hunting scene. Although it is essentially a two-dimensional visual depiction, an obvious effort was made to depict the fourth dimension by placing the images in sequence It is also believed that these paintings might have been instructional in nature—perhaps an iconic textbook providing tips to other hunters.

Most of the art of primitive cultures is content-intensive. Simple icons are used to depict or symbolize gods, spirits, myths, or legends of the tribe. The notion of using visual media to depict things imagined seems to date back to earliest man. One wonders at what point it occurred to someone to depict a mythological tale or character, or a figment of his or her imagination, as opposed to recording an actual event or story, like the hunting scene at Lascaux.

The ancient Egyptians used art to weave elaborate tales of gods, goddesses, kings, and queens. Their giant murals and frescos were cinematic in scope (scale is always an interesting factor in these things), populating their walls with a parallel universe combining history and myth. Although conventions of these paintings were visually very two-dimensional, this was apparently a stylistic approach rather than the product of a lack of dimensional sensibilities. Obviously the statues of ancient Egypt depict a high level of 3D sophistication. Yet the frescos feature a flattened form: the forward-facing bodies, with the profiled heads and feet. It may have been the flatness of the surface that threw them for a loop—although they could depict 3D in three dimensions, perhaps they could not translate it into two. You almost have the feeling that these characters are three-dimensional people trapped in Flatland. These images also possess a strong sense of linear time. As the characters march across the canvas, they appear to parade through time, creating an ongoing story being told on the surrounding walls.

An interesting approach to dimensionality was practiced by the Mimbres Indians of New Mexico 300-odd years ago. They used bowls as their painting surface and took advantage of the shape of the bowl to create three-dimensional scenes using relatively flat images. The bowl shape seems to suggest the valley environments the Mimbres inhabited. But what is most compelling is the scenes depicted and the way in which the round bowl surface is used to extend all four dimensions. Examples of Mimbre bowl designs include:

- Fish swimming in a circle interlocking with birds flying in the opposite direction (prefiguring MC Escher's interlocking animal designs).
- A woman giving birth in which you cannot tell which head is that of the mother and which of the child being born.
- People dancing in a circle holding hands.
- A scene of man and beast in combat in which the advantage of one over the other can be altered by changing the direction of the bowl.

All of these images and scenes embody a theology of the cyclical nature of time: life and death, mother and child, human and animal, bird and fish. In the world of the Mimbres, there is no top or bottom; no beginning, middle, and end. Everything is interchangeable within in a cyclical notion of time and space that can only be expressed on a round, concave surface.

In European and Western art, it is possible to follow a clear progression, or evolution of dimension, which clearly parallels both theological and cultural trends in history. In the middle ages, highly narrative images were rich in texture and decor, but decidedly flat. The use of forced perspective had not yet come into play, but the concept of creating objects in foreground and background had. There was depth, but not dimensionality. This was also a time of "illuminating" manuscripts with graphics (type treatments, decorations) and content-based illustrations. This is an early form of multimedia, in which two different media come together to create a new genre. (It is also interesting to note that the printing press all but eliminated illuminated manuscripts, a perfect example of media mortality caused by new technology.)

 THE LAWS OF CUMULATIVE MEDIA (p. 276)

This period, also known as "The Dark Ages," was a time when pictures were not all that were flat. It was also a time when the world itself was considered to be flat, and so the visual world, decidedly two-dimensional, echoed the general belief that the Earth itself was equally two-dimensional. Culturally, it was a time when most information and knowledge was diligently protected from the masses by the clergy. Only monks and royalty could read. Most of the world's great writings were in the form of these handmade manuscripts that were locked up inside of monasteries throughout Europe.

The Renaissance, the age of exploration and cultural expansion, brought us both a round world, and the added perceptual tool of perspective. The revelation that one could create depth by visual techniques of scale and orientation vitally changed the graphical landscape forever. A new level of realism was achieved by tricking the eye into seeing three-dimensional space where there was none. This included not only the use of perspective, but also a highly sophisticated approach to light. Indeed light, perhaps even more so than perspective, provided the extra ingredient to being able to depict greater realism of 3D environments and objects on a two-dimensional plane. This new addition of a third dimension to the eye was an integral part of a larger perceptual shift, which included everything from better education to economic prosperity, and eventually, with the rise of a non-royal gentry, to the movements that would lead to democracy.

The photograph changed everything once again, because it enabled the creation of a totally realistic depiction of objects, complete with light and forced perspective. By all appearances, the photograph eliminated the need for artists. But rather than eradicate artists, the photograph gave them new freedom. Suddenly, painters had an entirely new set of rules. No longer tied to the literal depiction of time and space, they began to experiment. The pointillists in essence invented the notion of a digital image. They broke down light into points and created a new way to trick the eye. The cubists followed up with a different perceptual take on 3D space. Pablo Picasso and Paul Klee, for example, created a new kind of three-dimensionality by trying to show all angles of an object simultaneously. Futurists such as Marcel Duchamp and expressionists such as Wassily Kandinsky experimented with animation on the canvas, adding a fourth dimension to the images.

ART IS A VERB (p. 29)

PICASSO: THE FATHER OF 3D GRAPHICS (p. 370)

If ontogeny recapitulates phylogeny (a biological axiom that states that the growth of an embryo is a microcosm of the evolution of the organism it will become), then the history of computer graphics is a microcosm of the history of perspective and visual perception.

Early computer graphics were, of course, extremely simple. The challenge was, once again, how to create the illusion of three-dimensional space on a flat surface, the computer screen. The capability to push pixels around led naturally to the conclusion that these things ought to be animated. In the 60s,

Ivan Sutherland, the father of Virtual Reality, developed the *Sketchpad*, which was a real-time interactive computer that enabled you to manipulate graphics in real time using a light pen. You could draw objects on a background, then move them in real time into the foreground or background. This eventually evolved into a more sophisticated system that integrated forced perspective. Sutherland and his contemporaries began to develop new techniques to create the sense of three dimensions.

In terms of the flat screen, these techniques involved using polygons that assembled together to create objects that appeared to be three-dimensional. Using principles of forced perspective, these images could appear as complex three-dimensional objects or topographies. Time was introduced as well, and the notion of "real-time" animation—images that moved around in response to user input—added a fourth dimension to the visual realm. The computer program calculated and re-drew polygons as you "moved" through the space, thereby creating the illusion that you were moving in relation to these objects, or that they were moving in relation to you. Both time and space were used to create the illusion of space. It is important to realize that the instantaneous feedback of such a system is crucial, and one of the great struggles in developing 3D graphics is that the more complex your image becomes, the slower your feedback. So you can move simple objects quickly or complex objects slowly; unless, as is increasingly becoming the case, you have enough firepower to move complex objects quickly.

Even while the graphics themselves were at a fairly simple level, Sutherland had another idea about 3D. He wanted to try to figure out a way to enhance the illusion of space by creating some form of depth in the display system itself. The early pioneers of photography developed techniques of stereoscopy which had even been attempted in cinema a few years prior to Sutherland's efforts. But Sutherland had something else in mind. It was something called a Head-Mounted Display. The objective of this creation was to immerse a person in an audio-visual sensorium to create a more immediate feeling of "being there." This was accomplished by placing two screens with slightly skewed images in front of their eyes. These screens would feed back the graphics in real time, depending on the person's position. Add to this a data glove for manipulating objects, and you would theoretically have a fully three-dimensional experience. Providing, of course, you didn't get a headache in the process.

 A BRIEF HISTORY OF REAL TIME: THE VIRTUAL REALITY LEGACY (P. 105)

Around the same time Sutherland was doing his thing, a filmmaker/ inventor named Mort Heilig was working on ways of making cinema more three-dimensional, beyond the traditional red-and-green stereo glasses used in movies such as his 3D film, *It Came from the Deep*. Heilig created a Head-Mounted Display for watching television, and a single-person contraption called a Sensorama, which gave you stereo vision, 3D audio, motion vibration, wind, and even smells. In response to the feared threat of television, Heilig and others also developed dome theaters at this time, as well as a variety of different sensory enhancement devices, none of which ever made it into the mainstream. Some did evolve into specialty theater technologies, and today can be seen in the form of dome and 360-degree theaters, 3D movies, and motion-simulator ride films.

This was also, mind you, the age of "hi-fi," a period where recorded audio was also starting to gain perspective. Stereo speakers enabled audio to fill the room, and experiments with binaural and 3D audio soon followed. Binaural audio is a technique in which you record three-dimensional sound by placing microphones into the perfectly sculpted inner ear of a full-scale sculpted head. You move the head around in the space and record sounds as if they were coming into a real head. Listened to on ordinary headphones, the results can be startling. The playback of binaurally recorded audio can be so real that you can actually find yourself feeling like you are getting a haircut, having a hat put on your head, or being whispered to in your left ear.

As with Renaissance painting, the secret ingredient for 3D in computer graphics was light. Modeling and surfacing became more and more sophisticated. But it was the development of lighting techniques that calculated the angle and intensity of light reflecting off a surface that took 3D graphics to the next level. With light, suddenly, the realism increased tenfold, and the images became so compelling that in some cases they could be made to appear nearly photo-realistic.

Back to the real world…don't forget, the Head-Mounted Display was invented the same year that man first walked on the moon. So, just as the world had become round during the Age of Exploration, now our explorations were taking us beyond our own small round world and into the galaxy. Sutherland's Virtual Reality devices were used in space and flight training, expanding our notion of three dimensions out into a broader sphere.

The World Wide Web is currently in the process of gaining perspective as well. The majority of the World Wide Web is, at present, Flatland. HTML (HyperText Markup Language) is a graphically enhanced, text-based medium—the modern-day equivalent to the illuminated manuscripts. The fourth dimension has been addressed to a certain extent in the form of animation, but up to this point, the web is predominantly a two-dimensional proposition.

The development of a 3D language for the web, called VRML (Virtual Reality Modeling Language) is bringing a new dimension to the Internet, ushering in what some are calling "The Second Web." The web is at about the same point today as the world was when Columbus boldly proclaimed the roundness of the world. To many, the web is still Flatland, and those accustomed to its two dimensionality, most often those who come from a print heritage, are baffled by the idea of 3D on the web. Just as Columbus said the world was round, so Mark Pesce and Tony Parisi, co-inventors of the VRML file format, have proclaimed the web to be round. Pesce has even gone so far as to create a simulated "Web Earth," which draws data from servers all over the planet to give 3D weather readings of the planet.

Eventually, the flat people will catch on. They will either adapt and grow into this new medium, embracing dimensionality and integrating it into their existing repertoire, or they will go the way of the illuminated manuscript, a beautiful but archaic form of illustrated text.

THE BIRTH OF CYBERSPACE: 3D COMES TO THE WEB (p. 97)

EINSTEIN, EISENSTEIN, AND THE SPACE-TIME CONTINUUM (p. 186)

VIRTUAL REALITY CHECK: WHAT IS VR ANYWAY? (p. 518)

GIRL GAMES: THE NEW FEMININE MYSTIQUE

I just got off the phone with a journalist who interviewed me for an article entitled "What Do Women Want?" about marketing interactive theme park attractions to women for the May 19 issue of *Amusement Business Magazine*. He posed a vexing question that is just now starting to be asked for the fist time, astonishingly. The question was: "What will it take to make products for women and girls?" When he first asked the question, I stopped short and had to think it through thoroughly. I ran off a couple of things, but finally came to the point: To create content that is female-friendly, the main thing that it's going to take is a massive change in attitude.

When I spoke at SIGGRAPH in 1994, one of the audience members got up during the question-and-answer period to respond to comments about the violence and male-bias of most computer games. The gentleman said, "We know that *Tetris* is the most popular game among women, but we don't know why." Speak for yourself. Of course *he* didn't know why, but that's because he, like most of his fellows in the computer game market, has never taken the time to *find out*.

Virtually every computer game company in the world has an army of playtesters who spend their afternoons playing games—sometimes for pay, but just as often, purely for the free access to unreleased games. Their job is to play games—play, play, and play—try to break them, try to beat them, and tell the programmers what they think of them. None of these people are ever girls.

The fact of the matter is, computer game companies just don't care about girls. Not only that, but they will tell you that to your face with no apologies. I once met with an executive at one of the biggest arcade game companies in America because one of his marketing managers had asked me to come and talk to them about creating games for girls. The executive said two things to me that on the one hand were no surprise, because I knew the overriding sentiment was universal in the game industry, but at the same time shocked me because he was so blatant about it. The first was, "Our job is to take lunch money away from 14 year old boys," and the second was "Girls? What do I care about girls? They're only five percent of my market." What really amazed me about both of these remarks was that they were as insulting to the poor hungry boys (no wonder all these computer game kids are so skinny!) as they were to the unfortunate and overlooked girls.

Things have changed quite a bit since that conversation, and I am pleased to say that, although only a small handful of people are *doing* something about it, more and more people are asking the question: What will it take to create a market for girls and women? Although I don't have any pat answers, I can tell you what has been done, what is being done, and what I personally have been doing to help shift the enormously lopsided mentality regarding this problem.

It is a popular misconception that women are not comfortable with computers, that they are in fact, techno-phobic. It's true that women are less interested in hardware, but if you go to any traditional office setting, you will find that by and large, it is the women, and not the men, who are most involved with the computers. Women are quite adept in the use of word processors, spreadsheets, databases, e-mail, graphics programs, and other software. Often, in fact, they are more adept at all these things than many of the men in the office. In the male-dominated executive suite, it is not extraordinary to find high-paid, high-ranking males who have never so much as touched a computer, let alone know how to use one; and even if they do, they use it seldom, instead relying on the highly developed computer skills of their executive assistants. Furthermore, because office administration and infrastructure is often under the domain of females, women are frequently the ones responsible for overseeing the purchase, setup, and maintenance of computers.

These kinds of misconceptions lead to peculiar ideas. In the old days when people were grappling with the notion of a home market for the computer, one of the ideas toyed with for a time was that women would use computers to store recipes. My friend Brenda Laurel, a VR expert, author of *Computers as Theater*, and the creative force behind the new Girl Game company Purple Moon Software (affectionately known as PMS), keeps one of the six computers in her house in the kitchen for recipes...in tribute to this absurd theory, no doubt generated by some guy in marketing.

Purple Moon, a spinoff of Paul Allen's Palo Alto-based R&D powerhouse, Interval Research, was developed in response to what was perceived as a gaping hole in the market for home consumer products. Females, after all, make up an estimated 53 percent of the population, making them the only minority that outnumbers the majority. Why then has the game and software industry blatantly ignored this huge potential market?

There can be no other answer but pure and simple ignorance. It is worse than gender bias—it is gender obliviousness. The male-dominated software and game industry is, like most of the entertainment industry at-large, a boy's club. But it is more entrenched in male values than any entertainment market because it has been so myopically focused on teenage boys, and because the people creating games continue to perpetuate this same market.

Much of the lack of appeal of games to females can be attributed to the enormous amount of violence that one typically sees in these products. If you ask game designers why video games are so violent, they will always say the same thing: "It's what the market wants." Or is it? What precisely is the market? Maybe it's what the marketers want, and what the designers want to make. In other words, maybe it's a self-fulfilling prophecy.

 It's Only a Game: The Birth of a Multi-Billion Dollar Business (p. 260)

Let's look at some hard facts. Recent studies have shown that women represent the majority of purchasers in all media with the exception of computer software, and even there, they exert a certain amount of control over the purchase of educational software for children. Women buy more books, rent more videos, and purchase more movie tickets than men do. Women also control leisure dollars, deciding, for example, where the family will vacation, and what kind of weekend activities they will do.

Furthermore, women have significant impact in the retail market. The typical mall has a shopping audience of *80 percent women*. Yet, mall owners, in an attempt to bring entertainment to retail centers, have begun installing video game arcades and male-oriented attractions such as *Virtual World's Battle Tech*, a Virtual Reality robot combat game, and laser-tag—products whose primary market is high school and college-aged boys. An arcade in a mall is like retail anti-matter. Not only do these attractions not appeal to girls and women, their core audience is actually a deterrent. Rather than fill the mall with teenage boys, why not create venues that will draw in the female audience? To date, there are no existing products designed to do this. As such, an enormous opportunity exists for attraction companies to fill this gaping hole in a market that is looking for something to do.

Another argument against creating female-targeted games is that computer games are inherently unappealing to women. In fact, among the earliest video games were two that were not gender biased in any way. *Pong*, the first computer arcade game ever made, had cross-gender appeal, and *Pac-Man*, still the most popular video arcade game of all time, did so well with females that a girl-oriented spin-off, *Ms. Pac-Man*, was created just for them—to my knowledge the only attempt made to tailor a game specifically to a female audience...at least until recently. Even as Americans continue their oblivion to the potential of marketing to women, the Japanese have begun to open the doors to the other half of the population. At a Family Entertainment Center conference in early 1997, I saw a two-player game called *Puzzle Fighter*. It was clearly geared to the girls' market, featuring cute little characters and a *Tetris*-like puzzle experience that included gemstones as playing pieces. Two girls could actually play this game together, having exactly the same pieces drop down from the top, but each doing something different with them in her own playing field. A year earlier, I had heard from a friend involved with SEGA that the new fad in Japan is fortune-telling games for young women and teenage girls.

To those who think there is no market for arcade games for girls, I suggest the following exercise. Go into your local arcade, preferably one that is in a venue with a mix of entertainment such as an amusement park, pier, or entertainment mall. If you look closely, you may notice that there are actually girls and young women in the arcade. Now look again and see how many of them are playing games. Chances are that hardly any of them are feeding quarters into those beautiful profit centers. So what you are really doing in this scenario is wasting bodies. These girls are already physically in the arcade; they go with friends, with their boyfriends, to meet boys, or what have you. They stand around and watch the boys play, and once in a while, they'll get on to a virtual motorcycle or ski simulator, but you won't see many of them shooting. Believe it or not, you see more of them at the air hockey table than any-where...and any time you introduce multi-user play into the scenario, you greatly increase your chances of getting female players. Unless, of course, the goal is to beat each other up or kill each other.

It's important to understand the psychology of why violent games do not appeal to women. A bit later in this chapter, I spell out some fundamental differences between female and male play styles, but just now I want to talk about the social dynamics of fighting games in an arcade setting. I am now, by the way, speaking primarily of the U.S., because I understand that the Japanese market is a little different. Let's say you are a teenage girl and you are out on a date with a boy. What is your objective? Well, your main goal is to impress the boy and get him to like you. Why would you want to play a fighting game with the guy you're trying to impress? If you lose, you look like an idiot; and if you win, you will appear overly masculine and threatening. But guys don't like to play games unless their opponent, whether it is the computer or another person, can challenge them. So for the young girl, this scenario is a no-win situation. As to playing with other girls, well there's no inherent interest, and similarly, the girl does not want to appear in any way threatening because it will hurt her chances of being liked—a big priority for girls in the arcade age range—mainly junior high and high school. Thus, the typical girl in an arcade will hang around, but her main activity will be to watch others play games and try to get the attention of male game players without seeming too forward or aggressive. There are some exceptions to this, and fringe groups of girls of course will totally reject this equation and do whatever they want. Whether we like it or not, much of the programming that girls get, and perhaps even a bit of their biology, will tend to lead to this kind of scenario.

Although the arcade market has all but shunned girls, the CD-ROM market has been a tad less unfriendly. *Myst* is one of a handful of CD-ROM blockbusters that also happens to have huge female appeal. Coincidence? I think not. Even so, no one has come out and stated that women may have had *something* to do with the success of *Myst*. There are certainly other companies that have attempted to create content for girls (Girl Games and Her Interactive among them), but none has yet to produce a blockbuster. In fact, the first female blockbuster in the CD-ROM market came from a very unlikely place.

On the heals of a dwindling CD-ROM market, the smash hit of the 1996 Christmas season was a title that was not only designed to appeal to girls, but was designed to appeal *exclusively* to girls. It outsold every other game that year and as of this writing in summer 1997, is about to hit the one million mark *within its first year of release*. This is an almost unheard of success in the hit-and-miss CD-ROM market. But in this case "hit" and "miss" go hand in hand, but not the kind of miss you think. The source of all this to-do? A product from a little outfit called Mattel entitled *Barbie Fashion Designer*.

Barbie has a lot going for it, including the fact that it is based on one of the world's most popular branded products for girls. But anyone who has spent any time studying female play patterns could have seen that this would be a blockbuster. For one thing, it is not a CD-ROM in the strict sense. It is actually a design tool that has a physical output. Girls use it to create fashions for Barbie, which they then print out on a special printer-friendly fabric and color by hand. Studies done by Purple Moon and other companies researching girl demographics found that most girls who use software cited paint and other creative programs as their primary computer activity. With this information in hand, *Barbie* addressed multiple girl issues—a popular female character, a creative activity, and the end result of the production of a material object, something that girls find very appealing.

Over the past few years, companies such as Girl Games and products such as *Makenzie & Company* have taken aim at the female audience. These companies and products are generally female owned and operated and often turn out to have primarily female employees. This is not a form of discrimination any more than the glaring lack of females in boy game companies is. It is merely a matter of culture; it is the rare male who has the experience or sensibility to understand, let alone even care about girls, their needs, and interests. *Barbie* is an exception, produced by Steve Schklair, the then director of Digital Domain in Los Angeles, the company that was sub-contracted by Mattel to design and produce the title. The Purple Moon product line, introduced in June of 1997, was based on two solid years of market research focusing on the 8–12 year-old-girl market. In addition to creating design criteria on what girls wanted, important in the formula was that these were also things boys clearly *didn't* want.

What is unique about Purple Moon products is that, like *Barbie Fashion Designer*, they resemble nothing that has been created for boys. In fact, at least in the children's market, creating content for girls is like dealing with a foreign country. It has necessitated the creation of entirely new genres that to boys, and the male game designers who produce boy-oriented games, would seem alien at best and unbearably dull at worst.

For whatever reason—family, society, or biology—girls and boys are just different. Books such as *Men are from Mars, Women are from Venus*, by John Gray or *You Just Don't Understand*, by Deborah Tannen describe some of these fundamental differences. The danger of such books is that they encourage polarity between the sexes; however, if we are sensitive to these issues, they can also serve as a bridge for mutual understanding. As a designer of interactive content, I find any study of gender culture useful; it expands my repertoire and helps me to better understand how to serve the full range of play and learning styles.

In the beginning of 1997, Purple Moon hired me as a consultant to design an ancillary product of their CD-ROM series. One thing that research revealed was that girls liked *things*. So a product line was developed for simultaneous release with the CD-ROM. It included bendable dolls as well as jewels. The assignment I received was to design a line of trading cards for each of the two CD-ROM series that could be treated as collectibles, but could also be used to play games. The game had to be self-contained, but also add another level of play to the CD-ROM or the Purple Moon web site. The cards were character-based. The first set, based on the *Secret Paths* series, dealt with the inner life of the girl, using real-life girl problems and folk tale parables to help girls find their way through common life challenges. The second set, based on a won-derful cast of characters developed by writer Pamela Dell, revolved around Rockett, a junior high school student who must face the social challenges of entering a new school. The Rockett cards in particular were designed for role-play. Girls could use them to act out different scenes from the CD-ROM. There were also Secret, Locker, and other cards that gave girls tidbits about the characters and what made them tick. Girls loved this kind of game because they are very interested in "backstory"—what motivates people to do what they do. For girls, gossip is a crucial tool they use to help understand others better.

Purple Moon was a great client across the board, but one of the things they allowed me to do was run some playtests during the design process, something I find is typically hard to convince my clients to do. Playtests always yield satisfying results, and the Purple Moon test was no exception. In one of the prototype playtests that we did, we found that younger girls repeatedly re-sponded negatively to anything they perceived as being boy-oriented. In fact, it was found that although the girls liked our cards, they did not like the *idea* of trading cards or the term itself because they considered it a "boy thing." One nine-year old girl said, "Boys think they're smarter and better at every-thing than girls, and that's why we hate them." By the way, it is characteristic of girls to express consensus; in this case, she was speaking on behalf of herself, her friend with whom she was doing the test, and presumably, her entire gender.

Based on Purple Moon's tests and other studies, there seems to be a need for children within a certain age range to separate and differentiate between genders. Girls think boys are gross, and boys think girls have cooties. Thus, from a play standpoint, it can often be better to actually segregate the two with game content distinctly designed for one or the other. Young boys, for example, hated colors they thought were girlie, like purple, for example. Girls like knowing that boys won't want to play the game, so anything that is a barrier of entry to the male makes a product more appealing to a girl. The "He Man Woman Haters Club," from the 30s film series *The Little Rascals* appears to be located on a two-way street. Anything that blends gender identification is offensive to both parties as indicated by Brenda Laurel's famous T-shirt of the icon that tested most poorly among both boys and girls: a Barbie doll wearing GI-Joe combat fatigues.

 Test First, Ask Questions Later (p. 463)

The following is a work-in-progress, a chart that I use in various forums to demonstrate some of the differences in play style that I have found to exist between males and females. These are of course grand generalizations. Most of them are things I've learned from my own research and observations, and from studying the research of others. I have seldom found much argument from anyone on any of these because they are all things that can easily be corroborated by observation. They make sense, and so that's why they can be very useful. Note that I place no value judgement on any of these per se. This is just factual information. The purpose of this information is not just to help distinguish between male and female markets, but particularly to help develop content that addresses both cultures. As we've seen from games such as *Pac-Man* and *Myst*, games with cross-gender appeal are ultimately those that do best in the marketplace overall. By understanding the differences, perhaps we can then begin to address the commonalities that will enable us to meet everyone's needs and expectations.

Males like...	Females like...
Shooting	Collecting
Eliminating	Constructing
Pressure, time limits	Open structure, exploration
Escalating skill curve	Cumulative content and story challenge
Finite goal	Ongoing goal or goals
Solving problems	Solving mysteries
Characters skills and qualities	Character motivations and personalities
Guns and gadgets	Characters and spaces
Science fiction	Natural beauty
Game	Story
Dying; it eggs them on	Do not like dying; they find it discouraging
Penalties	Rewards, encouragement
Winning conflicts	Resolving conflicts
Competition	Cooperation, collaboration
Achievement	Accomplishment
Independence	Interdependency

continues

continued

Males like...	Females like...
Individual experience	Social experience
Being King of the Hill	Creating level ground
Winning	Solving (winning can sometimes be a deterrent)
Ugliness, grotesqueness	Beauty, cuteness (such as friendly animals)
Danger	Safety
Dexterous challenge	Intellectual or emotional challenge
Strategy	Understanding
Advantage	Insight
Team play	Group play
Loud noise	Soft music
Feedback	Response
Individual games or activities	Overall context and ambiance
Good versus Evil	Inner life
Human-to-machine	Person-to-person

Reading this list, it doesn't take much to see why females like *Tetris* and *Myst* and don't like *Doom* and *Virtua Fighter*; but you can also see that both *Myst* and *Tetris* have elements that appeal to the male system as well as the female. Many of these qualities are not necessarily in conflict, and it is possible to actually merge them in various ways. Team play and group play, for example, are two different ways of describing essentially the same thing, but the language used simply conveys the difference in value systems that characterize how each gender might view the particular feature.

In *Virtual Adventures*, the game I creative directed for Iwerks Entertainment and Evans & Sutherland in 1993, we paid a considerable amount of attention and effort to creating a crossover experience. We incorporated many elements from the previous table to achieve a broad appeal. A few examples include:

- The game takes place in a beautiful underwater environment, but it is laden with treacherous sea creatures and prehistoric monster fish.
- The goal is to save the Loch Ness Monster's progeny by collecting her eggs.
- You can shoot non-lethal gel at your opponents or monster creatures to help you achieve this objective.
- The monster was designed very carefully—although she is a monster, she is a female monster, she is a mother, and she is in a predicament from which we must save her.

● Nessie was designed to be both beautiful and scary, friendly and intimidating. She is also quite large, and her lair is a dark and somewhat forbidding place, but also designed to have aesthetic appeal.

Virtual Adventures' B-monster-movie meets fairy tale scenario appeals across the board to males and females. The story content of saving a damsel in distress, even if it is a dragon, has a certain mythological attraction that clearly crosses over gender barriers.

Team play is crucial; it gives the men the sense of being on a team competing against another team, providing them with a bonding experience based on competition. For a woman, it is a group play experience that provides an opportunity to bond with the family through cooperation and a shared objective. For women, by the way, the goal might not be necessary. Females are perfectly content to participate in a non–goal-oriented shared experience. Males need something to motivate them, an objective, a time limit, and penalties to keep them going in the game. To appeal to men and women, the balance of penalties to rewards is crucial. If there are too many penalties, women will become frustrated and discouraged; too few and the men will become bored and lose interest. A proper balance can ensure that both groups will come away with a challenging and satisfying experience. For the most part, this seems to be the result when people play *Virtual Adventures*. *Virtual Adventures* is also designed to be both a story and a game, a ride, and a movie, and in that sense it crosses over barriers as well. For the hardcore gamer-type, it affords game challenge; for women, the game is put in the context of an overall plot within the context of a narrative structure.

 THE PRINCESS AND THE MONSTER: THE MAKING OF VIRTUAL ADVENTURES (p. 375)

An awareness of the dichotomies of male/female culture can therefore be used not to increase polarities, but to actually reduce them. In this way, we can begin to bridge the gap to the point where someday our arcade might actually be a place where men and women can play together in harmony.

One place where we see this occurring is on the Internet, with Chat and online communities, VR spaces, and other venues that utilize the computer as a social medium. Women are social creatures and have little interest in the kinds of individual entertainment experiences that are typical of male-oriented interactivity. Females almost always prefer their entertainment in a social context—as I mentioned earlier, they'd rather play air hockey than a video game; they prefer playing billiards to pinball.

One thing that I believe has been a major barrier of entry to female appeal of Virtual Reality is the self-contained immersion paradigm. Many people believe that women do not like Head-Mounted Displays because it will mess up their hair. As it turns out, one of the reasons is purely physiological: Women are more prone to motion sickness and therefore tend to get physically uncomfortable in HMDs. The other reason is psychological. *BattleTech*, which features individual pods, is not much more appealing to women than the HMD-based *Virtuality* arcade game; however, *BattleTech* has another aspect that women really dislike—physical isolation from others. Part of what made *Virtual Adventures* so appealing for women was that you were in a vehicle with five other people, able to talk to them, look them in the eye, and hear their voices only inches away from you. Women, who rely heavily on body language and vocal nuance for social cues, are more comfortable in a context where they can more easily "read" the teammates, or even their opponents, as in the case of air hockey or billiards.

Bearing all this in mind, my feeling is that the most important missing ingredient of female-friendly gaming is group play. As long as PC, arcade, CD-ROM, and Internet games are designed for a single user, they will have limited appeal to women. Why? Because the "masturbation" paradigm (note that the primary target market for arcade games is in the "wet dream" demographic) is not a typically female paradigm. In terms of entertainment, women tend to prefer group or communal activities over individual or isolating activities, which is one of the reasons why you find so many women online, but so few in arcades. It is not so much a fear of technology that deters women from participating in these experiences, but an inherent lack of interest in auto-entertainment.

In addition to the behavioral aspects in gaming, a number of physiological differences also affect male and female appeal when it comes to games. In a panel that I participated in at Amusement Showcase 1997 in Las Vegas, consultant Norma Lynn Cutler outlined a few of the physiological differences between men and women. Her research and studies showed that females are overall more sensitive than men in a purely physiological sense. Females have a more developed sense of taste, smell, hearing, sight, and touch. Women, for example, do not like to eat junk food because it tastes bad, while males may not notice the taste as much and are therefore less discriminating about what they eat. Color and design is crucial to women, and if they find a space to be an aesthetic assault, they are less likely to remain there for any length of time. Women like soft and textured tactile sensations, while men prefer things that are smooth and hard. Audio has an enormous impact on women. Roberta Perry, the panel organizer, described a sound system created for one of her clients that neutralized arcade sounds. This system could be used to control demographic mix; when it was turned on, at night and on the weekends, the sound was softened and women would come into the venue; as soon as it went off, allowing the loud arcade game sounds to leak through, female attendance dropped to almost nothing. Males find loud sounds stimulating, and also find it easier to ignore such distractions when playing a game. At that same presentation, Jill Bensley discussed research regarding skills. Certain motor functions had strong male/female differentiation. Men, for example were better at certain three-dimensional rotation problems, while women were better at navigation using landmarks, to name one characteristic.

Whether or not we understand the differences between males and females and how to appeal to them, if there is no effort made from the corporate side to address these markets, then everything will remain status quo. This lack of effort is not just coming from the corporate side either. Conferences, awards programs, and even the press continue to apply the male standard when evaluating interactive game products. *Virtual Adventures*, though highly acclaimed and a recipient of over half a dozen awards (none of which were from any conventional game industry organization), was criticized by some in the game and ridefilm industry as being "too soft." *Time* magazine called it "ethereal" and referred to it as the "Barney of VR games." Just as men will often refer to certain movies as "chick flicks," games that don't involve blasting people away are considered wimpy. Even if something is balanced, with a 50/50 male to female appeal level, it might be perceived, even by women, as more female than male. This would echo gender dialog expert Deborah Tannen's research. Tannen found that even if women speak less than men in a mixed group, which is almost always the case, both genders will have the impression that the women are speaking more. I once observed this phenomenon myself when helping Ed Schlossberg give a keynote address at a museum conference. We decided to create an interactive exercise as part of the presentation to demonstrate principles of perception. When quizzed in a handout as to whether women outnumbered men in the room, almost all the participants, both male and female, said yes. But when we did a head count, we found that the gender ratio was almost exactly 1 to 1.

To give you another example of how skewed this sensibility is, when I first arrived in Hollywood, the first thing I did was get an attorney. This is something you have to do in Hollywood; otherwise, it's too dangerous to try to have a career here. My attorney suggested that I might want to consider getting an agent, which to me (as an old-school nerd) was a near comical proposition. Only one of the agents I met with was a woman. After I showed her my reel, she sat for a moment in silence, a perplexed look on her face. She really had no idea what to make of me. Finally, a light bulb went off over her head and her eyes lit up. "How would you like to make *Doom* into a Theme park ride?" I said in theory it wasn't such a bad idea, except that I didn't develop violent content, that I had a reputation for designing nonviolent games, and I'd kind of like to maintain that. You should have seen the expression on her face. She raised her eyebrow in shock, as if I had just told her that I had sold my soul to the Devil. To date, her all-male roster of clients had been producing exclusively violent games. Needless to say, that was the end of the conversation.

The male-dominated sensibility is so ingrained in the entertainment industry, and particularly the game industry, that it will take a major paradigm shift for things to change. That I should be criticized, even ostracized to a certain extent, for choosing to make games that are not violent is absurd. Even if I choose to make these games, unless someone is willing to produce them, they are not likely to get made. It is a tribute to Iwerks and Evans & Sutherland that they were willing to take that risk and build a bridge to a new way of doing things.

I am looking to more products such as *Barbie Fashion Designer*, and new games such as *You Don't Know Jack* and *The Neverhood*, that do not propagate any particular gender bias, to show that girls and women constitute a real and present market. In America, where money talks, this is really the only way a change is going to be made. After it becomes apparent that there is profit to be made from women, you can bet you're going to see a massive change in attitude.

The other media have begun to catch on to this already, and perhaps the interactive media market, always a bit behind in some ways, will soon follow. I have been particularly encouraged of late because I have begun to see marketing to teenage and pre-teen girls in other media. A recent ad showing a gen-X girl in a huff proclaims "Talk radio is *not* just for guys." In addition, a bus bench campaign is currently running all over Los Angeles that shows an eight-year old girl kissing her friend with a logo for a product called *Friends*. A few years ago, record execs were known for rejecting new female acts with the absurd justification that "We already have a girl band." Now girl bands and female rockers abound in record stores and on MTV. So-called "chick flicks" are also getting a lot of acclaim and doing well at the box office.

Here's even more good news: the World Wide Web, with its emphasis on content over speed, multi-user environments, writing, and correspondence, has become a playground for girls and women. At home in its text-based milieu and attracted by its social possibilities, girls and women are right at home on the web. The only barrier of entry is, again, content. There is virtually no content for young girls at this writing, but by the time this book is published, a handful of companies will have launched new girls-only web sites. The Purple Moon site, structured as a members-only club in which each character from the CD-ROM has her own web page, is designed to create a fan culture among Purple Moon fans. Girls can use it to learn more about the game characters, but it also lets them send each other digital postcards and even online gifts (not to be confused with GIFs, a file format for pictures).

Based on existing social patterns between girls, this kind of web site addresses values and concerns specific to the 8–12 year-old-girl market.

Once girls this age begin to get online and become more involved in digital entertainment, things are bound to improve. First, as the audience increases, and so does the market, other companies will raise their heads, following in the footsteps of Mattel, Purple Moon, and others who have paved the path ahead of them. But second, and perhaps more important, a new generation of girls are going to be online. As these girls grow older, they may well become the next generation of interactive designers. The more women we see in the industry, the more likely girls' and women's needs are to be addressed. In the long run, women and girls are more likely to find a home either on the Internet or in out-of-home entertainment venues, due to their inherent multi-user infrastructures. And as they do, they will begin to create new genres and forms derived from their unique set of sensibilities and cultural values.

 Cyberfeminism, or, Why Women Love Cyberspace (p. 140)

Psycho-ergonomics (p. 404)

The Interactive Ecosystem (p. 233)

God Plays Dice with the Universe

In describing God, or the concept of God, most people use words such as "architect" or "author." "All the world's a stage," so Shakespeare said (he would), implying that God was a stage director. A modern day Shakespeare might liken the Creator to a film director who directs the cinematographer, the lighting designer, the art director, and all the actors. Instead of *Birth of a Nation*, it's called *Birth of a Universe*, an epic feature, the ultimate box-office blockbuster with a cast of billions, and a gazillion-dollar budget (George Lucas, eat your heart out).

I like to think of God more as a game designer (I would). And even though Albert Einstein was convinced that God does not play dice with the universe, he, of all people, should have known better. Because, as Einstein helped to demonstrate, the universe is not a linear story, but a highly dynamic interactive system. The universe is characterized by a variety of structural frameworks that allow for spontaneous interactions between all its components. For those who see God as a God of fate, of predetermined causes with no variation, then yes, he might well be the D.W. Griffith of the universe.

But consider this…if a game is a set of rules for spontaneous or improvised behavior, if it is a set of parameters for interactions, then cannot that same definition be applied to the universe? Could we not then look at the world in terms of a game—a structured play space in which anything, within reason, can occur? Was not Einstein himself merely figuring out the rules of this Cosmic Game?

 THE RULES OF THE GAME (p. 420)

THE RULES OF THE GAME (p. 420)

Traditional games are defined by a set of parameters that can be applied to almost any aspect of life and the universe, whether on the macro or micro level. Armed with an understanding of game logic, you can begin to re-formulate virtually anything you can think of as a game. This is a great exercise on a variety of levels. If you are an interactive designer, it will give you a whole new perspective on your craft, and if you are merely a player, it will help you to better appreciate your hobby. But it can also be used in other ways. If I were a science teacher, for example, I might have my students use this technique to reinforce their understanding of scientific principles. The simple tenets of game structure thus provide a template for understanding the structure of any dynamic system. To see how this works, let's try a few.

MOLECULE

Players are atoms and the goal is to stabilize polarities by hooking up with other atoms to create molecules. Changes in conditions, such as temperature, chemical reactions, or electrical charges, will alter the stability of the system. Atoms that are left with extra positive or negative charges must then search out other atoms whose charges will complement their own. The game is ongoing, like Monopoly. One thing about atoms is that there are always the same number of player pieces, even if they reconfigure into different molecules.

LIFE

Players take the roles of living organisms. The goal is to stay alive and procreate to generate more life forms. Obstacles are other players who either eat you or compete with you for resources. These obstacles can include anything from a virus, which eats away at you from the inside, or a carnivore, which swallows you whole. Resources are all the things you can absorb into your system to maintain life, including light, water, air, and food; they also include members of your same species with whom you can team up to procreate. If you are good at getting and managing resources, you are rewarded with prolonged life and a larger overall population for your species. If you use up all your resources unwisely, you may be penalized by running out. In addition, there is a lot of information in the system...everything from DNA to techniques for communicating with members of your species. Whoever maintains their life and the life of their species wins.

Ecosystem

In Ecosystem, the goal is to create dynamic equilibrium within a system. This means you want everything to be operating smoothly in an ebb and flow, the overall average of which is a state of balance. Variables, known as "perturbations" because they perturb the system, will intervene, attempting to upset the equilibrium. The natural systems must then adapt to these, working together to maintain balance.

As an interactive designer, I see all these systems as brilliantly designed games with simple goals, compelling and timeless logic structures that allow for a wide range of play styles and variable outcomes. Thus, the entire system, and each subsystem therein, can be viewed as a game, right on down to the day-to-day life of a regular person. Think of it. Doesn't your life seem like a game at times? Just for fun, take the list in the chapter, "The Rules of the Game," and see whether you can figure out your personal game, or the game you might be playing on a given day or in a given setting. I find this technique can be very illuminating, and it also takes the edge off when you're doing something challenging. Just think: You know, this is just like a really tough game of chess.

When looked at in this light, you can see that God plays dice with the universe—and Risk, and Monopoly, and chess, and Go. If you really analyze it, you will see that, as with all good games, the rules are perfectly fair, and if you want to play well, it's just a matter of picking the game that best suits your cognitive makeup and play styles. I'm lousy at cards, but I play a mean game of backgammon. So I figure I'll stick to the games I'm good at.

Every time I roll the dice, I'll think of Einstein, who, no doubt, could calculate for me the precise calculations of a rolling die. At such a moment, I might turn to him and say, "You know, Al...not only does God play dice with the universe, but he designed the dice, *and* the physical properties to make them roll." You really can't get any better game designer than that!

OM Meets OHM: Digital Oneness (p. 360)

Einstein, Eisenstein, and The Space-Time Continuum (p. 186)

A-Life of One's Own (p. 5)

GRATUITOUS INTERACTIVITY: MEDIA DISPENSERS AND THE ATM MODEL

So much of what is alleged to be interactive today is really nothing more than what I refer to as gratuitous interactivity. There is little point in creating something interactive purely for the sake of making it interactive. Yet in many cases, that seems to be the rule rather than the exception.

Gratuitous interactivity is easy to recognize. It leads to the inevitable question, what's the point? This approach to interactive design is characteristically gimmicky. You might see some cute tricks, but in the end, the interactivity leaves you wondering why you didn't just sit on the couch and watch *The Simpsons* instead. The problem with interactivity is that it asks you to actually *do* something, and unless there's a fairly good reason to do it, people would much rather take it easy and be spoon fed their entertainment and education.

The thing that really bothers me about gratuitous interactivity is that it gives interactivity in general a bad name. When people see some dumb "push-a-button-see-a-movie" kiosk, or go to a web site that offers choices that seem to lead down an endless path to nowhere, they shrug their shoulders and say, what's the big deal about interactivity? To them, these applications are the media equivalent of a Coke machine. Such gratuitous interactivity misses the finer points, which have to do with the idea of letting people have more control over their entertainment or educational destiny.

CHOICE IS OVERRATED (p. 127)

DECISIONS, DECISIONS, DECISIONS (p. 158)

In my interactive storytelling and game design courses, I am forever urging my students to avoid creating interactive experiences that are nothing more than "media dispensers," a kind of informational ATM or media vending machine. The purpose of the ATM (Automatic Teller Machine) is to take money from you, give you money, or transfer money. This is definitely an interactive transaction in the technical sense. But it is a very limited model: You put something in or you get something out. There is no conversation, no evolution, there is nothing unique about the way an individual person withdraws cash. The transaction is really the same for everyone. The experience of the "end user" is the same no matter if he or she is a rocket scientist or a jazz musician. Your particular play or learning style has no bearing on the ATM experience.

If you go up to an interactive kiosk in a typical museum, or use a typical educational application, generally what you will find is that you aren't interacting any more with it than you do with a bank machine. You have a choice whether you want to learn about medieval painting, Renaissance sculpture, or Greek architecture in the same way that you choose to withdraw $20, $40, or $80. After you've made the choice, the linear video, text, or other media is "dispensed" to you in a non-interactive, or non-reciprocal fashion. To use a metaphor from childhood, these experiences are best described as "Digital PEZ"—sweet enough but lacking in food value.

"Interactive" has become the trendy adjective of the decade. Everyone is "going interactive." But most of the time, they have no idea what this means. Clients come to me all the time because they want "something interactive," but they have given no thought whatsoever to what it is or why it would be useful or better than what they already have. Often, people want to add some level of interactivity that is essentially meaningless to the experience. More often than not, it is just a cheap trick or device that will enable them to say "This is interactive," even though from a cognitive and experiential standpoint, it is nothing of the sort.

Interactivity craves meaning. It needs motivation, and it longs for emotional, as well as intellectual content. It is difficult at best to convince a person that it would be a good idea to penetrate the fourth wall, to break the artificial boundary between man and media set up by the conventions of theater, film, and television. People are alternately intimidated or unmotivated by experiences that require taking risks. They don't like to make mistakes. They don't want to have unnecessary attention called to them. Think about the bank line scenario where everyone is avoiding one machine, even if they don't know why. How easy is it for some bold soul to break the pattern, step forth, and see if the machine truly is inoperative.

This example may seem mundane, but in its simplicity, it explains the challenge faced by interactive designers: What do I need to do to remove people's natural inhibitions and draw them into the process? How can I given them a good enough reason to take a risk?

If you want to understand the true meaning of gratuitous versus meaningful interactivity, spend some time playing *Monty Python's Complete Waste of Time*. As its name implies, it is a series of pointless interactive games and activities, held together only by the glue of Terry Gilliam's animated collages from the British Comedy group's famed television series and films. Designers at 7th Level meticulously disassembled Gilliam's original artwork to create a series of mini-animations that allowed for various levels of player intervention. *Waste of Time* is one of the few products in which repurposing content was not only acceptable, it was actually advisable. In fact, Gilliam's original cartoon bumpers were begging for interactivity. And they got it in spades.

Like most CD-ROMs, *Monty Python's Complete Waste of Time* is precisely that…but it is such an addictively delightful and satisfying waste of time that no one seems to care. The fact that it pokes fun at what it is (and indeed at its entire medium) makes it even more appealing. The reason it is so great is because it takes full advantage of its gratuitousness and pushes it to the limit. It is an interactive free-for-all. The payoff is twofold. First, there is the dynamic interaction with Gilliam's absurdist world, full of surprises and oddities; second, there is the laughter. Each time you do something, it makes you laugh. There are few things more motivating than laughter. Laughter is addictive, and so, once you start, you can't stop. The fact that what you are doing is a waste of time makes it even more funny and more addictive.

I use this example because, although it is quite sophisticated, *Monty Python's Complete Waste of Time* is actually very simple: Identify a body of popular assets that inherently lend themselves to interactivity, let the content drive the interactivity, create interesting and unexpected interchanges between media and player, and make sure you have a really good payoff. In this case, the content, the premise, and the payoff all feed back onto the motivation. Who doesn't want to waste time? Who doesn't want to laugh their head off? And who doesn't want to play around with Terry Gilliam's crazy vision?

As I've said before in other sections, interactivity is not about technology: it's about people and it's about experience. The most important aspect of an interactive experience is what goes on inside the head of the user. That's all there is to it. The way to avoid making interactivity gratuitous is to always understand this basic premise. If you consistently use the experience of the user as your measuring stick, you cannot possibly go wrong. To avoid gratuitous interactivity, you need to ask yourself questions such as these:

- Would my target user want to do this?
- Why would they want to do this?
- Why would they want to keep doing it?
- Why would they want to do it again?
- What can I do to spark insight and discovery?
- What can I do to create new connections in the players' minds?
- What can I do to surprise them?
- What can I do to scare them, make them laugh, make them laugh, smile, or cry?
- What can I do to let them make themselves laugh, smile, or cry?

- What are their motivations going in? And what is the payoff?
- Can I sustain an ongoing feedback loop of motivation/payoff?
- Is there enough variety to have different payoffs based on different actions?

These are just a beginning…but this is the interactive litmus, the "who cares" test that lets you know if you're on the right track.

The rest is a lot of good, fun, hard work. Do your homework. Don't go off half-cocked. If you don't know how to do it, find people who do to help you. Take classes. Read books. Don't be lazy. Pay attention. Interactive experiences are only as deep as the commitment and sensibilities of the people who make them. If you can't look wide and deep at the connection between your content and your user, then you will most certainly become guilty of gratuitous interactivity.

Here's the bottom line: you can't fool the audience. Hollywood would have us believe that the audience is stupid, but every once in a while, they prove themselves wrong. The interactive audience is not stupid, and they don't want to be treated as stupid. People who seek interactive experiences are by that very fact looking for experiences which are more intellectually stimulating and involving. They view themselves as intelligent and at the front end of the adoption curve; for the most part, they are right. In fact, odds are that most of them are smarter than you. Which is why you need to rise to the occasion.

I have found time and time again that no matter how much I plan for, no matter how many scenarios I anticipate, my audience always surprises me. They always invent new ways of doing things that I never imagined. That is what makes this job so fun. I am only one half of the creative process; the players are the other. The more I empower them to be creative and imaginative, the less gratuitous their experience will be. It is at that moment of discovery, that split second when the person's mind suddenly expands, when they see another side of themselves as reflected through a machine, where they lose their self-consciousness enough to jump into a new experience…that is the moment of meaning to me. That is the entire reason for doing any of this.

TEST FIRST, ASK QUESTIONS LATER (p. 463)

ACTION, REACTION, INTERACTION (p. 11)

USER OR PLAYER: THE CHOICE IS YOURS (p. 490)

HEISENBERG'S UNCERTAINTY

Heisenberg's Uncertainty Principle is a theory applied to experimental observation in physics. It consists of two parts. The first part states that, in a scientific experiment, you can never be certain about all conditions of the experiment at the same time. A simple way to explain this is that you can look at a three-dimensional object from any angle, but you can only see it from the angle you are facing, even though you know it has other sides. In other words, you can look at an object from any angle, but not from all angles at once. In terms of particle behaviors, it simply means that you cannot observe all aspects of a process concurrently. A typical statement of the Uncertainty Principle is that you can measure the direction or the position of a particle, but not both at the same time.

As you can see, this principle is very applicable to understanding media evolution as well as fundamental issues of interactive design. In Virtual Reality, for example, you must create the polygonal structure and behavioral algorithms for every angle of an object, but you cannot see all these elements at all times because the viewing portal is, of course, flat. Stereoscopy does not eliminate this problem, and neither does holography. Even though the image is in theory "there," you can't see it and therefore, you cannot prove that it is indeed there.

It doesn't matter much anyway, because the second part of Heisenberg's principle states that the very act of observing a phenomenon affects its outcome. To put it simply, turning the light on in a room changes what is occurring in that space. In interactive multimedia, not only is this the case, but it's actually the entire point. Interactivity, in a sense, turns Heisenberg inside out because it makes the observer an active ingredient in the experiment. Thus, the old question of the relationship between observer and observed is changed because now the observer is actually part of the phenomenon, and in the best of cases, the key activator of it. In traditional scientific experimentation, the observer is supposed to intervene as little as possible in the process; in this case, intervention *is* the process. The result is that not only does the nature of the experiment change, but so does the whole nature of experimentation itself.

Part two of the Uncertainty Principle also creates a very interesting problem for media in general, both interactive and so-called "passive" media. Note, for example, how the act of televising an event influences and even potentially reverses the outcome of historical events, as in both the Rodney King case and the O.J. Simpson case. Both events were characterized by a continuous and dynamic interchange between the observed and the observer. It fact, at a certain point, it is hard to say which was more influential in both cases—the participants themselves or the audience. There is no question, for example, that the audience prompted a total reversal on the King case; and it would seem that an irate nation convicted O.J. Simpson even though the criminal courts did not. His loss of the subsequent civil trial became the de-facto conviction that seemed to prove that which had been disproved only two years earlier. The Simpson trials are a case study for subjective reality and alternative viewpoints. It is the most celebrated case in history to have two contradicting verdicts. In a culture saturated with media in which history is controlled to a large extent by popular opinion, the very framework of our democratic system can be called into question. The Simpson case is a classic application of Heisenberg's Uncertainty Principle in the media sphere: we can never know all the facts, and the very act of observing the process affects its outcome.

There are many metaphors and concepts in science that are tremendously useful in the study of interactivity. Scientific principles concern themselves primarily with the interaction between systems, and with rules and conventions that seem to apply to events that might vary in a variety of ways. These principles, which can be applied to dynamic physical systems, enable us to begin to observe and define a set of consistent parameters that we can use in building interactive systems. This is why you will see axioms and natural laws throughout this book. Although theoretical in nature, they create a framework with which to understand patterns in the nature of media and its relation to both the individual and the culture at large.

As is the case with Heisenberg's physical world, in the media world, we can see a direct correlation between our methods of observation and measurement (our media) and the phenomena used to observe and/or measure (our culture).

As uncertain as Heisenberg might have been, there was one thing he was sure of: All things are affected by frame of reference, an observation that he shared with fellow physicist Albert Einstein. Both men's theories shed new light on the relationship of one dynamic system to another, and in shedding that light, of course, irrevocably change the systems they are illuminating.

What it really all comes down to is subjective reality. In both the uncertain and the relative world, there are no absolutes. Frame of reference is everything. We can never be sure of anything because we can only experience it from one, finite viewpoint. It is this singular, finite viewpoint that is the central experience behind Virtual Reality and spatial navigation interfaces— placing you into a dynamic, relative, uncertain, and decidedly subjective role relative to the world around you. In other words, it's a whole lot like real life, from both a philosophical and material standpoint.

VIRTUAL RELATIVITY (p. 524)

The notion of subjective reality has permeated all aspects of media evolution. One of the keystones of artistry and craft in the content of any new media, is the development of an understanding of the subjective paradigms that are best captured by the medium. Within the content of television, for example, the sitcom marked the creation of programs that were about people like the audience—ordinary middle-class Americans like Ralph Kramden and Lucy Ricardo became the "working class heroes" of the television medium. The film medium was catapulted into a new level of artistry by Sergei Eisentein, who, through the use of editing and cinematography, released the emotional power of film. There are a few artists and storytellers who have released that power in interactive media. Releasing that power is simply a matter of combining relativity, the notion that all events are relative to other events, and Heisenberg's notion that we always effect the outcome of what we observe. It is not so much the content, nor even the implementation of the content that matters. What is really critical is the relationship between the user and the content, and that is where Heisenberg comes in.

 EINSTEIN, EISENSTEIN, AND THE SPACE-TIME CONTINUUM (p. 186)

MIXED MEDIA, MIXED MESSAGE (p. 306)

GRATUITOUS INTERACTIVITY: MEDIA DISPENSERS AND THE ATM MODEL (p. 218)

THE HEURISTIC MAN: A PORTRAIT OF EDWIN SCHLOSSBERG

There was a running joke around the offices of Edwin Schlossberg Incorporated (ESI) that Ed's idea of an interactive kiosk was a device which, when you asked it a question, would respond by saying, "Look it up." This was often his response when asked to explain an obscure reference or tell you who or what someone was.

Ed is a fascinating and controversial character, an interesting person to work for, and a challenging boss. I consider him to be my first and still most influential mentor, and given his personality, he is and was definitely mentor material.

Ed is a very controversial guy. He is one of those brilliant people who, not unlike Bucky Fuller—one of his early mentors, tends to speak in a kind of poetic, free verse fashion. This manner of speech elicits a variety of responses from people. There was one camp within the company that was always playing a game of "Emperor's New Clothes" in the sense that they were always trying to understand what it was Ed meant. These people liked to put themselves in the position of "translators," because they thought they were in the know. It was always entertaining to watch their response to something Ed said, because the yarns that got woven would sometimes spin into comical proportions. There was a second group of people both in and out of the company (often including clients), who had no idea what the hell it was Ed was talking about, but thought for sure he must be saying something brilliant that they were just too dumb to understand. This group was kind of a second cousin to the first. There was a third group both in and outside the company that had no idea what he was talking about and thought it was all a big charade—truly emperor's new clothes—a metaphor some of these people actually alluded to from time to time. Finally, there was the fourth group of people who, like myself, believed that Ed's primary motivation in almost everything he said was to get people to think. I think what was most important to Ed was what *you* made of what he said, which might be why he frequently came off as somewhat smug—he was merely observing bemusedly all the bizarre and sometimes hilarious projections people put on to his words.

As a designer, Ed was what I call a brilliant problem maker. His main role in the company, as I saw it, was to direct not the solution to the problem but the problem itself. His philosophy was that if you knew the true nature of the problem, the solution would become evident. His world was full of metaphors and paradigms. (He once introduced me to a client as "The Paradigm Person.") He taught us how to look at the prepositional relationship between the user and the experience (are you in it, on it, around it, and so forth). Ed understood that all interactive experiences are driven by content. I have met a lot of brilliant interactive designers and thinkers since I went to work for Ed, but none has ever had quite his vision or perspective. He thought that users were everything, that they made the experience, that our job was to basically get out of the way and let them create their own world. He used to talk about "neural networks"—the idea of the connectivity between people's minds. He wanted to create interactive models that would help people better understand complex systems through active participation. He talked about role-playing, about how technology should be viewed as a mask and the interactive experience a masquerade party. He talked about the need for experiences that helped people to appreciate each other rather than exist in isolation from one another. He wanted people to be proactive, to instigate them, to inspire them to think. A word he used all the time was "insight." He wanted people to look in and act out, in a manner of speaking. He said that the primary goal of an interactive experience was to make people feel their own minds, to appreciate and understand their own intelligence. Interactive experiences aren't about how great the artist is; they are about how great the audience is.

Ed challenged us. He had no tolerance for slowness, for incomprehension, or for intellectual helplessness. His form of leadership was demanding. If you were a person who needed a lot of guidance, who needed to be told what to do, who required a boss who would somehow point the way, you were out of luck. The entire company was itself a heuristic environment, and being inherently process-oriented, Ed liked the office to be a microcosm of the world he wanted it to create. ESI was a do-it-yourself kind of place, a true autodidactic community. It is interesting to note, for example, that none of the first round of designers he hired on the IPL Game Pavilion projects were game designers or had any experience or training in this trade. It was only on the second round of hires that experienced game designers were brought into the mix.

Ed never wanted to hire experts. Indeed, he completely shunned the entire notion of expertise. He liked to find people whose skills he felt could be re-applied to another area. To design games, he hired architects, psychologists, sculptors, writers, and educators. I think he feared (and rightly so) that game designers would design games like existing games and that they would be married to a convention that he really wanted to bypass entirely. Ed wanted to create something of an entirely new genre and felt that hiring people unfamiliar with the craft would yield the desired result.

This caused a certain level of frustration as well as enthusiasm. The frustration arose because people sometimes felt insecure and unqualified to do these things they had never done before. I was certainly petrified in my first few months there because I felt like I had arrived in a foreign country without knowing the language; however, because of my upbringing and exposure to this *kind* of thing throughout my life, I kind of got it, even though it was all new to me. Also, I was a 21 year-old college dropout, so I didn't know any-thing—therefore, I had nothing to lose. I had no degree, nothing to prove, and no expertise to protect or reinforce. To a certain extent, I was a clean slate. All I wanted to do was learn, and I knew that I knew nothing, so as a result, I was like a sponge sucking up everything and processing it quickly and without prejudice.

Ed graduated from Columbia with a PhD in physics and literature. His thesis, which was published in a book, was an imaginary conversation between Albert Einstein, Samuel Beckett, and himself. I actually read this book. It was an extremely strenuous read. Ed's writing style can be very demanding, so you really have to concentrate, and you also have to understand that he expects you to fill in the blanks.

Comparing Einstein and Beckett was a fascinating study of the differences and similarities between two of the most brilliant minds of their day, each of whom focused his efforts in a different discipline. Here was the author of *Waiting for Godot* and *Endgame* in consort with the developer of the Theory of Relativity and the space-time continuum. Although Ed's thesis was a hard read, to be sure, it certainly opened my mind in new ways from which I have never entirely recovered, thankfully.

Ed wrote a few other books that were so divergent in theme, content, and style as to make one wonder whether there were not perhaps several different people writing under the pseudonym of Edwin Schlossberg. One of his early books was about CB radios, which fascinated him as a communication technology and a culture. In the 70s he wrote *The Pocket Calculator Game Book*, a collection of games you could play on an ordinary calculator. *The Philosopher's Game* was a kind of *Jeopardy* for meta-nerds in which you would have to match the philosopher to the philosophy vis-a-vis a certain situation or problem. One of my favorite of his early books was written under the pseudonym of Rebus Heaviwaitt, along with Gene Youngblood, author of *Expanded Cinema*, who went under the name Immanual Lighthanger. It was called *Projex* and was basically a satire of outlandish futurist proposals. Many of them poked fun at the ideas of Buckminster Fuller, such as bulldozing the moon into an icosahedron and building a tram system along its vertices. The book of Ed's that is still closest to my heart is a little poetry chapbook entitled *How I Learn How I Learn*. This book was closest to his art poems that had been influential on me as a teenager.

Ed is a classic New York intellectual and denizen of the New York art scene, hanging out with the likes of John Cage and Jasper Johns, among others. He had occasional gallery showings of his art works ("wall poems," as I called them) that often contained interactive elements—layers of transparent material, heat-sensitive liquid crystal paint, moving parts, letters that were broken into fragments that you would have to stand at a certain orientation to read. Most of the work was characterized by stenciled, or later, typewritten words on large surfaces, paper, cloth, parchment stretched across poles, or a shimmering hard linoleum-like surface. Like all of Ed's endeavors, they were somewhat enigmatic and didn't really fit into any pre-cast mold. Some of his critics thought that they were unaesthetic and therefore not meritorious as art. My impression was that they were really poems, not art, and that they were not meant to be an expression of any visual form, but more of a different way to read and experience words and particularly the vagueness of words. Ed's poems often consisted of double entendres or had words that overlapped or merged in some way and were very much what we used to call in the early 80s "language centered." Having been a poet myself, I always understood the frustration of being confined to the tiny page, so I found the expression of a poetical sensibility on a canvas or large-scale installation to be very satisfying.

Ed's foray in the museum world began in 1976 when he was asked to design a hands-on science exhibition for the Brooklyn Children's Museum. Ed created a series of scientific principle-based experiences for the children that was structured around the themes of air, fire, earth, and water. One of the principles was to show connections between things. The wave tunnel, for example, had a long waterway that you could manipulate to show different wave patterns. The tunnel itself, made out of wave-like corrugated metal, featured a neon wave showing the spectrum of light to show the parallels between water waves and light waves. It also included a giant climbing structure made of clear Lexan, coincidentally designed and built by my father, Peter Pearce. This 8 billion times enlargement of a diamond crystal allowed kids to "pretend they were electrons" bouncing around inside a giant crystal (see figure H.1).

Figure H.1

The 8 billion times enlargement of a diamond crystal at the Brooklyn Children's Museum

After the Brooklyn Children's Museum exhibit, ESI did a variety of children's museums and some early so-called "edutainment" projects, including Macomber Farm, the Funsonian at Hanna Barbera Land, and Sesame Place, a *Sesame Street*-themed edutainment center. These included some of the first uses of computer kiosks in museums, one of the first applications of live chromakey in which kids could put themselves into cartoons, and some very early laser disk exhibits. One of these exhibits enabled children to see themselves projected onto a grid next to a Muybridge clip of a horse. A treadmill connected to the laser disk player enabled the child to control the speed of the film clip and compare his or her own gait to that of the animal. ESI also developed animal empathy exhibits, including the first sight masks that simulated the vision of various animals. They also designed computer-based language games that helped you understand what chickens were saying to each other, and special interactive sensors that taught you the appropriate way to pet a live animal.

Macomber Farm is a perfect example of Ed's skills as a creative problem maker. The Massachusetts SPCA had come to ESI because it wanted to make an exhibition at a farm in Framingham about cruelty to animals. Ed and his team helped the client to realize that no one would go to such a museum, and furthermore, it would not necessarily yield the desired result of reducing cruelty to animals. Instead, Ed and his team suggested a museum about how to be kind to animals, an animal empathy experience that would put adults and kids in the "hooves" of various farm animals. Research showed that most urban kids knew nothing about farm animals, so it was also a way to show them where milk and eggs came from, for example.

The exhibit featured a series of components that enabled people to sense and do things as the animals would. Signs reading "I'm seeing like a cow," "I'm working like a horse," "I'm smelling like a pig," and so on adorned each exhibit (see figure H.2). These exhibits enabled children to simulate animal behavior and perception. One exhibit featured a pinball-style game that followed the progression of milk from the cow to the store. All these exhibits placed children and their parents into the subjective viewpoint of the animal—a perfect model for elementary school children, who are at the age where they relate very strongly to animals.

Figure H.2

Simulating the sight of sheep with a sight mask

The Macomber Farm project, which predated my joining the company, was always used as an example of how to reframe the client's way of thinking so that they can understand the problem they are trying to solve. Macomber Farm was the perfect case in which the client was trying to solve the wrong problem, and the outcome would have been a disaster. It's true that some clients were more fond of this approach than others, but there is no doubt that every design that ESI did was completely unique to the client, although some were more successful than others. Our biggest challenge was always that we had to meet the needs of two customers: the client and the visitor. Ninety percent of our difficulties arose when the needs and expectations of these two groups were at odds.

The thing I always loved about working with Ed was that he made me think. I never worried so much about "What Ed meant," because I'm not entirely sure it mattered. I think what he meant to do most of the time was to trigger our minds and ideas because a good percentage of the time, whatever we thought he meant was what he meant. Sometimes, of course, we would come in with a design thinking we knew what he meant and he would throw the whole thing out and ask us to start over; but I honestly think there was always about a 50/50 chance of that happening no matter what he said.

One really important thing Ed taught us was to think about relationships. He used to talk a lot about prepositional relationships, which always baffled the rookies. He would say, "Are we in it, on it, over it, beneath it? Is it bigger than us or smaller than us? Are we participants or observers?" These seemingly esoteric qualities turn out to be really critical in terms of interactive experiences, yet they are rarely addressed by interactive designers. Think about it. If I'm having an interactive experience, it's pretty important whether I'm in it, around it, on it, or observing it.

The most important thing was always the relationships of the people to each other. That was everything. When all was said and done, *everything* we did, all the high-tech gizmos and complex concepts, was really about that and only that. I think he felt the same thing toward the inner workings of the company as well—that it was all about the people and their connections between each other.

AUTOBIOGRAPHY OF AN AUTODIDACT, PART 2 (p. 58)

ART IS A VERB (p. 29)

SOCIAL COMPUTING (p. 434)

INTER-PLAY: IMPROVISATION AND INTERACTIVE THEATER

When I was in my late teens, my interest in theater led me to a study of improvisation. I shared a passion for both theater and film with my friend, Camden Morse, who later became an independent experimental filmmaker. Her mother, Dale Eunson, was director of a prominent L.A. improv group called Public Works that was based in Ocean Park, an oceanside artists' community in the heart of what is generally called "The People's Republic of Santa Monica." Public Works, and other various ensembles of its members, were very active in improvisation in the 1970s, and some continued into the 80s and 90s.

I can't even count the number of times I saw this group perform. In one show, I had the job of house manager—turning the lights on and off during inter-mission, making the coffee, handing out programs; I think I even took the money at the door. As a result, I got to see the play for free twice a week for its entire run.

Although forms of theatrical improvisation have been performed within different cultures throughout the ages, its birth in the context of modern theater can be traced back to the 1920s and 30s. Viola Spolin, who served as drama supervisor for a Chicago WPA (Works Progress Administrations) project, wanted to find a method for teaching theater that would cut across boundaries of culture and age. Based on her studies with Neva Boyd, a social worker who used games to teach leadership, Spolin combined theatrical conventions with principles of game structure to create a new method of theatrical training and performance. Called "Theater Games," these exercises were designed to unlock creative expression through spontaneous, intuitive, and collaborative experiences. Spolin used this technique in both training and directing amateur and professional actors. Her son, Paul Sills, went on to form the Second City Company in the 1960s, which became one of the most influ-ential improvisational theater companies in America.

The best interactive experiences are nothing more than a technologically enhanced form of improvisational theater. Improvisational theater has a long tradition of using game structure in interactive storytelling. Most improv skits begin with a game-like premise that enables the performers to make up the scene as they go along within certain parameters. Whether they are narrative or abstract, the idea is to create a set of rules that dictate a range of spontane-ous and unplanned actions and interactions between performers.

It's no surprise that modern improvisational theater came into being at the same time as abstract painting and jazz music, all of which are forms of improvisational free expression. Jazz, like improvisational theater, provides a structure within which intuitive, unplanned, and spontaneous events can occur. Jazz is also a game of sorts, with its own set of rules and parameters.

In improvisational theater, to make spontaneous actions narrative in their expression requires placing the actors into a situation, generally a set of circumstances or a conflict that must be resolved. As a student of improvisa-tion, I was typically put into situations such as the classic elevator trap, in which a group of people are stuck inside an elevator. This is a simple example, but more complex scenarios can also be developed.

For a glimpse of how this integration of game and story can result in spontaneous stories, check out the Comedy Central staple, *Whose Line Is It Anyway?* Using a game show format, this program actually pits actors against each other to see how clever they can be at extemporaneous narrative. A standard exercise that occurs in every show is the party scene. One of the performers is assigned to be the host, and all the others are given slips of paper with descriptions of characters. The descriptions are outrageous things such as "thinks he's a fish," "only eats food that is red," "is a hypochondriac," "nosy neighbor," and so forth. Each character arrives one at a time and the host has to guess what and who they are. Another standard improv exercise in the show is the mystery object. Two actors take turns trying to come up with feasible uses and functions of a mysterious item, intuitively spawned by their physical interactions with it. Narrative constructs can also be created by presenting the actors with a given situation in which each character has a certain objective. In the middle of the scene, the host calls out changes in the progress of the scene, to which the actors must instantaneously respond. Example: two male characters are in a hot tub; the host introduces the fact that one of them is gay and is going to tell his friend. A vacationing married couple at the top of the empire state building; the husband tells the wife he wants a divorce. I've made these up, but they give you the idea of the sorts of situations that might evolve in a such a game.

Whose Line Is It Anyway? is one example of how improvisation has become a staple of comedy theater. Improvised skits are common, and improv is a great source of humor because the unexpected outcomes often amuse the actors as much as the audience. Comedy is also very forgiving. Even an improvisational misstep or blooper can ultimately have the desired effect of making people laugh, so no harm done.

But not all improvisation need be comic. Public Works implemented improv and theater game style exercises in their stage performances, but unlike *Whose Line...?,* not all of them were meant to be humorous. They also integrated the audience members into the process, soliciting story ideas, or even dreams from the audience. The dream piece often ended up being quite abstract, treading a line between theater and dance; a collaboration with a performance artist resulted in a series of abstract props that could be used to represent real objects, or merely become part of a spontaneous movement. Word jams were also common, a form of verbal jazz.

A contemporary ensemble that uses audience interaction and forms of improvisation in its show is the New York-based *Blue Man Group.* The three men, who paint themselves blue for each performance, invite audience members onstage at various moments to become part of the action. One piece has two or three audience members wearing LED "Thought bubbles" over their heads. Each individual can see the others' thoughts, but not his own. At the end of the show, rolls of toilet paper are released from the balcony and the audience pushes them forward, eventually burying itself in a thick layer of tangled paper. They pass it onstage to the troupe, who move it onto the stage and off, finally clearing the space for the audience to leave the theater.

The Cirque du Soleil, in its *Quidam* show, integrated audience members into the show as well. A group of "soldiers," oddly robotic characters in white paper suits, milled around the audience before the show formally began. They captured several members of the audience, put them it paper suits, and forced them to join the parade.

These kinds of simple audience interactions can lend another dynamic to the show, even if only one or two people get to go onstage. The way in which the audience is brought in is crucial. In both of these cases, the performers gave the onstage audience members something to do which they could learn as they did it. No instructions were necessary. They were heuristic in nature.

Whether it is a full narrative scene, an isolated exercise, or a simple invitation to the audience to get involved, I have found that the success of improvisation, like the success of a game or interactive story, is almost always the direct result of a sound structure. The talent of the actors obviously plays a major role, but it is a good and solid premise that generally leads the way. In the same way that "the play's the thing," in the case of improvisation, the "gameplay is the thing" in the case of games. In other words, it is the well-formulated construct of the interactive experience that can make or break the success of the spontaneous interaction.

THE RULES OF THE GAME (p. 420)

ART IS A VERB (p. 29)

USER OR PLAYER: THE CHOICE IS YOURS (p. 490)

THE INTERACTIVE ECOSYSTEM

The whole idea that there is an interactive business is a bit of an oxymoron. What we really have here is far more of a delicate ecology than a robust economy. Although interactive media is *not,* as the *old* media would have us believe, in its infancy, it is certainly in its puberty, which is even worse. As one might expect from an industry that could be considered to be no more than 15 years old as a mass medium, the entire system is completely unstable. It's a dangerous business to be in, kind of like walking on moving ground, an undulating mosaic of plate tectonics; everything is constantly shifting, and just when you think you know where you are standing, you find you are in a different continent entirely.

In a natural ecosystem, the goal is to reach a state of equilibrium. In such a state, life forms eat each other; disease keeps population growth at bay, while procreation assures its replenishment; various events occur and conditions fluctuate, maintaining the overall balance of the system. Occasionally, something called a "perturbation" occurs, generally created by an outside condition of some sort—a flood or a fire, a virus introduced from outside, or the introduction of humans, whose role in the natural seems to be to disrupt equilibrium. In most mainstream media, from television to books to magazines to film to radio to consumer electronic games, we can clearly see that there is a relative state of equilibrium. This has been achieved over a period of time. Perturbations, such as cable television or audio CDs occasionally cause disturbances to which the system must adapt. Although trends still come and go, it can be said that overall, these media have a fair amount of stability as industries.

The interactive media industry, on the other hand, is characterized by one gargantuan perturbation after another. These perturbations are not just minor shifts in balance or changes in condition like cable television or audio CDs. Often they are characterized by major shifts in technology or intensely erratic and often unpredictable market trends. Much of this instability is actually self-induced in an industry characterized by trendiness, unsubstantiated hype, ignorant arrogance, naive greed, paranoid secrecy, and imprudent and counterproductive business practices. All this drama is layered against a background of technological innovation, inspired genius, adventurous creativity, and a certain amount of idealism. In other words, the entire industry acts just like a teenager, which is exactly what it is.

What follows are four scenarios of new media start-ups. These case studies have been compiled from watching actual new media companies in the wild. I live among them unobserved, as one of their own, adopting their habits and lifestyles so that I might better understand the inner workings of life within their native habitat.

SCENARIO 1: MUCH ADO ABOUT NOTHING

A group of friends get together and decide they want to start an interactive media company. It is de rigeur to start with a cool-sounding name, so let's just, for purposes of discussion, call our little new media start-up "Hype!Media." Now most of the people in Hype!Media have little new media experience;

there's probably a failed director or screenwriter in the bunch; one of them might have worked on a CD-ROM or web site or two; under the best of circumstances, there might even be a new media star in their midst. They are not untalented or unintelligent, just unprepared and uninformed. They print up a bunch of hip-looking business cards on somebody's home Mac system and are in business.

The first thing to do, they think, is get an investor or two—venture capital, or "VC," as we call it in the biz. If the start-up company is smooth enough, they can usually talk some poor equally uninformed person into throwing a couple million bucks their way. They've written up a business plan of course, but it's more like a work of fiction. If they're really naive, they'll base their entire business plan on the speculative success of one or another of the latest hip and new technologies—the newest set-top box, the latest Internet authoring tool, or what have you. Somewhere during this process, they hack up a little demo, just a sampler of what they want to do, something to show around to prove how cool they are.

Next thing they do is open up a really hip office. They spend a lot of money on a build-out, some kind of fancy sign, and a bunch of overpriced furniture. They hire a pack of hot shots from Hollywood and Silicon Valley at exorbitant salaries and give them all a piece of the action. Many of these people are likely to be refugees from recently failed new media start-ups. After that, the next sensible thing to do is throw an IPO (initial public offering) and go public. Once you're on the stock market, you can make a bundle.

In the meantime, somebody gets the cockamamie idea of maybe developing some content. Only problem is, all the money is spent. So the company decides maybe it might just be time to get a client. They start having lunch meetings with everyone in town—Microsoft, Disney, Sony, Viacom, Philips, Time Warner, and if they're lucky, they might even get an audience with Dreamworks SKG. Everyone smiles and shakes hands and says, "This is great; we have to find a way to work together." This goes on for months.

These new media start-up types travel in packs, but they also have the herding characteristic of assembling at conferences or new media "salons." When you run into them at these events, they always tell you they're really busy, working on some new big project, but "I can't say what." Or, they are in "discussions" with one of the major studios or software companies, "but I can't say who." They also talk about their "proprietary technology," something really cool that only they can do, "but I can't tell you or else I'll have to kill you." The ones that have really good publicity will make it on to the cover of *Inter@ctivity* or *Net Guide* or something like that. People might even start buying their stock if there's enough heavy hitters backing them.

Finally, they achieve ultimate multimedia stardom—they make the cover of *Wired* magazine. The caption reads "Hype!Media Next Big Thing or Another Smoking Crater?" I don't think I need to tell you the result. Did I mention that they eventually released a title? Did I tell you that it was a big flop? And hey—how about those falling stock prices! This situation has happened dozens of times. Every month, another company that was last year's darling bites the dust. It's a speculative market, based on poor planning, inexperience, and fallacious beliefs about what interactivity is and what the market will bear.

Fortunately for all concerned, this painful and costly process only took about two years to play itself out, so everyone can move on to their next venture.

The key factor in both the success and failure of a new media start-up of this sort is arrogance. You must believe that you know everything, and that you have a better idea than everybody else. You also must believe this even if you have no experience and are completely ignorant of every aspect of the craft and business of interactive media.

If the founders of Hype!Media are lucky, they will cash in on their stock when it was flying high, and can walk away from their dismal failure with cash-lined pockets. That's why you may find these cocky folks walking away from the smoking crater with smiles on their faces. Now, they can move on to the next new media start-up, or perhaps graduate to the ranks of executives at major studios, which would put them smack in the middle of Scenario 2...

Scenario 2: The Bigger They Are, the Harder They Fall

A major film studio, record company, or consumer electronics company decides it needs to get in on the new media act. Thinking that because it has a great track record at making consumer electronics or box-office hit films, the company thinks that it will be far better at creating new media than anyone with any actual experience. So instead of contracting out its products to people who are qualified, the company decides to start an in-house media division. Figuring it has the advantage of an endless supply of cash, the company hires everybody good that it can get its hands on, and designates a floor or two in one of its buildings to create a new interactive media division. Let's call this company "Dinosaur Interactive."

The first thing a big company does when it decides to form a new media division is to assign an executive to it. When you read about it in the trades, the headline will say something like "Dinosaur Studios starts Interactive Division to be headed up by Joe Sixfigures." This executive will generally fall into one of three categories:

- **Executive Category #1:** The VP Interactive is a woman, usually the highest ranked woman in the company; this is especially true if it is a record company. In this case, she will receive a staff totaling one, little or no funding, and constant haranguing from the higher-ups as to why she is not producing any content.

- **Executive Category #2:** The VP Interactive will be a man who has been an executive in some other completely unrelated industry, such as soap, or possibly another medium such as magazine publishing. It is imperative that he have an MBA, a marketing background, and know nothing about interactive multimedia whatsoever.

- **Executive Category #3:** The VP Interactive will have recently left an executive position at a now-defunct new media start-up or division. If you are seeking a job as a highly paid new media executive, it helps to be involved with several failing enterprises. In fact, the Peter Principle prevails here—it seems that the more companies you have assisted driving into the ground, the more appealing you might be to perspective employers. The best position to be in is to have five to fifteen years of experience and at least three bankruptcies under your belt. If you find yourself in such a fortunate position, don't be surprised if headhunters start knocking at your door…

On a few occasions, somebody really good and experienced is hired by one of these companies to head up its new media division. Now mind you, it's not entirely the company's fault that its top people are inexperienced; the fact is, there aren't very many experienced people at the executive level. The mistake these companies usually make is to hire an inexperienced executive rather than an experienced multimedia person. The conventional wisdom is that if you're an executive, you can just, well, figure it out. That's why you're paid the big bucks. You are better off hiring as your head honcho someone who has more experience in interactive media. The repurposed executive will work from old models and paradigms, which, as we've seen time and time again, simply don't apply.

So, let's say we have Joe or Josephine Sixfigures in place. Because Dinosaur is a studio, it is of course rife with content. Therefore, by executive order, no original products are to be generated. The process begins with the first assignment to repurpose content. This content will be either generated from recent or upcoming "hits" in other media, or it will involve pulling some ancient relic out of a dusty archive somewhere for which there is no clear and present market. In neither case does there need to be any kind of rationale as to why this content ought to be made interactive.

If Dinosaur Interactive is a well-funded division, it spends its first year producing a small handful of titles at an enormous expense. Every once in a while by some fluke of nature, one of these titles does well in the market place. If it is not a well-funded division, it produces one title in two years—with a ridiculously low budget—that makes little if any impact on the market.

Eventually, depending on how much rope the company has allocated with which to hang itself, within two to three years, the division is forced to fold, proving once again that there is not money to be made in interactive media.

SCENARIO 3: MIGHTY OAKS FROM SMALL ACORNS GROW

Two brothers in a garage in the northwestern mountains, let's call them "Acorn Media." On their own time and at their own expense, with a very small budget, they decide to hack out a little game that's kind of a cross between a fairy tale and a mystery. Echoes of *The Hobbit* and *The Name of the Rose*, a simple yet sophisticated idea, with a very low-tech engine. Beautifully drawn. Well thought out interactivity. Interesting *original* content. No hype. Just really nice content.

Self-published at first, it builds up a head of steam on reputation alone, finally landing a publishing deal with a major software company, and topping off the charts as one of the best-selling CD-ROM titles of all time.

SCENARIO 4: WE MAKE OUR MONEY THE OLD-FASHIONEd WAY: WE EARN IT

We return in essence to where we started, to visit another new media start-up. This one is called "Workhorse Interactive." The people who start it are not dissimilar to the people at the ill-fated smoking crater "Hype!Media," with the exception of one fundamental thing…they work for a living.

This company usually starts in the following fashion: Just for the hell of it, a bunch of friends—who may or may not have previous interactive experience, but are inspired and have a good idea—get together and decide to try a hack. They are really smart and each team member is good at what they do. So they get together to build this thing. Sometimes, they build it for somebody, sometimes, just for their own interest, for the love of it, and for the challenge. Nine times out of ten, the project is something that is not done for pay, but is just an art project or experiment that they want to do. It could be anything from a web page to a CD-ROM to a kiosk at a venue or an event, or something to be shown at a conference or exhibition.

The thing about this product is that it's really good. The team worked hard at it. They weren't in it for the money. They just had a cool idea and they wanted to try it out. But whatever it was they were trying to do worked. They win critical acclaim, perhaps an award, and suddenly, everybody is talking about this thing they did.

Now generally, this group does not have a company, but all of a sudden, they find that they have people calling them up wanting to be clients. They think it might not be such a bad idea to formalize things, so they form a little company. Using the same creative ingenuity they used to come up with their initial product, they work hard to put together an elegant corporate ID, one that will make clients confident, but not scare them with a lot of, well, Hype!

This company is very wary of VC. In fact, they avoid it like the plague. Instead, they do projects for clients. They have a lot of work. They are always busy. Each piece they do is added to their body of work and they begin to develop a style and a reputation. Occasionally, they get written up somewhere, and they may even make the cover of *Inter@ctivity*, but they rarely end up on the cover of *Wired*. Some of their clients are big, some are small. They shy away from big entertainment projects or anything that requires a lot of pointless schmoozing. They turn jobs down if they think they don't meet the company's overall mission. They refer jobs to other companies, even instigating associates to form companies to take projects that they themselves cannot or do not want to do.

These companies usually don't make a ton of money in their first or second year, but they manage to do something that most new media companies or divisions cannot: They stay in business. They break even, and after a while, they even start to make a bit of a profit. They stay small, with a maximum size of about 40 at the outside.

Once in a while, a company like this will take off on the basis of venture capital, but it is usually very cautious about where the money comes from and what they have to give up to get it. Even if it is a VC-funded start-up, the partners and employees spend most of their time creating product, and a lot less of it at photo shoots.

The stories you have just heard are true. The names have been changed to protect the innocent as well as the guilty. If you are in the business, please accept my humble apologies if I made you laugh or cry (you know who you are). You also know that although there are a few variables and exceptions, what I have just painted is a fairly accurate portrait of the new media industry. This is essentially the way individual organisms within the interactive ecosystem operate. I did not explore the lineage of the older, more established interactive companies, of which there are a small handful. They are the backbone of the ecosystem of course. However, their patterns are more predict-able and therefore less needs to be said of them. They are companies like Lucasfilm, Brøderbund, and LucasArts, to name a few, who have managed to keep a steady business going for over five years. Once you have passed the five year mark, you are a veritable institution in the interactive ecosystem.

Now I'm going to let you in on a known secret. The best technique for assessing the overall interactive ecosystem, the best way to take the temperature of the new media is by charting the conference circuit.

Let me explain. Some cultures are on a solar calendar; others are on a lunar calendar. The Chinese have their new year and the Jews have theirs. Some people are reviving the Mayan calendar, and many other cultures have their own calendars based on various events and significant markers.

In the interactive business, we observe the Conference Calendar. The New Year is in August—SIGGRAPH—the Mother of All Digital Conferences. Started in 1973, SIGGRAPH was originally a meeting of the Special Interest Group for Graphics of the Association for Computing Machines, or ACM, but is now larger than the ACM's annual convention. Between 35 and 45 thousand people from around the world attend this annual Mardi Gras of digital inno-vation. It has grown from a mild-mannered conference on computer graphics for hard-core nerds to a veritable carnival that features a trade show, papers, panels, and exhibitions. SIGGRAPH provides a venue for everything from high-tech medical imaging to the latest webcasting techniques to haptic and tactile feedback systems to high-end simulators to special effects features such as *Toy Story* and *Babe*. SIGGRAPH deals with every aspect of computer graph-ics, from the sublime to the ridiculous, from the trivial to the magnificent, and now includes not only graphics, but interactive techniques in its purview.

Most new products are released at SIGGRAPH. Scientists write their papers, researchers and students stay up all night, filmmakers seek a coveted spot in the Electronic Theater—a nightly showcase of the best work of the year, and an interactive venue that has been featured since 1992 showcases everything from garage VR to "SIGkids," an interactive studio for children where they can create their own computer art and virtual worlds. On the commercial side, companies sweat blood to finish the newest releases of their software to demo at SIGGRAPH on the gigantic trade show floor. SIGGRAPH is where everybody makes announcements: mergers, spinoffs, new products, and new versions of old products.

Believe it or not, it's also party central. One year in Orlando, we had a party at Treasure Island. All of us were dancing barefoot on a Disney-style simulated beach in our bathing suits and listening to San Francisco Techno-World-Music Goddesses D'Cuk-oo. Industrial Light and Magic (ILM), the Bay Area effects company started by George Lucas, is known for its SIGGRAPH party, and so coveted is an invitation to one of these events that clever computer graphics artists at the conference have been known to generate counterfeits with the latest desktop publishing technologies. Suffice to say that computer graphics geeks know how to have a good time, which is why I have nicknamed SIGGRAPH "Summer Camp for Tech Nerds." During that one particular week in August, if you call any organization or company involved in computer graphics or interactive media of any kind, chances are there will be about four people around because everyone is at SIGGRAPH.

If my theory holds true, and conferences are the barometer of industry-wide health, then I would have to say that SIGGRAPH is surely evidence that overall, computer graphics and interactive media are alive and well. Each year, the conference grows in scope and size, and no matter what happens in any branch of digital media, overall, SIGGRAPH is about as robust and healthy as a convention can be. Furthermore, each year is characterized by further growth in the interactive branch; although the specific medium or market may shift from year to year, there is always more, and never less, interactivity to be seen at SIGGRAPH. So this is good news for us all. Companies and platforms may come and go, but overall, we're in pretty good shape.

By charting events at conferences, we can get a feel for what's happening to the industry overall. Conferences give you a pretty good idea of what people are interested in, although it is not always the lack of interest of the conference attendees, but perhaps waning attention by the conference organizers that can also have an impact.

In 1996, I did an exhibit for the IntermediaWorld convention, the oldest CD-ROM conference in America. This conference took place in one hall of San Francisco's Moscone Convention Center while a brand new Internet conference was going on across the street in the other hall. Like passengers running to the opposite side of a sinking ship, people walked out of the CD-ROM conference to go to the Internet event. By the last day, the place was practically empty because people were clearly more interested in the Internet than in the CD-ROM market. Part of the reason the conference had gone downhill in 1996 was because all the major CD-ROM publishers had, for the most part, pulled out, forfeiting their usual preferred-status booths to save up for other conferences that they felt were more important. That was the last year of IntermediaWorld, and 1996 in general, was not a great year for CD-ROM conferences.

On the other hand, 1996 was the second year of E3, the Electronic Entertainment Expo, a gigantic computer game conference. So successful was this event that it had to move to Atlanta in its third year because the L.A. Convention Center was too small! (For those who've never been there, the L.A. Convention

Center is quite huge.) The Internet World, WWW, and Netscape Developers Conference have all been doing well as of this writing in the spring of 1997. Both 1997 San Francisco Bay Area VRML conferences, focusing on the new online 3D technology, sold out, even though they were within weeks of each other. Meanwhile, a traditional VR conference soon afterward lost both regis-trants and exhibitors only weeks before it opened. Thus, we see a shift from high-end VR to VR on the web.

The interactive industry is characterized by trendiness, fickleness, speculation, and fear. Much of this is accounted for by the fact that the vast majority of the people in the business have been in it for a relatively short period of time. A person with five years experience is considered a veteran of interactive media, and that person is likely to be holding a major decision-making position at the company. This lack of experience leads to knee-jerk reactions and extreme industry-wide mood swings. One month you'll talk to people and they will tell you they're putting all their bets on the new such and such technology, and five months later, when the such and such technology turns out to be vaporware, or nobody has really adopted it, they'll be the first to tell you why it was doomed in the first place.

In this business, there are three behavior patterns and belief systems that drive a lot of faulty decision-making, leading to widespread economic instability.

The first of these factors is impatience and the fickleness that goes with it. People expect instant gratification and if a product doesn't make money right away, they give up on it. "Next big thing or smoking crater?" is not a joke: it is the reality of the evolution of new companies within the interactive ecosystem. The toast of the town at one conference can end up toast by the next one.

The second fault in this industry's decision making lies in the strange belief that the next big thing is going to be "it," and that after that, nothing will change anymore. This is sort of contradictory, but it's truly what people think. This set-top box will be the one that sells; this Killer App will set new stan-dards. But the rapid evolution of new technology ultimately precludes any level of confidence in the capability of technology to sustain itself, which is why keeping an open mind and not getting too attached to anything is a really good idea. In fact, it's probably a good way to approach life in general.

The third factor is naivete. People just don't do their homework. They have no idea what happened before. So they ignore all the past mistakes and make them anew. This is the tragic flaw that has killed many a new media company before it was barely out of diapers.

One of the reasons for this last tragic flaw is that everyone in the business wants to be a pioneer, but it's too late for that. So instead of going to the real pioneers, asking them questions, getting advice, studying their successes and mistakes, there is this widespread denial, based mostly on the (again) adolescent belief that "we got here first." Those of us who've been around a while get to watch the next generation make the same mistakes made by the one before them and the one before them... Rather than learn about the wheel and invent the car, most people in interactive media would rather reinvent the wheel and pretend it was their idea.

This is particularly the case in Hollywood, where arrogance abounds. People do things they honestly believe are new or innovative because they don't realize that it was done 20 years ago, it just required a lot more computer power.

 NEW MEDIA IS OLD NEWS (p. 358)

The industry would be a lot better off if its culture wasn't so alarmist. This running back and forth from one side of the ship to the other is a self-fulfilling prophecy of instability. The skittish attitude that goes with it makes for a very volatile ecosystem that, from the outside, looks unsure of itself and thoroughly confused.

I tend to watch this process with mild amusement. People ask me what I think about this and that and I have to just shrug. CD-ROM was supposed to have died in 1985, but it seems to have survived until 1997, and I bet it has a few good years left in it. Taking the long view helps. Also helpful is taking the view that the main objective is to maintain some overall state of dynamic equilibrium. This means that things are going to change. To expect them not to is absurd.

One thing I will tell you from personal experience and watching this industry since before there was one, anybody who aligns himself with a single technology, anyone who imagines that a certain piece of hardware is going to be the "television" of new media, is doomed to failure. I have never seen a single company survive on a single-platform policy. If you are basing your company's success on the success of a certain platform or hardware solution, or a given technology, prepare for smoking craterdom. Those who succeed are the ones flexible enough to shift with the trends, to move freely from one platform to the next as technology evolves. I myself have never worked in the same platform twice, which isn't hard to do since none of the platforms that are all the rage today even existed when I started in this so-called business.

Beware too of the doomsayers and soothsayers. If they tell you the Mac or the CD-ROM is dead, look again; if they tell you Windows is the be-all-end-all and it's going to take over everything, look again. Nothing is that simple. It never has been, and it never will be. Just because something isn't the biggest and most profitable doesn't mean it won't survive in the market. In the strange blockbuster mentality of our day, if you're not at the top of the heap, you're in the manure pile, but this simply is not the reality. Just because a company takes a loss one year, or just because its stock drops one month, doesn't mean it's over. Likewise, just because stocks rise or the company has a boom year, or a great IPO (initial public offering on the stock market) doesn't mean it's going to do well. In fact, companies that come on strong with a highly accelerated IPO generally find themselves in trouble within a year because inflated values and unrealistic expectations lead to poor performance-per-promise—a business tactic guaranteed to end in disaster. In fact, one of the most common outcomes of an inflated IPO is that the founder of the company gets ousted by the board. If a company overpromises to its investors, it is essentially digging its own grave.

Thus, it is wise to avoid alarmist attitudes, to get married to new technologies, or to run like lemmings where the rest of the pack is running. Unless of course, you're in the mood to go for a swim.

Just a bit of research and some consultation with someone who might in fact know more than you can save you a lot of grief in the end. Or in the beginning. All you have to do is look backward and see what people looking forward were saying 15, 10, even 5 years ago, hell, even 5 months ago. This kind of overview will give you a new kind of perspective that will help you take things as they come, go with the flow, and remain on an even keel, even while everyone else is running to the stern and jumping overboard.

 THEORY OF MEDIA EVOLUTION (p. 468)

SOCIAL CAPITALISM (p. 425)

DANGER: KILLER APP (p. 152)

INTERACTIVITY IS SUBVERSIVE

No matter which way you look at it, interactivity is inherently subversive. The hierarchical status quo is a one-to-many, one-way broadcast paradigm that puts centralized control of the media in the hands of a powerful few. As we've learned over the past few years, he who controls media controls culture. No matter what its politics, every political system is built on an infrastructure of information. The policies and doctrines of that system are integral to the way that the society manages and controls the flow of information. Throughout history, revolutions have been lost and won on the basis of information. In the

Middle Ages, also known as the Dark Ages, control and social stratification were maintained by sequestering all information and books; no one could read except the monks, and all books were kept in monasteries and could only be reproduced by hand. The democratic system, on the other hand, was built on the foundations of the printing press—the capability to cheaply mass-produce information and distribute it unhindered.

Interactive media in general and the Internet in particular are the very antithesis of the centralized, broadcast media infrastructure. The Internet is completely horizontal and decentralized, free of hierarchy, totally accessible to anyone who can get on to a computer (most public libraries now have Internet stations), and virtually impossible to censor or control.

 CENSURING CENSORSHIP (p. 124)

The Internet culture is built on the core philosophy of the hacker ethic—namely, a belief that all information should be free to everyone. The computer gives us a way to multiply, store, and disseminate information at a scale heretofore unknown. The hacker ethic is one of ultimate democracy. Its tenets are as follows:

- You are only as good as your mind
- Information belongs to everyone
- The computer is a tool of empowerment

Just as the bohemian underground set up printing presses, and later Xerox machines, to disseminate all manner of art and propaganda, the hacker ethic is the arbiter of empowerment to the people. Furthermore, the hacker ethic encourages the adage "Question Authority." Hackers are smart. They can outsmart anyone. Here's a prototypical conversation I once had with a hacker friend. Me: "Can you bootleg this software for me?" He: "Is it copy protected?" Me: "Yes," He: "Well, that will make it a little harder." Hackers love to break in, they love to beat the system, they love to prove that all you need is a little ingenuity and the right string of code and you can do anything.

 STEAL THIS DATA: SHAREWARE AND THE HACKER ETHIC (p. 454)

The Computer Revolution is the ultimate revenge of the nerds. When I was a kid, computers were extremely nerdy, and anyone who understood them was doomed to spend his or her life a virgin. Today, being a programmer is about the coolest thing you can be, especially if you are programming hip content such as games or multimedia, or better yet, military flight simulation. "Billionaire Nerds" such as Bill Gates and the Steves (Jobs & Wozniac of Apple fame) are laughing all the way to the bank at those who poked fun at their pocket protectors and slide rules. In those days, guys with horn-rimmed glasses couldn't get a date, but in today's Digital Hollywood, blonde starlet-types can be seen hanging on the arms of would-be software moguls. Although I myself wasn't a computer nerd in school, I was definitely a bit too bookish and brainy for my own good. Today, I proudly refer to myself as a "geek girl."

The shift from industrial age to information age has had a major impact on the value system of this country. Because the primary system of values in America is based on profit and market demographics, the billionaire boy's club of tech moguls have changed the face of...well, *Forbes*, *Fortune*, and the *Wall Street Journal*. As little as 20 years ago, wealth was primarily generated by industrialists. Thus, the value of manufacturing and the machine age, and the need for mass-production labor, drove both the economic and the social milieu of the country. If you read the *Fortune 500* of the late 1990s, you will clearly see that the vast majority of wealth in this country is now being generated by either high technology or media content companies. Chip manufacturers, software companies, major studio/network conglomerates, and consumer electronics companies lead the pack of profitable companies in America. The electro-mechanical age has given way to the electronic age, which has precipitated a major shift in our cultural priorities.

I believe that interactivity represents a revolution. Just as the printing press created the tools for subversive propaganda over the past two centuries, interactivity is a tool of change and revolution for this generation. Interactivity is a reaction against the passivity of television, a medium that spoon feeds us images, information, even emotions; a medium that has created three generations of "couch potatoes"—the Al Bundys and Homer Simpsons of the world. This television-induced complacency is beginning to shift and change dramatically. Young children shoot at the TV now instead of just absorbing its output. These same children get their hands on computers... and you have the unthinkable. They turn away from their televisions because they actually *like* intellectual stimulation; they *want* to learn, explore, and take the reigns. Most kids, as it turns out, would rather be involved in an active interchange with the video screen.

 NERD VERSUS COUCH POTATO (p. 345)

As these children grow up, accustomed to more and more interactivity and responsiveness from their environment, they will come to expect it...they will come to demand a level of empowerment at every level. Even now, on the Internet, the passive models for both entertainment and advertising have failed miserably. The basic psychology and indeed the doctrine on which our entire media infrastructure is built neither understands nor has the capability to support a horizontal infrastructure based on individual empowerment coupled with a strong sense of community. Television is a tool of hypnosis for the capitalist machine. The computer, although it can be used for forms of hypnosis, is a tool of empowerment for the user. It was designed to be that on every level, from the word processor to the Internet to desktop publishing. Therefore, the computer will ultimately be a tool of change, a tool that is anti-establishment, or perhaps, one might hope, "re-establishment."

Marshall McLuhan said, "The medium is the message," and nowhere is this more true than in interactive media. The message is so profoundly built into the paradigm of the medium that it is pure folly to try to use it to carry any other message. The techniques of repurposing old media and trying to put passive paradigms into an interactive context have repeatedly failed. We should take note of this. The medium itself is trying to tell us something. It's trying to tell us that it doesn't want to be television. It doesn't want to be video on demand. It wants to be its own organism. As the centralized infrastructure of communications media tries to eat its way down from the top, spending millions of dollars, but never quite "getting it," the grass roots movement spreads from the bottom like wildfire. Few entertainment industry companies have been able to create anything on the Internet as wildly popular and successful as those things that are created by users themselves. The Internet is a user-built phenomenon. It is a venue in which people have come to enjoy entertaining themselves and each other. It's more like a party than a medium; it's a place and an environment where everybody gets to be a star, not just for 15 minutes, but for as long as he or she can sustain hits on a site. If the entertainment industry hopes to be a success in this new venue, it must evolve past its didactic, one-way mentality and understand that its job is not to feed entertainment to the audience, but to provide the audience with ways to entertain itself.

For 60 years, our culture has been influenced by the centralized media infrastructure of television, film, radio, and newspapers. The media aristocracy has told us how to dress, how to act, it has given us standards of beauty too high to reach, and standards of behavior too low to imagine. It has taught us that sex is obscene, but killing is not. It has elected presidents and acquitted murderers. It has babysat our children, instilling in them the very values that we ourselves shun, but accept nonetheless because we feel we have no control over their source.

The influence of media can and will change. Today, more and more families are sitting down in front of the computer rather than the television. Instead of watching *Married with Children*, a program that is disdainful of family life, a family will go to AlphaVille, build their own virtual environment, and get together with other families to make a stadium, a virtual "field of dreams," where everyone can play. Children will learn to talk by using voice-activated avatars. Instead of watching *Melrose Place*, young people are beginning to go online and create their own interactive melodrama, through collaborative role play games where they get to be the heroes and heroines of their own stories. Clueless, Hollywood continues in its old paradigm, going no further than the belief that the Internet is just a really good place to advertise movies.

 CYBERSPACE CADETS: VIRTUAL COMMUNITIES AND AVATAR WORLDS (p. 146)

The government is equally clueless. As the Supreme Court grapples with censorship, Netizens canvas their congressmen by circulating e-mail spams (large electronic mailings) and chain letters to thousands of their compatriots throughout the web. Interactivists form mailing lists and keep each other apprised of the latest civil action, the most recent human rights violations overseas, or this week's installment of the Internet censorship drama. Feminism is alive and well online as women's political groups form their own web sites and mailing lists to discuss pertinent issues and plot ways to harness the power of computers to empower themselves politically, socially, and technologically.

Don't get me wrong—the Internet is no Utopia. Much occurs online that reflects the darker side of subversion. Hate groups and neo-Nazis use the Internet to keep in touch and recruit new members. Timothy McVeigh, convicted and sentenced to death for mass murder in the Oklahoma City bombing case, was an America Online member who sported the moniker "MadBomber." The "Heaven's Gate" cult, which participated in a group suicide in March of 1997, made their income as web site designers on the Internet, and used their own web site to promote their cause and draw in new members. Along with subversion comes perversion, as sex peddlers use the web to promote kiddie porn.

Not only the web, but all interactive media has built into it an essential message of empowerment. Even something as simple as the Macintosh interface opened to an entire generation of artists and designers a level of technological empowerment that had previously been reserved for the military, research institutions, and big businesses. Turbo-charged with computers that understood them, creative types have been able to start up a variety of small entrepreneurial businesses in tiny home offices that used to require whole corporations to deploy. Anyone with these tools suddenly has the ability to push themselves and create in ways that were not available to us in the past. For less money than it costs to buy a new car, you can set up a digital studio in your home that would enable you to produce a magazine, a web site, a record album, a CD-ROM, or a video. Nonlinear editing systems, for example, which used to cost a minimum of $100,000, can now be bought for about 1/10th of that. It is so easy to make an album these days that most semi-serious bands are now producing their own home-brewed CDs. The best-selling CD-ROM title, *Myst*, was produced by two brothers in their garage. Now, we are beginning to see the next step—transmedia experiences that take digital assets and distribute them across all media simultaneously, from the Internet to CD-ROM to printed products to toys to television shows.

Distribution is control. In the published media, it is the distributors who control what is seen, and it is the distributors who make all the money. The same is true in broadcast media. But the new digital empowerment, in which you can produce everything yourself and distribute it yourself over the Internet, is going to radically change the politics of distribution. Rock bands no longer have to be dictated to by record companies, whose middle-aged marketing execs drive popular culture based on what *they* think kids will want. In the early 90s, the classic line from record company executives was: "We already have a girl band." Fortunately, now they are happy to take multiple girl bands, having made the mind-boggling discovery that the audience could actually accept more than one female artist at a time. This is the kind of attitude that exists within a centralized distribution infrastructure where a 45 year-old man who lives in a house in Beverly Hills decides what a 16 year-old grunge girl in the Valley wants to listen to. Now, she can decide for herself; and if she has a band, she can make a record and the hell with executive myopia.

The Interactive Revolution has been a long time coming, but it has finally arrived. Ironically, it is the Internet, originally developed by the government, that may in fact turn out to be its undoing. The military network that became the World Wide Web is now the madly anarchic hub of an international grassroots movement. No longer do we have to think globally and act locally; now we can act as globally whenever we feel like it. Even the boundaries between nations themselves become immaterial. The Internet is the ultimate *vox populi* (Latin for "voice of the people"), in which I can have friends in Serbia and in Santa Fe, and in which my community can span the globe based not on geography, or even nationality, but purely on common goals and interests.

Before the Internet, interactive revolutionaries had to work in relative isolation. In a certain way, I think we were all waiting for a way to break through…to reach out and to connect. Now, we have that. The moment that you have people gathering, whether in a public place or a virtual space, you have the potential for community and empowerment. In fact, all attempts to squelch revolutions are made on the basis of two things: limiting the ability of people to gather in large groups, and controlling the flow of information. The medium is the message. The Internet makes any control of either of these things impossible. Tiananmen Square can no longer occur; that same gathering can take place online and include people from everywhere on the planet who support the cause. Thus, revolutionaries can support each other on a global level.

DIGITAL SOCIALISM (p. 180)

William Gibson's tales of hacker heroism all revolve around renegade cyber cowboys breaking into the "Matrix" (a giant three-dimensionally depicted bank of data), and messing with the data banks of huge multinational corporations. What happens when the general public becomes its own multinational entity, when it turns out to be the hackers, and not the corporations, that control the digisphere, and they're all in this thing together?

If you are sitting there wondering, What's going to happen? What's she going to say? Forget it. I'm not in the business of predicting the future—I'm in the business of creating it. And you should be too. Think about it. Think about your own values. There are probably issues that deeply trouble you, social and political conditions that outrage you, creative problems that challenge your mind, ideas or movements that excite you. Instead of being a passive activist, an armchair pundit spending all your time talking to the television about the ills of the world, wouldn't you rather be an interactivist? Whatever you come away with from reading this book, I hope it will be this: That this is really all about you. That the Interactive Revolution is *your* revolution. That you do not have to let this happen to or around you; you can be part of it at a variety of different levels and in ways that manifest your own unique ideas, values, experiences, and abilities.

Maybe you will get the spark of that somewhere in the pages of this book. When that happens, that's the time to put the book aside (only temporarily of course) and sit down at your computer, stop by your local library or cyber café and see what's up. Maybe you can find a community of people with the same concerns and interests. Instead of watching the future come and go, do something about it. Because that's what this technology—and this book—are really all about.

 AUTODIDACTIC COMMUNALISM (p. 83)

STEAL THIS DATA: SHAREWARE AND THE HACKER ETHIC (p. 454)

BROAD OR NARROW: THE CASTING COUCH (p. 113)

IT'S NOT THE TELEVISION THAT'S INTERACTIVE, IT'S THE PEOPLE

When I was a young child, there was a program on that was, to my knowledge, the first real attempt at interactive television. It was called *Winky Dink &*

Me. This program involved buying a special kit that included erasable markers and a piece of plastic film that you placed over the television screen. At crucial points in the cartoon, Winky Dink would get in trouble. Your job was to draw the appropriate component into the scene—a net, a balloon, a bridge, or whatever was required to save Winky Dink. Of course, whether you drew it or not, Winky Dink was always saved, but it was fun trying to beat the clock and insert the appropriate piece to help him out. In addition to being fun, from a commercial standpoint, Winky Dink had a built-in ancillary product—the kit you had to buy to interact with the show. The program was discontinued because too many children were content to use available materials and draw directly on to their television screens with crayons and permanent markers instead of using the plastic film and special pen—perhaps Winky Dink had a little too much interactivity for the prevailing culture of the time (I don't think parents were too crazy about it either). As far as I know, this was the first in a series of unsuccessful attempts to bring interactivity to the television.

 Nerd versus Couch Potato (p. 345)

I believe that all attempts to date to make television interactive have failed for one simple reason: culture. Each and every one of them have ignored the cultural and behavioral context in which people watch and experience the television medium. The most common mistake has been to try to make the television act like a computer, such as Web TV. Compared to computers, televisions are essentially stupid machines; they have little intelligence built into them, so to make them function like a digital processor is misguided at best. Furthermore, they are built on a one way street, and there is little opportunity for reciprocal interaction with the audience. The second most common mistake is inherent in the content of the programming. Whether the television is trying to mimic a computer or not, virtually all interactive television launches have tried to introduce entirely new genres of content that have little or nothing to do with what people expect or want from their televisions. Because it is content that sells technology, the lack of acceptable content will always be a barrier of entry, even if the technology itself is viable.

All this notwithstanding, there are certain ways in which television is already interactive, even given its existing infrastructure. This interaction has been largely of a cultural and social nature. It is not about the audience controlling the content of the television via technical means, but influencing it through cultural movements. Thus, the relationship between "the audience" and the television can be studied as an interdynamic interaction which exists outside of the technology and within the bounds of the current television framework. It is ultimately the people and not the technology that carry the interactivity. Once we begin to see the ways in which people have created their own interactivity with their televisions, our jobs as interactive designers suddenly look a lot easier. We can let the viewer tell us how he or she wants to relate to the television and build our interactivity to suit reality.

The intimate relationship between Americans and their televisions started almost from the beginning. The sitcom, which was among the first genres unique to TV, was a comical homage to everyday life. The typical sitcom protagonist was an "everyman," or "everywoman" (in the case of sitcom innovator Lucille Ball) who bore a striking resemblance to the family into whose living room they broadcast every week. Game shows were also unique to the living room, which invites a certain level of audience involvement. Most game show contestants are "average Americans," the everyman and every-woman once again, and most include the proverbial "studio audience." As far as the at-home audience goes, who can watch *Jeopardy* from their living room sofas without calling out the answers? They have even introduced an ancillary product to address this most visceral of human urges—a handheld device that enables you to be a "virtual" contestant on the show. *You Don't Know Jack!* is a perfect example of how the inherent interactivity of a television genre can be effectively translated into an interactive experience. This enormously success-ful CD-ROM-cum-online game show departs little from the classic genre, enabling the player to live out the fantasy of being a game show contestant. The live broadcast (carried over from radio) also brought a level of immediacy to television programming that film certainly lacked, and married it with the visual absent from radio.

Television has evolved over the decades, but it was really in the 1980s and 90s that we have begun to see the boundaries of television's passivity pushed to the extreme. Much of this boundary pushing is being done by the viewers. The audience creates its own dynamic with the medium that leads to levels of involvement. The creators of television can be at times ill-prepared or in some cases even oblivious to these events. As "broadcasters," they are concerned with an interchange with the audience only insomuch as it involves the on off switch or the remote control. Whether premeditated or not, these phenomena demonstrate how fully integrated television is with our lives, and how much it has become a rallying point around which we all connect. Television is, as Marshall McLuhan pointed out, the electronic hearth, the media campfire around which we all sit to share our collective mythologies. What follows are a series of case studies that have, I believe, pushed the passive boundaries of television to the limit and revealed its potential for interactivity. In every case, it is not technology but people—whether they be creative innovators or restless viewers—who drive this process forward.

In the late 1960s, a program called *Sesame Street* revolutionized children's television. My sister and I, by that time already too old for the program, came home excitedly from school every day to watch it. It was the first educational television program that combined principles of education and entertainment, the first "edutainment" product, well before the term came into use.

Launching at a time of innovation in early childhood education, *Sesame Street* was a televised Montessori school, the Head Start of TV programs, and the first heuristic children's show. *Sesame Street* targeted pre-school children of all ages. It was multi-cultural and urban, hip, and sophisticated. It was also one of the first cases where television addressed the issue of English as a second language. Asian and Hispanic characters were featured, and sometimes, they even spoke in their native tongues!

Sesame Street was major departure from the standard educational children's fare of the time, which ran along the lines of *Mr. Rogers*, *Captain Kangaroo*, and *Romper Room*, all shows that to a certain extent or another were patronizing to sophisticated city-dwelling children. *Sesame Street* was educational without being didactic. It did not spoon-feed children educational content, but framed it within a playful world full of characters, sketches, animation clips, and music videos before there were really music videos. It was also the first children's TV show that was just as fun for adults as for kids. The Children's Television Workshop people realized that the parents were the ones turning the dial, so why not give them some added value as well?

Although *Sesame Street* is arguably the most influential educational television program of all time, it did more than revolutionize children's TV. It revolutionized the entire television medium. It did this by creating an entirely new television vernacular. The *Sesame Street* style was characterized by one outstanding quality: it was non-linear. The quick-cut montage style and total disregard for any sense of sequence set it apart as an art form unto itself.

Borrowing its style less from traditional TV programs than from the conventions of television commercials, *Sesame Street* influenced an entire generation with a completely different television aesthetic. *Sesame Street*, although it was a staple of commercial-free public television, was itself an advertisement for education. Its look and feel was aggressive and high-energy, rife with hip, multi-entendre humor, bright colors, fast animation, quick-cutting, catchy, rhythmic music, and memorable soundbites—all geared to the short attention spans of children. It was a great model, but one that might ultimately have resulted in a certain backlash—that many adults reared on *Sesame Street* still have the attention spans of children. Indeed, it was the first *Sesame Street* generation that created MTV, the ultimate in short attention span television.

One of the greatest leaps in television's evolutionary history was the advent of cable TV. We were the first on our block to get pre-remote-control cable (which tells you how long ago *that* was). In the beginning, cable was commercial-free (as it still should be, but don't get me started...). Early cable was like "the

People's Republic of Television." It had tons of educational programming, and a full spectrum of novelty children's shows, such as *Speed Racer* and the *Little Rascals*.

The weirdest things on cable were the public access shows created by viewers. At that time, there were not major networks on cable and it was not yet saturated with programming as it is today. So during downtime, our local cable station, "Theta Cable," rented out studio space and broadcast time. Anyone who wanted to could rent a studio for an hour and broadcast their own show. It was amazing what kinds of things you might come upon late at night or during that twilight hour of TV between 3:00 and 5:00 when all the latchkey kids were home unsupervised with their television-baby-sitters. That was around the time we began to see the first Infomercials, which in some ways could be viewed as an early attempt at interactive television ("Dial the number on your screen…"). Early cable was thus a bit of a free-for all, not like the early Internet. Anyone who wanted to buy studio time (at that stage of the game quite inexpensive) could go on TV and have their say—thus fulfilling Andy Warhol's contention that everyone was entitled to their 15, or in this case, 30 minutes of fame.

About 15 years later, long after cable was commercialized and co-opted by a new generation of networks, I was watching late-night television and came across one of these 70s-style public access shows. It was hilarious—two long-haired stoner kids jamming on their guitars and interviewing their high school math teacher. It even had its own crude title effects. The show was called *Wayne's World*, and it wasn't until the commercial break that I came to the realization that I was watching a *Saturday Night Live* sketch.

Another genre that has always had an interactive aspect is the TV talk show. In the 60s and 70s, my grandmother used to hang out with Merv after dinner every night, freely conversing with him and his celebrity guests throughout the hour-long salon visit (she never liked Johnny, I guess because he was always telling dirty jokes). Early talk shows focused on conversations with the rich and famous, but then in the 80s, a new breed of program emerged—the sensationalist talk show in which the hosts set up inflammatory situations that pitted guests against the "studio audience."

Most of these exploitation interview shows are exercises in moral intolerance. Audience members are encouraged to pass judgment on guests and to argue freely about what they ought and ought not do. Shows such as *Geraldo*, *Oprah*, *Sally Jesse Rafael*, *Rikki Lake*, and *Jenny Jones* (in order of de-evolution) are designed to hold our attention and keep us from switching channels during commercials. Tag lines such as "Gay bikers," "Women who dismember their men," and "Mother-and-daughter phone sex queens" are all designed to catch, grab, and keep your attention in a high-stakes game of remote control roulette. The interaction that arises from shows such as this can sometimes have fatal results. One man was murdered after it was revealed on one such program that he had a crush on a homophobic male coworker. It is just these sorts of freak events that reveal the gray area between television and "real life."

 ## Remote Control Group (p. 410)

Perhaps one of the most significant evolutionary leaps in television in the 1980s played an interesting trick in terms of media evolution. That innovation was "Music Television." Television had taken story away from radio 20 years earlier, and MTV took music back in trade. It also introduced a new form of nonlinear television. Before MTV, television was administered in 30-minute doses with 30–60 second commercial interruptions. MTV's fast-paced style and song-based content made it look like the programming was interrupting the advertising. The pop song took the place of the sitcom as the conventional unit of television and the music video was born.

MTV was one of the most daring things ever to happen to television. The convention of the song-based video opened the door for a level of creative expression that had been decidedly lacking in television fare up until that point. Music videos bore more of a resemblance to the experimental films of Stan Brakhage (*Dog Star Man*) and Maya Derien (*Meshes of the Afternoon*) than to anything else on TV. Because of its short form, each video could become its own little gem, its own audiovisual blast. Because they were based on poetry and not narrative, the opportunity for expression was vast. MTV made the video medium itself a pop art form, and became fertile ground for technical innovation as well. Music videos evolved an entirely new approach to the use of special effects, which has since infiltrated virtually every aspect of the video vernacular. Shaky angular cameras, cut-off frames, the use of a variety of filter effects, shooting black and white as a stylistic device, blending text with visuals—all of these techniques first made their appearance on MTV. The MTV bumper became an art form in and of itself. There is no question that MTV gave a rocket boost to the computer graphics industry.

It's important to recognize that MTV by no means invented video as an art form—it merely put it on television. One of the most influential video artists, and a man whose influence can be seen splashed all over the music video genre, is Nam June Paik. Paik, a conceptual artist and sometime member of the Fluxist movement, pushed the envelope of video in every direction, and continues to do so. His use of video as an abstract medium, and his rapid-fire collage style that integrated existing footage with abstract graphics, were perfectly suited to the task of supporting pop music songs. Paik also made the video wall an art form and was one of the first artists to do multi-site video performances.

ART IS A VERB (p. 29)

MTV had another unanticipated but not unwelcome side effect on the evolution of television. No one would have guessed it, but this strange new genre actually contributed to an increase in the overall quality of the television commercial. Competing with the audio-visually rich world of music videos, and borrowing from their high-intensity short-form vocabulary, television commercials actually started to get better. MTV was fun to watch not only for the music videos, but also for the ads. Huge companies like Nike and Coca-Cola began to address their advertising to a young, hip market; to capture that market, they had to speak their language. And their language was "MTV."

Now, you can certainly argue that MTV very possibly ruined the music industry as much as it fed it. It made it almost impossible to get a record deal if you didn't look like a fashion model. Attitude became as important as (if not more important than) the music. MTV could drive hit songs as readily, if not moreso, as the radio. Not coincidentally, the first video ever shown on MTV was called "Video Killed the Radio Star" by the Buggles.

MTV also spawned entire cultural and fashion movements. Would the grunge and Hip-Hop movements have become such widespread movements if not for the venue in which to parade their trademark sense of style? MTV became a theater of youth culture in which the music became even more of a metaphor than it already was for a certain lifestyle, aesthetic, and belief system. Because MTV was so incredibly profitable, it took youth culture out of the niche zone and legitimized it as a major market share. Before MTV, fringe youth culture existed on the fringe. MTV brought it to center stage, turning fringe into mass, alternative into mainstream.

I don't think it is any coincidence that the generations that spawned and embraced MTV were also generations that were raised on *Sesame Street*. The *Sesame Street* cadence really set the pace for the nonlinear MTV paradigm. I would venture to say that there is likely to be a great deal of influence coming from both of these movements into the interactive designs we see emerging now and in the future.

 THE ADD GENERATION (p. 17)

Continuing on our journey of interaction within broadcast television model, who can overlook the classic image of the sofa jock playing virtual coach to his favorite team. The phenomenon of audience involvement in sports events dates back to the gladiators and beyond, but nowhere does it stand out more than in the average American living room. There are few events on television which elicit such emotional zeal, and to see one or two people on their sofa leap three feet into the air at the sight of a touchdown is a remarkable and to some extent mind-boggling sight. Nowhere else in American culture do you see such passion or such identification. Most Americans have a stronger relationship with their hometown baseball, basketball, or football team than they do with their community, their job, their union, their religious group, and in some cases, even their families. I have seen no other instance where television has precipitated such a strong visceral reaction, and one that so blatantly begs for interaction. Imagine what it would be like if you could actually *do* something about the game. What if you really could kill the umpire or call a time-out and explain *your* defensive strategy to the team? Perhaps it's the very fact that you can't that makes the experience so compelling.

I once had an amazing experience that demonstrated the amazing power of televised sports in America. I was riding my bike down a New York City street around 10 pm one evening. I noticed that it was unusually quiet on the street for New York; it was as if everyone had decided to stay in for the evening. Everything was startlingly quiet. Then I heard this sound…it was like nothing I'd ever heard. It was the sound of screams of joy, hoots, whoops, and cheers coming out of apartments, storefronts, even cars and taxicabs. And then it dawned on me—it was the last night of the 86 World Series…the championship that pitted the New York Mets against the Boston Red Sox. I have never before or since seen (or heard) such a spontaneous eruption of unified emotion…and to think it was precipitated by the television.

There is more to television interactivity than just the programs or even our reaction to them. There is a whole other aspect to television that lives beyond the 30-minute increment. The most fascinating aspect of television is not what happens while we're watching the programs, but what happens in between. The vast majority of audience interaction with the television happens when it is turned off. I first became patently aware of this when I was in junior high school during a period when our family did not have a television set. I was already predisposed to feeling alienated and outcast, so this only added insult to injury. My peers would come to school literally speaking an alien tongue. For months they were greeting each other with the words "Nanu Nanu." Everyone seemed to know what this meant, but I felt left in the dark. I just played along, but I had no idea what was going on. Finally one night I happened to see an episode of *Mork & Mindy.* A young actor named Robin Williams played an alien from outer space for whom "Nanu Nanu" was the common greeting. Without access to these social cues, I felt that I was not a full participant in teen culture.

Many years later I had a similar experience, now seen through the eyes of an interactive designer, which further reinforced my awareness of the social dynamics precipitated by television. I was doing some freelancing for an architectural firm, and I happened to overhear a conversation between some of my coworkers in an adjacent cubicle. They were gossiping about some people they knew in common. They were talking about a friend of theirs—a girl who had either fallen or gotten pushed off a boat—and they questioned whether it was an accident, a suicide, or a murder attempt. There was nothing about the way they were talking that would have suggested that this was not an actual person they were talking about. They compared notes as to what had happened the way most people normally do when trading hearsay. It was only after nearly an hour passed that I realized they were talking about *Melrose Place*. The thing that really amazed me was that they had easily spent as much time discussing the show as they had watching it. Considering how many hours the average American spends in front of the television, it is a bit alarming to think that they may spend an equal amount of time talking about it.

This is certainly nothing new. An entire culture of dialogue has arisen around daytime soap operas, and early so-called "nighttime soaps." Viewers discuss these shows among themselves in between programs, and there are even entire magazines devoted to these shows. It's also worth pointing out the soap opera/ gossip culture is primarily a female culture, that nighttime soaps, at least in the early days of *Dynasty* and *Dallas*, were primarily targeted to a female audience. Women love the character-driven story and relish in tales of conflict, deception, and manipulation. They will spend hours psychoanalyzing fictitious characters, watching mystery shows, or reading mystery novels and trying to figure out "whodunit." They love examining and debating the whys and wherefores of people and their motivations. When evening fare embraces these paradigms, and crime, intrigue, and politics are added to the mix, men come to the party too and we have a spontaneous form of interactive television.

Most serialized drama uses this technique to create a fan culture whose main objective is to bring people back week after week. Leaving audiences in suspense is a high art form, and one that drives viewership in these genres. Shows such as *The X-Files*, *NYPD Blue*, and *ER*, and even some that don't have letters in their names, use the week-to-week cliffhanger to maintain show loyalty. A classic tactic is the "will they or won't they?" hook in which we keep coming back in pursuit of the question: will these two characters *ever* get it on, or are they going to just flirt forever??? (*Moonlighting, Friends, Caroline in the City…*)

Although this "in between time" interaction is what drives the popularity of many TV shows, few television directors have ever fully exploited this to its full potential. One exception is *Twin Peaks*, the delightfully surrealistic suspense-thriller-mystery series by filmmaker David Lynch. Lynch's cinematic mastery, as first revealed in the unsettling *Eraserhead*, has always been in creating characters and stories that leave you with more questions than answers. He departs from traditional film conventions by setting up conflicts that are never resolved and leaves you with a veritable tapestry of loose ends. Although this technique has varying levels of success in cinema where there is a certain expectation of resolution by the end of a 120-minute feature, it is a perfect paradigm for the episodic genre of television. Lynch leaves a lot up to the imagination, which can provide viewers with hours of fun-filled excitement before and after every show.

Twin Peaks was not just a television program, it was an event. It aired while I was working at Edwin Schlossberg Incorporated and living among a small village of interactive designers. The weekly ritual became a passion among the resident *Twin Peaks* aficionados. The day after the show, we would spend hours discussing what happened, trying to find clues, sharing insight from previous shows. Those who had seen episodes that others missed went into elaborate descriptions of the missed shows. Who was the "one armed man?" Why did the bird get shot? What happened in the cabin? What was in Laura Palmer's diary? We continued the discussion all week. Then, the day before the next show, we regrouped and tried to predict what might occur, or compared notes as to why certain things had happened.

For 29 weeks, all we talked about at work was *Twin Peaks*. It was our collective obsession as, each week, we tried to untangle this web of surreal and bizarre events and characters. What did it all mean? We all knew that we would never know for sure, but relished in the act of collective pondering. To me, there have been few other epiphanic moments in which I came to see that television was, after all, a social medium, even in its inherent unsociability.

Twin Peaks also had another hidden feature that was quite innovative. It was the first example I have ever seen of something that is now being called "transmedia"—using multiple media in conjunction with one another to tell a story. This is not the same as creating ancillary or "spinoff" products. Instead, the idea is to bury elements of the story in different media so that the viewer/ audience can put the pieces of the story together from different sources.

It is a shame that more people did not discover *The Secret Diary of Laura Palmer*. It was discovered during the series that the mysterious teenage murder victim Laura Palmer kept two diaries—one conveyed the normal teenage concerns, and a second was the alleged real diary of her innermost secrets. This second diary was in the custody of a strange, agoraphobic man whom Laura had met through her "Meals on Wheels" program. What few of the even most ardent fans realized was that this diary had actually been published in book form. By reading the secret diary *and* watching the show (the diary itself made no sense whatsoever by itself), you could actually solve the mystery and find out the answer to the riddle "Who killed Laura Palmer?" I knew, in fact, weeks before the final episode. The answer was not *revealed* in the book, mind you. It simply gave enough clues that if you were paying attention, you could actually deduce the solution.

I loved the idea of an integrated or transmedia experience. It captivated me for years, and I even tried to introduce it into a few interactive projects. For those still struggling with the notion of repurposing existing content to a new medium, however, it was a bit of a leap. It wasn't until 1997 that I finally had the opportunity to work on a project that utilized this technique. It was then that I designed a set of trading cards in conjunction with a CD-ROM and web site for Purple Moon Software, a company devoted to creating interactive content for girls.

 GIRL GAMES: THE NEW FEMININE MYSTIQUE (p. 202)

I use *Twin Peaks* as a model for how to think about interactive fiction because it reinforces the point that interactivity is really all between your ears and between you and other people. Though not interactive per se, *Twin Peaks* is a better example of interactive fiction than almost any CD-ROM I can think of. Lynch understood, on a profound level, the power of curiosity—that in fact, you can give the audience more by giving them less…that sometimes, it's not what you include but what you leave out that makes the story most compelling.

 BROAD OR NARROW: THE CASTING COUCH (p. 113)

NEW MEDIA IS OLD NEWS (p. 358)

DECISIONS, DECISIONS, DECISIONS (p. 158)

IT'S ONLY A GAME: THE BIRTH OF A MULTI-BILLION DOLLAR BUSINESS

The computer game industry is a multi-billion dollar industry. It currently outgrosses all other entertainment media, which is most remarkable when you consider that its primary market is males between the ages of 8 and 18. This narrow demographic is, without question, the world's most profitable niche market.

It is also remarkable when you consider how narrow the genres of consumer video games are. There are basically only about five different games. They just keep getting rehashed over and over again in a variety of different guises. I call these the "five food groups" of consumer gaming. They are as follows:

- Shoot
- Kick and Punch

- Race
- Obstacle Course
- Sports

Although these genres are all slightly different in terms of game play, they all have one thing in common: they are all based on a "twitch" model, which puts the player under pressure with a barrage of fast-paced assaults that require an instantaneous reaction.

Classic video games, such as *Super Mario Brothers* or *Sonic the Hedgehog,* fall into the obstacle course category. They are essentially an animated version of the classic children's board game *Chutes and Ladders*, which has existed in various forms for at least a hundred years. In these 2D animations, a background moves past, creating the illusion that the cartoon characters are moving through a linear environment. The characters are faced with a variety of obstacles that they must overcome to get to the next level, and another aggregate of game challenge. This sort of game can have a nonviolent theme, or it can involve dealing with violent and aggressive obstacles as you move along the linear path. To a certain extent, these follow the slapstick/comical violent aesthetics of Warner Brothers cartoons, in which the main character might be subjected to violence from which he, being an immortal cartoon character, can easily bounce back. These and other such games, for example, *Pitfall*, are now available in 3D versions, providing a three-dimensional take on this same genre. But if you look at content and game logic, they are virtually indistinguishable from one another. These games tend to appeal to younger children who have fun with the cartoon characters, the broad humor, and the comical obstacles they must encounter along their quest.

In the "Shoot" game genre, the standard logic is as follows: You are basically accosted by armed rivals that you must blow away to prevent from being killed yourself. If you succeed in not being killed, you get to go to the next level, in which meaner and more aggressive creatures/fighters/robots/spaceships will continue to torment and attack you. *Terminator* and *Doom* are two example of games in which shooting is a major feature. These games are little more than high-tech shooting galleries on steroids, except instead of shooting at ducks, you are responding to an assault from an army of Arnold Schwarzenegger-like cyborg clones hiding behind trash cans full of nuclear waste. In fact, if you look at the *Terminator* arcade game, its potential targets popping up at random in a 2D lineup make it look remarkably like a carnival shooting gallery, even with the film-based content. *Doom* actually offers players a Virtual Reality, 3D version of the shooting gallery, with evil creatures coming at you from all directions. 3D provides players with a high-quality means of killing and being killed, always with the goal of getting to the next level of killing.

Kick and punch games, which are a fairly recent entry to the genre pool, have become extremely popular, especially in arcades where two players can get together and duke it out, mano a mano, joystick to joystick. Hand-to-hand combat, perhaps the oldest sport known to man, has thus found its home in cyberspace. *Mortal Kombat* was infamous for providing graphic blood-and-guts feedback to the one-on-one fighter game, spurring a national controversy about the unrated gaming industry. People were beginning to wonder why computer game companies could create graphically violent content and target it to the very audience that is restricted from seeing it in movie theaters. In fact, at this writing, a rating system is finally being put in place that asks arcade owners and producers of consumer games to place stickers—giving various grades, the rough equivalent of movie ratings—on to games. It is, however, a cultural *phallicy* to think that a *red* warning sticker indicating that a game may contain graphic violence or sexually suggestive imagery would actually *deter* a teenage boy from stepping up to it. If the effectiveness of a similar ratings program used in the music industry is any indication, this entire system is bound to backfire. Again, the belief that it will not work is based on a measure of ignorance of the arcade culture, an environment notorious for its seedy culture, antisocial behavior, and illicit activity.

Fighting games have been enhanced by the development of high-quality Virtual Reality gaming systems for the home and arcade setting. These systems have become progressively more sophisticated. In fact, machines such as the Sony PlayStation and the Sega Saturn now have rendering capabilities that only a few years ago could only be achieved on a high-end graphics engine—at a cost of about $100,000. By all indications, these machines will only continue to get faster, better, and cheaper.

Virtua Fighter is one of the more popular of the 3D hand-to-hand combat games, and the new generation of this system features real-time effects and physics algorithms, that allow for features such as fluttering cloth, swinging hair, as well as gravity, adding realism to the thud of a fighter landing on his or her butt. The 3D quality also serves to enhance the muscular physiques of the male fighters, and the exaggerated bust measurements of the females. If anyone thinks that these female characters were created with the intent of appealing to a female audience, think again. The testosterone-inspired women of *Virtua Fighter* look more like pin-up girls than world-champion fighters. With skinny bodies and gigantic breasts, they do their dirty work scantily clad in what I call "combat lingerie," affording a better glimpse of thigh and cleavage as they kick, bend over, and double-flip their way into the hearts of teenage boys.

Video games can also be looked at as a metaphor for either eastern spirituality or drug addiction. Like Buddhism and Hinduism, most video games are built on a construct of getting to the next level. They almost always include a reincarnation feature. You can die so many times before getting knocked out of the game. If you manage to stay in the game, the reward is that you can get to the "next level." Of course in Buddhism and Hinduism, you are eventually reincarnated out of mortal existence into nirvana. With video games on the other hand, it's a lot more like *Waiting for Godot*. There is no ultimate resting place, just increasing levels of complexity and challenge which results in the addictive quality. The drug-like video game offers to satisfy but never does. Each new round is at attempt at getting "higher" than the last time. Like a junky, the video gamer pursues the high until he passes out (dies), but keeps coming back for more. Dying is not a deterrent, but a motivating factor, at least if you are male. According to several studies on gender play styles, boys and men find dying to be a good motivator, while women are discouraged by dying and will cease playing if killed.

There is ultimately no final reward in this type of game, just the ongoing jones for a better high. Because most of these so-called "twitch," or "thumb candy" games are geared to produce an adrenaline rush, it is very conceivable that this addictive quality is not only emotional, but also physiological. Gamers may, in fact, be catching a buzz off their own increased adrenal activity.

It is kind of mind-boggling to think that the place where we have put the most firepower in consumer computing opts to create the most visceral of experiences. We use our growing technical prowess to model successively more realistic simulations of Neolithic behavior. It is as if, as our technology increases, so does the need of our reptilian mind to exist on the most base of levels, in a mode of pure aggression in which our lower selves are the dominant factor. It is perfectly easy to be critical of this, and I certainly am, but I also have to ask myself what's behind it. Perhaps there is a deep need to find expression in this stuff, particularly for the group such games are targeted to. Perhaps that function is as much biological as it is cultural, a vestige from the days when teenage boys were just stepping out into the wild with their fathers to learn the hunting trade. Or perhaps these types of games are just easier to design…

 VICARIOUS EXPERIENCE (p. 504)

VICARIOUS EXPERIENCE (p. 504)

The set-top box paradigm of consumer computer games (Sega, Nintendo, Sony PlayStation, and so on) is completely the opposite of the cultural and genre paradigm of computer-based CD-ROM games. These games are characterized by an entirely different set of priorities. CD-ROMs are traditionally much more highbrow than set-top or arcade games. The first and foremost reason for this is that they are inextricably linked with the personal computer, which has a radically different demographic than consumer games. It also has to do with technical direction and constraints. Consumer games are built for speed, but

CD-ROMs are notoriously slow. They do not provide the adequate rapid feedback required for "twitch" games. In fact, until recently, CD-ROMs have been notoriously weak at most real-time functions, including Virtual Reality. Thus, CD-ROMs are designed more as multimedia products integrating text, animation, video, audio, and so forth. CD-ROM games, such as *Myst*, and series such as *SimCity* and its spinoffs (*SimCity 2000*, *SimEarth*, and so forth), *Carmen San Diego*, or *Indiana Jones*, are more oriented to mystery, problem-solving and role playing. CD-ROM, in large part due to the work of early content pioneers, is also viewed primarily as an educational medium. Its target market, 100 percent of whom are computer users, expects CD-ROM game products to have some level of intellectual or educational content. Witness the popularity of *You Don't Know Jack!*, a hard-core trivia game for adults. Mystery games such as *Seventh Level* or *Psychic Detective* are also typical of adult CD-ROM fare. It has not been until recently (recently being a relative term based on the time this book is being written, of course) that CD-ROMs have really had the firepower to support a game such as *Doom* or *Duke Nuke'em*, which are much more characteristic of the set-top game paradigm.

As always, whenever I'm thinking about current trends and where things are headed, I always find it useful to take a moment to reflect on the past a bit. A look at the history and evolution of computer gaming provides some insight not only into this industry as an isolated case, but also into how media evolve, where they come from, and how they become adopted into the popular culture.

 THEORY OF MEDIA EVOLUTION (p. 468)

The first computer games were invented, believe it or not, at MIT, the birth-place of modern computer science, and also, apparently, the birthplace of computer gaming. In 1959, John McCarthy, inventor of the term Artificial Intelligence, wrote a program that would enable the IBM 704 (also known as The Hulking Giant) to play chess. The 704 had no screen or CRT display, but some of McCarthy's students were even able to hack out a ping-pong type game (a predecessor to *Pong*) by using The Hulking Giant's blinking lights. Other early game-like programs included *Bouncing Ball*, which bounced a dot around on the screen, and *Mouse in a Maze*, which was a precursor to *Pac-Man*. Running on a TX-O computer, it enabled you to draw a maze with a light pen, place some cheese wedges in it, and then watch a mouse wind its way through. A VIP version featured martinis, and the mouse would get more and more tipsy, a great example of early skill-curve programming. Most of these programs' target market was the computer: The application was meant to get the computer to play the game moreso than the person.

In 1961, a year after Ivan Sutherland created *Sketchpad*, the first graphical user interface, the first generally acknowledged "real" computer game was created. It was a multi-user game called *Spacewar!* developed by a bunch of MIT hackers with a penchant for cheesy science fiction movies; their "day gig" was doing military-funded computer research. They got hold of a new computer—the PDP-1—which had everything they needed: speed, power, and most of all, a screen! Led by Stephen R. Russel, also known as Slug, this team hacked a multi-player game based on vectors, pretty much the only thing you could do with a computer screen at that time. *Spacewar!* included rockets, missiles, and a completely accurate starscape. It used real-time animation and input devices made from model-railroad switching hardware, enabling simultaneous, multi-player interaction. Naturally, the main objective of the game revolved around shooting.

Spacewar! notwithstanding, the consumer computer game industry did not start out with violent content. The first computer-based arcade game was developed in 1972 by Nolan Bushnell, the founder of Atari. Called *Pong*, it was a simple simulation of a ping-pong game. Using knobs that controlled paddles in a horizontal axis, *Pong* enabled up to four players to bounce a digital ball back and forth on the screen. It was a tabletop game and made its debut in everything from pinball arcades to pizza parlors. In 1974, when cheap microchips became available, a home version of *Pong* hit the market. *Pong* became the standard for video games and by the mid-70s, there were more than 60 different *Pong* "generics" on the market.

Nearly 10 years later, Atari set another standard with *Pac-Man*. With his circular head and wedge-shaped mouth, Pac-Man looks kind of like a happy face in profile. He serves as your cursor/playing piece as you move around on the screen gulping down cherries and other treats while trying to avoid unidentified critters for whom you yourself are a tasty treat. Fifteen years after it was introduced, *Pac-Man* is still the only arcade game that has a significant female following. It is also still the top selling arcade game of all time. Coincidence? I think not! It doesn't take a mathematician to see that opening the door to females doubles your potential market. *Pac-Man*'s appeal among females was so great that its makers were inspired to create *Ms. Pac-Man*, the first, and for many years, the only arcade game developed specifically with a female audience in mind. I call *Pac-Man* "the overeaters game," and it's kind of an inside joke that the appeal of *Pac-Man* for women is in its themes of food or, alternately, shopping. Beyond this simplistic conclusion are a number of reasons why *Pac-Man* has had such widespread female appeal, in sharp contrast to the bulk of other video games, whose audience is almost exclusively male. At this writing, some Japanese companies have begun to develop arcade games for girls; among them are variations on the enormously popular and female-friendly desktop computer game *Tetris*.

Girl Games: The New Feminine Mystique (p. 202)

If you look at a lineup of early computer games, you find that in the early days, violent games did not predominate as they do now. Although there was probably an equal ratio of violent and non-violent games in circulation by the 1980s, some of the biggest hits in first generation computer gaming were not combat or fight-based products. *Donkey Kong* (the sequel of which, *Super Mario Brothers*, is now of course a classic), *Pitfall*, *Boulderdash*, and *Breakout* provided a balance to shoot-em-up offerings such as the *Spacewar!*-like *Space Invaders*, and its sister product, *Asteroids*. There were even enormously popular text adventures, such as *Zork*, which sent you through a variety of puzzles, trials, and predicaments to create a surreal story-based experience.

A few other early arcade games are worth mentioning because of their significance in terms of evolving gaming conventions. The classic *Space Invaders* involved fending off the world from a barrage of invading spaceships. With *Space Invaders,* there was some actual strategy involved. Sometimes you had to sacrifice a city to save the world. The other interesting feature of *Space Invaders* was its self-adjusting skill level. The better you played, the faster the invaders came. *Space Invaders* was one of the first computer games to employ this technique to computer gaming.

Centipede, another early game, provided an interesting and unique logical structure. A multi-celled centipede squirmed around the screen and tried to eat you. You could shoot it, but then the pieces would break off and there would be more centipedes squirming around; and of course the speed of their ravenous attack would increase. While *Space Invaders'* self-adjusting skill curve had the computer anticipating the player's actions, *Centipede* employed a skill curve inherent within the game premise itself.

Another game that uses this technique is my favorite arcade game from adolescence—*Death Race 2000*, based on the seedy 70s thriller of the same name. In this very cleverly conceived game, you drive a car around an open field peopled by little tiny men who were so graphically crude they looked almost like needlepoint. Your goal was to run them all down as they walked around the screen. Whenever you hit one, it would let out a high-pitched, computerized yelp and turn into a tombstone. The result was that the target now became an obstacle. Therefore, the better you played, the more obstacles filled the screen, creating a natural, and rather elegant self-adjusting skill curve.

 THE RULES OF THE GAME (p. 420)

THE RULES OF THE GAME (p. 420)

Despite the increasing success of the industry, 1984 was, ironically, the year of the Great Video Game Crash. It seems that from that point on, computer games got progressively more violent. By the late 80s, violence in video games became a major controversy. Some of the companies had a very strong policy against it, but they were under heavy pressure from an increasingly competitive market to jump on the violence bandwagon. Eventually, even the most saintly of the video game companies succumbed to the pressure, and soon, violent content became the rule rather than the exception. The increase in violent video games has been a continued trend into the 90s, fueled, to a certain extent, by rapid advances in technology. As graphics get better, violence gets more graphic, and the cycle continues. In spite of increases in technical firepower, the content itself becomes progressively more homogenous. So even though we are seeing many new manifestations and variations of the five food groups, the games themselves continue to be cloned from other popular content.

> An interesting aside: *Pong* was the first arcade game, and it was also the first multiplayer game on the commercial market. After *Pong*, single-user play became the standard. It wasn't until several years later that multiplayer simultaneous play appeared again in arcades, but this time, in the form of combat-oriented games.

The video game industry is not unlike some other morally dubious businesses. Like the Cold War military/industrial complex, the tobacco industry, and the drug trade, it is built upon an economy of dubious ethics. Although it is hard to make a convincing argument in favor of violence, you would be hard-pressed to get most game developers to consider the alternatives.

You can no more tell a video game designer that it might not be such a good idea to let 10 year-old kids blow each other's guts out on a computer screen than you can tell a drug dealer to stop pushing crack to teenagers in the schoolyard. Regardless of whether they know it's wrong, they need to continue to justify it because they have so much to lose by saying, "You know, maybe you're right." The bottom line is…the bottom line. When talking about multiples of billions of dollars, few people are motivated to change course, no matter how many ethical questions are raised by their work.

Video game companies will do whatever it takes to retain their right to blood and guts. Three years ago, the computer game industry got together and created an entire conference devoted to their trade. This event was, in part, created to raise funds to fight game censorship and rating. Currently, every other form of entertainment besides computer games is subject to *some* kind of rating system. A 14 year-old boy cannot see a movie in which characters shoot each other or use profane language, but he can rip the guts out of a computer-generated character and splat its brains against the wall with impunity. He can't buy a copy of *Penthouse*, but he can engage in hand-to-hand combat with a virtual girl who wears less clothes than The Penthouse Pet of the Month.

There is only one thing that will assuage the preponderance of violence in computer games: market pressure and a concerted effort by developers to change the paradigm. The impetus to change falls on the game developers, not the government. But will they? Because of increasing pressure, some are starting to put some effort into non-violent games. We are beginning to see more things such as virtual skiing and racing. Some companies have seen the light and realized that there is more to the world than adolescent males. A small handful of developers have finally begun to see that there is a clear and present market for women; however, until there is some economic impetus to change direction, such as a massive boycott or major consumer action, we can expect to keep seeing a plethora of violent games on the shelves and in the arcades.

Just like drugs and tobacco, as long as people will buy violent-themed games, people will sell them. In spite of the ups and downs of the interactive industry overall, the consumer game industry continues to grow and is perhaps the most economically stable of all the interactive media. As is the case with any niche of the interactive market, its success can be measured by its conferences. E3 (Electronic Entertainment Expo) is now in its third year and going strong; in fact, they had to move the venue to the mother of all convention halls, the Atlanta Convention Center, because the Los Angeles Convention Center was too small! (For anyone whose ever been to the Los Angeles Convention Center, you will know what the exclamation point is for: It's quite gigantic.) For whatever reason, with a very narrow but ardent niche market, consumer games have managed to dominate the industry for more than 20 years. And it is this model, and the perceived expectation of inconceivable wealth, that fuels efforts in other interactive media, each hoping that it can someday achieve this same economic success. Nonetheless, other platforms come and go, and the "ultimate" consumer platform remains a moving target. Perhaps this will change over time, as new media grow and evolve.

THE INTERACTIVE ECOSYSTEM (p. 233)

DANGER: KILLER APP (p. 152)

THE MILITARY ENTERTAINMENT COMPLEX (p. 303)

Kiss My Asset: The Content Wars of the 1990s and the Birth of Transmedia

"Content" has become to the 1990s what "stock market" was to the 1980s. Everybody is cashing in on "properties," based on speculation and inflated values. After it became apparent in the late 80s that there actually might be a CD-ROM market, the going trend became the repurposing of content in new media, which meant it was a seller's market for licensed properties. By the early 90s, everybody was buying up content in a kind of purchasing frenzy. Hollywood met Silicon Valley in a second California Gold Rush. Hardware companies bought film studios; content companies absorbed other content companies; people were selling content for re-use in other media like it was going out of style. This led to the formation of megalopolies that resulted in such strange bedfellows as Walt Disney and ABC, Sony and Columbia, Viacom and AT&T. (Whatever happened to the Sherman Antitrust laws?) These corporate examples of big fish being eaten by other, bigger fish is reminiscent of the Russian nesting doll. As you open up each container, you find another container inside that, and another inside that. Look at this book, for example: Macmillan Technical Publishing, inside New Riders Publishing, inside Macmillan Publishing, inside Simon & Schuster, inside Viacom, which also owns Paramount, Blockbuster, MTV, Nickleodeon, and so on.

I find the whole notion of content as property to be totally surreal. In new media, we have the bizarre construct of intellectual property—the ownership of ideas and trade secrets, which may consist of anything from a vague concept to a company mission statement to a production methodology. These can often be intangible entities that are difficult to tie down because they might ultimately be impossible to copyright, patent, or otherwise protect in any way. As a result, the legal eagles resort to trying to protect such intellectual property by securing a flimsy assurance of confidentiality from the dozens and sometimes hundreds of people who have been exposed to it. Imagine how many Microsoft employees, not to mention partners and contractors, have had to sign confidentiality agreements...

If you look back over human cultural evolution, you find that the entire basis of almost every human conflict in history has revolved around the notion of property. The entire system of patriarchal rule and the misogynistic ownership of women was all based on the need to ensure that property could be passed down through the bloodline of the father. Thus, the womb became an heir manufacturing plant—assuming of course the woman could produce the requisite male heirs, or risk death if she could not. Even the Trojan War was fought over Helen being "stolen" from Paris. Many Hollywood action flicks revolve around the hero avenging either the destruction or theft of his female and/or familial property (sorry…just a little righteous outburst there). Without property, there would be no war…virtually all wars in human history have been fought over property, or a dispute of ownership of something, whether it be a country, or a county, a piece of land, a body of water, a gold mine, or a rainforest, a herd of cattle, or a harem of brides. Even religious battles are, at their core, territorial in nature. Indeed, you could make a viable argument that property is the root of all evil, not money. But in the realm of media property, money is, of course the entire point.

Individual properties, or media content entities, are also known as assets (although some content properties might be more like liabilities). After assets are digitized, they can then be migrated across all media, licensed, and repurposed to death. The conventional wisdom has, therefore, been to take content assets that are perceived to be of value, due to branding, star power, or some prior success (the blockbuster model again), and utilize it to generate new content. This approach is ironic indeed when you realize that most of what we refer to as new media has actually been an attempt to re-use old media in new ways. Perhaps a more apt term then would be "renew media." The theory behind this approach is that you can save money by not creating new content, and turbo charge your product's marketing by spinning it off of a well-known source with perceived existing market value.

This theory, though it sounds perfectly logical, actually falls apart in practice. First of all, there has been no indication whatsoever that using a licensed property actually has any advantage over creating original content. In the CD-ROM market, the majority of top sellers have been based on original content. *Myst*, *Doom*, *Seventh Guest*, and long-standing classics such as the *Sim* (*SimCity*, *SimEarth*, and so on) and the *Carmen San Diego* series (*Where in the World is Carmen San Diego?*, and so forth) have, for the most part been based on original content. The few cases where repurposed content has been used, such as *Barbie Fashion Designer* or the *Indiana Jones* series, the licensed property might have been what sold the product out the gate, but it is ultimately the product itself and the integrity of the experience that has been responsible for its success.

It also remains to be seen whether licensing property truly is cheaper. The amount it costs just to get the rights to a major film property could easily exceed the entire design and production cost of *Myst* hundreds of times over.

When you consider that a typical CD-ROM budget is under a half a million dollars, often as low as $100,000, and then reflect on the fact that you might be required to pay in excess of a million dollars just to get the rights to use a property, the numbers just don't add up. In addition, you can pay in the multiples of millions of dollars to get a license (not even a full purchase, mind you) to something such as the Hendrix estate or the songs of the Beatles. Furthermore, after you've obtained the property, there's no guarantee that you won't have to produce a lot of new assets anyway; and in fact, most licensed properties, in the end, require original assets even if they are based on existing characters or content.

This philosophy of repurposing content is generally proffered by people in marketing departments, who insist that you can't sell original content. Meanwhile, original content is being born and sold every day. The conventional wisdom (which is neither) sees this as a "safe bet," but in fact it is a much greater risk when you look at the facts. The reality is that even from a marketing standpoint, there is no basis in fact for believing that repurposed content sells, and much data exists to support that it does not.

The primary reason that repurposing content is ultimately an erroneous model for creating interactive products goes back to our old pal Marshall McLuhan. The medium is the message, and content seldom travels well between media. One of the reasons for this is because people have a fundamental misunderstanding of what an interactive product is. What you are selling when you create an interactive product is not content, but experience. Content—that is, the story, the characters, the assets, what have you—is merely a point of entry into the experience. But what keeps the audience coming back for more and what keeps them telling their friends and buying more units is ultimately *not* the content but the experience.

Barbie Fashion Designer is an excellent case of this. It is true that Barbie is what calls attention to the product. If this were the sole reason for its appeal, then why would other products based on high-profile content not do equally as well, for example, some of the recent Disney titles? No, what has made the Barbie title so popular is not the star power but the experience of designing clothes for Barbie, and then printing them on to real cloth and placing them on your real doll. This experience, no matter what the content, is a total winner for the target market of little girls. I have little doubt that even with a lesser doll, this product would have become popular, possibly even part of a synergistic marketing plan in which the CD-ROM was used to sell dolls. But you could make another product featuring Barbie, combining a successful property with a successful CD-ROM product, and end up with *Barbie Mortal Kombat*, for example. It doesn't take a marketing expert to imagine the results. But this, believe it or not, is the typical way that marketing people will conceive of new product. They will take a successful character or film, and a successful game, and in spite of the fact that there might be no clear or sensible relationship between the two, propose that two winners ought to add up to a double-winner. Whereas in this case, you are creating a double loser. Don't laugh. Products as preposterous as this are conceived of every day. I was once given a game script with the subtitle *Myst Meets Total Recall*. If you think *that* sounds frightening, consider this: The game was a vehicle for repurposing assets from Motown Records.

If you look at titles that have succeeded in repurposing content, what you will find is that there is something inherent in the content that makes it friendly to interactive media. Take *The Way Things Work*, a book that was turned into an educational CD-ROM. Not only was this an ideal migration of content to interactive media, in some ways, CD-ROM may be an even better medium than the book to tell this story. LucasArts' *Indiana Jones* takes an adventure film and turns it into an adventure *game*. The puzzles and mysteries that were part of the film series lent themselves perfectly to an interactive medium, CD-ROM in particular.

It makes no sense whatsoever to take a body of content, whatever it may be, and make it interactive just for the sake of making it interactive. Not all content wants to be interactive, and in reality, some ideas are better served by a passive medium. The first and foremost question you ought to ask when creating an interactive experience is, What's the point? What's the value in making it interactive? Is there an inherent interactivity to the content that is best conveyed through a participatory experience? These seem like simple and obvious questions, but if you look at current offerings in CD-ROM and on the web, you may wonder whether these kinds of questions are ever asked. If, as a participant or user of such an experience, you find yourself asking the question "What's the point?", it is no fault of yours, rest assured.

 GRATUITOUS INTERACTIVITY: MEDIA DISPENSERS AND THE ATM MODEL (p. 218)

When you encounter an interactive experience that makes sense, you know it. *Barbie Fashion Designer*, *The Way Things Work*, *You Don't Know Jack!*, *Myst*, and yes, even a horribly violent thing such as *Doom*…all of these products, whether based on original or repurposable content, are fully realized interactive experiences. We know this because they engage us completely, and because if we try to imagine the same experience being manifested in some other way, we cannot. *You Don't Know Jack!* would make a terrible film, as would *Myst*. *Barbie Fashion Designer* has no future as a television program, although I wouldn't be surprised if…

As you can see, the somewhat absurd flipside of this is, of course, spinning off linear content from interactive titles. I'll never forget seeing the ad for *Super Mario Brothers*, the movie. I also understand that *Mortal Kombat 2* is in production at this writing.

Absurd though it may sound, these films are in fact a mutant in the gene pool, an intermediary step to another level of evolution. This next step is being called "transmedia" by some of its proponents. Transmedia is a step beyond repurposing. It takes advantage of the cross-media potential of digital content by anticipating it, rather than treating it as an afterthought. Instead of repurposing existing content, new content is created to exist in multiple media concurrently. Furthermore, the interactive experience itself is spread across all these media. Rather than creating each experience as merely a spinoff of the last, pieces of the experience are woven into the content and interactivity of each medium. Character backstory may live on the web, while the core interactive experience might exist within a CD-ROM. Extending this interplay to traditional media, a television program may have an accompanying web site where clues to the motives of characters are buried. By developing the content with this transmedia approach in mind, you can then begin to create an entire content entity that is not necessarily centered in any one media, but lives across all of them. This is a prudent approach to take considering the inherent volatility of the market. This methodology is a failsafe against the comings and goings of technology. The focus instead is on the property itself, which is designed to move fluidly from one new medium to the next. The common factor will always be that the assets are digital, but if the CD-ROM market experiences a slump, you can energize the web site; if the characters and story premise take off, you can weave television shows and comic books from it. This platform-agnostic approach creates a property that can live independent of a specific technology. It can have ongoing life that builds on the inherent strength of the interactive market, which is not built on the fast-buck blockbuster, but on products and property with longevity and ongoing appeal.

The transmedia model will no doubt yield whole new forms of entertainment not yet imagined. Most of these will live at the intersection between media. For in fact, it is really the activities within the brain of the user that then become the glue that holds it all together. With that in mind, these interactions between media create another space for the player to create his or her own experience, and another level for a dynamic interactive experience.

IT'S NOT THE TELEVISION THAT'S INTERACTIVE, IT'S THE PEOPLE (p. 250)

THE DIGISPHERE (p. 168)

APPROPRIATION AND THE POST-MODERN ETHIC (p. 20)

THE LAW OF REDUCTIVE TECHNOLOGY, OR, NEVER SEND A MAN OUT TO DO A BOY'S JOB

"Never send a boy out to do a man's job." The Law of Reductive Technology reverses the old adage to make a point about chronic overuse of technology. It is a common error in judgement to use computers to do things that could be accomplished better, faster, and cheaper by other means. The tendency by most is to fall into a pattern of technological overkill. Sometimes a pair of scissors and some glue is faster than spending an hour trying to get your printer to center on your letterhead.

The analogy I use to illustrate technology overkill is with transportation modes. Presuming you live in a city such as New York, where they actually *have* public transportation, you can use the following formula. If you are going 10 blocks or less, you would walk. If you are going 10–50 blocks, you would ride a bike. If you are going more than 50 blocks, you would take the subway. Obviously, you would not take the subway if you were only going three blocks. That would be silly. Nonetheless, this is tantamount to what people frequently do with technology. They take the subway 10 blocks and then walk back seven to travel three blocks.

I like to take a reductive approach to technology. One of the ways I do this is by changing my definition of what technology is. A potential client once asked me what kind of project management software I used. I held up my pencil and said, "I use one of these." Apparently, that wasn't a good enough answer for him, becuase he later told me I wasn't "computer literate" enough to work for him. At that time, I had yet to see a timeline program that worked better than a pencil and the classic 11"-by-17" timeline graph paper. To me, the pencil is technology as much as the computer is.

What I like to do is figure out the minimum amount of technology I can get away with to solve a given problem. I took this to extremes once while I was working for Ed Schlossberg on the IPL project. We were developing a huge location-based entertainment site, a 45,000 square foot pavilion full of high-end multiplayer games. We had just received funding for the next phase of development, but it wasn't as much as we had asked for. So I was asked to reduce the production cost of the largest game in the site from $2 million to $1 million. I studied the specs and budget for a few days, and then came back to Ed and the management team and said, "The best way to cut costs on this game is to remove the computers." There was a hush in the room. My suggestion seemed outrageous. After all, weren't we supposed to be designing computer games? Upon further review, we realized that we were designing *interactive* games. The technology was there only to facilitate the interactivity. The elimination of the computers took nothing from the game. In fact, a deeper analysis revealed that they were unnecessary. We didn't need the network, because we discovered that the players themselves could perform the function of a network. The game took place in a large, themed venue. It was essentially a scavenger hunt in that players moved from one physical location to the next, collecting information which they would piece together into a final solution. There was no need to track their movements; all we needed to know was that they visited every location; and the way we knew that was that they came back to the start location after they collected all the information. We also discovered that that information could come in a variety of forms, and that the elimination of the computers acutally expanded our repertoire of media. Thus, we had to be more inventive and creative, and in the end, we had a much better experience because we weren't asking players to move from computer screen to computer screen.

People often approach a content problem with a preconceived technological solution. What you really have to ask yourself is, What story am I trying to tell, and what is the best way to tell it? The process should always begin with a vision of the experience you are trying to create. If you already have a technological solution before you have your experience in mind, or if the technology is driving your vision of the experience, think again…this is where you need to practice reductive technology.

I like to emphasize the *interactive* in interactive multimedia. It is the interactivity that is curcial—because you can just as easily make something interactive with a peice of paper as you can with a high-end flight simulator. It all depends on what you need to tell your story…and story always comes first. I am fond of saying that no amount of special effects in film can save a bad scrpt. Likewise, no amount of technology can save a poorly thought-out interactive experience.

Start with the person, develop the experience, and then ask yourself, What is the minimum technology I need to create this experience? From there, you can begin to build out, making sure that every decision you make is ultimately driven by the experience you want to create.

Gratuitous Interactivity: Media Dispensers and the ATM Model (p. 218)

Desgning for Technology (p. 161)

Biosphere Meets Digisphere: The Biosphere 2 Interactive Theater (p. 91)

THE LAWS OF CUMULATIVE MEDIA

The Laws of Cumulative Media, a sub-set of the Theory of Media Evolution, concern themselves with the dynamic influences that occur between evolving media. As new media emerge, they unavoidably impact the media that preceded them. The result is a constant interplay as each new medium emerges, attempts to co-opt or hybridize conventions of preceding media, eventually comes into its own, impacts the evolution of the media from which it sprung, and spawns still more media. These laws of cumulative media explore this phenomenon in an attempt to understand the interdynamics between different media as they evolve.

FIRST LAW OF CUMULATIVE MEDIA

Media is not reductive but cumulative; in other words, new media does not replace old, but merely expands the catalog of available expressions.

One of the most popular misconceptions of our day is the idea that new media *replaces* old. Each time a new medium is born, there is a reactive trend in which people proclaim that it will kill an older, more established medium. Nothing could be more absurd. There is no precedent for media killing each other off outright. Whenever a new medium is developed, it is added to the repertoire of media. It is very clear that television did not replace radio, as was anticipated when TV first came on the scene. Likewise, in spite of predictions of the declining literacy rates due to TV, film, and computers, there are currently more magazines and books sold annually than ever. And the Internet, lest we forget, is an entirely text-based system. Far from eradicating literacy, the online chat room has spawned a literary genre based on the newly formed art of two-way writing in real time.

SECOND LAW OF CUMULATIVE MEDIA

Each new medium strives to integrate and repurpose old forms of communication. In other words, when a new medium is first introduced, it begins as the "child" of existing media…striving to imitate or improve on accepted paradigms.

The television began as a form of "visual radio." Early TV shows resembled radio programs, used many of the same formats, and even used the same talent in many cases. On television, these accepted radio genres were then enhanced with a visual component. TV also borrowed from stage/variety show formats. Thus, early television was essentially a hybrid of radio and live theater.

A more contemporary example of a new medium is the Internet. The layout of many web sites is drawn from the conventions of the magazine page. Because it began as hypertext—a text-based system that enables links from one "page" to the next—it has been co-opted to a large extent by those from the print media accustomed to using text and still images. Even the language of the web—"page," for example—suggests a print paradigm. Others are attempting to use the Internet as a delivery system for streaming video (video delivered continuously off a server rather than downloaded entirely to the user's hard drive before playing). Again, this is an attempt to turn the web into television. Language evolved around this medium paradigm uses terms such as "net casting" and "channels."

Language is a good indicator as to the influences at play in a new medium. Metaphors from other media reveal which discipline areas are vying for domination. Eventually this process gives way into another level of the evolutionary curve...that in which the medium begins to take on a life of its own and develop its own unique paradigm.

Third Law of Cumulative Media

Every new medium has an impact on the evolution of the media that preceded it.

As a new medium evolves its own unique identity, it has the effect of changing the function of the media from which it emerged. Thus, the old media will have a tendency to move toward higher levels of specialization as the new medium becomes to take on some of their previous functions. This can have both a positive and negative effect on the preceding media. On the positive side, the new medium can free the old medium from certain more general tasks to focus on tasks for which it is particularly well-suited. Thus, media specialization trigger the development of new, more sophisticated genres, causing the old media to evolve as well. The potential negative effect, is, of course, the eventual extinction of other genres, resulting in the total extinction of entire art forms which have been co-opted or bettered by the new media coming in.

A good way to look at this is to imagine each medium before and after the medium that followed it. In this way, you can really begin to understand how a medium not only adds to, but transforms its predecessors. What follows are a few examples that illustrate this phenomenon.

One of the best examples used to illustrate the Laws of Cumulative Media is the effect of photography on painting. Prior to the invention of photography, the painter's job was not so much to interpret, but to record the visual world in an interpretive way. Many different styles were used to this end, and they changed radically over the centuries. But for hundreds of years, at least in Western culture, the main task of the painter remained the same—to depict and/or record a person, a landscape, an object, or a narrative (historical, biblical, mythological, and so forth). The emergence of photography afforded an accurate means of recording the visual world in still form. This released painters from the role of record-takers and freed them to express themselves more liberally. This freedom of expression led to an artistic explosion and "modern art" was born. Cubism, futurism, expressionism, and other new genres gave the artist a more specialized, and yet less constraining task: to create a highly personalized interpretation of the visual world. This individual interpretation could simply provide a new way of looking at the "real world," or it could go so far as to be drawn completely from the imagination of the artist. An amazing and diverse range of new artworks and genres blossomed due to the emergence of the photorealistic painting technology. The fallout of this was that photorealism became something of an endangered species. Note also the influence on language: Photorealism is the word we use today to describe a genre of painting that pre-dates, was co-opted by, and for the most part, has been eliminated by photography.

Another excellent example of cumulative media is the effect of television on radio. Prior to television, radio was largely a narrative medium. Radio's main repertoire consisted of news, audio plays, music, and variety shows. Because of its visual content, the television had greater strengths in both narrative and stage performance genres. Early television was a blend of radio, film, and live theater. Eventually it evolved its own formulae and genres unique to the properties of the medium.

As television evolved, radio took on a new shape and form. Modern radio focuses primarily on genres particularly well-suited to an audio format: news, talk shows, and recorded music. It is interesting to note that MTV borrowed back from the radio format and brought pre-recorded music to the television, a function it never had before. The other interesting evolutionary shift is the portable radio, particularly the car radio. Early radio sat in the middle of your living room, a position eventually taken over by the television. But if you listen to the radio in your home today, you will notice a majority of radio programming is targeted to the automobile driver, as well as the employee in the workplace. Just as photography did not kill painting but actually gave it more freedom to be more "itself," television did not kill the radio; TV helped radio to emphasize its unique strengths. The fallout, again, was the loss of radio drama, a genre that television all but eliminated.

What examples will we see of the Laws of Cumulative Media in the interactive age? It is hard to say now, because we are in the very midst of enormous shifts. As mentioned earlier, web pages on the young Internet have a tendency to look like magazine pages. Although many predict the Internet will replace the television, there is little to support this hypothesis. The Internet's biggest weaknesses are the very strengths of television—the instant transmission of video and audio. The Internet's biggest strengths are its updatability, its accessibility, its open distribution infrastructure, its multi-user capability, and most important, its interactivity. It is hard to imagine that the Internet will rob many functions from the television. In fact, there is little competition between the two. Where the Internet may ultimately take over is in the realm of updatable information, such as news and weather—CNN and the Weather Channel are among the most popular sites on the web. This, and the fact that many television shows and all the networks now have their own web sites, would suggest that the Internet and television are evolving in a symbiotic, mutually supportive relationship, rather than one that is mutually exclusive. The Internet is more likely to take over functions of the telephone and the post. The modem is more likely to rob from the fax than from the TV. And judging from the popularity of such things as online travel agents, certain kinds of telephone commerce are also being co-opted by the Internet.

The one thing the Internet may rob from the television is eyeballs. Although TV is still America's favorite pastime, studies show that "wired" children will spend more time with their computer than their television. Maybe the CPU is America's new baby-sitter. One can only hope that this trend forces the television to evolve. This would be a welcome and long overdue benefit to American culture at-large.

This kind of in-depth study is of great benefit to those attempting to anticipate future trends in media. In this way, we can begin to develop unique functionalities for new media, and in turn, bring new levels of specialization and sophistication to the media that preceded them.

Theory of Media Evolution (p. 480)

The Laws of Informational Entropy (p. 280)

Fear of Media (p. 193)

THE LAWS OF INFORMATIONAL ENTROPY

Entropy is the tendency of things to degenerate to increasing levels of complexity and/or chaos. The fact that chemical reactions generate heat, the fact that rocks will eventually become sand, that certain substances dissolve in water, and that your desk always seems to want to be more and not less messy—these are all examples of entropy in the physical world. Entropy is generally viewed as a tendency toward disorder, although you can certainly make an argument that it is nature's attempt at *creating* order (by her terms, of course). The erosion of mountains into sand can just as easily be seen as a move *toward* order as a move *away* from it, depending on your point of view. The following laws concern themselves with entropy, but not entropy of matter or heart. They are laws of *informational* entropy—the tendency of information to grow, expand, and become increasingly more complex.

FIRST LAW OF INFORMATIONAL ENTROPY

As information is passed from individual to individual, it multiplies in its raw form, and then goes through an interpretive process to create informational byproducts, which in turn become more information, thus creating an exponential and ultimately infinite explosion of information.

I often keep myself up at night with vexing philosophical riddles such as these: There is always more information, never less. Each day, more information is added to the universe. Some information is lost through erasure or entropy (fading ink, memory loss, and so on), but overall the volume of information is on the increase.

It's kind of like the child's game of Telephone. The first person tells a secret to the second, so now two people know. By the end of the game, everyone in the circle knows, and it is also likely that the information has broken down in translation. There is more information in the sense that the same information packet, not unlike a virus, has now spread throughout the group. In addition, that piece of information also mutates, spawning a new idea or thought (information) within the "host."

Beat author William Burroughs originally said "language is a virus." Cyberspace novelist Neal Stephenson absorbed this piece of information and integrated it into his novel *Snow Crash*. Stephenson postulated that information was a virus. Although not an entirely original idea, it merged in his fertile imagination with the notion of a computer virus, a piece of code that passes from computer to computer creating digital mayhem. Stephenson combined these two forms of informational parasite into the concept of a mental, informational virus that would cause the brain of the host to "crash," much as a virus-infected computer would.

SECOND LAW OF INFORMATIONAL ENTROPY

> The size of the information distribution infrastructure is always growing. As the information infrastructure grows, content multiplies to fill the space available.

Television began with few channels. More were introduced until there were about 13 channels to chose from. These were contained within the UHF bandwidth on your television (the radio equivalent to FM). VHF introduced numerous other stations, at least doubling the available bandwidth. Then came cable. You can look at UHF and VHF as the Roman numerals of television, and cable as the Arabic numeral system. Just as Arabic numerals provided merchants with more digits to make more money, cable provided more channel options resulting in more information.

This same rule holds true for all media. There are thousands of radio stations across the country, and tens of thousands of web sites. The World Wide Web, perhaps more than any medium, has created an information free-for-all, the likes of which has never been seen before. It is here, on the web, that the exponential explosion of information has had its most mind-boggling impact. E-mail is perhaps the best carrier of informational viruses, by virtue of its instantaneous delivery to massive numbers of people. Additionally, e-mail can give rise to flame wars in which random and semi-anonymous comments are sent back and forth between individuals who well may never have seen each other, and might not even know each other's name. This creates even further opportunity for the exponential increase in information in our culture.

These growth pattern in the information infrastructure do not necessarily occur in response to a demand for more information; rather, it might be that the growth of information is in part the fault of the growth in infrastructure. The World Wide Web, within its exponential growth potential, might grow infinitely. Both radio and television offer finite bandwidth, although the bounds of this are always increasing. The more URLs, channels, or stations that are created, the more content (information) will be generated to fill them.

THIRD LAW OF INFORMATIONAL ENTROPY

The more advanced, complex, and large our media and information storage and retrieval systems are, the more volatile they become.

Early information was carved or painted on stone walls or, later, building walls. This information was literally "set in stone"—unchangeable and un-movable. The Mesopotamians introduced clay tablets that were easier to work with. The malleable clay allowed for more ease of editing while the clay was wet, although, as with ink, once it dried, you were stuck with it. Tablets were also more portable than cave walls or stone tablets. Though certainly durable, the tablet technology introduced a new drawback—breakage. Thus, the advantage of making media easier to work with, more compact, and more portable had the byproduct of making it more fragile. Papyrus, the most portable and flexible of the ancient media, was flammable, prone to deterio-ration, vulnerable to water damage, and so on. Ironically, some of the oldest media created by humans might outlive newer media forms. Digital media does not have the shelf life of the cave paintings at Lascaux and might not even last into next week.

Digital media, the most advanced, flexible, and portable of all information formats is also the most volatile. As I write these words, I live in fear that my computer will crash, subsequently reducing my revelations to nothing but a memory...on my part, that is. So, although we can store much more informa-tion, do more with it, integrate it in new ways, and shoot it over high-speed networks, we do so at considerable risk. Digital media have, after all, a high mortality rate because bits and bytes are so easy to destroy. A magnet on a floppy disk, a crashed hard drive, a failure to save, or a spilled cup of coffee are enough to result in the total annihilation of information, ideas, and work. In the past, you had to burn books to destroy them. Now, all you have to do is put a refrigerator magnet on your floppy and it's toast.

FOURTH LAW OF INFORMATIONAL ENTROPY

The fourth law of informational entropy poses the question, Can we really handle all this information? Even as we are creating it, do we have the mental and emotional capacity to absorb it, understand it, and use it without going insane?

In the 70s, Alvin Toffler introduced the notion of *Future Shock*. His landmark book asked a crucial question that had not been addressed before in the race for technological superiority. Are human beings emotionally equipped to deal with the rapid acceleration of technology and runaway multiplication of information? The question arises as to whether the delicate instrument of the human mind can fathom the sheer quantity of information now available. If Toffler thought this was a problem in the 70s, he should spend a couple of years browsing the World Wide Web.

In the 1980s, Richard Saul Wurman's book, *Information Anxiety,* specifically studied the issue of people's emotional response to information. Wurman was himself a designer of "information graphics," a term that arose from an ergonomic movement toward more user-friendly design. In his book, Wurman looked at why people had negative reactions to information, and how we might deliver information in a less anxiety-producing way.

Knowledge is power, and access to information is considered to be inherently good in a democratic society. Through the Internet, emotionally unstable or anti-social individuals now have access to information that they might not be equipped to use responsibly. People like convicted Oklahoma bomber Timothy McVeigh, whose America online handle was MADBOMBER@aol.com (really!) can easily get access to formulas for high-level explosives that can result in the endangerment of lives. There is a great controversy raging today as to whether sites that publish dangerous information can justifiably be accused of reckless endangerment, as some upcoming lawsuits are suggesting.

Another example of information versus emotional capacity to handle oc-curred while I was writing this chapter: 39 web developers committed a ritual-istic, cult-induced suicide in San Diego (given the challenges of the web business, I'm surprised *more* web developers don't commit mass suicides!). A visit to their web page reveals all, including their plan to hitch a ride with aliens on a comet to a better world. In sharp contrast to the highly secretive Jim Jones cult suicide, this group was very public about their intentions. Yet because the Internet is so vast, it is easy for people like Higher Source and Timothy McVeigh to go unnoticed, even though they are upfront about their dangerous intentions.

What this demonstrates is not only the weakness of certain individuals to handle certain kinds of information, but also the weakness of a culture at large. The massive expansion of information allows more information to get buried. In some cases, as with both McVeigh and Higher Source, the discovery of that buried information might well have saved lives. This does not suggest that government intervention is a solution. What it does suggest is that our social consciousness, as well as our emotional fortitude, need to evolve in order to meet the increasing demands, opportunities, and dangers of the information explosion.

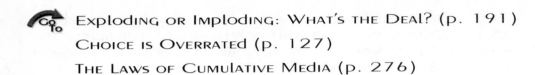

EXPLODING OR IMPLODING: WHAT'S THE DEAL? (p. 191)

CHOICE IS OVERRATED (p. 127)

THE LAWS OF CUMULATIVE MEDIA (p. 276)

MEDIA ARCHITECTURE

Perhaps because of my own background, I have always looked at interactive design as the discipline of media architecture. Interactive media, as it turns out, has a lot more in common with architecture than it does with other traditional media. This does not simply apply to architectural or spatial interface paradigms, such as Virtual Reality. In fact, the entire process of creating a new media product is much more like designing and constructing a building than it is like making a film.

Interactive designers/producers from a film/video would argue vehemently against this hypothesis, but hear me out. Like architects, and unlike filmmakers, interactive designers have to create an experience that is not finite. They must imagine many different variable uses of their application, just as architects must. Furthermore, the interactive designer must be able to translate creative content into mathematical and algorithmic formulae, in the same way that architects must translate their aesthetic decisions into engineering specifications. The discipline of taking a highly creative idea and translating it into a rigorous engineering document combined with the need to acknowledge myriad use patterns for the final product makes architecture, in many respects, a much better model for interactive design than traditional, linear media.

As I mentioned, I am admittedly biased in this area. It happens that I come from an architectural family, and that my frame of reference, literally and figuratively, is strongly rooted in that discipline. In my late teens, I worked at my father's space frame company, where I performed a good deal of research and also worked as an assistant project manager on a large, complex space frame project (for the uninitiated, a space frame is a building or structure consisting of a triangulated metal frame, such as a geodesic dome). This was in 1981 or 82 and we didn't have any computers to do materials handling. I had to fashion a matrix in which I manually filled in every single part of a structure the size of two football fields. Every bolt, every steel tube, every nut, every washer. All transferred by hand from drawings and added up with a standard 10-key adding machine. There were 504 different kinds of parts that had to be added up and then broken down into their common components.

From this master list, all the sub-parts for the members of this gigantic space frame would be ordered. My job was to make this list and keep it updated for every change. The master list was about 40 pages long, with about 15 columns going across the top to enable me to break down the components for each part ordered.

Ten years later, I had to write an interactive script for *Meet the Biospherians*, an interactive laser disk theater that I co-designed and project managed with Dennis Moore of Dennis Earl Moore Productions in Brooklyn. By that time, I had a computer; however, the script was written as a matrix, with the eight Biospherians (inhabitants of Biosphere 2) listed across the top, and all the questions (about 250 in all) listed down the left-hand side of the spreadsheet. I then ticked off which questions would be asked to which individual. This was the master script that was used to create a two-hour nonlinear documentary that distilled into a 10-minute simulated teleconference with thousands of possible variations.

 Biosphere Meets Digisphere: The Biosphere 2 Interactive Theater (p. 91)

I tell these anecdotes by way of pointing out the close relationship between architecture and computers. It is not by mistake that computer structures are frequently referred to as "architecture." Architecture is the structure of a building, and an "open architecture" in computerese refers to a structure that is flexible and interchangeable.

The technical and engineering similarities between architecture and computers are simple to see. What might take a broader leap is an understanding of the relationship of architecture in the design of multimedia. Having worked in both architecture and multimedia design, I find this leap fairly easy to make. Architecture is one of the few artisan forms that requires fairly equal doses of creativity and technical know-how. The same may be said of film, but I believe it is far more true of architecture. The architect must be both artist and engineer, and even the educational degrees, work credentials, and tests required to become a registered architect reflect the rigor of this interdisciplinary profession.

People who create data structures or computational infrastructures are frequently referred to as "architects." There is also a study of organizing information known as "information architecture." Information architecture can refer to how information is structured, or can deal more specifically with the craft of using 3D space as an organizing principle for information.

In a class I teach on 3D design, the course description states "This class could mean the difference between being a construction worker and an architect of cyberspace." I make this distinction because I think many of the current multimedia programs are training construction workers rather than archi-tects—people know how to build things but don't know how to *design* them, production workers conversant in software, but not in interface. Granted these are marketable skills, but there's more to designing multimedia than learning Macromedia Director. Designing really requires something more than just production skills—a sense of structure and form, some familiarity with the history of the craft, a working knowledge of psychology, as well as the aes-thetic sensibility needed to create any kind of interactive experience, whether it be VR-, animation-, or video-based.

Architects often make the best interactive designers because they completely understand these kinds of issues, and they grasp the interface between art and engineering. Nowadays, you are seeing quite a few formally trained architects beginning to create virtual reality environments, often along with their regular "real world" work. As you go browsing VRML sites on the web, you can clearly see who are the architects and who are the construction workers. The architects, at the very least, always have a sense of style and space. Hardcore VRML architects (VRML being the VR protocol for the World Wide Web) often eschew the use of texture maps in favor of pure structure and form. The use of excessive texture maps turns cyberarchitects into interior decorators. In tradi-tional architecture, interior *designers* poo-poo the work of interior *decorators* as superficial and unsophisticated, in the same way cyberarchitects frown on heavily texture-mapped environments as a sign of weak design sensibilities.

 ## ARCHITECTURE AS A NARRATIVE ART (p. 25)

Architects in particular love cyberspace because they get to break free of traditional constraints, such as gravity. You can toy with properties such as volume and scale in cyberspace. You can often recognize the work of conven-tionally trained architects by the preponderance of classic architectural ele-ments placed in surreal or scientifically unfeasible contexts such as floating walls, arches, and columns. The one self-imposed limitation I see with the work of highly architectural cyberspace design is that architects almost always want to build a space that has a floor and walls, that is somehow enclosed or contained like an actual building. Most of the work of the architecturally trained is characterized by the use of right angles and the intense need for a horizon line, some form of planar frame of reference.

On the other hand, fine artists working in cyberspace will often dispense entirely with any kind of real-world reference, or will put them in new and unanticipated contexts. I always enjoy the variety of styles and approaches to cyberspace design because you can see how different sensibilities affect the way that different designers might solve the same or similar problems.

To see some good compare-and-contrast examples of what I'm talking about here, purely in the arena of form (putting story and content aside for a moment), you could look at the work of Construct (http://www.construct.net), whose creative director, Mark Meadows, is an architect; Clay Graham (http://www.best.com/~cyber23/), trained as an information architect; and C. Scott Young (http://www.vrmlknight.com), a fine artist whose work defies any kind of traditional architectural paradigms, but certainly acknowledges and toys with them. Each of these cyberdesigners takes a markedly different approach; but note that they all avoid the use of texture maps, instead opting to work with their models as if with clay—putting the attention into the shape rather than its surface treatment.

There were also some fundamental architectural principles I learned working for my Dad, Peter Pearce, that really came into play when I got into VR. His obsession had always been natural structure, polyhedra, and creating structures that were both stable and efficient. He espoused a theory of economy of materials, which translated effortlessly into a fundamental understanding of the notion of a "polygon budget,"—a maximum number of polygons you can use to build a virtual space. Also, having had a lot of experience in my Dad's factory translating 2D manufacturing drawings into actual 3D objects, I understood how to read three dimensions onto a flat surface. This is a real challenge, as anyone who has ever tried to give an architectural presentation to a client knows. Most people cannot read plans or envision a building based on 2D images. This is why renderings, axonometric, or isometric drawings are used; however, even these can sometimes be misinterpreted. I understood how to take something flat and explode it out into three dimensions, because I'd had to do that with real stuff. Also, because my Dad was designing space frames, he was basically an expert in wire mesh, which is the technique that is used to create 3D models in cyberspace. As with space frame design, wire mesh modeling is based on using the least number of polygons to create the desired surface topography.

Peter Pearce wrote three different books, all of which I would consider to be required reading for the cyberspace designer. The first is a kind of manifesto called *Structure in Nature is a Strategy for Design*. This book, based on an enormous amount of research and experimentation, reveals the rationale by which nature spontaneously and consistently creates various kinds of structure—from the snowflake (see figure M.1) to the bee's honeycomb (see figure M.2) to the soap bubble (see figure M.3) to cracked mud (see figure M.4) to the dragonfly's wing (see figure M.5)—he found consistent rules and protocols to which virtually all forms of structure seem to conform. My father's observations led him to the amusing but provable conclusion that nature is essentially lazy because all natural structures are derived from the principle of finding the shortest distance between to points. After studying numerous natural patterns from the microscopic to the macroscopic, he further concluded that natural structure is based on the principle of triangulation. Natural forms tend to structure themselves using three-rate intersections, which would account for why we see hexagonal structures in so many places in nature. The triangle is of course both the most efficient and the strongest of the basic polygonal shapes requiring the least material for most tensile strength. It is therefore the basis for geodesic domes and other space frame structures. It wasn't until recently that I learned that in cyberspace, all polygons are ultimately triangulated—making the triangle the basic building block of all Virtual Reality. Everything in cyberspace, from a bicycle to an apple to a fish, is nothing more than a triangulated space frame.

Figure M.1

Snowflakes showing hexagonal pattern with infinite variations (photo courtesy of Peter Pearce)

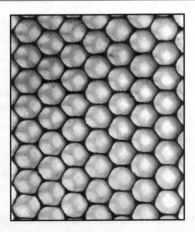

Figure M.2

Bees' ingenius hexagonal architecture mimics the hexagonal design of the snowflake (photo courtesy of Peter Pearce)

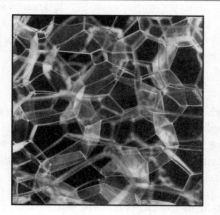

Figure M.3

Soap bubbles assemble in consistent triangulated configurations (photo courtesy of Peter Pearce)

Figure M.4

Cracked mud meets at three-rate intersections, bearing resemblance to the natural formation of soap bubbles (photo courtesy of Peter Pearce)

Figure M.5

The dragonfly wing reveals a pattern of three-rate intersections, not unlike those seen in cracked mud (photo courtesy of Peter Pearce)

My father's second book, *The Polyhedra Primer* is to VR designers what E.B. White's *The Elements of Style* is to writers. It is basically a guide to the grammar of polyhedra; each polyhedron is named and illustrated, starting from the most essential, and working up to the most complex. This basic guide to three-dimensional geometry is invaluable to anyone who is creating a world out of lines and vertices.

Experiments in Form, my father's third book, is based on a course that he taught at Cal State Northridge and California Institute of the Arts when he was Associate Dean of Design there. It is a series of experiments to teach students about form and structure. Among several exercises is one in which students create various randomly curved objects and then are asked to translate them into what is essentially a wireframe model; except the entire course was taught to architecture students and the objects were made out of wood, foam, cardboard, and plaster (see figures M.6–M.12). I have always felt that this book and the course that goes with it would be a revelation to anyone trying to figure out how to create curved and irregular objects in Virtual Reality.

Figure M.6

Experiments in Form: This random assembly of 30 cubes begins a sequence exploring different approaches to the same form (photos courtesy of Peter Pearce)

Image series continues

Figure M.7

Contoured sections incorporated into egg-crate model

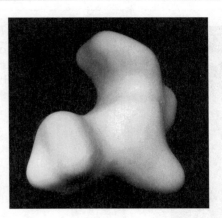

Figure M.8

This continuous surface version represents an optimized enclosure of the random cube assembly

Figure M.9

A triangulated polyhedral approximation of the shape

Image series continues

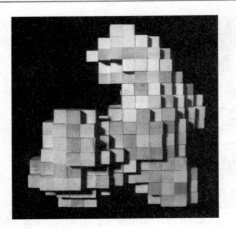

Figure M.10

A cubic grid using smaller units than the random assembly

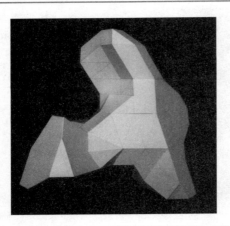

Figure M.11

An approximation of the envelope using closest packet equal shares

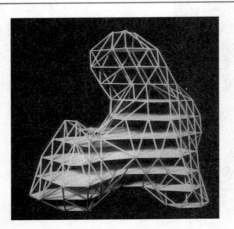

Figure M.12

Envelope expressed as a triangulated framework derived by connecting the centers of the spheres

Although originally developed for architects and industrial designers, these three books are invaluable to the VR designer; they provide a unique perspective, and also offer 3D designers a different way to think about modeling. By understanding fundamental principles of structure and form, borrowing from nature, and exploring a variety of means of sculpting 3D objects, designers can further develop their craft and become better at fashioning the alternate realities of their imaginations.

What I bring to this equation is a strange hybrid between content (film, storytelling) and this exposure to not only architecture, but the fundamental principles of structure. I suppose this makes me a kind of mutant form of storyteller/architect. I see both real physical space and virtual space as media, and I always have. To me, real space is a medium that uses actual objects, matter, materials, and measurable physical space as a context for experience; cyberspace uses the simulation or illusion of moving through 3D space as a medium for experience. There are certainly distinctions to be made between the two, but the essential principle is the same. So the question is not how do you design the space, but how do you design the *experience* that the space is ultimately going to facilitate. To do this, you need to effectively look at this as a new genre entirely, one that combines the crafts of story and game with the discipline of architecture to create something that can best be described as a story space, or as I like to call it, a narrative environment.

Mediaspace

Since the late 50s and early 60s, fine artists and media researchers have been experimenting with the notion of a media environment or mediaspace. If immersive Virtual Reality removes the fourth wall by sucking you into the media, then a mediaspace achieves the same effect by doing just the opposite: It sucks the media out into the physical environment.

Although mediaspace can have different meanings, depending on who's talking, I use the word to define a physical installation in a real environment that integrates media into a physical environment. These days, when you say the word "site," most people, at least in the Internet culture, assume you mean a web site. But when I say site, I mean an actual physical space. Mediaspace has its most direct applications in location-based entertainment, also known as "special venue," design, as well as fine art, museum exhibits, and public space. Mediaspace can also have some practical applications, as you'll see from some of the examples given in the following pages.

In the realm of video art, there is unquestionably no artist better known for creating mediaspace than Nam June Paik, a Korean artist whose work spans four decades. Paik, who is credited with coining the term "electronic super-highway," began building video installations in the 60s. He made robots out of television sets, created abstract video paintings, created some of the very first video wall art, and built entire rooms full of monitors that immersed you in a total video environment. One of his best known works is the *American Flag* videowall, a patchwork of moving images that creates a waving flag that is both beautiful in its fluid motion and illuminating in its content. The fusion of our nation's two most powerful archetypes, and the actual imagery Paik uses to create this flag, gives an irreverent and insightful glimpse into American culture. The influence of Paik's characteristically rhythmic video collage style, including fast-cuts, repeated imagery, montage of text, and visual and abstract graphics, can best be seen in the contemporary music video genre, where visuals become a form of musical expression rather than a means of conveying narrative.

Paik's playful and inventive work is rife with social commentary. He celebrates and exaggerates the power of television, while at the same time revealing its dangers and mundanities. In recent years, he has also begun to incorporate digital communication into his repertoire of social satire. As part of a 1996 exhibit at the San Jose Museum of Modern Art entitled *Superhighly*, Paik featured a piece called *E-Mail vs. Snail Mail*, showing his interpretation of a modern-day post office. An old-fashioned wall of P.O. Boxes reveals a window in which we see a video of a sleeping postal clerk; on the Information Super-highway, snail mail (as we digital types call it) is evidently a thing of the past. Paik also installed a fax machine in the exhibit. He posted the fax number as part of the exhibit, inviting visitors to fax in messages. They could then return to the museum and see their own faxes on the endless stream of fax paper issuing forth from the machine.

Paik was in with the Flux crowd, and actually made a variety of non-video installations as well. One of them was a goof on one of Paik's mentors, John Cage—known for his "treated pianos," in which he inserted objects between the strings or attached various items to the hammers. Paik's version, *Treated Toy Piano*, a miniature instrument covered with various objects, invites the same kind of playful interaction as Marcel Duchamp's bicycle wheel did 40 years earlier.

A number of artists, including Paik, also experimented with videospace as a social medium. Paik's remotely linked events, demonstrated McLuhan's hypothesis of a Global Village by closing geographical boundaries.

Within the interactive community, the Crown Prince and Princess of remote videospace and video as a social medium are Kit Galloway and Sherrie Rabinowitz. When I say videospace in this context, I refer to the shared space within the video environment, as opposed to the notion of placing media within a physical environment. During the 70s, Kit and Sherrie began to experiment with various remote video installations. In their 1977 piece *Hole in Space*, they linked together two locations by placing a large screen and video camera in store windows in New York City and Century City. This unmediated experience had no emcee and there were no instructions, no explanations. People thus evolved their own uses for this mysterious device. They began to create their own forms of interpersonal interaction through this new social medium, including phoning ahead and making appointments to meet at the *Hole in Space* (see figure M.13).

Figure M.13

Kit Galloway and Sherrie Rabinowitz' *Hole in Space* used live video to bring together people in Los Angeles and New York, 1977 (courtesy Electronic Café International)

For the 1984 Los Angeles Olympic Arts Festival, Kit and Sherrie created the first implementation of *The Electronic Café*, a multi-site installation throughout Los Angeles. *The Electronic Café* was a collaborative art space. Even though Kit and Sherrie were the artists, the art was not actually done by them; rather, they created the tools to facilitate the artistic expression of others. People in remote locations could thus draw and create original digital art together with *Electronic Café* participants in other, remote locations.

Kit and Sherrie eventually found a permanent home for *The Electronic Cafe*. With headquarters in Santa Monica, California (commonly known to Angelinos as "Multimedia Gulch"), Kit and Sherrie's constantly evolving international network of "cafés," have such unusual venues as a submarine which had been converted into a culture center in Denmark. *The Electronic Café* has become a regular hangout for digerati around the world, and is the site of an annual New Year's party, the only one I know of that spans time zones. At hourly intervals, a new city rings in the New Year, accompanied by the cheers and noisemakers of friends in another locale who have already rung in the new year or shortly will. For years, I have conducted a one-woman version of this: When I lived in New York, I used to have an annual tradition of calling my family in California just after midnight. Now that I live in California, I always call a friend on the East Coast at 9:01 to see how the New Year is going.

Kit and Sherrie have used their work in a wide variety of applications, some artistic, some social, and some clinical. A number of their projects have involved compositing together video from remote locations. They have hosted intercontinental jam sessions, provided a shared video stage for dancers in remote locations, and even brought deaf people together to communicate via sign language in a shared videospace (see figures M.14, M.15, and M.16, respectively). Kit and Sherrie have also helped people get over phobias of touching, helped resolve interpersonal conflicts, and facilitated what is probably the first actual examples of virtual sex. They have also experimented with videospace in a commerce application, in which a customer could try out new furniture by compositing it into her empty living room for a preview before making an electronic purchase. If anyone could be dubbed the host and hostess of cyberspace, it would have to be Kit Galloway and Sherrie Rabinowitz.

Figure M.14

An *Electronic Café* multi-site jam session (courtesy Electronic Café International)

 PLATE 42

Figure M.15

Shared video stage for dancers in remote locations (courtesy Electronic Café International)

PLATE 41

Figure M.16

Deaf teenagers in two different locations communicating via sign language (courtesy Electronic Café International)

PLATE 43

Myron Krueger is considered the father of interactive mediaspace. Krueger began creating "responsive environments," as he calls them, in 1969. Krueger's installation *METAPLAY*, first shown in 1970, integrated computer graphics with video, and had echoes of Ivan Sutherland's *Sketchpad*. A guest was projected on a large projection screen while "the man behind the curtain" (Krueger himself) drew computer graphics images on the screen from an unseen location. In one demonstration, he began by drawing outlines around a visitor's hand. Each time the visitor moved his hand, Krueger would draw a new outline. The visitor then began to draw in the air with his finger. Krueger, responding to the cue from the visitor, used the pen to follow the finger, thus allowing the visitor himself to draw on the screen. The visitor then passed the magic finger on to the next guest by touching her finger (see figure M.17).

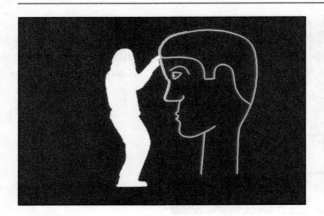

Figure M.17

Digital Drawing in Myron Krueger's *METAPLAY* (image courtesy of Myron Krueger)

Another installation, *CRITTER*, evolved this idea further by creating a computer-generated "intelligent" creature that would follow the player around on-screen (see figure M.18). Krueger discovered that if he captured the visitor as a silhouette, he could translate the visitor's outline into computer data. This enabled Krueger to create computer graphics that could interact with the visitor's shadow on a screen. *CRITTER* would follow you, cling to your leg if you tried to walk away, and crawl up the side of your shadow to dance a jig on the top of your head. If it crawled up again, it might do something different—somersault off your head into your hand, for example. Visitors had various reactions to *CRITTER* … some tried to avoid its attentions, while others (presumably animal lovers) would respond positively, petting it or trying to communicate with it.

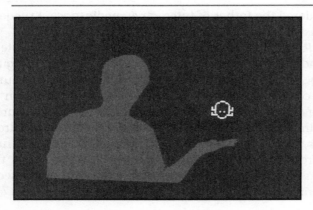

Figure M.18

CRITTER affords a playful metaphor for one of the central dramas of our time: the encounter between humans and machines (image courtesy of Myron Krueger)

These interactions, like many Krueger observed, were completely spontaneous and unplanned. Over the years, Krueger has done (and continues to do) many such installations, combining computer graphics, remote video links, and environmental effects to allow people to play together in what he calls "responsive environments" or "Artificial Reality." Characteristic of Krueger's body of work is an iterative and interactive process with the audience. Each new work seems to arise from some spontaneous reaction of a visitor to a previous work. So not only is the environment responsive, so is the artist himself, truly collaborating with the audience and crafting each new installation first and foremost as an experience derived from other experiences created by the visitors themselves. In this way, Krueger's entire body of work has itself been an evolving interactive process.

It is interesting to note the philosophical differences between Krueger's work versus that of Kit Galloway and Sherrie Rabinowitz. Kit and Sherrie are committed to working within the form of video. They believe that the literal depiction of the body is a powerful tool, so they have never done anything to abstract the physical body, nor are they particularly big fans of cyberspace avatars. They are interested in the risk and intimacy involved in exposing yourself and your body image in a media environment. Krueger, on the other hand, found that there are certain advantages to working with silhouettes. By reducing the human form to a monochromatic entity, you could translate it into computer; but also, he found that people behaved differently when they were no longer "themselves" in that immediate and intimate a way (see figures M.19 and M.20). I find it interesting that what began as a similar quest led to divergent paths, each of which has its own merits. In either case, both Krueger and Galloway/Rabinowitz have put a great deal of thought into their work, and collectively, know more than anyone about interactivity in a shared video space.

Figure M.19

Painting the town. The participant turns on lights in buildings using her fingers (image courtesy of Myron Krueger)

 PLATE 45

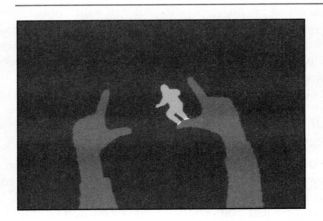

Figure M.20

A Tiny Dancer in My Hand
from Krueger's *VIDEOPLACE*
installation (image courtesy
of Myron Krueger)

 PLATE 44

Krueger also experimented with practical applications of remote video. *VIDEODESK* enables people in different geographical locations to collaborate in a shared video workspace. The video camera captures you and your partner's hands in silhouette, and then puts them into a shared videospace in which you can point at graphics on the screen, paint with your fingers, and manipulate or use your hands to sculpt graphical clay. This enables people in remote locations to create collaborative projects using a shared videospace. Today, Krueger's Artificial Reality Laboratory, located at the back of the Connecticut State Museum of Natural History, is an ongoing venue in which to experience Krueger's magical media worlds.

Several research institutions have also experimented with various kinds of mediaspace. The Media Room, developed at the MIT Media Lab by Richard Bolt, Christopher Schmandt, and Eric Hulteen, enables you to use voice and finger to move objects around in the space. By using the command "Put that," then pointing at the desired object, and then pointing at the desired location and saying "there," you can manipulate objects in a mediaspace with nothing more than your voice and finger.

Nicholas Negroponte's Architecture Machine Group, which later evolved into the MIT Media Lab, was created in the 70s to address ways in which computer technology could be integrated into the real world. Negroponte, like Krueger, envisioned a responsive environment of a more practical nature: a house that could respond to its occupants. Your house could know what you wanted and when, anticipate your every move, recognize your voice, protect you and your belongings, and assist you in a variety of ways, almost as if it were a living organism. This somewhat entertaining science fiction view of the future may seem amusing now, but all the technology currently exists to do this. It's just a question of who will step forward and begin to conceive of an architecture that is integral with media and technology. Negroponte's group have been innova-tors in nearly every arena of interactive technology, including the notion of a spatial interface, which simulate physical space through video or computer graphics. The term emerging for such work is called "spatial media," which is in a sense, the inverse of mediaspace. Mediaspace seeks to integrate media with the actual environment, while spatial media imitates the real environment within the digital or videospace.

 Spatial Media (p. 442)

In terms of Virtual Reality specifically, mediaspace is becoming an increasingly more popular way of relating to a virtual space. Variations on Krueger's *VIDEODESK*, known as "immerse-a-desk," create a flat or tiled surface on which you can manipulate 3D objects. This kind of technology is particularly well-suited for things such as CAD (see a 3D model of a car) or medical visualization (operate on a patient on the table).

The *CAVE*, developed at University of Illinois at Chicago's Electronic Visualization Lab, is a projection cube that you can stand inside to experience a different kind of Virtual Reality immersion than offered by the Head-Mounted Display. A group of up to eight can stand inside this space, where 3D computer graphics are projected on three walls and the ceiling. One person generally controls the orientation by wearing a head-tracker, but other interactions can be controlled by other visitors. Standing inside the *CAVE* is like standing inside a box of light, surrounded on all sides by high-end three-dimensional graphics, enabling you to literally get inside of a virtual space. It is ideal for three-dimensional mathematical and scientific visualizations, allowing you to go inside a geometric form, or a biological process, see inside a human body, or manipulate a molecule. It was also used by fine artist Rita Addison in her groundbreaking VR experience *Detour: Brain Deconstruction Ahead,* which used the *CAVE* to simulate perceptual anomalies she suffered as a result of brain damage.

 The Revelation of Rita: VR and the Power of Empathy (p. 413)

At the 1995 Interactive Media Festival (IMF) at Los Angeles' Variety Arts Center, there were three VR art pieces that took place in immersive mediaspace. One of these was Christa Sommerer and Laurent Mignonneau's *A-Volve*. It took place in a pool of water, whose bottom was a rear-projection video screen. Onto the screen were projected evolving organisms that had actually been created by participants. You could stand around the pool and rest your hand in the water as you observed these computer-generated life forms move about, procreate, eat each other, and so on. Thus, the virtual world intersected with the real world as a body of water both real and imagined. This simple yet highly effective tactile device served to dissolve the boundary between matter and media.

Another piece featured at the IMF was *Barcode Hotel*, by Perry Hoberman. I was particularly taken with this imaginative playspace because it utilized an input device that had long fascinated me and that I had always wanted to use in an installation: the bar code reader. That's right. An ordinary bar code reader, like the kind used in grocery or clothing stores. Three or four large tables faced a large screen, and each table was covered with bar codes. Each bar code had a direction for the virtual environment. Using hand-held bar code readers that hung from the ceiling, you could swipe the command of your choice and effect 3D objects in the virtual environment on the large screen. Large cubes on top of each table contained bar codes that enabled you to change objects. You could thus opt to be a bowling pin by swiping the cube, and then, by swiping various codes on the table, change your size, your surface texture, and direct your object to engage in certain movements such as bouncing or shaking. You could also mess with the little room the objects were playing in, changing the wall texture, or even causing an earthquake (a natural for the local Angelino participants).

Barcode Hotel was fun because it was simple and because it was for multiple users. It became a kind of digital dance floor where people could experiment with various controls and see the effect that their object might have on others. This is the sort of project that bridges the lines between art and entertainment, a new kind of collaborative playspace that, like Myron Krueger's work, offers the participant the opportunity to explore and experiment. *Barcode Hotel*'s simple and amusing premise becomes the impetus for a variety of different results within a fairly narrow set of parameters. As a game designer, I particularly liked its elegant, game-like structure. Of course, the idea of using a low-cost bar code as an input interface and bar code readers as input devices was brilliant to someone like me, whose biggest challenge in creating theme park attractions is how to have the most input at the lowest cost.

Another mediaspace piece featured at the IMF was created by Karl Simms and consisted of a row of screens, each of which had a sensitive pad in front of it. The computer generated abstract designs based on a genetic algorithm. By stepping on the different pads, you could select images you wanted to combine. The computer generated a new range of images based on combining the two selected images and processing them with the genetic algorithm. Participants could interactively instigate a graphical evolution as it "bred" new forms with each new genetic combination. One of the most interesting things about this piece is that Simm's code itself was part of the installation: the computer had a red-on-black text display and you could actually watch the code at work in real time as the experience progressed. Also geared toward multiple participants, Simm's work was a new genre of interactive painting, a collaboration between man and machine through a highly dynamic computational process. That computation was itself a work of art adds another angle of depth to this simple yet sophisticated piece. Hearkening back to the Flux movement, Simm's program is a kind of "score," a framework for visitor-created art. Simm's living code, like the scores of John Cage and Yoko Ono (to name only two well-known scorers) has a life of its own and becomes its own unique artistic statement, aside from its actual operation.

 ART IS A VERB (p. 29)

As is often the case with new technologies, it is frequently fine artists whose innovations leap forward most rapidly. Unhindered by nondisclosure agreements or the constraints of practicality to which most military, corporate, or academic R&D labs must adhere, artists have the opportunity to explore the "softer" side of interactivity. They can experiment more fluidly with the audience, see what they are going to do, and respond swiftly and effectively. The work of Krueger, Rabinowitz and Galloway, and Paik is particularly captivating when you consider that these artists often work with little or no budget, and for the most part, built or hybridized their own technology to achieve their visions. The need to work within limited resources inspires a level of inventiveness that often leads to unpredictable outcomes. Because the work of fine artists is in the public forum, artists have the opportunity to engage in a more dynamic dialogue and collaboration with the audience than the formal institutions currently exploring these innovations.

When looking to the future of technology, I tend to look first to the artists. I have noticed consistently that, although they generally don't always have the technological firepower of the big research institutions or commercial R&D facilities, they are the ones that pave the way for new forms of interaction. On the rare occasions when they *do* have that firepower—and believe it or not, it *does* happen—magical things can happen.

 V-ART (p. 494)

SOCIAL COMPUTING (p. 434)

NARRATIVE ENVIRONMENTS: VIRTUAL REALITY AS A STORYTELLING MEDIUM (p. 329)

THE MILITARY ENTERTAINMENT COMPLEX

My first assignment at my first interactive job in 1983 was to do research into gaming and simulation. I knew barely anything about games, and I had never even heard the word simulation before. In my research, I discovered that there were these top secret systems being developed by the military and the aerospace industry that were super high-tech and super cool. They cost millions of dollars to build, and they were beyond your wildest dreams of what technology could do. Only problem was, they were top secret military systems. Not only would we never have access to these amazing toys, but it was unlikely that we would ever even be able to find out what they were.

I remember discovering this and thinking how frustrating and ridiculous it was—that we would probably have to invent all these technologies from scratch; that we wouldn't have a fraction of the money the military had at its disposal; and that a lot of our ideas were going to be too expensive to implement. Why couldn't we get a hold of some of this military technology? After all, they were paid for with our tax dollars. But it was the Cold War. It was the military. There was no way around it.

Around the same time in 1983, I remember having lunch with one of my colleagues at Schlossberg and a friend of hers. He told me about this wild thing you wore on your head that would move pictures around in front of your eyes, and move sounds around your head at the same time so that you felt like you were in a real place moving around. He was developing this for NASA to use in training astronauts. It was totally wild, totally proprietary, and again, impossible to access.

After that, I never thought much about those military projects again until 10 years later when I got invited by Iwerks and Evans & Sutherland to help them put together *Virtual Adventures*. I really didn't know what I was getting into at first, because the first phase of the project was done remotely with no access to any technology. I didn't know we were using a flight simulator graphics engine. All I had been told was that it was "the coolest thing you've ever seen," according to Ed Newquist, Iwerks' then VP of Film, who I worked closely with on the project.

When I finally realized what was going on the first time I met with the E&S team in person, I must say it was nothing short of mind-blowing. All of a sudden this realization came over me that this was that thing that I had read about as a young interactive writer, those military systems that were totally and unbelievably cool, but that no civilian would ever be able to get their hands on. And *I* was going to get to play with this thing! It was one of those dream-come-true scenarios.

Virtual Adventures was a landmark project in many ways, but it was also a prototype of an alliance between an entertainment company and a military technology company. It was not the only such alliance at the time. In fact, there was a significant push going on at that time for military VR and high-tech companies to set their sights on the entertainment industry.

The reason was simple. The Berlin Wall was down. The USSR was no longer. No more was there a looming threat from the east, and so the government could no longer justify the billions of dollars of annual expenditures being poured into what was nothing short of a Cold War meltdown. Things were going to have to change. Cuts were going to have to be made.

This left the military contractors in a bind. They had been resting on their laurels for three decades, living off a seemingly infinite supply of paranoia money. And now, it was starting to dry up. Where could they turn? What other client besides the DOD could afford their exorbitant rates and support the level of high-tech wizardry of which they had become the masters? There was only one place to turn: Hollywood.

Thus was born "The Military Entertainment Complex." It's a funny cultural contrast, breeding peculiar alliances and strange bedfellows. In the early 1990s, if you went to a VR or high-end computer graphics conference, you were likely to see a strange contrast of types: you'd get your basic military nerd, a guy in one of those funky sweaters with the cotton reinforced shoulders; you'd have these San Francisco VR types, long hair and earrings, a Celtic tattoo here and there, maybe some green hair or combat boots; one guy always used to show up in a skirt; there were a few arcade guys showing their latest VR creations; and then you'd get the Hollywood types, mostly from theme park companies, scouting for new technologies to buy or steal from the military and research community.

Some of the earliest location-based entertainment (LBE—also known as "out-of-home") VR products were actually just military simulators that were ticketed on a per-ride basis. *Fighter Town* was one of the first of these. All they did was take a cockpit simulator and just rent it out for about 20 bucks a pop. Greystone Technologies, another military company, repurposed a flight simulator and went on to develop a variety of different gaming systems. A number of other military contractors have also been working closely with entertainment companies in Hollywood and Silicon Valley. One common result is that the military companies often lose their most creative people. After doing an entertainment project, they don't want to go back to reading a thousand page spec for a sub simulator. The entertainment companies often end up stealing the best people away from their military partners. Another scenario is that the creative team behind the big entertainment project will all exit stage left and form their own entertainment company.

Military companies are also trying go get in on the act with the film industry, marketing their 3D engines and image generators for film special effects. Up until the advent of high-powered PC workstations, nobody could really compete with SGI (Silicon Graphics Inc.) machines, which have been the standard in the film industry and have also been very popular for military projects, medical imaging, and other VR applications. Pretty much from the beginning, SGIs have been the main machine for high-end graphics in film effects and real-time 3D.

But faster, better, cheaper (cheaper, cheaper, cheaper) computers have been creeping up on SGI and starting to tug at their market share, forcing them to scale down from $100,000 workstations to $10,000 systems, to compete with the smaller, less expensive systems. The really amazing and even frightening thing is that you could do on a beefed up $10,000 PC in 1997 the same thing it took that $100,000 Onyx Reality Engine to do as little as two years earlier.

The PC workstation movement is not only giving SGI a run for its money; it's also having a big impact on The Military Entertainment Complex. Although those alliances continue to form and scouts from Disney, Sony, Paramount, and Universal continue to investigate ways of using high-end military technology in entertainment, the need for high-priced, high-tech is not as urgent as it used to be. It takes a lot less to do a lot more now than it did a few years ago, and people are looking to find ways to do high-end work with low- to mid-end systems.

In the meantime, efforts are still being made to forge weapons into plowshares, and I certainly hope these continue. It would be a shame to let all that taxpayer money go to waste.

Mixed Media, Mixed Message

Our time is a time for crossing barriers, for erasing old categories—for probing ground. When two seemingly disparate elements are imaginatively poised, put in apposition in new and unique ways, startling discoveries often result (Marshall McLuhan, 1967).

The preceding statement was made in the influential book *The Medium Is the Massage* nearly *30* years ago. McLuhan's visuo-textual satire of the now-famous quote from his previous work, *Understanding Media*, provided a hands-on, participatory elaboration of the principles embodied in his most famous insight. Standing at the heart of the spiraling vortex of multimedia, McLuhan's ideas take on even more meaning today than they did in the 1960s when they were first formulated. It is a testament to their perennial qualities that they continue to apply, even as new media emerge and converge. McLuhan imagined, and accurately, that eventually all media would merge into a continuous unified media field. Through digital technology and telecommunications, that is precisely what is happening today.

Interactive multimedia represents the ultimate convergence of media, combining everything from text to graphics to photo to video to music to computer technology. It is McLuhan's dream, and perhaps his worst nightmare. But the thing that is most compelling and most interesting about interactive multimedia is not that it is multimedia, but that it is interactive. Interactivity is the part of the equation that is the most touted but the least understood. I think McLuhan envisioned that this kind of electric environment, as he called it, would result in a new level of democracy and interrelation between individuals, communities, and nations. This might indeed come to pass, and in some arenas, is beginning to. At the same time, the Pandora's box of the computer has also issued forth such digital poltergeists as *Doom* and *Mortal Kombat*. Is this the empowerment that McLuhan had hoped would be available to an electrically savvy youth culture? Was he expecting that the "hot" media would ultimately leave us with a painful blister, even as it offers us new forms of community and insight? It was also McLuhan who pointed out that we were using old tools in the new media, and this is even more true with multimedia as it was with the monomedia that preceded it.

As is true of most brilliant insight, McLuhan's observation—"The medium is the message"—was at once revolutionary and self-evident. That the form of communication of ideas was as important as the content of ideas, and that, in fact, the media in which they were communicated was inextricably linked to the content, was like a light bulb going off in our collective consciousness.

 Theory of Media Evolution: The Four Axioms (p. 480)

McLuhan alerted us that certain modes of thought, certain ideas, would not have emerged had we not had the tools with which to communicate them. In fact, all media is an extension of our natural senses, and in turn these media influence evolution of these senses: The wheel was an extension of the foot, the book an extension of the eye. (I differ from McLuhan in that I think the written word is really a visualization of the voice, because it is derived from the spoken word and is not really a visual medium.) It is ironic that, just as Plato predicted writing would lead to the death of the oral tradition, McLuhan and other modern theorists predicted that the audio-visual media would lead to illiteracy in the text tradition.

 Bookmark: Interactivity and the New Literacy (p. 102)

Word to the Motherboard: Computers and Literacy (p. 530)

Indeed, new technology has always been met with alarm by arbiters of whatever happens to be the dominating medium. In the Middle Ages, the printing press, which made literacy possible for the so-called "masses," was seen as a threat to the status quo. All books until then were handwritten and few persons had access to the great works of literature, including the Bible. At that point, the Catholic Church controlled all the media, and granted access only to the aristocracy. This was a centralized, hierarchical system in which the medieval equivalent to a media conglomerate had total dominion over most of Europe's literary work. When the printing press arrived, it took the control of media out of the hands of the Church and aristocracy and into the hands of the people. In fact, it was the printing press that was partly responsible for the democratic revolutions and reformations in France, England, and the United States, all of which relied heavily on the printing press to disseminate their messages.

McLuhan observed that the early form of any new medium is characterized by a period in which we continue to use old techniques and old tools in the context of the new medium. I think that this is a natural and necessary phase in the progress curve for any medium. The first movies were filmed plays, and the first television shows were filmed radio programs, ad nauseam. You can view the maturity of a newly developed medium as a coming of age process, at which point it "comes into its own," developing its own forms, conventions, and standards. Until film became its own medium and not a documentation of another medium, it was an immature art form. When a medium is in this phase of immaturity, all it manages to do is add or subtract from the form that it mimics. Eventually, as artists begin to explore the qualities unique to that medium, a sense of craft is developed. As a result, the new medium becomes "greater than the sum of its parts," and then we have a mature medium.

 THE LAWS OF CUMULATIVE MEDIA (p. 276)

THEORY OF MEDIA EVOLUTION (p. 468)

It is ironic that it is almost never the generation that invented the new technology that masters and claims it as its own. The Lumiere Brothers, inventors of the film projector, are not considered to be great filmmakers, even though they were probably the first. The subsequent generations are those who are able to truly breathe life into the new medium. Some of the early filmmakers were truly brilliant. Sergei Eisenstein and D.W. Griffith were arguably the two most influential filmmakers in creating a new art form. Griffith is credited with inventing the "feature" film, the cinematic equivalent of the novel. Eisenstein introduced techniques of cinematography, editing, and montage that enabled film to manipulate time, space, and emotions. Prior to these innovations, most of Griffith and Eisenstein's contemporaries, even the best of them, did not get past the "filmed play" stage. After these explorers created new conventions, the pioneers could then come in and begin to develop craft around these new conventions and standards.

EINSTEIN, EISENSTEIN, ANd THE SPACE-TIME CONTINUUM (p. 186)

In this dialogue between artistic innovation and audience understanding lies the evolutionary leap that can bring a medium to fruition. In the age of convergence, this dialogue happens in real time; for in this new all-media, there is no longer a performer and an audience, but a conversation between the medium and the user or player. Indeed, we need to entirely rethink our concept of "audience." We also need to be in a constant interchange with the audience, each evolving in response to the other, so that we may reach a level of resonance in which everyone is on the same wavelength. This is, in a sense, the equivalent of learning that we don't have to run from the theater when we see the oncoming train. We need to develop new perceptual tools and new ways of integrating our media into our thinking and behavior process. This level of cognitive evolution must happen on the part of the audience, but it must happen even more on the part of the artist. It is truly the artist's responsibility to understand both the medium and the audience and find ways to bring the two closer together.

If the medium is the message, multimedia poses a whole new array of challenges. In addition to interactivity, which is in itself an entirely new way of thinking about the media experience, we also have to deal with the "multi" side of the equation. If the medium is the message, what do you do when you are dealing with quite possibly every medium there is within the context of a single medium? How do I integrate text, video, animation, and sound? How to I mix narrative with real-time 3D graphics. When we start to mush all these ideas and conventions together, we are faced with startling results. Some of these results startle us in a good way; others leave us wondering "what went wrong?" It is only through trial and error and experimentation that we can really hope to get the startling results we want. Sometimes we will fail, other times, succeed. Eventually (and hopefully), we will transcend the stage of derivative content and create experiences that are unique to both interactive media in general and to the specific media being converged.

The problem of "mixed media, mixed message," is largely the result of this derivative tendency. A great example of this is the web site *The Spot*. Everyone thought this was going to be the killer app on the Net, but it started out with several inherent flaws in its premise which predestined it to the novelty graveyard. First of all, *The Spot* was basically *Melrose Place* on the web. It was an episodic television series—the only problem was, it was all done with text and photos. Thus, the convention was borrowed from one medium, but the media itself was coming from something entirely different. This is a classic case of mixed media, mixed message. Within the conventions of television, we are accustomed to certain things, to a certain production value, to a certain level of performance and writing. By trying to copy television in a different medium, we are setting ourselves up for failure. The product will naturally be compared to that from which it was derived, and in this case, it cannot possibly measure up, even if the writing and graphic production values are exemplary.

There is nothing inherently wrong with co-opting conventions across media. This is done all the time, and much great work has been created in just this way; however, you should consider very carefully what conventions you repurpose and in what context. Eisenstein's early films, for example, were equated with poetry more than narrative. He was trying to capture rhythm and emotional content more than story. Griffith, on the other hand, was predominantly story-driven. Borrowing from poetry within the context of a visual art makes a lot of sense. It is different enough, and the expectations are divergent enough that the film medium only stands to benefit from such an exchange.

An example of a successful convention of co-opting is the recent CD-ROM hit *You Don't Know Jack!* In this case, the pre-existing television game show conventions from which the title is derived already lend themselves to interactivity. In fact, game shows are a great example of interactivity waiting to happen. In a game show environment both the interactivity and the choice of which media to combine made sense: text and audio are all that is needed to make this a really fun game. The whole experience happens inside the individual player's mind and between the competing players, which is exactly where it should happen.

Although "interactive movies" have been the panacea of multimedia, there are few more pointless exercises than trying to adapt film conventions to interactive media. Unlike television, which has an ongoing life of temporal events, film is the most profoundly un-interactive of media. Other than the remote control device, television does not offer much in the way of immediate interactivity; however, television has a certain amount of audience interaction within the frame of its ongoing content. Week to week, programmers respond, whether directly or indirectly, to the audience. They change content based on ratings, a form of audience feedback; news coverage frequently influences real-life events; weekly programs encourage audience dialogues between episodes; and most viewers will have a strong verbal interchange with a game show or a sporting event. Film, on the other hand, is completely unresponsive to the audience on every level. A film is made in a relative vacuum. It is not until it is complete and shown at previews that anyone has any idea what it will look like; and even then, not until it hits the theaters can we determine the audience response. There is no room to adapt, respond, or modify. It's a take it or leave it proposition. The film is released. If nobody goes it closes; if they do go, it stays open for as long as people will line up to see it. After that, it goes to video. End of story.

Filmmakers and marketers probably know less about their audience than any other media creators. Another barrier between creator and audience is that the convention of film itself is highly unresponsive. In a film, you are supposed to sit in the dark, be quiet, and just watch. Don't get me wrong, I am a total film nut. I believe movies are one of the greatest inventions of our time, but looking at them from an interactive designer's point of view, they are the furthest thing there is from what I want to create. Not to say I wouldn't try…because there is nothing I love more than to attempt the impossible. But I would be very cognizant of the pitfalls.

In looking at what conventions to borrow from where, it's very important to look first at your content. I am very frightened by people who talk about a medium when they don't even really understand what content they are trying to create. Within that, I would then look at two things:

- What existing media conventions fit that content, if any?
- How does this content lend itself to an interactive experience?

One of the things you need to consider is what you mean when you say "media." Most people think of media in terms of Hollywood, "the media." So when they look for conventions to borrow or upend, they are looking to the entertainment industry to define what is meant by media. But there are many other media. Books are a medium. Newspapers are a medium. Theater can be defined as a medium. I borrow most of my design conventions from arenas outside the conventional notion of media: board games and improvisational theater being two of the major influences. Game conventions are very useful for interactive designers to look at because they are already interactive. They provide many clues as to how to bring people into the process, and an excellent vocabulary for multi-user interactivity. Game structure also has a lot in common with story structure, so I have found that a method that works really well is to combine game conventions and story conventions as a way of creating interactive narrative.

If you borrow from straight story conventions, you will always be in a fight with yourself. Most of how story structure is taught precludes any kind of deviation from an authored plot. Games, on the other hand, begin with a premise while the plot itself is derived by the players. Thus, you can begin to converge conventions and create a new genre that is an evolution rather than a derivation of preceding conventions.

This is an important distinction to make. Rare is the case where a new convention is born out of thin air. Every convention in media is the offspring of one or more other conventions coming into harmony within the context of the new medium. The secret is to add the evolutionary push. History shows that trying to slap old conventions on new media results in failure; however, if you have the ingenuity to reformulate those conventions in a way that is appropriate for the new medium, then you are well on your way to making something that has a life of its own.

Conventions exist for a reason, and their formulation is an iterative process of co-evolution. The artist evolves to the user and the user to the artist until a mutually agreeable convention emerges that each can understand. This is never, by the way, stated outright, but exists as a subtle interchange over a period of years during which artists experiment with each new iteration of content. Conventions help the audience to understand a medium, and they also make it easier for an artist to create. The conventions of the sitcom television genre, for example, create a set of mutual expectations between audience and artists. We know it will be a half hour; we know it will feature the same characters and same locations every week; we know that there will be a certain style of story for a given show. *I Love Lucy* is a good example of an early, convention-setting show. Obviously, this show borrowed some conventions from film— certain camera moves, close-ups, reaction shots, and so forth. *I Love Lucy* also borrowed the half-hour comedy format from radio. Each *Lucy* show followed roughly the same plot convention: Lucy wants something and instead of asking Ricky directly, she comes up with some kind of cockamamie scheme to get it. When we sit down to watch the show, we know what's in store. When the writers sit down to write it, they know exactly what to do. This is what enables the genre of episodic television fiction to exist. If the writers had to write an entirely new original screenplay every week, this format would be impossible.

From a purely cognitive standpoint, we also have to look beyond the conventions and at the media itself. When we get into issues of convergence, as has been pointed out earlier, we need to address the emotional content of the media and how we can mix media without mixing up the audience. A great deal of multimedia is characterized by multiple windows of different media: text here, graphics there, video over here, audio coming in over the speakers that may or may not relate to what's on the screen. This kind of patchwork approach can be very disorienting. Even if you mix media, you want what you're doing to have some kind of holistic sensibility. You want the viewer feel like they are looking at one thing, not many. This can be done with several different media, but it needs to be carefully thought out. You want to avoid seams—abrupt transitions between media. Everything should flow together graphically and temporally. In general, I like to try to keep the parameters on my media as tight as possible. If I'm doing 3D, I like to just have nothing but 3D on the screen. If video is the primary format, then I stick to that, perhaps integrating effects that are appropriate to the experience.

No matter what kind of media "world" you are creating and no matter how many sub-classes of media are converging within it, the key is to have a sense of unity for the entire experience to have a consistency and integrity within itself. This is the case whether you are designing a high-end VR narrative environment or a card game based on a CD-ROM. Whether high- or low-tech, monomedia or multimedia, you never want the user to be conscious of the media. They should feel it, connect with it, and use it; however, they should never stop short with a thought like "oh, here comes the video," or, "this is so frustrating as text, I wish it was audio." Make the media fit the content, the interactivity, and itself. In this way, you can avoid giving the player, and yourself, a mixed message.

OM MEETS OHM: DIGITAL ONENESS (p. 360)

DESIGNING FOR TECHNOLOGY (p. 161)

PSYCHO-ERGONOMICS (p. 404)

MUSE-OLEUM: DEAD ZOOS AND LIVING MUSEUMS

A museum is a "place of the muse." But the traditional museum is more like a muse-oleum—a place of the dead muse. Granted, dead muses are great. There is no experience that compares to say, standing in a room with Monet's *Water Lilies*, or immersing yourself in the Renaissance splendor of the Uffizzi Museum in Florence. Art museums, like history museums, are generally a tribute to somebody else's muse, but it is the rare museum in which you can experience the living muse within yourself.

Indeed, most of the traditional museums are tributes to dead things. History museums commemorate and protect the artifacts of the past. Natural history museums are dedicated to the preservation and interpretation of past events. Or, as a child of one of my colleagues once put it, "Dad...do we have to go to the dead zoo again?"

Science museums offer a contemporary alternative. As a newer type of museum, science museums tend to devote themselves to theories, processes, and the physical properties of matter or life forms. Science museums tend to be the most interactive of museums, because it often requires a level of guest interaction to best illustrate some of these dynamic processes.

About half or more of the work we did at Edwin Schlossberg Incorporated during my tenure there was in the museum area, the rest in retail, commercial, and entertainment applications. One research project that I did was a fairly comprehensive history of museums, and particularly, the history of interactive museums, for a keynote address Ed was giving. Much of the information I got came from a book about the evolution of museums that was called *Museums of Influence* by Kenneth Hudson, which was a survey of the history of museums, and in particular, a look at museums of the 20th century.

Museums were originally developed to preserve the past, to store and care for artifacts of natural or human history, including the arts. They were not really designed for public use, and many early museums were not even open to the general public. Their main public audience consisted of researchers. Museums were for historians, archaeologists, naturalists, paleontologists, and so on. If you look at the typical interpretive materials in a classical natural history museum, you will find that the exhibits make little attempt to help the general public understand anything about the collections or artifacts, because this was never the intention. Art museums and history museums likewise have traditionally contained no interpretive materials. So although you could view the art or artifacts, there was little to help you understand them. Interpretive materials tended to consist of long blocks of text written by art critics or historians in a vernacular that was fairly incomprehensible to the average person. Ed used to call these didactic exhibits "walk-through books," in which the experts, in no language that you or I could understand, would give us a lecture on the items being exhibited.

The tradition of science and industry museums began in the first half of the 20th century as a result of the World's Fair movement and America's blossoming romance with the machine. The first of these in America was the Chicago Museum of Science and Industry, which was built in the old World's Fair facility in 1934, and showed innovations in science and technology of the day. In fact, many of the original science and industry museums in America are housed in former World's Fair venues. The Exploratorium is located in the Palace of Fine Arts, a former World's Fair site, and the New York Hall of Science is in the 1969 World's Fair site in Queens, New York.

For the record, the first interactive exhibition was created by the offices of Charles and Ray Eames in 1961. Called *Mathematica*, it explored principles of mathematics and physics through a series of simple, hands-on activities. With activities as simple as rolling a ball on a curve or dipping a wire frame in soap bubbles, people could get a firsthand experience of a mathematical principle as it applied to the physical world. They also created a giant moebius strip to demonstrate the idea of a single surface in three dimensions. Inspired by the work of MC Escher, the moebius strip featured an ant who could crawl around the strip in an endless loop. *Mathematica* also featured the first graphical timeline, which used images as well as text and graphics to tell the story of the history of mathematical discovery.

AUTOBIOGRAPHY OF AN AUTODIDACT, PART 1 (p. 45)

The Exploratorium, founded in 1969, is probably the most influential interactive museum in America. This giant loft-like space filled with hands-on exhibits became a blueprint for children's museums around the world. The heuristic exhibits were designed to demonstrate principles of physics and science. They consist primarily of handleable, mechanical, or electromechanical devices, and some computers, that teach children about wind, water, electricity, natural systems, light, the human eye, and so forth. The Exploratorium also includes interactive art exhibitions it its purview. Since the 70s, the Exploratorium has been producing *The Exploratorium Cookbook*, which gives instructions for other museums on how to assemble some of their classic hands-on exhibits.

A movement I read about that was popular in Europe in the 80s was the *eco-museum*, eco meaning "home." This kind of museum is really distinct to Europe because it deals with historical sites that are still active—in other words, medieval towns where people still live, or ancient ruins that are constantly visited. The eco-museum movement was an attempt to integrate interpretive elements into an actual site. You might, for example, start at a visitor's center in an historic village, and then be directed to tour the village. Throughout various locations, you come upon various interpretive signage and exhibits. Curators took this approach when an entire place was considered an artifact, and was implemented in several locations throughout Europe.

In America, we don't have very many medieval villages, and most of our historical sites are buried under layers of urban renovation. Our version of the eco-museum is the living museum in which an entire historically accurate site is re-created and peopled by live actor/docents in costume. These residents of history practice the skills and trades of the time and speak with visitors as they attend to the daily activities of a 17th century town. Old Sturbridge Village in Massachusetts and Colonial Williamsburg are two examples of this. Sturbridge, which prides itself in historical authenticity, has gone so far as to back-breed livestock, using modern breeding techniques to re-create actual oxen of the 17th century. Using real people in a history museum is always a great tact because it brings the period to life, particularly for kids, who respond very well to anything that helps them associate themselves with the past period.

The best exhibit I have ever seen about the Holocaust was done several years ago at the children's museum in Washington, D.C., and I understand that the Museum of the Holocaust in Washington has taken this idea to an even further level. The exhibition I originally saw put you in the role of a Jewish child in Europe during World War II. You would walk through each of the child's dwellings, from the nice middle-class house to the ghetto apartment to the concentration camp dormitory, all from the child's point of view. It was absolutely chilling, because suddenly the entire experience was totally personalized. This exhibit was an art studio/storytelling area where survivors would tell the stories, and then children could create their own special tiles for a mosaic commemorating those who died and suffered at the hands of the Nazis.

This to me is a perfect example of the power of an interactive or immersive experience. When you are put in the first-person in any situation, you find yourself having a whole different perspective. Suddenly, history means something, and it is hard to come away from such an experience without empathizing with the victim.

To me, empathy provides one of the most powerful potential uses of interactive media. There is no other tool better suited to create empathic experiences. In this way, we begin to move away from the role of observer and can actually enter into the mind and soul of the person, people, animal, or object whose story we are trying to tell.

 VIRTUAL REALITY AS A DRAMATIC ART (p. 508)

In addition to my research, I also got to work on wide variety of museum projects. Science or science-oriented museums were, of course, a staple of ESI's (Ed having designed his first science museum in 1976), but we also took on some interactive projects for more traditional museum environments. Introducing interactivity into the "dead zoo" or "art tomb" environment presented a unique challenge in each case. I thought it would be useful to provide a little case study of some of the museum projects and the challenges we faced in trying to "interactivate" them.

LIVING FOSSILS: A NATURAL HISTORY MUSEUM

The first museum project I worked on was a natural history museum in Georgia. This project provided ESI with a rare opportunity to build a natural history museum from the ground up. Ed, who had spent his formative years in the American Museum of Natural History in New York, often reminded us that this was one of those once-in-a-lifetime projects. I was assigned to this project as Assistant Project Manager/Content Director. In this role, I was responsible for corralling all the research, including quite a bit of study on child development from the work of Jean Piaget. The client wanted the feature exhibition to be "A Walk Through Time in Georgia," based on the premise that each of the seven regions of the state possesses evidence of each of the major epochs of natural history. Our solution was to create a walk-through diorama of present day Georgia in which you would come upon evidence of natural history— fossils in the rocks, dinosaur bones in the dirt, and so on. Each area of evidence led to a small gallery in which you would see various current theories about the evidence. Because scientific theory is always changing, we put the emphasis on interpretation so that the exhibit would not become obsolete. The exit of each of these galleries was an example of a "living fossil"—contemporary life forms that were the next-of-kin to ancient creatures whose evidence we just saw (for example, ferns, alligators, and so forth). This exhibit stemmed from two strong philosophical ideas:

- Natural history is still going on.
- You can only see the past through the eyes of the present. In other words, you can never really know what happened in the past, except through the modern-day evidence of it.

The museum also had a number of other exhibitions, including two children's areas. One was a scaled topographical map of Georgia geared for 7–12 year-olds. Kids could get "Explorer's Kits" on various topics and use this environment as kind of scavenger hunt zone. In most traditional children's areas, everything is in wooden drawers and there is no context for the isolated activities. Instead, we created a themed environment with activities integrated into it: hidden diorama peep holes; viewers that let you see the same scene in different seasons or times of day; fossil imprints embedded throughout the room that kids could find and use to make rubbings. It was an ongoing adventure that children and their parents could have and, by getting different kits every time they visited, come back many times and have a different experience with each trip. The other exhibit, geared to kids ages 3–6, was a fantasy forest in which children could dress up as animals and hide in a camouflage maze or use special feet to walk across a swamp maze.

The design of these children's areas was based on extensive research of Jean Piaget's levels of child development. I made a huge chart showing all the different qualities, interests, and beliefs that children had at varying ages. The client originally wanted only one room, but we felt that to address these different play and learning styles, there really needed to be two separate spaces. The fantasy forest was based on research that showed that between the ages of 3 and 6, children believe in "animism." In essence, they think that everything is alive and has feelings. At this age, kids relate particularly well to animals, so we used the animal role-play experience as a way to help them identify with and gain interest in nature and natural history.

Ed was very concerned about the misconception people had that natural history was over, so we talked a lot about "living natural history." We created natural history present and future areas, which included some simulation experiences that would help people learn about how to manage the environment. We designed an interactive theater that presented contemporary environmental situations, including all the different viewpoints on what should be done, and then let the audience vote on them to see the various possible outcomes.

The natural history project was challenging in terms of the scope of its content; however, as an interactive museum assignment, it was fairly easy in the sense that it was a new museum and that it did not have a huge collection, hence the emphasis was not going to be on artifacts. As you'll see later, a concentration on artifacts creates a whole plethora of problems in terms of interactivity. Fortunately, in this case, we started with a clean slate.

The biggest problem we faced with the Georgia natural history museum was a content issue that was essentially political. We were required to make the human evolution gallery optional so that Christians who did not believe in evolution could bypass it. I have never before or since heard of a science museum in which a content decision was driven by religious concerns, and you can imagine what our team of 20- and 30-something New York artist-intellectuals thought of that. But we were relieved that at least they didn't make us eliminate it entirely.

Sadly, this museum was never implemented as designed. The client hired another company to finish it, eliminating many of our more dynamic interactive components in favor traditional, didactic exhibits. In a final tragic blow, they decided to entirely do away with the gallery of human evolution.

 AUTOBIOGRAPHY OF AN AUTODIDACT, PART 2 (p. 58)

LIVING ARTIFACTS: A HISTORY MUSEUM

The next project, a conceptual design proposal for an interpretive layer to a history museum in New York, was a whole other animal than the natural history museum project. Nestled on the cusp of Harlem and the Upper East Side, it was a strange cultural amalgam on a variety of levels. I don't know what it's like now, but in 1988 when we were brought in to propose interpretive exhibits, it was a classic local history museum. It housed paintings of historical New York figures, furniture, silver collections, dioramas of the old Dutch Colonists, and the like. It was a very staid and quiet place set in the marble halls of a fancy old house facing Central Park. We were hired to develop a conceptual proposal for interactive interpretive exhibits at the existing facility.

The museum was in some respects a receptacle for all the heirlooms of rich New Yorkers over the last three hundred years. Most of what was there were estates that had been donated to the museum. In sharp contrast, the primary audience for the museum was kids from Harlem. They come in school groups or walked over from their neighborhoods after school and hung out there. As you can imagine, there was a bit of a disconnect there between the audience and the content.

The challenge of designing a history museum became a cultural struggle between the two dominant camps of the museum staff: the Educators and the Curators. The Curators believed that the mission of the museum was to collect and preserve artifacts. The Educators believed that the mission of the museum was to educate the public. It is interesting that the agendas of neither of these groups exactly matched that of the typical museum visitor, so it was our job to unify these three voices into a common set of objectives.

Some of the cultural baggage that we had to deal with was the struggle between the traditional Curators, who almost felt it was their job to protect the artifacts from the visitors, and the newly introduced Educators, whose agenda was to bring the artifacts closer to the visitors. One group was about Things, and the other was about People. And nary the twain shall meet.

The Curators viewed the whole notion of interactive exhibitions with suspicion. Given their priorities, the reasons for this are not surprising:

- Interactive exhibitions aren't artifacts.
- Interactive exhibitions detract from the importance of artifacts.
- For interactive exhibitions, hands-on means that at some point you are going to want to actually touch artifacts, and many of the curators were loathe to even show them, let alone allow them to be handled.

What we tried to do with our conceptual design was put an interpretive layer on the museum that constantly called visitors' attention back to the artifacts. Instead of telling the story of New York history, we proposed to tell the story of the interpretation of artifacts so that the museum became a kind of mystery treasure hunt in which visitors would be able to interpret objects and thus learn their stories. We did this in a variety of different ways, but in all cases, it was the artifacts that were to be the center of attention. The interpretation focused on looking at each artifact as the jumping off point for a story. We tried to make it fun. The proposed orientation exhibit, set in a Hollywood-like movie theater, was to be a short film about a New York artifact told from the artifact's point of view. The story followed a wedding ring that had been made in Old New Amsterdam and passed down from one generation to the next until it was given to the museum. In this way, we were able to put the life of this artifact in context of the history of New York—all told as a dramatic story revolving around this wedding ring.

We also proposed a unique way to get the Curators more involved in the exhibition. When we first started the project, we were given a tour of the "basement," in which we visited each Curator in his or her own little storage area. We really enjoyed this tour and found each collection and the Curators themselves quite charming. The way the Curators related to their collections was very interesting. One Curator showed us a collection of glass—a room filled from floor to ceiling with nothing but bottles and glass artifacts. It was amazing! We got to visit the costume collection, where we saw a collection of beaded handbags, and another of satin shoes, all carefully kept in special drawers.

We enjoyed this experience so much that we decided to propose an exhibition that attempted to replicate it. The concept was to create a Curator's gallery in which each Curator was given his or her own space, including storage equipment, that he or she used in the basement. They could then select their personal favorite items to exhibit and change their own area whenever they liked. Because most of the collections in the museum were from entire estates, they were among the best-documented artifacts in the city. Most of this material, much of it quite fascinating, was buried in filing cabinets in the basement. To take advantage of this untapped wealth of information, we suggested that the Curators' gallery include "research notebooks" containing copies of interpretive materials used to trace the history of the object: receipts, deeds, letters, diaries, photos, and so on. We also allowed for a little lecture area where Curators could give scheduled presentations of their collections. For most of our content-heavy projects, we tried to incorporate some kind of "behind the scenes" element because we knew it would be a big hit with visitors. Due to budgetary reasons, none of these proposed exhibitions were ever implemented.

LIVING ANIMALS: A LIVE ZOO

After designing a dead zoo, we later had an opportunity to design a live one. We were hired by a zoo in New Orleans to create a conceptual design proposal for interpretive exhibits, but this time, it was a collection of live animals. This was the first time I played the role of project manager, so for all intents and purposes, I suppose it marked a promotion. This project was a lot of fun because it was short and sweet, and the people we worked with were, pretty much across the board, excited by and responsive to our entire approach. We worked with the architects who were hired to do major renovation of the zoo. As part of this renovation, they wanted interpretive exhibits throughout the zoo. We turned this around and instead suggested an interpretive layer, which would manifest itself through a variety of components, both architectural and programmatic. In addition, we contributed to the zoo master plan, which we felt was an important part of helping to determine the visitor experience.

The idea for this project was to create various self-guided tours, but rather than being didactic walk-throughs like in traditional zoos or museums, they were set up as research expeditions. You would stop at carts throughout the zoo and pick a naturalist's kit. This kit included a kind of research dossier, and other items you might need for your research expedition such as binoculars, maps, field guides, and so forth. You could be a bird watcher, you could study endangered species, you could search for all the marsupials in the zoo, or focus your expedition on child-rearing techniques of different animals. At each of the animal exhibits, we proposed creating a walk-through diorama of the facility that a naturalist in that environment would use, such as a tent with field guides and a journal book for the African Wildlife area. The idea was to put people in the role of explorers, naturalists, and animal researchers so that they could learn and understand more about the animals. This design was never implemented, but it was a fun project. Because the client and the architects were really enthusiastic about our ideas, we had less controversy on this project than any other of this genre I recall working on.

LIVING MACHINES: A MUSEUM OF INVENTIONS

Another children's project we did was *The Innovation Station* for the Henry Ford Museum right outside of Detroit. The Ford Museum houses the largest collection, at least in the States, of machines and inventions. It's a gigantic warehouse full of everything mechanical, electromechanical, and so forth. There are cars, steam engines, appliances, and all manner of artifacts from the Industrial Revolution, the Machine Age, and the Automobile Age. Although there's not a lot going on in the way of organization, it's a real blast to see all these contraptions under one roof. Being located a stone's throw from Motown, it's a popular destination for locals and tourists alike.

We were hired to develop a single interactive exhibit for children to teach them about innovation and inventiveness. We wanted to create something very physical, something that would be at home among all these machines and devices. So we developed a big contraption that children had to operate. It consisted of four different colored balls mixed together, which children were supposed to separate by color. It was full of levers and pulleys and chutes and ramps, and the kids would adjust and move things around, trying to corral the balls each into their own segregated areas by color (see figure M.21).

Figure M.21

The Innovation Station at the Henry Ford Museum (photo courtesy ESI/Donald Deitz)

"The Innovation Station," which is still operating at the Henry Ford Museum as of this writing, is a machine that uses the kids as its engine. Because most of the other machines in the museum weren't actually operating in the museum, and certainly weren't interactive, we thought it would be great to have a working machine that people could actually operate themselves. In this way, we not only created a heuristic problem-solving activity, but we also let the kids have an immersive experience of what a machine is and how it works.

LIVING COMPUTERS: A MUSEUM OF INTERACTIVE MEDIA

When an interactive industry association in Washington, DC wanted to create a museum to showcase its members' work, ESI was one of the firms they contacted. Although the highest tech of all our projects, I found this project to be the least interesting design challenge of all our museum projects. This 10,000 square foot gallery space was the first museum devoted exclusively to the exhibition of interactive products. Instead of using interactive exhibits to interpret other content, this museum was *about* interactive applications themselves. Ironically, ESI was not to design any of the interactive content; our job was to create a context in which all of these different and changing applications could live. In addition to this challenge, we had to do this on a budget that, in any other circumstances, would have paid for little more than carpeting.

We did two things with this project that were interesting. First, to get away from a very techy environment, we decided to keep the environmental design very sleek and elegant and use a simple device to express the theme of each area that would simultaneously humanize the exhibit. We contracted a company in Brooklyn to do plaster life castings of people. In each area of the exhibit, we positioned these life-sized, white plaster characters, dressed in real clothes, to represent the different themes of the venue: In the school area, we had a sitting child raising her hand from a row of desks as a teacher pointed her way; in the home area, a mother in business attire drank her morning cup of coffee in a living room setting while her son played video games at a nearby desk; in the art area, an art student stood sketching as she faced a monitor in a giant ornate frame and a computer terminal on a Greek-like pedestal (all painted flat black for subtlety); and in the business area, two people at computer workstations at opposite ends of the room were talking to each other on the phone.

We also took a radical approach to the orientation exhibit, and one that we had to fight for. Because of their orientation toward technology, the client wanted something very glitzy and high-tech. For one thing, we could not afford anything high-tech with the given budget; and second, we felt that because the entire exhibit was high-tech, it would be much better to have a low-tech orientation experience. We talked about doing a history timeline, but that seemed awfully dull, so Ed suggested we use the metaphor of a parade. In the entrance of the museum we built a 20-foot long scale model diorama of a parade commemorating the history of communication technologies. The parade starts with a float that looks like an open mouth. Inside it, a cave woman is talking to her son. This float commemorates Speech. The second float features the caves at Lascaux and shows a scene of a cave man hunting, and then a cave painting of the same scene being looked at by other cave men. Each float, done in a cartoony style, used a scene such as these to demonstrate the way communication innovations changed or enhanced the way people relate to one another. Along the sidelines are plaques that identify the particular event that each float commemorates.

One of the things we were always big on was context. We hated kiosks or desktop computers or anything computer-oriented. Whenever possible, we liked to mix and integrate high-tech and high touch. We never liked the simple solution...but went out of our way to do the unobvious.

LEARNING FROM INTERACTIVE MUSEUMS

Creating interactive exhibitions for the museum, or for that matter, any other public context provides interactive designers with some very exciting challenges and opportunities. As you've seen, it is once again a matter of bringing the content into harmony with the interactivity. Scientific content, which revolves around processes and principles that are best expressed through physical demonstrations, lends itself to interactivity, and in some ways, even demands it. Civil history and natural history, whose conventions are more staid and passive, are a harder nut to crack. This being the case, you have to find something resonant within the content that brings it to life for the visitor and affords a logical and intuitive opportunity for interaction. Examples from the aforementioned projects include:

- Putting natural history in the context of the present; the continuity of natural history; the process of its discovery from present day evidence.

- Looking at history as story; using artifacts as a way to tell story; using the curator's perspective to explore the significance of collections.

- Interacting with live animals in the role of an explorer or naturalist; providing different layers of study of the zoo's contents.

- Letting kids become the engine of a machine to understand problem-solving principles, and the fundamental concept of a machine and its function.

- With an interactive computer museum, trying to place a human spin on the technology; emphasizing that technology is about communication between people and not about hardware.

These are just a few examples of ways to generate interactive content. Although they are applied specifically to museums in this chapter, they can certainly be applied to almost anything that lends itself to interactive content generation.

The second half of the museum equation is the public site angle. When I say the world "site" today, of course, many people think I mean a web site. But when I say site, I generally mean a physical place where people go to do something. Interactivity in a public place is very different from what you do in your home, subsequently, there are many things that you have to take into consideration. One of the most pressing issues is maintenance. Interactive exhibits can be hard to maintain and keep operative. Another is throughput: how many people can experience the exhibit per hour. Interactivity does not generally allow for high throughput, which always creates a problem in terms of public venues. Then there is the matter of motivation: will people do the experience? In a museum or other public site, most people will only spend a few minutes at an exhibit. Therefore, it needs to be immediately appealing and you need to be able to learn how to do it *while* you do it within those few minutes. You also need to consider who your audience is, and if you are designing for children, don't forget about the parents. Hygiene is also a major issue. Head-Mounted Displays, common wear for Virtual Reality, are almost entirely inadmissible in museums due to potential health problems. Then there is the matter of public visibility. Many adults do not want to do things that will make them stand out or embarrass them in any way; children are much more bold, and will often attempt to interact with things in ways that were not intended.

For these and other reasons, museum projects are an arena in which testing is an absolute must. Dangerous and costly mistakes can be avoided by creating prototypes and testing them on prospective visitors. Many cut this step from their budget, but more money has been lost than saved due to lack of testing.

Most of the fundamental principles that can be learned from site work can be reapplied to other types of interactive design. In fact, there is much to be learned from a study of interactive museums. Their heritage in understanding and implementing user-responsive environments, the research that has been done, and the mistakes that have been made, can provide those designing for the screen with a wealth of information to help them in designing better interactive media.

 TEST FIRST, ASK QUESTIONS LATER (p. 463)

THE HEURISTIC MAN: A PORTRAIT OF EDWIN SCHLOSSBERG (p. 224)

STROLLING THROUGH CYBERSPACE: SECOND NATURE AND THE VIRTUAL GALLERY (p. 457)

MYST-ICISM

I like to use *Myst* as a case study for some of the patterns we see in interactive multimedia because, in many respects, it represents a watershed moment on the curve of media evolution. *Myst* is a perfect example of second-generation, or Phase 3 development.

 THEORY OF MEDIA EVOLUTION (p. 468)

Myst's story goes something like this:

Two guys in a garage. Yes, that's right, the digital equivalent of Horatio Alger. The Brothers Miller decided to build a CD-ROM. They patently ignored all the so-called conventional wisdom and decided instead to invent their own paradigm. There were no software publishers involved, no movie studios, no venture capitalists or public offerings, no product developers, no marketing department. This was pure art.

They had almost no money, and they employed none of the high-end production techniques considered necessary for public acceptance. They used a tiny bit of video and animation, both considered de rigeur for interactive media.

Most marketing people say that you must have fast-paced action to sell a game. *Myst* had none of this. In fact, it had barely any motion at all. It had no violence, no mayhem.

Worst of all…it had no licensed properties. That's right, not one iota of *Myst* was repurposed content from any other medium. It was completely original. And what's more, it was an unlikely story to become a pop culture hit: a mysterious old man protecting his precious library against his duplicitous sons. In fact, if you took a proposal for *Myst* up against a committee of marketing and gaming people, they would have all given it the thumbs down. This is probably why the Brothers Miller didn't even take it to a big publisher, but instead published it themselves in the beginning.

Myst started out self-published with little or no marketing. It started small, but as it circulated, it began to build a groundswell by word of mouth. I remember hearing about it in 1993 from a friend who was utterly mad about it. Slowly but surely, people got wind of this cool new game, and it began to build an ardent following with scarcely any marketing or advertising at all. Finally, Brøderbund, publishers of the top-selling *Carmen San Diego* series and other popular edutainment titles, picked it up and gave it the full-on blast. After that, *Myst* quickly rose to the top of the charts and makes its name in history as one of the first blockbuster CD-ROMs. It's also very important to bear in mind that *Myst* was not an overnight success, but something that built up over time. This is the typical case with most CD-ROM titles.

One thing that *Myst* did, along with a couple of other titles that came out at the time, was introduce the idea of a spatial interface, or what I like to call "faux Virtual Reality." The spatial interface paradigm, which is of course the basis of Virtual Reality, is in many ways the most intuitive and transparent of interface paradigms. It most closely resembles the real world, and if properly designed and delivered, most users or players seem to know intuitively what to do in a simulated environment. Using this kind of spatial navigation as a way to interact with a story creates a kind of "narrative environment," a word I use to describe a physical or virtual space used to tell or experience a story. A narrative environment is sort of like a set into which you place components that precipitate story, whether they are clues to a linear story, such as *Myst*, or elements in a dynamic interactive story that you can affect, or roles and structures that enable you to improvise your own story.

 NARRATIVE ENVIRONMENTS: VIRTUAL REALITY AS A STORYTELLING MEDIUM (p. 329)

The Brothers Miller also went against all the typical high-tech aesthetics and instead opted for a medieval fantasy environment that borrowed more from *The Hobbit* than from *Star Trek*. They created a slow-paced world, in which was embedded a story. You had to search for the story in the form of various obscure and unusual clues. This process was not easy, taking upward of 40 hours for the average player to solve. This supported repeat play, which is crucial because repeat play is one of the key factors in building word of mouth. The more time you spent on *Myst*, the more you would talk about it, the more your friends would want to buy it.

 THEORY OF MEDIA EVOLUTION: THE FOUR AXIOMS (p. 480)

There is one other piece of information about *Myst* that is often overlooked. Unlike most other CD-ROMs and video games, *Myst* has perhaps the most diverse audience appeal of any CD-ROM that had been released to date. Most CD-ROMs are niche-oriented—children, teenagers, boys, and so on. *Myst* ignored the very audience that made the game industry into a multi-billion dollar business. Avoiding the thumb-candy paradigm in favor of aesthetic beauty and rich content, *Myst* opened the door for women and girls in a way that no other product had. In fact, *Myst* is the first CD-ROM game I ever heard adult women talk about. They loved it, and for some it became a downright obsession.

 GIRL GAMES: THE NEW FEMININE MYSTIQUE (p. 202)

IT'S ONLY A GAME: THE BIRTH OF A MULTI-BILLION DOLLAR BUSINESS (p. 260)

As defined in the *Theory of Media Evolution*, second-generation content is generally that which begins to set conventions for a new medium. *Myst* is a prototypical second-generation content creation because it broadened the audience while creating new conventions that soon went into popular use. Like most second-generation products, *Myst* was developed by artists unencumbered by industry assumptions. They were coming to the CD-ROM medium fresh and unbiased. The result was something totally original and unpredictable, which made its way into the popular mainstream to such an extent that it has become an adjective. Now you can't flip through a pile of CD-ROM pitches without seeing the words "*Myst*-like" peppered throughout.

This is definitely the indication that a title has become the guidepost for a new paradigm. Like all good second-generation artists, the Brothers Miller optimized the constraints of the medium and made something that was unique to the CD-ROM form. CD-ROM has never been very good at video, nor is it strong in fast-paced real-time animation, the mainstay of most video games. Over the years, designers had somehow tried to push CD-ROM to do things it just wasn't good at. The postage-stamp sized video window was decidedly unsatisfying, even if the content was interesting. Instead, the Brothers Miller built a rich world of still images that enabled you to navigate through a space one frame at a time, accompanied by a beautifully compelling audio track (see figure M.22). They took advantage of the strengths of the CD-ROM.

Figure M.22

The Path to the Selenitic Oasis from *Myst* (photo courtesy of Cyan, Inc. ©1993 All rights reserved)

Myst is by no means the only or even the best second-generation CD-ROM. The work of Jim Ludtke, whose *Freakshow* also set a new standard for CD-ROM design, has been cited for its creative innovation and superb exploitation of the medium. Similarly, Bill Barminski, Webster Lewin, and Jerry Hesketh of DE-LUX'O have created a series of CD-ROMs and web sites around Bill's irreverent art works, which also push the technology without knocking it down. British underground interactivist Andy Cameron produced *Anti-ROM*, a collaborative art CD-ROM title that became a cult classic in London.

These pieces are influential and in some ways better designed and implemented than *Myst*, but *Myst* has that one evasive quality so crucially important in America: profit. For the CD-ROM industry, *Myst* proved that you could make money without spending it. It is in the same vein as the recent sweep of mid- to low-budget independent films—paid for and owned by the author/ directors. They captivate the audience and become a pure profit center for all parties involved.

Myst showed the interactive industry that you can actually sell something of high artistic merit, with some level of intellectual content, that was not a carbon-copy of another successful product, nor a vehicle for repurposed content. As such, it set new standards for CD-ROM, which have opened the door for more evolved products to not only be made, but more importantly, published.

SPATIAL MEDIA (p. 442)

THE INTERACTIVE ECOSYSTEM (p. 233)

NERD VERSUS COUCH POTATO (p. 345)

NARRATIVE ENVIRONMENTS: VIRTUAL REALITY AS A STORYTELLING MEDIUM

Narrative environments is the term I use to describe physical or virtual spaces used to tell or experience. Narrative environments exist in actual and Virtual Reality, and I would say that the first commercial attempt to create narrative environments as an entertainment form were developed by Walt Disney for Disneyland.

Before Disney, amusement parks had no content. Roller coasters and other kinds of rides had little if any narrative built in. There might have been a haunted house-type ride before Disney, an implied story on a small scale, but it was really Walt who brought Theme to park. Walt was also probably the first person ever to re-purpose content, taking his popular cartoons and animated features, and building around them an elaborate three-dimensional world where people could visit and spend the day. Wrap the added revenue source of merchandise around that, and you have the prototype for a media asset empire.

 KISS MY ASSET: THE CONTENT WARS OF THE 1990S AND THE BIRTH OF TRANSMEDIA (p. 269)

Disney fused architecture and cinema and, for the first time, made environments that told a story. For any environmental designer interested in using spatial interfaces and creating narrative environments, I suggest a day at Disneyland over a week of CD-ROM and Internet surfing. *Pirates of the Caribbean* is one of my personal faves. A boat ride takes you through a series of vignettes that capture frozen moments in time that elicit a myriad of story possibilities. Think of the skeleton pirate with his pile of gold, or the lusty pirate chasing a wench around the balcony (I understand this latter scenario was recently redone to reflect a politically correct, less sexist sensibility). These scenes are only tidbits, but the world they weave sparks the imagination even in its ultimate linearity.

One technique that *Pirates* uses to great effect is the head-turner interface that surrounds you with 360 degrees of imagery and audio. You can't possibly take it all in at once. So where you turn your head (jogged in part by audio cues) determines which stories or vignettes you'll see. This is a great trick, because it ensures that the ride has repeatability. You can go back time and time again, and always catch a glimpse of something new. Considering that *Pirates* was one of the original Disneyland rides (opening in 1967) and you still have to wait hours in line to see it (I myself have seen it so many times I can't count), it's pretty obvious that this interface and general approach to narrative environments is a success by audience standards.

Another of the old Disney classics is the *Swiss Family Robinson Treehouse*. Although it does not have dynamic animatronic vignettes like *Pirates*, the treehouse uses strategically placed static props to tell a story. There is little text...just the occasional sign from time to time. Tourists wind their way through a series of handmade rooms as they progress up the stairs of a giant tree. Each room is made from a combination of natural ingredients and the leftover wreckage of a ship run aground. These rooms and scenes tell a clear story about the lifestyle of the family made famous in Robert Louis Stevenson's classic novel. Part of what is compelling about this environment is the ingenuity that it suggests. Various contraptions, such as the pulley system that brings water up into the tree, show you not only what these people might have lived like, but also how clever they were in adapting to their environment. Instead of viewing them as an unfortunate shipwrecked family, you see a portrait of a good-natured group who cheerfully and ingeniously turned a bad situation into a great deal of fun. Yet there are no characters, no words, nothing but the carefully crafted spaces that tell us this rather elaborate tale. While the "three acts" of the story are not presented in linear form, you can clearly see the classic narrative elements of conflict, transformation, and resolution embodied in the physical space. It's a great experience for families because it is a tale of family bonding with a moral—if we work together with a good and proactive attitude, we can do anything.

Snow White's Castle is a totally different kind of narrative environment. It is essentially a walk-through book, with a stop for each event in the story. This simple device of immersing a book in an evocative environment creates a great context to experience a well-known and well-loved fairy tale. There is nothing particularly challenging about it, except that you have an adventure following the characters and plot points through the authentic surroundings of the castle; however, the impact of the ambience of the space as a backdrop for a linear narrative should not be underestimated. A story told on the walls of an edifice has a very different impact than one read from the pages of a book.

In this sense, *Snow White* bears a resemblance to another, more traditional venue of visual storytelling: the Catholic Church. Centuries before Disney created narrative environments for entertainment, they existed for religious and educational purposes. In the pre-literate days of medieval Catholicism, the mass was not exactly geared for the masses. Recited in Latin (which only priests, monks, and noblemen understood), the stories of the Bible were transmitted to illiterate peasants through pictures...giant frescos and murals, statues and reliefs, and stained-glass windows that decorated the church interior (see figure N.1). It is through these vignettes, which combined to form a narrative environment of sorts, that illiterate Catholic peasants experienced the myths and parables of their religion. The Book was the Word, but to many uneducated in the so-called "Dark Ages," the Word was not a word at all, but Picture in Space, Image in Architecture.

Figure N.1

A picture painted a thousand words to pre-literature church goers attending a Latin mass

 PLATE 03

If you step back even further, into the ruins of ancient Egypt or Mesopotamia, you will see more examples of narrative architecture—pictorial storytelling that brings to life the lore and legend, history, and myth of these ancient civilizations. The Egyptians favored giant frescos that surrounded them with an ongoing timeline of significant events, movies frozen in time, a parade of characters that walked around them and among them in their daily lives (see figure N.2). Although historically the emphasis on narrative has always revolved around temporal communication, especially oral tradition, many cultures have practiced forms of narrative architecture as part of their storytelling tradition. Even in the caves at Lascaux, the earliest known evidence of cave painting, the artists attempted to embed a chronicle of events in their environment, perhaps even instructions on how to hunt a certain animal. The narrative environment, it seems, is as old as narrative itself.

Meanwhile, back at Disneyland... The newer *Toontown* area, a spin-off from the film *Who Framed Roger Rabbit*, creates a great backstory for beloved Disney characters. This zany little town, in which a falling anvil is a regular occurrence and vehicles have four different sized wheels, is the alleged dwelling place of Mickey, Minnie, Daffy, and all the rest of the Disney gang. Here you can visit the homes of your cel-painted heroes in a cartoon world where everything is a little off and interactive gags are found around every turn. You can turn on the stove in Minnie's kitchen and watch a cake rise, open the fridge and meet some dancing produce, or pinch the atomizer on a perfume bottle to smell Minnie's favorite scent. In Mickey's house, you work your way into the barn-like screening room where you see a retrospective of trailers of Mickey's movies as well as artifacts from his illustrious career (Mickey, the biggest star in *Toontown*, of course has the biggest house). And then there's the cartoon trolley car that bounces up and down as you ride around the little village. The entire experience immerses you into a world where you can become cartoon character yourself. Unlike the three previously mentioned Disney environments in which you are essentially a passive observer, *Toontown* invites you to become more a part of the action and is an excellent example of spatial interface design.

Figure N.2

The evocative narrative environments of the ancient Egyptians (image courtesy of Nigel Strudwick)

 PLATE 04

I tend to look to the real world more than the interactive world for clues on how to create compelling experiences. Narrative environments have been done to much better effect in real space than in cyberspace. Some CD-ROM products, such as the Miller Brother's *Myst* and their earlier product *Manhole*, Jim Ludtke and the Residents' *Freakshow* and *Bad Day on the Midway*, and Bill Barminski and Webster Lewin's *Encyclopedia of Clamps* all use navigation through a simulated physical environment as a way to get to content.

 ARCHITECTURE AS A NARRATIVE ART (p. 25)

Myst is a kind of sleeping world that you go through to look for clues to unlock the secret of what has happened here. *Freakshow* and *Bad Day on the Midway* (to an even greater extent) actually bring characters into the mix. In *Midway*, you are actually in an amusement park peopled by a bizarre cast of characters. As you walk through, you can change points of view and experience the world from each character's own unique perspective. Each character also has a dark ride associated with it, a kind of spatial manifestation of his or her inner world. This narrative environment is all the more compelling because it also uses a spatial metaphor to represent the inner workings of a character's psyche (see figure N.3). In *Freakshow*, you can tour the freaks' dressing-room trailers, peek through their drawers, and explore their home environments to learn more about the characters themselves (see figure N.4).

Figure N.3

A scene from *Bad Day on the Midway* (image courtesy of Jim Ludtke)

 PLATE 5 6

Figure N.4

A scene from *Freakshow* (image courtesy of Jim Ludtke)

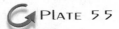 PLATE 5 5

Although not a narrative environment per se, *Encyclopedia of Clamps*, by Bill Barminski, Webster Lewin, and Jerry Hesketh of DE-LUX'O, is space-as-collage. In this surrealistic world, you move around hallways that contain imagery of Barminski's paintings and artwork. These works are highly stylized and irreverent indictments of consumer culture as told through the eyes of Cold War–era advertisements, inviting you to "Drink Crap" rather than Coke or "Enjoy Blatto Beer." You can click on icons and paintings or walk through doors to find yourself in surrealistic interactive worlds where you can do things such as place phonograph record icons on a little mono record player, make your own ad montages, or click on a spinning GI-Joe in a *Leave It To Beaver* kitchen. These vignettes have a certain amount of narrative content as Barminski and company spin a compelling world of mutant 50s advertising iconography. Interactive sound that includes sampled TV and radio ads combined with inventive jazzy Hip-Hop beats adds audio texture to a fun and unpredictable adventure.

Figure N.5

The space-as-collage narrative environment of *Encyclopedia of Clamps* by DE-LUX'O

 Plate 57

 Spatial Media (p. 442)

Although all these applications represent spatial interfaces and narrative environments, none of them is actually a Virtual Reality application—in other words, they don't use real-time navigable environments. In fact, from a storytelling standpoint, Virtual Reality is still something of a wasteland. Most entertainment-oriented VR applications up until now have concerned themselves exclusively with space, which is why they often come across feeling dry and lifeless. In the quest for three dimensions, the fourth dimension, time, is all but ignored. Perceived as a problem of architecture, not of narrative, most worlds in cyberspace are designed as raw space with no program, no theater, no activity, or agenda. This is particularly the case with multi-user spaces and online communities on the web. People go there, but there is nothing to do, no story, and neither content nor context. Upon entering these worlds, you find yourself wandering aimlessly through a digital ghost town. You feel as if the clock has stopped at some indeterminate time, neither past nor future, nor even present. You tend to come away from such environments, even the most beautifully designed of them, saying "So What?" You are left with an empty feeling, and rightly so, because you have been in an empty place. The result of this is that many think that Virtual Reality is an inherently unsatisfying and overhyped medium. Just as is the case with all media, however, it is not the medium itself, but the content that is to blame. There are very few VR experiences in the world today (even fewer available to a mass audience) that even begin to tap the great potential of this compelling medium which, though considered cutting edge, is perhaps the oldest of the "new media."

A Brief History of Real Time: The Virtual Reality Legacy (p. 105)

Virtual Reality Check: What is VR Anyway? (p. 518)

The few examples of narrative environments that *have* been created in Virtual Reality demonstrate the phenomenal potential of this new medium to entertain, educate, and illuminate us in new and radical ways. Most of them are site-based, or location-based projects, and almost all of them have only been shown on a temporary basis in galleries or exhibition spaces. There are a small handful, as you will see, that are seeping into the mass market, and I'm sure there will be more as time goes on.

Brenda Laurel, VR designer and author of *Computers as Theater*, along with VR artist Rachel Strickland, created one of the first narrative VR experiences called *Placeholder* in 1990. *Placeholder* is literally and figuratively, the Lascaux of Cyberspace. It is also an attempt to create the sense of spiritual environmental narrative in the Egyptian ruins and the Catholic Churches.

Virtual Reality as a Dramatic Art (p. 508)

Janine Cirincione, Brian D'Amato, Michael Ferrara, and Possible Worlds have created two well regarded narrative environments in Virtual Reality that have been displayed in art galleries around the world. Both *Imperial Message* and *Dead Souls* put you into a poetic and abstracted story through which you must navigate to effect an outcome. *Imperial Message* puts you in the role of a revolutionary on trial for subversive thinking. As you move your way around the village, you must be careful whom you align yourself with lest you indict yourself still further and end up a political prisoner or outcast. An impressionistic and lyrical experience, *Imperial Message* has the quality of making you the main character in a story in which there are fairly severe consequences to your actions. The terrain is dangerous, and if you don't watch your step, you could unwittingly make a wrong move with dire results.

Don Sanders of Learning Sites, Inc. and Eben Gay of ERG Engineering have been involved in a project to create virtual re-creations of ancient ruins. Developed for both research and education purposes, these re-creations enable you to take a tour of a photo-realistic replica of a South American or Egyptian temple as it appeared when built. These spaces provide historical narrative. They enable you immerse yourself in another time and place that no longer exists. In *Temple Gebel Barkal*, you can experience the grandeur of Egyptian temples as narrative environments—the giant frescos on the walls provide a first-person experience the scale and power of these huge pictorial stories (see figures N.6 and N.7). The environments can also have built-in interpretive components built into them, text that can be triggered by clicking on an object. As these worlds become available online through VRML and other 3D Internet tools, they can also include hyperlinks to web pages providing background information, research materials, or even the raw data from which the temples were assembled.

Figure N.6

Temple Gebel Barkal, the ancient Egyptian ruin, is brought back to life with Virtual Reality (image courtesy of Learning Sites, Inc.)

 Plate 01

Figure N.7

Interior perspective of the *Temple Gebel Barkal* (image courtesy of Learning Sites, Inc.)

 Plate 02

From 1993–94, four projects came on the scene, which in a sense set the pace for a new genre of narrative environments in VR. They were all very high-end, and had limited public access, but in their own right, set a new standard and opened the door for what might be possible. All four of these projects were showcased and/or debuted at the SIGGRAPH 94 computer graphics conference in Orlando, Florida:

- **Aladdin's Magic Carpet Ride:** by Disney
- **Virtual Adventures: The Loch Ness Expedition:** from Iwerks Entertainment and Evans & Sutherland
- **Detour: Brain Deconstruction Ahead:** by artist Rita Addison and Marcus Theibald at the Electronic Visualization Laboratory, University of Illinois at Chicago
- **The Dancer/Improv:** from the Media Research Lab, New York University

I will mention the Disney project first because it is the most obvious place to start, and also the best known and most accessible of the three projects. *Aladdin's Magic Carpet Ride* was developed under the direction of Jon Snoddy in a top-secret VR studio on the lot of Walt Disney Imagineering, the same people who brought you all the cool Theme park attractions described earlier. The story is simple: find the missing lamp. You have one half, and you must locate the other. As you fly about the streets of Agrabar in a VR simulation of the popular animated feature, you encounter various characters who respond to your actions, and guide you along through the world. This single-player experience is played with a Head-Mounted Display using a special interface designed to make you feel like you are flying on a magic carpet through the Middle Eastern landscapes.

Virtual Adventures/The Loch Ness Expedition, which I creative directed for Iwerks and Evans & Sutherland, is a very highly refined and structured narrative environment. It has a very clearly defined three act structure and is a hybrid dark ride, movie, and video game. In summary, the players get a four-minute pre-show, a "mockumentary" video featuring interviews with real witnesses who have actually seen the Loch Ness Monster, edited into a fictional news story about having discovered her eggs. Act One of the experience, the pre-show, sets the scene by revealing that volunteer scientists (you and your team of five other players) have been recruited to go under the murky waters and save the eggs from bounty hunters (other players who look like good guys to themselves and bad guys to you). The second two acts take place in the interactive pod, culminating with the discovery of Nessie and her eggs in a secret cave full of treacherous prehistoric aquatic monsters. After you gather enough eggs, and the game is over, you get to witness one of the eggs hatching in the lab via remote video monitor. *Virtual Adventures* was the first attempt to create a story-based, family oriented VR experience that did not have a combat-based goal. Packaged as a high-end Theme park attraction, it was geared to a broad audience, and was especially tailored to appeal to girls and women, a hugely ignored demographic in the VR and high-tech attractions market.

THE PRINCESS AND THE MONSTER: THE MAKING OF VIRTUAL ADVENTURES (p. 375)

GIRL GAMES: THE NEW FEMININE MYSTIQUE (p. 202)

The most compelling VR narrative I have ever seen, and perhaps the most importance evidence of the power of VR as a narrative medium, also showed at SIGGRAPH 94. It was a very high-end fine art installation that has only shown at a limited number of venues, but to my mind it is the Killer App of VR. *Detour: Brain Deconstruction Ahead,* is the real-life, first-person journey of Rita Addison, a photographer/psychologist who experienced severe brain trauma as a result of an automobile accident. With her vision and hearing permanently impaired, Addison set about trying to tell her story and after much searching, discovered the only medium that seemed to fit the bill: Virtual Reality. Her three act tale begins in a gallery of her photographs, showing her work before the accident. We then find ourselves on a dark highway where we hear a skid, a crash, and a scream. The next thing we know, we find ourselves inside Rita's brain as synapses are snapping and the damage is being done. We emerge into the same gallery where we started, except we now find ourselves trapped in a world of distortions, interference, visual anomalies, and auditory noise. We cannot escape, for everything we see is behind a veil of damaged perception. This before and after story gave me a chill when I first experienced it. It was the first time I had ever been *emotionally* moved in Virtual Reality space, and also the first time I had ever seen VR used as a tool for empathy. Because *Detour* is to me one of the most important VR pieces ever created, I also devote an entire chapter to it.

THE REVELATION OF RITA: VR AND THE POWER OF EMPATHY (p. 413)

Another example of narrative environment is the *Improv* project, which was introduced at SIGGRAPH 94 by Ken Perlin, head of the Media Research Lab at New York University. In a 1994 presentation, Perlin showed his dancer character, which combined traditional keyframe and procedural animations to create a self-operating and user-responsive character that clearly had personality (see figure N.8). *Improv* has since evolved into a full-blown personality engine that drives a simulated cast of characters to participate in different narrative scenarios. These characters are not designed to think so much as to respond to their environment. They can act based on internal algorithms that determine things such as moods and relationships to other characters, and react to each other as well as to external input from a user. They will look quizzically at a piece of self-ambulatory furniture, dance to your own MIDI-generated drum beat, or laugh at each other's jokes. These characters become user-responsive building blocks from which to create elaborate narratives in a virtual environment.

Figure N.8

Ken Perlin's procedurally animated virtual dancer

 Plate 27

 Artificial Intelligence and the Prosthetic Brain (p. 38)

All these projects are what I would consider to be second-generation, or Phase 3 content. They will set the standards for what is produced in the future. The one drawback they all share is that they will not be likely to meet a large audience. This is one of the fundamental obstacles that has prevented Virtual Reality from becoming a mainstream medium up until now. Most high-quality VR requires extremely high-end equipment and very elaborate and expensive interface devices to operate. It has therefore been confined to a narrow audience of digerati (digital culture mavens) who attend the conferences and electronic art shows where such projects are usually shown.

 Digerati: The Artificial Intelligentsia (p. 164)

Both *Virtual Adventures* and *Aladdin's Magic Carpet Ride* are probably the first high-end narrative VR products exhibited at public attractions and therefore accessible to a mass audience. In both cases, they were hosted at only one or two venues, and the throughput (number of people who can pass through per hour) is so low on the Aladdin ride that few people will ever have the opportunity to experience it, even though it is housed at a major Theme park.

There is still hope for VR, however. Another innovation was also featured at SIGGRAPH 94 that opened the door for ubiquitous Virtual Reality on the World Wide Web, VRML (pronounced "verm'l")—the Virtual Reality Modeling Language—is to Virtual Reality what HTML (HyperText Markup Language) is to text and graphics. HTML created an efficient way to display and exchange information, and a standard that enabled every site on the Internet to talk to and understand every other site. VRML does the same for VR. Using a language that boasts remarkably small file sizes (orders of magnitude smaller than the size of typical models on the high-end systems previously described), VRML provides a universal tool, a protocol as it's called, for creating efficient VR spaces on the Internet. VRML is, like everything else, evolving. The VRML 2.0 spec, which introduces protocols for animation, is evolving to incorporate shared avatar worlds and a myriad of other capabilities that will make the consensual hallucinations of William Gibson and Neal Stephenson a reality.

 THE BIRTH OF CYBERSPACE: 3D COMES TO THE WEB (p. 97)

CONSENSUAL HALLUCINATIONS: IS VR THE NEW LSD? (p. 137)

Currently, VRML offers several sites where you can go, don your "avatar" (Virtual Reality character), and mill about among the other avatars in a primitive form of cyberspace. These shared environments are a good start, but again, they are missing the element of time, the fourth dimension that is narrative. Entering them is not unlike walking into a mediocre cocktail party where you know no one and have no context for connection. This is an evolutionary phase that is a necessary part of the growth of this new medium and technology. It is, in media evolutionary terms, Phase 2, first-generation content (Phase 1 being the invention of the technology itself).

 THEORY OF MEDIA EVOLUTION (p. 468)

As of this writing, a small handful of first-generation companies and artists are paving the path for this new manifestation of Virtual Reality. VRML presents the first opportunity, beyond the 3D fighting games you see in arcades and on consumer game devices, to disseminate VR to a mass audience as a legitimate storytelling and entertainment medium.

Among the first artists in cyberspace to create narrative environments on the web is C. Scott Young, aka, "VRML Knight." Scott created *Idville*, a magical planet/world/island/space station. This beautiful latticed construction hovers in space, and is peopled with the charming and mischievous Idiom (see figure N.9). From each node of Idville, you can link to various scenes and vignettes featuring the Idiom. They have a story, a mythology, and a culture all their own that is constantly evolving and expanding. VRML is a low-polygon medium—in other words, you need to make efficient 3D models without a lot of faces or complex surfaces. Scott is a master at creating a great deal of expression with a small number of polygons. Texture maps are a popular tool of VR designers, but Scott eschewed these in the beginning because they were not available, but has since evolved texture-free models as stylistic devices (see figures N.10–N.12). Rather than taking the technical limitations as a hindrance, they have all but driven Scott's unique style of VR narrative, sculpture, and cyberarchitecture. The other feature that adds another dimension to VRML is its extremely short production cycle and easy updatability. VRML worlds do not have to remain static, but can constantly grow and evolve.

Figure N.9

C. Scott Young's *Idville* uses VRML to create a magical storyspace for adults and children alike

 Plate 37

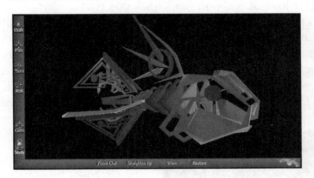

Figure N.10

C. Scott Young's VRML *CelFish* uses minimal polygons without texture maps to create a rich virtual sculpture

 Plate 38

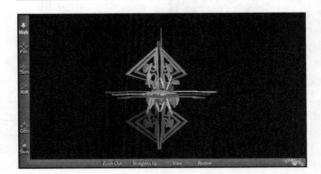

Figure N.11

C. Scott Young's *CelFish* appears more abstract when seen from the rear

Plate 39

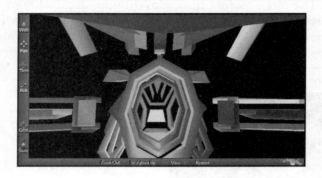

Figure N.12

A view from within C. Scott Young's *CelFish*, known as the "Jonah Viewpoint"

Scott has also created a world based on characters that he and his friends have developed through fantasy role-playing games they play on a regular basis. Scott recently unveiled one of the first VRML cartoons, *The Carrot Defender*, a serialized tale of vegetable superheroes (see figure N.13). Scott's worlds look like nothing you've seen. They are more Dr. Seuss than William Gibson. Thank God. As much as I love St. Gibson (as VRML co-creator Mark Pesce has taken to calling him), I can't imagine spending my free evenings hanging around "the Matrix." Other VRML pioneers include cyberarchitect Clay Graham, whose worlds are more architectural than narrative, and Mark Meadows, creative director of Construct. Mark created *Crutch*, an existential narrative, as well as a variety of landmark architectural pieces in VRML, along with co-founder Lisa Goldman, and their team of killer VRML designers.

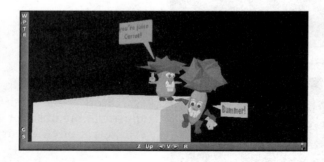

Figure N.13

C. Scott Young's *The Carrot Defender* hangs on for dear life

Motion-capture animation pioneer Brad deGraf and his company, Protozoa, Inc., have been creating a series of VRML characters based on performance animation techniques. Performance animation uses a body-suit that tracks body movements and gestures of a real person, then translates them into computer data to animate 3D digital characters. Protozoa has created a series of characters, among them the gruff but lovable amphibian Floops, produced by Jan Mallis and designed by Bay Raitt. Floops, who stars in his own weekly 3D animated comic strip, amuses us with a variety of antics (see figure N.14). From his sparsely decorated terrarium, he harasses the fish next door, who he feels has a much better deal, what with the mermaid and the castle and all. He begs for food and gets a drumstick larger than him from his doting but stupid human hosts. He admonishes us for peeking at him in the bath, and imagines he is hearing things when his rubber duck starts to talk. Floops' scenes, although linear, allow for total 3D navigation, and recent episodes, as of this writing, are becoming increasingly interactive. Eventually, one hopes to find an entire world of such entertaining creatures programmed to interactively respond to our presence and input. Protozoa is currently working on some top-secret characters that can actually be moved around in virtual space in real time with some very lifelike character traits, thanks to some ingenious animation tricks.

Figure N.14

Floops responds to a threat from within his VRML terrarium

 PLATE 33

At this writing, I am currently working with a team that is trying to bring the best of these techniques together to create characters that combine lifelike motion-capture animation with the flexibility of the *Improv* system. This will enable us to begin to develop highly dynamic interactive stories in which the player can interact with the virtual character, and characters can interact with each other in an ongoing drama—or comedy.

Cyberspace Cadets: Virtual Communities and Avatar Worlds (p. 146)

Cyberspace Cadets: Virtual Communities and Avatar Worlds (p. 146)

Jim Ludtke, who I mentioned earlier, designed a narrative environment using VRML. *Baby Sally* is a daredevil infant who we get to follow around as she makes her way through an obstacle course of classic childhood dangers. Much like the baby in the opening scene of *Who Framed Roger Rabbit*, Ludtke's adorable tot has a series of hair-raising close calls. It's a very entertaining world, and after all, perhaps VRML can handle a crawling baby (see figure N.15). Jim's baby is currently living at http://www.intervista.com, the home site for VRML co-creator Tony Parisi's company, Intervista. Intervista is also developing VRML characters, such as *Thud* (see figure N.16). A visit to their site will also gain you entry to a charming little three-ring circus, which is the first site I've seen with multiple animated characters (see figure N.17). The *VRML*

Circus provide us with glimpse of what a world might be like with many vignettes and events taking place all at the same time.

Figure N.15

Jim Ludtke's *Baby Sally* avoids dangers in a VRML world

 Plate 35

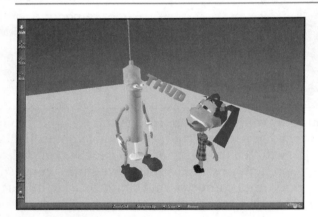

Figure N.16

Intervista's VRML character *Thud*

 Plate 36

Figure N.17

A barrage of events dazzle the viewer in Intervista's *VRML Circus*

 Plate 34

For my money, the future of VRML entertainment lies in multiplayer worlds and self-constructed narrative. Like good improvisational theater, cyberspace presents the opportunity for the audience to create its own characters and worlds, to weave its own plots and stories, and to essentially become the directors, producers, and actors within their own imaginary worlds. My ultimate goal, I suppose, is to make myself obsolete—to become an architect of sorts whose job is create the venue for narrative, provide the tools for storytelling, and then walk away and let the players create the content themselves. This is my vision of the web—a world in which the author becomes the gardener, and the audience is the garden.

NERd VERSUS COUCH POTATO

I appropriated the name of this chapter from Bob Cotton and Richard Oliver's comprehensive encyclopedia of the digisphere, *The Cyberspace Lexicon*. The expression describes the raging controversy between those who believe that the keys to interactivity are on the keyboard of a personal computer versus those who feel the sofa will be the final resting place of interactive entertainment.

The effort to bring interactive multimedia to the consumer market goes back about 20 years, when the first real attempts were made to marry digital technology with mass media. There are three interweaving stories that are integral to this evolutionary process. A bit of historical perspective on this process provides a better fix on where we are now (obviously a moving target since the "now" of writing this book will be "then" by the time you read this).

The first efforts to add interactivity to the television experience date back to the advent of the personal computer. It was at that time that two clearly divided camps began to form, and a third appeared hovering somewhere in the middle. It's important to realize that although the potential for PCs to become a mainstream item was fairly clear in the late 1970s and early 80s, the prevailing philosophy held that there was no significant market for PCs in the home. Time and time again, pundits and so-called industry analysts insisted that no one would be bringing a PC home anytime in the near future.

So the general belief was that, be it a broadcast model (interactive TV) or a consumer product model (such as CD-ROM), the solution to bringing interactivity into the home was the set-top box, an add-on device that would bring intelligence to your television (a dubious enterprise if you ask me). Although the broadcast people and the consumer product people worked pretty much completely separate, they both had the same basic philosophy. You have to make interactive television easy for the audience, and give them something that becomes a natural extension of that which is already the center of their lives—the television. Because nobody, after all, was going to want to buy a PC for the home.

On the opposite side of the spectrum, you had the "computer in every garage" school of thought, spearheaded primarily by Apple and Atari. The Macintosh computer was largely responsible for breaking down the barrier to home consumption because its easy-to-understand, user-friendly interface made it a much more companionable appliance for the home than the cumbersome, DOS-based PC. It certainly had always been the intention of Steve Jobs and Co. to create a device that was the computational equivalent of a toaster—something that one would expect to find in every American home. The Mac was kind of the Volkswagen of computers. The Macintosh was also designed to be an all-purpose computer, a crossover home/work/education/entertainment device, an odd combination if you think about it. This made it a very appealing choice for the self-employed and those who wanted to set up cottage industries at home, and also for individuals who saw its value as an educational device for children.

Somewhere hovering in between these two schools of thought was the consumer game market whose home arcade devices were already a fixture in popular culture by the mid- to late-70s. The consumer game industry wanted to appeal to the arcade market. They achieved this in one of two ways: by creating a set-top box that plugged into the TV (Sega), or by creating their own self-contained gaming machines (Atari). These machines were essentially one-trick ponies, toys rather than appliances, built for speed, but not for processing.

When the CD-ROM device first appeared on the scene, everyone said it would be dead in a year. Emerging around the same time as the audio CD invasion, it provided a way to store a lot of diverse information—not just video and audio, but actual computer data as well—in a small, compact storage unit. Indeed, anything digital could be stored on a CD.

Now you have to remember that up until now, the chief contender in terms of interactive video had been the laser disk player. It had a lot going for it because it produced high-resolution, broadcast-quality, and provided both random-access capability and superior quality to video tape. You could hold a lot of high-resolution, full-frame video and audio information on a laser disk, and you had the ability to access the content randomly from the disk. There was always a slight lag time while the device searched for the frame address, but this was a product of the simple mechanics that the stylus had to get from point A to point B on something the size of a vinyl record album. There were three major problems with laser disks:

- The players and disks were expensive.
- The disks could not store any digital information because laser disk is an analog technology.
- The disk player itself had limited intelligence and a poor interface (a remote control device to enter frame numbers on).

In other words, even though the quality was great, the high cost and limited functionality prevented laser disk technology from ever getting past the first leg of the adoption curve. It also suffered from lack of content, largely a problem of the constraints put on content and the expense of production (digital media is inherently more forgiving than analog). Video disk found its niche as a superior means of delivering video films and as high-end presentation medium for Theme parks and museums.

Although a small handful of titles were produced for laser disk, it never took off as *the* interactive medium for the home. Still, could CD-ROM overcome the obstacle of the obligatory computer? Furthermore, CD-ROM's poor video resolution, slow frame rate, and tiny video windows left developers accustomed to the high quality of laser disk feeling unenthused. Part of this reaction was based on the fact that in 1985, interactive multimedia was defined as interactive *video*. Indeed, the term multimedia had not even entered the picture yet. The marketing and business people felt that video was the panacea of interactive media, and that without it, there would be nothing. The only alternative was fast-paced arcade-style games, for which the CD-ROM was simply too slow. At that time, execs and pundits alike would have scoffed if anyone were to tell them that the interactive technology that would eventually put the mass in media would be text- and graphics-based.

The consumer product set-top box (as opposed to the broadcast set-top box) was based on the model of a "plug-and-play" device that contained both media retrieval and computing capability in a single unit that used your television set as its primary output. Users purchased individual titles to play in the device. This was an alternative to having the media broadcast into the home. A number of set-top box products were attempted during the 1980s, among them Sony's DVI (Digital Video Interactive) and Viewmaster's interactive box. Sony gave it a second go in conjunction with Netherlands-based appliance and light bulb giant Philips and the result was the CD-I player, perhaps the only viable contender for mass acclamation. Later, the 3DO device was introduced by Spectrum Holobyte, but it too quickly fizzed out. For a time, there was a bit of a face-off between CD-I and CD-ROM. CD-I was far better at delivering audio and video…it could run full-frame video at something that vaguely resembled, indeed exceeded, VCR quality. The sound was great as well, which gave it a real advantage. Unfortunately, CD-I was lousy at delivering animation. In fact, the animation resolution of the CD-I was one quarter that of the CD-ROM. Because animation is much easier to manipulate interactively than video, this put some major constraints on what you could do. Again it emphasized video, which is ultimately the least interactive medium.

CD-I used a remote control as its input device, eschewing the keyboard, which was, of course, anathema to the television paradigm. The keyboard controversy was a major theological argument at that time. There was this notion that you had to eliminate the keyboard entirely and replace it with a graphical, so-called intuitive interface. With CD-I, all you could do was point and click. Keyboard meant text, and text was bad. It was a kind of post-literate myopia based on the assumption that people do not or will not read or write. Hence, the dreaded keyboard had to be done away with because it was the precursor (excuse the pun) to text.

 THEORY OF MEDIA EVOLUTION (p. 468)

The fear of text, or aversion to it, is largely responsible for a lot of erroneous thinking about multimedia. Multimedia is just that—multimedia, which means that everyone should live happily together as one big family: text, video, graphics, sound, animation, and even real-time VR (can't we all just get along?). If everything is digital and it's all multimedia, then why does any medium need to be eliminated at all? Instead, let's embrace them all and take advantage of the very fact that we can. The truth of the matter is that while all these, excuse the expression, "vidiots" tried to focus the mass movement of interactive away from text, it was an almost completely text-based medium, in the end, which won. Namely, the Internet.

Interactive video is fundamentally an oxymoron. Anyone who has ever had any dealings whatsoever with video on the production level can tell you without a shadow of a doubt that this is perhaps the most linear of all media. Even film, with its cutting bins and splicers, moviolas and tape, is less linear than video. Nonlinear video editing has done a lot to change that, but if you edited video any time prior to say 1989, you were dealing with a linear nightmare all the way down the line.

Within the context of interactive multimedia, video itself is the least interactive of media. Once a video clip begins to play, the interactivity goes out the window. Now you can certainly make the video experience more active based on what is happening onscreen, but it's a decidedly undynamic interchange. Furthermore, because we are accustomed to video as a continuous story flow, to interrupt it with decision points seems awkward and unnatural. Nonetheless, for nearly a decade, most people in interactive multimedia felt that video was the most important thing. As it turned out, they could not have been more wrong.

Now let's look at the broadcast side of the equation—interactive television. I make it a policy not to make predictions about the future, but you need not look too far past the present to see what lies on the horizon. Although the television hegemony continues to attempt to master interactive media, the path to interactive media acclimation is littered with the bodies of failed interactive television attempts. Even the biggest companies fueled by seemingly endless funds have not been able to get this baby to fly. Yet interactive television continues to be a holy grail and I'm sure it will not go away. In spite of last 20 years of lessons learned, no doubt millions more dollars will get poured into this pointless exercise over the *next* 20 years.

A lot of people will not agree with me on this, but there is much evidence to indicate that interactive television is the ultimate in pointless exercises, a kind of eternal Godot of interactive media. Most people think the barriers of entry are technical, but nothing could be further from the truth. The biggest barriers of entry to interactive television are cultural and economic. The two greatest impediments preventing television from becoming interactive live in two places:

- In the production, distribution, and economic infrastructure of the broadcast medium
- In the living rooms of 200 million Americans and millions of other people around the world

One of the problems with new technology development is that it is usually done backward. It usually starts in the boardroom or the R&D lab, when it should start in the living room. Most failed attempts at interactive television can be traced back to a total lack of understanding of the context in which people use these devices. These devices are developed to be *sold*, not to be used. There is little regard for the end user, his or her needs or interests, lifestyle, routine, or culture.

Let me give you simple example that might seem obvious to you and me, but is not so clear to the corporate infrastructure of the media machines. What is the normal pattern of television watching in America? (This, by the way, is an exercise in psycho-ergonomics.) Let's first just look at the physical position. Television is generally viewed by the average person from a distance of about

4–8 feet. When watching TV, you generally sit on a sofa or comfortable chair. If you are a small child, you may sit on the floor only 2–4 feet away from the TV. It is also quite common to watch television in bed. Television is usually watched in a reclining position, with the remote control readily accessible for easy switching between channels. Furthermore, there is rarely a desk or table handy; perhaps a coffee table, but I have yet to see anyone watch the television with a flat surface that might accommodate a keyboard directly in front of him or her.

Now…here's what I want you to do. I want you to pay a visit to *every home in America*. Walk up and down every street in every town, no matter what kind of a neighborhood, from Beverly Hills to South Central L.A., from Westchester County to the Bronx, and while you're at it, *go to Europe*. Everywhere you go in the world where there is a television, you will be likely to see this exact same scenario: people reclining on a sofa and/or comfortable chairs facing a television set around a coffee table. In fact, this is often the focal point of the entire house, and many of the other furnishings and functionalities of the home will revolve around this salon setting.

Okay, now look again and ask yourself: *How* do people watch TV? Sometimes they watch it alone, but more often than not, they watch television together. Just think of all your favorite TV families—the Simpsons, the Bundys, the Cosbys…don't they all watch TV together? Doesn't your family?

Now, here is the $10,000 question. If most people watch television in a group, then why have the vast majority interactive television shows and set-top box titles been geared toward a single user? Why has it only been the last couple of years that even video games allow for more than one player? Even though the television is inherently a multi-person medium?

Now let's look at *motivations. Why* do people watch TV? Most people watch TV to relax, to vegetate, to be passive. *That's what it's there for, and that is all they want out of it.* You might give your commentary, or get aggressive during a ball game, but you really aren't there to be challenged, to be participatory, or to interact. In fact, quite the opposite. Most people turn to TV for relief from the need to act. After a hard day at work, you just want to sit around and be entertained. The fact that the entertainment has little or no intellectual content is part of its appeal. Some people watch to be informed, tuning in to the news, NOVA, or some educational program; however, even in those programs, no one ever expects or intends to get involved in the conflict in Bosnia or Einstein's Theory of Relativity. That's just not what you're there for.

Although there is little to suggest that people will soon be interacting with the television device, there are a variety of interactions that happen with the television on a cultural level. One way this happens is through the dynamic that occurs when viewers begin to affect real events through public opinion and ratings wars. The other way that people interact with the television is through fan culture. In fact, there is more support of television fan culture on the Internet than there is on the television.

It's Not the Television That's Interactive, It's the People (p. 250)

This brings us to the matter of infrastructure. The television is a one-to-many, mono-directional broadcast medium. There is no interactivity built into its infrastructure on any level. Technologically, it's a one-way street from broadcaster to broadcastee. People may argue that that is changing; now that television is going digital, it's all going to be different, but there's more to it than that. The entire *economic* infrastructure of television is based on advertising, which is inherently passive, involuntary, and can only work in a one-to-many broadcast scenario using content as its draw. The conventions and standards of television are as firm as conventions can be: programming in 30–60 minute increments interrupted with advertising in 30–60 second increments. Millions upon millions of dollars are poured into this system annually; it is a symbiotic relationship from which many people profit. Indeed, an entire economy is built on this relationship.

The programs generated within the television content culture and economy fit into certain conventions: sitcoms, day and nighttime soaps, TV news, Saturday morning cartoons, TV movies, talk shows, and all the new genres being developed on cable. Furthermore, the production methodologies for these shows are well-established. They all exist within an infrastructure, an ecology, and a symbiosis that is very healthy and well-defined. Why, then, would anyone within this system want to change it?

You don't have to be Marshall McLuhan to recognize that trying to make the television interactive is as ridiculous as trying to make movies interactive. People go to the cinema to sit for two hours and be absorbed, carried away, immersed, and taken through an emotional catharsis. Cinema is the direct descendent of Aristotle's ritual dramas and Shakespeare's popular theater. Nobody wants to screw around with that. It's worked for thousands of years, and everybody loves it. So if it ain't broke, don't fix it.

It is understandable why marketing executives *want* television to be the answer. There are a hell of a lot of TVs out there, which is exactly why this formula won't work. Television has already evolved to its level of stability, and once that happens, its tough to change things. But here's a little secret you may have already figured out if you've read the chapter entitled "The Laws of Cumulative Media." Once a medium is adopted into the mainstream culture, only one thing can change it—the introduction of another medium that takes over some of its functions. In other words, the thing most likely to alter the way people watch television is not the television itself, but another appliance entirely. Furthermore, if the Laws of Cumulative Media are true (and I stand by them), this new medium will by no means replace the old one but merely urge it to a greater level of specialization. Plenty of evidence supports this hypothesis.

THEORY OF MEDIA EVOLUTION (p. 468)

THE LAWS OF CUMULATIVE MEDIA (p. 276)

I think we all know by now who the new kid in town is. It's that little beige box in the corner of your den, or up in the kid's room, or in that funny little anteroom that used to house an urn or statue. If you're paying attention, you may have noticed that your kid is now spending more time with it than with his or her old baby-sitter, the television.

Which brings us full circle from where we started. Throughout a decade of ill-fated interactive television attempts, and constant predictions of its imminent demise, "The Little Platform that Could"—CD-ROM—has maintained a slow but steady gain on all the coming and going "set-top boxes."

Why did CD-ROM survive for so long? The answer is simple: It's the content, stupid! It makes no difference whether the platform itself is good or bad; the problem has always been lack of content. Nobody will buy a piece of hardware for $800 if there is only one or even three titles for it. *In order for a platform to become commercially viable, it must have a critical mass of content.* It is a crucial piece in the curve of media evolution. If critical mass of content is not achieved within a certain period of time, you are essentially dead in the water. You might be able to hang on for a while, like CD-I did, but that was only because Philips had a seemingly infinite amount of money to spend to keep this ailing patient alive.

THEORY OF MEDIA EVOLUTION: THE FOUR AXIOMS (p. 480)

While people were pouring millions of dollars into R&D to make the television interactive, humble little CD-ROM companies operating on shoestring budgets were just plugging away making content, content, and more content. Some of the early CD-ROM developers included Voyager, Electronic Arts, Brøderbund, LucasArts, and Sierra, to name a few. Eventually, these companies were joined by others until, by 1993, there were numerous CD-ROM developers worldwide and hundreds of titles available to CD-ROM owners.

We've spent some quality time with the couch potato, now let's spend a few moments with the nerd.

As stated earlier, it is axiomatic that a CD-ROM owner is also a computer owner. So right away, we are looking at a very different demographic than that of the television. We can assume, for example, that the average computer owner is probably better educated and more affluent than the average TV owner. We can also assume that most computer owners also own televisions. Most home computer owners purchase computers with several uses in mind—functional software, education, and entertainment.

The CD-ROM culture has always been oriented toward educational content, even within its entertainment products. The first CD-ROMs produced by Voyager, were, after all, classical music appreciation titles. Can't get much more highbrow than that. Not only that, but among the best-selling products are CD-ROM encyclopedias and reference titles.

It should not be surprising that the vast majority of popular CD-ROM games have been either "edutainment titles," such as *SimCity*, *Carmen San Diego*, and *Indiana Jones*; games that are intellectually challenging such as *Myst*, *Seventh Guest*, and *You Don't Know Jack!;* or products that are creatively challenging, such *Barbie Fashion Designer*. It was probably around 1993 that we began to see a preponderance of more arcade-like games, such as *Doom* and *Duke Nukem*. Mercifully, there were several years when the CD-ROM technology was just too slow to support so-called "twitch" games. Now, as the mainstream TV consumer game encroaches on the CD-ROM culture, we see more and more of these types of games. But they are balanced out by the *Jacks* and *Barbies*, which prove that death and mayhem are not a prerequisite to profit.

In the beginning, CD-ROM acclimation was limited to a fairly narrow target market; but as old titles continued to maintain popularity, and new, more exciting and accessible titles emerged, something very strange began to occur. The old prediction that no one would buy CD-ROMs because no one would buy computers suddenly inverted, and between 1992 and 1995, there was an explosion in purchases of home computers. Why? Most people were buying them because they wanted to be able to use CD-ROMs. In other words, rather than the computer discouraging people from buying CD-ROMs, the CD-ROM was encouraging people to buy computers. By the end of 1995, all computers came with CD-ROM drives and most came with titles "bundled." CD-ROM titles were used to sell computers.

It was around this same time that something else happened that further opened the door for the computer as a mass medium. In 1993, the Internet opened its doors to the public at large. Up until this time, the computer-based interactive culture had not had an equivalent to interactive television. While interactive television had been a costly and expensive uphill battle, the Internet exploded overnight, the impact of which can be felt in virtually every aspect of our culture.

DANGER: KILLER APP (p. 152)

To understand the culture of the Internet, it's important to take a look at is origins. It has always been, and continues to be, a tool for research and education. It was originally created by the military to facilitate a more efficient exchange of information between universities, research institutions, and military R&D facilities. In some ways, the Internet is the world's biggest public library. That it has been co-opted by entertainment companies is really an afterthought. There is still more information than entertainment on the Internet, and when you consider that one of the most successful commercial sites on the Internet is an online book store, you can quickly see the difference between the nerd and couch potato mentality. After all, when was the last time you saw a book advertised on TV?

One thing that remains clear is that, in spite of its entertainment applications, people still use the computer for utilitarian functions—word processing, bookkeeping, desktop publishing, and so on. So, apologies to Alan Kay, the computer might be a medium, but it is also a tool, which gives it added value for the typical household. The computer is a highly flexible device. Unlike the television with its narrow functionality, the computer affords a seemingly infinite and expandable realm of possibilities. The geography of the digisphere is indeed infinite in all directions.

Voyager's slogan is "Bring Your Brain," which is really the definition of computer culture. People come to their home computers with their brains. Even if they are merely playing games, the expectation of computer users is to be challenged, to be pushed, to learn something new, to develop a new skill, to garner some new information, or to be entertained in an *intellectually challenging way*. Even if you play *Doom*, you are still looking for a challenge, because that is the nature of the device.

Inversely, the television is not typically a device that asks you to think. The user expectation of intellectual stimulation from a computer is one reason why it's so much harder to produce good interactive content than good television content. If the interactivity is meaningless or doesn't challenge or illuminate us in some way, if it isn't clever, and if it doesn't force us to think, we feel shortchanged. Interactive multimedia asks you to do the work, to meet the content halfway; but if you get there and the content isn't walking up to you and shaking your hand, you have to ask yourself: Why bother? I'd rather be on the couch and have my stupidity spoon-fed to me than have to work to get it.

Furthermore, the computer has not traditionally been a medium of commerce. Advertising is an inherent part of the television infrastructure and has evolved to the level where it's really the entire point of television. There is no similar economic precedent for the computer. Because the number of eyeballs you can capture with a computer is now at about 10 percent of those you can capture with television, its value as an advertising medium is dubious at best. Not only that, but the Internet culture by-and-large frowns upon advertising. A few years ago, it was considered a sin to actually try to sell anything on the Internet. If you attempted any kind of blatant advertising, you were shunned, and in some cases, might actually receive extreme negative retribution. You could get away with advertising if you were offering some kind of added value or information. The only exception was the early e-mail service Prodigy (started by Sears and Nynex), which had blatant advertising, and was always considered somewhat lowbrow to the larger computer community.

Nowadays, advertisers are trying to get in on the act, but they are learning very quickly that they can't get anywhere by creating commercials. Whatever they do, it has to have some kind of informational value or intellectual challenge, which is why you see so many games and contests on web sites. Nobody's going to go to a commercial of his or her own volition. People watching TV try to get *away* from commercials. That's what the remote control is for.

 REMOTE CONTROL GROUP (p. 410)

Now that we've talked about the cultural milieu, let's look at the usage patterns of the computer, in the same way we did the television. Let's take a visit to the dens of the 20 million or so Americans who currently have computers in their homes.

The standard setup for a computer in home setting is as follows. The computer generally sits on a desk or a computer workstation. It is seldom found in the living room, but more often in a den, office, or even a bedroom. In many homes, you might even have to look in the kid's room to find the computer, although some households might have more than one. On the desk, you will usually find a keyboard, a mouse, a CD-ROM drive, a model, and occasionally, a joystick or track ball.

The typical computer user sits upright at a desk, in an office-style chair, at a distance of 12–24 inches from the screen. Most people use computers alone, although children may play a game together, or parents sit with their kids to play with an educational title. There are very few multiplayer CD-ROM games, but in the case of such a scenario, for example, the desktop game show, *You Don't Know Jack!*, a group may sit around and play together.

I found it very interesting to recently discover that the Evelyn Wood speed reading program advises readers to never read in a passive position, but instead, sit upright with the book resting on a desk and seated in a comfortable upright chair. This more active posture is supposed to increase both speed and comprehension. On the other hand, the prostrate sofa or bed position tends to encourage intellectual laziness and physical drowsiness in the reader. What this suggests is that both the passivity of the television and the engagement of the computer are as much a product of physical posture as they are of cultural and mental orientation.

Now we've looked at the *how* of computer use, let's examine the *why.* Where the TV watcher looks to the TV as a source of passive recreation, the computer user goes to the computer for information, stimulation, or activity. This may take any number of forms, and indeed, the possibilities are countless. At the computer, you may be doing anything from checking your e-mail to doing research for a school project to designing a party invitation to browsing the web for information or entertainment to writing a book. If you have a task in mind, your intentions might be fairly deliberate. You might just sit down to play without a clear idea of which game you will play, or you might have a current obsession with which you fill up all your free time. Perhaps you are even playing an ongoing game in which you must pick up where you left off last time. You might go online to check the news, check your mail, randomly browse, look for something very specific, or just visit your favorite web site or chat room and see what's up. Nowadays, with the plethora of easy-to-use web tools, who knows, you might even go to the computer to work on your own web site.

Although this is generally a solitary experience, some of what you do online might be social in nature. Whereas the TV provides a form of passive sociability in a shared space, the Internet provides remote but active social interaction with people in other locations. Although there has been a lot of concern expressed about this latter manifestation of web culture, I'd be hard pressed to say which scenario is preferable. At least online people engage each other in dialogue, even if they aren't in the same place while doing it.

 SOCIAL COMPUTING (p. 434)

Most computer owners have a much stronger relationship with their computers than they do with their TVs. The investment of time, effort, money, and attention required by a computer is much greater than that of the television. Computer owners are forever buying new software and hardware, upgrading, and generally fussing over their computers like they would a fussy child. The television, conversely, just sits there, and no one pays much attention to its well-being until it starts to fail.

People take their computers seriously, which might be in part because their computers take them seriously. A machine that responds to me, that serves as a tool for me to be productive, that provides an educational or entertainment experience based on the inherent assumption that I am uniquely intelligent is a very different prospect than a device that coddles to the lowest common denominator and doesn't care whether my name is Neilsen or Juarez. The computer treats me with a certain amount of respect and dignity. By owning one, I am essentially saying that I'm a relatively bright, productive, and educated person; I care about my kids' education; and I have things I want to do besides going to a 9-to-5 job and veging out in front of the boob tube.

Now that you've seen the contrast of nerd versus couch potato culture, ask yourself this question: Now that I've established this great reciprocal relationship with my computer, knowing it is intelligent and that it assumes I am intelligent, do I really want to sit back in my rolling office chair and watch *Married...with Children* in a Microsoft Internet Explorer MPEG video window?

Conversely, am I going to go to my couch after work, lean back in the Lazy Boy with a beer and a bag of chips, plop a keyboard on my lap and check my e-mail on a screen that's six feet away?

As absurd as these scenarios sound, this is precisely what entertainment companies have been trying to do. If you ask anyone in the mainstream media what is the future of interactive technology, they will all tell you the same thing: The computer and the TV are going to merge into one device. Having seen the differences between the computer and television, the nerd versus couch potato culture, I think you can draw your own conclusion.

Let's talk about Einstein for a minute. Let's talk about the Law of Inertia. The Law of Inertia states that things at rest tend to want to stay at rest and things that are moving tend to want to keep moving in the same direction they are already going in. To stop, move, or redirect something in a state of either static or ambulatory inertia is an energy-intensive proposition. It's really a matter of rowing against the tide, an apt example, because it's really what people continue to try to do. Why not instead have a look where the currents and the winds are blowing and train our sails accordingly?

 Einstein, Eisenstein, and the Space-Time Continuum p. 186)

No matter how much power the megalomedia infrastructure thinks it has, there is one thing that has a lot more power: the general public. All you have to do is recall the famed "New Coke" incident or revisit the Rodney King or O.J. Simpson trials to see that. The public is a mighty force, and although the media might try to manipulate and control it, it is really the audience, and not the media, that is in control. Just ask the Neilsens. They might spend money, advertise, manipulate the market, and control the channels of distribution, but the powers that control the media will never get America to redesign its living room.

To me, the answer to any kind of success in new media is not to invent something entirely new, but to look at what's already there and build up from there. We can already see clear directions with both television and computer media. The way to succeed is to follow the Law of Inertia, to continue to move in those directions and leverage the existing culture to create new forms and genres. If more people obeyed the laws of nature, the world would be a better place. Instead of rowing against the tide, try sailing for a change. It's just as challenging, but it's a lot more fun and you can get a hell of a lot further.

 Broad or Narrow: The Casting Couch (p. 113)

God Plays Dice with the Universe (p. 215)

Interactivity is Subversive (p. 244)

New Media is Old News

Certain terms are temporal in nature. New is one of them. I always thought it odd that people would use "new" in a name, because things are only new for so long. New York (formerly Old New Amsterdam), the New School for Social Research, and New Math are all old news. As is "new media."

The term "new media" came into use in the early 1990s, and the term, as far as I can tell, originated in Hollywood. At the time, I found the term new media disconcerting. Interactive media was not new in the early 1990s, and just because nobody knew about it in 1983 doesn't mean it didn't exist. Having been at it since then, I guess I could just as easily call it "knew media." At one point, I was even thinking about calling my company Pneumedia, just for a hoot. I believe that the term "new media," which superceded "interactive multimedia" (which came into use in the mid-80s), was created by the "old media" industry in order to put it the context of what they did. This is not atypical of the arrogance of Hollywood, which, for at least a dozen years all but poo-pooed interactive media as not worthy of their attention. Then, when they suddenly realized what it meant to them, especially to those companies that had reusable assets, the term "new media" suddenly became hot.

Understand this—interactive media is not new. In fact, calling it new reinforces a serious problem with the way interactive media is thought of and taught—with total and utter lack of awareness of historical context. As anyone will tell you, those who ignore the past are doomed to repeat it. If you consider the plethora of naive and erroneous predictions that have been made about computers and media over the past 35 years, it would seem that those who ignore the future are doomed to repeat it as well.

The Interactive Ecosystem (p. 233)

Nerd versus Couch Potato (p. 345)

There is a strange kind of mass amnesia in which everything is about the present and future. In the culture of computers, we act as if nothing ever happened before today, because we are all so busy trying to frantically keep up with the so-called future and hold our ground in the so-called present. As a result, we've created a monster in the form of something called new media. This monster has forgotten about radio, television, computers, the printing press, language, iconography, culture, communication, and all the elements that have gone into creating the media culture we live in today. It has forgotten that 30 years ago people were actually thinking about this stuff, writing about it, and trying to understand why it was important. We can remove the blinders by opting to be a little more deliberate about what we're doing and realize that we are not creating new media at all, but, in the post-modernist tradition, re-combining all the old media in new ways to create something better defined by the term "interactive multimedia."

Mixed Media, Mixed Message (p. 306)

Although it's a mouthful, I prefer the term "interactive multimedia" for two reasons. First, multimedia is a much more accurate description of what we do—it's putting all the media together and trying to create new hybrids of media that we already know. The second reason, and this is key, is that little word up-front; that strangely deceptive, seductive yet misunderstood quadra-syllabic icon of our age—interactive. Interactivity is at the heart of all this so-called new media. Most of what's being done is an attempt to give the audience more control—more involvement and more input. In fact, inter-activity is what distinguishes the concept of an audience from the concept of a user or player. The audience and/or viewer sits passively while information, education, and entertainment are being fed to them. The user or player is a person who takes control and command and has some effect on what he or she is seeing, hearing, and doing.

New media is really an oxymoron as well as a misnomer. It is an oxymoron in the sense that there is nothing new about media itself—the only thing really new is interactivity. The label "new media" is also misnomer because it leaves out the most important thing that distinguishes so-called "new media" from "old media"—interactivity.

A BRIEF HISTORY OF REAL TIME: THE VIRTUAL REALITY LEGACY
(p. 105)

THE PEDAGOGICAL MOUSEPAD, OR, HOW IT ALL GOT GUI
(p. 365)

USER OR PLAYER: THE CHOICE IS YOURS (p. 490)

INTERACTIVITY IS SUBVERSIVE (p. 244)

OM MEETS OHM: DIGITAL ONENESS

The synthesis of all media into a single medium, a medium which is both one medium and all media, has profound cultural and spiritual implications beyond the obvious technical and creative ones. When all things are digital, text, movies, and audio are really all the same medium and what we have created is a single, all-encompassing omni-medium.

It has always been a source of vexation to me, particularly as a writer, that the term "multimedia" is used interchangeably as both plural and singular. We talk about "multimedia" as a medium, yet media is plural. In spite of the obvious grammatical conundrum that this presents, it accurately represents the reality we are faced with, which is equally vexing: We have created a single medium that integrates all media and therefore is properly both plural and singular. When you begin to integrate all media and create a kind of omni-medium that unifies virtually all content, information, art, music, film, and text into a single continuous all-media medium, the implications go beyond merely the economic, the creative, or the mechanical. After you have a state of what amounts to "digital oneness," you begin to open up theological issues as well. This continuity of all media and information calls to question the very nature of consciousness and thus the nature of the individual.

Marshall McLuhan came to this conclusion in 1964 when he wrote about the "Information Age":

> ...might not our current translation of our entire lives into the spiritual form of information seem to make of the entire globe, and of the human family, a single consciousness.

Although McLuhan did not live to see the full realization of his prophecy, 30 years later, this statement echoes loud and clear against the backdrop of integrated media. We live in a world in which all information has converged in the guise of the Internet and virtually everything we encounter, even our very selves, will eventually have a parallel existence in the digisphere. We live in a world where revolutions are fought and won with fax machines and laptop computers, movies become CD-ROMs, video games become movies, and where a picture paints a thousand K and is so easy to manipulate that photographs become suspect as trial evidence. The ramifications of this on the level of human consciousness are almost too much to fathom. McLuhan's statement suggests a level of cognitive unity, the creation of a single collective human mind, a bitstream into which we can all dip to share information, ideas, and emotions from a single, unified source.

Aldous Huxley, author of *Brave New World* and *The Doors of Perception* is another highly influential prophet of the digital age. These two Huxley works have certainly had a major impact on digital culture, but I think his most compelling work is his treatise on comparative theology entitled *The Perennial Philosophy.* The basic thesis of this book is that the core belief of all religions is essentially the same: All things in nature are part of a unified "higher truth," which is God. Mostly through a collection of quotes by Hindu, Buddhist, Muslim, and Christian spiritual teachers, Huxley demonstrates that any doctrine of separateness is inherently unholy and anti-God. The "perennial philosophy" to which he refers comes across in this simple statement by the Indian poet Kabir: "Behold but One in all things; it is the second that leads you astray." In other words, a sense of autonomy, individuation, and separation from this unified sphere of divinity is the greatest danger to the human soul. It is also another way of saying that the ego, which seeks to separate, control, and place itself above others and outside the unity of the divine, is the seed of destruction.

These same notions are echoed in the work of Jesuit priest Pierre Theillard de Chardin, whose work sought to integrate spiritual and scientific principles. De Chardin, who wrote in the 1960s, believed that the dichotomy between religion and science was false, and that principles of physics, biology, and evolution only supported the notion of universal divinity. Because computer science is indeed a science, de Chardin's influence is strongly felt among artist/scientists who seek to utilize computers to further bridge that gap.

In some respects, the Internet is the ultimate spiritual plane where there is little room for ego, because we are all reduced to bits of information in the datastream. The chat rooms on AOL are the most democratic place in the world. Everyone is an equal, and everyone is anonymous. No one can ever take control or be in power. There are no mechanisms for domination, and so in a very pure and simple way, the Internet can be perceived as a highly spiritually evolved technology. The digisphere of the Internet is one of the few places that we can exist in a totally egoless and spiritual state among others, as McLuhan pointed out. Egotism thrives on boundaries; it is nourished by isolation and separation; it derives strength from systems of hierarchy in which power-hungry ego feeds on the false belief that one individual can have dominion over another. In fact, the very word "Avatar," (originated by Farmer and Morningstar who created *Habitat*, the first online avatar-based world) is taken from the Hindu word, meaning an incarnation or embodiment of a god on earth. These creators of the first cyberspace community thus saw the avatar-based world as a channel of human divinity.

Cyberspace Cadets: Virtual Communities and Avatar Worlds (p. 146)

In the real world, it is a rare thing to interact with another human on an egoless level. Most of the social and economic constructs created in our culture are based on hierarchy, power, and control. Not so online. On the Internet, it is almost impossible to operate from an ego-driven stance at all. Even celebrities can have different lives online. On the one hand, they can interact with their fans on the level of ideas and information. At the same time, celebrities have the opportunity to become anonymous—the Internet enables them to mingle with people in an environment that is inherently equalizing.

The entertainment industry is an economy based entirely on ego. It is a cult of personality built entirely on an ego-feeding system that can ultimately cultivate the most monstrous side of the human character. Neuroses abound in Hollywood, not because people are more neurotic, but because a world built on an ego-based infrastructure is guaranteed to make anyone crazy. Even the most even-tempered and humble soul is challenged by an environment in which one person can garner a salary for single film that could easily support a hundred families in a respectable fashion. It is a system that coddles and nurtures the worst in us, the greedy, self-centered and childish aspects of human nature that tenets of religion and morality have tried so hard to discourage. It should be no surprise that the result of this system is widespread addiction to drugs and sex, alcoholism, suicide, and even murder. Few people, even the best of us, would have the psychological acuity to withstand such a system. It is the very antithesis of virtually every system for human spiritual harmony.

The Internet on the other hand is totally ego-less. The great and the small have equal domain. The dinosaur has as much chance at survival as the mouse, perhaps moreso. Cyberspace is about community, "com-unity," and "comp-unity." If offers a medium of transaction that is completely horizontal and thus propagates a much more spiritual kind of interchange. This is why the entertainment industry has no idea what to do with it. They try to utilize it to propagate the ego-based culture, but they are baffled by an environment that does not support a star system, and indeed, even shuns it.

In his clinical research, observation, and study, psychologist Carl Jung identified a secondary plane of consciousness, the subconscious mind. In studying the subconscious, particularly as manifested through dreams and mythology, Jung discovered certain archetypes or universal symbols that seem to transcend culture and conscious thought. In the dreamscape, Jung saw a portal into this subconscious thought, and through that portal there seemed to exist a continuum, an inexplicable sphere of consciousness that almost appeared as if it were shared between all people, regardless of age, race, culture, or any other externally imposed factors.

In his book *Man and His Symbols*, Jung tried to observe and identify the common language of the subconscious through archetype and symbol, and in so doing created a vocabulary for a neural network or shared mind that existed beyond the level of consciousness and traditional forms of human communication.

If McLuhan was right, the Internet is the manifestation of Jung's unconscious metaplane; for in it we find a shared mind that works on both the conscious and subconscious level; a unified field of thought that becomes the collective creation of all those who enter it. Like Jung's system of symbol and archetype, this sphere transcends geographical and cultural boundaries and offers us an extension of the human mind and soul that all but dissolves the boundaries between us.

That spiritual overtones exist throughout cyberspace is no accident. In fact, there is a significant faction of interactive and Virtual Reality designers who are very consciously trying to integrate spiritual principles into their work. Brenda Laurel and Rachel Strickland's influential 1993 art installation *Placeholder* was a ritual space in which users took on the roles of animal spirits represented by petroglyphic spirit animals of the Anasszi Indians. The highly acclaimed *Osmose*, by Char Davies, has been described as a "virtual meditation space." Rita Addison's stirring before-and-after account of sensory anomalies caused by a brain injury has profound spiritual ramifications. The exquisitely serene artificial life environments of Christa Sommerer and Laurent Mignonneau seduce the visitor into a highly spiritual interchange with a simulated natural environment. Other interactive artists whose work have had a profound spiritual effect on participants include Karl Simms.

 V-Art (p. 494)

T_Vision, an ambitious project by Art+Com, creates a unified digital Earth by drawing from all the world's databases into a single, high-resolution model of the earth at every level of magnification. Their goal is to eventually get access to models of every country, every building, even every human on earth and integrate them into this parallel universe that represents the ultimate unity of our entire planet.

T_VISION: SPACESHIP EARTH MADE VISIBLE (p. 460)

The "architects of cyberspace" have been highly influenced by spiritual principles. Mark Pesce and Tony Parisi, co-inventors of the Internet VR protocol VRML, have strong spiritual groundings in their work. Pesce appeared on the cover of the "Techno Pagans" issue of *Wired* in 1995, and has numerous spiritual references in his books, classes, and lectures. Mark has also created *Web Earth*, a scaled down version of *T_Vision* on the web that enables viewer to have an overview of the entire Earth and access data about it from a variety of sources. Like Mark and Tony, many of the pioneering VRML artists have included strongly spiritual themes in their work, borrowing from Hindu philosophy, mythology, and even creating ritual space and virtual temples in cyberspace. Many of the digerati gather in an annual celebration called *Burning Man*, a giant pagan ritual and camp-out which takes place in the Nevada desert each summer. The connection to nature and the commitment to use computers to improve our relationship is a major part of the philosophy of many cyberspace designers today.

THE BIRTH OF CYBERSPACE: 3D COMES TO THE WEB (p. 97)

DIGERATI: THE ARTIFICIAL INTELLIGENTSIA (p. 164)

I myself have been concerned with these issues, as indicated in this chapter and in other chapters throughout this book. I see interactive media as a potential tool for social change. I therefore try to integrate principles of spirituality into all my work. This does not mean religion, but rather, the idea that a medium of discovery and empowerment can lead to various forms of revelation and transcendence.

In 1996, I hosted a panel for the SIGGRAPH computer graphics conference entitled *The Soul of the Machine: The Search for Spirituality in Cyberspace*. Its participants included Mark Pesce, Char Davies, Rita Addison, and composer/musician Paul Godwin. Its theme was the exploration of VR as a medium for spiritual transcendence. Each artist presented their work and the philosophy behind it. Paul gave an interactive presentation in which he had the audience chant along with a dial tone. Later in the day, he facilitated an online exercise in musical collaboration—an online intonement/vocalization with people in remote locations. This is another example of the use of the computer as a ritual space and its potential as a vehicle for unity and deeper understanding between people.

Consensual Hallucinations: Is VR the New LSD? (p. 137)

The Soul in the Machine (p. 439)

God Plays Dice with the Universe (p. 215)

The Pedagogical Mousepad, or, How it all Got GUI

We've all heard the story (or should I say legend) of the birth of the graphical user interface. Like all legends, we will no doubt hear it many more times. It is a story about a modern-day Prometheus who dared to steal fire from the gods and give it to the masses, resulting in his being lashed against the rocks in perpetuity for his arrogance. That's right. I'm talking about Steve Jobs.

If you know this legend already, you can skip this part. Or, you may want to hang on for the ride just to get my side remarks along the way.

The graphical user interface, known in the Land of Acronyms as GUI, was the brainchild of one Alan Kay, an esteemed member of the research staff at Xerox PARC (Palo Alto Research Center) in…you'll never guess where…Palo Alto, California. Let's just call it Mount Olympus. Kay, like just about anybody who did anything cool during the first 20 years of computing, came out of ARPA, which was a defense R&D program.

A Brief History of Real Time: The Virtual Reality Legacy (p. 105)

Xerox was clever enough to fund and support Kay and his team in their efforts to create this new kind of interface, but not clever enough to market it to a mass audience. Enter Prometheus…Apple Computer co-founder Steve Jobs—the madly passionate garage-hacker-turned-mad-genius-entrepreneur. It was love at first sight. On his initial tour of Xerox PARC, Jobs saw in the graphical user interface a revelation: A realization that the power of the computer was not in hardware, nor even in software, but in the dialogue between the user and the machine. What he realized at that first viewing was that there could actually be a way for normal, non-geeks to operate a computer with ease. This was the missing ingredient he needed to support his vision of the Digital Volkswagen, the computer-as-appliance, the notion that everyone should have a computer and should not have to have a Ph.D. in Mathematics to use it.

Some say that Steve Jobs co-opted the graphical user interface from Xerox PARC, but he could just as easily be seen as the Robin Hood of personal computing. After his first visit, Jobs returned with his team from Apple, against warnings from some of the Xerox PARC people, who could see the writing on the wall (or the monitor, as the case may be). This young team of hotshot hackers scrutinized the GUI in detail so that they could return to their secret workshop and create what would become the first commercially available, mass market, GUI. Unencumbered by bureaucracy, secrecy, and the snail's pace of the research culture, Jobs' team carried this torch outside the sanctuary of knowledge to light the flame of personal computing for the common man.

The Prometheus connection is apt. The ancient Greek myth tells the story of a Titan who empowers humans with something which, up until then, was only found in the domain of the gods themselves. Fast forward to Christian mythology, watch, and listen as a guileless serpent coerces Eve (a woman, no less) to eat the…that's right…Apple of knowledge. Both myths tell a similar story, and in both cases, the perpetrators are punished for their alleged arrogance.

The entire tale of the graphical user interface presents a moral dilemma that would lend itself to a very intriguing interactive experience: What if you wanted to change the world? What if you saw something really cool that you knew was going to have a major impact on the world? What if the people that invented this amazing thing did not seem to have any interest in making it available to a large audience? What if they were just, well, sitting on it? What would you do?

Now I'm a pretty straight up kinda gal, but I can easily see what these guys were faced with. To anyone who thinks they were wrong, I put forth to you the notion of karma. Twenty years later, the idea that Apple emulated so successfully from Xerox PARC had now been co-opted once again by Mr. DOS himself in the form of the Windows interface.

So let's talk about the GUI, about why it's so important, and about how and why it changed everything.

Before Macintosh, there was basically one paradigm for personal computers: DOS. DOS, of course, stands for the very catchy Disk Operating System. It was purchased for a minuscule amount of money by a couple of other guys named Gates and Allen, also known as Microsoft. Microsoft turned around and sold it to IBM and it quickly became the standard operating system for IBM PCs, and later what came to be called "clones" or IBM-compatible machines. DOS was fairly low level, meaning it was close to the machine, as opposed to the Macintosh operating system, which is high level—far from the machine, separated by several layers of code. The simple equation here, by the way, is that the closer you get to the human, the further away you have to get from the machine. The simple reason for this is that the machine just doesn't speak any common human language, so you have to learn some kind of computer code or language to talk to the computer at a low level.

DOS wasn't designed to be particularly user-friendly. In fact, it wasn't designed to be friendly at all. Though functionally quite sound, DOS leaned toward the side of user-unfriendly. You had to know everything before you even sat down at a DOS machine. A C:\ prompt would appear on the screen, and assuming you knew what C:\ stood for (generally some disk drive or other), you would type in "dir," meaning directory, and then you would get a list of documents, each of which had to have a maximum of eight letters, followed by a suffix, such as .doc, meaning document, or what have you (see figure P.1). If you wrote the word delete, followed by the name of a program or executable file or document, it would delete it. Just like that. No fail-safe, no dialog box, just boom, it's gone, kaput.

Figure P.1

The user-unfriendly DOS interface

How would you open one of these documents? Well unless you knew how, you couldn't. Generally, you had to run a program by typing in its name after the prompt. After the program came on, you selected from a series of function keys (F1–F12) that ran along the top of the keyboard that you had to memorize. The functions of these keys were, of course, completely different for every program. If you memorized the function keys for one program, you had to re-memorize them for another. If you weren't careful, you might find out that F7 meant save in one program and erase in another. Then, to make it even more fun, you could also memorize a bunch of combinations of keys, by pushing down something such as a Control key and a letter key at the same time, which again, if done accidentally, could precipitate some irreversible process, the impact of which you might not even realize until much later when you went back and tried to find the missing data.

All this happened on a beautiful black screen with either orange or green letters on it. What you saw on the screen was a stream of text and symbols that had little or nothing to do with what you would see after you printed the screen contents. If you used the green screen for long periods of time, you would get "pink eye," a state in which you literally saw the world through rose-colored glasses—your eyes compensating for the direct exposure to the green light of the letters.

I know I sound like I'm whining, and I'm sure some of my older colleagues would look at me the same way my Dad does when he talks about walking five miles to school in the snow and says, "Oh, yeah...well try programming with a punch card."

Suddenly, the Macintosh computer comes on to the scene. The screen is... white. White. Imagine that! When you type on the white screen, the letters all appear in a row, the way they would look on an actual piece of paper. The carriage returns where it's going to return on the actual page. The typeface is the same as it will be in the final document.

But that's not all! You didn't have to memorize *anything* to use a Mac. All you needed to know were a few basic parameters. You clicked the mouse on a pull-down menu to display choices of what to do. In plain English. Fancy that (see figure P.2)! You could cut or paste text just by highlighting what you wanted to edit. If you pressed the Delete button, it would ask you whether you were *sure* you wanted to do that. The environment was user-friendly. You didn't have to be an MIT grad to use it. It was *easy*.

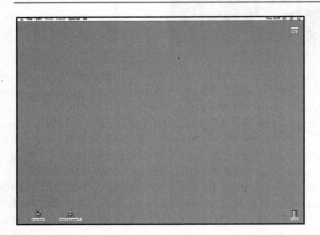

Figure P.2

The easy-to-use Macintosh interface

CONFESSIONS OF A MACINTOSH CONVERT (p. 132)

The Macintosh interface is a perfect example of a heuristic learning tool. It is a tool that teaches you how to use it through its use, an educational paradigm in which the user can ultimately teach him or herself, a tool that supports autodidactic, or self-taught, learning. The creation and mass dissemination of such a paradigm into the popular culture is single-handedly responsible for transforming the computer into a mass medium. Had DOS maintained the predominant position in personal computers, the world would be a very different place today. The graphical user interface as co-opted, developed, and marketed by Apple invited the rest of the world to the party.

The Macintosh was the first computer that artists could use. Even now, as its market share has progressively waned, the Macintosh is still most often the machine of choice of graphic designers, artists, and filmmakers. The DOS interface was a left-brain proposition. It served a very narrow target demographic. But by adding a graphical interface, you could suddenly connect with a different part of the user's brain. The WYSIWIG (What You See Is What You Get) capability of the Mac meant that you could build your content around visual cues instead of mathematical cues.

There was also the safety factor. The Macintosh's user-friendly protocol made it more difficult to make horrible mistakes. Every time you went to delete something, the computer would ask you to confirm if you really wanted to do that. You began to trust the machine, to feel as if you were having a relationship with it. Even the happy face that comes up on the intro screen at startup conveyed the notion that the computer was, to a certain extent, personified, that it was a thoughtful machine, and that it actually cared about you. If you are a Mac user, you will know what I mean when I say the Macintosh interface has a personality. One of its character traits is that it is supportive and it always anticipates my next move. Another trait is that it knows what kind of mistakes I might make and helps me avoid making them.

I once read a great humor piece that compared a dog to a computer. They were talking primarily about the Macintosh, because in some ways, it has many of the same traits as a loyal and intelligent canine.

I find it fascinating that, although the Microsoft Windows interface is, for all intents and purposes, the same thing as the Macintosh interface, what it lacks is personality. It is missing some seemingly simple things, but they are essential in gaining my trust and in making me feel safe and comfortable, as if my feelings are being taken into account. It's as simple as the fact that on the Macintosh, I can use any file name I want, with as many characters as I want, so I can recognize my files. In Windows, I still have to use the eight-character protocol. To me this is a constant reminder that what I'm dealing with is really DOS in sheep's clothing.

The reason I am going into such a level of detail here is to make the essential point that computer interface design is a matter of psychology more than anything else. It is not the elegant graphics of the interface that make it valuable, it is the emotional bond that we have with the interface.

On a wider scale, this level of bond, this trust, and this sense that the computer liked artists and wanted to help them had a massive impact on the culture at-large. A society of artists armed with computers is a beautiful and dangerous thing. Like the Gutenberg Press, the Macintosh paved the path for desktop publishing. Suddenly, you could produce high-quality graphics and text at home. Many graphic designers began to set up home studios, and small companies began to publish their own newsletters. Individuals were empowered to do things it used to take whole companies to do.

Because the graphical user interface was so friendly, it also did something else remarkable—it made computers accessible to children. It is a great tribute to the Macintosh GUI that it can be used by a digital media professional to do high-end video effects and editing, and by a small child to play a game or learn how to read. Its simplicity is expandable—easy enough for a child, but sophisticated enough for an adult. The heuristic, self-teaching GUI means anyone from my three year-old nephew to my 80 year-old grandmother can use it.

This is why the GUI is the ultimate power tool—because it can be used by virtually anybody to do virtually anything; and they can teach themselves how to do it every step of the way. Thus the computer has truly become, in Marshall McLuhan's words, an extension of man, a way to be bigger than we are, no matter what our size to begin with.

AUTOBIOGRAPHY OF AN AUTODIDACT, PART 1 (p. 45)

AUTODIDACTIC COMMUNALISM (p. 83)

ARTIFICIAL INTELLIGENCE AND THE PROSTHETIC BRAIN (p. 38)

PICASSO: THE FATHER OF 3D GRAPHICS

The notion of trying to capture three-dimensional worlds in a two-dimensional space predates the realization of computer graphics by some years. Almost as soon as photography was invented, 3D photography was explored through the use of stereoscopy. Two images slightly offset, each seen by a different eye, could create the illusion of three dimensions.

It was really the cubists, and most particularly Pablo Picasso, who began to explore the notion of knowing all sides, all aspects, all facets if you will, of an object at once. By unfolding a three-dimensional object and laying it out on the flat surface of the canvas, Picasso was trying to do the seemingly impossible—to show you both front, back, and sides of an object at once. Virtual Reality goes one step further or one step back, depending on how you look at it. Because we can interact with the canvas, we no longer have to see all sides at once because we have the liberty of circulating around the object. Picasso understood, in what he was trying to do, the essence of the 3D computer graphics: the idea that objects exist in three dimensions and that there must be a way to translate that into a two-dimensional plane.

When looked at this way, the best Virtual Reality experiences are interactive paintings, dynamic canvases that can be penetrated and explored. The example of Picasso reinforces my opinion that it is artists, not businessmen or technologists, who are going to realize and manifest the interactive media into what they should truly be. The best Virtual Reality is as captivating as a Picasso painting, and tells us as much about our environment it does about our perception of it.

The job of the artist (at least of the modern artist), is to provide us with new modes of perception. It is said that when Picasso was criticized because his portrait of Gertrude Stein didn't look like her, he responded "It will." What Picasso was painting was not so much a facsimile but an avatar; he was creating a portrait of Stein's persona, not her physical appearance. The evolution of perception is key to the evolution of culture and intellect. In fact, the history of our evolving group mind can be seen as the evolution of perception. Prior to the 20th century, this can be traced as an evolution of perspective, as we become better and better at conveying three-dimensional space on a two-dimensional canvas.

Throughout the 20th century, we were no longer concerned with conveying real space, but with conveying various forms of psychic space. Fine art in Picasso's day was no longer about *what* we see, but about *how* we see. From Albert Einstein, who pointed out that there is no absolute measurement and all events occur relative to other events, to Sergei Eisenstein, who brought subjectivity to film, this process of evolving perception is a key to understanding our relationship to our culture, to ourselves, and most of all, to our media.

GAINING PERSPECTIVE: THE EVOLUTION OF DIMENSION (p. 196)

VIRTUAL RELATIVITY (p. 524)

EINSTEIN, EISENSTEIN, AND THE SPACE-TIME CONTINUUM (p. 186)

ART IS A VERB (p. 29)

POP VR: JARON'S WORLD

Jaron Lanier is, without question, the most recognizable icon in Virtual Reality. He is probably the closest thing we have to a VR pop star. And he looks the part. Soft-spoken, and sporting a huge outcropping of blond dreadlocks, Jaron's eerily transparent blue eyes can almost lead one to believe that he is looking beyond you into a parallel universe. In fact, he has devoted his illustrious, if not sometimes rocky career to creating these parallel worlds, and more importantly, making them accessible to the public. Within the digital community, he is a pop culture icon who tried to make VR a pop culture medium.

A BRIEF HISTORY OF REAL TIME: THE VIRTUAL REALITY LEGACY (p. 105)

It's no wonder that Jaron looks like a rock star. He is, in fact, a musician. A drop-out-turned-programmer (pretty much the archetype for the hippie/geeks of his generation), he began as a programmer for Atari Games in the early 80s. At that time, Jaron had the idea to create a tool that would enable non-programmers to write computer code. In 1984, a mock-up of his visual programming language, called Mandala, appeared on the cover of *Scientific American*. Instead of using alphanumeric code, Jaron's language enabled people to program using playful graphical icons on a musical staff. Mandala began as a means of creating experimental music, but as Jaron developed his ideas, he realized that this iconic system could be used in a variety of other applications.

One of the unique ideas behind Mandala was the interface device. Jaron envisioned that people could manipulate these icons and objects with the use of a glove, creating a natural and intuitive means of human/computer interaction. In 1983, Jaron met another musician/engineer, Thomas Zimmerman. Zimmerman invented a data glove, not as a means to interact with computer environments in 3D space, but as a way to play "air guitar." Zimmerman's data glove was meant to be a more natural way to interface with a synthesizer, using gesture to control sound and music…not unlike the ideas that had been percolating inside the multifaceted mind of Jaron Lanier.

Under the auspices of Jaron's VPL Research, Inc., this team of musician/ magicians created the first commercially available Head-Mounted Display and Data Glove system, as well as the software engine to make it all fit together. The system was commercially available, but cost-prohibitive. What it did was open the door for Virtual Reality to move to another level. Jaron, with his visionary philosophy and bashful rock star demeanor, became a kind of spokesperson for VR and is still perhaps the most recognizable of mainstream VR acolytes.

VPL had its VR sights aimed toward multi-user collaborative spaces. VPL debuted one of their demos at a trade show in January of 1989 at the same time that Autodesk (another Northern California company) unveiled its high-end CAD (Computer-Aided Design) VR system. Autodesk's system, a far cry from the rough and primitive wireframe models that preceded it, had solid objects and lighting, creating a new level of quality for the VR environment. In VPL's collaborative digital workspace *Day Care World*, multiple participants could enter a virtual environment and work together to design the layout for a day care center. One of the cool features of *Day Care World* was that the designers could change their scale with relation to the environment, allowing them to see the day care center from the perspective of the children it was designed for. VPL's system had even better resolution and was even more refined than Autodesk's. Both systems marked a kind of springboard for VR to leap from its Ivory Towers and Armored Fortresses into the popular culture. 1989 was the beginning of a new generation of VR.

1990 heralded the release of the very first public Virtual Reality attraction opened in a mall in Chicago. Dubbed *BattleTech*, it was a sci-fi VR game developed by role player/engineers. Players enter a pod vehicle used to control a giant virtual robot. The goal of the game is to run around a cyberdesert and blow everyone else away, limb by limb. *BattleTech* was one of the first public accessible VR attractions.

While *BattleTech* provided a Virtual Reality in a full attraction venue, one of the first VR products for arcades was *Virtuality*, which featured a game called *Dactyl Nightmare*. It's a rather baffling game logic, but the goal is, of course, to kill the other player. You stand on a small circular platform wearing a Head-Mounted Display and playing a game of "shoot your friends" in a somewhat uneventful cyber grid. Each time you get shot, you blow into a million pieces, then reassemble somewhere else in the grid. The Dactyl part comes in when giant pterodactyl dinosaurs come flying down, pick you up, and drop you in a different location. My problem with this game was always that the thing was the most fun was being picked up by the Dactyl, and the second most fun thing was getting blown up.

Today, of course, you can see various forms of VR entertainment in locations as diverse as the corner arcade and your living room. Most of the games, sad to say, are variations of the *BattleTech* and *Virtuality* theme: "shoot your friends." We are now seeing some evolution toward more sports-oriented games, such as motorcycle simulations and skiing games.

1994 marked another landmark year for pop VR. At this time, two major high-end VR attractions were introduced: Disney's *Aladdin's Magic Carpet Ride* and Iwerks and Evans & Sutherland's *Virtual Adventures*. Both of these products provided high-end game/story experiences that enabled visitors to experience the best available VR technology coupled with very high-quality content. Again, one was vehicle-based, the other used a Head-Mounted Display. *Virtual Adventures* took place in a six-person submarine, while *Aladdin* used a single-player simulated carpet with a stereo helmet.

Both these products, though well-received and popular with audiences, had limited success due to cost and context. When I say context, what I mean is that neither game fit into any known paradigm of how to present such an attraction. *Virtual Adventures* was, erroneously, marketed as an alternative to roller coasters, while *Aladdin* was placed in Disneyland, in the context of a location famous for its high-throughput dark rides.

We are now seeing more and more VR games appearing in arcades, and it has reached the point where 3D has become the rule rather than the exception. Most of the arcade audience has come to expect it, and so, although the game remains the same, the technology gets more sophisticated.

In the future, I hope that we can create more games like *Aladdin* and *Virtual Adventures*, but at a price point that is feasible for the mass market. I also hope that the marketing people responsible for getting these products to the public can take a little more risk, be a little more adventuresome, and invent new ways to make these products viable.

 NARRATIVE ENVIRONMENTS: VIRTUAL REALITY AS A STORYTELLING MEDIUM (p. 329)

One huge potential market for high-tech VR entertainment is malls. Many malls are trying to draw in customers with entertainment. Movie theaters are now de rigeur in mall and promenade settings, but real estate developers are looking for interactive products to include within a retail/entertainment mix. Unfortunately, there are very few products out there, and even less that are affordable.

Another place where we are going to see significant movement in the VR/LBE arena is in casinos. *Virtual Adventures* is featured in Iwerks' entertainment zone at the Foxwoods Casino in Ledyard, Connecticutt, and Las Vegas has become a mecca for new and unconventional entertainment.

The third location we will be seeing more VR now and in the future is in a new generation of high-tech attractions or special venues such as the SEGA Gameworks project. A joint venture of Universal Parks, SEGA, and Dreamworks SKG, SEGA Gameworks is a venue for SEGA products, as well as other high-tech entertainment. A number of other companies are also developing high-tech "black box" attractions that are specifically designed to facilitate such products as Virtual Reality games and experiences.

IT'S ONLY A GAME: THE BIRTH OF A MULTI-BILLION DOLLAR BUSINESS (p. 260)

DIGERATI: THE ARTIFICIAL INTELLIGENTSIA (p. 164)

V-ART (p. 494)

VIRTUAL REALITY AS A DRAMATIC ART (p. 508)

THE PRINCESS AND THE MONSTER: THE MAKING OF VIRTUAL ADVENTURES

In the entertainment industry, artistic integrity is seldom a requirement, but if you're lucky, it will sometimes be tolerated, and on a rare occasion, even encouraged. Artistic integrity often only arises out of a sheer force of will on the part of the artist against seemingly insurmountable odds. At other times, it is an accident that occurs because the Powers-that-Be are unaware that it is happening. The best place to achieve artistic integrity is outside the industry itself, where, unfettered, the artist can create something wonderful. After the artist's creation gains public acceptance, the industry can then—vulture-like—encircle and exploit it, applauding itself at the end of the year by bestowing with awards that which only a year before they said would never fly.

Although at heart I am an artist, for reasons of which I am not quite certain, I have placed myself square in the middle of the entertainment industry and all that goes with it. This is partly fate, party conscious choice (I like to entertain people, just as a matter of course), and partly because I have a passionate conviction that the more people get ahold of this stuff the better. I guess my philosophy is that the best way to change the world is through mass media, and the best way to propagate a subversive agenda is to make it entertaining. I love the fine arts and support all the work done in this area, but for my agenda, it does not afford a broad enough audience. At my first interactive job, with Edwin Schlossberg Incorporated, I was raised on family values: children's museums, Theme parks, zoos, even malls—places where families could go and have fun and learn together...so I guess that sensibility kind of stuck with me and never quite went away. I've never been much of an academic and I just don't have the wherewithal to deal with the art world...although I'm not sure that would be any harder than dealing with the entertainment industry. Anyway, for whatever reason, the entertainment industry is where I landed, and so here I am.

I am not sure how many of the people at Iwerks ever really knew what I was doing, but I think at the very least they believed that I knew what I was doing, and that was all it took. They had the right idea and they were excited, idealistic, adventurous, and willing to put their money where their mouth was. Most important, they were willing to take the kind of bold risk necessary to make something new in the world...and they certainly took a bold risk on me. They knew both what they knew and what they didn't know, and they were willing to trust me to provide them with some direction. Overall, helping the Iwerks and Evans & Sutherland teams to join forces and create *Virtual Adventures* was one of the most enjoyable and satisfying creative challenges of my professional life. It was an extraordinary opportunity to create something really great, and it's one of the things I'm most proud of in my career, not just because I feel it is among my own best work, but because it is among the best work of a really excellent team of people that I had the opportunity to work with over a 12-month period. The *Virtual Adventures* project was the right thing at the right time with exactly the right people at the right moment in history with the right attitude. It all fell into place and we made something really great.

So enough of the commentary, here's the whole, beautiful tale. It's kind of a fairy tale really, about a digital princess who, instead of getting swept off her feet and falling in love with a prince, or even a frog, fell in love with a monster, a friendly dragon endowed with magical powers...and it goes something like this...

It all started, believe it or not, in the Netherlands. It was the annual TILE conference (Technology in Leisure and Entertainment) in 1992. Two fortuitous things occurred at this event. The first was that Stan Kinsey met Michael Mascioni. The second was that Stan had his first encounter with the people from Evans & Sutherland. Kinsey was the co-founder of Iwerks Entertainment, one of the top three ridefilm companies in America. A former Disney-ite,

Kinsey began having his own visions and spirited away the Crown Prince of special format films, Don Iwerks, whose father Ub Iwerks—Walt Disney's principal partner and the mastermind behind much of the Disney Theme park technology. Stan was the *seer*; Don was the *doer*. Stan went around the world to speak at conferences. Don, a tall, mild-mannered man who seemed like nothing could ever irk him, worked diligently at his drafting table to come up with all these killer ways for people to experience cinema.

At TILE, Stan started schmoozing with Evans & Sutherland and somehow or another something got drawn on a napkin (really...no joke) and the next thing everybody knew, they got this cockamamie idea that they would take Evans & Sutherland's world renowned flight simulator technology and marry it with Iwerks world-renowned theatrical skills and something magical was bound to happen.

The impetus for *Virtual Adventures* was a "what I did on my summer vacation" proof of concept hacked out by a visionary artist/engineer at E&S named, rather aptly, Kellan Hatch (the final content implementation revolved around collecting eggs). Kellan took a couple of weeks off and put together a castle...it was actually a great little demo. It started in a little kid's room, and the castle was actually a miniature castle sitting on a table. Using something that was roughly derived from a submarine simulator (it had a periscope), the demo simulated a tiny helicopter that you flew into the castle. Inside the castle were a series of rooms with flashing blades and flickering candles and bats and a huge pool of lava with a gigantic dragon in it that you could subdue by shooting ice cubes at him, causing him and his molten bathtub to freeze up into an icy blue (you had to pick up the ice cubes from some kind of giant ice machine in another room). You could deal with various obstacles by shooting balls of green slime at them. If you hit the bats, they would fall to the ground and twitch around before getting back up and going at it again.

Kellan Hatch is without question the unsung hero of *Virtual Adventures*. He created the bulk of the models and images that went into creating the database of exquisite images, and oversaw the rest of the team who implemented it. He was the secret weapon that made *Virtual Adventures* fly.

The other driving force behind *Virtual Adventures* on the E&S side was a gentleman by the name of Mike Ryder, who was heading up E&S's efforts to get into the entertainment industry. He had an uphill battle to fight against the Powers-that-Be: brilliant engineers enamored of the entertainment industry and seduced by its potential profits, but also characteristically conservative and unimaginative, having spent over two decades building nothing but military simulators and gigantic cockpits. So, the people at Evans & Sutherland were on a mission of sorts...they were trying to find a way into the entertainment business because they thought maybe they were on to something.

Now if you have any kind of memory at all, you are probably asking yourself the key question: Who in the hell is Michael Mascioni and where does he come in? Well, quite simply, it's his fault that *I* got sucked into all this in the first place.

The first conference I ever spoke at was something called Intertainment 89 in New York when I was working for Edwin Schlossberg Incorporated (Intertainment was also, coincidentally, the name of ESI's top-secret entertainment project at the time). Ed had been asked to speak and he asked me to go in his stead. The panel was entitled something like: "Is Location-Based Entertainment the Next Goldmine in Interactive Media?" The title itself was quite ironic, because the answer was and still is—not yet. Michael Mascioni was the organizer of that conference. Over the years, he and I kept in touch and he would occasionally ask me to speak at a conference or panel he was putting together.

In October 1992, I got the call from Michael that would drastically alter the course of history…mine anyway. He was adamant. He had just returned from the Netherlands and met this guy named Stan Kinsey. He said that I needed to call him because he was doing something amazing, and Michael had told him that I was the perfect person to work on it. He gave me the number and just insisted that I call this guy Kinsey. Seeing as Michael was one of the few individuals who knew what the hell it was I did, I figured if he thought this was a good fit, he was probably right. A couple hours later, I happened to flip through the most recent copy of *Millimeter Magazine*, and lo and behold, there was this guy Kinsey. So I picked up the phone right then and there, actually looking at the picture of him at the time, and phoned him.

We had a long and very amicable chat with a lot of humor and seemed to hit it off just fine. I lived in New York at the time, but planned to be in L.A. in a few weeks for some holiday or another, so I made an appointment to see him.

One of the indicators I use to tell whether a meeting is going well is when it turns into a "hot potato" interview—each person who meets with me immediately wants me to meet somebody else. I got to the interview and met with Stan for about 10 or 15 minutes; he got very excited, left the room, and brought in Eddie Newquist, VP of film; he got excited, left the room, and then went and got somebody else. By the end of the interview, I think I met about seven or eight people. Everyone was very excited, especially me, and I left to go about my holiday business.

I went home to New York and heard nothing for several weeks. Then, sometime in January, I got a mysterious call from Eddie Newquist who ran Iwerks film studio at the time. He wanted to send me something to see what I thought. They paid me a nice little consulting fee for a day to just read this stuff and give my comments. Eddie Newquist is one of the most enthusiastic people I have ever met. He looks and acts just like a little kid, with the high-energy Peter Pan quality of someone who spends his time making family entertainment. In this first phone call, Eddie told me about this thing they were doing, that it was really *cool*, that I had never *seen* anything so cool, and that it was going to *blow me away*. Now, you have to understand that I was a bit jaded. I had seen a lot of vaporware come and go, and up until this point, I had been duly unimpressed with Virtual Reality to the point where I had all but ignored it. I had vaguely heard of Evans & Sutherland, but I didn't really get the connection, even though I knew since the early 80s about the fancy flight sims the military had been making. So when I heard Eddie going on about how cool this thing was, I was thinking to myself "yeah, yeah. I've heard all the hype. It probably looks like 3D *Pac-Man*. Whatever."

The next day I received a mysterious FedEx package, and this began what I termed the "Mission: Impossible" phase of the project. During the first six months, I never met with anyone, and barely even had a conversation with anyone. Every few weeks, I would get a call from Eddie telling me he was sending me something. The next day, a FedEx package would arrive. I'd have to comment, or write something, or do a treatment. It was never more than a couple of days of work at a time, but each time it would get to be a little longer and more involved. I would complete the task at hand and FedEx or fax it back, and then I'd wait. Weeks would go by. I'd hear nothing. Then another call. This same routine continued for a about six months.

The first round of materials focused on the product itself aside from content. My contribution at this point had to do with the issues around the product's multiplayer functionality, from both a design and economic standpoint, but also in terms of social dynamics. Some of the areas I was involved in included the following:

- The number of players in the game/experience, including number of people on a team, and number of teams competing with each other.
- Seating positions for players relative to each other.
- The best combination of controls to facilitate team interaction within this vehicle.
- Creating interdependence between players without making it too easy for one person to ruin it for everyone else or dominate the game.
- Balancing throughput (number of players per hour) with user experience. This was an issue of finding a balance between economic and play concerns.
- Designing a non-content–specific vehicle that could transform into different vehicles for different games or experiences.

In addition to reviewing these factors, there was the content itself (various submitted game ideas) to review and return with comments. I evaluated the content for audience appeal, game structure, story content, and so forth.

Finally, I got the call to write a treatment. With his characteristic excitement and enthusiasm, Eddie game me the following assignment:

> Come up with a game about the Loch Ness Monster. Borrow whatever you want from the other ideas, or come up with stuff from scratch… whatever you want, as long as it's about the Loch Ness Monster.

My response was uncharacteristic silence. When I first got this assignment, I must confess I thought: This is ridiculous. How cheesy, how *National Enquirer*, how totally lowbrow. It was the weirdest thing I'd ever heard and I was tempted to suggest something different, but I decided to give it the old college try to see what would happen.

In retrospect, I now believe it was a fit of genius that led Eddie Newquist to this premise. As a rule, Iwerks tended to prefer working with licensed properties, particularly hit feature films because they believed that familiar content had a better market. So for *Virtual Adventures*, they wanted something familiar and recognizable, but they also wanted something they wouldn't have to pay for, something in the public domain. The Loch Ness Monster was a great solution because Loch Ness itself is a constrained body of water, and on top of this, you had a legendary monster to add the dimension of both mystery and character.

I've always had a fantasy of becoming a detective, so I took on this albeit dubious concept with the relish of Nancy Drew trying to track down the latest suspicious occurrence. I started at the New York Public Library. There wasn't much, but whatever there was, I read it: articles, a small handful of books on inexplicable phenomena—monsters and the like, the kind of thing you might see on *In Search of…* in between the heads of Easter Island and giant petroglyphs in the desert sand.

Once I got into it, I really fell in love with whole idea of the game proposal. The kitschiness of it became an asset rather than a liability. I liked that the content fit the lowest common denominator (or "LCD" as I call it). I told Eddie I wanted it to be a B Horror movie with an *In Search of…* kind of feel. He thought his approach was very hip. We both agreed that it made the game accessible, while still giving it a sophisticated edge.

I started to find out some interesting things. I found out, for example, that animals similar to Nessie had been found in other bodies of water similar to Loch Ness (deep, cold mountain lakes and fjords); that, as far as anyone could tell, these creatures had been sighted at those locations for hundreds of years, as documented through various drawings and written accounts; and that they all seemed to fit roughly the same description: a giant, snake-like creature that slithered through the water. On further investigation, I discovered that, at various times, scientists or hobbyists managed to capture this creature on film or radar, and in the majority of these cases, Nessie did not appear snake-like at all, but as a large pear-shaped creature with fins and an extraordinarily long neck, which could easily cause it to be seen as serpentine. In fact, its silhouette and general size (between 20–40 feet from head to tail) was strikingly similar to an aquatic dinosaur known as Elasmosaur, perhaps related to modern-day aquatic reptiles such as alligators. In light of the enormous popularity of dinosaurs at the time, I realized I had found my angle.

Upon further investigation, I discovered that most of the more "serious" Nessie aficionados believed that there were actually multiple creatures, that they procreated, and that they had lived in Loch Ness for hundreds of years. But it was the famous sonar picture—of what appeared to be a mother and two babies, with roughly the silhouettes of the Elasmosaur—that really sparked my imagination. Baby dinosaurs, I thought. Now what could be more appealing than that? I submitted the initial treatment, and this went back and forth, getting more and more fleshed out, maybe one or two times. Then there was a long silent period. Finally, one day, I received from Eddie the revised version of my script, and a request for comments. It was one of those moments I can't describe…a moment of abject horror. I read it and was baffled. The script had evidently undergone some radical surgical procedure by committee, sort of like a facelift being carried out by ten people at once. Suddenly, there were aliens coming from outer space and new components added to the game structure that made the game unwieldy and the story convoluted and confusing.

After reading it, I sat vexed for some time. The revised script was awful. And it wasn't just because I wrote the original that I felt it was awful. I'm used to working collaboratively, so that wasn't the issue. The script they sent me was a dud. I knew there was only one thing to do—the same thing I would have done if they'd sent it to me in the original batch of concepts: Tell them the truth, and lose the job. At this point, mind you, I didn't know that there was anything more to this for me than being the writer; however, I knew that there potentially might be a lot more work with the company. I also knew that with this memo I was going to be signing my death warrant with Iwerks, but I just couldn't see any other option. I outlined in detail, how, what, and why the thing as revised would not work. It was rational. I gave sound and accurate reasons. I faxed it to Eddie early in the day and then waited for the fateful call telling me that I was fired.

It was a horrible afternoon. Just hanging around the house, waiting for the phone to ring, waiting for the axe to fall, realizing I had just shot myself in the foot, but also that there had really been no other alternative. Finally at about 7 pm New York time, the phone rang. It was Eddie Newquist. He was perky as ever...even more perky. His first remark to me was "I want to thank you. You made my day!" My jaw dropped. The long and short of it was that he had been arguing with the Powers-that-Be about this stuff for weeks, and it was my memo that made them see the light of day. Without skipping a beat, he put forth his next question: "Are you available to come to Los Angeles and creative direct this project?"

I was flabbergasted. This was not at all what I had expected. I was delighted as well because I realized that we were getting off to a damn good start. The chances of this kind of interchange coming to this kind of conclusion in Hollywood are slim. I said sure. It just so happened that I was looking for an excuse to go to L.A., and so far, things seemed to be going great with these guys.

In the meantime, Eddie asked me to do a fleshed out script. I did some more research and returned with a more detailed script, which included background materials—images I collected from the New York Public Library's extensive picture collection, some books on dinosaurs, and some videotape of actual eyewitness interviews with people who had seen the Loch Ness Monster (we actually ended up using some of these very interviews in the final product's pre-show video).

After that, there was another hiatus. I didn't hear anything for a few weeks. Then the call came. "What are you doing on Tuesday?" Eddie asked me. "Can you come to San Jose so I can introduce you to the team as creative director of this project?" I didn't have anything else particularly important to do, so I said yes.

And so it was that in May of 1993, at the Meckler VRWorld Conference, I stepped into the world of Virtual Reality. At that time, I was essentially a VRgin. Due to my background in custom technology for Location-Based Entertainment, I had never worked in the same platform twice. While at Schlossberg, I had some exposure to spatial interfaces, navigation within a simulated space, and using a real physical space to create narrative, but I had never worked with Virtual Reality per se. I also had some familiarity with military technologies, and maintained a vague fantasy that I would someday create something with one of these fancy simulation systems. Even with this preliminary background, I really had no idea what I was in for when I arrived in San Jose that day to begin my own virtual adventure.

 A BRIEF HISTORY OF REAL TIME: THE VIRTUAL REALITY LEGACY (p. 105)

AUTOBIOGRAPHY OF AN AUTODIDACT, PART 2 (p. 58)

When I arrived, I was immediately introduced to the team, some of whom were in military garb if I recall correctly. Eddie introduced me formally as the Creative Director of the project. I took that to mean he was making me an offer (one thing I always liked about working with Ed Newquist was that he always just got right to it…he always cut to the chase). The first thing they did was pop in a video tape. You recall my earlier impressions of VR and my reaction to Eddie's ranting about this system, so I wasn't expecting a whole hell of a lot. What I saw on the screen literally took my breath away. It was an absolutely beautiful underwater environment, with goldfish, green seaweed, and pink coral. It was utterly exquisite. They explained that this was what would be shown on the screen to the players…only it was real time and you could actually navigate through it. I was totally speechless as I sat and watched this thing. It was as beautiful as a Disney animated feature. I was so taken by this gorgeous imagery that it wasn't until I got my breath back that I realized what I was looking at—a visualization of the treatment I wrote three months earlier. It was at that moment that Eddie Newquist's first words to me—*this is going to blow you away*—came to pass. It was, as he had said, truly awesome.

I don't remember all the details of that first meeting, but I believe those in attendance included Eddie Newquist, the Project Manager Kirsten Fossen (who was about to become Kirsten Newquist-Fossen), and soon-to-be Product Manager Mike Haimson. I don't remember whether Michael Dulion was present at this time, but he was the President of Attractions and Technologies, the division that the product was developed under. Stan Kinsey was not present either, but he obviously played a key role in the project as well. From E&S came Mike Ryder, Jeff Edwards, and others. The people heading up the technical team included Kellan Hatch and Joyce Mellus. Kellan was in charge of The Image Generator (in other words, all the graphic components). Joyce Mellus oversaw the operation of The Host (or Hostess, as I came to call it), which was the master brains of the system. The Host tracked where everything was supposed to be and what it was supposed to do and told The Image Generator which images to generate, when, and where. Kellan and Joyce handed me about four pages of diagrams and bulleted lists that amounted to "The Complete Idiot's Guide to VR." It was amazing. Everything was super clear. This is a polygon, this is a behavior, this is a texture, this is how it all fits together; you have a polygon budget, which means you can only have so many polygons on the screen at a time, so you have to take that into account when deciding what imagery to put on the screen. Having been, as I like to say, "raised by wild polygons in the woods," I had no problem understanding the manual. For years, my dad had indoctrinated me in The Way of the Triangle, and the importance of economy of materials in building structures. The space frame and dome that I knew so well were easy for me to translate into digital terms, and it didn't hurt that these people were extraordinarily clear and concise. They had avoided the classic engineering trap of either explaining too much or deliberately obfuscating to make the whole thing seem impossibly difficult. In other words, they spoke English. This, I recognized at once, was going to be fun.

AUTOBIOGRAPHY OF AN AUTODIDACT, PART 1 (p. 45)

BUCKMINSTER FULLER AND THE DIGIDESIC DOME (p. 116)

MEDIA ARCHITECTURE (p. 284)

Two weeks later, I settled into my little freelancer's nook in some back storage room at Iwerks, with the worst computer they could find, and began a six-month odyssey that was about the most fun I've ever had in my entire life. "Mission: Impossible" had become a full-blown operation and we had six months to make it a reality. *Virtual Adventures* was a wild ride in more ways than one!

My first task at hand was going to be further refinement and development of the script. From the beginning, I set up *Virtual Adventures* as a product of three different media rolled into one:

- It had to be a great movie.
- It had to be a great game.
- It had to be a great ride.

It was really through the process of creating *Virtual Adventures* that I began to develop my theories about the connection between story structure and game logic, which have since become the underlying philosophy of all my work, as well as curriculum for training that I do in game and interactive story design.

THE RULES OF THE GAME (p. 420)

The premise of the story for *Virtual Adventures* was that Nessie's lair had been discovered and players were part of a team of scientific researchers sent down to investigate. The players' goal was to collect Nessie's eggs and the reward was to see them hatch. We went through several rounds as to why you were collecting the eggs. A major problem we faced in trying to come up with a viable premise was that we were dealing with three teams of six. Initially, the teams were all working together toward a common goal. But this team dynamic didn't provide for competition, which would make the game exciting. We decided a good premise would be that there were a group of bounty hunters trying to *steal* the eggs. We would make a bounty hunter ship preprogrammed to do battle with the player teams. But this was going to be a technical nightmare.

PSYCHO-ERGONOMICS (p. 404)

One day I got this really goofy idea. I asked the programmers whether it was possible to make the submarine vehicles look different depending on your viewpoint. In other words, I wanted to know whether I could make a ship look like a good scientist ship to the players in it, but like a bad bounty hunter ship to the players seeing it. So basically, each ship would look like a good guy to its own crew, and a bad guy to everyone else. Yes, they said, we can do this, as long as the ships had the same polygons. All we had to do, therefore, was create two different texture maps to make the ships look different enough, and from there, it was a no-brainer.

This premise turned out to be a winner. I had already learned on earlier projects that creating inter-player competition provides a structure that can support diverse game play based on the play styles and skills of each team and its individual members. All this without burdening the game itself to provide all the challenges. This is the ideal in any game: Let the players do all the work.

One of the things that was great fun about *Virtual Adventures* was that it was a truly collaborative process, involving many people, each of whom had a really strong specialty. Because of the nature of the project, it was imperative that we all work together on everything. Teamwork has always been really important to me. I was trained to do interactive media in a very team-oriented, non-hierarchical setting in which people were encouraged to be interdisciplinary as well as specialized. Furthermore, the drive in my early working environment came from a sense of team pride instead of a huge system of ego-reward. This sensibility of team pride is what I am most comfortable with in a working environment.

It took six different companies, only three of which were located in Los Angeles, to create *Virtual Adventures*. The principles were its partners, Iwerks in Burbank and Evans & Sutherland in Salt Lake City. In addition, a company in West Los Angeles designed the vehicle. Pat Downes, out of San Diego, designed all the interactive controls as well as the software that drove the 3D audio system. A sound specialist from SoundDeluxe's Florida office provided the music and sound effects. Another company based in Hollywood executed all the video production for the pre-show and the tutorial.

My job as Creative Director of the project was to be the glue that held all these pieces together. Each team had a fair amount of autonomy within its own scope, but it required a single person to contain the entire project in her head and make sure that all the pieces fit together. This person was me. My right brain was a guy named Matt Codd who was the Art Director for the project. I referred to us as the "two-headed monster." I wrote the script, got everybody's feedback, revised, and refined, and Matt put eyes on the story. He was a master. A Cockney-accented Brit who drove an old Cougar that was forever breaking down, Matt always showed up late for our collaborative brainstorming sessions wearing a baseball cap and Doc Martens. I'd hand him piles of pictures—color Xeroxes from all that great stuff I collected at the New York Public Library, and tons of images from all the dinosaur books I'd collected. We figured out which ugly, mean-looking fish were going to be in the underwater cave of Nessie's lair, and exactly what Nessie was going to look like. We looked to classic underwater movies for inspiration—Disney's animated feature *The Little Mermaid*, *The Abyss*, and *20,000 Leagues Under the Sea*. We also spent some quality time with the work of Jacques Cousteau and some other underwater documentary materials because we were looking for bizarre underwater creatures to re-create in this imaginary world. And of course, there were the weird documentaries about monsters and underwater phenomena from which we drew our eyewitness accounts of the real Loch Ness Monster.

Virtual Adventures was produced on a highly condensed schedule. From the time I arrived, we had less than six months to complete the project for its November 1993 debut. A typical CD-ROM project, to provide an example, takes about 18 months to produce, so we had to accomplish this, a much more complex project, in about a third that time. Furthermore, we were repurposing an old technology to do new, untried things. No one knew quite what would happen. On top of this, the creative team was completely new to the technology. It was clear from the start that in order to get the job done, the creative team would have to work with the engineers every step of the way. This team dynamic was just fine with me, because I needed them to help me understand the technology.

My first meeting at E&S was kind of hilarious actually. I heard later from the team there that they had been anticipating my arrival with some trepidation, that they were, for some reason I'm not sure why, intimidated by me, I'm sure no more so than I was by them. When I arrived for the meeting, I immediately started cracking jokes and making them laugh. They later told me that they were totally surprised and relieved, and after that they figured this was going to be a lot of fun.

One thing that was fun for them was working in the creative context of an entertainment project. I always insisted on bringing the engineers into the creative process upfront, because I think the idea that creative people should design everything first and then feed it to engineering is ridiculous. It takes more time, degrades team spirit, and ensures a much lower chance of success. I have a saying that goes: "There's nothing worse then a good idea badly implemented; with the possible exception of a bad idea implemented well." My point is that without proper engineering input upfront, the chances of implementing a project badly are much higher.

The traditional approach of segregating the creative and the engineering is tantamount to giving your team a lobotomy, separating its left brain from its right. My friend (and VRML co-creator) Mark Pesce refers to the myopic engineer as having "two left brains," but this is really not necessary. The fact is that most engineers are, in fact, highly creative, but not always in ways that so-called creative people recognize. It's really a culture gap. By keeping these two sensibilities separate, you really do a disservice to everyone involved, most of all the end user for your product. The more you can get the creative people to see the engineering viewpoint, and in turn, the more you can get the engineers to think creatively, the better the outcome will be. Everyone I know who has worked on a successful high-tech project will vouch for this, I assure you. If you hear creatives complaining about engineers or engineers complaining about creatives, dig a little deeper, and you'll find out that some form of segregationist management is behind it.

You have to remember what I was stepping into here. These were military contractors. Not only were they hardcore deepgeeks (and I mean that with all due respect and reverence), they were military geeks. So I knew that there was going to be a culture gap, but I also knew it was going to work in my favor. Let me just say that I'd rather walk into a military contractor with an entertainment project than to walk into an entertainment studio with a military project. In this sense, therefore, my job was going to be easy. Rather than pulling the "I'm the creative, follow my orders…" attitude that a lot of entertainment industry people have, I came in with a completely different attitude, which was "Listen…I don't know anything about this totally amazing technology, so you guys gotta help me out here." Instead of dictating how it was going to be, I asked them to tell me how it was. I told them what I was trying to accomplish, what I wanted the experience to be like, and then we talked about ways to make that happen.

When I first got there, they wanted a spec. That was what they were used to, and it was what they expected. Their typical procedure was that they would get a spec from the DOD, which was basically a legally binding document to which they had to conform or risk…I don't know what…court martial? I'm not sure. Anyway, The *Spec* was *Law* to these guys. I didn't have a spec. How could I write a spec for a technology I'd never worked in before? Furthermore, we had six months. To write a full spec would take about two, which would leave them with only four months for production. It was necessary to start production immediately, which meant that creative and engineering would have to work in tandem. Personally I think this was great. The time frame actually helped the overall quality of the project because it eliminated the possibility of a spec, which really would have been a dictate from Us to Them, a situation that would most certainly have ended in disaster.

I'll never forget the expressions on their faces when I posed to them questions like:

- How can we make the water look more buoyant?
- What kinds of things does this system do best?
- How many different colors of fog are there?
- What are the coolest tricks?
- What little pet project have you been doing on your own that never found a home before?

I started brainstorming sessions with these kinds of questions. I told the engineers what I wanted, and they told me what they could do, and there was a back and forth, which involved them making creative suggestions as often as I might propose engineering solutions. Because we were just creating illusion, things didn't have to be literal. I didn't need things to be actually random, as long as they *looked* random. They didn't need to be 3D, as long as they *looked* 3D. I was perfectly happy to give up an idea if the engineers had a better one that could be easily implemented. So it was a highly iterative process.

 DESIGNING FOR TECHNOLOGY (p. 161)

I wrote the specs incrementally, generating about one mini-spec a week. I'd write the player control spec, then the ship spec, then the animal spec, then the environment spec, then the Nessie spec, and so on. As each spec was completed, it would go out for review and I'd immediately start the next one. When the review came back, I'd release the new spec, and make revisions to the proceeding spec, finalizing it for production. At the same time, Matt Codd would create the sketches that went with each spec and submit them accordingly. After this process, the E&S people would send me stuff back. First, they'd send printouts or videos of the wireframe models for us to review. Then, they'd draw the texture maps and send us color copies for approval. Then, they'd slap the texture maps on the model and send us a video and we'd sign off on that. This process went enormously smoothly, and we were able to get a lot done in a very short period of time through this syncopated technique.

Here is one of the many reasons why I love my job: We had to have shooting in the game, but it was agreed that the shooting would not be destructive or violent. The tricky part was coming up with some kind of ammunition that would not kill or hurt anyone or anything. Because I hate violence anyway, this was an easy task. I wrote up a list at the time called "101 Non-Lethal Uses for a Projectile" as part of an exercise in how to shoot in a non-violent fashion. The one that we settled on was actually the next level of evolution from the green blobs that had been in Kellan's original demo. It's official name was

"Non-Lethal Immobilizing Gel," but the document describing it came to be known as the "gloop spec." The gloop spec was around 7–10 pages long and it described in detail every possible thing that could happen to the gloop—what it did when shooting it, what it did when hitting a flat surface, what it did when hitting a curved surface, what it did when hitting an animal, and so forth. It also included a list of gloop sound effects for each of these conditions.

Whenever the E&S team would hit a technical snag, I'd come in and do what I called "creative solutions to technical problems." There are two stories about this. The first one has to do with gloop.

Every time the gloop hit the windshield of a ship, it would stick on the windshield until removed by the windshield wiper. Thus, one of the gloop's offensive functions was to obstruct the other players' views through their windshields. It was really important, therefore, that the gloop appear to splatter on the windshield in a semi-random fashion; however, technically, we could only have a single gloop splat shape. We could change the color of the gloop, giving each ship its own unique gloop color, but we had to have the exact same gloop splat every time. Obviously, I vexed over until I finally got an idea. I asked the programmers whether it was possible to put a spin on the gloop so that even though it was always the same shape, it would always land at a different rotation. That way, we could trick the viewers into thinking they were seeing different splats just by making sure the gloop always landed at a different rotational orientation. No problem. Then I had to deliver the splat. I kept trying to sketch it, but it wasn't coming out right.

Einstein once said that genius was one part inspiration and 99 parts perspiration, but he left out the part about luck. One of the guys at Iwerks moonlighted as a dee-jay for a local college radio station. That afternoon, I came back from a meeting to discover a bumper sticker from the station on my desk. Its logo happened to be a giant splat of black ink. I immediately Xeroxed it, blacked out the station's call letters with a marker, and faxed it to Utah. (Pop quiz for trivia nuts: Which L.A. radio station's logo was the model for the gloop splat in *Virtual Adventures*?)

The windshield wipers posed another potential problem. A couple of weeks before completion, the E&S guys came to me and said they weren't going to be able to finish this feature. I was kind of upset because it meant taking one entire control functionality away from the Commander, which would make that position less interactive in the game. I told them it was okay if they couldn't pull it off, but if they could, it would really be great. So I had pretty much given up on it, and the plan was that the gloop would fade after a few seconds. The day I came in for review of final sign-off, two of the engineers were whispering to each other, and one asked the other "Did you tell her?" "No…not yet," the other said. For the first time, I got to play the game all the way through, with all the pieces linked together, and lo-and-behold! there were the windshield wipers! They had stayed up all night getting them to work. What can I say? It was a killer team.

 PROGRAMMER AS ARTIST (p. 399)

Another example of "creative solutions to technical problems" came about when we were dealing with bubbles. The first problem was how to make bubbles look random. We accomplished this by taking two layers of something called "a stamp." A stamp (also known as a billboard in some circles) is a flat image, a texture map that always turns to face you no matter which way you turn. Originally, we were going to make actual 3D bubbles, but spheres take up a lot of polygons and therefore are not desirable to have in a 3D database. Instead, we decided to use these stamps, figuring that because the bubbles were spheres, you could just draw a flat one that looked 3D, and as long as it was always facing you, it would look like a bubble. To create a realistic sense of movement, we made two transparent layers of bubbles that moved up from the bottom of the lake at different speeds so that they would not appear to all behave in a uniform fashion. By staggering the movement, we were able to make the bubbles appear random.

Everything seemed like it was going to be fine with this strategy, but then another problem arose. When you got too close to a transparent or translucent surface, the image generator overloaded and crashed the system. The engineers were panicked and insisted on cutting the bubbles. So I thought about it and said, "Wait a minute. What do bubbles to in real life when you bump into them? They pop! As soon as the ship gets close enough to crash the system, make the bubbles go away!" Voilá, another problem solved, no injuries, no harm done.

I also had a great time with Pat Downes on the controls. Pat would come up from San Diego with these boxes full of stuff that he had picked up from various military contractors selling post Cold War surplus. We ended up using a number of actual military surplus items in the final product because they were sturdy, easy-to-get, and cheap. Among them were an actual Cessna steering yoke and an actual helicopter joystick. Pat was a tinkerer extraordinaire, and he always amazed me with his ingenuity and resourcefulness. We had a blast together trying to figure out the best way to interface people to our virtual world.

Pat also designed the proprietary 3D audio system that we used for the project. There were four speakers and an under-the-set sub-woofer in the cab. The audio effects were attached to objects in the environment that would sound like they were moving around you, closer, further away, and so on. The system also enabled you to build in physical properties to the space, such as size of the room and surface properties so that you could have natural resonance to create a sense of the size and quality of the space. The sound specialist at SoundDeluxe designed the sound effects and wrote the score which consisted of a musical bed—a completely linear orchestral theme that played through-out the story with interactive themes that sat on top of it. The four-minute piece had two movements, one for each of the two in-vehicle "acts." Each of the in-vehicle acts took place in a different environment. Each zone within an environment and each autonomous element in that environment had its own theme that would slowly swell in or fade out as you entered the zone or encountered the element. The linear quality of the music was really crucial to building tension in the story and to reinforcing the three-act structure of the game. The object-specific themes enabled us to create a fully interactive, textured soundtrack.

I could write an entire book about creating *Virtual Adventures*. It was an amaz-ingly fascinating process for me, and I never get tired of sharing it with other people. But I'm sure by now you're dying of curiosity about the final product. What the hell was it? How did it turn out in the end?

So without further ado, I give you, *Virtual Adventures*, the final product:

> *Virtual Adventures: The Loch Ness Expedition* is a game for 24 players, divided into four teams of six. Each team takes the controls of an under-water vehicle, a small yellow submarine, in the roles of volunteer scien-tists who have been sent to the depths of the Loch Ness to rescue the eggs of the legendary Loch Ness Monster from evil bounty hunters. The goal is to collect as many of Nessie's eggs as you can and bring them back to the lab, where they will then be hatched and cared for until they can be safely returned to their mother. *Virtual Adventures* is designed to be a story, a game, a ride, and a film. Its three-act structure is as follows:

Act 1

A bogus newsstrip or "mockumentary" that you watch while waiting in the queue tells the story of the recent confirmation that the Loch Ness Monster does in fact exist, and that she has eggs. Actual interviews with real witnesses and Loch Ness researchers (people who have done legitimate scientific explo-ration of the area) are intercut with images of the main character, Dr. Deadre Mackalby, who is heading up this research effort. The problem with this research is that it has now fallen into the wrong hands: Dr. Jack D. Wripper, a notorious bounty hunter has located the eggs and means to obtain them for his own financial gain. With his team of henchmen, he has headed into the depths of Loch Ness to obtain the eggs. Your job is to go down in a specially designated research vessel and get the eggs before the evil bounty hunters succeed in their vile plot. You step into the briefing area and receive your assignment and instructions. The positions include the following:

- **Pilot.** Responsible for piloting the sub; uses a yoke steering mechanism to turn right or left, or tilt the ship up or down; a foot throttle controls speed and a red reverse button held down continuously backs the sub out of a tight spot.

- **Claw Operators.** Located on either side of the Pilot, the two Claw Operators have two functions: to provide defense to the ship by shooting non-lethal immobilizing gel at bounty hunters or hazardous creatures, and, to pick up any eggs they find in the environment using their robotic claw devices.

- **Commander.** The Commander sits between the five other positions, at the center of a five-pointed star. The Commander is in charge of coordinating the efforts of the team and is the communication hub. The Commander has a touch-screen map showing positions of ships and eggs in the Loch. The Commander controls the windshield wipers and has a "gloop torpedo" for use in an emergency. The Commander is also responsible for the very important task of retracting the claws into the ship after the Claw Operators actually grab the eggs. In other words, the Claw Operators cannot bring the eggs onboard without the help of the Commander. The Commander also has a live microphone that enables communication with the Commanders of the "bounty hunter" ships.

- **Periscope Operators.** The up and down periscopes are located to the right and left rear of the ship, behind the Commander. The periscope interface is a bicycle-style seat that the player or players straddle. The seat is large enough for a parent and a small child or two children. Periscope Operators hold handlebars on either side of a small screen and rotate the entire unit to get a 360-degree view of the Loch. They can also shoot immobilizing gel to protect the ship.

This team of six dons 3D glasses (not Head-Mounted Displays, but regular 3D glasses) and enters the ship to embark on their rescue mission, a four-minute interactive adventure inside a simulated 3D world.

The inside of the ship is made of gray fiberglass, with a curvaceous interior. It could be a submarine or a spaceship, and it was designed to be flexible enough that it could become any one of a variety of vehicles, depending on game content (see figure P.3).

Figure P.3

The inside of the *Virtual Adventures* Pod with players in position (image courtesy of Iwerks Entertainment and Evans & Sutherland)

 PLATE 15

ACT 2

Once inside the ship, you and your team explore a beautiful underwater world. Fish of gold and blue swim around in the turquoise waters between rays of sun and delicate bubbles; a sunken ship teems with treasure; an old castle turret rests in the depths of the Loch; you glide through the skeleton of a giant fish. Moving around might trigger surprises, such as a huge sandworm that suddenly pops up from the bottom or an ominous stingray that slides above the sand beneath you. There are a small handful of eggs, as well as bounty hunters present, attacking you by splattering colored gloop all over your windshield; the swipe of the windshield wipers clears it away as you look for eggs. You can also utilize special scout units. If you attach to them with two claws, these scout units will take you directly to the eggs. But you have to be careful, because some of these are booby traps that will blow you to the surface.

Suddenly, a hole opens up in the lake bottom and you find yourself being sucked into a whirlpool, along with everyone and everything else in the area—fish, other subs, and all...

ACT 3

The whirlpool drops you into a dark, underwater cavern. Your headlights are on, but you can hardly see anything except what's immediately in front of you. The water is murky and green; there is no sunlight here and strange forms and silhouettes swim in and out view. As you sink down into this treacherous zone, you suddenly catch sight of the great spectacle for which you are searching: a giant beautiful aquatic dinosaur sitting atop a stone nest (see figure P.4). You have found Nessie and her lair. Scattered all around are giant reptile eggs. Nessie cries out in fear as giant predator fish swim around her eggs and bounty hunters move about trying to snatch them up (see figure P.5 and P.6). She cannot fight them all off by herself; she needs your help. While fending off bounty hunters, you quickly scurry to gather up the threatened eggs as the oxygen monitor on your screen slowly ticks off to zero and the music reaches its final crescendo.

Figure P.4

A close-up of Nessie (image courtesy of Iwerks Entertainment and Evans & Sutherland)

 PLATE 18

Figure P.5

The player ship battles off fierce monsters to protect Nessie (image courtesy of Iwerks Entertainment and Evans & Sutherland)

 PLATE 16

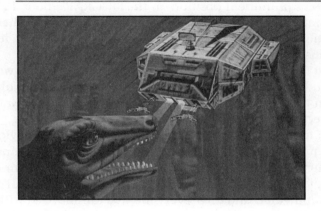

Figure P.6

An evil bounty hunter ship threatens Nessie and her eggs (image courtesy of Iwerks Entertainment and Evans & Sutherland)

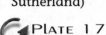PLATE 17

As you exit the ship, you enter a post-show area. There you see a status screen that shows how each team and each individual player did. But the real highlight is on the adjacent monitor: A brouhaha is erupting in the lab as Dr. Mackalby, with reporters chasing close behind, heads into the nursery. We cut to a close up of a watery incubator where the first of Nessie's babies begins to hatch. Everyone applauds as the newly hatched Nessie breaks its way out of the reptilian egg and peeks its head out. As soon as the bounty hunters can be cleared of the area, the babies will be returned to safety with their mom in the Loch.

 VIRTUAL REALITY AS A DRAMATIC ART (p. 508)

Virtual Adventures was launched in November 1993 in the Iwerks booth at IAAPA (International Association of Amusement Parks and Attractions), the largest annual amusement park convention in the world, in Anaheim, California. It was mobbed the entire week and was one of the most talked about products at the show.

It was shown again in the Evans & Sutherland booth in August 1994 at SIGGRAPH, the largest computer graphics show in the world. I went to SIGGRAPH that year to speak about it, and having been off the project for some six months, I had no idea it was going to be such a prominent feature of the show.

I stopped short after entering the Exhibit Hall to find that Evans & Sutherland had somehow managed to get a front-row seat, prime position by the main entrance, one of the most coveted pieces of real estate in the trade show floor. They usually have a pretty good spot, but this was unprecedented. The center-piece of the booth was *Virtual Adventures*, whose tickets were a highly coveted commodity for the duration of the convention.

Surprised as I was at E&S's prominent position on the SIGGRAPH floor, I really wasn't prepared for what happened the night I went to the Electronic Theater. This is a showcase of the best computer graphics of the year. Ordinarily, it is a strictly linear affair, consisting of short clips from a variety of different projects. I heard from a few people that *Virtual Adventures* was in it, so I was expecting to see it included in the usual three-minute video clip format along with everything else. In this particular year, they decided to include an interactive feature in the Electronic Theater. They brought Loren Carpenter's famous paddle system: audience members used plastic paddle input devices about the size of a tongue-depressor, with a green reflector on one side and a red reflector on the other (see figure P.7). By holding the paddle in the air and rotating it 180 degrees, you could send a binary signal to the computer. Four thousand people were in theater, and after everyone was familiarized with the paddle device, suddenly the world's largest game of *Pong* appeared onscreen. The audience was divided in half down the middle, and by turning the paddles to indicate an up or down paddle movement, 4,000 people were able to effectively play a game of *Pong*. This was followed by a well-known skiing simulator featuring an egg on skis. Now the audience could, as one unit, turn right and left to keep the poor egg from crashing. It was kind of amazing, but it actually worked.

Figure P.7
The Loren Carpenter paddle system allows for interactivity with a large-scale audience (image courtesy of Cinematrix, Inc. Interactive Entertainment Systems®)

Then the screen changed a third time, and on it, about 40 feet across, was the underwater environment of *Virtual Adventures*. They hooked the image generator up to the projector. When I realized what was about to happen, I almost started to cry. There I was in the third row watching 4,000 people work together to try to pick up one of Nessie's eggs. Needless to say, it was a mindblowing experience, one of those career moments that everyone dreams of.

Since it was introduced, *Virtual Adventures* has won eight awards, among them the first Academy of Interactive Arts and Sciences Award for Best Virtual

Reality in 1985, and several Governer's Awards from the California Governer's Conference on Technology and the Arts. As of this writing, it is installed in three locations, two public and one private: The Nauticus Marine Park in Norfolk, Virginia; Cinetropolis at Foxwoods Casino in Ledyard, Connecticut; and the original demo system located at Iwerks' offices in Burbank, California, which is only used for private marketing demonstrations.

Virtual Adventures is magic to me in a lot of ways. For one thing, it was the ultimate in interactive alchemy. Science and wizardry came together to create something much greater than the sum of all its parts. It's a fairy tale and a B-monster movie; it's a legend retold in modern terms; it's the story of a friendly dragon hiding deep in an underwater cave in a Scottish Loch. *Virtual Adventures* is also, interestingly enough, a natural environment. Far from creating the stereotypical sci-fi VR experience, or from following the traditional model of a game whose entire goal is the destruction of other players or simulated life forms, we tried to create a beautiful natural environment that was teeming with life, and a story about rescuing and rejuvenating life.

 V-ART (p. 494)

Even though I wrote the story, I'm still not sure I really totally understand it. People tell me things all the time, observations and insights that continue to illuminate an experience which now remains somewhat mysterious even to me. I think it was my dad who first pointed out to me that *Virtual Adventures* is an Easter egg hunt, which prompted me to dub it "*Godzilla* meets *The Little Mermaid* meets an Easter Egg Hunt." The fact that it is a magical dragon story only occurred to me as I was writing about it for this book. Many people have commented to me on the highly feminine themes of motherhood and fertility, and the emotional focus of helping a mother to rescue her babies as the motivation that propels the story forward. Make no mistake, I've been teased about this as well. *Virtual Adventures* is probably the first commercial VR game with a feminist subtext. It's not an accident that it also has a female as its main human character. The emphasis on female characters is part of the reason why women find the game so appealing. For me, the female characters are not a deterrent, and in fact, the affable Dr. Mackalby adds a friendly touch. She is a kind of cross between Jane Goodall and Jacques Cousteau. The objective in *Virtual Adventures* is not a military maneuver, but a naturalist's rescue mission.

Virtual Adventures was designed to have something for everyone. That the game is about collecting is also not an accident. The combination of collecting and shooting was a deliberate design choice made to appeal to the typical play styles of both women, who love collecting, and men, who love to shoot. It offers heroism in the guise of maternal protection. It offers beauty for the girls and monsters for the boys. It offers game for the guys, and story for the gals. It offers gradations of more active to more passive positions, enabling people to interact at a variety of different levels if so desired. Believe it or not, everybody does *not* like to drive!

Time magazine called *Virtual Adventures* downright ethereal and referred to it as "The Barney of VR Games." It's been criticized for being too violent and for not being violent enough. It's received critical acclaim for bringing interesting story, original gaming, and sophisticated aesthetics to a medium plagued by adolescent and unimaginative content. It has also been the source of much skepticism because its high price has prevented it from achieving the mass-market dissemination its content could clearly support.

There is no good reason why this product should not have been a huge hit. In the places where it installed, it's extremely popular; however, there are not that many installed. Much of its lack of commercial success, I believe, is based on a faulty marketing strategy that places unrealistic expectations on a new medium. Because the creators were experienced in the ridefilm arena, they were accustomed to marketing their products as roller coaster alternatives. By force of habit, they applied this same approach to *Virtual Adventures*; however, traditional amusement park operators have no context for understanding this product, least of all to replace a known entity such as a roller coaster.

Another unrealistic belief was that the product had to make back its ROI (return on investment) based on a pay-per-play ticket scenario. Anybody with a pocket calculator could have figured out that this was simply not possible. Furthermore, it's the exact opposite of how high-end theme park rides generate revenue. Disneyland makes its money first from retail, then parking, then food, and finally from the gate ticket. The rides are viewed as a draw for the other revenue generators. In this scenario, all that is expected of the rides is to get people into the park and keep them there, funneling them into retail venues, and reinforcing brand identity and cross-media appeal. I always thought that *Virtual Adventures* belonged in a mall, alongside retail or food as a draw, perhaps even inside a theme-based restaurant. Not surprisingly, neither of the two sites that are up and running as of this writing are Theme parks, and one is a casino. Another ideal location for this product would, of course, be Las Vegas.

Perhaps someday, *Virtual Adventures* will find a way to reach the broad audience it was designed for. In the meantime, I am delighted for each and every person who gets a chance to experience it. Everything we did in that 12-month period to bring this wild idea to reality is for them.

The Military Entertainment Complex (p. 303)

Narrative Environments: Virtual Reality as a Storytelling Medium (p. 329)

The Interactive Ecosystem (p. 233)

Virtual Relativity (p. 524)

Programmer as Artist

I would no sooner call a computer programmer an engineer than I would call a cinematographer a technician. Few people are aware of the creativity involved in programming a computer. Programming is not unlike architecture in that it involves a strong balance between creative vision, inventive problem-solving, and technical accuracy.

In some respects, the task of programming is even more challenging than architecture. In spite of its volatility, the computer is less forgiving than the two-by-four. One misplaced number or bad string, one colon off, one parenthesis left unclosed, and your whole program can go kablooey. In architecture, one wrong nail does not necessarily lead to the collapse of an entire building.

Having worked with many programmers, I find that each has his or her own unique style. I liken programming to a genre of cryptic poetry, but poetry in which the essence of the poem is in its operation rather than its actual text. Not unlike in a play where the text is merely a set of instructions for actors to follow, the code's the thing. The code is what makes the dream a reality.

Much like a poet, a programmer has to find his or her own "voice," a unique way of working and writing code that distinguishes him or her from other hackers. Some are systematic and methodical and write their code in an orderly fashion. Some programmers, on the other hand, write binary "free verse" in which this algorithm points to that algorithm, but there is no overall coherency. Some programmers have elaborate annotations alongside their code, describing what it's doing so that other programmers can make sense of it; others leave no bodies and take no prisoners.

Some programmers like to show you their code and explain its intricacies. Ken Perlin of NYU gave a talk at SIGGRAPH 94 in which he displayed an entire program on a giant projection screen and explained what it was doing line by line. I have another friend who won't let anyone see his code, keeping it to himself like a secret diary, as if to say "Pay no attention to the man behind the curtain."

If you want to understand what's involved in making computers "think," or at least act like they do, then you ought to spend a good hour or two watching an ace programmer at work. You would be stunned to know, for example, that really good programmers can type up to 70 or 80 words a minute—in C++! It's quite something to watch, really.

When I was a young game logic analyst at Edwin Schlossberg, Inc., I used to ask the head of my department, Craig Southard (who later worked with LucasArts), to let me see printouts of code. He was a bit baffled by this. "You won't understand it," he'd say. But I wasn't looking for meaning. I was looking for structure. I wasn't trying to understand the words. I was looking at the brackets and the colons and the tabs. I was trying to understand the geometry of the language. I was trying to "groc" (understand deeply) the process. I wanted to understand the way that programmers think. I always liked C best because it looked nicest on the page. BASIC was too…too basic, too stupid really, it didn't seem to have any deep structure. It was just sort of well…there. Pascal I barely remember, and I think there was some FORTRAN running around then too. But I know that I could understand C, and I could get the gist of the logic flow, and I could even understand some of the commands.

At that time, it was important to me to see code, because I was learning how to do flow diagrams, and I felt that understanding the structure of code would help me do better flow diagrams. The way I learned to do flow diagrams was actually quite ingenious. Craig (who also taught me how to use a word processor, God bless his soul), showed me how to make a basic flow chart and then as an exercise, asked me to make a flow diagram of an elevator. Twelve years later, when I first started going to Denmark to teach, the head of the *Space Invaders* multimedia program told me that his first logic assignment to his students was to diagram an elevator.

 MEDIA ARCHITECTURE (p. 284)

I could never program. I don't have the patience for it, and it is a lonely job that requires keeping bizarre hours and eating an unnatural amount of pizza. I am, however, a logician at heart. I understand the basic principles of the algorithm: a set of commands or instructions for dynamic, interrelated events and processes.

A programmer does not necessarily have to be a mathematician. I was abysmal at arithmetic and couldn't add or subtract to save my life, but I was great where there were tables involved. The nine multiplication tables were my favorite. To this day, I do multiples of nine by using the nine tables. When I got into geometry, I was an ace. I was great with things such as powers of two, and I was especially fond of imaginary numbers. I was a poet, and imaginary numbers were of course imaginary, so they were cool, but there was also something both nihilistic and at the same time existential about an imaginary number.

In case you have no idea what I'm talking about, imaginary numbers are the square roots of negative numbers. The reason they are imaginary is that negatives multiplied by negatives are positives, and so are negatives multiplied by positives. Therefore, there cannot be any negative number that has a square root. I guess because I hated numbers, I got a certain measure of glee from the idea of a number that defied numeric logic.

I'm not a programmer myself, and I would venture to guess that there are many programmers who are mathematicians, but the best programmers I ever met were painters, photographers, musicians, and English majors. Long live the literary programmer! If you think about it, it makes sense. Programming is a form of writing, and you are learning a language, so language skills are really crucial. Writers sit in front of computers all day, so do programmers. From a mathematical viewpoint, computers have made arithmetic obsolete. As arithmetically impaired as I am, I once wrote a program in BASIC that added up numbers, which is about the easiest thing for a computer to do.

When it comes to programming, it's really logic and problem-solving that prevail. Some of the best programming is intuitive as well as logical, or perhaps it starts intuitive and ends up being logical. What is really fun about programming is the idea that you are creating something from nothing but a bunch of on/off switches. You start with these little tiny things, and you end up with these elaborate expressions. This construct is really exciting for me because, when I work with programmers, what they're doing is trying to algorithmically realize something I thought up in my head. I find that to be a lot of fun. The code is a bridge between my imagination and reality. So to me, programming is a magical process where the programmer is the magician that breathes life into my imagination.

When I worked on *Virtual Adventures* with Iwerks and Evans & Sutherland, I remember having these long elaborate sessions with the programmers where we tried to figure out how to create the various effects I wanted. At first, I baffled them because, coming from a military simulation background, they were accustomed to working from elaborate military specifications. I was coming in and saying, "I want it to feel buoyant," and they responded with, "What are you talking about?" What I did with them was a kind of give and take, which I loved, where I told them the general effect I wanted, and then we'd figure out how to do it together. A lot of times I'd ask, "Well, what can you do that's similar?" or "What tricks do you have up your sleeves already?" and then we'd work it out.

My favorite story regarding *Virtual Adventures* is about the gel that players would shoot at each other's windshields. When the gel (or gloop, the technical term) landed on the windshield, it was in "splat" mode, as we called it. But the problem was that the splat mode could only be one shape, in which case you would see this same splat shape on your screen repeatedly, which we hated. So I suggested that the way we solve it was to put a spin on the gloop when it left the turret so that it would always land at a random axis point. In this way, we were able to make it look like a different splat every time, even though it was the same. This collaborative process is the kind of thing I love about my job— finding creative solutions to technical problems and technical solutions to creative problems. For me, the programmers are demigods, wizards who can make impossible things happen by just jotting down a few incomprehensible lines of text.

Some programmers come from the Land of Cant—a place where anything you ask for "can't be done." What I find is that a lot of these programmers will say, "No," to begin with, but then later, they'll stay up all night with a warm pizza and try to do it anyway. There is a certain code ethic, a kind of hacker machismo that states that anything deemed impossible is worth attempting. Most of the good programmers I have worked with have this ethic. It's really great, because many times they achieve feats even *they* didn't know they were capable of. The *Virtual Adventures* programmers stayed up all night the day before a product launch to program an element of the game they said could not be done. It was really great because they had decided not to tell me because they wanted to surprise me. When I came in for the final review— there it was. That's the sort of thing that makes me think of programmers as my heroes.

THE PRINCESS AND THE MONSTER: THE MAKING OF VIRTUAL ADVENTURES (p. 375)

The advent of authoring tools, a luxury we didn't have when I was first starting out, has changed the face of programming as we know it. Many people can now, in essence, do what it used to take fleets of programmers to accomplish. Macromedia Director has made it easy for the lay person to turn hacker, for creative people to program without really knowing the language. Maybe I'm old fashioned, but I'd rather have a real-life code hacker than be an auteur trying to work it all out myself by using some predetermined toolkit. Because I have never worked on the same platform twice, authoring tools don't do me a hell of a lot of good. Even if I were working in the same medium, I'm not sure I'd go for authoring tools, because, much of the time, applications are designed by the tool instead of the designer. Part of what's really fun about the whole process is me, the technically inept, joining forces with programming wizards, because what we come up with is actually greater than the sum of its parts. The auteur using Director or what have you has only his or her own personal skill sets to pull from. I personally think that on a creative level, you're better off breaking it up so that you can benefit from both sides of the brain. Also, everyone knows that real-code programs are better than authored ones. First of all, they're faster because they don't have all that cumbersome authoring tool code slowing them down. For another thing, they're more robust because with authoring tools, you're always trying to get them to do something they weren't designed to do, and that's when you get in trouble. A lot of authoring tools try to think for you, which is a problem if you think differently than the person who wrote the tool. For my money, Macromedia Director is too linear, so it encourages a linear way of thinking and designing. Tools such as mTropolis, which is object-oriented, enable a more flexible, less linear way of thinking and working. People who are skilled at using these tools can often push them to their limit, but the problem is, the tool is only as good as the imaginations of the people who designed it.

Personally, I still prefer to do things "the old-fashioned way" (and no, I don't mean punch cards). I like the process of making something from nothing, and I like working together with a team of people who are smarter than I am (programmers are always smarter than everyone else...and they usually know it too).

One thing I notice and have found somewhat disturbing is the way Hollywood handles programmers. The code culture is very different from the entertainment culture. Entertainment people are notoriously arrogant; so are coders, except they are generally a lot smarter than entertainment industry people, so they can get away with it.

I was once talking with two other interactive designers, one of whom was new to the craft, having come from a traditional film and TV directing background. The second designer, who was more experienced, asked him how directing for interactive media was different from other media. The one thing that was different, said the rookie, was programmers. He found them difficult to work with. I told him that had not been my experience, that I had always had good experiences with programmers. He continued by saying that on set, you can just say something such as, "Get that chair the hell out of there. Go make it look distressed or something." With coders, however, you have to coddle them, saying something like, "That is the most beautiful chair I've ever seen...can you add a texture map to it...maybe a little shadow?" After his comparison, I remarked, "Oh, I see what the problem is...that's how *I* treat *everybody*." I found it absurd that he would talk about programmers as if they were set decorators. I didn't particularly like the way he talked about set decorators either, for that matter. The fact remains that people who write code may be eccentric, they might even be sociopathic at times, but stupid they are not. Programmers deserve a certain amount of respect. To me, they are nothing short of heroes, entering a dark and mysterious world to tackle a beast that I cannot even fathom. They do it somehow, and when they do it well, it is truly awesome to behold.

Although most of my experiences with programmers have been great, there is the occasional prima-donna-programmer-from-hell. This poor soul, both arrogant and insecure, insists on lording his intelligence over others, and feels it is his duty to constantly remind others of their status as lesser human beings. These are the worst of the worst, and in some respects, worse than the classic arrogant Hollywood types. Far from harmless, these coders can pose a real and present danger to your product. They have this unseemly habit of holding code hostage. I have seen programmers repeatedly threaten to walk off jobs, and I have even seen a programmer refuse to finish his code a week before deadline unless another team-member was fired. The scary thing about prima donna programmers is that, precisely because they are so smart, they know how to hit you hard where it hurts. The biggest problem with these guys is that they usually get coddled…and this makes them even worse. So my advice is, never submit to the wrath of a progammer/terrorist. Just fire him and get someone new. Who needs that?

The prima donna programmer has, for me, been the exception, rather than the rule. I continue to cultivate good relations with programmers and enjoy the dynamic tension between creative ideas and robust technical implementation. I have fashioned myself as "The Code Fairy." I always wear a computer chip medallion around my neck and by rubbing the surface of the chip, I generate "code dust." The purpose of code dust is to help in the debugging process. It sounds silly, I know, but it actually works. Virtually every time I have done it, the problem was solved within 10–15 minutes. It's kind of like pixie dust for debugging. It even works over long distances, it just may take a little longer to kick in. I have been known to help debug code in Boston from Los Angeles. Anyway, code dust is my way of paying homage to the people who make this all possible, the people who literally make my dreams come true.

DESIGNING FOR TECHNOLOGY (p. 161)

STEAL THIS DATA: SHAREWARE AND THE HACKER ETHIC (p. 454)

PSYCHO-ERGONOMICS

Ergonomics is the study of human factors in industrial design, especially in the area of furniture, office equipment, and appliances. Introduced in the 50s and

60s, the inclusion of ergonomics into the design process led to the development of products and furniture that, for the first time, truly took the physical makeup of the user into account. Chairs and desks were designed with proper human dimensions and geometry in mind; the idea being that if "form follows function," the chair should fit to the form of the sitter.

Psycho-ergonomics is a term I developed that relates to the study and consideration of human factors of the mind for systems of communication that accommodate not only the way we think, but also our emotional makeup. The development of the graphical user interface (GUI) is an example of a psycho-ergonomically responsive product. The GUI design accounts for the human factors of thought and emotion involved in the relationship between human and machine.

The study and understanding of human psychology is the most important skill that an interactive designer can possess. Graphics, storytelling, and game design skills take a backseat to an interactive designer's knowledge of and sensitivity to such issues as play style, cognitive style, developmental levels at various ages, gender differences, values, and perceptual variations. A concentration in these areas is the key to creating an effective interactive experience. Whether by intuition or intention, or through research or experience, the best interactive designers are first and foremost students of the psychological craft.

Recent psychological research has shown that EQ (emotional quotient) can play a greater role in personal success and happiness than IQ (intelligence quotient), which is the standard measurement we use to evaluate intellectual ability. EQ tells us not about the intellect, but about the emotional makeup of a person—how he or she approaches a problem, responds to a challenge, communicates, and relates to others—all values that have not traditionally been considered "skills." Recent studies are finding that in certain positions (management roles, for example), EQ is as important, if not more important than IQ. Hypothetically, a manager with good people skills is generally more effective than a brilliant engineer in a management position.

EQ plays an essential role in the psycho-ergonomics of cyberspace, because it drives such functions as communication with others, understanding information, identifying choices, and making decisions, and the capability to figure out how to affect the various functions of the system. These are the basic issues of comprehension—what people see when they look at the screen, how they interpret what is seen, the feedback they receive when they take a certain action, and what motivates them to take the next action. There is a tendency to think of the "user" as a generic everyman with no outstanding or unique characteristics, but this is an erroneous way of thinking. The result of this mentality is a kind of vanilla interactivity that in no way addresses the wide variety of approaches different users might take to the same choices and opportunities. As an interactive designer, your job is to engineer a dialogue between your application and the user. To make that dialogue more meaningful, more authentic, and more accessible, you must "get to know" each and every *person* with whom you will be engaging in that dialogue.

Although there are numerous issues in developing a psycho-ergonomically sound design (these vary widely with the application and audience), there are a few general issues that are fairly universal across all products and all audiences:

- Accessibility
- Learning Curve
- Motivation

It's important to make your application accessible to the audience. The primary key to accessibility is making a system "friendly" so that there is a minimum intimidation factor. This is a very important function because many people are natural technophobes. Also, many people are reticent when encountering something new. Therefore, user-friendliness can help people get over the obstacle of anxiety because fear is the greatest impediment to engagement, learning, and play.

Removing fear clears the way for the second most important aspect of psycho-ergonomics—learning. How do you learn the rules and protocol of the application; how do you explore and discover; how do you assimilate information and integrate it into your own internal database; how do you progress from a place of ignorance (in the simple sense of "lack of knowledge") to a place of knowledge and understanding?

People have vastly differing learning styles that determine the way they adopt and acclimate information. The ideal psycho-ergonomically designed interface contains features that respond to a variety of different learning styles. Some people, for example, learn better with text and language as their key entry point; others derive better understanding from visuals; some are adept at understanding spatial relationships, while others tend to see the world in terms of logical equations. Different people have different values which ultimately dictate how they will interface with an interface. By values, I don't mean "family values" or "religious values." I mean informational or psychological values. Do I crave safety or adventure? Do I find ambiguity enticing or frustrating? Do I look for affinity through a human character, or am I more interested in how a machine works?

Motivation is the third aspect of psycho-ergonomics. Motivation is critical to any interactive experience. Nonetheless, it is often baffling to designers. A big issue these days is not how to get people to a web site on the Internet, but how to keep them there. The success of almost every CD-ROM is built upon its capability to support repeat play. This is where motivation comes in. Motivation is the "why" of interactivity. In an interactive game, motivation is crucial. To create and maintain motivation is one of the game designer's most pressing tasks. This is also the case in any kind of goal-oriented interactive experience, whether for the purpose of entertaining or learning or both. Within the arena of motivation, different styles and different personality types respond better or worse to different types of motivation. If you study gender differences, for example, you will find that women respond better to rewards, while men tend to derive more motivation from being penalized. In gaming, for example, women do not like to die, whereas men find dying to be highly motivating.

GIRL GAMES: THE NEW FEMININE MYSTIQUE (p. 202)

In most areas of psycho-ergonomics, feedback is essential. How the system responds to the user can make the difference between motivating the person to go forward and discouraging them to do so. Designers should not expect the user to conform to their constructs, but should respond to every possible choice or action taken by the user. When I worked for Ed Schlossberg, we developed a basic rule of design: no error messages. The design criteria stated that if the player could make a mistake, something was wrong with the design. One way that designers try to address this matter is to issue horrible-sounding audio cues when you do something wrong. An error message is unmotivating, jarring, and does not ultimately serve the interface. The correct philosophy to adopt is that an error message is the result of an error on the part of the designer, not on the part of the player.

There are three basic methodologies that you can use to develop a deeper understanding of psycho-ergonomics as applied to interactive applications. These are as follows:

- Research
- Observation
- Testing

Instead of making up things from scratch, I recommend taking advantage of over a century's worth of highly respected research. In terms of education and psychology, I recommend the work of Jean Piaget and Maria Montessori, both of whom did extensive study of learning and play styles among children. Howard Gardner's *Education Ecstasy* also provides insight into the learning and discovery process.

There are a wealth of books on architecture and design, among them, Christopher Alexander's *A Pattern Language* is an in-depth detailed study of the psycho-ergonomics of architecture which can be applied not only to spatial interfaces, but also to interface design in general, because architecture acts as an interface to the environment. Edward R. Tufte has authored several interesting books, including *Envisioning Information, The Visual Display of Quantitative Information,* and others that study the use of graphics and icons to communicate information. Richard Saul Wurman's *Information Anxiety* provides insight into the widespread fear of information, and provides clues as to how to make information more accessible and manageable. *The Psychology of Everyday Things* is another book that can give insight into how people relate to their environment.

In terms of psychology, I recommend consulting the work of Carl Jung, who identified a system of common archetypes and symbols that characterize human psychology. Jung also did extensive research on the subconscious mind and dream life which can be very useful to storytellers, especially when drawing upon familiar themes and symbols for inclusion in an interactive experience. The book *EQ* explores how emotional makeup affects success and effectiveness in life, and how this interfaces with the intellectual skills to create unique character traits. Several books are also out now on the study of gender differences that, like it or not, are real and come into play in interactive design to a huge extent. One pop psychology book that I have found very helpful on this theme is Deborah Tannen's *You Just Don't Understand*, a study of men and women in conversation. This book explores the different value systems of males and females and how they affect the way they relate to each other and the world.

There are also a number of good books specifically about interactive design. Books with a particularly strong bent in terms of the behavior and psychology of interactivity are Brenda Laurel's *The Art of Interface Design* and *Computers as Theater* and Myron Krueger's *Responsive Environments* and *Artificial Reality.*

This is by no means a comprehensive list, but it is important to explore and investigate to find the work that best applies to the specific work you are doing.

 MEDIOGRAPHY (p. 537)

In addition to consulting founded research, the second thing that will be very useful in the study of psycho-ergonomics is observation. Much of what Piaget and Montessori learned derived from merely observing children, watching them teach themselves through various self-motivated play activities. When I first started designing computer games, I spent a lot of time in arcades hanging around and watching people play. I observed how they learned, and noticed, for example, that a lot of kids learn to play video games not only by watching other kids play, but also by coaching each other. At Edwin Schlossberg Incorporated in the early 1980s, we had a weekly board game club in which we used ourselves as guinea pigs. Each week, we played a different game, analyzed the logic and structure, and observed how they affected our behavior and interactions with each other. Social interaction is a very important factor in any kind of multi-user experience, and one that can never be fully understood through hypothesis. Observation will usually provide the best clues as to the social dynamic that might occur within a given structural premise.

One technique I use in the observational study of psycho-ergonomics is to ask a lot of questions. Whenever I see an interactive application in a public site, I will ask people what they think of it. If I see people using an interactive kiosk in a museum, for example, I'll observe them, but I'll also ask them what they think of it, or what they'd like to see improved. I once stood in front of an exhibit at the Smithsonian Air and Space Museum and watched as people consistently walked away from a computer exhibit without completing the experience. They were discouraged and frustrated because the system had taken them into a dead-end from which there was no escape. You can derive a lot of information from observation and inquiry. Because few people to date have done comprehensive studies of the psycho-ergonomics of interface design, and fewer have made their findings public, the best way to find out about the intricacies of psycho-ergonomics is to do your own formal or informal studies and find out what people *really* do before designing an interface that might or might not work.

Perhaps the most underutilized technique for assuring audience appeal and design integrity is user testing. I can't overemphasize this enough. Design testing, or as they call it in academic circles, formative evaluation, is utterly crucial when developing psycho-ergonomically sound interactive experiences. The moment you have a concept, test it. Before you immerse yourself in a concept, find out whether it even works as a premise. I'm not talking about marketing or focus groups, I'm talking about understanding and resonance. If you tell 20 people about your basic concept or construct and they all look at you like you're speaking Esperanto (a supposedly universal language that nobody understands), you may have a faulty premise from a strictly psycho-ergonomic standpoint.

At each step in the design process, you can test various aspects of your project in isolation to see whether they are sound. Testing can be done cheaply and does not necessarily require a huge sampling. But I will tell you this, I have never seen a case where an interactive design didn't require user testing; it was just a question of how late in the process it happened, and how many changes had to be made *after* production. In fact, the number of post-production changes in a product is inversely proportional to how much advance testing was done. I have a friend who is fond of saying "you always build a prototype; it's just a matter of whether or not you sell it." In fact, most user testing is, erroneously, done at the end of the production cycle when it ought to be done at the very beginning. I will tell you this from my own personal experience: The most tested product I ever worked on came out perfect from a design standpoint and required no interface revisions after it was programmed. Conversely, the game I designed that included no design testing had to undergo some major redesigns after the product was introduced, something that was much more costly than it would have been to test the game before it was completed.

I can't emphasize enough the importance of testing because until you test with potential users, even your initial ideas, everything else is just hypothesis. It's a dangerous business because one false move in an interface design can often lead to the death of a product. A dead-end like the one I described in the Smithsonian Air and Space Museum took a perfectly good idea and rendered it completely impotent, something that could easily have been avoided with simple prototype tests.

REMOTE CONTROL GROUP

Let's take a moment to talk about the television. Specifically, I want to talk about the television remote control, the magic wand that made the joy of channel surfing possible. This little palm-sized wonder has had a lot more impact than meets the infrared-insensitive eye. The really mind-boggling thing is that, in 20-odd years of attempts at creating interactive television, we are only now on the verge of coming up with something more sophisticated than the remote control.

The impact of the remote control device on the content and form of television cannot be overemphasized. In the pre-remote control days, there were a lot less channels. It would be impossible, in fact, to process the number of channels we have today with the old-fashioned "don't touch that…" dial. The dial offers a very limited bandwidth by virtue of the fact that it only has so many numbers, and even with the UHF/VHF switching option, it offers a finite number of viewing options.

The remote control is the friend of Attention Deficit Disorder (ADD). It brings to mind a *Saturday Night Live* gag with Garret Morris—"News for the Hard of Hearing"—in which Morris appeared in a small circle in the bottom corner of the screen. Following the report, he repeated each news item, yelling out each story with hands cupped over his mouth. Remote control is TV for the hard of concentrating. All television could easily be classified with the name of an old Comedy Central show, *Short Attention Span Theater*. It not only accommodates impatience, but indeed, encourages it.

The remote control has brought new meaning to the term instant gratification. It has given us a way to alleviate boredom before it even takes hold. Television can no longer rest on its laurels for even a moment. The show must draw you in and keep you in so that you don't flick to another station. Think about what television commercials were like before the age of remote control. Now, TV commercials have to be eye candy to keep the consumer from pointing his magic wand at the screen and zapping them into demographic limbo.

 THE ADD GENERATION (p. 17)

I'm not usually too pronoun conscious, but in this case, I very deliberately say "his," because the rapid-fire channel-surfing style of television watching is a classically male viewing pattern, and can set up an interesting male/female dynamic: The guy holds the remote and he switches briskly between channels, while the woman wants to stop here and there for, say, five minutes to perhaps get the gist of some character interaction or developing story line. Obviously, there is the control issue. "Who controls the remote" is definitely part of the power structure of any family or relationship. The fact that only one person can operate the remote control at a time means the person in control in effect becomes the "Big Brother" of the household media. Whoever holds the remote controls what those around him are seeing and hearing. In this setting, the person with the remote can censor or proliferate whatever he likes. It is very disconcerting to have your entertainment or information hijacked in midstream. So in a certain sense, it is not only a way of controlling the group entertainment experience, but also a way of actually controlling the mind of the other individuals.

Unlike other slightly more complex interfaces, the remote control interface is simple and very flat in its structure. The decision making is arbitrary. Part of the reason for this is that in most menu-driven interfaces, you are making a choice to go *to* something, but with the remote, you are more often motivated by the desire to go *away* from something. In some cases, the viewer knows where he's going, but the typical channel surfer switches not because he wants to see anything in particular, but because he is bored with the current offering. This is a peculiar and backward way to propel a decision-making process if you think about it. What if we made all other life decisions on this basis. "I married Susie because Lorna was dull." "I went to that restaurant to get away from the boring food at the restaurant down the street."

The tremendously compelling motivation of boredom, coupled with the capability to instantaneously accommodate lack of interest, is perhaps the great malaise of our culture. What is doubly peculiar about this phenomenon is that, although you might be propelled into action by boredom, the end result of all this channel surfing is essentially a sensory overload in which you are bombarded with an inordinate amount of information—most of which, if you really think about it, is gratuitous. By some strange occurrence, the following has become a self-fulfilling prophecy: The more boring TV there is to get away from, the more we need more boring TV to escape to, and so forth.

The remote control is supposed to offer us an escape from the prison of boredom, but in the end, the remote control has become its own prison—the prison of choice. And the choices it offers are essentially meaningless because the remote control only offers an escape from the cell, not from the jail itself. It is as if the jailers opened all the bars and invited us to move around freely from cell to cell, when what we really want to do is step out in the sunlight and be able to become an active part of the world again.

In interactive media, we need to invert this "escape from boredom" mentality. We need to offer enticing choices, choices that have some meaning and consequence. The frustration of the remote control is that, ultimately all roads lead to Rome. Whether we watch the TV or not, change the channel or not, it makes no difference. In interactive multimedia, the choice should make a difference, the outcome should vary based on choice. Furthermore, the choice itself should have some inherent interest. As a user or player of an interactive product, what I want is to be propelled forward because I am chasing discovery, not because I am escaping boredom.

CHOICE IS OVERRATED (p. 127)

GRATUITOUS INTERACTIVITY: MEDIA DISPENSERS AND THE ATM MODEL (p. 218)

The remote control has really been the only means we have of interacting directly with the television. Even so, just that one little flick of the clicker has a somewhat empowering effect. It makes you feel that you are in more of a dialogue with the TV. In fact, the remote control generation is much more vociferous with their television. At the same time, isn't this interaction more disempowering? Why? Because you are presented with an essentially mean-ingless choice. The bottom line is, no matter how many times you shoot your television, it will never know that you are bored, and it doesn't care what you like and dislike. You can shut the story off, but you can't affect the outcome.

Based on this mentality, it should be no surprise to anyone that "video on demand" has been considered some kind of panacea for interactive television. The furthest the television broadcast sensibility can seem to go with inter-activating its media is to let you actually chose *when* you get to experience your passive media. There's got to be more to it than that!

In spite of the limits of remote control, if you look at the television in a broader way, as an integral part of our democratic society, you can clearly see that there is a dialogue between the audience and the medium. This dialogue manifests itself on both a large scale, in our day-to-day lives as individuals, and in our relationship to the larger whole of culture and politics. A look at this relationship demonstrates that, in reality, people really do interact with their televisions, but in a much more significant way than merely changing channels. Instead, what people want to change, and indeed have changed, is the content of television itself. Because television is the portal into modern culture, changing the content of the TV consequently means changing the content of culture, and ultimately, of history.

Broad or Narrow: The Casting Couch (p. 113)

It's Not the Television That's Interactive, It's the People (p. 250)

Nerd versus Couch Potato (p. 345)

Theory of Media Evolution: The Four Axioms (p. 480)

The Revelation of Rita: VR and the Power of Empathy

Imagine walking into a box of light, a tiny eight-by-eight foot room, which you share with seven other people. You are walking down the glowing hallways of a gallery. Hovering before the white luminescent walls, between marble columns, are large photographs of nature—beautiful scenes of trees reflecting off glistening water, a dusk sky blossoming with color over a rippling sea, vast deserts and intimate forests, the sound of water lapping on a shore, of birds singing, and wind gently rustling the trees. These bucolic and serene images create a sense of peace and solace as you turn and take a closer look at these windows into the natural world (see figure R.1).

Figure R.1

Detour: Rita Addison's nature photographs as they appeared to her before her brain injury

 PLATE 05

As you head down the hallway, the photographs fade and give way to a dark highway—yellow lines flash by as they shoot toward you out of a thick fog, the sound of screeching brakes and skidding tires, a woman's agonizing cry. Broken glass shatters before you.

You move toward and enter a human brain floating in the blackness (see figure R.2). You hear the echoey sound of a heart beating. Synapses break in half with the electrical flash of a lighting bolt, accompanied by an eerie sizzling sound punctuated by a loud snap (see figure R.3)! You can see the brain being literally fried. The prognosis comes from a man's voice in the distance: "I'm afraid she's going to have problems…"

You wake up, as if from a dream, or is it a nightmare? Or are you entering a dream or nightmare? You can't be sure. The scene is familiar…the same glowing gallery…the same photos…the same exquisite images of nature…but there's something wrong. Each time you turn to look at one, your vision is impeded: a big black spot appears in the middle of your field of view; a white gooey haze seems to be smeared across your eyes; colors seem to invert, as if you are looking at a negative of the picture; an image seems to ripple as you move closer to it; strange reversals of depth and tone; color distorted or lost (see figure R.4). Behind it all, a constant noise, not deafening, but persistent… crackling…screeching…sounds creating interference between your perception and the audio environment. You are trapped inside a compulsory hallucination, beautiful in its organic abstraction, but terrifying in its relentlessness. You are trapped inside the mind of Rita Addison, a world where sight and sound are perpetually distorted by a series of sensory anomalies—a veil between you and the world that never goes away.

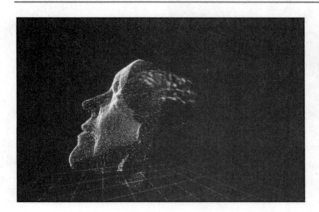

Figure R.2

Detour: Cyberscan of Rita's head. An animated close-up of the brain portrays the brain injury as it occurs

 PLATE 06

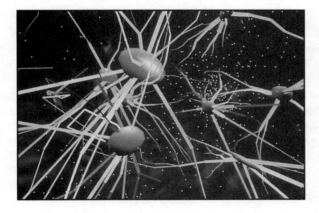

Figure R.3

Detour: A model of neurons intended to demonstrate brain damage at the cellular level

 PLATE 07

The scene dims. The low lights slowly come up. At that moment, you are somehow numb; something unbelievably profound has happened to you. You turn, and there she is, facing you: Rita herself. You cannot look at her or speak with her now without an incredible sensation coming over you. "I know how she is seeing me. I know how she is hearing me. I can see myself through her eyes." She smiles and shakes your hand warmly as you try to find the words to express the inexpressible. As you stumble out into the "real world," you take a moment to adjust and absorb the sheer magnitude of what you've just experienced: being inside another person's mind.

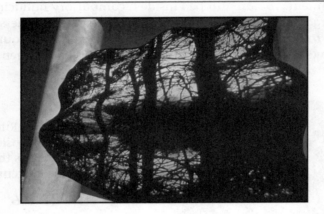

Figure R.4

Detour: Rita's own photographs distorted by visual anomolies caused by brain injury

PLATE 08

For me, *Detour: Brain Deconstruction Ahead* was both the answer to a prayer and a response to a fundamental question that had plagued me for a long time. Is there a God in cyberspace? *Detour* answered the question clearly: Yes, and it has a human face.

For some years I had been plagued by this question: I knew that interactive media had enormous cognitive power; I knew that as an educational tool it was invaluable; I knew that heuristic learning, and the sense of complete involvement made possible with the use of spatial interfaces, had tremendous impact on intellectual development. I knew that these responsive media could make you *think,* but why, I had to ask, did they not make you *feel*? Until I saw *Detour,* I had never seen an interactive experience that had the emotional impact of a film, or even a book. I had never gotten the wind knocked out of me by a computer application. I had never seen a VR world that made me cry. *Detour* was the thing I had been waiting for—VR as catharsis. VR as mimesis. VR as an empathic art.

It is a gross understatement to say that *Detour* is the ultimate interactive drama, but it's a good place to start. It is deceptively simple, a "before and after" story, as Rita herself puts it. Its purpose is to tell a simple tale of a person's life turned upside down by circumstances beyond her control. The catharsis occurs on two levels: in the heart and mind of the viewer experiencing *Detour,* and in the soul of the artist, who found a way to turn a personal tragedy into a glorious triumph.

The real catharsis is in the intersection between the experience of the viewer and Rita's experience. This collaboration demonstrates the unique power that Virtual Reality has to communicate that which cannot be communicated, to express the inexpressible. Rita's experience is unthinkable. It's the ultimate horror, perhaps the most frightening thing that could happen to anybody. In the introductory monologue, she expresses her desperate quest: "I have to find my way back to my brain." She accomplishes this by finding her way to yours. In the transference of her brain to yours, Rita creates the ultimate cathartic experience by breaking the boundaries of subjective perception. She opens your mind by opening her own, by peeling back the shell and showing you the inside of her brain, both as an entity (the second act in which the brain itself is being altered) and as a state of perception.

From VR's very inception, artists and philosophers alike have seen its potential to express altered states of consciousness. Aldous Huxley's classic study of hallucinogenic ritual and transformation, *Doors of Perception*, is something of a biblical text among VR artists and theorists. Pop culture icons of the movement Huxley's work spawned, such as Timothy Leary and Terrence McKenna, embraced Virtual Reality as another means of opening those doors. The emphasis among this school of thought was on creating a "consensual hallucination" (in the words of William Gibson), which could enable the kind of experience you have through the use of hallucinogenic drugs to then be shared.

Detour surprised everyone by opening an entirely different door. The very thing that the McKennas and Learys were trying to emulate with VR becomes, for Rita, a perceptual prison that is hauntingly beautiful yet inescapable and ultimately alienating. What most proponents of hallucinogenics were trying to create, Rita was trying to break out of. *Detour* enabled Rita to open a door to perception in the *opposite* direction, not for the conscious mind into a plane of hallucination, but as a way out for a mind trapped in a compulsory hallucination. Rita's door swings both ways: One way for us to see our way in and another for her to see her way out.

Detour speaks to us on such a profoundly human level. To my knowledge, it is the first autobiographical, narrative VR experience that tells the true story of a highly personalized experience. Other VR experiences have offered a personal perspective, and even a cathartic mindspace, but never a real life story. As Brenda Laurel demonstrates in *Computers as Theater*, the expression of drama as a means of empathic catharsis goes back to Aristotle and further still. *Detour* creates that cathartic drama, made even more compelling because it's real.

Detour resonates on a variety of levels. Rita begins by taking our breath away with her beautiful photos of nature…a bridge to the ultimate reality. Rita's relationship with nature is clear and immediate: It is a love affair of the eye, a lavish sensory exchange. Rita's photos express a deep spiritual and emotional connection with the natural world, in a very classically "right brain way"—neither intellectual nor philosophical, but deeply intuitive and sensual. You can see that she relishes in the seductive beauty of nature with passion and reverence.

For such a person to have her senses interfered with in such a dramatic way is something that to anyone would be seen as a tragedy. The opening act of *Detour* establishes that this is a woman whose eyes are everything to her. There is no worse thing we can imagine than the loss or distortion of this sense of sight and perception. And so the empathy is created...a simple story with poignant drama that anyone can understand on a visceral, emotional, and spiritual level. Mimesis. Empathy.

Remarkably, it is with the very eyes that Rita has lost that she regains her power, by creating a new visionscape that acknowledges the terror and in so doing, dispels it. This is where the catharsis occurs. By expressing the intense feeling of isolation she experiences within her "deconstructed brain," by sharing the most intimate view you can have of another person—the naked brain, the pure perceptual experience—she propels you into her consciousness.

 CONSENSUAL HALLUCINATIONS: IS VR THE NEW LSD? (p. 134)

It is interesting to note that the story of *Detour* is linear. In other words, you cannot affect the outcome. Under normal circumstances, this would pose a serious conflict within the context of an interactive narrative experience; however, because it is not a story about choice, but about having a situation forced on you, the inability to effect the outcome of the story is an integral part of the experience. In this world, you have the freedom to have a sense of autonomy, but the dramatic event itself is utterly beyond your control, just as it was beyond hers. By putting you in the role of a victim whose fate is not of your own making, Rita puts you in the position of powerlessness that she experienced.

You can clearly see from the outcome that this is a tale of the triumph of the human spirit. In the face of this insurmountable tragedy, Rita was able to find a way out, and that way out is you. You know that as you walk out of the space, and you look into her smiling eyes, full of warmth and gratitude and reverence...you realize that it is you, perhaps a stranger, or as was the case with me, a future friend...you realize that *her* way out is through *your* eyes. Not only is she there to move you, but you are there to move her. For each person that experiences the reality of Rita's world, she is that much less alone, and that much less trapped. Thus, the doors of perception open for everyone, and the healing process, which is mutual, continues for as long as any other person walks around with Rita's eyes inside his or her own head.

The story of how Rita came to make *Detour* is worthy of a documentary, and I hope someday, someone will either make one, or give me money to do it.

After the accident, Rita found herself in a state of rage and frustration. Her greatest passion in life, capturing nature on film, was taken from her. She was frustrated by people's apparent lack of empathy for her situation. She tried time and time again to explain what was going on in her head, how she was seeing and hearing things differently, how unbearable it was to be trapped in this new brain that she didn't like. Yet people seemed to turn a deaf ear on her. They trivialized her experience in that way that people do when confronted with a reality so horrifying they don't want to even face it lest they would somehow open themselves up to a reality too terrible to consider. It is the same reason people turn their heads from the homeless or blame a rape victim—because it is too painful to consider the alternative, that they too could some day end up a victim. This strange form of denial and fear created a barrier that would not enable people to let the reality of Rita's situation seep in without the risk of having to imagine themselves similarly afflicted. Rita fell into a state of despair and alienation, lost and confused, yearning to create, but unable to escape the reality that, through no fault of hers, her brain was no longer her own. But then somewhere something snapped.

Motivated by a potent mix of righteous anger and the kind of creative passion that can only be born of a highly personal struggle, Rita determined to find a way to express herself come hell or high water. One day at a convention, she had her first encounter with Virtual Reality. At that moment she knew that she had found the medium in which to tell her story.

She began hoofing the pavement. Being based in the Boston area at the time was a real benefit because Rita was right in the lap of MIT, the home of computers and one of the birthplaces of VR. Rita paid a visit to David Zeltzer, who had run the infamous "Snake Pit," the former Virtual Reality department at the MIT Media Lab, and was now running a different VR lab on another part of campus. Zeltzer led her to Tom de Fanti, Dan Sandine, and the *CAVE*. She joined forces with her collaborator Marcus Thiebaux, got an ARPA grant to do the project at University of Illinois at Chicago, and began the task of telling her impossible-to-tell story in the one-and-only medium it could be told in.

 A BRIEF HISTORY OF REAL TIME: THE VIRTUAL REALITY LEGACY (p. 105)

THE MILITARY ENTERTAINMENT COMPLEX (p. 303)

Rita's story has been an inspiration to many because it not only demonstrates the power of technology to communicate and to heal, but it is also one of those amazing tales of a courageous individual who turned a devastating tragedy into a triumph, not only for herself, but for us, and for an entire medium. More than anyone else, Rita brought her personal struggle to cyberspace, and it is in her telling of this simple before-and-after story that she unleashed the power of VR as a medium of empathy and understanding.

 V-ART (p. 494)

VICARIOUS EXPERIENCE (p. 504)

VIRTUAL REALITY AS A DRAMATIC ART (p. 508)

VIRTUAL RELATIVITY (p. 524)

THE RULES OF THE GAME

At my first interactive job in 1983, the first assignment I received was to learn as much as I could about games. Furthermore, my job was to write descriptions of multiplayer interactive games that were in the design process with a diverse team of creative people, none of whom were game designers. I knew nothing about games at the time, and as each new game idea arrived at my desk in its own unique form—everything from text, to sketches, to foam core— I kept asking myself these same questions: Is this a game? Why is it a game? What *is* a game anyway? I began to embark on a massive research project in order to answer these fundamental questions. I spent several weeks playing and analyzing games, pondering every quality and nuance, trying to understand what the hell we meant when we talked about designing games.

 AUTOBIOGRAPHY OF AN AUTODIDACT, PART 2 (p. 58)

Now this may seem a bit mundane. After all, doesn't everybody know what a game is? Well sure, it's easy to recognize a game when you see one, but what is it that makes it a game, and what are the properties that all games share in common? My mission was to discover the answers to these questions so that when the designers I worked with, most of whom had never designed a game before in their lives, came to me with their zany ideas, I could look them in the eye and say, "Yes, this is indeed a game." As a result, I became the self-appointed game police, the quality assurance department, making sure that each game concept we generated fit the criteria to be properly called a game. I have since refined this list and now use it in my teaching, so...

Here now, for your edification and amusement are "The Rules of the Game."

Definition: A game is a form of structured but spontaneous play. A game has a logical structure that is defined by a set of rules, which afford a wide variety of variable outcomes within the parameters of that structure. A game, to be a game, must have the following components:

- Goal
- Obstacles
- Resources
- Consequences: Rewards and Penalties
- Information
- Rules/Structure

Goal

A game must have a clear goal or objective known to all players at the outset. Many games also have sub-goals that can aid in the achievement of the primary goal. For instance, chess has the following goal and sub-goal:

- **Goal:** To capture opponent's King
- **Sub-goal:** To make your Pawns into Queens to improve chances of capturing King

Obstacles

A game wouldn't be very challenging without obstacles. In fact, without obstacles, it wouldn't be a game at all, but an activity. Obstacles are rules or elements that impede your progress toward achieving your goal. They can come in a wide variety of forms. In multiplayer games, you can look at other players as one of the primary obstacles between you and your goal. Chess, for example, has the following obstacles:

- Opponent's pieces guarding his or her King
- Opponent can capture your pieces
- Opponent's objective is to capture your King first

Resources

Resources help you achieve your goal and overcome obstacles. Sometimes, a resource can be a reward for a sub-goal. Some resources in chess include the following:

- Different playing pieces with different move options
- The ability to capture and remove other players pieces from the board

CONSEQUENCES: REWARDS AND PENALTIES

Rewards are positive consequences for successfully overcoming obstacles or achieving certain sub-goals; rewards can often come in the form of resources that help you to overcome obstacles. Rewards can come in the form of resources to yourself, or penalties against your opponents. Again, the game of chess affords some good examples of rewards in a game:

- Capturing opponent's pieces decreases obstacles to capture of his/her King (offensive reward/resource), and decreases the number of pieces available to capture your King (defensive reward/resource).
- You can turn a Pawn into a Queen by moving it to the far side of the board, thus increasing your ability to capture our opponent's King.

Penalties are negative consequences that can be the result of unsuccessful actions, or the successful action of an opponent. Penalties generally take the form of obstacles, and can often translate into rewards for other players. In chess, a poor move can lead to piece captured by opponent, resulting in less protection for the King (defensive penalty) and fewer pieces to capture the opponent's King (offensive penalty).

There are very seldom neutral consequences, that is, consequences which neither reward nor penalize *someone*. A neutral consequence is often the sign of a flawed game structure—consequences must be significant to have any impact on the players or the course of the game.

INFORMATION

Within the game, there is a variety of information that can include, but is not restricted to the following:

- **Information known to all players:** In chess, this would consist of the rules of the game, board layout, and piece movement parameters.
- **Information known to only one player:** In gin, this would be the cards in your hand.
- **Information known to the game only:** In gin, this would be unused cards in deck. In *Space Invaders*, this would be the paths and frequency of alien space ships.

⬤ **Randomly generated information:** In backgammon, this would be the roll of the dice.

RULES/STRUCTURE

The preceding five elements exist within the logic and structure of the game. All the moves and activities of the game must be performed within these constraints. One of the key factors that distinguishes a game from an activity is the fact that you must perform the actions of the game within the framework of the rules. Any deviation from that framework is generally considered cheating or breaking the rules. The examples in the following bulleted list show some of the game parameters of chess. These parameters create the constraints within which the spontaneous play can occur. Most of the structural parameters you see listed here are provided to create a level playing field so that the game will be "fair" and the outcome determined by skill and luck, and not by any lopsided logic within the game.

⬤ The checkered playing board
⬤ The designated position of the pieces
⬤ The movement parameters of each of the pieces

This list was developed initially in 1983. I'm not sure exactly how or when it happened, but 10 years later when I was working on *Virtual Adventures*, and attempting to develop something that was both an interactive story and a game, I accidentally stumbled upon a stunning revelation about the relationship between game structure and story structure.

 THE PRINCESS AND THE MONSTER: THE MAKING OF VIRTUAL ADVENTURES (p. 375)

To understand this better, let's look for a moment at the tenets of traditional story structure. You need look no further than high school English class to remember these simple principles. A story consists of the following:

⬤ A character with a **goal** or **objective**
⬤ **Obstacles** that come between the character and his/her objective
⬤ **Resources** that help the character overcome obstacles toward his/her objectives
⬤ **Consequences** of the character's actions toward meeting his/her goals or objectives; these consequences may be negative—**penalties**—or positive—**rewards**
⬤ **Information:** How much of it does the character have? How much of it do we the viewer have?

● Story or plot **premise**, including the **parameters** of the culture within which the character must carry out his or her journey toward the objective.

An example of how this applies concretely to a story might be one I use in the chapter "Decisions, Decisions, Decisions"—the film *Groundhog Day*. In the film, Bill Murray's objective is to get out of Punxsutawney and to get Groundhog Day over with as quickly as possible. The obstacle put before him is that he keeps waking up on the same day over and over again. As each situation of the repeating day presents itself, he relies on his inner resources, which evolve as the story unfolds, transforming him from a jerk into a decent person. During this process, his goals actually change; after giving up on achieving his primary goal, he develops a new goal: to get laid. He figures out how to use his knowledge of that day to manipulate people to get what he wants. But he is repeatedly penalized for this self-centered behavior. At first, he tries to impress the object of his affection, again, being penalized in ways which put him further away from his goal. Because this approach doesn't work, he finds himself getting a crush on Andie MacDowell's character, and now his goal becomes to get the girl. As he does good deeds in the story he is rewarded with qualities that become resources—knowledge of the people and events of the day, new skills such as piano playing and ice sculpture. As he begins to let go of his self-centered and childish values and adopt better values as a person, he is rewarded in the form of resources that help him achieve the goal of getting the girl, which releases him from his purgatory in Groundhog Day and sends him back out into the world a changed man. The pattern of story is as follows:

● Objective + Obstacles = Conflict
● Resources used in meeting obstacles determines character
● Drama is in the character's decision-making process and the consequences (rewards and penalties) of his/her actions
● Pattern of rewards and penalties lead to climax, resulting in transformation of character
● Transformation results in resolution of the conflict; this can take the form of character achieving primary goal, or, more often the case, changing goal entirely

Groundhog Day is a prototype for a linear story that bears the seed of interactivity. A tale such as this could easily be translated into a game/story experience wherein the player must repeatedly face these same situations and make different decisions about what to do. In this scenario, story becomes game, and game becomes story.

BUILDING CHARACTER: THE SOUL OF DRAMA (p. 119)

DECISIONS, DECISIONS, DECISIONS (p. 158)

One day when I was writing these elements of game/story on the white board during a class, one of my students burst out with: "But that's just life, isn't it?" Therein lies the secret. Life can be viewed as both a story and a game; and there doesn't necessarily have to be a winner. In fact, if you look at the parameters of game structure, there is no rule that says there has to be a winner. A goal could just as easily be infinite as finite. There is no reason why a goal has to result in closure, and as you can see from the previous analysis of story structure, more often than not, the character can change goals in mid-stream, also permissible, albeit less common, within the boundaries of a game structure.

The fact is that virtually everything in life can be seen as a game. Using the preceding parameters, you can define virtually any aspect of life as we know it, from raising a child or fighting off a virus, to keeping an ecosystem in equilibrium, as a game.

A-Life of One's Own (p. 5)

God Plays Dice with the Universe (p. 215)

Inter-play: Improvisation and Interactive Theater (p. 230)

Virtual Reality as a Dramatic Art (p. 508)

Social Capitalism

Social capitalism is a little oxymoron I invented to describe what I consider to be the next-generation business model. Social capitalism combines the entrepreneurial spirit of capitalism and a free market economy with the community spirit of social democracy. It marks a trend away from competition and toward cooperation. Its archetype is the cottage industry of the global village. It is interactive and its horizontal structure defies hierarchy. The widespread influence of social capitalism can be seen as far as the European Union, and as close as the Internet. In fact, the supreme court decision that deemed the "Information Decency Act" indecent proves that social capitalism is alive and well in America.

The 1980s was a time of intense capitalism in this country. It was a period of enormous prosperity, much of which turned out to be superficial at best. The economic growth of the 80s, as propagated by Reaganomics, was really a matter of the Emperor's New Clothes. The stock market was a place where people were trading nothing more than pieces of paper whose value could be manipulated by crafty market traders. This form of financial vaporware ultimately led to a massive stock market crash, setting off a real estate crash, which triggered a Savings and Loan scandal. This chain reaction devastated the corporate culture and the American economy, resulting in corporate downsizing and massive vacancies in commercial centers.

Out of the ashes of this disaster arose the Information Age and the Digital Revolution. Supported by a new generation of powerful personal computing tools and a survivalist guerilla mentality, people began to regroup. A certain faction of refugees from the corporate culture began to create a new economic entity, a "virtual class" of freelancers and consultants who created their own subculture within the capitalist framework.

The term "virtual class" was coined by Londoners Andy Cameron and Richard Barbrook of Westminster University's Hypermedia Research Centre in their *Mute* magazine article, "The Californian Ideology" (*Mute*, Issue 3, Autumn 1995). In the article, they describe, with some disdain, a virtual class of high-priced California consultants whom they see as part of a digital elite comprised of disciples of Marshall McLuhan and readers of *Wired* magazine. Their major criticism of digital culture in California is that it is based on a doctrine of technological determinism and a decidedly post-political posture. These guys are, of course, my pals, so I fashioned a friendly reply, a companion article entitled "The Californian Ideology: An Insider's View" (*Mute*, Issue 4, Winter/Spring 1996). In my article, I describe the socio-economic and cultural conditions unique to America, which have precipitated this "virtual class."

In America, there are no politics: only economics. Everything here is driven by economics, pure and simple. The classic tenets of social democracy as practiced to varying degrees in most of the stable European countries are utterly anathema to the American ideal of dog-eat-dog, every-man-for-himself. Class consciousness and a sense of social responsibility are markedly absent from the American scene. The next best thing we have to offer is so-called "family values," a thin veil for the political and social agenda of the far far far right. In England, or the highly developed social democracies of Scandinavia, for example, there exists a built-in belief that it is the responsibility of the individual to watch out for the culture as a whole. In America, all we want to do is keep our taxes from going up. There is little concern for the welfare of the nation as a community; indeed the very word welfare, which once meant simply "health, happiness, and prosperity," in America has come to stand for "lazy poor people of color with lots of illegitimate children using up our tax dollars." Furthermore, support for the arts and especially the arts in technology has waned down to the point where we ought to be embarrassed to call ourselves a civilized nation. In Europe, artists can actually get funding, not to mention public appreciation. Many American digital artists have to turn outside the U.S., to Canada and

Japan, for example, to get support for their projects. For the full text of these articles, visit http://www.metamute.easynet.co.uk.

Digerati: The Artificial Intelligentsia (p. 164)

The issue of class stratification brought on by the rise of an elitist computer culture is certainly a valid concern, but there is another way to see it. First of all, most revolutionary movements, even those started on behalf of the poor, are seldom led by them. It is almost always a middle class, educated elite that leads a revolutionary movement. Most of the time, fueled by a fairly strong liberal orientation, they will end up bringing the poorer groups with them. Democracy was by no means architected by the poor, any more than socialism was, but both movements sought to create a fairer system that would ultimately benefit all. One can only hope that the new virtual class will carry on this tradition. Furthermore, all revolutionary movements are in fact driven by economics rather than politics. It was the rise of the merchant class that ultimately led to the French Revolution, a group that was not part of the gentry or royal class, but had gained substantial economic power.

So what is the new "virtual class" and what is the new economic structure it is evolving within?

Let's start with computers. For many years, there was a strong conviction among the computer science community that there would never be a home market for personal computers. If personal computers were to thrive, they would do so strictly in the workplace, and only the rare technophile would ever have the need for one at home (this was in the DOS days of course). What this group of prophesiers didn't bargain for was that there might be a market in the *home office*, and that is really the seed of both the home computer revolution and of the rise of the virtual class.

When the Macintosh computer came out, with its easy to use interface and innate friendliness toward creative types (simple word processors, easy-to-use graphics programs, straightforward spreadsheets…even that little pocket calculator thing), many of the early home computers were bought not for the purpose of entertainment but by individuals who were setting up home businesses. Eventually, enough software was available to expand the PC market still further as a household appliance and home entertainment center.

As an engine for home business, a computer is a creative power tool. Today's computers enable you to do things at home that it used to take a huge office infrastructure to create. Desktop publishing, project management, and graphics tools enable people to do almost anything they want at home. In fact, many of these digital cottage industries that formed in the early 90s were the product of post-recession fallout. People who had been using computers throughout the 80s in the office were going home and realizing, "hey, if I had one of these babies in my den, I could do everything I did at work—and charge a lot more for it. Thus, the virtual company was born.

A virtual company can take a lot of different forms. In its simplest definition, it is a person or persons who form a company that has no central physical plant. Generally, these individuals or small groups adopt a fictitious business name. They usually set up at home, with a couple of phone lines, a fax machine, and a computer or two. They print up some business cards, usually self-designed with the help of the computer once again, each with the home phone, address, and e-mail of the bearer. They set up a web site, and voilá! a "virtual company" is born. Depending on the ebb and flow of projects, this virtual team may hire other independent contractors or virtual companies to help them with larger, more complex projects; but at bare minimum, this will be a lean, mean, low-overhead machine. In fact, many digital artists and engineers work this way today. I myself have operated in this fashion since 1990, and in fact, you will find that a significant number of top people in digital media will no longer consider any other lifestyle. Headhunters may come banging on our doors, but we prefer to camp out at home, where we can come and go as we please, work the notoriously strange hours characteristic of computer hackers and artists, and be able to spend at least a tad of time with our friends and families. Most of us have peculiar working habits, and we find that we work better in unconventional settings, whether it be in a room full of tie-dye and batik, or, as is the case with me, the garden patio of the local cyber-cafÉ.

In Silicon Valley and Hollywood, a significant number of creative people are now working this way, forming "virtual companies" that can expand and contract to meet the workload, but operate with extremely low overhead. It is now possible for a graphics designer to have a mid- to low-end SGI computer, a high-end PC or Mac workstation, or a beefed-up post-production studio at home for between $10,000 and $25,000, not too shabby when you consider that such an individual can have an earning potential of upwards of $100,000 annually, significantly more than he or she could make on staff at any one of the major studios or software companies.

When full-fledged companies do form out of these small virtual companies, they tend to remain fairly small. The optimal size for a small digital studio, content provider, or software shop is about 30. These companies also rely heavily on freelancers and other virtual companies to fill out their own internal skill sets. To accommodate different types of projects, many of these full-fledged and virtual companies will form alliances based on complementary skills, thus creating a kind of community of small entrepreneurial entities.

The economic system emerging from this corporate culture is what I define as "social capitalism." A classic social capitalist construct is a community of individuals or virtual companies loosely associated with each other who share resources, skills, and projects. Instead of forming a large company, which would require that all members of the group take on the same collective goal, they have developed a working relationship that is horizontal in nature. All these people own their own small companies, and are each others' clients as well as each others' contractors. Furthermore, the classic law of the jungle of capitalism—competition—becomes not only moot, but really counterproductive in this kind of milieu. The industry itself is so volatile that the sense is that we are all in this thing together. Although there is still much secrecy and proprietary design, there is also a greater spirit of mutual cooperation than ever before.

In these communities of virtual companies, there is no overall hierarchy, but a short-term hierarchy might be formed to accommodate a particular project. When you are working on my project, I'm the leader and vice versa. This is a very nice way to work. Unlike in the corporate environment where the hierarchy is clear, defined, and set in stone, with this model, everyone gets a chance to be boss sometimes. There are some excellent benefits to this. One benefit is that everyone gets a chance to *be* managed. This is always bound to help one's own management skills, but it is also a relief to know that you don't *always* have to be in charge. Another benefit is that these people are autonomous and work on a contractual basis, which means there are no feudal ties, such as those that exist within a company. There is no "big brother" telling you what to wear and how to work or what sort of cubicle you are entitled to given your station in life. People might come and work out of your office for a limited duration, or, more often, they will work to a large extent at home, communicating with you via e-mail or a shared "extranet" (an intranet that connects remote locations). The whole point is that the relationships are more fluid and no one is, in essence, under anyone else's control.

This new model of social capitalism, in which each person contributes according to his or her abilities and takes according to his or her need, is a very productive management model. These small companies are indeed so effective at what they do that many of the huge corporations actually contract much of their content work out to these smaller entities. Just around the time I was writing this book, a number of large companies either closed or downsized their CD-ROM departments. Part of the reason is the ebb and flow of media platforms, but the other is that the typical large company cannot support the kind of small budgets and gruelling time schedules that can more efficiently be dealt with by smaller companies with a more horizontal structure. After spending millions of dollars with little success, these giant media moguls are turning to smaller companies built on the model of social capitalism.

Many virtual companies and entrepreneurial alliances happen between individuals and companies that are not in the same geographical location. Because of the evolution in communications technology, it is now possible to have incredibly productive and close collaborations remotely. I can write a document and e-mail it to someone as far away as Denmark, he can edit it and send it back to me. He can fax me translations to proofread, and I can fax back my comments. Programmers can modem code back and forth. This adds another level of flexibility to the arrangement. This means not only can you work at your own pace how and where you want, but you don't even have to be near any commerce center to be part of commerce. Many programmers and digital artists are nature-lovers and prefer the isolation of a country dwelling to a busy urban setting. So the outdoorsy programmer or artist type can have her ranch in the middle of nowhere, and as long as she has a modem and can "hook in," she can work with whomever she likes wherever she likes without ever having to leave the woods or even see anyone for that matter. Some of these high-tech jockeys go so far as to get high-speed T1, T2, or ISDN lines installed in their country cabins for faster transportation to desired digital locations. It's not unusual to find people who have Internet servers sitting in their homes.

 COMPUTER TERMINAL VERSUS COMMUTER TERMINAL: TELECOMMUTING AND THE NEW ECONOMY (p. 129)

Some would say this working paradigm encourages isolation, which it does to a certain extent, but what it also does is enable a broader array of interaction types. This kind of remote communication also has the reverse effect in that it allows people more freedom to move. I am writing on my PowerBook in the airport. If I wanted, I could go to a payphone and ftp this draft of my manu-script to my editor before I get on the plane. Or, I can go write in the woods and send drafts to my editor from the Adirondacks. The point is that remote communications enable collaborations that could not happen under any other circumstances, and it also means that you can truly pick the best people for the job without having to worry about whether they happen to be local. Even though I live in Los Angeles, the majority of my clients and collaborators are located elsewhere.

The old management paradigms have become obsolete. The old model for management is orchestral, consisting of a large group of musicians, each with a predetermined score, and a single conductor whose role it is to provide centralized leadership. Alternatively, the new management model looks more like a jazz ensemble. There is no bandleader, but rather a group of musicians who agree to play a composition together. The system is small and more horizontal. Each musician has an opportunity to play with the group, and also to improvise and have his or her own solo. The musicians take turns, allowing each other the maximum opportunity for creative expression. This leads to a system that is once more individualistic and more collaborative, with no centralized hierarchy and a much broader repertoire.

Another major change brought on by social capitalism is a shift in attitudes about competition. Competition is necessary in a free market economy. It is part of what keeps people innovating and what drives the evolution of technology. Competition has also been the scourge of the computer revolution. Because of its roots in the military, this entire industry grew and evolved within an environment of extraordinary secrecy, competition, and paranoia. Non-disclosure agreements, intellectual property, and lawyers abound, creating a milieu that has been known to reach ridiculous heights of absurdity. The standard joke in the business is, We'd like to tell you what we were doing, but then we'd have to kill you. You can often find yourself at a cocktail party or industry function and when you ask people what they are doing, everyone will say "I can't really talk about it." The trouble is, when people say that, it can only mean one of three things: They are doing something top secret and presumably really significant; they are in negotiation on something top secret and presumably really significant; they are doing nothing at all but they want to make it *look* as if they are doing something really significant.

In my opinion, the interactive and digital industries in general have suffered enormously from all this secrecy and competition. In fact, I think this industry could be 10 years ahead of where it is today if this were not the prevailing culture. Each time a new project appears, everyone has to reinvent the wheel, because no one is willing to pass the torch of unused ideas or share lessons learned from failures. Because everything is proprietary, each company would rather invent its own system from scratch at enormous expense, with no guarantee of success, than find someone who's already figured out how to do it well and just license his or her technology. The same precise projects have been done over and over again, with the same often disastrous results, because the proprietary culture of digital media makes it impossible for us to learn from each others' mistakes. As a result, collectively, we keep repeating the same mistakes again and again.

Kiss My Asset: The Content Wars of the 1990s and the Birth of Transmedia (p. 269)

Many dire errors in judgement have also prevailed under this veil of secrecy. The creators of the legendary Xerox PARC graphical interface, which became the impetus for the Macintosh interface, had no immediate plans to share it with the rest of the world. It was only due to the vision of the people at Apple, who had the wherewithal to "borrow" it, that it was able to spawn the personal computing revolution.

To realize the destructive impact of competition, we need look no further than at the intense rivalry between Apple and Microsoft for domination of the PC market. Had Apple licensed its system for the PC in the first place, and had Microsoft worked in cooperation with them, both companies would have prospered, the industry would not be perceived as unstable, and the consumer would have more confidence and more options. Today, the battle between these companies has ultimately hurt everyone, from the companies themselves to the software houses that produce applications for both PC and Mac platforms. The group that pays the greatest price for this destructive competition is the consumer, and ultimately, the culture at-large.

 THE PEdAGOGicAl MousEPAd, OR, How iT All GoT GUI (p. 365)

In moments of utopian fantasy, I often imagine what the world would be like today if everyone in this business had pooled his or her resources all along to create a collective intelligence base. Each entity could have its own expertise, but could learn from and build on the work of the others. In this way, we could all evolve in a harmonious and collaborative fashion, in a spirit of cooperation and civic-minded well-being, rather than living in isolated ignorance, and repeating each other's mistakes time and time again.

Creating this level of collective prosperity is not hard to do. Today, a new generation of developers is taking a different tack. The model really has its roots in HTML (HyperText Markup Language), the file format that makes up the basic building blocks of the Internet. This simple standard language, which enables all web sites to find and understand all other web sites with the use of an HTML browser, could easily have been produced as a proprietary, licensed entity. Instead, its creators opted to give it away. This awesome act of offering for free that which could have been sold at a profit has resulted in nothing short of a "multiplication of the loaves." The exponential amount of prosperity that has resulted from this initial act is astounding. By giving something away, HTML's inventors created an entire economy.

Mark Pesce and Tony Parisi, who developed VRML (Virtual Reality Modeling Language), a protocol like HTML that supports Virtual Reality and real-time 3D animation on the web, have taken this spirit further still. Beginning with an initial demo and a preliminary specification, they opened the entire process up to the 3D graphics community at large. Thus, the first and second VRML specs were created by a collaborative team consisting of everyone from the major software and hardware companies to independent programmers, artists, and renegade hackers. The spirit of the entire process has led to a shared tool that has been created to service an entire industry free of cost to anyone. Parisi and Pesce could have ostensibly created VRML themselves, and made a small fortune trying to market this thing as a proprietary, for-profit item, but they opted instead to practice social capitalism. Instead of creating a single entrepreneurial entity, they opted instead to create an entire industry; now that this industry has been created, Pesce and Parisi can find their entrepreneurial niche within it.

 The Birth of Cyberspace: 3D Comes to the Web (p. 97)

One of the things that characterizes the VRML industry, such that it is, is the spirit of cooperation that exists within this community. Because of this unprecedented move, a collective R&D project by a multiparty consortium, the VRML community is characterized by a surprising lack of competition. There are rivalries of course, but rivals can stand side by side in friendly competition and, to a certain extent, mutually supportive competition. This is the kind of healthy competition/cooperation strategy that will build a strong economy and benefit everyone in the end. Because the VRML community is so small, the general perception among VRMLians is that for the industry to succeed, they all must succeed. This is the essence of social capitalism. Following a philosophy similar to that of social democracy—that the individual is responsible for the culture as a whole and the culture is responsible for the individual—these companies understand that if the industry as a whole does not flourish, all will suffer. Because they are trying to create a mass medium, they understand (obviously a level of evolution from the previous generation) that a massive saturation of content will be required for the technology to be adopted into the mainstream. If you go to any VRML conference (at least at this point in VRML's progress), you will see that the mission for everyone is to get as much stuff out there as you can because at this point, we can only succeed if we *all* succeed. If any one of us goes down, it will make us all look bad. The industry is now just too small for everyone to be fighting. It is at a point where everyone knows each other personally; those whose ethics are questioned usually feel it in a big way. The older, wiser companies mentor the smaller companies, all aware that the ecosystem is at the point where it just needs more of every life form to become viable. A totally viable scenario, and one that would be rare in another environment, is a company that turns down a major project and then asks some associates whether they would start a company so that they could feed that and other projects to the new start-up. What this established company essentially does is create a source of potential competition; but what they see themselves as doing is maintaining their objectives of creating a certain kind of content, while helping to grow the industry as a whole. No one harmed…everyone profits.

 The Interactive Ecosystem (p. 233)

VRML is at the front end of its adoption curve at the writing of this book, but within a few months, all Internet browsers will come bundled with a VRML browser. With the creation of more content, and the refinement of the spec and browsers, VRML stands a damn good chance of making it into the mainstream. If it succeeds, it will create a new paradigm for how business can be done, and perhaps social capitalism will become the most viable economic paradigm for the 21st century.

SOCIAL COMPUTING

I can't remember the first time I heard the term "social computing," but I know that it rang loud as a bell to me. Due in large part to an early indoctrination at my first interactive job, I was trained to believe that the sole aim of interactive technology is to provide a venue for social interaction. Drilled into me in 1983, this philosophy wasn't too hard to subscribe to because I somehow understood it intuitively and naturally…it seemed somehow obvious to me that this was the best and most interesting use of a computer…as a way to connect people.

In 1983, Ed Schlossberg told us that interactive multimedia (which didn't really even have a name then) would never become a mass medium until it was recognized and cultivated as a social medium. I waited through a long incubation period for the CD-ROM (an inherently single-player device) to run its course, and watched with gratification when, in 1993, the web hit the mainstream like a gale wind. I must say, after waiting 10 years, the force with which the Internet seemed to skyrocket was a little dizzying even to me, a person better prepared than most for something like this to happen. But perhaps it was precisely the fact that I had been waiting so long that made the sudden explosion of interactivity so shocking. I remember a period of time when I could not help but burst forth with a yelp every time I saw an URL appear on my television screen. It was mind-boggling.

Most evolutionary curves are slow on the uptake and end with a burst of activity. The small mammal explosion of the Jurassic period was such just a burst of activity which subsequently led, in part, to the extinction of the dominant species of the day. In spite of their diminutive size, these tiny, quick, diversified species acquired a taste for dinosaur eggs, and the rest is, well... natural history. One can only hope that the Internet represents a parallel trend—perhaps the small but agile denizens of cyberspace will eventually devour the dinosaur conglomerates of mass media.

When asked what it is about the Net that gets everyone acting so crazy, all I can do is smile and say "social computing." People love it. They love communicating via cyberspace. They love the adventure of meeting new people, making new friends, the safe danger of exploring relationships that they might not explore in the real world. They love e-mail and Chat. Even if there is nothing to talk about, people love talking on the computer. Not since the telephone has anything really given us such a compelling social tool, and like the telephone, people use the Internet to communicate not only for practical reasons, but just as often, merely for the sake of communicating.

Some say we live in dangerous world. I can't see that our world today is any more dangerous than it was, say, during the Spanish Inquisition, or the American Revolution, or the Second World War for that matter. The world today *looks* more dangerous because it appears *smaller,* thanks to a contracting media universe. We see more of the world's dangers, and in more graphic form, than we ever have before. So, in a world perceived as dangerous, cyberspace creates a place of safe danger—a sanctuary where you can see, say, and do outrageous things with a certain measure of impunity. You can join in a kind of shared mindspace—a world where ideas and words take precedence over economic position and physical appearance, the things that seem to be of so much value in the so-called *real* world. In cyberspace, you can exist purely as a personality, or a persona...and you don't even have to leave the house.

I have a friend who says that he likes the Internet because it keeps people off the street who wouldn't be on the street anyway. Some critics insist that the Internet is leading to isolationism...but please, let's try to keep some perspective here. It is probably true that there are people who stay home more now that they are online, but there are a couple of other things to consider. Children who have both televisions and computers now spend more time at their computers than in front of their TVs. Granted, they're still not getting outside, but at least they are doing something to stimulate their minds rather than stagnate them. Even aggressive "twitch" games prove to be more conducive to brain development in children than television. Furthermore, as you measure the time of people who spend less time out and more time in, think about the people that were always in. The Internet has actually given a social life to those who "wouldn't be on the street anyway." Sociopaths, nerds, and even people whose isolation is involuntary, such as agoraphobics and shut-ins—who can suddenly get out of the house in a whole new way. The Starbright Foundation uses networked Virtual Reality in hospitals as a way to get terminally ill kids to play together in simulated space, "get out" as it were, and do things in cyberspace that their disintegrating bodies can no longer do in the real world.

 VICARIOUS EXPERIENCE (p. 504)

Furthermore, members of the so-called "digerati"—the denizens of digital culture, many of whom are the creators of these worlds—use the Internet to facilitate real-world socializing through mailing lists that keep people up-to-the-minute on various live events. The growth in webcasting creates a new way to bring live events to a wider audience, but also enables viewers at home to participate with the people at the real party or event.

 DIGERATI: THE ARTIFICIAL INTELLIGENTSIA (p. 164)

Avatar-based environments, most of which are still primitive and devoid of form and content, provide the capability to create and manipulate a virtual persona that can express different aspects of your personality. Such experiences have the potential to enable players to become players in the dramatic sense, creating their own theater and narrative environments.

 CYBERSPACE CADETS: VIRTUAL COMMUNITIES AND AVATAR WORLDS (p. 146)

Multi-user dungeons (based on the role-play game *Dungeons & Dragons*) have long been a mainstay of the Internet, before there was a World Wide Web, when you still had to be able to practically write code to get online. MUDs are text-based games in which each player uses a self-created character, with special traits and magical powers, to interact with other players/characters in a fantasy environment. This kind of interactive fiction, in which players create their own characters and write their own stories, has been a popular pastime among a small but avid group of gamers since as far back as the late 1970s. In fact, when I first started in the interactive industry, my assistant play test director, Athomas Goldberg, was a very active *Dungeons & Dragons* (D&D) player. He went on to create the virtual actors of *Improv*—autonomous characters that are preprogrammed to react to each other and actual humans to create dramatic improvised narrative experiences. Thus, the tradition of interactive, user-created fiction dates back to the early days of the Internet, and you can see its influence everywhere in the creations of interactive designers and storytellers today.

 VIRTUAL REALITY AS A DRAMATIC ART (p. 508)

ARTIFICIAL INTELLIGENCE AND THE PROSTHETIC BRAIN (p. 38)

Collaborative environments also provide another kind of venue for social computing. *Cityspace* from Digital Circus, is a collaborative VR city created by children. Computer technology, because it is active and interactive, acts as a catalyst for a much more creative audience environment than any other medium. In fact, if you look at the sale of software, the biggest moneymakers are not content-oriented titles, but creative tools. Several surveys have shown that women and girls in particular are more interested in the computer as a creative tool than as an entertainment medium…and here, perhaps, lies the secret. It should be no surprise to anyone that a title that combines creativity with entertainment, *Barbie Fashion Designer*, became the top-selling CD-ROM overnight, addressing a hungry market whose needs have been all but ignored.

 GIRL GAMES: THE NEW FEMININE MYSTIQUE (p. 202)

Women and girls in particular thrive in the social environment of the web. For women familiar and comfortable with both the telephone and the written word, the chat room is a natural. One of the things I and others have found in studies and tests is that women are not interested in experiences that isolate them. In fact, many women I've spoken to report playing *Myst* with other people, even though it is, technically a single-player game. But for women, the computer comes alive as a tool of creation and a tool of communication. Thus, when presented with the opportunity for social creation, they can and will readily find a niche in which they are completely at home, and perhaps even at an advantage.

 CYBERFEMINISM, OR, WHY WOMEN LOVE CYBERSPACE (p. 140)

In spite of all my rantings about the web as a social tool, I will always favor the social experiences that occur in a shared physical space. Multi-user interactive attractions in Theme parks, malls, and museums use technology in a social context without isolating us. The multi-user game model in arcades and the home consumer game market all focus on competition, on cultivating the computer as an anti-social medium. I prefer environments in which the social interaction is positive and collaborative in nature. In *Virtual Adventures*, for example, the cooperation between the players in a given submarine was the primary interaction of the game; the competition with other teams was secondary, and its main purpose was to create a challenge in the game, and to create more impetus for teamwork within the cooperating group. As a result, people came out of the game with a sense of connection with their team, more than a sense of competition with other teams.

 THE PRINCESS AND THE MONSTER: THE MAKING OF VIRTUAL ADVENTURES (p. 375)

Creating this sense of connection is a sharp contrast to a game such as *Battle Tech*, a VR attraction featured in several malls around the world. The goal of *Battle Tech* is to shoot your friends. You enter individual pods and take the role of giant killer robots with the sole purpose of annihilating everyone else in the game. The social highlight is at the end, when you emerge to the instant replay area to review as a group who killed whom when and how many times. This has been the overriding paradigm for social interaction in arcades and attractions since the 80s.

Out-of-home experiences such as *Virtual Adventures* enable people to get out of the house and come to a place where they can experience a level of social computing not available at home. Like going out to a movie, interactive entertainment becomes an event. We can enjoy high-tech entertainment and still be able to look each other in the eye and be part of an exciting theatrical experience. A variety of fine artists and cybercommunity organizers have also found ways of using computers as a social medium. Kit Galloway and Sherrie Rabinowitz have been using video and digital technology to bring people together since 1977. By compositing people together, they have created shared video space in which people can collaborate through dance, music, sign language, or just to hang out. They have also created collaborative digital art studios where people in remote locations can create art projects together. Their *Electronic Café* in Santa Monica (and its numerous international nodes) has become a headquarters for out-of-home social computing worldwide.

Myron Krueger is another artist who uses the computer to create shared social space. He converts video images of audience members into digital silhouettes that can play with each other, with him, and with autonomous creatures in a shared digital environment.

Virtual Reality and digital artists such as Christa Sommerer and Laurent Mignonneau, Perry Hoberman, and Karl Simms, to name a few, have all created diverse experiences that enable people to collaborate and play in evocative digital environments.

 MEDIASPACE (p. 293)

V-ART (p. 494)

Cyber-cafÉs, like the one I am sitting in as I write this, provide an interesting hybrid for those with cabin fever. I can go out and cruise the web in a social context, get on a C-U, See Me system with someone in a cyber-cafÉ halfway around the world, bring my friends down to show them my web site, and schmooze among fellow digital denizens while I sip a yogi tea with soy milk. Most cyber-cafÉs, by the way, are open until 2:00 am or later to accommodate the restless vampire-like lifestyle of many computer geeks. Cyber-cafÉs are a clear demonstration of the desire to connect, and to mingle among both humans and computers in a shared physical environment.

Whether safe at home in New York or North Dakota, hobnobbing with insomniacs at L.A.'s Cyber Java or London's Cyberia, there are an increasing number of options for social computing. What it has to offer on a cultural level is new ways to relate to each other, whether through the veil of the Internet, or face to face. New modes of communication and collaboration can open up new doors of perception beyond that of the individual mind and into the realm of a shared consciousness which ultimately cultivates our individuality while providing us with greater connectivity.

Cybersex and the Literary Renaissance (p. 144)

Danger: Killer App (p. 152)

Word to the Motherboard: Computers and Literacy (p. 530)

The Soul in the Machine

> Mechanization was never so vividly fragmented or sequential as in the birth of the movies, the moment that translated us beyond mechanism into the world of growth and organic interrelation.
> —Marshall McLuhan, *Understanding Media*

The film projector is perhaps the crowning achievement of the industrial age, because in form, it is the most mechanical and in many respects soulless of devices, but in content and expression, it is the most powerful art form yet devised by man. The relentless rhythm of frame after frame, 24 frames per second, speeding past a beam of light as it slips through socket grips, seems as heartless as anything you can imagine. It is also deceptively simple. In spite of its hard, mechanistic nature, the film projector issues forth some of the most emotionally compelling, moving, and soulful experiences created by the human mind.

To me, the computer also has the capacity to have that kind of power on the soul level. If we can create the same kind of emotionally powerful experiences on computers that we create on the movie screen, so that each individual can begin to not only feel the experience, but also to feel his or her own presence in it, then we have succeeded in breathing life into the beast. The power of the computer lies not it its capability to dazzle and engulf us, as with the cinema, but in its power to extend our natural talents and perceptions and make meaningful connections with others.

It is not that the machine has a soul in and of itself—quite the contrary. The soul of the machine is really just us. The machine is a medium in the same way that a fortune teller is a medium—it acts as a channel for spiritual entities to transact with the temporal world. The same is true of the computer. You can see the computer as a medium, an empty vessel through which meaning and soulfulness can transpire. As such, it is probably the most powerful tool we have yet created, but at the same time, the most challenging. In fact, I think everyone knows this, which is why, for some of us, using the computer to create meaningful transactions has become something of an obsession. But we struggle, as did the early filmmakers, with finding that soul, with uncovering the "arcanum," the ultimate answer that unlocks its power. Eventually, I believe this will happen. I believe that people will begin to create new paradigms in the same way the early filmmakers began to do so. A small handful of artists and content creators have already begun to pave the way. After a set of paradigms—a vocabulary, a set of shared understandings—has been established, and this is slowly beginning to happen, then we will have ourselves a machine with soul, in the same way that the film projector has soul.

Both the projector and the computer are instruments of light. The film projector projects light through a translucent film. The computer projects light directly at us from the screen. I think that in the interest of being media-conscious, we should take note of this in both its similarity and its difference. The medium derived from light passing through something is a very different medium than that in which the light is coming directly into your eyes without the benefit of an intermediary. In this case, we are looking directly into the light. In fact, in film, the light source is actually behind us, and the image bounces toward us off a reflective surface. By necessity, the light source in such a configuration must be at a far distance from us. With the computer, the light source is literally at arm's length.

 EINSTEIN, EISENSTEIN, AND THE SPACE-TIME CONTINUUM (p. 186)

The television is also light-emitting, but it is hypnotic. The distance from it, its orientation to us as we recline on a sofa or, perhaps more aptly, a Lazy Boy, is that the light transfixes us, holds us in place, immobilizes us to a certain extent. Sometimes, this passivity is desirable because it creates the sensation of relaxation, or forces us to be passive when we might have spent the rest of our day in a very active and aggressive mode. But the television has the power to hypnotize us even when we aren't necessarily seeking a passive role. Think of what happens when you are sitting in a bar, for instance, where a TV is playing. Suddenly you find yourself transfixed, even though in actual fact, you came there to visit or meet people; instead, you are suddenly sucked in;

even if the show is something you have no interest in; even if the sound is turned off, the television seems to somehow seduce the eyeballs with its mesmerizing flicker.

Remote Control Group (p. 410)

In sharp contrast with the film medium, which has the power to transport and transform us, the television seems like a rather soulless device. It is a rare moment when you derive from television the sort of transcendent experience you can derive from a good film. Movies certainly lose a certain measure of their zing in video format. Even on video, the content conventions of film—the two-hour feature—still seem to pack more of a punch than those of television. The sheer scale and visual quality of film absorbs us. The movie theater is a cathedral of sorts, a darkened ritual space of quiet and focus. That, and the fact that we devote a good two hours of our time to it, all make the film a more engrossing experience. The home-based television is less special some-how, and its content rarely has the cathartic power of the cinema. Because it lives with us in our house, its function seems mundane, a part of our daily routine, just another appliance, like our microwave or dishwasher. Perhaps if looked at in Aristotelian terms, we can see the television as a campfire and the cinema as the amphitheater. The television is more intimate and less cathar-tic, while the cinema is an event, a ritual, the modern-day equivalent of the large public theatrical productions of the Greeks, or even of Shakespeare's Globe Theater.

Nerd versus Couch Potato (p. 345)

There is a certain poetry to the technical framework of the computer. By simply manipulating ones and zeroes, by switching pixels on and off on a computer screen, by processing input through an elaborate construct of mathematical orchestrations, you can create a seemingly endless array of experiences and functionality. This simple atomic structure provides the essential building blocks to create the digital equivalent of the Sistine Chapel, or, using the film metaphor, *Battleship Potemkin*. As you manipulate the light and color on the screen with these seemingly soulless mathematical equa-tions, you suddenly break open a hole in the universe and out through this dry and logical contraption leaks a moment of epiphany.

The people who have been most effective at achieving this epiphany are, as always, artists. In the case of digital media, they are also alchemists—magi-cian/scientists who combine the rational and the supremely mysterious to become engineers of transcendence.

 V-ART (p. 494)

MEDIASPACE (p. 293)

OM MEETS OHM: DIGITAL ONENESS (p. 360)

SPATIAL MEDIA

The idea of a spatial interface—that is, a system for information navigation based on the metaphor of physical space—is by no means a new idea. Indigenous and professional architects have been using it for thousands of years. Any study of virtual space should begin with a study of real space. For indeed, most architecture is, to a certain extent, a form of interface design, whether the architect is aware of this or not.

 ARCHITECTURE AS A NARRATIVE ART (p. 25)

Temples, churches, and other religious edifices are perhaps some of the most content-rich forms of architecture we know. The design of sacred space in most cultures is based on a very sophisticated system in which every stone laid has some spiritual significance—the direction the building faces, its height, the location and orientation of the entrances, and so on. Within the interior spaces, everything is thoroughly planned according to a variety of conventions that might be more or less strict depending on the tradition and its guidelines.

Sacred spaces often contain some narrative elements—visual cues that either explicitly tell stories, such as the giant stained glass window picture books in a Catholic or Greek Orthodox Church, or implicitly convey them, such as the more minimalist cross you might see in a modern Baptist Church. In addition to narrative, sacred spaces also contain social cues that tell us what we are expected to do in that space, and set up certain hierarchical relationships between the people who use that space.

The Catholic tradition provides an excellent example of how to use space as an interface for information. The spatial interface within the church is really a highly developed form of information architecture—including not only pure content, as in the stained glass window, but also social cues that serve to reinforce culture, convention, and ritual.

Consider the traditional Catholic Church layout. Rows of pews face forward to a raised altar that is divided from the congregation by a low railing. For centuries, this was the standard layout for a Roman Catholic Church. Vatican II changed all that. In 1971, the leadership of the Catholic Church met in Rome in response to modern pressures that ultimately resulted in a variety of initiatives to formalize a more populist church theology. One outcome of this event was that the mass, which was formerly read in Latin, was now to be read in the vernacular language of the congregation. Another, lesser known change that occurred during this conference was in the actual layout of the worship space. Under Vatican II, the pew layout is actually in a semi-circular form, with the altar actually jutting out into the space and surrounded by pews. The railings were eliminated. Most Catholic churches built after Vatican II use this "altar-in-the-round" layout. In older churches, the mass is often performed in front of the railing, or the railing is removed entirely. The railing was originally used for people to lean on as they knelt to receive the communion, which was administered by the priest from behind the railing. Today, "lay ministers"—that is, specially ordained members of the congregation—serve the Host into their brethren's hands with both parties standing eye to eye at floor level. This sets up a very different dynamic and social hierarchy than what a priest friend of mine used to call the old fashioned "guppy" system— with the congregation kneeling supine, open-mouthed, waiting for the priest to insert the Blessed Sacrament.

Changing the mass from Latin to popular languages also had a strong, though less obvious, effect on the physical layout of the church. Traditional medieval and Renaissance churches are full of narrative content. This is not merely for decorative or even for inspirational purposes. It is because at that time, most of the congregation could not understand what was read during the mass. The images on the wall, a form of informational graphics, provided them with a visual map of the content of their religion. Thus, these archetypal images were not only there to represent theological concepts, but also to depict events so that the illiterate churchgoer could, quite literally, follow the story.

Perceiving physical space as a form of information navigation enables you to better understand how and why "virtual space" can be a very effective way to manage and relate to information and content. You need only enter a public library to see how a space can become a form of information architecture.

There is a strong pedagogical basis for using space to navigate information that dates back as least as far as Aristotle, who developed the concept a "virtual house" to aid memory. During the Middle Ages and the Renaissance, several philosophers, including John Dee, Robert Flood, and Mario Piti developed more elaborate constructs for using the visualization of physical space as a way to enhance memory. Mario Piti developed the notion of the "The Memory Palace." Based on the observation that objects in physical space could provide strong triggers to memory, these mental interface designers developed a system of memory recall based on visualizing a physical space into which they could place information. By using this "information space" within their own minds, they could then increase and enhance their own memories. Robert Fludd, a Jesuit priest, used this method to memorize biblical and religious texts for a missionary journey to China, for which carrying a library of books would have been untenable. He thus made himself into a human library. Perhaps this could be considered an early form of portable computing.

Even these medieval philosophers had a sense of the power of physical space as a metaphor for the mind and a method for managing information. At the turn of the century, educational innovator Maria Montessori created three-dimensional heuristic toys for preliterate children, designed to teach principles of mathematics, logic, organization, and even language. Through this "hands-on" approach, Montessori discovered that by using other parts of the mind—parts that deal with kinetic involvement, tactile feedback, and spatial rotation and navigation—children could learn fairly complex principles at an early age. These heuristic devices were placed in the context of a highly developed physical layout that organized these experiences by content, and used visual cues, such as outlines on shelves, to teach pre-school children how to maintain order in their environment. Because the understanding of navigation through physical space is perhaps the most primitive form we have of interfacing with the world, it was no wonder that this was the best method for teaching a small child. In fact, even laboratory animals can be taught to navigate physical space and to remember and recognize "zones" that represent certain events, such as being fed or receiving a mild electrical shock. Thus, it is fairly clear that this understanding of space, and the use of space as a signifier of information and memory, is shared by many ambulatory creatures. Even non-ambulatory creatures have a have a certain sense of space. Plants lean toward the sun, gravitate toward water, and in the case of vines, find their way to the nearest clinging surface. Who knows, even rocks may remember where they've been.

The graphical user interface that is a convention on most personal computers today is based on the metaphor of a desktop. Although the metaphor is a bit stretched in my opinion (I would look for a stapler and a telephone on my desktop, as well as a cup of tea and pictures of my family, but anyway...), it is clear why the implementors arrived at this desktop idea.

 THE PEDAGOGICAL MOUSEPAD, OR, HOW IT ALL GOT GUI (p. 365)

Think about your own actual desk at home and you will begin to understand the power of spatial perception and memory. What would you do if you needed, say, a pencil, or a hole puncher? Think about the location of that letter you have to answer, or where you reach to grab your dictionary. If you pay attention, you will realize that most of what you do at your desk has become a reflex. You do not have to think about your actions each time. You don't have to try to remember where you put the dictionary, or where the pencils are. Even if you can't see it, your hands know that the dictionary is 23 degrees over your right shoulder—you simply grab for it, and there it is. You can put this to the test in the following way: Get someone to call you from your desk some time and try to tell him or her where certain things are located. Look at your own process of remembering. Most of the time, you will visualize the space, and even imagine yourself reaching for the item in question. There are likely to be instances in which you know exactly where something is, but you are at a loss as to how to explain this to someone else. Once in your own space again, of course, you can find it with no trouble.

Driving a car is another obvious way to be aware of the unconscious ways in which your mind and body works integrally to understand physical space. Have you ever had the experience of driving for a period of time and becoming lost in thought? At a certain point, you regain awareness and find that you have progressed a certain distance with no conscious memory of how you got there. While your mind is preoccupied with other things, your body and senses can still navigate and maneuver the vehicle safely. Now, think about this: a day or week later, you drive that same route. Although you might have no memory of the directions, your body seems to know the way, even if your conscious mind does not. In this case, you might find that any attempt to describe this "forgotten" route to a third party would be impossible, and yet you know exactly how to get there. How many times have you given inaccurate directions to a location that you yourself could get to with your eyes closed?

 BEEN THERE, DONE THAT (p. 86)

If you have children, watch them. Watch them as babies as they begin to crawl around and explore; observe as they begin to understand and remember their environment, as they become more agile in their interactions with it.

As you become more sensitized to the way people relate to physical space, you will begin to understand the tremendous power of Virtual Reality. Of all interface paradigms, VR is the most primitive, the most intuitive, the most authentic, and the most like "real life." In theory, even a laboratory rat could navigate a Virtual Reality system, and a small child certainly could.

There is a popular misconception in today's "be here now" digital culture that spatial interfaces and Virtual Reality are a "new technology," but this is completely false. In fact, the 3D Virtual Reality interface actually pre-dates the 2D graphical user interface by about five years.

A BRIEF HISTORY OF REAL TIME: THE VIRTUAL REALITY LEGACY (p. 105)

I want to elaborate a bit on what I mean when I say spatial interface, because not all spatial interfaces are Virtual Reality. The CD-ROM products *Myst* and *Seventh Guest*, to use two easily referenced examples, use a spatial interface metaphor. Neither of these applications is, however, Virtual Reality. VR is defined as "real-time 3D animation." This means that in theory (technology notwithstanding), you can move smoothly through the space as if it were real. As you navigate, everything changes position in relation to where you are located, and each time you change position, the world and its contents respond by changing their relative position to you.

 VIRTUAL REALITY CHECK: WHAT IS VR ANYWAY? (p. 518)

VIRTUAL RELATIVITY (p. 524)

There are numerous examples of spatial interfaces that are not VR in the classic sense, yet have been quite effective. Perhaps the best known of these spatial interfaces is *The Aspen Project*, which was done at MIT in 1983 and became the impetus for the MIT Media Lab. Like many high-tech projects, and virtually all early VR, this show was made possible by a generous grant from the Department of Defense.

The Aspen Project was developed as a research project for training soldiers, although the actual application itself was peaceable enough in its implementation. Nicholas Negroponte's team set about to create a model of Aspen, Colorado, selected based on its small size and straightforward layout. The team traveled through the city with a video camera attached to an automobile and videotaped, in increments, every street, intersection, building, and so on. These images were shot in such a way that they could be linked together to create the illusion that you were moving freely through the space. Interestingly enough, the entire project was delivered via laser disk through a fairly elaborate system of branching.

The Aspen Project used route mapping as a way to navigate Aspen and to get information about the town. You could enter, for example, the Police Department, and hear from the town sheriff, see his office, and get a look at the most recently posted fugitives.

The spatial interface of *The Aspen Project* could be used to access anything from the books in the library to newspaper clippings to historical information about the town. So instead of reading a book, or even seeing a film about Aspen, you could learn about the town through a simulated tour that resembled a real tour of the town. This application also had the added value of providing a front end for information that you could not access by navigation through the actual town of Aspen.

Vicarious Experience (p. 504)

In the 1980s, Kathleen Wilson of the Bank Street College of Education created an educational demo for an early consumer set-top box platform. Like *The Aspen Project*, *Palenque* used a branching system based on photographs of a real site. People could visit and explore the ancient Mayan ruin, and through it, they could then access historical information, see relics, and understand the physical site in its cultural context. Because of the failure of the platform it was written for, *Palenque* never made it to a broad market, but it was shown at many conferences in the museum world at that time as a prime example of how interactive media could be used as an educational tool for museums. A decade later, VR researchers began creating fully immersive real-time models of ancient ruins, in this case, using VR to reconstruct them as they originally appeared, complete with indigenous events, such as sacrificial offerings.

In 1993, *Myst* brought attention to the spatial paradigm in the CD-ROM entertainment medium. Although spatial interfaces had been used before in entertainment titles, most were decidedly 2D. *Myst* uses a well-orchestrated network of beautifully rendered stills. The three-dimensional quality of the images, combined with ambient audio and moodiness of the content, provides a compelling experience of physical space with relatively few technological pyrotechnics. It's not just that the environment of *Myst* is a physical space, but that it has a sense of place. Along with *Seventh Guest*, another spatially based CD-ROM product of the same period, *Myst* introduced a new interface convention: a cursor/pointer that enables the player to navigate through space, turning left or right by moving the cursor to the desired part of the screen. The cursor changes form depending on where it is on the screen to let you know what your options are. In *Seventh Guest*, the interface uses a skeleton hand that beckons to you and points the way to the available options. Neither of these games use text prompts of any kind, nor is there any interruption to the story flow. They are not "nonlinear" stories in the traditional sense. Both titles also have the eerie quality of a deserted world. In *Myst*, of course, the deserted environment is part of its charm and mystery: Where did all the people go? *Seventh Guest* has the occasional arrival of actors, a cast of characters, but their intermittent and somewhat out-of-context appearance can sometimes seem abrupt and awkward. In any case, both titles brought the idea of a spatial interface into the consumer realm in a big way, adding a new convention to the repertoire of interactive designers.

 Myst-icism (p. 325)

Spatial interfaces have a number of advantages, but as pointed out earlier, perhaps the greatest of these is their universal accessibility. *Myst* manages to have probably the broadest appeal of any CD-ROM game, which is probably due in large part to its spatial interface. The spatial interface seems to work equally well for everybody, although there are certain styles of real-time interaction that might be stronger or weaker for different market segments.

One of the most narrow but profitable of these market segments is of course the adolescent male and the consumer/arcade game market. Traditionally, arcade games took place on a fairly flat landscape. Classic "twitch" games such as *Sonic the Hedgehog, Donkey Kong,* or *Super Mario Brothers* are based on a kind of animated version of the classic board game *Chutes and Ladders.* Although there was the occasional 3D game along the way, it wasn't until about 1994 that the arcade industry began to add dimensionality to their standard bag of tricks. This began a widespread trend that led to an evolution in arcades where the vast majority of new games coming out use a real-time, 3D paradigm. Although the games themselves have changed little, fighting games such as *Virtua Fighter* and *Mortal Kombat* bring a new level of realism to the combat genre.

 IT'S ONLY A GAME: THE BIRTH OF A MULTI-BILLION DOLLAR BUSINESS (p. 260)

From *Myst* to *Mortal Kombat* is quite a leap, but it brings home the point that spatial interfaces are as diverse as they are accessible. They can be fast or slow, beautiful or ugly, narrative or twitch. They can exist as navigational space or narrative environment. They can be used as an entry point for educational content or for pure entertainment.

When you get into real-time VR (covered in more depth in another chapter), you will see that the early VR applications focused primarily in two areas: design tools and simulation training. Early CAD (Computer Aided Design) systems enabled automobile designers, for example, to make a model of a car and simulate drag coefficient by using wind algorithms. Today, all commercial airlines use VR as the primary training tool for new pilots. The military also uses VR extensively for military simulations including war games, tank simulators, and other forms of military training. Finally, VR has been used for many years to train astronauts for space travel; for this it is particularly ideal because VR enables the creation of conditions that you could not otherwise re-create in the real world.

The medical profession uses real-time 3D modeling (a form of Virtual Reality) for training as well as for visualizing and understanding physiological systems. Navigable models of the human body create three-dimensional views of anatomy that are nearly impossible to view through any other means besides dissection. The capability to shift scale and viewpoints also allows for views that even dissection or surgical procedures cannot provide. These navigable models can also be combined with tactile feedback systems that enable surgeons to learn a procedure not only by sight, but also by touch. Models such as these enable students and doctors alike to become familiar with the human body without actually having to crawl inside it.

In a more abstract way, 3D can also be used to manage and explore data. Information architecture in its purest form deals with the notion of using space as a metaphor for ideas. Most of the applications of real-time 3D that I've been talking about are content-driven experiences that create a literal or fantastical 3D world. All these worlds, for example, contain buildings and people, or people-like creatures (as in the case of *Mortal Kombat)*, or models of actual objects; however, 3D metaphors and systems can also be used as a way to structure datasets.

William Gibson, in his short story collection *Burning Chrome*, gave us the first glimpse of a data architecture system. He called it "The Matrix"—a giant network that linked together all information in the world through an elaborately constructed virtual city consisting of blocks of data, security walls, and bit-eating viruses. Gibson's characters, many of whom were themselves augmented through computer chip implants, could wire themselves directly into this Matrix in pursuit of various data, or purely malicious intent, or both. In Gibson's scenario, brainwaves and bits are interchangeable, creating a neural network in which the boundaries between computer and human become very fuzzy.

Although the Matrix represents a highly abstracted dataspace, some information architects find it useful to utilize metaphors and techniques from real architecture in their information spaces. One such company is Construct whose abstract virtual architecture suggests a Matrix-like environment on the web (see figure S.1). Another information architect working on the Internet is Clay Graham. A pioneer of VRML-based (Virtual Reality Modeling Language) 3D on the web, Graham brings a strong architectural sensibility from the real world into the world of information navigation. He uses many traditional architectural conventions of spatial orientation and organization as a way to organize information and data. These information structures, with their elegant and simple form, offer the user a navigation metaphor that is familiar without being literal. As a result, information can be organized in a way that creates a sense of place, as well as a way to both present and gain access to information (see figures S.2–S.5).

Figure S.1

Construct's virtual architecture (image courtesy of Construct)

 PLATE 48

Figure S.2

ArtSpace, a virtual building showing a clear path and goal relationship, links to essays on space, place, symbol, and sign

 PLATE 52

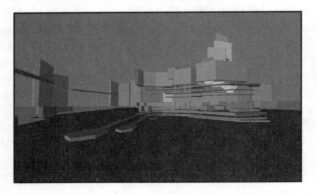

Figure S.3

In the *Virtual Playground*, Clay Graham combines elements of Le Corbusier with embedded information layers using VRML

 PLATE 51

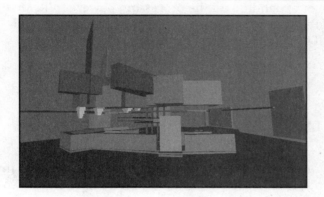

Figure S.4

The absence of texture mapping in early VRML forced Clay Graham's *Virtual Playground* to focus on three-dimensional form

Plate 5 3

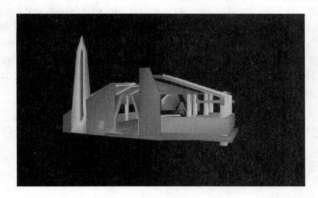

Figure S.5

This virtual building, designed by Clay Graham for Autodesk, suggests an almost church-like ritual space

Plate 5 4

Clay and other information architects use Virtual Reality to visualize information in a wide variety of ways. While at Silicon Graphics (manufacturers of high-end 3D graphics computers), Clay created an information space representing the personnel at the company. Each employee was represented as a column in the space. A horizontal axis provided a dateline and each column had a start and end point based on that individual's tenure at the company.

Navigational interfaces, or "spatial media," really constitute an entire class of experience within the interactive sphere. The following describes several genres that can be classified under the general heading of "Spatial Media."

Spatial Interfaces

Games such as *Myst* are not Virtual Reality, but use what I call a "spatial interface," a form of faux Virtual Reality. You cannot move through the spaces nor manipulate images in real time in *Myst* and therefore it is not VR. There are many other ways to exploit the advantages of a spatial interface without going to all the trouble or expending all the processing power of VR. *Myst* would not be greatly enhanced by real-time interaction; its series of well-crafted still shots are all that's required for the desired effect.

 GAINING PERSPECTIVE: THE EVOLUTION OF DIMENSION (p. 196)

ARTIFICIAL REALITY

Artificial Reality is a term first coined by artist/engineer Myron Krueger in the 60s. Krueger's pioneering "responsive environments" were not Virtual Reality in the Sutherland sense, but were an attempt at creating an immersive environment through media and computation. Krueger made his own contraptions and merged media in a variety of different ways to merge the real world with the artificial. Much of his work revolved around play and audience involvement, multi-user applications, and breaking the fourth wall between media and reality. People were videotaped and placed into simulated worlds where they could change the lighting and sound in an actual room by merely walking on the floor.

 MEDIASPACE (p. 293)

AUGMENTED REALITY

Augmented Reality is a term used by Nicholas Negroponte and denizens of the MIT Media Lab to describe applications such as *The Aspen Project*. *The Aspen Project* used a navigational system based on branching between videotaped segments of drives down each street in Aspen, Colorado. Created on laser disk in 1983, the video added to the realism of the tour, but it was impossible to go off the beaten path, as you most certainly can in VR. Although I will no doubt get tomatoes hurled at my head for saying this, I find the term "augmented" reality to be misleading. Augmented means, essentially, enhanced, not simulated. To me, Myron Krueger's digitally enhanced installations feel more like reality that is augmented than a video-based simulation of a town. Be that as it may, this is the term that has been applied to this kind of work by its developers, so being a purist and all, I won't say much more than that.

Simulations

Simulation is a general word that comes up a lot in discussions of VR. A simulation is, quite simply, a model of a system. It is not necessarily a 3D model, but it can be, and there are many ways that computers can be used to model systems, and some can even exist purely in the form of data without any graphical correlation, such as simulating environmental impact of a new real estate development or calculating birthrate statistics against such things as diet and economic development to anticipate future population growth. The classic desktop computer game *SimCity* simulates systems within a city environment where you can build factories and bridges, rezone for new residences, change environmental restrictions, and see the results as the computer calculates all the variables of your input with the simulated processes under way. Simulations don't necessarily require computers either. Predating *SimCity* by some 15 years was *The World Game*, a giant board game played on a world map designed by Buckminster Fuller to simulate resource management on "spaceship earth." Ivan Sutherland and his partner Dave Evans designed some of the first computerized flight simulators, but there were actually mechanical flight simulators used prior to this that enabled pilots to practice before taking off. In general, simulation is a great tool for teaching and research, and it can also be highly entertaining.

Whether abstract or literal, metaphorical or archetypal, content-driven or data-driven, spatial interfaces provide a compelling and practical means of communication between human and machine. Although it is still difficult to get a computer to understand a human, an understanding human with a strong sense of design can act as a translator, giving the computer user an easier port of entry. Thus, spatial media and navigational interfaces, drawing from real-world paradigms and metaphors, provide an elegant and effective way for a computer to speak to the human in his or her own language.

Narrative Environments: Virtual Reality as a Storytelling Medium (p. 329)

Psycho-ergonomics (p. 404)

Cyberspace Cadets: Virtual Communities and Avatar Worlds (p. 146)

V-Art (p. 494)

Mediaspace (p. 293)

STEAL THIS DATA: SHAREWARE AND THE HACKER ETHIC

The birth and rise of digital technology is an amazing tale rife with wild characters, wonderful anecdotes, and dramatic legends of heroism and demise. It is a classic tale of "revenge of the nerds." The people who created this multi-billion dollar business are often the same people you made fun of in elementary school. Billionaire hippie geeks abound, and the least likely characters are likely to end up as legends.

You can track the history of computer evolution as an ongoing back and forth between two diametrically opposed cultures. On the one hand, you have the Department of Defense, who provided the substantive research and funding support to make it all happen in the first place; and on the other hand, you have the subversive hacker element, with its ruthless cleverness and rebellious disregard for convention. Between these two cultures, a spark was lit, and a movement was born.

In the academic and defense realm, eccentric hackers abound. Students at the first MIT computer lab would fight for punchcard time, sneaking in at all hours of the night, and giving birth to the pizza/Coke lifestyle. These obsessive geniuses relished in the knowledge that they were more clever than the establishment, even though they flourished within it. They were constantly pursuing crazy projects, such as getting the computer to play chess with numbers, or designing games such as *Spacewar!* and *Mouse in a Maze*. Although these guys might not have been in the picket lines with their hippie counterparts, they certainly shared many of the same qualities, not the least of which was a total disregard for authority.

 THE PEDAGOGICAL MOUSEPAD, OR, HOW IT ALL GOT GUI (p. 365)

The hacker movement and the current Digital Revolution owe a lot to the 60s and the hippie movement. The stereotype of the long-haired, drop-out genius coder is very much based in fact, and if you think about it, it makes perfect sense. The hippie movement got off to a good start, but got tripped up by a rapid-fire series of events that were essentially the hose on a bonfire. These included the assassinations of Dr. Martin Luther King, Jr., John and Robert Kennedy, and the subsequent resignation of Richard Nixon in the mid-70s in the face of a national scandal. All these events took the wind out of the sails of what otherwise might have been a true revolution. The messages sent out to the populace were:

- If you try to do anything good within the traditional means, by government or civil action, you will be killed.
- Corruption in government will prevail.

I believe that these events precipitated what some say is the Post Political Age—the age when politics is no longer considered a valid or viable means to affect social change.

For the title of this chapter, I co-opted (bootlegged?) Abbie Hoffman's suggestion to "Steal This Book" ("Steal this slogan?") because it echoes loudly through the corridors of cyberspace, where shareware and the idea that information should be free, just like the air we breathe, is the prevailing ideology of the hacker ethic and the Digital Revolution.

The rise of the PC mythos is really a story of hippie hackers gone haywire. Bill Gates, Paul Allen, Steve Jobs, and Stephen Wozniak were all hippie hackers. Each of the "opposing teams" built an empire based on "stealing this data"— Jobs on the graphical user interface he reverse-engineered from Xerox PARC; Gates on the operating system software he bought for a song from a tiny outfit and resold to IBM as DOS; and now Microsoft Windows, the lowbrow version of the Macintosh interface. No one can fail to see the irony of these former hacker/plagiarists going on to become license mongers of the "We Own Everything" variety.

 ## Kiss My Asset: The Content Wars of the 1990s and the Birth of Transmedia (p. 269)

The hacker ethic states that you will get more by giving something away. Hackers like to show off and they like to share. The best example I can use to talk about this idea today is HTML. For those unfamiliar with the term, HTML (HyperText Markup Language) is the standard protocol for the World Wide Web and the Internet. It is this simple across-the-board standardization that enables any web page in the world to connect to any other web page because they are, in essence, speaking the same language. VRML (Virtual Reality Modeling Language), a protocol for VR on the web, enables standardization and interchangeability of 3D models and environments. Both HTML and VRML were not created as commercial products, but as standards for use by anyone, anywhere, totally free of charge. The result is pretty clear. The inventors of these protocols succeeded in creating an entire economy, indeed, an entire virtual country, by giving something away. Imagine what would have happened if you had to pay a licensing fee to get or use HTML. In short, the Internet would still be a communication device for the military and educational institutions.

If you look at how people deal with the shareware ethic within the constraints of a licensing agreement, you will see a different pattern. I see a fair amount of evidence in favor of the argument that bootlegging software has actually helped the industry, and helped the economy. I doubt very much that the rise of Apple would have been as strong if they didn't make it so damn easy to install, and therefore, bootleg software. People who might not otherwise have bought hardware were spurred on to buy computers because they knew they could get the software from friends. When we were buying computers in the mid-80s, the idea was to buy the computer that ran the software you wanted. So if you knew you had access to the software, then the hardware purchase became a lot more attractive, and in some cases, feasible.

I am a great believer in software bootlegging. As an independent consultant without access to huge corporate software budgets, I would never have been able to have or use a computer if I were forced to purchase all the expensive software I need to run my business. I find it very difficult to feel sorry for Bill Gates or Paul Allen, both of whom, if I'm not mistaken, are in the Fortune 500. I don't have the sensation that I am taking food out of the mouths of starving children by using a bootlegged version of MS Word.

 APPROPRIATION AND THE POST-MODERN ETHIC (p. 20)

As a tool for enabling large-scale democracy, the computer is the direct descendent of the Gutenberg Press. In fact, McLuhan and others argue that perhaps there would be no democracy if not for print media. The printing press enabled us to *replicate* information for the first time, which is precisely why it's called *mass* media. For those who don't know, some of the earliest applications of print were not as items for sale, but propaganda created for mass distribution. It is exactly this ease of replication, this explosion not only of information, but of information *reproduction and distribution*, that is responsible for the current Digital Revolution. I believe this revolution will have as much of an impact on our so-called democracy as the printing press did on the feudal and monarchic systems.

In my opinion, the social and economic benefits of piracy far outweigh the economic losses incurred. In fact, you could make a sound and verifiable argument on the premise that piracy is actually *good* for the economy at large. Software bootlegging actually creates jobs. It creates businesses. It facilitates a spirit of entrepreneurship.

The idea of passing software tools around, contributing to their multiplication, and spreading them like a happy virus from machine to machine is a beautiful and subversive thing. Besides, there's not a hell of a lot that can be done to prevent it.

The hacker spirit is alive and well on the World Wide Web, where shareware and freeware are regularly offered up for public consumption. On the Internet, hackers roam free, mostly having a good time, but every once in a while, committing acts of digital terrorism to keep us on our toes.

Whether you are a hacker, a surfer, or a web-spinner, you can benefit from the essential spirit of the hacker ethic: that all information should be free, that knowledge is power, and that if you have a computer and know how to use it, you can do just about anything.

 SOCIAL CAPITALISM (p. 425)

AUTODIDACTIC COMMUNALISM (p. 83)

INTERACTIVITY IS SUBVERSIVE (p. 244)

STROLLING THROUGH CYBERSPACE: SECOND NATURE AND THE VIRTUAL GALLERY

At SIGGRAPH 95, I produced an interactive community-based project called the lounge@siggraph which included *The Virtual Gallery*, an original demo project in collaboration with a military research center at Utah State University in Logan, Utah called Space Dynamics Laboratory (SDL). SDL's Dean Garlick contacted me after SIGGRAPH 94 to see if I was interested in putting a demo together with them. They came up with an interesting idea for an interface and wanted to know if I'd like to develop a game demo for it. It wasn't until February of the following year that I finally got the chance to come see these guys (Logan, Utah, about two hours out of Salt Lake City, is not the sort of place I frequently find myself).

These guys, you have to remember, specialize in very high-end military satellites, and this group in particular, focused on creating computer models of the earth's topography using infrared mapping and 3D computing techniques. But they came up with this really cool idea for an entertainment product, and they didn't quite know where to turn. The interface used a treadmill that enabled you to navigate through a virtual world by simply walking. When they first presented the idea to me, they had not yet fully conceived how you would turn in the space. At first, we considered a hand-control device on a bar in front of the monitor. But then we decided that one of the criteria for this thing would be that it would involve no hand-held controls, no gloves, and best of all, no Head-Mounted Displays. We explored a number of different options—video input, full body infrared tracking, and so forth, and came to the conclusion that the easiest thing would be to isolate a body part that we felt could cue us into the user's desired direction. We tried shoulders, hips, I think they even experimented with knees, and finally arrived at a solution that was so simple it seemed almost preposterous: when people want to turn, the first thing they do is look in the direction they want to turn, and when they look in the direction they want to turn, their head turns. So all we had to do was use a very small infrared tracker to measure very subtle head movements and we could get a very accurate positioning to determine direction. To facilitate 3D audio, I ended up finding a cool audio dome system by Brown Innovations that hung a couple feet above the player's head and delivered 3D audio without requiring a worn head set.

After we resolved the interface problem, it was time to develop some content. I proposed an idea to SDL that I had been mulling around with for a while which was called, for lack of a more original name, *The Virtual Gallery*. It was based on my own experience of going to museums since childhood: I would stand transfixed in front of a painting for as much as a half an hour at a time, trying to imagine what it would be like to live inside the world depicted by the painter. The idea of *The Virtual Gallery* was to create an art gallery where each painting was actually a window or portal into a 3D environment that housed a VR interpretation of the painting. This idea was inspired by viewing several virtual museum projects in which all the art was flat. It seemed to me that if you were in a 3D space, the art you were looking at ought to be 3D too, and since it's Virtual Reality, you could blur the line between the two in a really interesting way.

All of the models were built by SDL staff and students, with the exception of a world based on MC Escher's multi-directional staircase room which was created by Eben Gay of ERG Engineering in Boston. We made models of Renaissance landscapes, paintings by Paul Klee, Magritte, and Van Gough. We built an entire house out of Matisse interiors. It consisted of five different paintings, each of which was a portal into one of five rooms in the house. You could walk from one room to the next and then walk out of it through the painting of the room you'd just entered. Marita Isaksson was also associate curator on this project, helping to select the paintings and coordinate production activities; Geer Madsen creative directed the sound design and also did the linework for the logo of the product, which was called "Second Nature."

The Virtual Gallery has some interesting features, some yet-to-be implemented. One of the issues was layout. We had a bit of a problem because there were quite a few paintings, and if you put them all in a single story, it would seem vast and unwieldy; this was of special concern because we were asking people to literally walk across the room, and they would get tired (which they actually did). So we decided to create a multi-level gallery. But we also wanted people to be able to see all the paintings from anywhere in the room, which proved to create a problem. So first, we decided to get rid of the walls and instead had the paintings floating in space; and second, we decided to get rid of the floors. The gallery was a large enclosed box with multiple levels and stairs leading between them, but which also had transparent floors. This layout evoked the sensation of walking on air, and if you wanted to change levels, you could just go up the stairs. To make exits out of the paintings back into the space, we provided a painting of the gallery within each painting world; thus, you could walk about of the painting through a painting of the gallery, if that makes any sense.

Eventually, I want to implement some other features. In a multi-user application, I want to create avatars for each space that are stylistically in keeping with the painting. In a Magritte space, for example, everyone would be seen as a floating bowler hat. Matisse guests would be rendered as 2D dancers or other Matisse paper-doll like characters.

I want to say a few words here about this treadmill interface, because as always, there were a number things about it that really surprised me. I intuitively knew it was a good idea when the SDL team first pitched it to me, because obviously walking is the way people normally get around. It was almost scary how obvious and simple an idea it was. That's why I called the product "Second Nature," also referring to creating a second universe (by the way, I've since found out that there is also a company with this name, so apologies to them if there is any confusion here). Anyway, it was clear that walking is about as intuitive as it gets. But it wasn't until the treadmill was installed and running for a week that I was able to really observe people on it and learn more about the subtleties of it. For most people, the physical exertion of walking, and the ease of use of the interface completely overshadowed the fact that they were seeing the image on a monitor, and not through any kind of so-called immersive device. In fact, most people completely forgot they were on the treadmill at all, and got totally absorbed in the experience. This fully supports my theory that immersion is a state of mind not a hardware device. The comment that surprised me most, and that I heard from almost everybody who gave it a whirl, was that they felt tired afterward. And they liked it. They enjoyed the fact that they had to exert themselves. It made the experience more realistic and absorbing, and really felt like they had traversed through physical space. This was a physiological by-product of the interface that we had not anticipated, although SDL has also marketed it as an exercise machine. The conclusion that I came to was that the psychological effect of the physical exertion was in part responsible for the suspension of disbelief that people experienced when they used it.

Although it has not yet been mass-produced as a commercial entertainment product, we hope somebody will create a VR attraction technology out of this device. The capability to produce high-end real-time graphics on lower-end computer equipment may someday make this a viable attraction product.

V-ART (p. 494)

PSYCHO-ERGONOMICS (p. 404)

APPROPRIATION AND THE POST-MODERN ETHIC (p. 20)

GAINING PERSPECTIVE: THE EVOLUTION OF DIMENSION (p. 196)

ART IS A VERB (p. 29)

T_VISION: SPACESHIP EARTH MADE VISIBLE

It is truly unfortunate that neither Marshall McLuhan, Buckminster Fuller, nor Charles Eames lived to see the design and implementation of *T_Vision*. *T_Vision* is perhaps the most comprehensive project to date that attempts to create a single, unified vision of the Earth. It is in essence, the realization of Fuller's conception of "Spaceship Earth," and McLuhan's notion that connected media creates a "global village." Interestingly, the project was inspired in large part by the Charles Eames film *Powers of Ten,* which takes the viewer through a progression of scales to the power to 10 as expressed through a view of the Earth. Starting at the macro level, the film and its companion book take you from the starscape to the molecular level. You start with a view of the galaxy and work your way "down to earth," ending up inside the hand of a picnicking human. *T_Vision* combines the vision of all three of these great men to create the Spaceship Earth Global Village to the Power of 10.

AUTOBIOGRAPHY OF AN AUTODIDACT, PART 1 (p. 45)

BUCKMINSTER FULLER AND THE DIGIDESIC DOME (p. 116)

In 1969, humans had their first stunning glimpse of their own planet from space. Reports back from the first moon landing were of a transcendent experience, both literally and figuratively, of seeing our planet as a tiny blue orb, a single and complete entity. It is ironic that the United States space program itself was, in large part, fueled by the utter disunity of Cold War techno-machismo, which required that we "keep up with the Kruschevs" or whatever. The fact was, this vision from space manifested the Earth as a single entity.

T_Vision's premise is so remarkably simple that it is one of those projects that was inevitable, like the invention of the lightbulb. Visitors stand and look at a projection screen. A large globe-sized sphere serves as the input device. As you rotate the sphere, you can orient it to your position on the earth as seen on the screen. You can also use buttons on the interface to change your orientation (that is, angle toward the earth) and to move backward or forward (see figure T.1).

Figure T.1

T_Vision: Viewing the earth onscreen via the globe/sphere interface (image courtesy of ART+COM)

The image you see on-screen is a virtual model of the earth that constantly pulls data from all the world's major earth databases in real time. At a distance, you can get up-to-the-minute weather maps showing cloud positions all around the world; as you move in, you begin to see specific weather data, such as temperatures on various parts of the planet. The system uses something called "levels of detail," or LOD, a method used in Virtual Reality to add detail as you move closer to an object. You can move in toward the Earth, and begin to make out the boundaries of continents. The imagery combines topographical models with satellite photographs to create as realistic as possible a depiction of the planet. As you move in closer, you get a bird's-eye view of a city or region (see figure T.2). You can switch between image types, a satellite image, to a photo, to a 3D model. You also have the opportunity to move through time via aerial views of the city at different periods in history. Camera icons on the city indicate places from which pictures were taken at various times. Click on one of these icons and you can see an image of that street a year ago or 20 years ago.

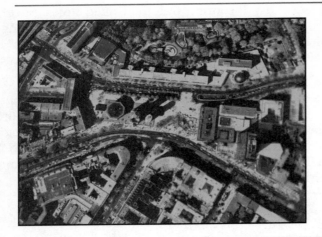

Figure T.2

T_Vision: The LOD system affords a satellite view of a city (image courtesy of ART+COM)

You can even enter a 3D model of the ART+COM office itself (see figure T.3). Click on the video camera in the window and you get a live feed of the clock on the church tower just outside—enabling you to check the current time where ART+COM's offices are located.

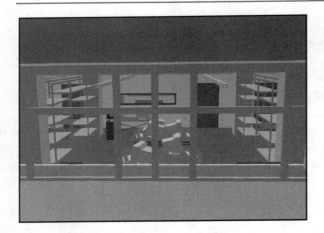

Figure T.3

T_Vision: Viewing a 3D model of the ART+COM office interior (image courtesy of ART+COM)

T_Vision, supported by both Germany and Japan, uses a high-end computer graphics engine and high-speed networking lines to grab images on the fly from databases all over the world. So when you look at the *T_Vision* planet, you will see the most current, high-quality imagery found anywhere in the world. The long-term goal of this wonderfully ambitious project is to eventually have access to data about every aspect of the earth at every level of scale (the system will go down to a viewing area of a few centimeters on the Earth's surface), perhaps all the way into the hand of a picnicker.

T_Vision is so vast in its scope that it is hard to imagine what it *can't* be used for. Its creators see it as a planning tool for World Powers…a dynamically interactive globe that ultimately provides access to virtually any data anywhere on the earth. *T_Vision*'s educational applications are obvious. As we create and accumulate more and more data about the Earth, and go about the business of digitizing everything, *T_Vision* can become a hub from which to access this information in a holistic and integrated way.

 SPATIAL MEDIA (p. 442)

THE DIGISPHERE (p. 168)

T_Vision makes visible that which we somehow all sense on a profound intuitive and spiritual level: Everything is one and as we go from macro to the micro, we see patterns of connectivity that span all the apparent boundaries that we live within on a daily basis. *T_Vision* uses a worldwide network to put the world in a single, manageable space, enabling the Earth to paint a self-portrait through technology.

When I hear people decry the evils of technology, seduced in part by the paranoid elaboration of Hollywood-induced melodrama, I want to invite them for a visit to a small planet via *T_Vision*. This project is as grand as it is simple, and in its grand simplicity, is perhaps the simplest statement that can be made of the potential wonders of technology put to good use. For in it, we see ourselves interconnected in a single continuum.

This is really the fruition of three major visionaries of the 60s, who, 30 years ago, brought us metaphors and structures for understanding what *T_Vision* so vividly illustrates: The earth can now be seen as a single entity brought together by technology that dissolves the boundaries of geography, scale, and understanding.

 EXPLODING OR IMPLODING: WHAT'S THE DEAL? (p. 191)

V-ART (p. 494)

A-LIFE OF ONE'S OWN (p. 5)

OM MEETS OHM: DIGITAL ONENESS (p. 360)

TEST FIRST, ASK QUESTIONS LATER

I cannot emphasize enough the importance and value of playtesting. I am not talking about the kind of playtesting where you let a bunch of teenage boys have a go at it two weeks before a project's done. What I'm referring to is design testing, preproduction testing, or what we used to call in the museum world "Formative Evaluation."

A couple of years ago, some friends of mine worked on a very expensive CD-ROM game. They didn't create any prototypes or perform preproduction tests for the game. They shot hours of expensive video and wrote thousands of lines of code. Two weeks before the programming was supposed to be completed—in other words, after it was far too late to do anything about it—they started testing. There were problems and it didn't matter because none of them were solvable at that point in the production path. So they might as well have not done the testing in the first place.

It was while I was working for Ed Schlossberg that I learned the importance of prototype and preproduction testing. I intuitively knew that with an interactive experience, there was no real way to know what was going to happen unless you figured out a way to simulate the game and let people do what they were going to do. Because you have no control over the outcome of the experience, you have to rehearse all possible outcomes, to make sure you haven't made some horrible, deadly error in either logic or gameplay...*before* you let the programmers at it.

In those days, mind you, there were no authoring tools, so there was no easy way to prototype software. Coding something was sort of like building a house. You wrote a spec, got a bid, and for some astronomical amount of money, these really smart guys who made everything seem impossibly complicated, would write the code for you, let you review it a couple of times, and then that was that. Despite the enormous amount of money you shelled out, half the time the programmers would only grant you a license, meaning that even though you paid for the code, they owned it. At ESI, we were doing all custom hardware configuration, so there was the expense of R&D and building the contraptions on top of the programming. Therefore, I wanted to avoid spending all that money before we knew if people really liked the games.

My partner in crime in this endeavor was an NYU film student and avid *Dungeons & Dragons* player named Athomas Goldberg. He was 18 years old and smart as hell and seemed to know exactly what to do without being asked. (It's always good having really smart young people around who haven't yet been ruined by college, and haven't yet been taught to believe in limitations.) After a stint as a set and lighting designer, Athomas went on to join Ken Perlin's group at NYU and co-developed *Improv*, a computerized drama engine consisting of autonomous characters that could interact with the user and each other.

ARTIFICIAL INTELLIGENCE AND THE PROSTHETIC BRAIN (p. 38)

VIRTUAL REALITY AS A DRAMATIC ART (p. 508)

The games we created at ESI varied wildly in style, logical structure, and player count, so each test required a completely custom design. We also learned from one of our mentors that it was dangerous to try to test everything at once. Instead, you need to pick specific things that you're concerned about and test them in isolation. Therefore, we tested some games multiple times, each time to study a different aspect of the game. After you isolate what it is you're going to test, you then come up with a test objective, basically a question you are asking that the test should answer. After you formulate the question, you need to ask yourself, What am I going to do with the information? You need to be prepared for that. If there's nothing you are going to do to change the game if the test results don't come out as expected, it's a waste of time.

We would develop step-by-step procedures for how to implement the test, and then bring in playtesters. Sometimes, particularly for test issues that were totally structural or logical in nature, we would just test with our own staff. But more often then not, we would bring in people from a list we had accrued of various supposedly "normal" subjects, mostly young adults from 18–35, which seemed to be our primary target market.

Note that these were not market tests and they were never intended to be. They were playtests, the purpose of which was to see what people would do within the game context. Many people shy away from testing because they think it has to be some kind of formal market test, or they follow the popular misconception that you need to test 1,000 people to get an accurate read. This is true for thorough market testing, but in terms of playtesting, it's not necessary. Most of the time, if a game's a dud, you only need about three player groups to figure that out. Depending on the game, how concerned we were about it, and what aspect we were testing, we would typically test anywhere from 4–10 groups.

We mocked the games up in a variety of forms. Some of the games that were more physical or mechanical in nature required building prototypes. We made the prototypes out of everything from two-by-fours to foam core to fishing poles. We tested one game that utilized full-scale elevator simulators in a scaled-down version first, to make sure it was a good idea, and then we did a full-scale mock up with cardboard and foam core to see how it would work. We tested the games that were more computery and less mechanical as card or board games, or in one case, as a kind of nonlinear book. An eight-player game that required heavy trading over a computer network required eight test administrators who would physically carry cards back and forth between players to facilitate trades. By doing this labor-intensive test, we inadvertently created a model of how many networked transactions per minute we could expect to have in the game, which helped us to better evaluate the game's technical requirements.

My favorite test was for a 40-player mystery game that was set up as a scavenger hunt. We rented out a fancy, if not somewhat dilapidated 19th century townhouse in New York's Gramercy Park, and invited 40 people up to play a mocked-up version of the game. It was great. We had all these people milling around trying to solve these mysteries, so we were really creating a simulation not only of the game structure, but of the social milieu of playing a game in this fashion.

We ultimately built three full prototype games in something we called "the mini-site," a small-scale version of the 45,000 square foot pavilion into which these 20-odd games would eventually be installed. Built as a promotional demo, this top-secret little venue was viewed by dozens of people throughout the 1980s, many of whom went on to develop their own LBE (location-based entertainment) products of their own. Although it was never completed, as far as I know, it was the first real attempt at creating such a venue.

We used this mini-site for testing as well as demoing, and in the course of two evenings, took over 200 people through. The second evening included repeat visitors because repeat play is a crucial aspect of the longevity of any interactive experience.

In this and all the other tests we did, we developed a pretty formalized system that consisted of the following steps:

1. We initiated the test with a proposal, which would be reviewed by the game designers, software and hardware teams, and so forth, who added any issues they wanted to test.

2. Observers at the test took notes on what people did. We followed each test with both a verbal and a written evaluation from the players.

3. In the case of full prototype tests, we had some diagnostic capabilities built into the game so that we could, for example, get a printout of how many trades were made during a game and by whom.

4. We then took all the data and generated a test report, which included the original goal and intent of the test, the procedure, the observations of the test team, any diagnostic data, player responses, questionnaire results, and so on.

5. Finally, we wrote a summary of our conclusions, and followed up with a list of recommendations for specific design changes we thought should be made based on the test data.

When we finished the entire testing process, Athomas and I wrote a document that outlined all the general things we learned from testing, and rules of thumb that could be applied across all our game design efforts.

I would have to say that of everything I've done in my life as an interactive designer, the process of testing these games was probably the most valuable episode in my autodidactic communalist education. Because it was during this time that I learned to be a psychologist. I learned about play styles. I learned what people liked and disliked. I studied the differences between males and females in a gaming environment. I learned about what it took to get people to interact with strangers (most of the people we tested didn't know each other), and what it took to get them to get over their passive or inhibited states into pro-active or interactive states. I learned about what confuses people. I learned how people learn, and how important it is for the *game* to teach them the rules, not the tutorial (one thing we discovered in our testing was that people almost never read directions). Most important, I learned how to make them forget about everything and just play.

 Psycho-ergonomics (p. 404)

I am sad to say that in the intervening years since I left ESI, I have had few clients receptive to my incessant demands for testing. One who did was Dennis Earl Moore, who hired me to project manage and co-design an interactive theater for the Biosphere 2 Visitors Center. Another was a recent client, Purple Moon, for whom I designed two card game products based on a CD-ROM. *Virtual Adventures* was inadvertently tested at a trade show, unfortunately, and had to undergo several significant modifications *after* it was released as a result. I begged them to let me have a schedule and budget for testing, but it never happened, even though all agreed it was important. As Steven Meyer (my technical director at ESI) used to say, "You always make a prototype; it's just a question of whether or not you sell it."

 Biosphere Meets Digisphere: The Biosphere 2 Interactive Theater (p. 91)

Girl Games: The New Feminine Mystique (p. 202)

The Princess and the Monster: The Making of Virtual Adventures (p. 375)

THEORY OF MEDIA EVOLUTION

To better understand the acclimation of media into the popular culture, I developed a theory of media evolution. This theory of media evolution recognizes a typical pattern of invention, dissemination, and acclimation of media into popular culture. In other words, this theory provides an overview as to how a given medium or media evolve over time. The theory helps to better understand the attrition rate of media, and the relationship between hardware, content, culture, and economics. It's particularly useful to content creators because they begin to form a diagram of what needs to happen for a new medium to come into it's own and develop its own unique genres and expressions. By no means is this the only such theory, but it comes from a unique the perspective: that of an "in the trenches" interactive designer trying to understand the cultural context of how media are adopted into the popular culture. By reviewing these past trends, I can then understand how my creations fit into a bigger picture, and avoid some of the pitfalls that result from ignorance of these fundamental patterns. Because content is the driving force beyond the acclimation a medium, content producers in all media should be especially concerned about these trends and patterns.

Several other sets of what I call "natural laws of media evolution" are associated with the theory of media evolution. These natural laws are subsets of the theory of media evolution that deal in more detail with certain aspects of media development. These subsets include the following:

- Theory of Media Evolution: The Four Axioms
- The Laws of Cumulative Media
- The Laws of Informational Entropy
- The Law of Reductive Media
- The Interactive Ecosystem

Media evolution is a very tricky business, if not more tricky than the evolution of living organisms. At each step in the process, any number of factors can conspire toward the ultimate failure or success of a "species" of media. The process might look something like a flow chart in which each crucial point can either send the medium to the next level or pass it on into extinction or obscurity. (In new media, we call this a niche market.) If a media species can make its way through each of these trials, it becomes, like a living organism, stronger and more likely to succeed. The process of Evolution occurs in the following phases:

- **Phase 1: Invention:** The physical invention of the media device.
- **Phase 2: First-Generation Content:** Early attempts at content, mostly derivative or generated by device inventors.
- **Phase 3: Second-Generation Content/Adoption:** Content watershed in which the medium begins to form its own conventions; market begins to adopt the new medium.
- **Phase 4: Third-Generation Content/Acclimation:** Medium fully realized with own unique content, standards, and conventions; mass market acclimation achieved.

PHASE 1 : INVENTION

Almost every new medium begins with an invention. Few new media start with content—they are generally initiated with hardware. This is ironic because—though invention is the necessary first step in media creation, a spark of electricity in the primordial ooze—it is invariably the content that makes or breaks the medium in the end. Nonetheless, the first step on the path is the device, and everything else emerges from there.

One thing we see a lot of in interactive media is a phenomenon called vaporware. Whether hardware or software, a technology qualifies as vaporware if it exists only as hype in the mind of its creators. It's not at all uncommon, say, for a hardware company to market a device that does not yet exist in operable form. It's not that hard to market vaporware, it's just impossible to sell it.

A new innovation has to have certain character traits to have a snowball's chance in hell of succeeding. The key factors involved are as follows:

- It has to work. Well.
- It has to be manufacturable.
- It has to be manufacturable in such a way that the first generation will be expensive but below a certain price threshold to support the first leg of the adoption curve, and then after a certain number of units can be produced, the price can drop significantly.
- It has to be content-friendly, which means flexible, capable of supporting a wide variety of different content, and relatively easy to produce quality content for.
- The content itself must be producible at a price threshold that will enable the medium to be profitable.

Even if you meet all this criteria, all you will have at the end of Phase 1 is basically a dumb machine—an empty vessel waiting for a raisón d'être. If this machine can accomplish all these things, however, it passes through its Paleolithic period, the equivalent of a Stone Age, and into the next phase of its evolution…

PHASE 2: FIRST-GENERATION CONTENT

It is often the case that the very first generators of content for a medium are the same people who invented the media device. This is necessary in order for them to "demo" their technology and prove to the world that it works (the Lumiere Brothers of film are a shining example). Although you are likely to see first-run content created by inventors, it is a rare thing to see an invention that was created by content producers. This is definitely a case where the chicken must precede the egg. So the next major hurdle the medium must get over is to seduce content producers into creating for it.

Generally, content producers for a new medium are brought in from other media. The first generation of content is almost always derivative—generally a matter of repurposing existing media or hybridizing other media to create new forms. The reason for this hybridization is that people will generally start from what they know. So if I am, for example, a director of stage plays, my first attempt at movies will naturally be something that looks very similar to a stage play.

Most early content in a new medium will be primitive and seem awkward—like a teenager who hasn't grown into full adulthood and doesn't quite know who he or she is yet. But it's very crucial that the medium has appeal to content producers, and that they are willing to step away from that which they already know (and are presumably successful at) and step into something new. It is often something inherently seductive in the technology that enables this to occur, but it can also have a certain amount to do with the personalities of the people or companies involved. Short-sighted technologists can kill an otherwise excellent medium by not opening the door wide enough to content producers; and some technologies, although weak, can prolong their life spans if their inventors can create enough incentive for producers.

Media producers at this point will generally divide into three camps regarding a new media device: those who don't care; those who are opposed to the new media; and those who are fascinated by it. It is often not the most successful artists from the old media that gravitate to the new. They have no motivation to do so because, well, they are already doing well at something that is a known quantity, so why rock the boat? There are always a few exceptions, and those are the artists who will always innovate no matter what comes their way. But to give an example, look how few film directors migrated to television; a few more radio people migrated over, but they weren't making as huge a leap in doing so.

It is often the second tier of "old media" people who will embrace a new medium. They tend to be younger, people who haven't achieved enormous success yet, but who are looking for a new path, a new arena to shine in. They might be more avant-garde, more experimental, and they will often come from an interdisciplinary background, rather than a high level of specialization, which enables them to adapt to and create new paradigms. Some are truly sparked by the new medium and its potential beyond that of other media, and these are the artists who generally pave the path for second-generation content.

A characteristic of this period is the variety of "novelty" applications. An excellent example is the infamous oncoming train clip which had audiences fainting and running out of theaters at the turn of the century. This is a classic example of a novelty piece which is at once an experiment in production, but also a way to test the audience and see how they respond to or adapt to the new medium.

In the meantime, another crucial factor comes into play at this point in the process is the introduction of a distribution channel. It is not enough to have a film and a projector. You must have a theater, too. It is not enough to have a TV and a program, you need to create a conduit between the two. After you develop a smattering of halfway decent, if immature, content, you need to figure out how to get it to the public. Lack of distribution can often be the death of a new medium, even if it follows all other paths of success previously indicated.

Almost any moderately good medium with the right price point can support a small early adoption curve niche market; however, this must expand fairly rapidly for the medium to go anywhere. Different media move at different rates. Movies, which started out at the turn of the century, weren't really in the mainstream until the 1920s. The CD-ROM market, for example, took a good 10 years to build up any kind of mass market momentum. The Internet took off in less than three years. One thing seems evident though: Looked at in a larger, historical context, the adoption curve time frame seems to be getting shorter and shorter with the introduction of each new medium.

Now, here's the really tricky part: You need to reach a certain level of critical mass to go to the next level. Why? The primary reason is economic. Up to this point in the process, people will have spent a lot of money with little return on their investment. Therefore, there has to come a point where there is money going back into the system for the system to evolve. If this does not occur, the medium will essentially starve to death, unable to compensate itself for past R&D, or support future development. A medium in its infancy is a money pit.

With money going in, you can then evolve the technology to the next level, specifically taking content into account. Before this point in time, the medium is designed as a container for something that doesn't exist yet. Once that container begins to be filled, even a little, you can revisit the technology with an eye toward better content, as well as better performance and cost-effectiveness.

Finally, if at this point in the process, the price point does not begin to drop significantly in response to a need for mass production or distribution, you can pretty much kiss your new medium goodbye. Early adopters can only take a medium so far; after their market has been saturated, you have to bring your price point down to the next level or you will either die, or, if you have a really killer technology, you may be able to survive as a niche market item. This isn't such a bad outcome, but it only works if your product is of extremely high quality. Also, niche markets are delicate ecosystems that can fall victim to deadly perturbations (disruptions in equilibrium) that lead to unexpected extinction.

All this said, it's very important to understand at this phase in the process the axiom that software sells hardware. No piece of hardware, no matter how fantastic it is, ever made it without having a significant amount of quality content to back it up. Just as in biological evolution, it is the number and diversity of a species that is the best assurance of survival. A weaker device can often prevail just by the virtue that it has more and better content.

PHASE 3: SECOND-GENERATION CONTENT/ ADOPTION

Second-generation content is the first indication that a medium is beginning to have a mind of its own. This type of content can be defined as the onset of craft. One of the hallmarks of this phase of development is the emergence of conventions and standards that become adopted into popular use. With his landmark 1915 film, *Birth of a Nation*, D.W. Griffith created what is widely credited as the first feature film. Griffith gave birth not only to a nation, but also to the mythos of "director" and to a set of conventions that have stayed with us to this day. Prior to this development of conventions, film formats were all over the place. They varied in length. One variation was the serialized film, derived from the episodic novel genre that were popular in periodicals of the day. More like a TV show than what we know today as a film, this short film form was an action adventure or soap opera that invariably ended in a cliffhanger to ensure the audience would come back for more. Cinema of the period also borrowed heavily from theater and vaudeville, employing stage sets and the stiff theatrical performance style of the stage, further exacerbated by lack of sound, which meant still more overacting. Most editing was done in-camera and there were few changes in camera angle. Griffith introduced a new narrative form, a film approximately two hours in length that encompassed an entire, well-developed story, and included a greater variety of sets and cinematic techniques. Just as the novel became the storytelling convention for books in the 17th century, the feature film evolved as the storytelling convention for film in the early 20th century.

The other characteristic of second-generation media producers is the development of techniques unique to the medium. Russian filmmaker Sergei Eisenstein introduced a new level of film craftsmanship when he incorporated a variety of editing techniques into his 1925 masterpiece *Battleship Potemkin*. Even without sound, Eisenstein was able to develop a breadth and depth of techniques that enabled film to become at once a more fluid and a more powerful medium. His background in experimental theater and engineering enabled him to integrate the artistic with the technical, creating a kind of visual poetry through the use of advanced editing and cinematography. His conventions were thus added to Griffith's to create an expanded cinematic repertoire.

When you talk to developers of interactive media today, you will frequently hear a statement such as, "We can't do that because the technology isn't there yet." They use the constraints of the current technology as an excuse for producing unadventurous or mediocre content. D.W. Griffith no more balked at the lack of sound in film than did Eisenstein at its lack of color. Artists who transcend such restrictions ultimately *push* the technology to its next level by demanding of it more than it can deliver. Such leaps in craft and artistry dazzle audiences, inspire producers, and unlock the potential of a new medium, subsequently demanding that the technology evolve to better serve the content.

I want to talk for a moment about the notion of conventions and standards. Conventions are techniques or tricks within a medium that characterize that medium as unique. Standards are collectively agreed on and formalized specifications that everyone within a medium agrees to adopt.

Conventions are generally developed by content creators. The feature film is both a convention and a standard. Various conventions of film editing include long shots to provide an overview, establishing shots to set a scene, reaction shots to show the interpersonal dynamic of a scene, and close ups to provide more focus on a single character. Conventions are not necessarily formalized, but once established, are difficult to break. Some conventions can evolve into standards, such as the feature film. The half-hour duration of a television program is both a convention and a standard. A good way to think about it is that a convention facilitates content creation, and a standard facilitates distribution.

Creative conventions make the producers' jobs easier. Standard narrative conventions mean that writers don't have to "reinvent the wheel." Imagine how insane it would be if a film could be any length. The sitcom provides a formula that can be filled in with story week after week in a tight time frame. There are also production conventions—for example, every film generally has a director, a producer, a cinematographer, actors, an assistant director, and on down the food chain. This enables people to specialize in a position so that once they are on set, everyone knows what is expected of them. These conventions of form and process make it easier for content people to not only conceive of content for a medium, but also to go about the grisly business of producing it.

Conventions are also good for the audience. The audience learns conventions and learns to adjust to them. When editing first came into play and suddenly distorted the perception of time, it took a little getting used to, but everyone did, and we now all know what it means when there is an establishing shot, a cutaway, or a flashback in a film.

Conventions in interactive media are still hard to pin down. Arcade games are most deeply steeped in convention, with fixed genres that most game designers feel they must design to. In the CD-ROM environment, it's a little more evasive. *Myst* created certain conventions, as has *Doom*. On the web, there are certain conventions that are generally used, such as underlining a hypertext link and changing its color after it is selected. Though this might seem simple and mundane, it helps users better understand what to do and how to interact with the computer. The Macintosh interface is an excellent example of what happens when you have strong conventions in place. The consistency of the interface enables the user to focus his or her attention on the use of the application rather than its mechanics.

Although conventions are adopted and universally used, they are not necessarily written into law. A film can be any length, have actors or not, have a director or not, and eschew with any of the previously mentioned conventions; however, if, in doing so, the film also dispenses with the standards, it will radically effect its capability to be distributed. Standards are the officially sanctioned rules that dictate protocol within the distribution infrastructure in any given medium. These can take a variety of different forms. In film, the use of 35 millimeter film, color, and sound is a standard. Imagine how impossible it would be to make a film if, say, every director had to invent his own projector, or formulate his own film stock. What if the means of laying sound to film were unique to each movie. If this were the case, the film industry would be long gone. Television would be impossible if there were not a standard length or increment for programs. Imagine what would happen if shows were different lengths and didn't start on the hour or half hour. The whole thing would be a complete mess. These standards help the medium get to the audience and the audience to get to the medium. The adoption of HTML as the standard file format and the World Wide Web as the network infrastructure for the Internet are what have enabled it to become a mass medium virtually overnight.

Here's where the adoption part comes in. Adoption curve is a term used in marketing that refers to the rate at which a new product is acclimated into the market. Most adoption curves begin with "early adopters"—adventurous and affluent individuals who lead the way for the more cautious general public. Early adopters are the trendsetters who start the momentum going on a new product; but acclimation can also stop there, with the early adopters serving as little more than a niche market. Early adopters are willing to pay more for new products. Subsequently, they pay exorbitant prices for new technology, well beyond the manufacturing costs which, in turn, enables the technology companies to support past R&D, and further develop the product for a mass market.

In order to have adoption, you must have distribution, and in order to have distribution, you must have standards. If you have not developed at least a first pass at standards by this point, you are essentially dead in the water.

A good sign that adoption is beginning to occur in Phase 3 is the emergence of critics. Although critics are the bane of most content producers' existence, their appearance generally marks a certain level of maturation of the medium. When people care enough about a medium to write about it and read about it, this is a clear step toward mass acclimation. Like the bird that sits atop a hippopotamus and keeps him well-groomed, the critic is a secondary life form that lives off and through a larger form, keeping it healthy while it feeds itself. It matters little whether the criticism is good or bad, as long as something is being said. To paraphrase from Oscar Wilde, "The only thing worse than being talked about is not being talked about."

One thing that is always interesting to observe is the rise of genres in one medium that talks about another. Film and TV are covered by the print media, film by the television medium, but there is almost no coverage of print on television. You seldom see a book review on TV, but you can read them weekly in your local paper. If you were to remove all the magazines about entertainment from your local newsstand, it would look decidedly empty. Likewise, if you banned entertainment reports from the television news in Los Angeles you'd have, well, nothing. It is fascinating now to look at the Internet and how much of its content is actually about other media. Online newsgroups and bulletin boards enable television fans to share thoughts on their favorite shows; one of the largest Internet commerce sites is a book store; and it is pretty much de rigeur for every newly released feature film to have its own URL. There are even Internet sites about the Internet, trying to help them make some sense of the chaos and direct them to sites that might be of interest.

Phase 3 content is also characterized by the development of good content production tools. The easier and better the tools for content, the more content producers will be drawn to the medium, and therefore the more content will be generated. The downside of this is that it is often characteristic of Phase 3 content to be driven by available tool sets. Early tool-driven content often leads to inadvertent conventions that are a product not of creative ingenuity, but of the limitations of the tools themselves. Many early CD-ROMs, for example, are easily recognizable as products of the Macromedia Director tool. "When you have a hammer, everything looks like a nail," and so early tool-users will often let the tool design for them. The reason many web sites are so dull is because they are designed by HTML authoring tools.

Although all of the features previously mentioned are crucial to the evolution of second-generation content, there is one final step that must occur for the medium to jump the hurdle into Phase 4 and mass market acclimation. The craft reaches a certain point, the tools reach a certain point, standards and conventions begin to emerge, but all this is moot without content saturation. It is true that all of these elements are interdependent, but unless there is enough content at a certain point to drive the sales of media devices to early adopters, everything will fizzle out. It doesn't even matter whether the content is good. There just has to be a lot of it. As long as some of it's great, and some of it is pretty good, the medium has a vague chance of surviving. If this is not the case—if there is little content, or it does not reach out to a broad enough audience, the medium will either die or settle into a comfortable niche market. Despite this, even a niche market needs content saturation because it is the continual creation of content that keeps the medium alive on an ongoing basis.

PHASE 4: THIRD-GENERATION CONTENT/ ACCLIMATION

Phase 4 brings the medium to its full level of maturity, both technologically and in terms of craft and content. At Phase 4, the medium has "arrived." This is the point where it can truly be called a "mass medium." Although a medium may continue to evolve from this point on, by this time, it is stable enough that it can expect to have a long and healthy life span. Assuming the creation of content continues and technology responds to demands from the content creators, a medium at Phase 4 is in good shape.

One of the signs of full acclimation of a medium is its capability to support itself, and to support higher production, marketing, and advertising budgets. The success of a mass medium can generally be gauged by the outrageous amounts of money spent on production. Furthermore, when a medium is advertised in other media, it is a clear sign that it is on the verge of, if not fully ensconced in, Phase 4 development. After a medium reaches this point, the amount spent on development is usually a fairly accurate measure of the amount being made.

There might be a number of technical perturbations within the medium that will bring on various shifts. The audio recording industry, for example, has gone through several iterations in terms of delivery. From the phonograph, to the hi-fi, to the CD player; from reel-to-reel, to 8-track to cassette. These changes also meant major changes in standards, but because they occurred well into Phase 4, when the medium had full saturation, the market could withstand these perturbations without hurting the medium as a whole. Most of these transformations actually turned out to be quite profitable for the music industry. The replacement of the LP with the CD player, for example, forced three entire generations to retool in terms of both hardware and content.

Sometimes these shifts in technology can precipitate a shakeout of skill sets. Certain art forms and skills within the medium might become obsolete. For example, many directors and actors were unable to make the crossover from silent movies to "talkies." The same thing might occur on the Internet as it breaks out of its derivative relationship with print. Some print artists who flourished on the early web, might, in the face of more sophisticated technology such as VRML and Java, be left out in the cold. Other such shifts are occurring in other arenas of digital media, not necessarily just interactive media. Television is allegedly going digital in the near future. Whether it has done so by the time you read this or whether the consumer has accepted such a shift, I cannot predict. Digital effects have also precipitated radical shifts in skill sets in the film industry, although it is all still ending up (for the most part) on good old-fashioned, 35 millimeter, 24-frames-per-second celluloid.

A Phase 4 medium is also characterized by another dynamic—its relationship with other media. As the new medium reaches mass dissemination, it will naturally impact everything else. What you will see is a ripple effect through other media. It is always the case that as a new medium evolves, it has an impact on other media, although the popularly held belief that a new medium will kill other media has been proven untrue time and time again.

Television by no means killed radio, but it certainly altered it irrevocably. At the same time, other new media that arise will impact the Phase 4 medium. This phenomenon is what I call "The Law of Cumulative Media." Because it pertains not to any single medium, but to the relationship between them all, it has its own section covering its own set of rules and patterns.

There are four axioms that also go with the Theory of Media Evolution. They are, in a sense, the essential ground rules that dictate all of the aforementioned patterns and trends. These axioms look at media evolution in a current context, and provide some guidelines for launching new media into the marketplace and the culture.

THE EVOLUTION OF INTERACTIVE MULTIMEDIA

Now, here's the bad news. Although all of these patterns can be applied to the evolution of interactive multimedia, it also has some properties of its own that make it difficult to ascertain precisely where it stands in its evolutionary curve. Part of the reason for this lies in the "multi" part of the equation; the other part has to do with an important distinction between a platform and a medium. Interactive multimedia is, as we've seen, a hybrid of all media. Although it is based upon the standard of digitization, the various platforms in which this digital media exist are at various levels of standardization. The high acceleration of technology has meant that some platforms have a very high attrition rate—they emerge and die off very quickly—while others seem to hold steady.

Consumer and arcade games head the list in terms of mass market acclimation, and they have accomplished the prerequisites of conventions, and mass distribution. At the same time, the hardware seems to be a moving target, with completely new game machines being released every year. Nonetheless, this planned obsolescence hasn't hurt this voracious market any. Like the shifts in audio hardware, the game industry seems capable of withstanding major hardware shifts in light of its huge market share.

When CD-ROMs first appeared in 1985, pundits and soothsayers predicted the medium would be dead in two years. Twelve years later, in 1997, most major record stores and consumer electronics stores now have extensive CD-ROM sections. Even after over a long and arduous adoption curve, the CD-ROM medium seems to be hovering somewhere between Phase 3 and 4. It has accomplished a certain level of standardization, established certain conventions, and reached a broad enough market to be considered a mass medium, but not broad enough to be self-supporting. It also has not reached full maturation in terms of craft.

As of this writing, the DVD (Digital Video Disk) is threatening to wipe out the CD-ROM. But don't expect this "Invasion of the CD-ROM Snatchers" scenario to pan out to quickly. Planned obsolescence notwithstanding, CD-ROM still has one major factor in its favor, and one that is hard to overcome: content saturation. 1997 has been the year the Internet ate CD-ROM, with several CD-ROM developers closing down or significantly downsizing. Even if everyone were to stop producing CD-ROMs tomorrow, consider this: there are still enough titles out there to keep people stocked up for another couple of years. Because CD-ROM is largely a repeat-play medium, people might just continue to play with the CD-ROMs they already have for a good long while.

I'm actually pretty happy about the CD-ROM shakeout. I think it will lead to better products: In 1993 everyone and their brother were setting up CD-ROM studios, and most of the major studios and record companies were jumping on the bandwagon; however, many of these people, with endless cash but little vision, had no business in this business. The departure of these ill-founded ventures merely makes more room for the serious CD-ROM producers, both new and old, to move this medium into Phase 4. Now that we're past the gold rush, we might stand to see some real gems as the true craftspeople continue to hone their skills.

The following list contains what I consider to be some good examples of content that is pushing CD-ROM toward Phase 4. This list is by no means complete, but it's a start:

- *Myst*
- *Barbie Fashion Designer*
- *Bad Mojo*
- *You Don't Know Jack!*
- Jim Ludtke and the Residents' *Bad Day on the Midway* and *Freakshow*
- DE-LUX'O's *Consumer Product* and *Encyclopedia of Clamps*
- *Monty Python's Complete Waste of Time*

These titles succeed because they do not try to make the CD-ROM do something it is inherently bad at. Instead, they take its inherent attributes and build an experience around that. Each title is very straightforward and focused in what it is trying to do, and it has a consistency and integrity within itself. Each title also has a very strong intuitive interface, compelling content, and a well-developed graphical aesthetic. They all push the envelope, but they push it *toward* the audience. Although these titles were totally unique and innovative when released, they had immediate resonance with the audience and built a strong following largely on word of mouth and critical acclaim. Not all of them are bestsellers, but I think they should be.

At this point, the vote is still out on the Internet. I believe it is hovering between Phase 2 and 3. Much of its content is still what I would classify as first generation, but at the same time, its rapid adoption is unprecedented. Compare the first three years of the Internet to the first ten of the CD-ROM and you'll see what I mean. In spite of standardization and content saturation, the conventions of the Internet are still somewhat wishy-washy, and it is far from achieving Phase 4 craftsmanship. The Internet is also still evolving in terms of technology. The advent of 3D on the web will be the online equivalent of the birth of film "talkies," and will no doubt bring about another major shift before true Phase 4 status is achieved.

THEORY OF MEDIA EVOLUTION: THE FOUR AXIOMS

There are certain fundamental rules that dictate the way media evolve over time. *The Theory of Media Evolution* observes some patterns of media evolution that enable us to better understand and predict the process of introducing and acclimating new media to the culture. The following are axioms of the Theory of Media Evolution. These axioms provide a very clear blueprint for how and why new media and technologies succeed or fail in the complex relationship between medium and audience.

FIRST AXIOM OF MEDIA EVOLUTION

Software sells hardware.

Perhaps the greatest error made in the marketing of new media and communications technologies is the peculiar belief that people will buy hardware for its own sake, regardless of whether there is something tangible for them to do with it. Anyone who has paid any attention to the dynamics between hardware and software will tell you that you cannot sell a delivery system without something to deliver.

By way of proving my point, I will use three parables—two from the music medium, and one more directly related to computers and multimedia. The first is a little-known tidbit of history that I have always found fascinating. The second is a mass media overthrow, to which everyone in America was party, either willingly or unwittingly. The third parable follows the path of a failed hardware platform as a case study for the importance of software and content in the battle for interactive domination.

Parable 1: The Introduction of the Phonograph to Rural African Americans

Once upon a time, there was a brand new invention called the phonograph, a new device that enabled people to listen to prerecorded music for the first time. In the 20s, phonographs were being sold out of music stores throughout the rural south. These stores were successful at selling phonographs to many white customers, but there seemed to be absolutely no market for the phonograph among African Americans at the time. This was particularly vexing because it was clear that there was a huge music market there, and there was an enormous amount of local talent with a huge following; however, this rich musical culture was not reflected in the pre-recorded offerings of the local stores. Their passion for music notwithstanding, few rural blacks were interested in the music of Bing Crosby or Sophie Tucker. A few enterprising store owners, recognizing this disconnect and the opportunity it presented, got a really great idea. They set up low-budget recording studios in their back rooms and recorded the local artists. But here's the amazing thing: In the beginning, they actually gave the records away for free with the phonographs. This is the first known instance of "bundling."

Bundling, as many in the software and CD-ROM business are aware, is the practice of distributing free software as a means of promoting the sales of hardware. Most new PCs, for example, are "bundled" with the Windows 95 operating system and one or two other programs, such as Microsoft Office or an e-mail program.

Parable 2: The Compulsory Audio CD Act of 1989

I'll never forget it as long as I live. It was like *Invasion of the Record Snatchers.* Someone had come in the night and planted pods that swallowed up all the vinyl record albums and replaced them with these little shiny things in plastic boxes. Before you knew it, you couldn't find a new piece of vinyl to save your life. I remember walking into Tower Records on Broadway and West Fourth Street in New York City and asking the clerk, "Where are the records?" He just looked at me blankly like an alien zombie. They had come, they had conquered, and now we all had to go out and buy a CD player if we ever wanted to listen to any new music again.

As someone who has a tendency to resist progress, I sat strong, like the old woman on her porch unwilling to let her house be torn down to make way for the freeway. As others caved in to this clear and obvious market manipulation, I stood steadfast by my hi-fi stereo. Between 1989 and 1992, I managed to triple my record collection because all my friends who had been brainwashed turned their entire album estates over to me. I liked records. I still like records. I like the clicks and pops. I like the big, beautiful, unbreakable record covers (those confounded jewel boxes are always getting cracked), I like the readable lyrics, and I like watching the round black disks spin around on the turntable.

In 1993, I finally caved in because they simply stopped releasing any more vinyl albums, and there were actually a few contemporary artists I liked. I've become accustomed to CDs, but there will always be a cherished place in my heart for the original vinyl renditions of The Beatles' *White Album* and Hendrix's *Electric Ladyland*—both of which had great posters that folded into fourths and fit perfectly into the sleeve—and that old scratchy copy of *Derek and the Dominoes* with the double-thickness vinyl and that one leftover pot seed caught in the spine I could never quite get out.

Many contemporary music artists are equally blue about the death of the "licorice pizza." Both vinyl veteran Neil Young and CD-mavens Pearl Jam have been trying to start a vinyl revival, perhaps a "re-vinyl," by pre-releasing vinyl in the larger format prior to a CD release. Many artists today throw samples of record pops or scratches on their CDs and a few have even added a spinning record-groove sound to the end of a record just to give it that old-time vinyl flavor.

Parable 3: How to Kill a Medium

With respect to computers, I first learned about hardware selling software firsthand in the mid-80s when I was ready to buy my first computer for the home. Remember that at this point it was generally believed that no one ever was going to buy computers for the home. I asked all my techy friends what to get, and they all said the same thing: Buy the hardware that runs the software you want to use.

This has been an axiom for PC and Mac purchasers since the dawn of the digital age. The wisdom of this, however, seems to somehow have escaped the manufacturers of home multimedia equipment. My last tale is a cautionary tale, and only the tip of the iceberg, but here goes. Note that the characters and situations are factual. Any resemblance to vaporware is purely coincidental.

One major company in particular has paid the price and paid it dearly for not heeding the all-powerful first axiom of media evolution. The company was Philips New Media and the device was CD-I. CD-I was not a bad technology. In fact, it was in many respects superior to CD-ROM. It also had the added advantage of being a "set-top box," meaning that it was a self-contained unit not requiring connection to a computer. As far as audio and video were concerned, in the late 80s, it could deliver both better than CD-ROM, which was notorious for its poor video resolution and low frame rate. Conversely, CD-I technology could deliver broadcast quality audio and video. It was also incredibly reliable, and later, Philips added a feature that enabled CD-I to double as an audio CD player.

CD-I had everything going for it, except for one minor thing: content. When the CD-I player was released, there were only about five titles for it. Most of them were actually not too bad. But at $800 a pop at CD-I's initial launch, the titles didn't have enough content to justify the purchase for most buyers. Thus, it remained a luxury item, condemned to the eternal limbo of early adoption niche hell, where it made a slight swell, but never really gained momentum. It did a little better in Europe, where CD-ROM sales were slow due to a slower computer adoption rate. Even with a price point of $500 and significant hardware improvements, CD-I never quite made it past the first arc of the adoption curve. Philips eventually realized that they had to support the CD-I with content development and started a software division to create CD-I titles. Unfortunately for them, it was too late by this time. The platform had too little market saturation, and it was also notoriously difficult to produce for. In order to lure content developers in, Philips offered them co-development deals for CD-I *and* CD-ROM. This ultimately defeated the purpose of creating software to support hardware sales. Meanwhile, the weaker CD-ROM technology took over, not because the platform or its titles were necessarily any better, but because there were just more of them…a lot more…and therefore, CD-ROM won the race.

Furthermore, the increase in popularity of CD-ROMs during the mid 1990s was a major factor in the sales not only of CD-ROM players but also of computers. A 1995 study revealed that the sales of CD-ROMs had gone so far beyond what was anticipated that analysts had to restructure their models to accommodate the astronomical growth curve of this technology.

But don't hold your breath. Even as we speak, in the summer of 1997, the Internet is looking more and more like the Tsunami that ate CD-ROM. As many CD-ROMs as there are on the shelves of Frye's and Blockbuster, there are ten times that number of web sites. If content saturation is the primary criteria for acclimation of a new medium, then the Internet has it over everything—there are close to an infinite number of Internet domain names available. Market researchers estimate that the Internet will take over as the predominant distribution method. So once again, we see that software continues to sell hardware.

 NERd VERSUS COUCH POTATO (p. 345)

SECONd AXIOM OF MEdIA EVOLUTION

It's the content, stupid!

In January of 1990, I attended the annual "industry outlook" meeting of the IICS (International Interactive Communication Society). These kinds of meetings were old hat to me by now, standard fare for an industry that typically focuses too closely on its future, at the expense of learning from its past. Annual industry outlooks usually involved a panel of analysts who, even though they were wrong about all their predictions the year before, are, nonetheless, invited back again to misguide us year after year.

Each of the speakers got up and said their piece; as always, each focused on the technology—CD-ROM was going to do this, interactive television was going to do that, Sony and Philips bla bla bla, IBM and Apple bla bla bla. But then something unusual happened. One of the speakers got up and said something *else*. All he said was one word, but it woke me up from my trance, and made me realize that there was indeed hope. His name was David Traub and all he said was: "One word—content." That's right. Content. In sharp contrast to the heavily technological bent of the other panelists, Traub, who was a journalist, consultant, and new media pundit, quietly informed us that it was all about content; that hardware had nothing to do with anything, and that what was going to drive forward the success of interactive media was the content and the people who produced it.

Although content was not a new word to me—it was also the central focus of the work I did at Edwin Schlossberg Incorporated—I had never heard someone outside of the company even mention it. I had always been at a loss for words when asked to describe what it was I did, but when I heard David Traub utter the word content, it was like a light coming through the ceiling and a choir of angels singing. I wanted to rise to my feet and cry, "Hallelujah! I now know what I am! I'm a content person! Praise the Lord!"

There is no question that content is driving the bus. If hardware is the bus, content is the driver, and if nobody is there to drive it, the bus will just sit there and rust. There was a time when all anybody talked or thought about was hardware. This era was necessary because every medium must begin with invention, and invention equals hardware; however, if the medium stays at the invention level and does not graduate to content, it will become the proverbial abandoned vehicle sitting in the empty lot with grass growing between its seats. Can I get a witness! If you watch the progress of any medium, it is always the quality and quantity of the content that leads to success. There is nothing else, and anybody who tells you otherwise is just plain blind.

Gratuitous Interactivity: Media Dispensers and the ATM Model (p. 218)

Decisions, Decisions, Decisions (p. 158)

Now's the time when I get to contradict myself. Here goes: But didn't your hero, McLuhan, say that the medium is the message? What does that mean? Doesn't that somewhat go against what you are saying about content? Isn't he saying that the hardware does count for something?

Indeed it does…and yes, and guess what! That's what the Third Axiom of Media Evolution is for!

Third Axiom of Media Evolution

Content is everything, but experience is everything else.

"The medium is the message" is just another way of saying "the experience of the medium is inherent in its content and vice versa." This is especially true in interactive media, where the experience is in the hands of the user. Experience is crucial because we have to look at any media experience not as an isolated case of content delivery, but within the entire context of the content delivery experience, right down to the popcorn and sticky floors.

That sounds like a good place to start…in the movie theater. Think about the experience of going to the movies. You go out, perhaps even get dressed up (if you're old-fashioned like me). You wait in line to buy a ticket. You have to go during a narrow time window because movies are only out for a short duration. If you're really excited about the movie, you can't wait, and so you try to get tickets on opening night. If you're crazy (like the second generation of *Star*

Wars gazers were), you'll camp out overnight to get a ticket for opening day. You hand over your ticket to a pimply teenager in a suit. (In the old days, the Grauman's Chinese ushers walked you to your seat and wore wool military-like uniforms, even in the summer). And there's that smell. Popcorn. Coca-Cola. Bon Bons. You stop by the concessions counter and get some. You don't want to miss the previews. You cuddle up in a dark room next to your loved one and 500 of your closest friends as you wait for the curtain to rise, an unnecessary but nonetheless unwavering convention. The lights dim and everyone knows what's in store. Two hours of total immersion in 30 feet of light on a giant movie screen with surround sound. The experience of watching a movie is as important as what happens on the screen. In spite of predictions that video would kill cinema, Americans have yet to lose their passion for the big screen.

If the medium is the message—that is, experience=content—in traditional media, then it is doubly so in interactive media. An interactive experience is more about the experience than it is about the content. More accurately, the experience *is* the content, because ultimately, the content is created by the player. In traditional narrative, character is story, story is character. In the same way, in interactive experience, player is content and content is player.

As an interactive designer, I always make it my business to design experiences uniquely suited to their media. Ineffective interactive products often fall on their faces purely on the grounds that they were produced in the wrong medium. If the medium is the message, it is absolutely essential to pick the right medium for your message, even if it means giving up some assumptions about what you are trying to do. Think carefully about that next time you are debating whether to go web or CD-ROM, video or VR. Your story can fall on deaf ears if not told in the right voice.

As interactive media evolve, this sensibility can and should become an increasingly important part of the development of craft. Interface design is another way to think about experience, but interface is only half of it. Interface is the end of experience, not the beginning. It is characteristic of interactive designers, especially those from the graphics disciplines, to think that interface *is* experience. But the experience should be designed before the interface; the interface is merely a way to facilitate an experience.

 PSYCHO-ERGONOMICS (P. 404)

It is common for people within a given discipline area to adamantly believe that their discipline is the key. At a salon I once attended, an audience member addressed the speaker with a rant about graphics and how they were the missing ingredient from most interactive titles. "Graphics are the most important thing," he asserted. I had to break in at this point: "You're wrong," I said, more aggressively than I might have intended. "The most important thing in an interactive experience is what happens in here," and I pointed at my head.

To me, the key about experience is that it happens between the ears of the player. It is not a design problem, but a psychological one: How do you create content into which the individual can project his or herself to a unique and personalized experience? The best quality of an interactive product is that it prompts you to feel that your experience is totally unique, whether it is the actions you take, how you arrive at those actions, or merely what goes on in your mind as you play. In the end, the experience has to be uniquely the player's. Most linear media is really about the experience of the artist and about our interpretation or projection into that. But interactive media is about your own experience, the unique version of this story that only you can tell or influence, whatever it is.

As an interactive artist, my job is to read the minds of my players...all of them—to put myself into their shoes and minds, to anticipate their every move, and to create a full, well-rounded experience that will resonate inside them. In order to do this, I have to begin every project with a thorough under-standing of my audience. I do a lot of research. I look at behavioral qualities of the group in general on a demographic level. Then I look at the specific group I am addressing. This is especially important with attractions or mu-seum work because you have to address regional and economic issues that are very specific to that location. I try to learn as much as I can about the intellec-tual and emotional makeup up the group, its interests, and what it is already doing. I get as much information as I can about the prevailing culture.

Next, I look at the content. What kind of experience will this group relate to that can connect it to the content. Here's a great example. For the Museum of the City of New York, a project I worked on while at Edwin Schlossberg Incor-porated, we had to create an experience that would connect elementary school kids from neighboring Harlem with a collection of 400 years of artifacts from some of New York's richest families. The client, by the way, was baffled by the fact that its major audience was young black and Hispanic kids. Aside from public school visits, these latchkey kids often came by after school or during the summer. The museum was free to them, was heated and air-conditioned and provided a preferable hangout to the streets. But there was little there to address the experiential needs of this group, or to connect it in any significant emotional way with the content.

One way the museum accomplished this was by setting up exhibits that would put a contemporary spin on New York history. One of their most successful events was a street games exhibit, in which they had kids all over the museum playing 400 years' worth of children's games. Families came from all over the city and the local kids loved it.

When we proposed our own interpretive exhibits, we introduced the idea of emphasizing the "story" in history. We used narrative to explore the significance of artifacts. Most museums describe artifacts by revealing information about them. Our idea was to conceal information, to provide visitors with a way to explore and unearth information so that their visit could be more exploratory. This was in keeping with the self-guided experience of the local children, who loved to discover new and unusual collections, or visit the same exhibits over and over, in search of new details. We also let visitors see the museum from the point of view of the curators, providing a behind-the-scenes glimpse into the process of collection and scholarly interpretation.

If I could say only one thing about the relationship between content and experience, it is to repeat what I touched on previously. The point of the experience is to create a resonance within the player respecting the content. It is not about understanding information or navigating through an interface. It is not even about having a well-developed story or script. Granted, you need these things to create a good experience, but they do not make a good experience. What makes a good experience is that people care about what they're doing. A good interface and script enables them to do this. If giving people a reason to care is not your primary objective, then don't be surprised if they don't. If you look at everything in these terms, asking yourself "Does this feature give the player a reason to care about what they're doing?"—a good script and interface will naturally follow.

 TEST FIRST, ASK QUESTIONS LATER (p. 463)

FOURTH AXIOM OF MEDIA EVOLUTION

Word of mouth is the best marketing tool.

The fourth axiom of media evolution is most explicitly targeted at interactive media, but in fact, it applies to all media across the board.

Although it is true that you can orchestrate a box office hit through advertising and promotion, even if the product itself is weak (case in point, *Independence Day*), it is also true that in reality, the primary marketing tool for all media is word of mouth. In the book world, people buy books because the books are being talked about and read. In the film world, an unlikely contender such as *Shine, Slingblade,* or *The English Patient* can be the most talked about film of the year while its over-marketed competitors, with their moment in the box office sun, are soon forgotten.

Interactive media is, perhaps more than any other medium, based on a word of mouth market. Although it has grown enormously over the past few years, interactive media still has a relatively small market, too small to support the huge advertising budgets typical in media with a larger audience. With typical CD-ROM budgets at about $100,000, and high-budget CD-ROMs at around $3 million, just purchasing the ad space for a TV commercial can strip the product's total production budget. With these kinds of rations, few interactive designers can hope to see significant advertising money thrown at their project. But even if they do, don't hold your breath.

The *Johnny Mnemonic* CD, published by Sony Imagesoft, is a classic example. Ever hear of it? Probably not. Here's why. This product was a shoo-in to be the CD-ROM hit of the year. It launched with a big bang at E3, the testosterone-drenched consumer game mega-conference, in 1995. *Johnny Mnemonic*, the biggest attempt to date to make an interactive movie, boasted all the ingredients of a surefire combination: a successful game designer; a successful music video director, a story by cyberspace icon William Gibson; a simultaneous co-release with the film, starring Keanu Reeves and directed by painter Robert Longo; great production value with virtually full-screen video; a big production budget (estimates range between $3 million and $5 million, depending on who you talk to); and a big advertising budget. The CD-ROM was produced by Propoganda Code, the interactive division of one of the top music video and commercial studios, published and paid for by Sony. With all this in its favor, the product took worse than a nose dive. It went almost entirely unnoticed. Nobody played it. Nobody bought it. Nobody talked about it. End of story. With all these factors in its favor, how could a project like this, with so much firepower behind it, have been such a dismal failure? It's the content, stupid! And not only the content, but the experience.

In sharp contrast, let's look at what makes a successful CD-ROM. The prototype is, of course, *Myst*. One of the top-selling CD-ROMs of all time, *Myst* had a fraction of the budget of *Johnny Mnemonic*. It was produced by two brothers in their garage. The Miller Brothers, who created *Myst*, are the Wright Brothers of multimedia—proving to the skeptical Powers-that-Be that yes, indeed, CD-ROM could fly. Originally self-published, *Myst* built up enough of a head of steam on word of mouth alone to land a major publishing deal. By the time it had an advertising budget, it had already built up a big buzz, so the ads served as a turbo-charge, leveraging its self-propelled popularity. The greatest thing about *Myst* is that it is content- and experience-heavy and technologically mundane, proving once again that content and experience are everything and you can do a lot with a little if you use your head.

 MYST-ICISM (p. 325)

More recently, we have seen the stellar ascent of the interactive game show *You Don't Know Jack!* This game, which is a jacked-up, GenX version of

Jeopardy, has taken America by storm. What it has going for it is a simple, winning game formula, great writing, and a hell of an attitude. The CD-ROM took off, and now the web site has been building nothing short of a cult following.

Talk is cheap...but it's also profitable. It's the best advertising value for your dollar. As any book publisher (or at least mine) will tell you, the main thing you need to sell a book is content. People read the book, they talk about it, and more people buy it. Critics review it. They like it, or they fight over it, whatever. It gets talked about. That's all you want. No matter how much money you spend on advertising and promotion, in the final analysis, the way to sell units is to be the talk of the town. The best way to be the talk of the town is to produce something worth talking about.

THEORY OF MEDIA EVOLUTION (p. 468)

THE LAWS OF CUMULATIVE MEDIA (p. 276)

THE LAWS OF INFORMATIONAL ENTROPY (p. 280)

MIXED MEDIA, MIXED MESSAGE (p. 306)

BOOKMARK: INTERACTIVITY AND THE NEW LITERACY (p. 102)

USER OR PLAYER: THE CHOICE IS YOURS

I have always been uncomfortable with the term "user." In theory, the user is supposed to be the individual empowered by interactive media. But the term user comes with a plethora of negative connotations. In human affairs, a user is a person who is opportunistic, exploiting others for his or her own personal gain. In our culture, "user" is one of the least complimentary things you can say about another person. Most of us would like to avoid being defined as a "user" in a social context.

User is also closely related to the word usury, which refers to the practice of loan-sharking. Usury is considered a sin in the Christian rule book, which of course led to one of the many cultural rifts between Gentiles and Jews. Only Jews practiced usury because Christians were not allowed to do so, thus perpetuating the negative stereotype of the "Jewish Banker." In Christian terms, usury is right up there with adultery. Well maybe not quite as bad, but close.

Within some circles, the word user is often preceded by the word drug, where "use" has come to represent substance abuse. You could certainly apply this meaning to the addictive game-playing patterns encouraged by many consumer and arcade games, but in other contexts, it does not apply.

In addition to the word user is the very ominous term "end user," which sounds more like the name of a Samuel Beckett play than a term describing someone who interacts with a software application. There are other even more dubious connotations, but I want to publish this book without a parental warning sticker, so I won't get into that here.

The concept of "use" is worth exploring for a moment. Use is a very generic term referring to virtually anything you can do with a tool. If the definition of a user is "one who uses," and "use" means "the act of practicing or employing something," or "to put into action or service," this term could really be applied to virtually anything, but is more suggestive of interaction with a tool than with an entertainment or educational application. It makes sense to call a person who is employing or putting into service a word processor or spreadsheet a "user," but it doesn't quite work to say a person is *using Myst*.

People enjoying *Myst* are more often called players. Player has a variety of different connotations which, looked at in different ways, offer us some interesting metaphors for interactive experiences. The word "play" and its derivatives take up over one entire column in the dictionary, which suggests that the word has many different potential meanings. Just for fun, let's take a look at some of these definitions.

Play in the context of game play has been used for many centuries and its meaning is very specific. A player in this context is anyone who is playing a game. Play is also defined as child's play, meaning a non-goal–oriented activity, which is a little different than a game.

 THE RULES OF THE GAME (p. 420)

The term "player" can also have a negative social connotation, referring to someone who is dishonestly scheming or exploitative (not unlike a user), such as the main character in Robert Altman's film, *The Player*. A player can also be a person who engages in flirtation and promiscuous sexual activity. There is also "a play on words," which involves twisting language in a humorous way, and also "play" in the sense of teasing or joking around. There is a mechanical meaning of play, as in, "this lever has a lot of play," and then there is the media term "airplay," meaning broadcast time or media exposure.

On the machine side, players are the devices that play media—a record player, a tape player, a CD-ROM player. It is interesting to think of the device in the context of game play...I wonder whether the CD-ROM player has as much fun when it "plays" a game as the human player does?

Then there are the dramatic connotations of play. "The play's the thing," the staged representation of an action or story." In this context, play is both a noun and a verb and "player" is defined as a performer or actor "playing" a role. One way to apply this to interactive media is to view the person using the application as a performer who is, in a sense, on stage performing the "application." This interpretation suggests a level of creativity and craft that is different from that implied by "game player," and certainly more than the generic and rather un-fun "user."

INTER-pLAY: IMPROVISATION AND INTERACTIVE THEATER (p. 230)

My favorite metaphor for interactivity within the realm of play is what musicians do with musical instruments. This paradigm acknowledges that there is a device involved, and it also suggests that the player possesses some skill or craft, much as the actor in a play. For a musician to play an instrument he must be able to understand it and really work it and make it do interesting things that are unique to the individual "player." This interpretation frames multimedia more as an instrument than a tool, which I think is really heading in the right direction. A really good multimedia experience should be more like a piano than a hammer if you ask me. The idea that you can create such an instrument which itself never changes but which produces variable "performances" at the hands of different "players" is really the ideal paradigm for how to view interactivity.

Furthermore, you can play a composition as well as an instrument. There is a great quote from the lead singer of Counting Crows who said that he liked his band members because "most guys play instruments, but these guys play songs." This puts the emphasis not on the device but on the content. I am not just playing the computer, I'm playing the game, playing the story, playing the composition. As a "player," you can play the same composition in an interpretive way, you can improvise within the parameters of that composition, or you can make up your own original composition. It is an act of creation that brings together an "instrument" with content. This really puts the user/device/software transition in a whole new light.

The idea of a "score" as a way to facilitate interactivity has been used in avant-garde art since as early as the 1920s. Both the Dada and the Fluxus movements were based in large part on interactivity with the audience, and a score was a creative way of directing audience participation while allowing for spontaneous improvisation. John Cage applied such scores to his experimental music, but artists such as Yoko Ono and Alan Kaprow created scores for performance art pieces. To these artists, art and play were synonymous, and their work can also provide interesting models for meaningful forms of interactivity.

Art is a Verb (p. 29)

Computer semiotics, a fairly new academic discipline, is the study of sign and symbol within the computer. Computer semioticians have caught on to some of these same subtleties. Because semiotics, which traditionally concerned itself with film and literature, is concerned with meaning and interpretation, semioticians are very aware of the connotations of the terms they use. Computer semioticians derive their terminology from the words interact and interaction, but there is also a suggestion of theatrics, no doubt drawn form cinematic references. The term "interactor" describes the person who is acting on the system, and the term "actor" describes the objects or elements being acted on. Being from Los Angeles, I have my own associations with the term actor, which inspire me to put forth questions such as: Is the interactor an interwaiter by day? Would the female be an interactress? Will a new movement arise that involves "method interacting?" Will actors within the computer have bit parts? Please stop me before I hurt someone…

In spite of my uncontrollable urge to parody the actor/interactor approach, I think it has some validity in that it provides an accurate description of what's going on, but I find the words themselves and the way they are defined a bit dry and academic. The current interpretation of these word constructs defines the user as if he or she were an engineering problem. Because play is at the heart of interactivity, I am in favor of play over action as a way to look at how people are going to relate to their experiences.

Psycho-ergonomics (p. 404)

If you've followed me this far down this path, this is probably the point where you are asking yourself, Isn't all this just semantics? Who cares? It might not be very important for television to distinguish between *audience* and *viewer*, but this distinction is crucial in interactivity. Interactivity is the intimate relationship between this person—the user, the player, the interactor, what have you—and the software—the composition, the hardware—the instrument, and in the case of multi-user activities, other people—the jam session. Thus, creating clear language and a strong metaphor for that relationship is critical to truly understanding the dynamics of interactivity. We can also borrow from these other established disciplines, using them as our inspiration or jumping off point into more sophisticated human/computer/human interaction.

In 1989, I went to the fifth anniversary symposium at the MIT Media Lab. The most memorable moment for me was hearing Gloriana Davenport, head of the interactive cinema group, give a talk entitled "My Storyteller Knows Me." She told the story of the introduction of the television to an American Indian tribe. The tribe was given the use of a television in place of their traditional story circle. After a couple of weeks, they gave it back. The reason, said the chief, was that although the stories were interesting, in the story circle, "My storyteller knows me." In other words, the story is addressed to the specific person hearing it.

As an interactive designer, it is my job to know my audience. It is my job to consider all the various ways they will interpret and want to affect the experience. As a result, there are many different people I have to know.

TEST FIRST, ASK QUESTIONS LATER (p. 463)

Interactivity should be a conversation. It should require the players to stretch themselves, and the computer to bend and sway in whatever direction is necessary to respond to the player. The player should be a creative and integral part of the process, and should be able to become completely absorbed in the experience of playing. The end result should feel more like being a player playing a guitar than being an end user withdrawing money from a bank machine. The player should have the sensation of a musician who has mastered his "axe," having an epiphany each time he picks it up to play.

WHO IS THE AUTHOR? (p. 528)

CYBERSPACE CADETS: VIRTUAL COMMUNITIES AND AVATAR WORLDS (p. 146)

NARRATIVE ENVIRONMENTS: VIRTUAL REALITY AS A STORYTELLING MEDIUM (p. 329)

V-ART

Although the military has been the driving force behind the development of technology and infrastructure in interactive media, I believe it is the artists, particularly fine artists, and, to a certain extent, commercial artists, who are the driving force behind content and application. Fine artists, have been playing around with the audience since at least the beginning of the 20th century and by varying accounts, long before.

 Art is a Verb (p. 29)

Fine artists have an advantage over scientists, researchers, military technologists, or even commercial artists because they are not bound by the constraints of functionality which makes them free to express themselves and their interests in a variety of ways. Because artists are often sensitive to the *emotional* issues, the more "right brain" matters, shall we say, they are often more attuned in an instinctive way to the finer points of human interaction.

An artist might learn in a gesture or with a passing experiment, or merely by observation or even intuition what a scientist or researcher requires empirical data to prove. True, the best scientists intuitively know what will and will not work, but by their trade, they are required to prove it. Artists must prove nothing. They don't even have to be understood. They can essentially do anything they want. As a result, when artists begin to venture on to interactive soil and explore collaborative and interdynamic relationships with the audience, they often arrive at revelations beyond the reach of traditional scientists and researchers.

For artists, particularly techno-artists or performance artists, Virtual Reality can be enormously captivating. What artist does not wish to entirely absorb his or her audience in a fully immersive experience of some kind? If you are an interactive artist, VR can become the most marvelous canvas imaginable because its capacity seems limitless. It is literally the stuff that dreams are made of. It opens up, in the words of Aldous Huxley, "new doors of perception" that, to an artist, represent the endowment of near magical powers.

Virtual Reality is the most expensive paintbrush available to an artist. It is the rare artist indeed who has both the requisite artist/scientist temperament/ passion, and access to the resources that enable them to explore this powerful medium. Due to the low accessibility of high-end VR, few artists have really been able to create full-blown VR installations. In addition, because of the enormous expense of the equipment needed to effectively deliver VR content, the audience is limited. Even outside the realm of VR, artists continue to contribute to the spatial media in general in a very significant way. In addition, the advent of 3D on the web through VRML, Java, and other technologies, has opened the virtual door to a much larger community of artists. It is often the fine artists who, led by something beyond empirical research, pass over a threshold into realms harder to pinpoint. They find their way into the subconscious and unleash the human power of the technology.

Myron Krueger is a pioneering digital artist whose home-brewed computer-video hybrid mediaspaces have provided outstanding insight into human behavior. Dubbing these "responsive environments," Krueger's body of work, spanning nearly two decades, is an ongoing collaborative experiment with the audience. Krueger's work is delightfully simple in its experimentation, but its playful dynamism created the groundwork for most of the VR and user-responsive art we see today. Krueger also showed that after you introduce the audience to the process, you can create very simple structures, almost game-like in their elegance, and the players will create their own art, sometimes spontaneously inventing new forms of expression not imagined or anticipated by either the artist or the player. Although many define Krueger's work as Virtual Reality, I would not use that term. By the strictest definition, Virtual Reality describes a system of three-dimensional models depicted in a navigable space on the computer. Most of Kreuger's highly refined work does not fall into this definition. Krueger's immersive installations fall into the class of what I call "media environments" or "mediaspace." A more detailed account of Krueger's work can be found in the chapter exploring the mediaspace genre.

 MEDIASPACE (p. 293)

VIRTUAL REALITY CHECK: WHAT IS VR ANYWAY? (p. 518)

Between 1993 and 1995, a number of fine artists had the opportunity to use classic VR in the Ivan Sutherland sense—that is, high-end, real-time 3D environments—as a canvas for artistic expression. A small handful of these emerged as defining works, garnering artistic acclaim, as well as earning several awards and citations. Although there is no doubt more great VR art yet to emerge, these brilliantly conceived and crafted alchemic creations merge art and science, magic and engineering. These V-Artists and their work demonstrate the power of this medium to reach beyond the simple function of expressing an artist's vision into a new realm of artist/viewer collaboration and first-person immersion in an alternate reality.

Although these pieces are all markedly different in their approach and implementation, they rather remarkably have two things in common. First of all, they utterly defy the classic VR-sci-fi-psychedelic-horror stereotype. Far from taking us to an abstract and disembodied hallucination or into a sterile futuristic world, all these pieces, without exception, revolve around themes of nature. Physical embodiment and consciousness of self within a natural context, rather than escape from reality into a synthesized world, is the resonant theme shared by all these pieces. The second interesting and perhaps not entirely coincidental fact is that all the pieces described here were created by women artists and male/female teams.

Brenda Laurel and Rachel Strickland's 1993 installation, *Placeholder*, at the Banff Centre in Alberta, Canada was a ritual space that put people in the roles of petroglyphic animal spirits of the Anasassi Indians. Two people at a time using Head-Mounted Displays as their interface (see figure V.1), took the roles of a snake, a spider, a crow, or a fish. Each role had its own distinct traits:

the snake would add a hiss to your voice; if you were the crow, you could fly by flapping your wings. The experience took place in an environment inspired by the stunning natural landscape in the surrounding Banff National Park in the Canadian Rocky Mountains. Visitors could move around this natural environment, play and converse with each other, move objects, and leave behind recorded fragments of their own narratives in the three different locations—a cave, a waterfall, and a formation of spires. *Placeholder* thus became a kind of virtual Lascaux, in which, rather than leaving behind petroglyphs, visitors were petroglyphs leaving behind their own disembodied voices of the animal spirit world. Ancient oral and visual traditions in storytelling were thus merged in this audio-visual cave painting (see figures V.2–V.4). *Placeholder* was an exploration of ideas about ritual space and narrative environments set forth by Brenda Laurel in her book, *Computers as Theater*. With *Placeholder*, she explored the role of theater-as-ritual, and the importance of drama as a form of archetypal catharsis.

Figure V.1

Entering the world of *Placeholder* via a Head-Mounted Display (image courtesy of Interval Research Corporation)

 Plate 11

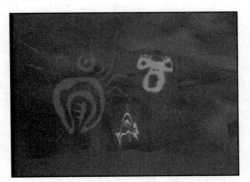

Figure V.2

Navigating the cave world of *Placeholder* as a spider (image courtesy of Interval Research Corporation)

 Plate 12

Figure V.3

Navigating the spires in the *Placeholder* environment as a crow and interacting with a fish (image courtesy of Interval Research Corporation)

PLATE 13

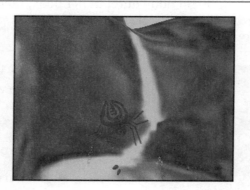

Figure V.4

Navigating the waterfall in the *Placeholder* environment as a spider (image courtesy of Interval Research Corporation)

PLATE 14

VIRTUAL REALITY AS A DRAMATIC ART (p. 508)

INTER-PLAY: IMPROVISATION AND INTERACTIVE THEATER (p. 230)

I first saw Rita Addison's *Detour: Brain Deconstruction Ahead* debuted at SIGGRAPH 94 in Orlando. This compelling autobiographical piece used the artist's own breathtaking photographs of nature to tell the before-and-after story of perceptual damage from a brain injury caused by a 1992 automobile accident. *Detour* was the first example I had ever seen of VR-as-autobiography. *Detour* provides the user with a first-person perspective to experience Rita's shift in perception as a result of an accident. All this is told through the simple device of viewing a gallery of her photographs as seen before and after the accident. Though the images are the same, the sensory anomalies that are simulated in the VR world create a drastic contrast to the clarity of vision seen in the "before" segment. This intensely personal experience is both disturbing and illuminating. The photographs themselves are images of nature that Rita took over the course of her career as a photographer prior to the accident. Thus, again, nature becomes the unifying theme through which to experience Virtual Reality. Taking place in a large projection space, called the *CAVE*, eight people at time can experience Rita's world, through the eyes of her camera and her love of nature.

THE REVELATION OF RITA: VR AND THE POWER OF EMPATHY (p. 413)

At the 1995 Interactive Media Festival in Los Angeles, the French team of Christa Sommerer and Laurent Mignonneau presented *A-Volve*, an experiment in artificial life and audience collaboration. In *A-Volve*, you walk up to a touch screen where you can draw the shape and profile of an abstract object. Entering a dark room, you are surprised to find yourself standing around a pool where you can actually reach in and rest your hand in the water (see figure V.5). Below the surface is a projection screen showing the life forms within the pool, 3D organisms based on the simple line drawings you and other visitors created before entering the space (see figure V.6). These simulated life forms interact with each other—cross-breed and procreate, eat each other, and so on—with a little help or hindrance from their creators, who can intervene in the process by merely resting their hands over the desired organism. The serene environment is meditative and the tactile involvement created by the simple device of using real water made this a Virtual Reality experience that provided a strong ground-ing in physical reality in a simple yet enchanting way.

Figure V.5

Interacting with the artificial life of *A-Volve* (image courtesy of Christa Sommerer & Laurent Mignonneau ©1994)

 PLATE 19

Sommerer and Mignonneau have also created several other artificial life art works, including *TRANS PLANT*, an environment in which you see yourself on a video screen and can grow trees and grass depending on where you step. Another piece, called *Interactive Plant Growing*, uses real plants as interface devices. As you come near the plants and even stroke them, they pick up electrical charges from your body and send them back to the computer, causing it to generate a computer-simulated version of the plant on a large screen (see figure V.7). Again, the tactile sense is a major factor, providing a new way to literally "get in touch" with nature. In *Phototropy*, visitors use a flashlight to affect the growth patterns of virtual moths on a screen. In the dark, they form cocoons and remain at rest, but when a visitor turns the light on, the moths burst out of the cocoons, following the light for nourishment. Move the light around and the moths grow and multiply, but if you leave it in one place too long, you will burn and destroy them. The light is turned off and they return to their cocoon form, waiting for the next visitor to come along and shine a light on the situation (see figure V.8).

Figure V.6

A computer-simulated evolution scale of *A-Volve* life (image courtesy of Christa Sommerer & Laurent Mignonneau ©1994)

 PLATE 20

Figure V.7

Interactive Plant Growing uses real plants as interfaces (image courtesy of Christa Sommerer & Laurent Mignonneau ©1993–1997)

 PLATE 22

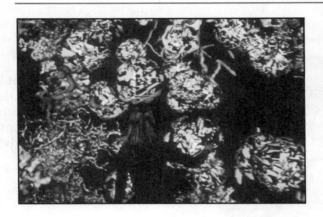

Figure V.8

A visitor interacts with the moths of *Phototropy* via a flashlight (image courtesy of Christa Sommerer & Laurent Mignonneau ©1994)

Plate 21

A-Life of One's Own (p. 5)

In 1995, Char Davies unveiled the stirring *Osmose*. The only single-user experience of these nature-centered works, *Osmose* uses the metaphor of scuba diving as an interface into a virtual world. As with underwater diving, your breath controls your rise and fall in the abstract natural world, and gentle movements from side to side control your direction. It is a brilliantly simple device because it takes you into a parallel universe while at the same time drawing your attention back to your body and your breath. This scuba diving interface very effectively addresses two classic navigational problems with VR. First, it is a perfect way to deal with the problem of cumbersome HMD equipment—from the standpoint of a diver, heavy gear is a matter of course, and thus the awareness of it not only does not detract from the experience, but actually adds to it. Second, the scuba metaphor solves the navigational problem of the floor/walls/ceiling conundrum. *Osmose* is not a room, but a continuous space; it has no "ground" and so a walking paradigm would not work for its ethereal, floating spaces. Most VR spaces feature a floor, which means walking…or in the case of the HMD, walking in place. This can get very confusing to the user because it is giving a mixed message: walk/don't walk. Char's diving interface gives only one message: float. The result is that the visitor can be free of the mechanics of the device, and experience total immersion in the virtual world (see figure V.9).

Osmose, as I mentioned, is one of the few VR worlds anywhere that has no floor. Like an underwater world, it seems to have no boundary, and leaves you with no clearly defined sense of scale. *Osmose* has been described as a meditation space. It is an abstraction of a natural environment, but it is deeply organic and in some way even sexual in its imagery. Small glowing, sperm-like objects either fly or swim (you can never be quite sure which) among branching structures that could just as easily be arteries as trees; and a central tree-like structure suggests the Tree of Life; or it could be the central heart of a living organism (see figure V.10).

Figure V.9

A participant dons an HMD and breath measuring apparatus to immerse himself in *Osmose* (image courtesy of Char Davies/ Softimage)

Figure V.10

Osmose's Tree of Life (image courtesy of Char Davies/ Softimage)

 PLATE 09

Other environments intermingled with this world of swimming lights and quivering translucent leaves include a maze of code, and a poetry world consisting of pure text (see figure V.11). In *Osmose*, you can be a cell, or an embryo, a fish, or a bird, you can be inside it, or it could be inside you. Because it is a virtual space, it is undefined and unscaled and thus it becomes an aggregate of every level of scale, and of every natural process. In this way, it also bears a relationship to Charles and Ray Eames' classic film and book

Powers of Ten, and *T_Vision*, the VR interpretation of a world at every level of scale, detail, and magnification. *Osmose* ends by pulling you out of the environment, a glowing seed, egg or cell, that you can see growing smaller and smaller as you move into darkness. Some describe the departure from it as a mournful exit from the womb; others left *Osmose* saying they no longer feared death. There is no question that for those who have embraced this mystical immersive experience, it is both cathartic and transcendent, a kind of digital nirvana, that takes people to a place they never expected to be taken by technology.

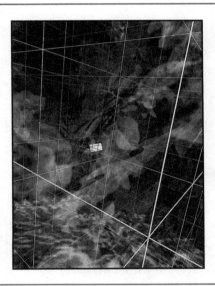

Figure V.11

Osmose's Matrix (image courtesy of Char Davies/ Softimage)

 PLATE 10

My own project, *Virtual Adventures*, came out during the same three-year period as *Detour*, *A-Volve*, and *Osmose*. Although not a fine art but a mainstream entertainment project, *Virtual Adventures: The Loch Ness Expedition* also takes place in a richly immersive natural environment. It is a story of man protecting nature from man. In particular, *Virtual Adventures* also shares two characteristics with both *A-Volve* and *Osmose*—it takes place in a beautiful, immersive underwater environment, and it deals with themes of birth and procreation.

All of these works together seem to form a suite, and I have regularly included these artists' work in various showcase exhibitions and panels. We have also been able to exchange ideas and philosophies toward understanding the commonalities and differences between our work. For whatever reason, we have all chosen to utilize this phenomenally powerful technology to tell stories about the human connection with nature. As you'll see in some other sections, quite a bit of VR and digital art concerns itself with nature in one form or another. It is interesting to note that, more than any other genre of interactive media, women seem to have a very strong presence in the arts and entertainment side of Virtual Reality. At least half of the high-end V-Artists seem to be female, which may be a little surprising considering the male skew in high-end technology. For whatever reason, a healthy percentage of women artists have been given the opportunity to bring their own unique sensibilities to this high-tech art form. The pieces discussed in this chapter set themselves apart, perhaps because they all approach the VR environment in terms of the human emotional connection with nature, as told through deeply personal, intuitive, sensory, and spiritual experiences.

OM MEETS OHM: DIGITAL ONENESS (p. 360)

THE SOUL IN THE MACHINE (p. 439)

VIRTUAL RELATIVITY (p. 524)

WHO IS THE AUTHOR? (p. 528)

T_VISION: SPACESHIP EARTH MADE VISIBLE (p. 460)

VICARIOUS EXPERIENCE

"Isn't all of this just vicarious experience?" This was a question posed by an audience member at the end of a panel session on Virtual Reality I gave in 1994. "Of course it is" I said, "That's the whole point."

The entire purpose of Virtual Reality is to enable you to do things you wouldn't or couldn't do in real life. I also pointed out to this audience member that vicarious experience is nothing new. In fact, you could argue that novels are the original Virtual Reality.

Many people decry the apparent trend that people are craving more and more vicarious experience in lieu of real experiences. The 1995 film *Synthetic Pleasures* (featuring a guest appearance by the vicarious king himself, Timothy Leary) explored the increasingly elaborate forms of substitute reality. People want to be able to do things without really doing them. In Japan, for example, you can go to an entirely artificial, indoor beach complete with sand, waves, and surfing. In addition, the Japanese developed a totally enclosed driving range for owners of utility vehicles to enjoy off-road adventures in complete safety. On-hand emergency crews rescue drivers who overturn their vehicles or get themselves into a tight spot. I heard one story of a driver who wrecked his car six times in one of these high-class playpens, but kept coming back for more (his insurance rates must be astronomical).

If I might wax philosophical for a moment, a brief review of human history indicates that vicarious experience is not only integral to the development of human culture, but can actually be used as a measuring stick for cultural evolution. Indeed, the evolution of a culture can be seen in terms of the level and quantity of vicarious experience that people have access to, which is another way of saying communication tools and genres. What is communication but the ability to transmit vicarious experience? If you think about it, aren't the cave paintings at Lascaux really an attempt at creating a vicarious experience? Oral history from the tribal campfire to Homer is a vicarious experience. In fact, the whole idea of recorded history in any form is merely an attempt to create still more vicarious experiences.

Through communication technologies and techniques, we can have the effect of certain experiences without really having them. We can go to places and times to which we could not be physically or temporally transported. We can even enter the minds of other people. All media, in fact, is about vicarious experience. When experiences are "broadcast"—whether by a TV station or a blind poet—so that many people can share the same experience, we begin to develop a collective memory. By conveying experiences beyond our own personal memory, we are able to, in a sense, expand our own memories to those of other people. Human culture has this sense of growing out of control because each person's individual memory is augmented by the memories of every other person or medium he or she encounters. Therefore, we all have an accumulation of vicarious experiences in addition to our authentic or so-called genuine experiences. In fact, many of our genuine experiences are strongly colored and influenced by the vicarious experiences we store in our "database." In some cases, a vicarious experience might even turn out to be more "real" in memory than an actual experience.

Dreams, myths, and fairytales are also forms of vicarious experience, only instead of recreating the memory of actual events, they offer a portal into a different level of consciousness. Psychologist Carl Jung found many parallels between our dream life and our mythologies. In his research, he discovered that the subconscious draws from what appear to be universal archetypes that, in many cases, cross cultural boundaries. In his extensive analysis and study of people's dreams, he found that even without any prior conscious exposure to classic fairytales or myths, the subconscious seemed nonetheless to draw from this pool of collective archetypes. This collective unconscious, according to Jung, is a kind of invisible fabric that holds the fabric of human experience together in ways of which we are not aware.

For the individual, dreams can be among the most cathartic of vicarious experiences. Drawing from principles of Aristotelian drama, the dream can be seen as a kind of personal mimesis, or cathartic transformation, for the individual. Dreams often provide us with stories and scenarios that our conscious minds could never "dream up." This subconscious plane is also the place that Aldous Huxley, Timothy Leary, and Terrence McKenna were trying to extend to the conscious level through hallucinogenic drugs, another form of vicarious experience.

 ## Consensual Hallucinations: Is VR the New LSD? (p. 137)

One of the research projects I always wanted to do is a study of the relationship of real and vicarious experience. Virtual Reality simulators, for example, have been used as a training tool in various forms for about three decades now. One of the great benefits of these systems is that they not only enable people to practice and learn in as close to a real situation as possible, but they also help people get over the fear and intimidation factor. At Motorola, for example, factory workers trained in VR to work on high-end machinery made less mistakes because they were less afraid of real machinery after having practiced in the simulator. Researchers at the HIT Lab (Human Interface Technology) in Seattle use Virtual Reality to cure phobias, such as fear of spiders. Taking the phobic patient through a vicarious encounter with the object of the phobia, enabled the patient to face and overcome her fears. The use of a real mechanical spider that mimicked the spider's movements in the virtual environment enabled the patient to not only see, but also to touch the spider, encountering her fear in a safe environment. Researchers have also used VR to teach autistic children how to notice and track moving cars and stop at a crosswalk Stop sign. Using a VR environment enabled the children to perform functions that they could not ordinarily do, and which would be extremely dangerous for the child in a real life setting.

The notion of "safe danger" is a key factor to vicarious experience. In interactive experiences, whether educational or entertaining, the benefit of these kinds of systems is that they enable people to experience the emotional impact of danger without actually being in a dangerous situation. This type of experience also enables people to practice dangerous tasks, such as flying a plane or piloting a submarine, in a setting that has no fatal consequences. The capability to thus "rehearse" a real-life situation in a safe context removes a certain measure of inhibition and fear, a natural barrier to learning.

Vicarious experience can also have other psychological benefits. Kit Galloway and Sherrie Rabinowitz of Electronic Café International have used their shared video space experiments to help people overcome social inhibitions, such as fear of touching others. Compositing people together in a videospace creates the opportunity for new kinds of interactions and social dynamics which can have enormous clinical benefit.

Virtual Reality in particular has also been used to offer people alternative realities to a physical condition that limits their abilities. A Virtual Reality system that uses a wheelchair as its interface enables paraplegics to move through a virtual space and experience different planes of reality. This same system is used for the non-wheelchair–bound as an educational tool to enhance understanding of the limitations such a situation creates.

The Starbright Foundation is one of the groups creating digital playspace for hospitalized and terminally ill children. Enabling children to do things such as fly in Virtual Reality not only improves their mental health, but as a result, also seems to have a positive effect on their physical health. Some of these systems offer collaborative playspaces that enable children in relative isolation to develop social connections with other ailing children through play and conversation, other activities believed to improve physical health.

Artist Rita Addison created what may be the ultimate vicarious experience with Virtual Reality: a simulation of perceptual anomalies caused by a brain injury she received in an automobile accident. This, like many other of the preceding projects, is a vicarious experience that could only be expressed through this uniquely subjective medium.

 THE REVELATION OF RITA: VR AND THE POWER OF EMPATHY (p. 413)

Vicarious experience gets a lot of hard knocks, but I personally think it's great. It's mind-expanding, and at its best, it opens up new mental frameworks and perceptual opportunities. As we've seen, the very basis of human history and cultural development is, to a large extent, a measure of evolving vicarious experience. Whether it is a petroglyph or the Sistine Chapel ceiling, a novel or a feature film, a religious ritual or a virtual environment, all vicarious experience boils down to is a chance to get a glimpse of the world through another's eyes. The more of it we have, the more opportunities there are for expanded awareness and understanding. These experiences also give us an outlet for expressions that we might not otherwise have. Whether we are guests at a costume party, players in a game of Monopoly, or video game jockeys blowing away simulated aliens, vicarious experience enables us do things that might be considered unacceptable in the real world. For a moment, we let go of our inhibitions and experiment in a setting of safe danger where anything goes. Hopefully, after we've step out of such an experience, we might find expression for our darker sides…subsequently freeing repressed emotions so that we can function more smoothly in the realm of social constraints.

 SOCIAL COMPUTING (p. 434)

CYBERSPACE CADETS: VIRTUAL COMMUNITIES AND AVATAR WORLDS (p. 146)

One of the things this book attempts to do is offer you a vicarious experience of interactivity. Throughout this book, I describe interactive experiences which, for whatever reason, might not be accessible to you. Some of them are just not available to the general public. Others require a trip (such as my own project, *Virtual Adventures*), and you may be constrained from experiencing some of the publicly accessible projects listed here by technical limitations, or even lack of access to a computer. Through this book, I offer you a way to vicariously experience these vicarious experiences through my own account of them. Strange though this may seem, it perfectly illustrates my point. Through the medium of text, combined with your own imagination and a few visual cues, you can have at least an impression of what it might be like to be in a fully immersive virtual environment, to experience VR on the web, or be part of an online community.

This simple twist offers a window through which to understand what vicarious experience is and can be. Interactive technology, unlike other media, brings us the power to affect the outcome in such experiences. With other media, we are subject to fate—the story will always be the same, and we are not at liberty to interject our own influence on it. On the other hand, a vicarious experience that is interactive, as we've seen, places us in a completely different relationship to our media. Now we are the masters of our own fate in a simulated world, whether real or fantastic. This affords us a new kind of freedom which, at its best, can ultimately lead to more freedom and power in the non-vicarious world of actual reality.

BEEN THERE, DONE THAT (p. 86)

VIRTUAL RELATIVITY (p. 524)

VIRTUAL REALITY AS A DRAMATIC ART (p. 508)

SPATIAL MEDIA (p. 442)

V-ART (p. 494)

VIRTUAL REALITY AS A DRAMATIC ART

In her 1991 book *Computers as Theater*, Brenda Laurel suggested the computer as a dynamic theatrical space that could provide the ultimate vehicle for dramatic experience. The responsive computer and Virtual Reality, she argued, are ideal media through which to activate the Aristotelian notion of "mimesis," the intangible sense of emotional resonance at the core of drama and storytelling.

Virtual Reality, as a medium, contains qualities that lend themselves to drama, narrative, and storytelling. First, it forces the viewer into a highly personalized, first-person viewpoint. No longer alienated from the action by an invisible fourth wall, you are suddenly sucked in, invited to become an active participant in the dramatic interchange—like Alice through the looking glass, or the infamous wardrobe of C.S. Lewis's classic *Narnia Chronicles*. Not unlike Gumby walking into the pages of his favorite book, you can literally enter the drama as a full-fledged character rather than a passive spectator. This first-person viewpoint elicits *empathy*, which is another way of saying mimesis. The first person perspective inherently creates empathy, subsequently enabling VR as an empathic medium, a quality it shares with no other existing medium. Dynamic interaction becomes a vehicle for including me as an active participant, or *player* in the interactive drama or *play*. Implementing both empathy and dynamic interaction creates a winning combination with enormous potential to create entirely new and compelling narrative genres.

 ## USER OR PLAYER: THE CHOICE IS YOURS (p. 490)

Although some may trivialize drama as mere entertainment or distraction, its historical importance in the evolution of culture would suggest that it has a much more integral role in human development. Like dreams, which provide catharsis on the individual, subconscious level, drama provides catharsis in a social context. This catharsis provides a means to process emotions, fears, conflicts; to understand the meaning of life; and to explore and share common life themes and struggles with others. Theater, oral and literary traditions, as well as cinema and television, provide various forms of catharsis through narrative. It seems to be a fairly universal axiom that there is a clear and present need for this kind of narrative catharsis in every human culture. From the caves at Lascaux to Shakespeare's Globe Theater, the desire to tell and share stories and dramatic narrative appears to be as old as human communication, and might, indeed, even be its impetus. Early storytelling might have been a matter of survival, explaining through anecdote how to hunt a bison or avoid a predator. As human culture evolved, we began to develop mythologies, archetypal dramas to explain the nature and origin of things. As Jung recognized, many of these archetypes, though manifested in different ways, are common across all cultures and appear in mythology, folklore, and even in our dreams. Joseph Campbell, expert in comparative mythology and star of the highly acclaimed *Power of Myth*, provides an engrossing tour of the world's religions in terms of myth, narrative, and archetype, from Earth-centered pagan myths to Catholicism to *Star Wars*.

Throughout history and even pre-history, the dramatic acting out of cathartic scenes and stories as a form of religious and social ritual, has been practiced and cultivated in a variety of ways.

Psycho-ergonomics (p. 404)

OM Meets OHM: Digital Oneness (p. 360)

Along with mimesis and catharsis, the primordial drama is also characterized by suspension of disbelief—meaning that the audience member becomes absorbed and immersed, suspending whatever inhibitions or rational boundaries he or she might impose between his or her own mind and the essence of the drama. Suspension of disbelief can be a product of implementation, but it can also be as much a product of content. A really compelling story can be implemented simply, and perhaps even poorly, but if the characters and events are believable and consistent within their own reality (whether Mount Olympus or the bridge of the *Starship Enterprise*), the story will successfully achieve suspension of disbelief. The audience will forget that they are in the Acropolis—or on the couch—and achieve mimesis, a connection to the story.

In the early 80s, Brenda Laurel and some of her colleagues at Atari began to explore the idea of creating a virtual drama-world, what I call a narrative environment, a space in which players could enter and become participants in a story.

The idea of a shared story space has been part of digital culture from the beginning, and also has its roots in live role-playing games such as *Dungeons & Dragons* (*D&D*). Players in a networked MUD (alternately, "multi-user dungeon" after *D&D* or "multi-user dimension") create unique characters and enter into a live text-based Chat or self-generated serialized drama. In a MUD environment, various skills, magical powers, and personality traits of characters create an elaborately structured infrastructure for improvised drama. This unusual form of real-time fiction integrates traditional elements of drama, text-based story, theater, improvisation, and role-playing to create evolving, user-created worlds and stories. Denizens of *D&D* do the same thing around a gaming table, often creating elaborate illustrations of their characters, and developing extraordinarily sophisticated stories and plot lines. Most *D&D* and MUD environments are mediated by "Dungeon" Masters or "Wizards." Computer-based games can also include computer-generated characters or "bots" that are designed to serve or assist players with preprogrammed responsive algorithms.

The Rules of the Game (p. 420)

Since the mid-80s, a variety of different researchers have explored various experiments for creating interactive drama. Laurel and colleague Joseph Bates at Carnegie Mellon University developed a structural framework for creating drama in cyberspace. Starting with a text-based infrastructure, the goal was to eventually link these systems to a fully rendered, real-time 3D environment, or Virtual Reality. In 1993, Laurel, along with co-director Rachel Strickland, was able to implement her ideas about Virtual Reality as a ritual space with an original project entitled *Placeholder.* This immersive world of myth and mystery put players in the roles of animal spirits represented by Indian petroglyphs. Participants could play with one another and objects in the space, and leave the equivalent of audio petroglyphs behind as a record of their experience. *Placeholder* took place in a natural setting based on a real setting: The Banff National Park in Alberta, Canada surrounding The Banff Centre, where the piece was shown. *Placeholder* demonstrates how Virtual Reality can have the added benefit of enhancing an appreciation of reality, in this case, nature.

 V-Art (p. 494)

Strolling Through Cyberspace: Second Nature and the Virtual Gallery (p. 457)

One of the more interesting projects focused on interactive drama is *Improv* out of New York University's Media Research Lab. Ken Perlin initiated the project with a virtual character known generally as *The Dancer.* Where previous simulated character projects were built upon an Artificial Intelligence model, *The Dancer* was an experiment in behavior. Perlin didn't particularly want the character to think. Perlin was more concerned with simulating personality than creating emotions or thought. The idea relied on the development of a set of algorithms that dictated gesture and movement of a 3D, computer-generated character in real time, which consequently enabled the creation of a convincing character. The character contained no innate intelligence, but could merely *act* intelligent (I will refrain from drawing any corollaries with real life actors here…). The dancer could walk across a room, do several dance movements, and basically "cop an attitude," which might appear to be alternately friendly, flirtatious, stand-offish, or downright rude, based on a variety of gesture parameters that Perlin—or anyone for that matter—could control in real time.

 Artificial Intelligence and the Prosthetic Brain (p. 38)

I first saw *The Dancer* demonstrated at SIGGRAPH 94. It was one of those presentations where you sit with your jaw hanging open. I saw so-called artificial characters before, but all of them *appeared* artificial. Their jerky movements and unconvincing interactions with their surroundings did nothing but illuminate the natural complexity of the human organism and its utter defiance at emulation. Perlin, who made a name for himself with a little universally adopted graphical algorithm known as "Perlin noise code," applied some of the same ideas of creating a level of "noise" (apparent randomness required to make things appear natural) to his gesture animation. The result of this combination was a virtual character that actually elicited an emotional response from the audience.

What I didn't know at the time of this presentation was that one of the new researchers on Ken's team was Athomas Goldberg, who had worked with me on the playtesting effort at Edwin Schlossberg Incorporated 10 years earlier. Goldberg, who spent several years in the theater as a lighting and set designer, with particular expertise in dynamic lighting of dancers, was originally hired to light the dancer and provide art direction to the character and the scene. The lighting provided a dramatic effect that added to both the dimensionality of the scene and the believability of the character. Goldberg's initial involvement as the resident production designer evolved as he brought his experience in theater, computers, and interactive design to bear on this new art form.

As a result, Goldberg became a principle researcher at the MRL and eventually developed *Improv* into a full-blown authoring and animation tool for creating interactive fiction and all-purpose real-time animation. The key to *Improv* is that its characters are truly actors...not actually AI, intelligent beings, but creatures designed to *behave as if* they are intelligent, in a believable way.

Improv is an exercise in body language. A typical *Improv* scene features a number of characters who, through procedural animations, are able to interact with one another in real time. Using a very simple interface, an operator can make subtle adjustments to the character's demeanor to indicate certain emotional states. A character can be, for example, confident or unsure, aggressive or meek. By recognizing each others body language, these characters can play off of each other, in the same way pantomime actors will play off each other in an improvised scene. Two characters might be aggressive and end up in a fight; a character might be sensitive and become offended by another's joke (see figures V.12–V.14). Characters can also react to foreign objects introduced into the environment. If the user starts moving objects around in the room, the characters will respond with different reactions such as curiosity, fear, surprise, and so forth. A typical *Improv* demo includes a scene in which the characters are responding to a bat. At SIGGRAPH 95, the bat was hooked up to an interface that enabled visitors to the show to control the bats by flapping their arms. Depending on where they flew in the room, the characters would react to them in different ways based on their current moods or attitudes. Another experiment that was done with *Improv* is virtual dancing. By hooking a character up to a MIDI interface, the user can actually make the character dance to a different drummer. In other words, based on tempo or other variables (including personality), the character can actually dance to user-generated improvised music.

In addition to getting characters to interact with each other and a live player, Goldberg also wanted the characters to be able to interact with and use inanimate objects. Instead of using the classic Artificial Intelligence construct of having the simulated characters learn how to use objects, Goldberg came up with a completely different approach. Why couldn't the objects themselves tell the characters how to use them? Each object's instructions were self-embedded. When a character encountered the object, the object told the character what to do. When the character walked away, it carried no memory of the transaction; however, the character might handle the object in a different way based on mood or attitude.

Figure V.12

Improv: Gregor & Friends engage in simulated social dynamics

 Plate 28

Improv is, as you might imagine, deeply influenced by principles of improvisational theater. The work of Viola Spolin, in particular, inspired Goldberg to integrate theories of spontaneous drama within the repertoire of his repertory. As a director of interactive virtual narrative, I rate *Improv* as one of the best tools around, primarily because it is designed with both the creator and user in mind.

Figure V.13

Improv: Botanica Virtuale—
entering the Graveyard
(SIGGRAPH 96)

 PLATE 29

Figure V.14

Improv: Botanica Virtuale—
Juke Joint (SIGGRAPH 96)

 PLATE 30

Improv's virtual actors are not paid to think—they're paid to act. As a director, I can work with these characters to create a variety of different narrative scenarios. I can, just as a real director would, direct their attitudes and actions, and their relationships to each other, myself, props, and other outside or internally driven influences. I can program them to respond in different ways to different situations—to improvise within a set of given parameters. In this way, I can create dynamic theatrical experiences that break the fourth wall between audience and exhibit but still maintain a sense of narrative structure.

 INTER-PLAY: IMPROVISATION AND INTERACTIVE THEATER (P. 230)

BUILDING CHARACTER: THE SOUL OF DRAMA (P. 119)

1994 was a seminal year for VR Drama. At that same SIGGRAPH conference where Ken presented *The Dancer*, three other projects were introduced that broke new ground for Virtual Reality as a narrative art:

- *Aladdin's Magic Carpet Ride*
- *Virtual Adventures: The Loch Ness Expedition*
- *Detour: Brain Deconstruction Ahead*

Walt Disney Imagineering (the people who brought you *Pirates of the Caribbean* and *Swiss Family Robinson Treehouse*) produced a project based on the film *Aladdin*. Players donned an HMD (Head-Mounted Display) and manipulated a yoke that created the sensation of flying a magic carpet. The goal was to reassemble the broken magic lamp by finding its missing pieces scattered throughout Agrabar. Disney's game, creative directed by Jon Snoddy, featured "Disney-quality" (an actual adjective in the theme park biz) animation, including a mix of traditional animation techniques (all the shadows were hand painted rather than rendered with lighting algorithms) and a hint of AI (characters responded to your presence and egged you on down the path). Although Disney made several other attempts to create VR in their top secret R&D facility in Burbank, this was their first publicly unveiled (and one assumes, the first successful) attempt at a Virtual Reality experience. Needless to say, the Disney booth was among the most crowded exhibits on the tradeshow floor.

 Narrative Environments: Virtual Reality as a Storytelling Medium (p. 329)

The second ground-breaking VR entry, also a location-based entertainment project, was the product of a joint venture between the company that invented VR—Evans & Sutherland, and a Burbank ridefilm company called Iwerks Entertainment started by former denizens of Walt Disney Imagineering. The product was called *Virtual Adventures: The Loch Ness Expedition*. Based on the legend of the Loch Ness Monster, this VR ride took the narrative element even further by adding dramatic structure, game logic, and multi-user interactivity to the mix. In *The Loch Ness Expedition,* players embark on an underwater mission to rescue the Loch Ness Monster's eggs from bounty hunters (other players, who look like good guys to themselves but bad guys to everybody else). *The Loch Ness Expedition* combined a three-act structure with basic tenets of game logic to create a hybrid movie/ride/game in which players became the heroes of the story. *Virtual Adventures* was also the first VR game to involve cooperative team play, and, other than the Disney ride, the first to target a family audience (up until that point, VR had been strictly the domain of testosterone-ridden teenagers and college boys). *Virtual Adventures* was, by the way, my first foray into high-end Virtual Reality. I creative directed the project.

 The Princess and the Monster: The Making of Virtual Adventures (p. 375)

Virtual Adventures and the *Aladdin* VR ride set a new standard for VR content. No longer was VR relegated to sci-fi robot gladiators in cyberdeserts, or hyper-realistic military combat simulations. Here was story-based VR content for all ages, content that brought a level of narrative as well as aesthetic quality to VR in the realm of commercial entertainment. Although both exhibits suffer from cost prohibitions, they set new standards for VR attractions as a main-stream entertainment genre.

Detour: Brain Deconstruction Ahead was another landmark in VR drama that was first presented at SIGGRAPH 94. I had been hearing about it all week. "Did you see the brain thing?" people were asking me, and I remember one person referring to it as "The Broken Brain." When I got there, I was not expecting what I saw. *Detour* was an autobiographical story told in a CAVE or VROOM (Virtual Reality Room). Developed by fine artist Rita Addison and designer/programmer Marcus Thiebeaux, *Detour* told the dramatic tale of a car accident that left Rita with brain damage which altered her senses and perception. Although I talk about this project at length in other chapters, I want to speak of it here in the context of interactive drama and as it relates to these other projects.

First of all, unlike any other VR application I'd seen, *Detour* was autobiographical. It was also factual, and in some respects, scientific. Like *Virtual Adventures*, *Detour* followed a three-act structure. The story itself was linear; there was no way for the viewer to have any impact on the narrative, but *Detour* immersed the audience in a first-person sensory experience, an unusual dramatic premise, even for VR. In this application, you were put in the role of a specific, real person. To my knowledge, this was unprecedented for VR. The passivity of the narrative might have been unproblematic in almost any other situation, but this is one of those rare cases where it makes perfect sense. *Detour* is a tale of sensory entrapment, a first-person account of events beyond the control of the main character. Part of its very drama is in the fact that you cannot control the outcome. Just as the artist herself lost control of her life, and her brain, so we the viewer must also lose control to get the full impact of the experience. What we do get to do is navigate the world through the eyes of the main character as if we were her.

The interaction itself and the premise of *Detour* are both quite simple. We start in a gallery of Rita's work, which establishes her character and sets up the story: she is a photographer, in love with the lush sensorium of nature. Act 2 pulls us out of the light and serene gallery into a dark highway, a skid and a crash, and a tour inside of Rita's broken brain. Here, we change viewpoints, but actually enter into a model of the brain as it incurs damage. It's a horrify-ing experience, made all the more eerie by the fact that this is the only depic-tion we see of Rita herself: her face in wireframe as we move into her brain coming unglued. We are then returned to the world, the gallery, now faced with the irreversible fate that Rita herself experienced: brain damage and the sensory anomalies that go with it. No matter where we turn, the world becomes distorted, and we are trapped inside a world in which we no longer have control. The poignancy and catharsis of this is driven home in the sharp irony that the vehicle for experiencing these anomalies are Rita's own photos, the works of art she can no longer create. The resolution of this drama lies in the fact that we are also seeing the rebirth of her art through a new art form. Thus, *Detour* takes us full circle, and the photographer who lost her eyes is reborn as a pioneer of Virtual Reality art. If Aristotle's concepts of mimesis (empathy) and catharsis (transformation) are the criteria by which we measure drama, then *Detour* is one of the best realizations of Virtual Reality as a dramatic art.

The Revelation of Rita: VR and the Power of Empathy (p. 413)

One thing that is amazing about *Detour* and the other narrative pieces previously described is that most of these experiences are less than ten minutes in length; however, they are able to tell a powerful story in ten minutes that it might take a film two hours to tell. Because of the constraints of technology and throughput, few Virtual Reality experiences can afford to be much longer than this. As a result, the genre of VR storytelling has been condensed into a very short form. This is also a tribute to the inherent qualities of VR immersion: you can say a lot in a short period of time because it's a very dense medium. Because it is so intense, and because it is to demanding on the senses, it is unlikely that immersive Virtual Reality experiences such as these will ever get much longer than this. It is also interesting that the majority of these products tend to fall into increments of four or eight minutes. This is not a convention that anyone decided on, it just seems to be a natural length for immersive drama.

In addition to these genres of high-end, immersive VR drama, there is also a 3D revolution underway on the web. VRML (Virtual Reality Modeling Language) is opening the door for an entirely new different form of VR content. If the aforementioned projects are the cinema of VR, then VRML is the television. Already, VRML "episodics" exist—animated comic strips or cartoons with 3D characters. C. Scott Young, a pioneering VRML artist, created some of the first VRML comic strips with his serialized tale of vegetable heroics, the *Carrot Defender*. His *Idville* and other VRML worlds created prior to the advent of animation are a form of narrative sculpture—navigable statuary with a story built in. San Francisco-based Protozoa's award-winning *Floops* has become the first real VRML celebrity in cyberspace, and Protozoa has been at the forefront of character animation in VRML. Mark Meadows of Construct recently released *Crutch*, and other story-based VR is no doubt imminent. Multi-user avatar-based worlds are gaining in popularity, but as of this writing, none have really incorporated drama. Because of my fascination with multiplayer interaction and improvisational drama, I am looking forward to exploring the potential of this new medium further.

THE BIRTH OF CYBERSPACE: 3D COMES TO THE WEB (p. 97)

CYBERSPACE CADETS: VIRTUAL COMMUNITIES AND AVATAR WORLDS (p. 146)

DECISIONS, DECISIONS, DECISIONS (p. 158)

VICARIOUS EXPERIENCE (p. 504)

VIRTUAL REALITY CHECK: WHAT IS VR ANYWAY?

Although it was first invented in the late 60s, Virtual Reality was really introduced to the popular culture in the early 80s by William Gibson and the so-called "cyberpunk" fiction movement (Gibson is credited with inventing the term "cyberspace"), but did not gain access to a larger audience as a concept until the early 90s when sci-fi films such as *Circuitry Man*, *Lawnmower Man*, and *Total Recall* brought VR to a mainstream audience. Many other films and television programs featuring Virtual Reality have since emerged, but most fictional depictions of VR focus on its darker side—as a tool of combat, manipulation, or intentions gone awry. I'm sure a large part of this has to do with VR's roots in the military.

A BRIEF HISTORY OF REAL TIME: THE VIRTUAL REALITY LEGACY (p. 105)

Though the popular media would have us believe that VR started in the early 1990s, this so-called "new technology" has been in use for nearly 30 years. VR was originally developed for flight training, military simulation, aerospace training, and Computer Aided Design (or CAD) systems. It has also been used as a research tool in the sciences, as a way to model and visualize biological systems, to train doctors and simulate surgical procedures, and to create visual models of mathematical and scientific principles and processes. Most of this work required an enormous amount of computing power, and due to the high level of secrecy of the military and the relative isolation of the academic research community, these applications were virtually unknown to anyone beyond their immediate practitioners.

By the late 1990s, Virtual Reality made its way into the popular vernacular in both America and Europe. When you talk about Virtual Reality to the average, non-technical person today, he or she will invariably have heard of it. But if you ask them the question "What is Virtual Reality?" few people would be able to give you an answer. Those who can answer are likely to be under 12 years of age. On the other hand, if you ask the same question of VR experts, you will get as many different answers as people you ask, and they will differ widely. From a poetic and semantic level, Virtual Reality is both an evocative and yet seemingly meaningless concept. Because it has achieved the status of hype, there is a tendency to use the term very loosely to apply to things that really are not VR. The term is often used erroneously in the same way that people use "interactive" erroneously, merely because it's the cool thing to be.

It is unfortunate that a good deal of mainstream journalism on the subject of Virtual Reality is often backed up with less research than science fiction. Much of the confusion about VR among the general public can be attributed to a press which has glommed onto "Virtual Reality" as the buzzword du jour. It is unfortunate that erroneous information often goes into public record as statements of fact. Such misinformation can even get written in stone as historical information, even if it is retracted later. Also to blame are the opportunistic marketers and publicists who will hype as Virtual Reality that which is not, merely because the term has become "wired." I can't tell you how many people I've talked to at conferences who make claims at creating Virtual Reality when they are doing nothing of the sort.

Being a purist and something of an armchair historian, I like to stick with the term as defined by its original creator, Ivan Sutherland. Sutherland created what is generally acknowledged to be the first Virtual Reality system in 1969, and also is credited with coining the term itself. Call me old-fashioned, but I figure if it's good enough for Ivan, it's good enough for me. Actually, it's not very complicated at all. The following is my simplified, paraphrased version, but I think it pretty much sums it up in a sentence:

> Virtual Reality is a simulated, computer-generated world through which a user can navigate in real time (with immediate feedback) as if he or she was moving through a real three-dimensional space. Virtual Reality is, by definition, interactive.

To be more specific, in a Virtual Reality environment, the computer knows the shape, size, and properties of every object in the database. These objects are constructed of "polygons," or enclosed shapes, such as a triangle, that can be assembled to make objects such as a house, a tea pot, a tree, or even a simulated animal or human. To make the object appear more realistic, a texture map is applied. A texture map amounts to digital wallpaper laid on to the three-dimensional polyhedron made of polygons. It is sort of like making a papier-mâché sculpture—you create the frame first, and then you lay a surface treatment on to it. After you create the objects, you can endow them with other physical properties, such as weight, density, and so on. You can also program physics into the environment, such as gravity, or climate characteristics, such as wind and fog. You can also endow objects with properties as they relate to each other—for example, what happens when wood hits metal versus when wood hits sand. A system called "collision detection" determines when two objects hit each other and what happens as a result (without collision detection, you can literally walk through virtual walls). Proximity detection, a variation of collision detection, enables you to know when objects are near each other in order to trigger certain responses. You can also add animations; either keyframe animation, which is essentially linear, or procedural animation, which is responsive to the environment and user input. You can also program behaviors, which are algorithms that enable spontaneous interaction between objects and with the user. Virtual Reality environments are greatly enhanced by lighting, which lends a sense of depth and volume to the space. Details such as shininess and shadows derive from calculations based on the direction and intensity of the light as well as the surface treatment of the object. As most designers of traditional media know, sound and music can often make half or more of an experience. 3D, or spatial audio systems, that create real-time music and sound effects can add a level of believability to your 3D visuals. You can even add acoustical properties to your space to create realistic resonance within a simulated environment.

Virtual Reality is most commonly associated with a Head-Mounted Display (HMD), a contraption worn on the head, and a wired "data glove" for manipulating objects in the virtual space. The HMD is a kind of immersive interface device involving as many of the senses as possible, ideally filtering out any outside input. In addition to pioneering the computational aspects of Virtual Reality, Ivan Sutherland also originated the Head-Mounted Display as an interface device for Virtual Reality. A typical HMD generally contains two small screens, one for each eye, showing two slightly offset views of the same image; this stereoscopic viewing device tricks the eye into thinking it is seeing a two-dimensional scene in three dimensions. An HMD usually contains some kind of tracking device that sends a signal back to the computer telling it the movement and rotation of your head; the computer in turn generates real-time animations in response to your movements. As you move your head, the computer-generated graphics in the two tiny screens move accordingly, relative to your viewpoint, or position in the simulated space. Many HMDs include binaural or spatial audio systems that use stereo techniques to create the illusion of audio space. Based on the relative position of a sound source to your head, the effect is calculated so that that the sound seems to emanate from the object, wherever it may move. The HMD is generally seen in the company of a data glove—a wired glove that enables the computer to calculate the position of the hand and fingers so that you can interact with the environment, opening doors, touching buttons, and picking up objects.

VIRTUAL RELATIVITY (p. 524)

Head-Mounted Displays have become very controversial. Hard-core VR purists consider the HMD to be de rigeur for fully immersive VR. Studies show that HMDs have certain educational benefits—people trained using them seem to learn better due to the immersive quality of the experience. Unfortunately, HMDs have also been known to cause a variety of undesirable side effects. One is that the stereoscopic eyepiece causes temporary confusion to the depth perception system. Pilots trained with a stereo VR system are not allowed to fly real planes for a minimum of 24 hours after using the system. HMDs can sometimes induce headaches, dizziness, and motion sickness (especially in women, who are physiologically more susceptible to motion-related discomfort). In addition to all these side effects, the heavy weight of the head mount can cause headaches, neck aches, and general discomfort.

Aside from the HMD, there are many other immersive systems. Alternatives to Head-Mounted Displays, such as the Fakespace boom and push systems, still use stereoscopic systems but do away with the cumbersome head mount. Simulated cockpits or submarines created by Evans & Sutherland and their competitors are common in military and commercial applications. Several companies, including Evans & Sutherland, have also developed dome theaters for VR; and the University of Illinois, Chicago's Electronic Visualization Laboratory developed the CAVE, a rear projection cube that places about eight people in an enclosed box of light. All these systems enable various forms of sensory immersion, each suited to different applications. Other enhancements include tactile response, also known as "forced feedback," a popular area of research because it affords an even stronger sensory experience.

Forced feedback systems such as SensAble Devices' Phantom, are electrome-chanical devices that enable you to relate to the VR world through the sense of touch. Some of these systems are so effective, they can simulate objects that are rough or smooth, hard and soft, moving or stationary, and can even create the tactile illusion of something as subtle as stickiness. Smell is perhaps the greatest bafflement of all. Due to its strong association as a sense-memory trigger, some feel that it is a highly underrated element in creating simulated sensoria. But the technical difficulty associated with creating aromas, not to mention getting rid of them, has made this the toughest nut of all to crack. Few of these systems are currently available to the general public; most are too expensive and delicate to be used in public venues, and few artists and designers have been able to develop content for these various devices. They are used primarily in research, military and training applications, some therapeutic applications, and occasionally for entertainment and fine art applications.

VICARIOUS EXPERIENCE (p. 504)

Although most high-end systems are not accessible to the general public, Virtual Reality applications have nonetheless managed to slip into the mass culture in other forms. Walk into any video game arcade today and you will no doubt see driving simulators where you race along a virtual racetrack. These days, you can pay a dollar to ski down virtual slopes, and even ride a bicycle through a VR landscape at your local gym. Games that simulate hand-to-hand combat— what I like to call Neolithic VR, such as *Virtua Fighter, Mortal Kombat,* and *Tekken*—have found their way into both arcade and home game systems.

IT'S ONLY A GAME: THE BIRTH OF A MULTI-BILLION DOLLAR BUSINESS (p. 260)

If you prefer a less vigorous form of VR, you might want to boot up your VRML (Virtual Reality Modeling Language) browser and cruise through the realization of William Gibson's hypothetical cyberspace. For those familiar with the World Wide Web, VRML is to VR what HTML is to text and graphics. It is a universal protocol, or generally accepted standard, that enables you to create Virtual Reality environments on the Internet. VRML enables VR and VR creation tools to come to the average desktop, and is deliberately designed to be easy to use so that virtually anyone can create his or her own 3D worlds on the web. As desktop PCs become faster and more powerful, these VR worlds on the Internet will become more and more of a reality for the average computer user.

THE BIRTH OF CYBERSPACE: 3D COMES TO THE WEB (p. 105)

Now that we know what VR is, let's take a look at what it's not. VR is not:

- **Ride simulators and motion-based film:** Being passive, they clearly do not qualify.
- **3D movies:** These are also passive.
- **3D special effects for film:** These effects are what is called "rendered," meaning that the models and animations are pre-processed and output as linear animations; VR is real-time, which precludes pre-rendered, linear animations.

- **Virtual sets:** These are only VR to the people producing with them, but for the viewer or user, they are merely another form of 3D effects.
- Any interface based on an architectural or spatial metaphor that does not involve real-time 3D animation. Such applications can, however, be placed under the broader classification of spatial media.

 SPATIAL MEDIA (p. 442)

The most important thing to know about Virtual Reality is that it is not a technology, but a medium. There are many different ways to implement VR, many different applications and approaches to it. Just like film or video, VR is merely a means of conveying content, and an interface through which to connect people with interactive experiences on computers. Any value judgement of VR itself is somewhat silly, because it is not the medium itself that is good or bad, but the content generated in it.

As a popular medium, VR is at the front end of its evolutionary curve. Narrative environments (my term for VR worlds that facilitate story) are just beginning to be explored, and the revolutionary innovations of VRML make it possible for people to not only experience VR on a daily basis, but to create their own VR worlds and experiences and make them accessible through the web.

 NARRATIVE ENVIRONMENTS: VIRTUAL REALITY AS A STORYTELLING MEDIUM (p. 329)

As a designer and content creator who has worked with a wide variety of interactive media, from military flight simulators to playing cards, I find VR the most satisfying medium to work in because it is the most interactive. Of all interactive media, it enables the most user responsiveness and flexibility. I can use it for both games and stories. If done well, VR can be graphically rich. It sparks the imagination and is an ideal venue in which to weave fantasy worlds, reflect on reality, and interact with others. It is inherently dynamic, and rather than nonlinear, it is really omni-directional. As a storytelling tool, VR has tremendous power because I can use it not only to create participatory stories or environments for the player, but I can also create environments in which players can create their own stories. With VRML and new VR content creation tools, cyberspace will become a collaborative construction of its participants. In this scenario, everyone will become an interactive designer, creating collaborative and personal worlds to share with each other. Because my mission is and has always been to use my own creativity to facilitate the creativity of others through participatory experiences, I can think of nothing better than a world in which everyone is an interactive designer. There really could be nothing more interactive than that.

VIRTUAL RELATIVITY

I doubt very much that Virtual Reality could ever have happened without Albert Einstein's general Theory of Relativity. The theory states simply that everything happens relative to everything else. In terms of movement, for example, Einstein demonstrated that you could just as easily say that the train was standing still under a moving earth as that the train itself was moving. In cases where velocity is constant, in fact, the standard Newtonian laws of gravity and motion behave as if the object is standing still. This is very fortunate for those of us who are residing on a constantly rotating planet. In fact, if you look at the earth and its contents as an example, it is impossible to say what is moving relative to what. If a train is moving at the same velocity as the earth in the opposite direction, is it standing still?

The theory of relativity creates the basic groundwork for Virtual Reality. Whether Ivan Sutherland and Dave Evans realized it at the time, they were in essence creating the ultimate manifestation of relativity: The principle behind Virtual Reality is to make you feel like you're moving through a simulated three-dimensional environment by moving *its* position relative to you. In other words, if you stand still and turn your head while wearing an HMD (Head-Mounted Display), the objects on the screen will be constantly repositioning relative to your head to create the illusion that you are moving through the space. This same technique is used at a much simpler level in old-fashioned 2D animation: the camera is trained on the supposedly moving object as the background speeds by. You can also give the appearance that something is falling by moving the background in the vertical axis. By manipulating the relative position of objects to each other, you can thus create the illusion of movement from a third-person perspective. With a first-person orientation in a 3D world, you can use the same technique to create the sense that you yourself are moving through space, but within a plane that has three axes rather than two.

The computer creates this illusion by containing a full mathematical model of the object in the scene. In sophisticated systems, this not only includes the models or object forms themselves, but also lighting and behavior algorithms, such as level of detail or collision detection. As the system senses your movement, whether it is with the motion tracker on an HMD, through mouse-based navigation, or the movement of a steering wheel, the system constantly recalculates its orientation to you.

If you consider this in a fully rendered world, you can see how complex this might become, and why, until recently, it took an enormous amount of computing power to do these calculations. Each time you move your head, the computer must go through the following relativity calculations:

1. Redraw all the polygons (enclosed shapes) on the screen to reorient the object to you; this involves using forced perspective such that you always feel as if you're at the correct angle with respect to the object; and it must be done for each frame so quickly that you barely notice the delay between your movement and that of the screen image.

2. Recalculate all the lighting angles; find the light source relative to both you and the object so that the shadows and reflections are properly placed.

3. If there are textures on the surfaces, the system must calculate how their orientation has changed relative to the viewpoint.

4. If there is collision detection, the system must determine whether the movement will result in any contact between objects, including the user's own avatar or digital representation; if the object has different properties, the system must decide what to do about the collision. Do the objects bounce off each other, or do they land with a dead thud?

5. A realistic world, even if it is fantastical, will probably require programming some physics algorithms. Gravity, mass, momentum, bounce, air currents, and a variety of other physical properties can be attributed to objects in a virtual environment. These also need to be factored in when calculating movement.

6. Levels of detail are used as a way to make this process more efficient by making an object less detailed the farther away it is from you, much as it would be in real life. When you see something from a distance, you make out less detail. As you approach it (or it approaches you… relativity and all you know), it appears more detailed. This principle is also applied to VR, making the scene more convincing to the eye. If level of detail is included, the computer must determine when and how to load the various detail data for each level of magnification.

7. A very active world requires the inclusion of some pre-set animations that are different from behaviors because they are essentially linear. Thus the animation sequence runs continually throughout the scene; and as you move around in the space, calculations are needed to determine how your movement affects your view of the animations.

8. Now, what if you want the objects in your world to have dynamic behaviors. When you approach the object, does it react to your presence? Does a school of fish swim away from you when you go toward it? Does a character speak to you when you are within a certain distance? The computer must recognize each of these interactive triggers, and then generate the desired behaviors accordingly.

9. The importance of audio is matter of common knowledge to content creators in all media. Thus, for added realism and believability, you might want to include some spatial sound. This might include audio effects triggered by collision, the voice of a character, or even interactive music. A whole variety of relative calculations must be performed to find the sound in an audio database, play it at the right time, and calculate its location relative to you. Resonance algorithms in the space will add a measure of acoustic authenticity, requiring an additional set of calculations to create the right spatial quality.

A key concept in this scenario is the notion of viewpoint, and this is where the relativity comes in. The viewpoint is simply the point of view from which you see the environment.

A very important thing to understand about Virtual Reality is that you are always in a first-person point of view. You might be observing events, but because the 3D space somewhat dissolves the fourth wall (in theater and film, the invisible wall between audience and performance), you always have the sense that you are seeing the world in the first person. This is radically different from any other existing medium. As much as people have tried, for example, to give film or video a subjective feeling, the effect is never quite resolved because of the linear nature of the output and the unremitting presence of the fourth wall.

The fourth wall is really another way of saying that, to the performers, the audience doesn't exist. Therefore, you are always in the third-person objective reality of anonymous observer when watching a play or movie. If you are playing an interactive video, even if there is an attempt to make you feel as if you are in the first person, the lack of dynamic reciprocity inherent in the video medium creates a built-in fourth wall that is hard to overcome without a significant amount of craftsmanship. Although books can often make you feel as if you are the main character, the non-reciprocity of the book medium, the fact that you, the observer, are neither known to or acknowledged by the author, reinforces the fourth wall paradigm.

INTER-PLAY: IMPROVISATION AND INTERACTIVE THEATER (p. 230)

The Theory of Relativity is a scientific principle that reinforces the notion that there is no such thing as objective reality. In fact, this also relates to Heisenberg, whose Uncertainty Principle says that the act of observing affects the observed, and that a lone observer can only observe a limited amount of information about a system. Both the Theory of Relativity and the Uncertainty Principle drive home in a very scientific context the philosophical axiom that there is no absolute reality and that everything is, ultimately, subjective.

HEISENBERG'S UNCERTAINTY (p. 222)

EINSTEIN, EISENSTEIN, AND THE SPACE-TIME CONTINUUM (p. 186)

Most media suggest quite the opposite—that there is an absolute reality. Omniscient narrative, the all-seeing eye of God, is the starting point for most media; however, in Virtual Reality, there is no omniscience (except of course if you are the designer or programmer). Virtual Reality locks you into a subjective viewpoint, and a dynamic one at that.

VR's subjective viewpoint is enormously powerful, and can sometimes be as frightening and disorienting as it is inspiring and empowering. Putting me in a pro-active first-person relationship to my media experience essentially includes me in the action. The power of the sense of inclusion to the human psyche cannot be underestimated. Isolation and a sense of "alone-ness" have been proven to be both psychically and physiologically detrimental to the human organism. Inviting me, the viewer, to the party includes me as an integral part of the action. No longer am I the anonymous or ignored outsider, instead, I now have a valid viewpoint, and even a recognizable impact on the media experience.

VIRTUAL REALITY AS A DRAMATIC ART (p. 508)

VICARIOUS EXPERIENCE (p. 504)

Such a first-person perspective provides me, as the user, with a new tool of empathy. I can even change my the point of view to that of a different character, enabling me to experience the same event from different perspectives.

The power of subjectivity is enormous because it gives us a sense that our presence in this world actually matters. At the same time, in a virtual world, we also have the awareness of being a part of something larger than ourselves—the classic metaphor of consensual hallucination in which we share a world of ideas, images, information, story, fantasy, empathy, and so on...but each gets to experience this shared sensorium from his or her own unique perspective and add his or her own subjective elements to the whole.

Spatial Media (p. 442)

Virtual Reality Check: What is VR Anyway? (p. 518)

A Brief History of Real Time: The Virtual Reality Legacy (p. 105)

Narrative Environments: Virtual Reality as a Storytelling Medium (p. 329)

Gaining Perspective: The Evolution of Dimension (p. 196)

Who is the Author?

In reading about the works of Foucault recently, I was struck by a discussion on the idea of authorship. Roland Barthes, the book stated, said that "The author is dead," to which Foucault retorted, "Who is the author?"

I wonder how Foucault would have addressed this issue when presented with the added dimension of interactivity. Interactivity rather undermines the entire concept of authorship on a variety of levels. First of all, the author of an interactive experience seldom becomes a media personality. Historically, game designers or interactive designers are not viewed with the same regard for authorship as, say, film directors or even book authors. Although they might receive the occasional magazine interview, and there are certainly "stars" in the industry, you will seldom find a cult of personality surrounding an interactive designer the way you do in other media.

In interactive media, there is also another author: the player. All interactive media is really a collaboration between the player and the "author." In the game I creative directed, *Virtual Adventures: The Loch Ness Expedition*, for example, the author creates the story, but the players are responsible for developing the characters and the precise progress of the story line in real time.

The Princess and the Monster: The Making of Virtual Adventures (p. 375)

This new angle on authorship requires authors to give up a certain measure of control—something that most of them will be unwilling to do. The beauty of interactive authorship is that you trade in control for something much more enticing: the challenge of creating a structure that allows for a variety of outcomes, a story that is many stories. As author, you construct the framework, and then step back and let the player create his or her variations within the framework *you* have created.

The more interesting Virtual Reality environments are often entirely user-created. Construct's stratus enables any user to display his or her artwork in a VRML Virtual Gallery (see figure W.1). Another great example of this is a children's project called *Cityspace,* which is a virtual city created by kids. Hosted at San Francisco's Exploratorium and SIGGRAPH, among other venues, *Cityspace* brings together children's creativity with powerful graphics tools and lets them create their own imaginary world together. Another project of this nature is *The Nerve Garden*, a VRML site that enables to kids plant and cultivate a plot of digital soil in an A-Life garden. They can plant seeds and care for these creatures, maintaining a balance of water and light, as well as harmonious coexistence with other children's life forms. This ongoing natural drama plays out over time and helps children to understand natural systems in a creative and dynamic multi-user environment. Other VRML and avatar-based worlds provide a venue for players to create their own stories, and even create their own whole entire cybernations.

Figure W.1

Sample gallery created by a user from the Stratus online museum project

 PLATE 49

 A-LIFE OF ONE'S OWN (p. 5)

CYBERSPACE CADETS: VIRTUAL COMMUNITIES AND AVATAR WORLDS (p. 146)

In interactive design, there is always a lot of talk about content: how to create it, how to manage it, how to control it, and how to distribute it. I have no immediate answers to these quandaries. Some Internet designers have introduced "webisodics," weekly soap operas with evolving plot lines. The challenge with webisodics is that you have to produce a new show every week, which includes writing new stories, creating new plot lines, and getting actors (if there are any) to play out new scenes. What a hassle! Maybe I'm just lazy, but the ideal scenario for me would be to let the player create the content. Just as the evil executive in *The Player* suggests trying to find a way to do away with writers, I'd like to find a way to do away with authors in the interactive world. The notion of an "authorless" environment accounts for why I like Virtual Reality so much. VR can become more of a space to create content than content itself. The way I see it, my job is to come up with a really good premise for a piece of improvisational theater designed to be performed by the audience. This approach is really where the magic is for me...not in how much I can create, but in how little I can create, and inversely, how much I can get the audience to create themselves. My ideal interactive experience is a well-structured multiplayer environment in which the players create and nurture their own stories. Then, I can just retire and enjoy the show!

INTER-PLAY: IMPROVISATION AND INTERACTIVE THEATER (p. 230)

VIRTUAL REALITY AS A DRAMATIC ART (p. 508)

EINSTEIN, EISENSTEIN, AND THE SPACE-TIME CONTINUUM (p. 186)

INTERACTIVITY IS SUBVERSIVE (p. 244)

WORD TO THE MOTHERBOARD: COMPUTERS AND LITERACY

When people use the term "computer literacy," they mean it to describe the state of being conversant (as in able to converse, or have a conversation) with the computer. But the word literacy is defined, quite literally, as "the ability to read and write," or, in a more broad sense, cultured and educated as defined by being well-read. Literacy, in other words, is directly related to literature, or in its simplest form, the written word.

There is a peculiar misconception by some that the computer is somehow contributing to the decline in literacy in America, but all trends would indicate quite the opposite. There is little doubt that television has certainly contributed to the deterioration of literacy, but it doesn't take a cultural pundit to see that in spite of this, the written word is currently in the midst of a major nationwide revival.

The entry point of computers for most people, both in the home and in the office, is writing. Word processing is the predominant skill that most people possess on the computer. The power of the word processor should not be underestimated. It has all but revolutionized literacy on a whole variety of levels.

I first began to get a glimmer of how powerful the word processor could really be when I worked at Edwin Schlossberg Incorporated in the early 80s. Many of the people I worked with were trained as industrial designers and architects, and were virtually illiterate when I started working with them. They would turn in illegible documents, sometimes (if I was lucky) rendered on a typewriter, but more often than not, scrawled across odd-sized pieces of paper from the drafting supply cabinet.

All the people to whom I refer were, by the way, men. The women, even those not trained as writers, were all able to type and write fairly clearly. The men, although quite intelligent, college-educated, and (many of them) well-read, had a much lower literacy rate overall, and few of them were trained in touch-typing. The single largest influence on these men was the introduction of the Macintosh computer into our work place. One of the men, trained as a fine artist, described it to me as a process of sculpting. When the words went into the computer, they weren't done yet...like wet clay, he could move them around, manipulate them, refine them until he liked the form, and then print out the end result, the equivalent of putting it in the kiln. But not quite, because even then, you could get feedback and further refine. Suddenly, the fear was gone, and the malleability of the words opened the door to people previously baffled by this process. For men, who traditionally are weaker than women in verbal skills but excel at the mechanical electronic and spatial navigation, the computer has actually evened the odds with respect to writing.

The other example of computer-induced literacy I like to use is that of my sister, Aleta. As a child, she was severely dyslexic, so much so that she had to be held back a year in elementary school. This was at the time when they didn't really know what dyslexia was and many children who suffered from this learning disability considered "slow." Aleta was extremely bright and articulate, and in matters of spatial orientation, mechanics, and manual dexterity, she was downright extraordinary. She was also quite articulate, but she had great difficulty reading and even more trouble writing.

In her early 20s, Aleta discovered the Macintosh computer. My sister easily adapted to the Mac's seemingly fool-proof heuristic interface and machine-like nature (she was a mechanical whiz). This combination made her feel right at home. The computer provided Aleta with a tool that enabled her to deal with words with the part of her brain that was strongest—the mechanical, visual, and spatial. Again, no paper. Spelling was not an issue. Now she could just write the words and ideas in her head without worrying about reversing letters or spelling things phonetically. After Aleta got all her thoughts down, she could go back and clean up the mechanics of the words. Since then, she has edited several books, including significant editorial contributions to this one, and has also become a database expert.

 THE PEDAGOGICAL MOUSEPAD, OR, HOW IT ALL GOT GUI (p. 365)

When I first began working in the interactive field in 1983, I did not know how to use a computer. In fact, my first year or so at the offices of Edwin Schlossberg Incorporated, I did all my writing on an IBM Selectric. For those of you who were born after 1970 (a scary thought in and of itself), this is a sort of typewriter that was, when it first came out, the cutting edge in text generation. The Selectric used a ball-shaped typing element instead of heavy hammers, enabling a quicker response time to the touch, hence speeding up the typing process significantly. During the early 80s, I also had some encounters with early attempts at word processing. One was the memory Selectric, which could memorize a sentence or two, not a particularly useful feature. Another improvement was the Wang, which I always liked because of its name (I was 19!). I can barely remember the Wang, but I seem to recall it had a tiny little display that would show you a couple words at a time before it printed them out with a daisy wheel. The one thing that stands out about the Wang was that it was quite huge, bigger than any PC today, but without the monitor.

I have been writing since I was eight years old. I began typing at about 16, thanks to my stepmother's insistence that if I wanted to be a writer, I had to learn to type. From a writer's point of view, there are a number of significant differences between using a typewriter and using a computer. First of all, there is the psychological aspect. The blank page, a seductive yet daunting object, has always been the writer's best friend and worst enemy. The classic image of typing a few words, ripping the paper out of the machine, and beginning again, was for many years the archetype of the writer's experience. I fell prey to this on many occasions when trying to write stories or poems. I even wrote an entire play once that was a conversation between my paper, my beer, and my cigarette, each complaining about my abuse of them; but the paper was the most distressed, because just when it thought it was actually going to become *literature*, I would cry out in disgust, rip it from the (manual) typewriter, and send it in a crumpled wad into the trash. Many writers over the years have written about the process of writing, and especially about their feelings toward the blank page.

Ernest Hemingway started *A Movable Feast* with the line: "Begin with the perfect sentence." Today, in the age of word processing, it's not necessary. There is no blank page. Now it's the blank screen. In many respects, the blank screen is a much less daunting foe for the simple reason that with a piece of paper you are committing to something immediately. With a computer, you are merely "floating it" in some transient limbo, wherein it can be massaged, modified, and toyed with before it becomes The Written Word.

The word, once written in stone, is now malleable. It is this malleability of computer text that has totally transformed the writer's process. As with all things, there are advantages and disadvantages to this. The advantage is that it is much easier to write. The computer has cured me of virtually any sign of writer's block, other than just plain old laziness, which I suffered from quite severely when I wrote on a typewriter. It has also become much easier for people who do not classify themselves as "writers" to write because they have more flexibility both in terms of the way they write and their ability to edit and change things with ease. I know many people who are writers today because of the computer.

The malleability is mixed blessing for the writer. While ease of writing is an advantage, ease of editing means that things can be easily changed—by other people. In the old days, every change to text meant that the text had to be retyped. Now, people feel free to change things endless times, and this lack of commitment exacerbates the perfectionist tendency to keep tweaking things ad infinitum. I once wrote a concept report that was edited something like 20 times. This would never have happened in a typewriter-driven world, but with the computer, you can get feedback quicker and make changes faster, which, as with all things, is both a blessing and a curse. Furthermore, it is much easier for people who are not the original writer to go in and muck around with your words. To any self-respecting wordsmith, the very idea of this is abhorrent.

In my opinion, by far the most powerful aspect of writing on the computer is the ability to multitask and write in a nonlinear fashion. The typewriter has an inherently mono-task, linear construct. One page at a time. One line at a time. I, on the other hand, have always been a very nonlinear, omni-directional thinker. As a student, I had to write all my essays on index cards because my ideas seldom came out in the correct order. After I got all the basic concepts out, I would put them in the correct sequence and write out the linear text. My life changed dramatically merely with the ability to write two documents at the same time. Using a multitasking environment is the equivalent of having five typewriters on your desk and being able to work on five documents simultaneously. For me, this was a tremendously freeing experience. I was never able to think linearly in the first place, which is part of why I had such severe writer's block. I felt constrained by having to think in a straight line and finally gave up trying to write novels, and even stories, at a fairly young age. I could not maintain one stream of thought without getting distracted by another. Instead, I devoted by recreational writing to poetry and songs, which were more manageable for my short attention span. As you can imagine, I was uniquely well-suited for a career as an interactive writer and designer. The flow diagram made much more sense to me than the straight narrative. It was a much more accurate model of the way my mind worked.

This is my first book. I could never have written this book on a typewriter. This book was not written linearly, nor is it meant to be read linearly. I wrote this book in soundbytes, as it were, in bits and pieces based on the topics and areas I wanted to explore. The reason I couldn't write this as a continuous linear text is because there are too many interconnections between things. I cannot say that one idea naturally leads to the next because there are numerous ways to traverse the landscape of ideas contained here. I called my publisher up one day in a tizzy because they had asked me to make a table of contents. I had tried to do so for nearly a week, but every time I came up with a series of parts that made sense, the next moment I was fashioning a different set. I finally called my editor and said: What do I do? After several go-rounds, we finally settled on alphabetical order because in the final analysis, it seemed like the most arbitrary, and thus the most interactive approach. Let the reader make up his or her own table of contents. That was the basic premise behind this decision.

Because of this battle I have with linearity, it was a very conscious choice on my part to write a book. I could have made a CD-ROM or a web site instead. But I liked the challenge of taking something as simple and linear as a book and trying to use it a medium for interactive content. In a certain way, I wanted the content to *fight* with the medium. I wanted this to be a self-conscious process. In doing this, I hope to expand your understanding of interactivity in a very concrete and experiential way. To write a linear book about interactivity seemed anathema. I sincerely hope that you do not resort to experiencing this book merely in its predigested sequential iteration, but that you will also explore the tangents and parabolas offered here. As I mentioned in the introduction, I also encourage you to and hope that you will (as I do with virtually every book) write your own annotations in the margins. There is an entire second book written in the margins of my copy of *Understanding Media*.

The character of the computer is inherently nonlinear and omni-directional. We no longer deal in terms of linear chains of cause-and-effect. The term "web" is apt because the computer creates three-dimensional geometry of interconnections in which the cause and effect are instantaneous and sometimes even concurrent. The matter of "which came first, the chicken or the egg," suddenly comes into clear focus with the computer. The answer is simply that the chicken and egg exist in a recursive loop of reciprocal cause and effect, with no beginning, middle or end. It doesn't really matter which came first, we only know that you need one to generate the other.

Nothing has blasted open the writer's process like networking. With networking and shared workspace, we suddenly open up an entirely new domain that is dramatically jarring to the writer's sensibility. Writing is and always has been an essentially solitary act. It has been this way since the days of clay tablets, through quill pens, and well into the computer age. The fluidity of the computer has created new forms of writing in which there is no clear single author.

As we develop tools for instantaneous collaboration, we must redefine the very definition of the term "author." It is now possible for people to work on the same document or visual image at the same time, either within a Local Area Network (LAN) or Wide Area Network (WAN). The dramatic effect this is going to have on the very nature of writing has yet to be determined. It has already had a tremendous impact in the form of chat rooms on the Internet, where instantaneous textual communication has spawned an entirely new literary form. Suddenly, the ability to write in "real-time" is a cherished skill, which no one had any use for in the past. People participate in and write role-playing games that really amount to a very sophisticated form of collaborative fiction. These multi-user fiction experiences are quickly evolving into a new art form as more artists and writers begin to explore the possibilities of collaboration. The Dadaists experimented with multi-user art with their game, *Exquisite Corpse*, in which each writer would add his or her image, and then fold the page back leaving lines for the next artist to draw his or her own inspiration from. This same game can also be played with text, with each writer leaving the last word of his or sentence exposed for the text writer to follow. Even with the dynamics of interactivity, this process is still fairly linear. With multi-user role-playing games, you can have concurrent sub-plots going on as you create a form of multileveled, live, text-based improvised theater.

Who is the Author? (p. 528)

Inter-play: Improvisation and Interactive Theater (p. 230)

Social Computing (p. 434)

Beyond the physical act of writing, the computer has also changed the process of publishing. As the path between writer and reader narrows through self-published periodicals and even moreso with the World Wide Web, writers are less and less beholden to the distribution infrastructure that controls the circulation of content to a larger audience. Any poet can publish his or her poetry online. You can read the news almost as soon as it happens. Cults can even publish their manifestos on the web. After the distribution path is no longer clogged by all these middlemen (apologies to my publisher!), writers can begin to experience a new level of freedom.

There is more to this new level of freedom than mere control of the distribution channels. McLuhan talks a lot about the printing press creating a highly linear aesthetic that has driven our culture up until the Information Age. At that point, according to McLuhan, text was usurped text by sound and vision, both of which have a much less linear and more ephemeral nature. The World Wide Web suddenly brings a new kind of texture to text, often accompanied by other media…sound…visuals…animation, and so on. Multimedia, the synthesis of multiple mediums, brings new power to text. In *The Medium Is the Massage*, McLuhan and Quentin Fiore used graphics to lend new power to the written word. The influence of this book can be seen throughout the pages of *Wired* magazine, where text and image begin to merge, creating a new way to look at words. On the web, text can become more dynamic with the help of hyperlinks, animation, audio, video, and 3D. The CD-ROM/web trivia game, *You Don't Know Jack!*, is a classic example of what can happen when you truly mix media with interactivity. For designers who understand the inner dynamics and inter-dynamics of interactivity, the turbo-charged text opens the door for a whole new genre of literature.

CONFESSIONS OF A MACINTOSH CONVERT (p. 132)

BOOKMARK: INTERACTIVITY AND THE NEW LITERACY (p. 102)

MIXED MEDIA, MIXED MESSAGE (p. 306)

THEORY OF MEDIA EVOLUTION (p. 468)

MEDIOGRAPHY

Most books have a bibliography, but this seems rather limited, because this is really a book about all media. Thus, this mediography covers the gamut of reference materials in all media that pertain either directly or indirectly to the contents of this book. Many of the items listed here are specifically mentioned in these pages, others I provide for the purposes of augmentation and edification. This list is by no means comprehensive: there are many other wonderful references from which to draw. My hope is that this book whets your appetite for more knowledge and inspires you to venture forth to explore a rich body of film, television, literature, and interactive media that will provide further insight into the subject of interactivity and interacive multimedia.

Books: Required Reading

The following books are on my "required reading" list for anyone with aspirations toward interactivity. There are so many books that can contribute to a fuller understanding of interactivity that I cannot possibly list them all here. This book consists of my personal favorites, and a few I haven't actually read, but which have become classics or standard fare among interactive designers and producers. Further pursuits will no doubt reveal still more highly illuminating texts on the subject.

Art of Human-Computer Interface Design

Laurel, Brenda (Boston: Addison-Wesley Publishing Co., 1990)

An early classic on the psychology and aesthetics of interface design.

The Art of War

Tzu, Sun (Oxford, England: Oxford University Press, 1963)

The perennial classic by the Chinese General/philosopher is among the oldest known treatises on the art and science of warfare.

ARTIFICIAL LIFE: A REPORT FROM THE FRONTIER WHERE COMPUTERS MEET BIOLOGY

Levy, Steven (New York: Dell Publishing, 1992)

A fairly comprehensive survey of various experiments in artificial life.

ARTIFICIAL REALITY

Krueger, Myron (Reading, MA: Addison-Wesley, Revised Edition 1997)

The classic book on Krueger's theories of simulated realities, artificial worlds, and mediaspace.

AVATARS! EXPLORING AND BUILDING VIRTUAL WORLDS ON THE INTERNET

Damer, Bruce (Berkeley, CA: Peachpit Press, 1977)

An in-depth study of avatar worlds on the web by Bruce Damer, our resident expert on A-Life and cyberspace cadets.

BEHAVIOR IN PUBLIC PLACES

Goffman, Erving (New York: Macmillan Publishing Co. Inc., 1963)

This study of social interaction in physical space is an indispensible guide to those creating online communities and avatar worlds.

BEING DIGITAL

Negroponte, Nicholas (New York: Alfred A. Knopf, 1995)

Based on his essays from the back of *Wired* magazine, this book provides a useful history of computers as told from the point of view of the founder of the MIT Media Lab, the world-famous high-tech research facility. Check the "Spatial Media" chapter in this book for a detailed description of *The Aspen Project*.

APP A

BIOSPHERE 2: THE HUMAN EXPERIMENT

Allen, John (New York: Penguin Books, 1991)

An in-depth description of the Biosphere 2 project discussed in the "Autobiography of an Autodidact, Part 3" and "Media Architecture" chapters of this book.

BURNING CHROME

Gibson, William (New York: Ace Books edition, 1987)

In this classic collection of cyberpunk short stories, Gibson first introduced the "Matrix," and coined the term "cyberspace."

CHILD'S CONCEPTION OF THE WORLD

Piaget, Jean (Littlefield Adams, 1975)

Piaget's early work in child development and heuristic learning were the impetus that spawned the graphical user interface movement and the personal computing revolution. Piaget wrote numerous books on cognition, most of which can be found at Amazon.com.

COMPUTERS AS THEATER

Laurel, Brenda (Boston: Addison-Wesley Publishing Co., 1993)

As discussed in the chapter "Virtual Reality as a Dramatic Art," Laurel's classic dissertation explores ways in which principles of traditional theater and ritual space can be applied to the creation of compelling virtual narrative experiences.

THE CYBERSPACE LEXICON

Cotton, Bob and Oliver, Richard (London, Phaidon Press Ltd., 1992)

Every interactive designer should have this indispensible reference book on his or her shelf. It's the *Webster's Dictionary* of cyberspace. Plus, it has a very hip design by graphics innovator Malcom Garrett.

DIGITAL HARMONY: ON THE COMPLEMENTARITY OF MUSIC AND VISUAL ART

Whitney, John (Boston: Byte Books/A McGraw-Hill Publication,1980)

John Whitney is considered the father of computer animation. This dissertation on his theories of using paradigms of musical structure to create abstract animations is considered a classic in the literature of computer animation.

DIGITAL ILLUSION

Dodsworth, Clark, Ed. (Boston: ACM/Addison-Wesley Publishing Co., 1997)

Clark Dodsworth's rich anthology includes essays by some of the top people in computer graphics and location-based entertainment (including yours truly). Here, you can read about many of the seminal projects in ride simulation, Virtual Reality, fine art, and high-end film effects from the perspective of the people who have, themselves, created these digital illusions.

DISCOVERY OF THE CHILD

Montessori, Dr. Maria (Madras, India: Ballantine Books, 1948, 1958, 1962)

This classic, first published in 1948, outlines Dr. Montessori's theories of discovery-based learning and describes the basic template for both the Montessori classroom and the autodidactic devices she created that paved the way for today's heuristic computer interfaces.

THE DOORS OF PERCEPTION AND HEAVEN AND HELL

Huxley, Aldus (New York: Haper & Row, 1954–1956)

The real *Brave New World* is the human mind. This classic book on alternate perceptual realities was a bible to the hallucinogenic generation and has found a new audience with denizens of virtual reality. Also, don't miss Huxley's other classic, *The Perennial Philosophy*.

Einstein for Beginners

Schwartz, Joseph and McGuiness, Michael (New York: Pantheon Books, 1990)

This classic provides an introduction to the Theory of Relativity and Einstein's ideas about space and time, as covered in "Einstein, Eisenstein, and the Space-Time Continuum" and "Virtual Relativity." Einstein's own writings on the subject are far to numerous to list here. I recommend a visit to Amazon.com for a full list of his work.

Envisioning Information

Tufte, Edward R. (Graphics Press, 1990)

Edward R. Tufte's books can be seen on the shelves of virtually every print graphics and interface designer in America. The fundamentals presented in this book create a universal vacabulary for visualizing and communicating information graphically. Also see his newer *Visual Explanations: Images and Quantities Evidence and Narrative.*

Evolution's End

Pearce, Joseph Chilton (Chicago: University of Chicago Press, 1992)

Pearce (no relation) takes an in-depth look at the evolution of the human brain and espouses his theories about how different media actually affect the physical development of the brain over time.

Expanded Cinema

Youngblood, Gene (New York: E.P. Dutton Company, 1970)

A classic book of media theory and experimental cinema. Includes some of the earliest analysis of computer animation and video art, including the work of John Whitney and Nam June Paik. With an introduction by R. Buckminster Fuller.

EXPERIMENTS IN FORM

Pearce, Peter (New York: Van Nostrand Reinhold Co., 1980—out of print)

A curriculum originally developed for industrial and architectural designers. As described in "Media Architecture," this book takes students through a series of exercises in form by asking them to build several diffent versions of an abstact shape using square, triangular, and spherical grids. A great book for 3D modelers and VRML world builders.

THE FILM SENSE

Eisenstein, Sergi (Orlando, Florida: Harcourt Brace & Company, 1969)

The classic text on the art of cinema by the master himself, director of the classic *Battleship Potemkin*. Check Amazon.com for other books by Eisenstein.

FLUXUS CODEX

Hendricks, John (Waterbury, Connecticut: Harry N Abrams, 1988)

A comprehensive survey of the Fluxus art movement. This book has provided me with endless inspiration and amusement and much of the material for my slide lecture entitled "Dadabase: A History of Interactivity in Art," has been drawn from this book.

FRANKENSTEIN

Shelley, Mary (New American Library)

The classic tale of human-created humans, technological ethics, and the dangers of bad parenting. Became the impetus for an entire genre of fiction and film.

FUZZY LOGIC

McNeill, Daniel and Freiberger, Paul (New York: Simon & Schuster, 1993)

A personal fave which I would have written about in this book if I'd had time and space. A fascinating study of the principle of fuzzy logic, a new school of set theory that deals with gradations rather than absolutes. Really useful in thinking about both artificial intelligence and interface design.

GRAPEFRUIT

Ono, Yoko (Owen, out of print)

Yoko Ono's classic collection of Flux scores. This magnificent piece of interactive poetry has provided me with years of inspiration and insight.

HACKERS: HEROES OF THE COMPUTER REVOLUTION

Levy, Steven (New York: Vintage Books, 1984)

The classic chronicle of the pioneers of the digital age. A highly informative and entertaining read. Don't miss it.

THE HITCHHIKER'S GUIDE TO THE GALAXY

Adams, Douglas (Harmony Books, 1989)

This brilliant radio play is considered a classic among the digital set. Both the tapes and several different editions of the book are available on Amazon.com.

I SEEM TO BE A VERB

Fuller, R. Buckminster with Jerome Agel and Quentin Fiore (New York: Bantam Books, 1970)

Designed by Quentin Fiore, who gave McLuhan's *The Medium is the Massage* its graphic look, this visually dynamic text and image collage is rife with philosophical insight and its call-to-action tone will leave readers well-equipped to handle an interactive world.

INFORMATION ARCHITECTS

Wurman, Richard Saul (Graphics Press)

Richard Wurman's work in information graphics, including his earlier book *Information Anxiety*, have provided new insight into the graphical expression and organization of information. Although most of Wurman's *Information Architects* are not involved in interface design, the book is an invaluable look at effective graphical communication.

JOHN CAGE: DOCUMENTARY MONOGRAPHS IN MODERN ART

Kostelanetz, Richard, Ed. (New York: Praeger Publishers, 1968)

A great collection of essays by and about the work of John Cage, grandfather of art concrét and avant garde composer. (Interestingly, the book is dedicated to Buckminster Fuller.)

THE LIVELIEST ART

Knight, Arthur (Hanover, New Hampshire: Mentor Books, 1957)

A classic history and analysis of the cinematic arts. They made us read it in high school film class. A must-read for students of media theory.

MAN AND HIS SYMBOLS

Jung, Carl G., Ed. (New York: Dell Publishers, 1964)

A collection of essays on Carl Jung's notions of archetype and symbol, edited by and with an excellent introduction by the world-famous psychologist. Highly accessible reading for the layperson.

MARCEL DUCHAMP

Libel, Robert (New York: Paragraphic Books, American edition, 1959)

A great book on the life and work of Duchamp, including writing by Duchamp himself and others on his work.

THE MECHANICAL BRIDE: FOLKLORE OF INDUSTRIAL MAN

McLuhan, Marshall (Boston: Beacon Press, 1951, 1967)

Pre-dating his landmark book on media theory, *Understanding Media*, by 13 years, this collection of biting essays provides an insightful analysis of the visual vocabulary of advertising, pop culture, and mass media. The notion of a mechanical bride is especially timely in this day and age of cyborgs and avatars.

THE MEDIUM IS THE MASSAGE: AN INVENTORY OF EFFECTS

McLuhan, Marshall and Fiore, Quentin (New York: Random House,1967)

This illustrated companion piece to *Understanding Media*, designed by Quentin Fiore, created the TV-inspired print graphics aesthetic that dominates media-savvy publications such as *Wired, Mondo 2000*, and *Raygun*. This deft montage of text and image created a new visual vocabulary whose influence can be seen at every level of modern interface design.

MICHEL FOUCAULT

Shumway, David R. (Charlottesville: University Press of Virginia, 1989)

This book explores the life and work of philospher Michel Foucault, and discusses Foucault's concerns about the nature of authorship and "the empty space left by the author's disappearance," as discussed in the chapter, "Who is the Author?"

NAM JUNE PAIK: VIDEO TIME, VIDEO SPACE

Paik, Nam June; Stoos, Toni; and Kellein, Thomas (Waterbury, Connecticut: Harry N. Abrams, 1990)

A book on the work of pioneering video artist Nam June Paik.

NEUROMANCER

Gibson, William (New York: Ace Books, 1984)

Following on the heels of Gibson's short story anthology, *Burning Chrome*, this is the classic novel of cyberspace cowboys going up against multi-national corporations on the yet-to-be-created Internet.

ON EDGE: PERFORMANCE AT THE END OF THE TWENTIETH CENTURY

Carr, C. (Hanover, New Hampshire: Wesleyan University Press, 1993)

A survey of conceptual and performance art in New York during the 1980s by *Village Voice* art critic C. Carr. Much of this work includes a high level of audience interaction and I frequently read from this book in my slide lecture, "Dadabase: A History of Interactivity in Art."

A PATTERN LANGUAGE

Alexander, Christopher (London: Oxford University Press, 1977)

This book and its companion piece, *Timeless Ways of Building*, are considered the bible to many contemporary architects. Exploring the way that humans interface with their real physical environment, it provides a wealth of information that can easily be reapplied to interface design, spatial media, and Virtual Reality.

PEDAGOGICAL SKETCHBOOK

Klee, Paul (Faber & Faber, 1985)

German painter Paul Klee penned this delightful book on drawing, a great favorite of mine, and the inspiration for the name of the chapter "The Pedagogical Mousepad, or, How it all Got GUI."

THE PERENNIAL PHILOSPHY

Huxley, Aldous (New York: Haper & Row, 1944, 1945)

Forget about *Brave New World*...Huxley's real brave new world was the inner spirit. This book has been called one of the best books on comparative religion of all time. Referenced in the chapter "OM Meets OHM: Digital Oneness," a must read for those who care about the spiritual side of digial media.

POLYHEDRA PRIMER

Pearce, Peter (Palo Alto, California: Dale Seymour Publications, 1978)

From point, to line, to triangle, to truncated dodecahedron, this book is the ultimate guide to the polygonal world; an indispensible reference tool for 3D modelers and designers.

THE POWER OF MYTH

Moyers, Bill and Campbell, Joseph (Doubleday, 1988)

The classic book of mythology based on the Bill Moyers interview with comparative religion expert Joseph Campbell is a comprehensive guide to myth and archetype invaluable to storytellers in any medium.

PUTTING YOUR TALENT TO WORK

Capacchione, Lucia and Van Pelt, Peggy (Deerfield Beach, Florida: Health Communications, 1996)

One of a number of books by the author's mother, as mentioned in "Autobiography of an Autodidact, Part 1." An excellent book for those contemplating a career change.

SNOW CRASH

Stephenson, Neal (New York: Bantam Books, 1992)

This second-generation cyberpunk sci-fi classic has become something of a bible for denizens of cyberspace.

STRUCTURE IN NATURE IS A STRATEGY FOR DESIGN

Pearce, Peter (Cambridge: The MIT Press, 1978, 1990)

Considered a classic in architectural circles, this book provides an in-depth anaysis of forms in nature. A great reference for creators of A-Life, fractal geometry, L-systems, and other natural algorithms, as well as 3D modelers looking to refine their technique. The moral of the story: triangulation rules!

TIMELESS WAYS OF BUILDING

Alexander, Christopher (Oxford: Oxford University Press, 1987)

Christopher Alexander, the architectural guru, explores fundamental and perennial principles of architecture. This and his earlier classic, *A Pattern Language*, provide guidelines that can easily be reapplied in the creation of narrative environments and simulated architectural spaces.

UNDERSTANDING MEDIA: THE EXTENSIONS OF MAN

McLuhan, Marshall (Cambridge: MIT Press, 1964, 1994)

Required reading for anyone using or creating media of any kind; this landmark book introduced the notion of media theory to a mass audience and forever changed the way we look at media and ourselves.

VIRTUAL REALITY

Rheingold, Howard (New York: Simon & Schuster, 1991)

A comprehensive survey of the history and development of Virtual Reality, and a source for much of the VR research in this book.

Visual Explanations: Images and Quantities Evidence and Narrative

Tufte, Edward R. (Graphics Press, 1997)

Tufte's latest book on informational graphics provides much insight into the visual language of interface design. His earlier book, *Envisioning Information*, is considered a classic among graphic artists and interface designers.

VRML: Browsing & Building Cyberspace

Pesce, Mark (Indianapolis: New Riders Publishing, 1995)

VRML co-inventor Pesce's book provides practical how-to information interspersed with historical background and witty philosophical insights. A classic for VRML designers and a great book for beginners.

VRML: Flying Through the Web

Pesce, Mark (Indianapolis: New Riders Publishing, 1996)

A comprehensive guide to VRML browsers by the co-inventor of the technolgoy that made William Gibson's cyberspace a reality.

Yoko Ono: Arias and Objects

Haskell, Barbara and Hanhardt, John G. (Salt Lake City: Peregrine Smith Books, 1991)

An insightful and comprehensive study of the work of Yoko Ono, conceptual artist and interactivist extraordinaire.

World Wide Web Sites

The following are web sites showing work that is mentioned in this book, as well as some of my personal faves, just for good measure. I have also listed a couple of sites that are good resources for finding other content, such as books covered in the previous section of this mediography.

AMAZON.COM

http://www.amazon.com

Currently one of the most profitable commercial sites on the web, Amazon.com is a great resource for finding most of the books listed in this mediography. It is also evidence of my theory that the Internet is leading to a renaissance in the popularity of traditional books.

AMERICAN FILM INSTITUTE (AFI)

http://www.afionline.org

Check out AFI's multimedia courses, including my classes on interactive storytelling and interactivity in art.

BIOTA.ORG

http://www.biota.org

Visit Biota.org to see examples of some of the projects mentioned in "A-Life of One's Own." A great resource for people interested in artificial life, and the home of *The Nerve Garden*.

bLITCOM

http://www.blitcom.com

This is the site for the new company that I've started with VRML co-creator Mark Pesce, and Jan Mallis, producer of *Floops*. On this site, you should be able to see my first VRML character, "bliss.com." Because the site will be brand new when this book hits the shelves, there won't be much on it, but stay tuned...

CITYSPACE

http://www.cityspace.org

This ongoing collaborative children's project has been featured at such events and venues as SIGGRAPH, the Interactive Media Festival, and San Francisco's

Exploratorium children's museum. Visit their web site to check out the virtual city created by kids.

Contact Consortium

http://www.ccon.org

Devoted to the study of artificial life, this consortium of companies and artists hosts the annual Avatars conferece and is developing projects that can be seen at www.biota.org.

Construct

http://www.construct.net

One of the pioneering companies in VRML and virtual architecture. See the color signature of this book for examples of their work.

Damer, Bruce

http://www.damer.com

Personal web site for Bruce Damer, head of the Contact Consortium and author of *Avatars! Exploring and Building Virtual Worlds on the Internet.*

De-lux'o

http://www.deluxoland.com

From the people who brought *you Bar-min-ski: Consumer Product, Encyclopedia of Clamps,* and *Cyclops Boy.*

Detour: Brain Deconstruction Ahead

http://www.evl.uic.edu

The University of Illinois, Chicago's Electronic Visualization Lab is the home of Rita Addison's *Detour,* the CAVE, and a variety of interesting VR projects.

THE EAMES OFFICE

http://www.eamesoffice.com

The official web site of the office of Charles and Ray Eames, creators of the first interactive museum exhibit and first multimedia slide presentation.

Edwin Schlossberg Incorporated

http://www.esidesign.com

Visit the ESI web site to see the work done by the company where I got my start, including a few projects that I worked on, as described in "Autobiography of an Autodidact, Part 2," "Test First, Ask Questions Later," and "Museoleum: Dead Zoos and Living Museums."

Electronic Café

http://www.ecafe.com

The Elecronic Café International, and its founders Kit Galloway and Sherrie Rabinowitz, have been at the forefront of the interactive revolution since the 1970s, when they started bringing people together into a shared media space via video satellite. Check out the VRML model of the café's Santa Monica Headquarters, creative directed by yours truly.

Floops

http://www.sgi.com

Silicon Graphics, Inc., hosts *Floops*. Visit on Tuesday and Thursday to see new installments in the webisodic VRML show.

Fuller, Buckminster

http://www.bfi.org

http://www1.netaxs.com:8080/~cjf/buckyrefs.html

There are dozens of Buckminster Fuller sites on the web. The first URL listed here is the Buckminster Fuller Institute; the second is called Chris Fearnley's list of Buckminster Fuller References. Thanks Chris.

GRAHAM, CLAY

http://www.best.com/~cyber23

Clay Graham, cyberarchitect extraordinaire, has created a unique vocabulary for information architecture in VRML. Samples of his work appear throughout this book and in the color signature. Visit his site to see more work and read Clay's essays.

HYPERMEDIA RESEARCH CENTRE

http://www.hrc.wmin.ac.uk

The Hypermedia Research Centre at the University of Westminster in London; a great program and one of the institutions where I speak. The HRC is at the heart of the new media scene in London.

IMPROV

http://www.mrl.nyu.edu

To learn more about *Improv*, check out the Media Research Lab's web site at New York University.

INTERVISTA

http://www.intervista.com

The company started by Tony Parisi, co-inventor of VRML. Intervista created the Worldview VRML browser, which is included with Microsoft's Internet Explorer.

KRUEGER, MYRON

http://www.iamas.ac.jp/interaction/i97/artists.html#Krueger

Visit the site for the International Academy of Media Arts and Sciences that features a sampling of Krueger's work in artificial reality and mediaspace.

LEARNING SITES, INC.

http://www.learningsites.com

The home of the *Temple Gebal Barkal* model, among other archaeological projects.

LUDTKE, JIM

http://www.primenet.com/~jludtke

See more wonders from Jim Ludtke, creator of *Freakshow* and *Bad Day on the Midway*.

MIT MEDIA LAB

http://www.media.mit.edu

The world famous media research center at MIT, founded by Nicholas Negroponte.

MOUSEHOUSE, DENMARK

http://www.mousehouse.dk

The Danish multimedia production company and educational center that spun off the Space Invaders multimedia education program.

MUTE MAGAZINE

http://www.metamute.co.uk

Check out the *Mute* magazine web site for articles by yours truly, including "The Californian Ideology: An Insider's View," as discussed in the chapter "Digital Socialism."

NANOTHINC

http://www.nanothinc.org

To learn more about Charles Ostman's nanotechnology, as discussed in "A-Life of One's Own," visit the Nanothinc web site.

Osmose

http://www.softimage.com

Visit the Softimage web site to learn more about Char Davies' *Osmose*.

Parisi, Tony

http://www.intervista.com

Intervista is the company started by VRML co-creator Tony Parisi. Also see Intervista.

Pearce, Celia

http://www.momentum-media.com

A work in progress, this is the web site for my consulting firm, **momentum media group**.

Pesce, Mark

http://www.hyperreal.org/~mpesce/mark.asc

VRML co-creator Mark Pesce's personal web site.

Placeholder

http://www.interval.com

Visit the Interval site to learn more about Brenda Laurel and Rachel Strickland's *Placeholder*.

Protozoa, Inc.

http://www.protozoa.com

The creators of *Floops* and other exciting VRML characters.

PURPLE MOON SOFTWARE

http://www.purple-moon.com

Brenda Laurel's *Interval* spinoff on the forefront of the Girl Games movement. Check out the friendship cards, designed by the author.

REAL WORLD STUDIOS

http://www.realworld.on.net

Visit the Real World site to find out more about the *X-Plora* CD-ROM mentioned in "Been There, Done That."

SAN FRANCISCO STATE UNIVERSITY, MULTIMEDIA STUDIES PROGRAM

http://www.msp.sfsu.edu

San Francisco State's Multimedia Studies Program where I teach Exploring Spatial Media.

SIGGRAPH

http://www.siggraph.org

SIGGRAPH holds the largest annual computer graphics show in the world. Visit their web site for more information on the organization and the conference.

SOMMERER, CHRISTA, AND MIGNONNEAU, LAURENT

http://www.mic.atr.co.jp/~christa

The web site of V-Art team Sommerer and Mignonneau contains information about their work, as seen in the color signature of this book and described in "V-Art."

SPACE INVADERS MULTIMEDIA EDUCATION PROGRAM, DENMARK

http://www.invaders.dk

The Danish multimedia program where I teach; check out the outstanding student work.

T_VISION

http://www.artcom.de

Visit the Art+Com web site to learn more about the *T_Vision* global database project.

YOUNG, C. SCOTT

http://tcc.iz.net/mymind/open.htm

http://www.vrmlknight.com

An early pioneer of VRML art, C. Scott Young has mastered the art of the low-poly world and sculpture. Check out the real-time versions of the fanciful *Idville, The Carrot Defender*, and the *Celfish*, featured in the color signature of this book.

FILM, VIDEO, AND TELEVISION

The following lists films and videos mentioned throughout this book, as well as a few others thrown in for their value and insight. Again, by no means complete, but certainly a start to get you on your way.

2001: A SPACE ODYSSY

Stanley Kubric's monumental sci-fi classic features HAL, the Mother of All Digital Frankensteins. Few would argue that this is the most important science fiction movie ever made. (Film; available on video)

BATTLESHIP POTEMKIN

Sergei Eisenstein's 1925 classic has been called "the best film ever made," and is certainly the most influential. A must-see to understand the roots of modern film editing, cinematograpy, and narrative technique. (Film; available on video)

BIRTH OF A NATION

Although credited as the first feature film ever made, the power of D.W. Griffith's classic epic has been tainted by its racist overtones. (Film; available on video)

BLADE RUNNER

The cyberpunk classic, based on a story by Philip K. Dick, considered the other father of cyberspace. (Film; available on video)

CIRCUITRY MAN

This entertaining and unusual cyberpunk flick features some interesting twists on androids, memory, computer-chips-as-drugs, Virtual Reality, and post-apocalyptic Los Angeles. Staple fare for late-night sci-fi channels. Also see the sequel, *Circuitry Man 2*. (Film; available on video)

THE COMPUTER WORE TENNIS SHOES

This quaint and dated comedy features a very young Kurt Russel as a dim-witted jock who accidentally gets a mainframe computer downloaded into his brain. A real hoot, espcially when looked at through the perspective of modern computing. (Film, available on video)

GROUNDHOG DAY

This story of a man who is forced to live the same day over and over and over is a perfect model for an interactive experience. (Film; available on video)

LAWNMOWER MAN

A Digital Frankenstein story of the potential ills of Virtual Reality, which transforms the "backward" and abused lawn mower of a small town into an evil, deadly genius. (Film; available on video)

MAX HEAdROOM

The achetypal Digital Frankenstein, Max is a computer-generated talking head that lives inside your TV. Don't miss this highly entertaining series rife with social commentary and excellent satire. (Television series; available on video)

REMAINS OF THE DAY

This film about a man who cannot make a decision provides a great deal of insight into the power of decision-making in traditional drama, and how this can be leveraged for interactive drama. (Film, available on video)

SESAME STREET

The landmark children's television show has influenced three generations of media-savvy kids. (Television series)

SHORT CIRCUIT

Ally Sheedy and Steve Gutenberg star in this comedy about a friendly military robot on the run, as described in "Digital Frankensteins." (Film; available on video)

SlAckER

This existential look at the laid back youth of Austin, Texas uses a structure that naturally lends itself to interactivity. (Film; available on video)

STAR TREK

Although I myself am not a "Trekkie," the *Star Trek* television series in all its various generations and iterations is enormously influential among creators of digital media. A great study of a very active fan culture that can form around an otherwise passive medium. (Television series)

TOTAL RECALL

Arnold Schwarzenegger as a man whose mysterious past leaves him caught between the real and the virtual. (Film; available on video)

TRON

Credited as the first "Virtual Reality" movie, this film about people trapped inside a computer game was less than a smash hit, but is today considered a cult classic by some. (Film; available on video)

TWIN PEAKS

This landmark series brought a moment of art to the boob tube. The weekly conversations had by its fans demonstrate the culture that can arise from television shows. (Television series; available on video)

VIRTUOSITY

In this Digital Frankenstein tale, a computer-generated über-villain designed for training police officers escapes into the real world to wreak havoc on the populace. (Film; available on video)

WAR GAMES

This cold war classic is a sleeper with a twist: the massive military computer, with its built-in learning curve, comes to the conclusion that nuclear war is as pointless as a game of tic tac toe, all with the help of the very adorable adolescent Matthew Broderick. (Film; available on video)

COMPUTER GAMES AND CD-ROMs

This list consists primarily of a small handful of defining titles, including a few classics mentioned in this book. It is by no means comprehensive, but gives a sampling of works that I think point the way.

ANTI-ROM

CD-ROM designed and published by Hypermedia Research Centre, University of Westminster.

This hard-to-get experimental British CD-ROM as created by a collaborative of underground artists in London. Completely brilliant. I'm not sure if it's still available, but you can rad about it at the Hypermedia Resarch Centre's web site (see the preceding web sites).

BAD MOJO

CD-ROM designed and published by Pulse Entertainment.

Like Kafka's *Metamorphosis*, *Bad Mojo* puts you in the role of a man who has been turned into a cockroach, faced with a series of trials you must overcome to have your humanity restored.

BARBIE FASHION DESIGNER

CD-ROM produced by Digital Domain under producer Steve Schklair; published by Mattel.

This CD-ROM woke the world up to the reality that girls represent a viable market for computer entertainment. The brilliant idea of letting girls design clothes for their Barbie dolls and print them out on real cloth is a model for understanding what girls want from their computers.

BAR-MIN-SKI: CONSUMER PRODUCT, ENCYCLOPEDIA OF CLAMPS

CD-ROM designed and published by DE-LUX'O.

Created by Los Angeles artist Bill Barminski, director/producer Webster Lewin, and programmer Jerry Hesketh, this cult classic breaks new ground for CD-ROM interface design and interactivity. Every screen is literally a work of art. It's also one of the most entertaining and witty CD-ROMs around. Also see their companion piece *Encyclopedia of Clamps* and check out their web site listed in the web site section of this Mediography.

CENTIPEDE

This early classic computer game created by Atari has a built-in skill curve in that each time you shoot the ravenous centipede, you break it in two, thus creating more creatures from which to flee.

DONKY KONG, SUPER MARIO BROTHERS

The classic *Donky Kong* and its successor *Super Mario Brothers* created by Nintendo created the oft-imitated paradigm of chutes and ladders–style twitch gaming that has now become a convention.

DOOM

CD-ROM produced by Williams Electronics.

I am loathe to list *Doom* here because I think it's so heinous, but it does have some historical significance in that it brought real-time 3D to CD-ROM. Too bad it had to be in the form of shooting and killing.

FREAKSHOW, BAD DAY ON THE MIDWAY

CD-ROM designed by The Residents with Jim Ludtke.

These two titles broke new ground for narrative environments and the use of space to to tell a story. *Freakshow* has been cited as the next level of evolution in narrative, at the opposite end of a timeline that starts with Aristotle.

INDIANA JONES SERIES

CD-ROM designed and published by LucasArts.

These deftly written and designed CD-ROMs for children based on the popular film series provide hours of adventure with seemingly endless variations.

MONTY PYTHON'S COMPLETE WASTE OF TIME

CD-ROM published by 7th Level.

Without question, one of the all-time best CD-ROMs ever made, and certainly the funniest. A perfect example of re-purposed content used to greate effect. Terry Gilliam's classic Python animations are transformed into comical games and pointless sight gags.

MYST

CD-ROM designed by Cyan, Robyn and Rand Miller; published by Brøderbund.

Myst is credited as the first commercial CD-ROM to create a new paradigm for this medium. An unlikely blockbuster, it is completely outside of the convention of what is supposed to sell, and proved that people really do want a level of artfulness in their interative experiences.

PAC MAN AND MS. PAC MAN

Arcade game designed and published by Atari.

The classic game of eat or be eaten is still the most popular arcade game of all time, and due to its popularity among girls and women, spawned the "Eve" of computer games, *Ms. Pac Man*.

PITFALL

Video game produced for the Atari set-top system by Activision in 1982.

Similar to the chutes and ladders paradigm, but instead of jumping from one spot to the next, you swing. A lot of fun, for a twitch game.

Putt Putt Series

CD-ROM designed and published by Electronic Arts.

Don't laugh. These titles for very young children are simple but utterly delightful. Integrating simple stories with neat little games, puzzles, and tasks, kids love the delighful series based on the adventures of a cute little car.

Rockett's New School and Secret Paths in the Forest

CD-ROM, and ancillary products produced by Purple Moon Software.

These two titles are the first in a series by girl game company Purple Moon. Based on years of testing and research, they address concerns and play styles that are uniquely female.

SimCity and the Sim Series

CD-ROM designed and published by Maxis.

This perennial classic and its spinoffs are a perfect example of what interactive media can and should be. The ability to simulate and intervene in dynamic systems is one of the strong suits of computer technology, used to great effect in this entertaining and educational games. Still as strong today as they were when first published.

Space Invaders

Desktop computer game designed and published by Atari.

The classic computer game that introduced fast action and complex skill curves to computer gaming.

Tekken

Arcade game designed and published by Namco.

The popular fighting game allows players to beat each other up using beautifully rendered 3D characters.

Urban Feedback

CD-ROM published by Perfect Indigo.

Produced by London artists Sophie Greenfield and Giles Rollestone, this amazing interactive video collage combines video, graphics, poetry, and sound to create an entirely new kind of experience. You can literally "jam" with it as you make various choices that create a rich montage of site and sound expressing the fragmentation of urban life.

Virtua Fighter

Arcade game produced by Sega.

This high-end 3D fighting game uses virtual reality to model neolithic behavior, but its production values and technical effects are extraordinary.

You Don't Know Jack!

CD-ROM and web site designed and published by Berkeley Systems.

So deceptively simple, most interactive designers are kicking themselves for not having come up with this irreverent interactive game show (**http://www.berksys.com**).

Locations

Because location-based entertainment is such an important part of my story, I thought it would be helpful to list some of the locations I describe in the pages of this book. This is not a complete list, but it at least points you to a few interesting and/or significant sites mentioned herein.

Disneyland and Walt Disney World

Anaheim, California and Orlando, Florida.

Anaheim is home of the *Pirates of the Caribean*, the *Swiss Family Robinson Treehouse*, and *Toontown*, as described in "Narrative Environments: Virtual

Reality as a Storytelling Medium." When visiting Orlando, I particularly recommend Typhoon Lagoon and the MGM/Disney Park.

ElECTRONIC CAFÉ INTERNATIONAL

Various locations with headquarters in Santa Monica, California

The international network of cafés hosts all types of events that bring people together into shared media space using analog and digital video. Check their web site http://www.ecafe.com or give them a call for a listing of upcoming events.

THE INNOVATION STATION

Henry Ford Museum, Michigan

This exhibit, which I worked on with Edwin Schlossberg Incorporated, helps kids to understand fundamental ideas of problem-solving and ingenuity by trying to figure out how to sort balls of different colors using a giant interactive machine.

MATHEMATICA

Museum of Science and Industry, Los Angeles

This landmark interactive exhibition, opened in 1960, is still fully operational today, with the addition of computer kiosks. When I visited it with my class in 1995, my students felt it was better executed than any of the other, newer exhibits in the museum.

UNIVERSAL STUdIOS TOUR

Universal City, California

The classic Hollywood theme park of filmmaking has a variety of interesting and compelling narrative environments, and a handful of interactive and/or immersive venues.

Virtual Worlds

Various locations, including: Chicago, Illinois; Walnut Creek, California; Pasadena, California; London, England; and Las Vegas, Nevada.

The original VR attraction features the classic "shoot your friends" VR paradigm, but is historically signficant in that it was among the original mall-based attractions and the first mass-market VR attraction.

By the Author

Just for reference, the following is a partial list of my own work, including interactive applications, articles, products, and and where you can see and/or find them.

bliss.com

VRML character debuted at SIGGRAPH 97, Los Angeles Convention Center for Silicon Graphics, Inc./blitcom

bliss.com is the VRML celebrity spokesperson I creative directed to represent our new company, blitcom. Originally created for Silicon Graphics to demo their new browser, our long-term goal is to build a webisodic show and a variety of worlds and characters around her. Bliss can be accessed via **http://www.blitcom.com** or **http://www.sgi.com**.

The Californian Ideology: An Insider's View

Mute magazine, Issue 4, Winter/Spring 1996

Article I wrote in response to Andy Cameron and Richard Barbrook's scathing inditement of Californian digital culture, entitled "The Californian Ideology." For a full text of both articles, visit *Mute*'s web site at **http://www.metamute.co.uk**.

CREATIVE:CODE:CULTURE

Mute magazine, Issue 3, Autumn 1995

Tips and anecdotes on collaboration between artists and programmers. **http:// www.metamute.co.uk**.

E-MAIL FROM ABROAD

Irregular column for *Mute* magazine

In my irregular column for London-based *Mute* magazine, I send back e-mail reports from stateside, mostly covering various digital events, interspersed with gossip and social commentary.

THE INS AND OUTS OF NONLINEAR STORYTELLING

Article in *ACM SIGGRAPH Computer Graphics*, Volume 24, Number 2, May 1994; also featured in *Digital Illusion*, edited by Clark Dodsworth (Reading, Massachusetts: Addison-Wesley, 1997).

Written to accompany my SIGGRAPH 94 panel talk of the same name, this article has become the basis of a seminar I have teach at interactive media programs around the world.

LOUNGE@SIGGRAPH

SIGGRAPH 95, Los Angeles Convention Center

Temporary installation for Interactive Communities at SIGGRAPH 95, hosted in the Los Angeles Convention Center

This week-long exhibit showcased a handful of the CD-ROMs and web sites mentioned throughout the book. This exhibit created a small buzz which ultimately led to our being asked to do *The VR Garden*.

MEET THE BIOSPHERIANS

Interactive Theater at Biosphere 2 Visitors Center, produced in conjunction with Dennis Earl Moore Productions.

This 80-person interactive theater creates a simulated conversation between a host and the former crew of this prototype for a space colony/greenhouse. Located in the Biosphere 2 Visitors Center, Oracle, Arizona.

SECOND NATURE/THE VIRTUAL GALLERY

Prototype/Demo developed in conjunctoin with Visual Insight, Space Dynamics Laboratory, Utah State University Research Foundation, Logon, Utah.

This VR product has been showcased at a small handful of exhibitions. Visitors walk into 3D models of famous artworks using a treadmill interface and infrared tracking system to alleviate the need for cumbersome immersion devices. I helped develop the hardware interface and creative directed the content. Product currently available for use in entertainment and commercial applications.

SEGA GAMEWORKS

Arcade/Attraction developed in conjunction with The Jerde Partnership.

I contributed to the intial conceptual design on this Dreamworks SKG/Sega/Universal joint project, and from what I understand, many of my contributions actually made it into the final product. Currently opened in Seattle, Washington and other locations around the country.

SHOOT YOUR FRIENDS: A CALL TO ARMS IN THE BATTLE AGAINST VIOLENCE

Article written for *Digital Illusion*, edited by Clark Dodsworth (Reading, Massachusetts: Addison-Wesley, 1997).

My manifesto on the roots and culture of violence in computer gaming and a plea to the industry to expand its use of alternative genres.

VIRTUAL ADVENTURES

Virtual Reality attraction developed in conjunction with Iwerks Entertainment and Evans & Sutherland.

Described in "The Princess and the Monster: The Making of Virtual Adventures," I creative directed this 24-player game which uses high-end Virtual Reality and feature-film quality production values to create a hybrid ride/game/interactive movie. Currently installed at Foxwoods Casino in Ledyard, Connecticut and Nauticus Marine Park in Norfolk, Virginia.

THE VR GARDEN

Temporary installation developed in conjunction with Reed Exhibitions for IntermediaWorld 96, held at the Moscone Convention Center in San Francisco.

Although this exhibition had a short run at a relatively small conference, it got written up in several print and online reports and I understand that a search on the web will reveal several sites that discuss it.

INDEX

D

E

F

G

J-K-L

M

N

U-V

W

X-Y-Z

Plate 01

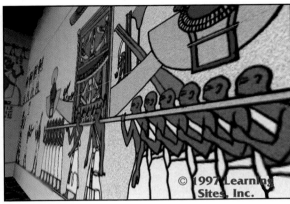

Plate 02

Plate 03

Plate 04

Plate 05

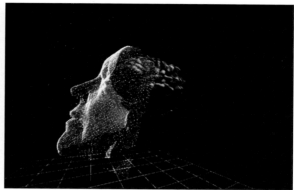

Plate 06

Plate 07

Plate 08

Plate 09

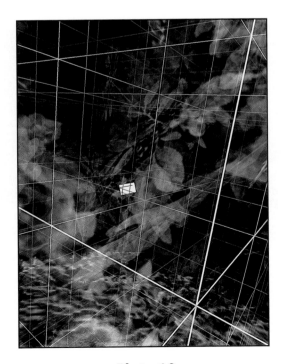

Plate 10

Plate 11

Plate 12

Plate 13

Plate 14

Plate 15

Plate 16

Plate 17

Plate 18

Plate 19

Plate 20

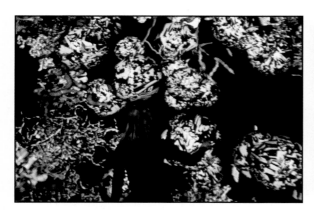

Plate 21

Plate 22

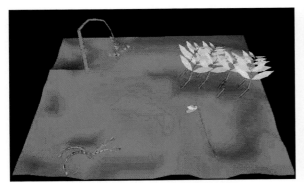

Plate 23

Plate 24

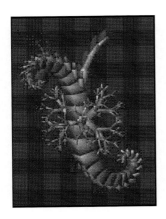

Plate 25

Plate 26

Plate 27

Plate 28

Plate 29

Plate 30

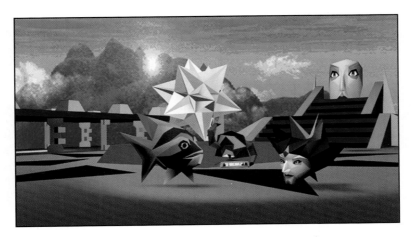

Plate 31

Plate 32

Plate 33

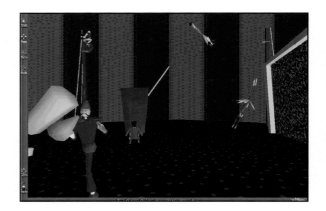

Plate 34

Plate 35

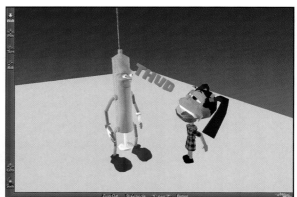

Plate 36

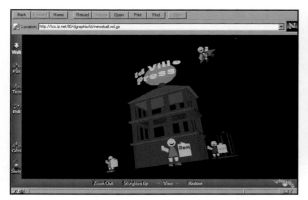

Plate 37

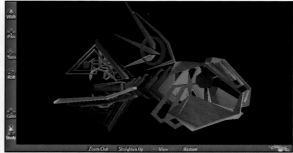

Plate 38

Plate 39

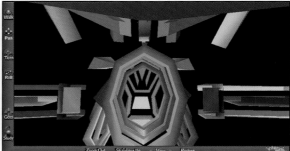

Plate 40

Plate 41

Plate 42

Plate 43

Plate 44

Plate 45

Plate 46

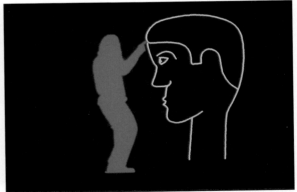

Plate 47

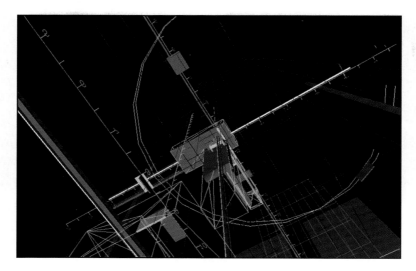

Plate 48

Plate 49

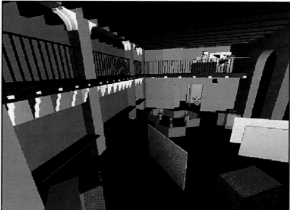

Plate 50

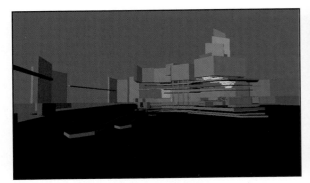

Plate 51

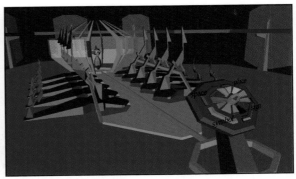

Plate 52

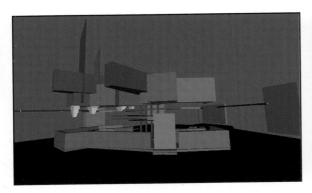

Plate 53

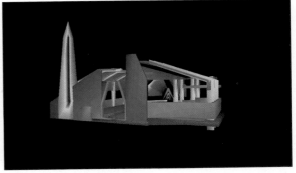

Plate 54

Plate 55

Plate 56

Plate 57

Plate 58